BASIC ECONOMICS

BASIC ECONOMICS
FIRST CANADIAN EDITION

EDWIN G. DOLAN
GEORGE MASON UNIVERSITY

ROY VOGT
UNIVERSITY OF MANITOBA

HOLT, RINEHART AND WINSTON OF CANADA, LIMITED • TORONTO

Canadian Cataloguing in Publication Data

Dolan, Edwin G.
    Basic Economics

Based on the 2d American ed. by Edwin G. Dolan.
Includes index.

ISBN 0-03-920123-6

1. Economics. I. Vogt, Roy. II. Title.
HB171.5.D58 1980   330   C80-094649-9

Printed in Canada
1 2 3 4 5 85 84 83 82 81

Credits and Acknowledgments

Photo of Gerald Bouey, page 194, courtesy of CP Picture Service. Photo of Ronald H. Coase, page 359, courtesy of the University of Chicago Law School. Photo of James Coyne, page 194, courtesy of CP Picture Service. Photo of Milton Friedman, page 240, by C. G. Bloom, courtesy of the University of Chicago Office of Public Information. Photo of John Kenneth Galbraith, page 480, courtesy of Professor Galbraith. Photo of Samuel Gompers, page 539, courtesy of the AFL-CIO. Photo of Harold Adams Innis, page 9, courtesy of the Robert Lansdale Photography Ltd. Photo of William Stanley Jevons, page 341, courtesy of Historical Pictures Services, Inc., Chicago. Photo of Harry G. Johnson, page 241, courtesy of Times Newspapers Limited. Photo of John Maynard Keynes, page 136, courtesy of the Bettmann Archive. Photo of Oskar Lange, page 595, courtesy of United Press International. Photo of William Arthur Lewis, page 585, courtesy of Princeton University. Print of Thomas Robert Malthus, page 575, courtesy of the Bettmann Archive. Photo of Alfred Marshall, page 40, courtesy of Historical Pictures Services, Inc., Chicago. Photo of Karl Marx, page 594, courtesy of Miller Pictures Limited. Print of John Stuart Mill, page 125, reproduced from the collection of the Library of Congress. Photo of Louis Razminsky, page 194, courtesy of CP Picture Service. Photo of Joan V. Robinson, page 464, courtesy of Ramsey & Muspratt Studios, Cambridge, England. Photo of Paul Anthony Samuelson, page 165, courtesy of Professor Samuelson. Photo of Theodore W. Schultz, page 585, courtesy of Theodore W. Schultz. Photo of Joseph Alois Schumpeter, page 481, courtesy of the Bettmann Archive. Print of Adam Smith, page 6, reproduced from the collection of the Library of Congress. Photo of Graham F. Towers, page 193, courtesy of CP Picture Service. Photo of Freidrich August von Hayek, page 34, courtesy of Wide World Photos. Photo of Ludwig von Mises, page 601, courtesy of United Press International.

P R E F A C E

Teaching economics in the 1980s is more of a challenge than ever before. A recent poll taken by *Fortune* magazine found that two out of three economics professors feel there is a sense of lost moorings in economics. Three out of four feel increasing doubt about the accuracy of macroeconomic models. Seven out of eight have less confidence than they used to in government programs as solutions to economic problems. The result is that 98 percent of all professors polled said they were now teaching economics differently from the way they taught it five years ago.[1]

Despite this sense of uncertainty, most economists realize that the last decade has been very productive in terms of economic knowledge. In macroeconomics, great strides have been made in understanding the dynamics of inflation and unemployment, the role of monetary policy in the economy, the operation of the labor market, and the importance of expectations as a determinant of economic behavior. In microeconomics, such established fields of study as industrial organization and regulation have taken on a new life. Government involvement in business and the impact of foreign investment on business behavior are topics that are justifiably receiving greater attention than in the past.

All this means that teaching economics in the 1980s requires a new kind of textbook—one that brings into the classroom the new learning and new controversies of today's economic science. Students have an uncanny ability, from the first day of classes, to pose exactly those questions that are being debated in the latest professional journals. They deserve the best answers that can be given; and, in cases where there is no universally acceptable right answer, they deserve honest explanations of why disagreements persist. They must also have some understanding of the historical roots of our problems. That is why Canadian economic history receives more than usual attention in this text.

Here, in brief, is the strategy used in *Basic Economics, First Canadian Edition*, to meet the challenge.

MACROECONOMICS

The effects of monetary and fiscal policy have always been a central theme in teaching macroeconomics at the principles level, and this emphasis is continued in *Basic Economics*. However, the macro section of the book reflects a major shift in economists' perceptions of how fiscal and monetary

---

[1]Walter Guzzardi, Jr., "The New Down-to-Earth Economics," *Fortune*, December 31, 1978, p. 77.

policies operate. As the late Arthur Okun put it: "The evidence of recent years suggests that through its fiscal and monetary policies the federal government can control — within a reasonable margin — the total growth of GNP measured in dollars. But it cannot control the division of that growth between increases in output and increases in the price level."[2]

In accordance with this view of how the economy works, *Basic Economics* introduces early in the macroeconomics section (Chapters 6 and 7) the crucial distinction between nominal quantities, measured in current dollars, and real quantities, adjusted for changes in the price level. The text then portrays the multiplier effects of fiscal policy and the effects of monetary policy as having their primary impact on nominal GNP; it also offers the continual reminder that changes in nominal GNP may represent changes in either real output, or the price level, or both (Chapters 8 to 14). Because of the important role played by the foreign market in Canada's economy, imports and exports are built into the multiplier from the very beginning. A "simple" multiplier without a foreign sector is not an option for the Canadian economy, and there is no reason why students should be given the impression that it is an option. Chapters 8 to 14 build the foreign sector into the multiplier, and a separate chapter (Chapter 15) is used to illustrate general equilibrium conditions in both domestic and foreign sectors of the economy. We believe that we have accomplished this without an overly complex technical apparatus. To answer the crucial question of how changes in nominal GNP are split up between inflation and changes in real output, the book turns to the supply side of the economy. Chapter 16 introduces the Phillips curve and draws initial distinctions between demand-pull and cost-push inflation. It also deals with the labor market and the determination of the unemployment rate in terms of job search theory. Chapter 17 discusses the short-run dynamics of inflation, with special emphasis on the role of inflationary expectations and the phenomenon of inflationary recession. Finally, it explains the major policy alternatives to traditional fiscal and monetary fine-tuning. The result is a thorough integration of the traditional theory of income determination with modern theories of inflation and unemployment.

MICROECONOMICS

Microeconomics, like macroeconomics, has a traditional core, represented by Chapters 18 to 23. These chapters give a careful exposition of the theories of consumer behavior, production, cost, and perfect competition. Chapter 22 examines the extent to which the performance of the Canadian economy may have been affected by foreign ownership and control of Canadian business enterprises and resources. Similar topics of current concern are discussed in Chapters 24 to 28. Chapter 24 discusses pure monopoly, a traditional topic, and then applies the theory to the case of cartels, a type of market organization receiving greatly increased attention in these days of OPEC. Chapters 25 to 27 explain a wide variety of market forms, organized around the question of when perfect competition is required for satisfactory market performance and when rivalry among a

[2]Arthur Okun, "An Efficient Strategy to Combat Inflation," *Brookings Bulletin* 15 (Spring 1979), p. 4.

relatively small number of competing firms is enough. The chapters place considerable emphasis on recent empirical work supporting each side of this question. Chapter 28 deals with anticombines policy and with other attempts by government to limit and control the growth of private monopoly power. The role of government as both regulator and producer is carefully examined.

APPLICATIONS

Basic Economics contains a number of chapters that put students' newly acquired theoretical tools to work on problems of contemporary policy. After a discussion of how various types of income are determined in theory (Chapter 29), two chapters (30 and 31) deal with such issues as collective bargaining and income inequality. Chapter 31 examines the economics of poverty and highlights recent empirical research into the effects of antipoverty efforts. Finally, in Chapters 33 and 34, alternatives to our own economic system are described and examined in some detail. There is no better way to confront the student with both the potential and the problems of a capitalist economy than to compare that economy with alternative models, and with actual alternatives such as the economy of the Soviet Union. These last chapters should therefore not be considered optional.

TEACHING AND LEARNING AIDS

The substantive content of a textbook is only part of what makes it usable in the classroom; for the book to be effective, its content must be taught by instructors and learned by students. Therefore, this book pays particular attention to teaching and learning aids.

The Cases According to a time-honored principle, each generalization should receive a specific illustration, and each illustration should lead to a generalization. Following this principle, numerous short case studies are included in the book. Some of them illustrate general statements about economic policy with specific episodes—for example, Canada's experiment with wage and price controls. Other cases introduce empirical material supporting the discussion in the text—for example, inflation-unemployment trends or data on economies of scale. All cases are placed directly in the text, where they will do the most good, not at the ends of the chapters. Thus they serve as an integral part of the learning process, not just as entertainment or digression.

Readability In *Basic Economics*, readability means three things. First, it means a lively writing style that draws students into the subject matter. Second, it means complete control of the level of difficulty, as measured by standard readability formulas; the book corresponds to the actual reading abilities of today's undergraduate students. Third, it means elimination of the "alphabet soup" style of textbook writing. When terms such as "average variable cost" and "marginal propensity to consume" occur, the text uses the actual words, not a thicket of AVCs and MPCs that bewilder students.

Vocabulary For many students, vocabulary is one of the stumbling blocks to learning economics. This book uses a three-level reinforcement technique to handle the problem. First, each new term is printed in boldface at the point it is first used and defined. Next, the term and its definition are repeated in the margin of the same page. Finally, the term appears in a complete alphabetical glossary at the end of the book.

Graphs   For the benefit of students who may not be used to working with graphs, an appendix on the subject has been added to Chapter 1. This appendix does more than simply explain techniques. It also addresses the most common problems students have in working with graphs. One of these problems is the tendency to memorize graphs as meaningless patterns of lines. Another is the inability to draw original graphs when they are needed in note-taking or on examinations. The Chapter 1 appendix warns of these pitfalls and carefully explains how they can be avoided. As an added bonus throughout the book, the large page size and single-column format make it especially easy to put graphs exactly where they are needed in relation to the text.

Chapter Support Materials   Each chapter is preceded by a brief statement of learning objectives and a list of terms for review. Each chapter is followed by a concise summary and a set of review questions, and most have an annotated list of suggestions for further reading.

Study Guide   A comprehensive *Study Guide to Accompany Basic Economics*, published separately, completes the package of learning aids. Each chapter in the student guide consists of four elements: a list of learning objectives (somewhat more detailed than those given in the chapter openings in the text), a programmed review requiring active student involvement and problem solving for immediate reinforcement, an application taken from a Canadian newspaper or magazine and accompanied by discussion questions, and a self-test. (The self-test items are carefully coordinated with the test bank in the *Instructor's Manual* in terms of format, coverage, and level of difficulty. Answers to self-test items, with explanations where necessary, are at the end of each chapter in the study guide.)

Instructor's Manual   The text is accompanied by an instructor's manual written by the authors of the text. This manual contains answers to the text's end-of-chapter questions. It also contains a special section entitled "What's Different Here, and Why." This section highlights the unique terminology and underlying models of *Basic Economics*, to help instructors who have used other books in the past convert their courses and lecture notes. The manual also contains additional discussion questions, and suggested answers to the application questions in the students' *Study Guide*. Most important, perhaps, for many instructors, it contains a *test bank*. The test bank has a number of features that make it a powerful instructional tool. It is divided into two sections, A and B, each containing ten true-and-false and fifteen multiple-choice questions for each chapter (seventeen hundred test items in all). The two sections are parallel in coverage and level of difficulty so that they can be used in alternate semesters or in different sections of the same course and still allow comparability for grading. The test items are distributed as evenly as possible among three levels of difficulty: recognition and understanding, simple application, and complex application. Individual items are coded for level of difficulty and topic covered. The test items were developed by the authors of the text and Elizabeth Craig of the University of Delaware.

A WORD OR TWO OF THANKS

We have been extremely fortunate in getting help of many kinds from many quarters while writing this book. It is a pleasure to acknowledge that help here.

The greatest debt is owed to David E. Lindsey, who provided the theoretical inspiration and many of the technical details for the underlying macroeconomics model of this book—an approach he developed over many years of teaching at Ohio State University and Macalester College.

Next we must thank the many reviewers who commented on various drafts of the manuscript and suggested countless improvements. In Canada these include Douglas Auld, University of Guelph; Gordon F. Boreham, University of Ottawa; John D. Boyd, University of British Columbia; Beverly J. Cameron, University of Manitoba; Norman Edward Cameron, St. John's College, University of Manitoba; Brian Hull, Canadian Foundation for Economic Education; Lionel L. Ifill, Algonquin College; Sadat Kazi, Vanier College; M.S. Shedd, University of Calgary; and Brian Truman, Mohawk College.

Last but not least, Roy Vogt would like to thank the editors of Holt, Rinehart and Winston of Canada, particularly Dennis Bockus, for providing excellent assistance in the preparation of the manuscript. Thanks are also extended to Beverly Cameron for her work on the *Study Guide*, to Frieda Unruh and Karen Vogt for typing assistance, and to other members of the Vogt family—Ruth, Kathleen, and Paul—for their patience and understanding.

CONTENTS

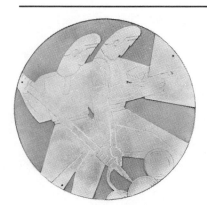

PART THREE / THE THEORY OF PRICES AND MARKETS

CHAPTER 18 / SUPPLY AND DEMAND: BUILDING ON THE BASICS

CHAPTER 19 / THE LOGIC OF CONSUMER CHOICE

APPENDIX TO CHAPTER 19 / AN INTRODUCTION TO INDIFFERENCE CURVES 340

CHAPTER 20 / THE NATURE OF THE FIRM

AN OVERVIEW OF THE MARKET ECONOMY

C H A P T E R 1

WHAT ECONOMICS IS ALL ABOUT: THE CANADIAN SETTING

WHAT YOU WILL LEARN IN THIS CHAPTER

As economists struggle to understand the dramatic economic events of recent years, they are placing increased emphasis on the basics: how individual markets work and how individuals react to changing economic conditions and policies. This chapter will begin explaining these basics with a discussion of the concepts of economic scarcity and choice. It will distinguish between economics as a science and as policy. Interpretations of Canadian history that have been offered by some of our economists will also be examined. The Appendix to Chapter 1 will introduce the use of graphs in economics.

The 1970s were years of dramatic change for the Canadian economy. Unemployment and inflation struck in combinations that not so long ago would have been thought flatly impossible. Energy and environmental quality, long ignored or taken for granted, became subjects of national debate and targets of sweeping programs of governmental regulation. The international monetary system was revolutionized, and Canadians watched their dollar lose much of its value on world money markets.

Not surprisingly, all this change and turmoil pushed public interest in economics to new heights. Enrollments in economics have never been higher. Newspapers and television have greatly increased their coverage of economic affairs. The specialized business press has prospered. People want to understand the economic events they are witnessing, and they expect economists to explain them.

Economists are trying hard to do so, and this book is part of the effort. Together with the course of which it is a part, it will help readers become more perceptive of economic news and more constructive participants in discussions of economic issues.

Economics has been undergoing a revolution, part of which has been an increase in modesty among economists. Economists are beginning to understand why the theories and forecasting methods of which they were once so proud came to grief in the 1970s, but they are not fully agreed on what to replace them with. They are beginning to understand why economic policies of the past have not always had the intended effects, but they are not fully agreed on how to design policies that will do better.

There is, however, one thing that economists today seem to agree on:

more emphasis on the basics is needed. That means paying more attention to how individual markets operate and how individuals react to changing economic conditions and policies. This emphasis will be very much in evidence throughout the book. The discussion will begin with two of the most basic economic concepts of all: scarcity and choice.

SCARCITY AND CHOICE IN ECONOMICS

Learning economics means learning to look in a special way at what people do, singling out some features for close attention and placing others in the background. In this respect, economics is much like other social sciences, each of which has its particular way of looking at the world. Psychology emphasizes how people's motivations and personalities shape their behavior toward one another. Political science takes special note of how people's actions are shaped by power relationships within formal and informal political institutions. Economics emphasizes how human actions are influenced by the fact of scarcity and the necessity of choice.

Scarcity

In economics, *scarcity* means that people do not have as much of everything as they want. Economic scarcity is a subjective concept; it is not measurable by any objective, physical standard. A geologist might say that tin ore is scarce but that iron ore is abundant, meaning that the earth's crust contains much more iron than tin. But an economist would say that both are scarce because people do not have as much of either as they want. An environmentalist might say that sperm whales have become scarce, meaning that there are now barely enough of them to maintain a breeding population. But an economist would say that sperm whales are less scarce than they once were. A century and a half ago, before the discovery of kerosene, whale oil was much in demand as a lamp fuel; today, there are relatively abundant substitutes.

Scarcity as an imbalance between what people have and what they want is sometimes said to be artificial. If people could only learn to limit their wants, then they would solve the problem once and for all. But scarcity is inescapable. Suppose, for example, that you limited your material desires to a single bowl of rice a day and went out into the wilderness to meditate. As soon as you began looking for twigs to build a fire to cook your rice, you would discover that twigs are scarce. You would have to take time off from meditation to look for them. You would build your fire carefully, in such a way as to boil the water without wasting fuel. And in so doing, you would be drawn to meditate that your behavior in the wilderness was shaped by scarcity, much as it was in the world you had left.

Choice

Economics accepts scarcity as a fact of life, but what makes life interesting, economically speaking, is not scarcity itself so much as the necessity of choosing among ways of coping with it. Earthworms must live with a scarcity of good soil in which to dig their burrows, but they have no choice but to dig. As a result, economists find earthworms nowhere nearly as interesting as people, who can earn their sustenance by burrowing in the soil, by fishing in the sea, or by lecturing on economics to the burrowers and fishers.

As soon as the element of choice is added to that of scarcity, a whole world of economics opens up. How does a person decide how much time to spend fishing and how much to spend farming? Why does one person specialize in farming and another in lecturing on economics? Why is one service more highly rewarded than another? All these questions relate to the way people's lives are shaped by the choices they make among alternatives for coping with scarcity.

Factors of Production

The limits to our range of economic choice are set by the **factors of production**. Factors of production are the basic components used in the production of all goods and services. They include (1) **natural resources** — land with its original fertility and mineral deposits; (2) **capital** or **capital investment** — manufactured productive resources, such as tools, industrial equipment, structures, and artificial improvements to land; and (3) **labor** — the productive contribution made by people working with their minds and their muscles. Sometimes a special form of human activity, **entrepreneurship**, is identified as a fourth factor of production. An entrepreneur is someone who recognizes new business opportunities and organizes technology and labor to take advantage of them.

Improvements in the quality of factors of production permit the expansion of production possibilities. The quality of labor done by a given population improves as people become healthier and better educated. The quality of capital increases dramatically as technological change improves equipment and brings new methods of production. Only natural resources do not undergo qualitative improvements; in fact, many actually decline in quality as they are depleted by use. So far, in Canada, the increases in quantity and quality of other factors have more than made up for the depletion of natural resources.

Factors of production The basic elements of natural resources, labor, and capital used in the production of all goods.

Natural resources As a factor of production, land and mineral deposits.

Capital As a factor of production, all manufactured productive resources such as tools, industrial equipment, structures, and artificial improvements to land.

Labor As a factor of production, the contributions to production made by people working with their minds and their muscles.

Entrepreneurship A unique form of business activity that consists in inventing new ways of doing things, being alert to new opportunities, taking risks, overcoming constraints, and developing new products and organizations.

Specialization and the Division of Labor

Individual units of labor, capital, natural resources, and entrepreneurship are different from one another. Units of labor — individual human beings — are the most diverse of all. Because people are not interchangeable parts, we must pay careful attention to the **division of labor** — who gets which job — if we are to do well in our struggle against scarcity.

Suppose that for some reason or other we chose to devote half the nation's labor power to producing education and half to producing other goods, but that we used the wrong half in each place. Skilled production workers would awkwardly mumble their way through lecture notes on Greek history while professors got their thumbs jammed in delicate factory machinery. We would not produce as much as possible of either education or manufactured commodities. Simply by arranging to have the production

Division of labor The division of the production process for a commodity into numerous specialized functions.

workers and the professors change places — by using the proper division of labor — we could increase the output of both manufactured goods and education. That is, production could be increased by *specialization.*

More than two hundred years ago, Adam Smith began the most famous economics book of all time with an example emphasizing the importance of the division of labor. Smith had visited a pin factory and had seen that when one worker specialized in putting heads on the pins, another in sharpening the points, another in placing them on cards, and so on, they all could produce a hundred times more than could the same number of people working separately. Smith went on to show how free markets and private enterprise solve the problem of the division of labor simply by attracting people into the occupations where their potential earnings are greatest. Beginning with Chapter 2, this book will spend many chapters doing the same thing and will have time left over for a look at how governments sometimes try to improve on the market by substituting their own judgments concerning the division of labor.

Adam Smith (1723–1790)

Adam Smith was born in Kirkaldy, on the east coast of Scotland. He studied first at Glasgow University and then at Oxford. In those days, the universities of Scotland were greater centers of learning than those of England, so Smith returned to the north after finishing his studies at Oxford and obtained a chair at Glasgow. It was not, of course, a chair in economics. Economics had not yet been invented as a distinct discipline, and besides, it was not yet Smith's major interest. His specialty was moral philosophy.

During his long career, Smith wrote just two books. It was his good fortune, however, to have both bring him immediate fame. His first book was *The Theory of Moral Sentiments*, published in 1759. His second, *The Wealth of Nations*, appeared seventeen years later, in 1776. David Hume, a friend of Smith's, commented that "the reading of it necessarily requires so much attention, and the public is disposed to give so little, that I shall still doubt for some time of its being at first very popular." Hume, however, was wrong. The book sold well from the start.

The task Smith set himself first of all was to explain the workings of the economic system — that is, the sources of the "wealth of nations." The greatest source, he discovered, was the division of labor. Chapter 1 opened with the observation that "the greatest improvement in the productive powers of labor, and the greater part of the skill, dexterity, and judgment with which it is anywhere directed, or applied, seem to have been the effects of the division of labor." He then went on to give his famous pin factory example.

It was not enough for Smith just to describe the division of labor, however. He wanted to explain how it came about. His explanation was highly characteristic:

This division of labor, from which so many advantages are derived, is not originally the effect of any human wisdom, which foresees and intends that general opulence to which it gives occasion. It is the necessary, though very slow and gradual consequence of a certain propensity in human nature which has in view no such extensive utility; the propensity to truck, barter, and exchange one thing for another.

Here, for the first time in the book, Smith emphasized the importance of the unintended consequences of human action: each person acting in the marketplace has only narrow ends in mind, but the joint result of the actions of everyone is a general benefit that none intended.

As *The Wealth of Nations* progressed, Smith added another theme, that of the benefits of economic liberty. The free, spontaneous interaction of people in the marketplace is not just one way to bring about the general benefit of mankind; it is the best way. Government attempts to guide or regulate the market end up doing more harm than good. Smith especially attacked the privileges of legally protected monopolies, the

Poor Laws (which he saw as inhibiting the mobility of labor), and the apprenticeship system (which worked against free entry into occupations). All such restraints on the market tended to force trade into "unnatural" and less beneficial channels.

Smith's book has meant various things to various people. To some it has been a handbook of laissez-faire liberalism. To others, it has been the fountainhead of economic science. Still others have found it, not without reason, to be unoriginal and crammed with errors. Whatever its faults, it is a book that continues to be read and debated. In 1976, its bicentennial brought leading economists from all over the world to Glasgow to pay tribute to the professor of moral philosophy who had lectured there so long before.

AN OVERVIEW OF EARLY CANADIAN ECONOMIC HISTORY

Much of this book is devoted to providing tools and ideas that help to explain the operation of modern economies in general. Throughout this text, however, we will also examine economic institutions and phenomena that distinguish the Canadian economy from others. Canada's early economic history and the way it has been interpreted by leading Canadian economic historians will be outlined in the following pages; more recent developments will be discussed in later chapters.

Canadian economic historians stress the role played by geography in Canada's economic development. It should be noted first that North America faces Europe. Its Atlantic coastline is generally more accessible to landing and settlement than its Pacific coastline. Its climate more closely resembles that of northern Europe than that of the Asiatic countries. Aggressive European merchants settled North America, and their technology and markets gave the impetus to economic expansion in the New World.

Geography also dictated the types of settlements that took root in Canada, and their relative success. The early settlements on the Atlantic coast depended on the fisheries, supplemented later by trade in timber and furs, for their existence. They were forced to compete with European fishing interests and with rivals along the New England coast. A vast, densely wooded hinterland cut them off from the more vigorous settlements developing along the St. Lawrence River.

Commercial ventures setting out from the St. Lawrence penetrated deeply into what later became the United States, because travel from the Great Lakes south via the Mississippi River was much easier than the journey westward over the precambrian rocks. Initially, the Appalachian Mountains separated the interior from the New England colonies along the eastern seaboard; however, the colonists were soon motivated to overcome this barrier and to expand their own commercial ventures into the Ohio valley and across the trade routes of the Montreal merchants. In 1783, after the successful revolutionary wars against England, the American states laid claim to the land west to the Mississippi, and traders from the St. Lawrence were forced to pursue their trade in furs north of the Great Lakes, to the Red River settlement in what is now Manitoba and beyond.

Economic historians differ as to whether this movement occurred in defiance of or as a natural outgrowth of North American geography. W.A.

Mackintosh, for many years a highly regarded scholar at Queen's University, took the former view. He noted that throughout most of North America, rivers and mountains encourage movement north and south. He stressed the difficulty of moving goods and people overland north of the Great Lakes. That the commercial empire of the St. Lawrence was eventually linked up with the western prairies, and that from this linkage there developed a viable nation, occured, in his opinion, in spite of nature. On the other hand, H.A. Innis, a notable economic historian, was impressed by the watersheds of both the St. Lawrence and Hudson Bay, and by the technology used by the early traders to penetrate quickly and deeply into the Canadian hinterland. Consequently, he concluded that Canada emerged as a nation because of its geography.

Despite differences of opinion about the role of geography, virtually all Canadian economic historians have stressed the importance of staple products in Canada's economic development. A **staple product** is a commodity on which an economy concentrates much of its labor and capital. In Canada's history a succession of staple products — fish, timber, fur, pulp and paper, minerals, wheat, and oil — have provided the impetus for its economic growth. This level of specialization has had serious implications for the stability, organization, and independence of the Canadian economy.

Staple product A commodity on which the economy of a settlement or region concentrates much of its labor and capital.

Given the abundance of land and the relative scarcity of labor and capital, early Canadian settlements answered a European demand for their goods by concentrating on the export of natural resources, or staple products. This set a pattern for Canadian economic strategy for centuries to come. In good times, foreign markets have made exports the leading sector of the Canadian economy, generating new investment in the home production of raw materials and in the further processing of finished goods. However, dependence on foreign markets has also made our country extremely vulnerable to recessions and changes in policies in the countries to which we export. Some regions in Canada have also fallen into what is known as a "staple trap," meaning that they concentrate so much on the export of a few products that they fail to develop other industries. The neglect of a more diversified economic base makes it all the more difficult for the economy of a Canadian region to counteract the negative effects of recessions originating outside the region or country.

The very nature of the staples affected Canada's development. When furs were in great demand, the ease with which fur-bearing animals were caught led to rapid depletion of local supplies and thus to rapid penetration of the Canadian hinterland by traders seeking more pelts. A vast, but frail, economic system evolved linking eastern headquarters to their sources of supply. Increased amounts of capital were required to overcome the transportation problems created by the great distances over which goods had to travel. This requirement favored strong organizations like the Hudson's Bay Company and led to the growth of monopoly in what had been an extremely competitive industry.

Later, in the nineteenth century, when a nation-state was created on the foundations of this far-flung economic base, massive government subsidies were required to build the canals and railways that were necessary to link the various regions of the country. In the decade after Confederation, when the Canadian population was less than 4 million, the federal government committed more than $60 million to the construction of two railways, linking Central Canada to the Atlantic and the Pacific.

It was the nature of our staple production, therefore, that created conditions of foreign dependence, government assistance, and regional instability, all important features of the Canadian economy to this day.

In recent years the "staple approach" to Canadian economic history has been criticized by some economic historians, but scholars like Melville Watkins of the University of Toronto have argued that on the basis of both new theoretical work and empirical research the staple approach remains one of the most original and useful keys to understanding Canada's economic development.

Many Canadian scholars regard Harold Adams Innis as the most original and influential economist this country has produced. He brought to the study of Canadian economic history a restless and original mind, and the theories he expounded were supported by thorough empirical research. He influenced a wide range of social scientists through his prolific writings and his teaching and leadership at the University of Toronto.

Innis was born near Otterville, Ontario in 1894. He studied at McMaster University, which was then in Toronto, and later did graduate work in economics at the University of Chicago. There he studied with such well-known economists as Frank H. Knight and J.M. Clark, but he was most influenced by the economic historian C.W. Wright. Under Wright's direction he chose to write his doctoral thesis on a history of the Canadian Pacific Railway.

After his graduation in 1920, Innis turned down several offers to teach in the United States, preferring to return to Canada to teach economics at the University of Toronto. Here he plunged into the study of Canadian economic history. He traveled throughout the country, even making a hazardous journey down the Mackenzie River, learning about Canada firsthand and gathering original source materials in private and public archives.

Harold Adams Innis (1894 – 1952)

His three major works were published at ten-year intervals: *The Fur Trade in Canada: An Introduction to Canadian Economic History* in 1930, *The Cod Fisheries: The History of an International Economy* in 1940, and *Empire and Communications* in 1950. He wrote dozens of other books and articles, but these three works illustrate most clearly the richness and the development of his approach to economic history.

In his book on the fur trade, Innis examined the factors that shaped the growth of one of Canada's earliest industries and, in turn, how the development of this industry influenced the creation of a unique Canadian nation. He emphasized the role of geography and technology in the rapid westward expansion of the fur trade, the importance of foreign markets, the high overhead costs involved in creating an effective transportation system, and the way in which the physical characteristics of the furs traded affected the organization and stability of the economy.

This interpretation of economic and social change was carried further by Innis in his other major works. In his study of another staple industry, the cod fisheries, he again focused on the dependence of the industry on foreign markets; the impact of new technology, in this case such things as iron, steam, and refrigeration; and the search for protection after periods of vigorous competition.

Following his work on the fisheries, Innis planned to make a similar study of another major industry, pulp and paper. However, the more he examined this industry the more he became impressed with the profound impact that communications media such as newspapers have on society, and the less he felt able to deal with the industry in a purely economic way. During the 1940s he plunged into an intensive, far-ranging study of how communications media have influenced the growth and decline of civilizations.

For example, in media such as stone and parchment he detected what he called a "time bias." Societies using such media tended to restrict the enlargement of their boundaries and fostered traditions and political organizations that favored stability over time. Eventually such societies might be successfully invaded from outside by societies that favored media with a "spatial bias," such as papyrus, paper, and printing. The use of such media encouraged civilizations like the Roman Empire and our own to move quickly over space, conquering territories devoted to stability and "time." However, these more aggressive societies made themselves vulnerable to new forces emerging at the boundaries of their far-flung empires. Internally, their neglect of time and tradition forced them to adopt measures favoring greater social cohesion, political centralization, and monopoly.

Innis documented these ideas in his last major work, *Empire and Communications*. After his death in 1952, these ideas continued to influence scholars in numerous disciplines. In particular they formed the basis for the famous work of Marshall McLuhan. McLuhan's well-known statement, "The medium is the message," is closely linked to Innis's observation that the physical nature of a staple product or communications medium profoundly affects the economic, social, and political life of society.

ECONOMIC SCIENCE AND ECONOMIC POLICY

A great part of what one reads about economics in the newspapers or hears about it on television is focused on specific problems of economic policy. Should the federal government spend more money and run a larger budget deficit? Should price controls on oil be lifted in the hope of increasing production and decreasing consumption? Should the government encourage or discourage exports of Canadian natural gas? If we are to learn the economic way of thinking, we must learn how economists think about policy issues as well as how they think about pure theory.

The mention of economic policies such as price controls or budget deficits tends to set little lights labeled "hurrah" or "ugh" flashing in our minds. Sometimes our mental circuits work so fast that we do not notice that, between the mention of the policy and the flashing of the lights, a chain of thinking somewhat like the following must occur:

1. If Policy X is followed, Outcome Y will result.
2. Outcome Y is a good (or bad) thing.
3. Therefore, hurrah (or ugh) for Policy X.

In order to understand the contents of this book and how to put them to work, it is important to understand the logic of the three-step chain of thinking. To that end, we will go through it one step at a time.

Positive Economics

Economic science cannot foretell the future, but it can offer predictions of the "if, then" form: "If A occurs, then B will occur, other things being equal." An economist might, then, make the assertion: "If government spending were increased, then unemployment would decline, as long as no other changes in economic conditions occurred in the meantime." Such a statement is sometimes called a **scientific prediction**. It is a statement of cause and effect but one that is valid only under specified conditions. In making scientific predictions of this form, economists rarely attempt to foretell

Scientific prediction A conditional prediction having the form "if A, then B, other things being equal."

whether A will actually occur or whether other things will actually remain constant.

When economists limit their attention to statements that are pure scientific predictions, they are said to be practicing **positive economics**. All sound analysis of economic policy must begin with positive economics as step 1.

Resolving Disagreements Of course, economists sometimes disagree about whether a certain scientific prediction is valid. In fact, a great deal of the day-to-day work in which economists engage is directed toward resolving disagreements on matters of positive economics. Some scientific disagreements concern matters of pure theory and are much like the disagreements among mathematicians concerning whether some unproved theorem is true or false. These disputes can, in time, be resolved by a process in which each party tries to state the reasoning as carefully as possible or to detect logical errors.

Frequently, economists try to resolve disputes over matters of positive economics by using **empirical** methods. That means looking at evidence — statistical or otherwise — based on observation of past experience. Much of this work is done by specialists in the statistical analysis of economic data who are called **econometricians**. Suppose that the scientific prediction in dispute said: "If government spending were to increase, then unemployment would decline, other things being equal." An econometrician might enter the debate with the announcement that, according to a study of postwar data on the Canadian economy, an increase in government expenditure has, in fact, been consistently associated with a decline in unemployment, taking into account the probable influence of other factors. Or the econometrician might assert that the data reveal no systematic association at all between government spending and unemployment when advanced statistical techniques are used to eliminate the influence of other changes in economic conditions. Questions of this sort are not usually resolved by a single empirical study, but repeated studies and the gradual accumulation of evidence serve to narrow areas of disagreement and contribute to scientific progress in economics.

Normative Economics

A positive economic statement of the type "if Policy X, then Outcome Y" cannot by itself resolve the issue of whether Policy X is desirable. To come to a conclusion on the desirability of the policy, one must decide whether Outcome Y is good or bad. When economists make statements of the type "Outcome Y is good," they are engaging in **normative economics**.

Most economists do not consider themselves experts in ethical theory, and few would be prepared to defend their normative statements with the same rigor and clarity they would use to defend their positive economic analysis. Nonetheless, economists who wish to speak persuasively on the subject of economic policy should be able at least to point to some general ethical principles on which their normative conclusions might plausibly be based. Economists who base their like or dislike of a particular policy on arbitrary whims are less likely to be listened to than are those who speak in

Positive economics The part of economics limited to making scientific predictions and purely descriptive statements.

Empirical A term referring to data or methods based on observation of actual past experience or on controlled experiments.

Econometrician A specialist in the statistical analysis of economic data.

Normative economics The part of economics devoted to making value judgments about what economic policies or conditions are good or bad.

terms of consistent and well thought out values. With this in mind, we will look at a few basic ideas that frequently arise in discussions of normative economics.

Efficiency The property of producing or acting with a minimum of expense, waste, and effort.

The Efficiency Standard The standard of **efficiency** occupies a prominent place among those standards by which economists judge the performance of the systems they observe. In its most general sense, the word *efficiency* means the property of producing or acting with a minimum of expense, waste, and effort.

Efficiency and Equity Most economists think that efficiency itself is a good thing. This does not mean, however, that any policy promoting efficiency is automatically a good policy. Other norms and values must be introduced into policy analysis to supplement the efficiency standard. Among the most important of the supplementary standards are those referred to in everyday speech as equity, merit, and justice.

The standard of equity has two roles to play in relation to the standard of efficiency. First, it may be used to supplement the efficiency standard in cases where the choice is between policies that are equally efficient. Efficiency alone defines not a single, unique pattern of economic life but only a range of possible patterns. Different but equally efficient patterns often involve different distributions of welfare among specific individuals. In one efficient state of the world, Jones may be rich and Smith poor; in another, Smith may be rich and Jones poor; in a third, Jones and Smith may be equally well-off. When such alternatives confront us, we may be led to reason like this:

1. Policies X and Y produce equally efficient outcomes but imply different distributions of individual welfare.
2. The distributional outcome of Policy X is more equitable.
3. Therefore, let us undertake Policy X.

A second possible use for the criterion of equity is to override the criterion of efficiency. For many people, efficiency is a goal that should not be pursued at the expense of equity but that should, if needed, be sacrificed to the pursuit of equity. In such cases, the logic might run as follows:

1. Policy X would be bad for efficiency but would help achieve greater equity.
2. The loss of efficiency is unfortunate, but the gain in equity outweighs it.
3. Therefore, in the absence of a policy that will serve both goals at once, go ahead with Policy X.

A Difficulty Whichever way it is used, the concept of equity plays an important role in policy analysis. Using it, however, involves a difficulty that did not occur in the case of efficiency. The difficulty is that equity has no universally agreed-upon meaning. It means different things to different people, depending on the values they hold and the ideologies they profess. Few things are more harmful to intelligent debate on questions of economic policy than for the parties to a discussion to use the same word to mean different things. The word *equity* and the associated words *merit* and *justice* may be the cause of more misunderstandings than any other terms in economics.

In the interest of avoiding such misunderstandings, we might wish to establish beyond doubt that a particular meaning of *equity* is the right one. But to attempt it would take us deep into details of philosophy and far from the main subject of this book. Instead we will simply suggest two meanings of the equity concept (or two classes of meanings within which are many minor variations) without choosing between them.

Equity as Distributive Justice　The first meaning of *equity* equates it to **distributive justice**. The phrase "from each according to abilities, to each according to needs" gives a rough idea of what the principle of distributive justice means. The concept is based on the idea of innate merit; that is, all people are presumed — solely by virtue of their birth, their existence, and their common humanity — to merit some share of the total stream of goods and services turned out by the economic system. An improvement on the phrase is "to each according to innate merits."

Distributive justice The principle of distribution according to innate merit. Roughly, the principle of "from each according to abilities, to each according to needs."

Just what each person's innate merits are is a point that gives rise to many variations on the idea of distributive justice. For example, some people believe that all economic goods should be distributed equally among all members of society. Others think that a person's innate claims on economic goods ought to be limited to some minimum standard of living and are willing to see any surplus above this minimum distributed according to other principles. Still others conceive of innate merits as being limited to certain specific types of goods. Each person might have, for example, an innate claim to a share of food, shelter, medical care, and education, but no such claim to even a minimum share of tobacco, imported wine, or manufacturing services.

Equity as Market Justice　The second meaning of *equity* makes it equivalent to what can be called commutative justice, or more simply, **market justice**. The justice of the marketplace is *value for value*; market justice is based on the idea of acquired merit. Individuals have no innate claim to a share in the total economic output but merit only whatever share they acquire through production, exchange, or voluntary donation.

Market justice The principle of distribution according to acquired merit. The observance of property rights and the honoring of contracts. Roughly, the principle of "value for value."

The idea of market justice gives a special significance to the concepts of property and contract. Suppose that the entire mass of economic goods is divided up as the properties of specific individuals (or voluntary associations of individuals), so that for every loaf of bread, some person stands ready to say, "This bread is mine — my property to use and to exclude others from using." Then the central meaning of *market justice* becomes the movement of property from hand to hand only by fair contract (except for voluntary gifts). *Fair contract* means that each party must be satisfied that the value to him or her of the property received is at least as great as the value of the property given up. So market justice can be summed up as the observance of property rights and the honoring of contracts.

Economic Ideology

Each person carries out the job of policy analysis, whether in a systematic or a casual way, within a personal framework of thought that can be called

Economic ideology A set of judgments and beliefs concerning efficiency, market justice, and distributive justice as goals of economic policy, together with a set of prejudices or beliefs concerning matters of positive economics.

an **economic ideology**. An economic ideology includes a person's judgments concerning the relative priority (and exact interpretation) of distributive justice and market justice and attitudes toward the relative importance of equity and efficiency as goals of economic policy. Often, it also includes a set of prejudices and more or less rationally founded beliefs concerning matters of positive economics. Liberalism, Marxism, libertarianism, conservatism — these and many other "isms" are the labels we use to refer to economic ideologies.

To deal with every policy issue from all possible ideological points of view would be too much to attempt in this book. Instead, we will content ourselves for the most part with pointing out the implications of various policies in terms of the standards of efficiency and equity just discussed. People will have to reach their own conclusions on the ideological level.

Why Distinguish between Positive and Normative Economics?

When policy analysis is broken down into a three-step process in which positive and normative elements are clearly separated, orderly debate on important economic issues is made easier in several ways. First, the breakdown of policy analysis into positive and normative components makes it clear that disagreements on policy questions can arise from two different sources. If you and I disagree as to whether Policy X is good or bad, it may be either because we disagree on the positive issue of whether Policy X will, in fact, result in Outcome Y or because we disagree on the normative issue of whether Outcome Y is good or bad. Our analysis also indicates that a particular sort of spurious agreement could arise between us: You might think that Policy X will cause Outcome Y and that Y is good, whereas I might think Y is bad but that X will not cause it! This sort of thing occurs surprisingly often. In any event, it is clear that intelligent policy analysis requires careful thinking.

Second, if a positive statement is associated with an unpopular normative position, it is less likely to gain acceptance. Critics must be persuaded that both are valid. People are less likely to pay serious attention to the claim that fluoridation of water harms their bodies when its opponents also claim that fluoridation is an evil communist plot. A positive statement divorced from any normative view is not disadvantaged in this way.

Third, when a positive statement is associated with a popular normative position, it may be accepted too uncritically. Why? Because reactions to value judgments are much more pronounced than are reactions to positive statements, so that value judgments surreptitiously tend to dominate thought. People are all too likely to accept a "what is" statement from someone who agrees with them about "what ought to be." This natural reaction helps explain the inability of economists to persuade politicians that increases in the legal minimum wage have worsened the employment opportunities of poor people. Politicians say they want to help the poor and resent being informed that a method they support has not worked. Perhaps they even suspect that economists critical of minimum wages do not share their values. They apparently believe that minimum wage laws help the poor simply because they believe that the poor ought to be helped.

CONCLUSIONS

In a once-over fashion, this chapter has tried to give some idea of the kinds of things to which economists are sensitive when they look at the world around them. It has shown that economists think in terms of scarcity and choice. It has described the impact of some early features of Canada's economic history—particularly the concentration on staple production—on current economic problems and institutional behavior. It has explained how to distinguish between positive and normative economics and why that distinction is important. What can be said now to sum it all up?

If there is one single feature of overriding importance about the economic way of thinking, it is this: *economics is about people*. Individuals are the units of analysis in all economic theory. Every economic principle developed in this book must be a statement about the way individuals make choices, struggle with the problem of scarcity, and respond to changes in their environment. And all economic policies must be judged in terms of their impact on the welfare of individuals.

This does not mean that economists are all rugged individualists, in the sense that they are indifferent to social issues, or that they are political know-nothings who do not care about the national interest. What it does mean is that economic science (and all valid social science, for that matter) is based on the recognition that society and the nation have no existence and no importance apart from the individual human beings of which they are composed. Society is not a super-being, and the nation is not a sentient creature capable of feeling pain when a pin is stuck in the national thumb. *Society* and *nation* are only the names of groups of which all people are members. *We* are what economics is all about.

SUMMARY

1. Learning economics means learning to look at human actions and interactions in a special way, singling out some features for close examination and placing others in the background. The economic way of thinking places particular emphasis on how people's actions are influenced by the fact of scarcity and the necessity of choice.
2. All economic decisions can be described in terms of scarcity and choice. Limits on our choices are imposed by the availability of factors of production and our ability to take advantage of their most efficient combination.
3. The choices made by Canadians have been shaped by their economic history. Emphasis on staple production has resulted in regional instabilities, dependence on foreign investment and consumer markets, and considerable economic involvement by governments.
4. Positive economics cannot foretell the future, but it can offer scientific predictions in the form "if A occurs, then B will occur, other things being equal." Disputes in positive economics can, in principle, be resolved by reasoned discussion or by the examination of statistical data.
5. Normative economics is concerned with statements about what ought to be. Most economists think that efficiency is, in itself, a worthy goal of economic policy. The efficiency standard must, however, be supple-

mented by considerations of equity when policy decisions are to be made. There is no universal agreement on what equity means. Some economists maintain that equity is primarily a matter of distributive justice; others emphasize market justice. Partly becuase of such disagreements on the meaning of *equity*, economists try to distinguish carefully between their positive statements and their normative statements.

6. Economics is about people. All economic principles must be framed in terms of the way individuals make choices and respond to changes in their environment, and all economic policies must be judged in terms of their impact on the welfare of individuals.

DISCUSSION QUESTIONS

1. Suppose you want your grades to be as high as possible this term; yet your time and abilities are limited. Would it be possible to look at the way you spend your time as an economic problem? What constraints and alternative activities do you face?

2. Suppose you won a lottery prize of $20 million. Would this solve all your personal economic problems of scarcity? Explain.

3. Does Canada still rely heavily on the production of a few staple goods? If you think so, what products would you list as staples?

4. Can it be said that economics is about money or about goods and services rather than about people? Explain.

5. Do the animals in a forest face an economic problem? What are their objectives, constraints, and alternatives? What has happened to their economic problems as people have impinged on their habitat? Is economics about nonpeople too?

6. Should we all be entitled to our fair share of the earth's produce? Would this question be better stated if we replace "the earth's produce" with "the goods and services that Smith and Jones and Jansen and M'Boye and Li Ha Ching and... (listing all the earth's 4 billion people by name) produce"? To make it still easier, suppose that Smith and Jones are the only two people on earth. Is Smith entitled to a fair share of what Jones produces and vice versa?

APPENDIX TO CHAPTER 1
WORKING WITH GRAPHS

HOW ECONOMISTS USE GRAPHS

At one of our country's well-known colleges, the students have their own names for all the courses. They call the astronomy course "stars," the geology course "rocks," and the biology course "frogs." Their name for the economics course is "graphs and laughs." This choice of names indicates two things. First, it shows that the students think the professor has a sense of humor. Second, it shows that in the minds of students, economics is a matter of learning about graphs in the same sense that astronomy is a matter of learning about stars or geology a matter of learning about rocks.

To begin, then, we can say that economics is not about graphs; it is about people. It is about the way people make choices, use resources, and cooperate with one another in an effort to overcome the universal problem of scarcity. Economics is a social science, not an offshoot of analytic geometry.

The skeptical reader may reply, "If economics is not about graphs, why are there so many of them in this book?" The answer is that economists use graphs to illustrate the theories they develop about people's economic behavior in order to make them vivid, eye-catching, and easy to remember. Everything that can be said in the form of a graph can also be said in words, but saying something two different ways is a proven aid to learning. The purpose of this appendix is to show how to make maximum use of an important learning aid by explaining how to work with graphs.

PAIRS OF NUMBERS AND POINTS

The first thing to learn is how to use points on a graph to represent pairs of numbers. Consider Exhibit 1A.1. The small table in that exhibit presents six pairs of numbers. The two columns are labeled *x* and *y*. The first number in each pair is called the *x value*, and the second is called the *y value*. Each pair of numbers is labeled with a capital letter A through E. Pair A has an *x* value of 2 and a *y* value of 3; Pair B has an *x* value of 4 and a *y* value of 4, and so on.

Next to the table is a diagram. The lines placed at right angles to one another along the bottom and the left-hand side of the diagram are called *coordinate axes*. The horizontal axis is marked off into units and is used for measuring the *x* value, while the vertical axis is marked off into units for measuring the *y* value. In the space between these axes, each lettered pair of numbers from the table can be represented as a lettered point. For example, to put Point A in place, go two units to the right along the horizontal axis to represent the *x* value of 2 and then three units straight up, parallel to the vertical axis, to represent the *y* value of 3. The other points are placed the same way.

Usually, the visual effect of a graph is improved by connecting the points with a smooth line or curve. When this is done (as shown in the diagram), it can be seen at a glance that as the *x* value increases, the *y* value also tends to increase.

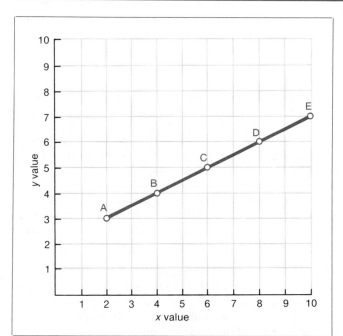

Exhibit 1A.1

Pairs of numbers and points

Each lettered pair of numbers in the table corresponds to a lettered point on the graph. The *x* value of each point corresponds to the horizontal distance of the point from the vertical axis, and the *y* value corresponds to the vertical distance from the horizontal axis.

	x	y
A	2	3
B	4	4
C	6	5
D	8	6
E	10	7

COMMON ECONOMIC GRAPHS

Economics is interested not in abstract relationships between x's and y's but in relationships concerning people and the things they do under various conditions. This means that graphs in economics are labeled in terms of the ideas used in putting together economic theories. Exhibit 1A.2 shows three common ways of labeling coordinate axes. Each of these will be encountered many times in this book.

Exhibit 1A.2a represents the relationship between the price of subway tokens in some city and the number of people who choose to ride the subway each day at any given price. The table shows that as the price of tokens goes up, fewer people choose to ride the subway. The graph shows the same thing. As a matter of tradition in economics, whenever a graph involves both money values and quantity units, the vertical axis is used to measure the money value (in this case, the price of subway tokens) and the horizontal axis to measure the quantity units (in this case, the number of riders per day).

Exhibit 1A.2b uses quantity units on both axes. Here, the problem is to represent the various combinations of milkshakes and hamburgers that can be bought at the local carry-out when milkshakes cost $.50 each, hamburgers cost $.50 each, and the buyer has exactly $2.50 to spend on lunch. The table shows that the possibilities are five burgers and no shakes, four burgers and one shake, three burgers and two shakes, and so on.

The graph offers a visual picture of the "menu" to choose from, given limited money to spend. The points from the table are drawn in and labeled, and any can be chosen. A diagonal line has been sketched in to connect these points, and if the purchase of parts of hamburgers and milkshakes is allowed, the buyer can choose from among all the points along this line (for example, 2.5 burgers and 2.5 shakes). The buyer who wanted to have some money left over could purchase a lunch represented by a point within the shaded area, such as Point G (which stands for two burgers and one shake and costs just $1.50). But unless the buyer gets more money, points outside the shaded area cannot be chosen.

Exhibit 1A.2c illustrates still another kind of graph frequently used in economics — one showing how some magnitude varies over time. This graph indicates what happened to the unemployment rate of young males over the years 1969–78. The horizontal axis is used to represent the passage of time and the vertical axis to measure the percentage of young males officially classified as unemployed. Graphs like this are good for getting a quick idea of trends over time. Although young male unemployment has had its ups and downs in recent years, the trend during the last four years was clearly upward.

SLOPES

When talking about graphs, it is frequently convenient to describe lines or curves in terms of their *slopes*. The slope of a straight line drawn between two points is defined as the ratio of the change in the y value to the change in the x value between two points. In Exhibit 1A.3, for example, the slope of the line drawn between Points A and B is 2. The y value changes by six units between these two points, while the x value changes by only three units. The slope is the ratio 6/3 = 2.

When a line slants downward like the line between Points C and D in Exhibit 1A.3, the x value and the y value change in opposite directions. Going from Point C to Point D, the y value changes by −2 (that is, it decreases by two units), while the x value changes by +4 (that is, it increases by four units). The slope of this line is the ratio −2/4 = −1/2. A downward-sloping line such as this is said to have a negative slope.

The slope of a curved line, unlike that of a straight line, varies from point to point. The slope of a curve at any given point is defined as the slope of a straight line drawn tangent to the curve at that point. (A tangent line is one just touching the curve without crossing it). Consider the curve in Exhibit 1A.4. Applying the definition, the slope of this line at Point A is 1, and the slope at Point B is −2.

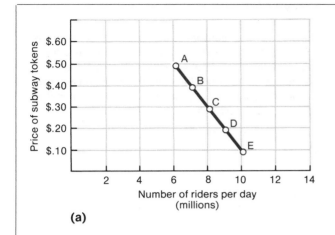

(a)

	Price of Subway Tokens	Number of Riders per Day (Millions)
A	$.50	6
B	$.40	7
C	$.30	8
D	$.20	9
E	$.10	10

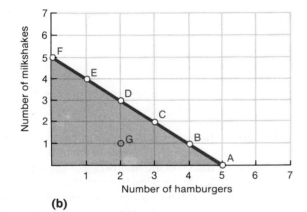

(b)

	Number of Hamburgers	Number of Milkshakes
A	5	0
B	4	1
C	3	2
D	2	3
E	1	4
F	0	5

(c)

Year	Unemployment Rate Males, 15-24 Years Old
1969	8.3%
1970	11.2
1971	12.0
1972	11.9
1973	10.0
1974	9.6
1975	12.5
1976	13.3
1977	14.9
1978	15.1
1979	13.4

Exhibit 1A.2

Three typical economic graphs

This exhibit shows three graphs typical of those used in economics. Part a shows the relationship between the price of tokens and the number of riders per day on a certain city subway system. When a graph shows the relationship between a price and a quantity, it is conventional to put the price on the vertical axis. Part b shows the possible choices open to a person who has $2.50 to spend on lunch and can buy hamburgers at $.50 each or milkshakes at $.50 each. Part c shows how a graph can be used to represent change over time.

Source: Part c is from Department of Finance, *Economic Review,* April 1980, p. 196.

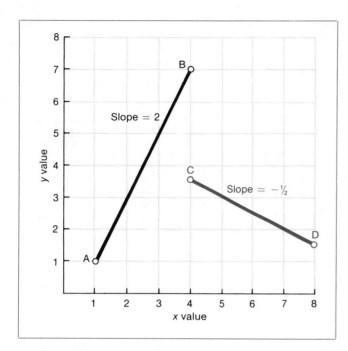

Exhibit 1A.3
Slopes of lines
The slope of a straight line drawn between two points is defined as the ratio of the change in the *y* value to the change in the *x* value between the two points. For example, the line drawn between Points A and B in this exhibit has a slope of +2, whereas the line drawn between Points C and D has a slope of −1/2.

ABSTRACT GRAPHS

In all the examples so far, we have had specific numbers to work with for the *x* and *y* values. Sometimes, though, we know only the general nature of the relationship between two economic magnitudes rather than specific numbers. For example, we might know that when people's incomes rise, they tend to increase their consumption of meat rapidly at first. But then, as they reach very high incomes, their meat consumption levels off. If we want to represent a relationship like this without caring about the numbers involved, we draw a graph like that shown in Exhibit 1A.5. The vertical axis is labeled "quantity of meat consumed per month," without any specific units. The horizontal axis is labeled "income," again without specific

Exhibit 1A.4
Slopes of curves
The slope of a curve at any given point is defined as the slope of a straight line drawn tangent to the curve at that point. A tangent line is one that just touches the curve without crossing it. In this exhibit, the slope of the curve at Point A is 1, and the slope of the curve at Point B is −2.

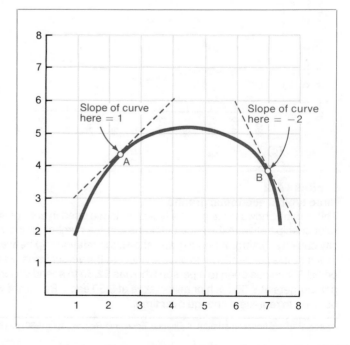

Exhibit 1A.5

An abstract graph

When we know the general form of an economic relationship but do not know the exact numbers involved, we can draw an abstract graph. Here, we know that as people's incomes rise, their consumption of meat increases rapidly at first, then levels off. Because we do not know the exact numbers for meat consumption or income, we have not marked any units on the axes.

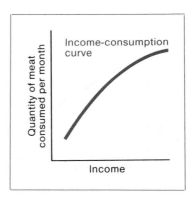

units. The curve, which rises rapidly at first and then levels off, tells us the general nature of the relationship between income and meat consumption: when income goes up, meat consumption rises, but not in proportion to the change in income. We will use abstract graphs like this one very frequently in this book. Abstract graphs express general principles, whereas graphs with numbers on the axes summarize specific known information.

STUDY HINTS FOR GRAPHS

When you come to a chapter in the book that is full of graphs, how should you study it? The first and most important rule is not to worry about memorizing graphs. I have never taught economics without having at least one student come to me after failing an exam and say: "But I learned every one of those graphs! What happened?" I always tell the students that they should have learned economics instead of learning the graphs.

Here are some specific study hints for working with graphs: after reading carefully through a chapter that uses graphs frequently, go back through the graphs one at a time. Place your hand over the explanatory note that appears beside each graph and try putting what the graph says into words. If you cannot say at least as much about the graph as the explanatory note does, read the text over again.

If you do all right going from graphs to words, half the battle is won. Next, try covering up the graph, and using the explanatory note as a guide, sketch the graph on a piece of scratch paper. If you understand what the words mean and can comfortably go back and forth between the words and the graphs, you will find out that the two together are much easier to remember and apply than either would be separately. If you "learn the graphs" as meaningless patterns of lines, you are lost.

CONSTRUCTING YOUR OWN GRAPHS

For some students, the hardest kind of question to answer on an exam is the kind that requires construction of an original graph as part of an essay answer. Here are some hints for constructing your own graphs:

1. Put down the answer to the question in words. If you cannot do that, you might as well skip to the next question without wasting time on the graph. Try underlining the most important quantities in what you have written. The result might be something like: "The larger the *number of students* who attend a university, the lower the *cost per student* of providing them with an education."

2. Decide how you are going to label the coordinate axes of your graph. In our example, because it is conventional to put money values on the vertical axis, we label the vertical axis "cost per student" and the horizontal axis "number of students."

3. Do you have exact numbers to work with? If you do, your next step should be to make a table showing what you know and then to use that to sketch your graph. If you do not have numbers, you will be drawing an abstract graph. In this case, all you know is that the cost per student goes down when the number of students

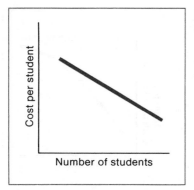

Exhibit 1A.6
Constructing a graph
To construct a graph, first put down in words what you want to say: "The larger the *number of students* at a university, the lower the *cost per student* of providing them with an education." Next, label the coordinate axes. Then, if you have exact numbers to work with, construct a table. Here we have no exact numbers, so we draw an abstract graph that slopes downward to show the cost goes down as numbers go up. For graphs with more than one curve, repeat these steps.

goes up. Sketch in any convenient downward-sloping line (as in Exhibit 1A.6), and you will have done as well as can be done.

4. If your graph involves more than one relationship between pairs of economic quantities, repeat steps 1 to 3 for each relationship that you want to represent by a line or curve. When sketching graphs with more than one curve, pay particular attention to points where you think two curves ought to intersect (which will happen whenever both the *x* and *y* values of the two relationships are equal) and where you think they ought to be tangent (which will happen whenever the slopes of two curves are equal).

5. After your graph is completed, try translating it back into words. Does it really say what you wanted to say?

A REMINDER

As you work through this book and are introduced to various specific kinds of graphs, turn back to this appendix now and then. Do not commit the fatal error of memorizing graphs as meaningless pictures. Remember that if you can go back and forth between graphs and words, the underlying theory that both are trying to express will stay with you more vividly than if you rely on either graphs or words alone. Remember that economics is about *people*, not graphs.

SUGGESTIONS FOR FURTHER READING

Easterbrook, W.T., and Aitken, Hugh G.J. *Canadian Economic History*. Toronto: Macmillan, 1956.
Though published more than two decades ago, still (1980) the most comprehensive treatment of Canadian economic history.

Easterbrook, W.T., and Watkins, Melville (eds.). *Approaches to Canadian Economic History*. Toronto: McClelland and Stewart, 1967.
Contains interesting essays by a number of economic historians, including Harold Innis, on the interpretation of Canadian economic history. Part One includes several useful descriptions of the staples approach to our economic history.

Heilbroner, Robert L. *The Wordly Philosophers*. New York: Simon and Schuster, 1980.
A popular, well-written, and reliable guide to the thought of leading economists, past and present.

Koopmans, Tialling C. "Economics among the Sciences." *American Economic Review* 69 (March 1979) pp. 1–13.
A thought-provoking presidential address to the American Economics Association organized around several fascinating case studies.

Robbins, Lionel C. *An Essay on the Nature and Significance of Economic Science*. 2d rev. ed. London: Macmillan, 1935.
The classic treatment of the topic.

C H A P T E R 2

THE BASIS OF TRADE, THE PRICE SYSTEM, AND THE MARKET ECONOMY

WHAT YOU WILL LEARN IN THIS CHAPTER

This chapter will explain the basis for specialization and trade within and between modern economies. It will introduce the role played by markets in determining what is produced, how it is produced, and for whom it is produced. The chapter will explain each of three functions of markets: transmitting knowledge, providing incentives, and distributing income. It will show how the price system broadcasts information on opportunity costs and relative scarcities to buyers, how prices at the same time provide incentives to resource owners and entrepreneurs to put resources to best use, and how the incentive system operates to determine individuals' incomes. It will also introduce the questions of whether the market distributes income fairly and why it does not always operate perfectly. These questions will recur frequently as the discussion of economics progresses.

FOR REVIEW

Here are some important terms and concepts that will be put to use in this chapter. If you do not understand them, review them before proceeding.
- *Scarcity and choice (Chapter 1)*
- *Factors of production (Chapter 1)*
- *Positive and normative economics (Chapter 1)*
- *Market justice and distributive justice (Chapter 1)*

OPPORTUNITY COST AND THE PRODUCTION POSSIBILITY FRONTIER

When economists speak of the **allocation of resources**, they mean the determination of *what* will be produced, *how* it will be produced, *who* will produce it, and *for whom* it will be produced. In Canada people can choose from a wide range of occupations and produce a variety of goods and services. Because of scarcity of time and resources, the decision to pursue a particular vocation or produce a particular good involves the sacrifice of other possible activities and goods. Economists call this **opportunity cost**. The opportunity cost of doing something is the loss of the opportunity to do the next best thing instead, with the same time or resources.

How much, for example, does it cost to go to university? The direct, out-of-pocket expense for tuition, books, and room and board might come

Allocation of resources Determination of what will be produced, how it will be produced, who will produce it, and for whom it will be produced.

Opportunity cost The cost of doing something as measured by the loss of the opportunity to do the next best thing instead, with the same amount of time or resources.

to about $5,000. However, if attending university meant the sacrifice of a job yielding $7,000 for the seven-month study period, the real opportunity cost of attending university would be $12,000. In addition to the $5,000 of past income sacrificed, an additional $7,000 of potential income would be lost during university attendance. It is clear that in any decision we make, we trade off one opportunity or good for another. This is as true for a business firm or a national government as it is for an individual.

To see this more clearly, assume that a particular region of Canada, the Maritimes, can produce only two goods, grain and fish. Given existing factors of production, the Maritimes can produce various combinations of these goods.

Even if all people in the Maritimes devoted all their time and resources to fish, there would be a limit to the quantity of fish that could be produced each year. For the sake of illustration, suppose that this limit is 20 million pounds. The extreme possibility of producing 20 million pounds of fish in one year and nothing else is shown by Point A, in Exhibit 2.1 Assume that the maximum rate of output of grain if no resources at all are put into fish is 1,000 million bushels, shown by Point B. Between these two extremes is a range of possibilities for producing fish and grain in combination. These intermediate possibilities are represented by points such as C and D, which fall along the curve in the diagram. This curve is the **production possibility frontier**.

Production possibility frontier A curve showing the possible combinations of goods that can be produced by an economy, given the quantity and quality of factors of production available.

It is a frontier because it is a boundary between the combinations of fish and grain that can be produced and the combinations that cannot possibly be produced. Points A, B, C, and D, which lie right on the curve, represent combinations of fish and grain that can be produced. A combination such as that represented by Point E, in the shaded area within the production possibility frontier, can be produced even if some factors of production remain unemployed or are used wastefully. For example, labor is used

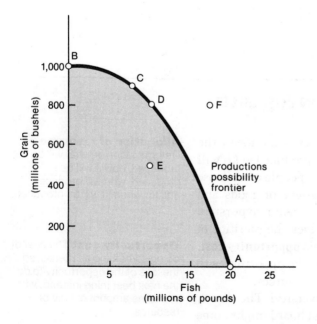

Exhibit 2.1
A production possibility frontier for fish and grain
This diagram shows a production possibility frontier for fish and grain. Point A represents the maximum production of fish if no grain is produced, and Point B represents the maximum production of grain if no fish are taken. A, B, C, D, and all other points along the frontier, as well as points such as E in the shaded area under it, are possible. Points such as F, outside the frontier, are not possible given the quantity and quality of resources available.

inefficiently if people are used for jobs to which they are not suited, or if their use is temporarily halted by strikes or limited by monopolies which restrict entry to a particular labor market.

In contrast, a combination of fish and grain such as that represented by Point F cannot possibly be produced in one year without increasing the population, developing new resources, or improving the technology of the region. Therefore, at a given point in time all combinations outside the shaded area are impossible.

At any point along the production frontier, there is a trade-off between fish and grain. More of one cannot be produced without giving up some of the other. For example, suppose we began at Point C, where 8 million pounds of fish are produced each year and 900 million bushels of grain are produced. If we wanted to increase the output of fish to 10 million pounds per year, we would have to give up some grain and use those resources to build extra ships, nets, and processing plants. That would move us to Point D, which represents 10 million pounds of fish and only 800 million bushels of wheat.

Now we can see how the production possibility curve allows us to visualize the concept of opportunity costs. In moving from C to D on the production possibility frontier, 2 million extra pounds of fish can be obtained at the opportunity cost of 100 million bushels of grain. Putting this on a per-pound-of-fish basis, the opportunity cost of fish production in the range between C and D is approximately 50 bushels of grain per additional pound. Geometrically, the opportunity cost of fish in terms of grain is given by the slope of the production possibility frontier.

Why is the Production Possibility Frontier Curved?

Why is the production possibility frontier a curve rather than a straight line? If it were a straight line, this would mean that the opportunity cost of producing an additional pound of fish, measured as a loss of grain production, would be the same no matter how people chose to divide their efforts and resources between fish and grain. When opportunity costs are constant, each additional unit of output of one good requires a specific and unchanging amount of sacrifice of other goods, as resources are shifted from one use to another. For the analysis of some problems, it is useful to assume constant opportunity cost, but it is highly unlikely that this situation would occur in actual practice. Why?

The answer is that factors of production are not **homogeneous**. That is, individual units of any factor are not all alike. Some are suited to specializing in the production of one thing, others are suited to something else.

Homogeneous Having the property that every unit is just like every other unit.

To see why this puts a curve in the production possibility frontier, imagine that starting today the Maritimes wanted to increase the output of fish. The first thing it would need would be more fishermen. The opportunity cost of getting the first few fishermen would be low. Farmers on marginal land, not very interested in farming, could be recruited. Later, however, people and resources more suited to farming would be transferred to fishing. The opportunity cost of fishing would rise, and the production possibility curve would begin to bend as we moved along it.

Soon we would have to start calling in people who were not at all qualified to be fishermen, even though they might be doing a good job at farming. A man who had spent his life tending fields and who had never been in a boat or worked in a fish processing plant might be expected to be much more productive on a farm than in the fishing industry. As more and more unqualified people were moved to fishing, the production possibility frontier would bend still more sharply. In short, differences of ability and specialization among people as well as differences among units of other factors of production can be counted on to give the production possibility frontier its typical bowed shape.

The swelling out of the production possibility frontier from the origin illustrates what economists call the **law of increasing costs**.

Law of increasing costs As resources are shifted from one use to another, an additional unit of output of one good requires an increasing rate of sacrifice of other goods as greater and greater shifts occur.

Economic Growth and the Production Possibility Frontier

It is important to note that the limits on our range of choice illustrated by a given production possibility frontier apply only as long as available quantities and qualities of factors of production do not change. If such factors improve with time, the frontier will expand and shift to the right, as shown in Exhibit 2.2.

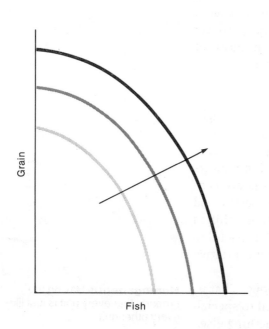

Exhibit 2.2
Expanding production possibility frontier
The position of the production possibility frontier at any point in time depends on the quantity and quality of the factors of production available. As time goes by, population grows, new capital is accumulated, and technological change takes place, permitting the production possibility frontier to shift outward, as indicated by the arrow in this diagram.

The quality of labor and entrepreneurship characteristic of a given population improves as people become healthier and better educated. The quality of capital increases dramatically as technological change improves equipment and brings in new methods of production. Only natural resources do not undergo qualitative improvements; in fact, many actually decline in quality as they are depleted by use. So far, the increases in quantity and quality of other factors have more than made up for the depletion of natural resources in advanced industrial countries.

In less developed countries it is sometimes extremely difficult to shift the production possibility frontier to the right. Given the scarcity of resources, increases in capital investment require some sacrifice in consumption. But in nations where consumption is already very low, no further sacrifices are possible. Economic growth remains for such nations a frustrating dream.

SPECIALIZATION AND TRADE

Regions like the Maritimes are able to produce a wide range of goods besides grain and fish, but economic theory can be used to show that it might pay them to specialize in the production of a few goods, and obtain other necessary goods through trade.

To illustrate this, let us create a simplified model of Canada, made up of two regions: the Maritimes and the Prairies. Both regions are assumed to have farms and fishing resources, but the more moderate climate of the Maritimes and their proximity to Atlantic spawning grounds happen to make both their farms and their fishing beds more productive than those on the Prairies. The number of labor hours required to produce a ton of each product in the two regions is shown in Exhibit 2.3. For simplicity, we shall consider only labor cost in this example. We shall think of other costs as proportional to labor costs. Further, we shall assume per-unit labor costs to be constant for all levels of output.

Exhibit 2.3
Labor hours per ton of output in the Maritimes and the Prairies
The figures in this table show the number of labor hours required to produce each ton of fish and grain in the Maritimes and the Prairies. The Maritimes have an absolute advantage in the production of both goods.

	Maritimes	Prairies
Fish	2	5
Grain	4	5

Absolute Advantage and Comparative Advantage

Exhibit 2.3 reveals two kinds of differences in the cost structure of the two regions. First, *both* fish and grain require fewer labor hours to produce in the Maritimes. The Maritimes are said to have an **absolute advantage** in the production of both goods. Second, there are differences in the opportunity costs between the two regions. In the Prairies, producing a ton of fish means foregoing the opportunity to use 5 labor hours in the fields. A ton of fish thus has an opportunity cost of 1 ton of grain there. In the Maritimes, producing a ton of fish means giving up the opportunity to produce 1/2 ton of grain. In terms of opportunity costs, then, fish are cheaper in the Maritimes than in the Prairies. On the other hand, in terms of opportunity cost, grain is cheaper in the Prairies—where 1 ton of grain requires giving up 1 ton of fish—than in the Maritimes—where 1 ton of grain costs 2 tons of fish. The region in which the opportunity cost of a good is lower is said to have a **comparative advantage** in producing that good.

Absolute advantage In trade theory, the ability of a region or country to produce a good at absolutely lower cost, measured in terms of factor inputs, than its trading partners.

Comparative advantage In trade theory, the ability of a region or country to produce a good at lower opportunity cost, measured in terms of other foregone goods, than its trading partners.

Pretrade Equilibrium

If no trade takes place between the Prairies and the Maritimes, equilibrium in the fish and grain markets in each region will be established independently. We have simplified things by ignoring all costs but labor costs. Further, to keep the example clear, we have assumed that these costs are constant, even though, as we have seen on p. 25, this is an unrealistic assumption in real-world situations. In pretrade equilibrium, the ratio of the price of fish to the price of grain in each region will thus be equal to the ratio of labor inputs needed to produce the goods. In the Prairies, where a ton of grain and a ton of fish both take the same labor to produce, the price of fish will be equal to the price of grain. In the Maritimes, where a ton of fish takes half as much labor to produce as a ton of grain, the equilibrium price of fish will be half the price of grain.

Suppose that each region has 1,000 labor hours available for production of fish and grain. This information allows us to construct a production possibility frontier for each region, as illustrated in Exhibit 2.4. The straight-line frontiers reflect the special assumption of this example that costs of the goods in terms of each other remain constant as labor resources are shifted from one good to another in each region.

Exhibit 2.4

Production possibility frontier for the Maritimes and the Prairies, assuming 1,000 labor hours for each region

With 1,000 labor hours the Maritimes can, in the extreme, produce 500 tons of fish or 250 tons of grain. The Prairies with the same amount of labor can produce 200 tons of fish or 200 tons of grain.

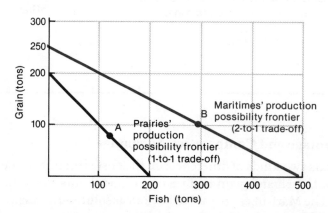

Since it takes 2 hours of labor in the Maritimes to produce a ton of fish, and 4 hours of labor to produce a ton of grain, the Maritimes can produce a maximum of 500 tons of fish or 250 tons of grain, or a combination of the two goods as indicated by the production possibility frontier. Because the Prairies require 5 hours of labor for each ton of grain or fish, producers there can produce, at a maximum, only 200 tons of fish or 200 tons of grain, or a combination of the two goods as indicated by their frontier. The slopes of the production possibility frontiers reflect the trade-off (opportunity cost) between the goods in each region. One ton of grain can be traded off for two tons of fish in the Maritimes, while a ton of grain can be traded off for a ton of fish in the Prairies.

The amount of each good produced in each region, before specialization and trade, will depend on demand and consumer tastes. Suppose that demand conditions are such that in the Prairies 80 tons of grain and 120 tons of fish are produced (Point A in Exhibit 2.4), while in the Maritimes 300 tons of fish and 100 tons of grain are produced (Point B in Exhibit 2.4). The quantities produced and consumed in pretrade equilibrium are noted in Exhibit 2.5

Exhibit 2.5
Pretrade equilibrium production of fish and grain in the Maritimes and the Prairies
If the Maritimes and the Prairies do not engage in trade, each region will have to meet all its needs from its own resources. The quantities of goods produced in each region depend on the strength of regional demand. The relative prices of the two goods in each region will be determined by their labor costs, as shown in Exhibit 2.3.

	Maritimes	Prairies	Total for Country
Fish (tons)	300	120	420
Grain (tons)	100	80	180

The Possibility of Trade

The stage is now set to consider the possibilities for trade between the Maritimes and the Prairies. A superficial look at labor costs might make us think there were no possibilities for trade. Prairie consumers might like the opportunity to buy some of those cheap Maritime goods, but why should Maritimers be interested? After all, can they not produce everything in their own region more cheaply than it can be produced in the Prairies? If so, how could they gain from trade? A closer look will show us.

Imagine that an enterprising merchant in the Prairies decides to send a carload of grain to the Maritimes. The Maritimers have been used to giving 2 tons of fish for 1 ton of grain. Prairie farmers have been accustomed to getting only 1 ton of fish for 1 ton of grain. Any exchange ratio between 1 and 2 tons of fish per ton of grain will seem attractive to both parties. For instance, a trade of 1 1/2 tons of fish for 1 ton of grain will make both the Prairie merchant and the Maritime fish producer better off than they would have been had they traded only with others from their own region. Absolute advantage turns out to be unimportant in determining patterns of trade. Only comparative advantage matters.

Gains From Specialization and Trade

The opening of trade between the Prairies and the Maritimes will soon begin to have an effect on patterns of production in the two regions. In the Prairies, fishermen will discover that instead of working 5 hours to catch 1 ton of fish, they can work 5 hours on a farm and exchange the 1 ton of grain they get for 1 1/2 tons of fish from the Maritimes. In the Maritimes, people will find that it is no longer worth their while to spend 4 hours on the farm to produce 1 ton of grain. Instead, they can fish for 3 hours to catch 1 1/2 tons of fish to exchange for 1 ton of grain from the Prairies. In short, Prairie people will find it advantageous to specialize in grain and Maritimers will find it advantageous to specialize in fish.

Suppose now that trade continues at the ratio of 1 1/2 tons of fish per ton of grain, until both regions have become completely specialized. The Maritimes no longer produce any grain and the Prairies no longer produce any fish. The Prairies grow 200 tons of grain, 110 tons of which are shipped to the Maritimes. Maritimers in turn catch 500 tons of fish, 165 tons of which are traded to the Prairies. Exhibit 2.6 summarizes their posttrade situations.

Exhibit 2.6
Posttrade production and consumption of fish and grain in the Prairies and the Maritimes, in tons
It is assumed that they traded 1 1/2 tons of fish for 1 ton of grain. Both are completely specialized. In comparison with pretrade output, shown here in brackets, production in the country has increased, and each region's consumption has increased.

		Maritimes	Prairies	Total for Country Posttrade	Pretrade
Fish	Production	500	0	500	(420)
	Consumption	335	165	500	
Grain	Production	0	200	200	(180)
	Consumption	110	90	200	

A comparison of Exhibit 2.6 with Exhibit 2.5 reveals three noteworthy things. First, it shows that Prairie people are better off after trade than before. They have 45 more tons of fish to eat, and 10 more tons of grain. Second, it shows that Maritimers, too, are better off. They have 10 more tons of grain to consume, and 35 more tons of fish. Finally, the last columns of the tables reveal that total national output of both grain and fish has risen as a result of specialization and trade. In short, everyone is better off.

Generalized Mutual Advantage

The principle of mutual advantage from specialization and trade applies to different countries as well as to regions within a country. It is the rational economic basis for international as well as domestic trade. Wherever one country has a comparative advantage over another in producing some good, specialization can increase consumption in each country, and both national and international output can be increased.

It will be observed in several places in this book that Canada's international trade plays a vital role in its economy. Our nation undoubtedly derives great benefit from it and is also subject to some special pressures and problems because of it. There is, however, no need for a special *theory* of international trade. In our previous illustrations, the names of entire countries, such as Portugal and Canada, could have been substituted for the "Maritimes" and the "Prairies," and the same results would have been obtained. That is because the same principles apply. It makes no difference whether buyers and sellers live on the same or opposite sides of political boundaries, as far as the application of the theory of comparative advantage is concerned.

Trade and Markets

One major precondition for trade of any kind has not yet been examined. If people are to be able to specialize and trade with each other, there must be a coordinating mechanism that brings buyers and sellers together. In the Canadian economy, markets play a central role in providing the necessary coordination. **Markets** are the various arrangements people have for trading with one another. They may be elaborately organized, like the Toronto Stock Exchange or the Winnipeg Commodity Exchange, which match up the sellers and buyers of respectively, corporation securities and basic agricultural and mining commodities, or informal, like the word-of-mouth network that puts teenage babysitters in touch with people who need their services. But however markets are organized, they perform certain common functions: transmitting information, providing incentives, and distributing income. In the following section, case studies will clarify the way widely varied markets carry out these functions.

Markets All the various arrangements people have for trading with one another.

THE FUNCTIONS OF MARKETS

Information and Its Value

Information is the most precious good in any economy. Economic prosperity depends on putting resources to their best uses, and, to do this, the people who make decisions on how resources are to be used must know which uses are best. Like water, economic information is taken for granted when it is cheap and abundant. Its importance becomes apparent only when it is scarce, as the following case study illustrates.

Case 2.1
The Role of Information in the Bazaar Economy

At the foot of the Atlas Mountains in Morocco sits the ancient walled town of Sefrou. Once an important stop on the caravan route from Fez to the Sahara, it has been, for about a century now, an important *bazaar*, or market center, for some 15,000 to 30,000 people. Since the mid 1960s, anthropologist Clifford Geertz of the Institute for Advanced Study has been observing the bazaar at Sefrou. What he has discovered is instructive.

According to Geertz, information in the bazaar is poor, scarce, maldistributed, inefficiently communicated, and intensely valued. The level of ignorance about everything from product quality and going prices to market possibilities and production costs is very high. The name of the game in the bazaar is the search for information a person lacks and the protection of information a person has. As in any other economy, capital, skill, luck, privilege, and hard work contribute to individual success; but in the bazaar they do it not so much by increasing the efficiency of production as by enabling a person to secure a strategic location in the market's communications network. The primary problem facing participants in the bazaar is not to balance options but to find out what they are.

Geertz interprets the central features that distinguish the bazaar from a modern, industrialized market economy as responses to the scarcity of information. One of these features is bargaining. In a system where virtually nothing is packaged, standardized, or regulated, every transaction must be preceded by elaborate bargaining over price, quantity, quality, and credit terms. During the bargaining, buyers and sellers naturally try to conceal their minimum acceptable terms from one another, but at the same time they must manage to reveal enough information to form a basis for a mutually advantageous trade.

At this point, the efficiency of the bazaar is apparently improved by a second characteristic feature, which Geertz calls "clientalization." By this he means a tendency of buyers to return repeatedly to the same seller to engage in intensive bargaining rather than to search quickly but extensively among many sellers for the best price. Evidently, repeated bargaining within a stable client-seller relationship improves information exchange by enough to offset any loss of information resulting from frequent examination of alternative sources of supply.

In Geertz's view, the whole structure of the bazaar can be viewed as a set of communications channels designed to serve the needs of people whose interests are opposed in the act of bargaining but joined by the need to coordinate their economic activities. The same is true of any economic system; but since information is relatively scarce in the bazaar, its value is more prominently displayed.

Source: Based on Clifford Geertz, "The Bazaar Economy: Information and Search in Peasant Marketing." *American Economic Review* 68 (May 1978) pp. 28–32. Used by permission.

The Price System

In the Canadian economy of today, bargaining and client-seller relation-ships are by no means unknown. Their importance as channels for the transmission of information, however, is completely overshadowed by another mechanism that exists only in rudimentary form in the bazaar economy. This mechanism is the *price system*. In the modern economy, prices typically are not subject to bargaining on a one-to-one basis between buyer and seller every time a transaction is made. Instead, they are widely advertised and published as an invitation to any buyer to enter the market on equal terms with other buyers. The price system is essentially a system for broadcasting information on opportunity costs and on the relative scarcity of various goods and services. A rise in the price of any good relative to the price of other goods signals increasing scarcity of that good. A fall in the price of any good (or, in times of inflation, a failure of its price to rise as fast as the prices of other goods) signals increasing abundance. Buyers can adjust their behavior accordingly.

The following case, supplied by Nobel prize-winning economist F. A. Hayek, brings out the contrast between the price system and the bazaar system. In Hayek's example, prices are the cheap and easily available source of information used by buyers to adjust to complex events occurring far away.

Case 2.2
Information and the Price System

Assume that somewhere in the world a new opportunity for the use of some raw material, say tin, has arisen, or that one of the sources of supply of tin has been eliminated. It does not matter for our purpose—and it is very significant that it does not matter—which of these two causes has made tin more scarce. All that the users of tin need to know is that some of the tin they used to consume is now more profitably employed elsewhere, and that in consequence they must economize tin. There is no need for the great majority of them even to know where the more urgent need has arisen, or in favor of what other needs they ought to husband the supply. If only some of them know directly of the new demand, and switch resources over to it, and if the people who are aware of the new gap thus created in turn fill it from still other sources, the effect will rapidly spread throughout the whole economic system and influence not only the uses of tin, but also those of its substitutes and the substitutes of these substitutes, the supply of the things made of tin, and their substitutes, and so on, and all this without the great majority of those instrumental in bringing about these substitutions knowing anything at all about the original cause of these changes. The whole acts as one market, not because any of its members survey the whole field, but because their limited individual fields of vision sufficiently overlap so that through many intermediaries the relevant information is communicated to all.

Source: Reprinted by permission from F. A. Hayek, "The Use of Knowledge in Society," *American Economic Review* 35 (September 1945) pp. 519–530.

By informing people of the value and scarcity of tin, wheat, forklift trucks, and hundreds of thousands of other commodities, the price system reduces countless decisions to the level of pure economizing. Producers and consumers can observe market prices, combine them with their own knowledge of local circumstances, and arrive at valid judgments about the advantages and disadvantages of various production and consumption activities. To be sure, there is more to economic decision making than pure economizing, and the price system does not supply the answers to all economic questions. But entrepreneurial talents and energies, which in a bazaar economy are used up merely in finding out how much things cost, are now liberated to deal with the problem of finding new and better ways of doing things.

Incentives in the Market Economy

Knowledge of the best use of resources is a necessary condition for efficient coordination of economic activity, but it is not by itself sufficient. In addition to knowing the uses to which resources should be put, the people controlling them must have incentives to devote them to the known best use. Providing those incentives is the second major function of markets. As Adam Smith wrote more than two hundred years ago:

It is not from the benevolence of the butcher, the brewer, or the baker that we expect our dinner, but from their regard to their own interest.... Every individual is continually exerting himself to find out the most advantageous employment for whatever capital he can command.... By directing that industry in such a manner as its produce may be of the greater value, he intends only his own gain, and he is in this, as in many other cases, led by an invisible hand to promote an end which was no part of his intention.

The market offers different kinds of incentives to different people. Consumers who keep themselves well informed and spend their money judiciously are rewarded by the satisfaction of more needs with their limited budgets. Workers earn higher incomes if they stay alert to job market opportunities and work where their productivity is highest. Real estate brokers earn higher commissions the more efficiently they match suitable buyers and sellers. In every case, people who acquire economic information have an incentive to act on that information and not just file it away.

No doubt the most famous of incentives in the market economy is the profit motive. Profits make up a relatively small part of all income received by individuals. As officially measured by government statisticians, wages and salaries outweigh corporate profits by more than ten to one. But profits have an importance entirely out of proportion to their magnitude because they are the reward earned by entrepreneurs for properly coordinating the contributions of workers and other resource owners. A business firm earns a profit by buying inputs at their market prices and using them to produce a product that can be sold for more than the cost of all the inputs. And just as the market rewards firms that use resources productively, it penalizes those who use them wastefully. If the value of the inputs a firm buys exceeds the value of the product it makes out of those inputs, that firm will suffer a loss and will eventually disappear from the market.

**Friedrich August von Hayek
(1899–)**

In 1944, a slim volume entitled *The Road to Serfdom* burst onto the world's best seller list. This book warned that an enthusiasm for economic planning and strong central government was leading Western democracies down a path that, if not checked, could end in Soviet- or Nazi-style totalitarianism. The author of the book was as surprised as anyone to find it a best seller. He was Friedrich von Hayek, then a professor at the London School of Economics.

Hayek, born and educated in Vienna, by 1944 already had a first-class international reputation as an economic theorist. He had written widely on monetary theory and on the subject now know as macroeconomics. In contrast to many of his contemporaries, he did not believe that the Great Depression of the 1930s signaled the final failure of the market economy. The market would and could work, he held, if it were freed of the distortions introduced by ill-advised government policies. Most of all, what the economies of the world did not need as a cure for their troubles was comprehensive economic planning. Planning could never replace the market as a method for utilizing knowledge and guiding the division of labor. The attempt to make it do so would lead only to a loss of political freedom, not greater economic prosperity.

In 1950, Hayek left London for the University of Chicago, where he taught for twelve years as professor of social and moral science. Much of his time he now spent writing on broad issues of law and social philosophy. His major work of the University of Chicago period was *The Constitution of Liberty*. In this book, he defended the classical liberal ideal of the limited state based on a free market economy and a written constitution.

In 1962, Hayek saw that the University of Chicago's mandatory retirement age was fast approaching. Retirement seemed such an impossible idea to him that he returned to Europe, where professors could serve for a lifetime. He is now visiting professor at the University of Salzburg in Austria and professor emeritus of the University of Freiburg in Germany. In 1974, the name Friedrich von Hayek was back in the international headlines once again. The Swedish Academy of Science had awarded him the Nobel Memorial Prize in Economics—the highest professional distinction there is. A fitting time to retire from a distinguished career? Not for Hayek. The first volume of his new work, *Law, Legislation, and Liberty*, had just appeared the year before, and there were two more volumes to complete. Asked what he would do when the job had been finished, Hayek indicated that he would then, after a detour of many years, be ready to get back to some unfinished problems of economic theory.

Distributing Income

As a by-product of providing incentives, markets distribute income and wealth. People who possess skills and talents or who own resources that are scarce and highly valued get richly rewarded for putting them to their best use. People whose talents or resources are less scarce or of poor quality get less well rewarded even if they use what they have as wisely as possible. Entrepreneurs who take risks and guess right make large profits; entrepreneurs who take risks that looked just as prudent at the outset but who have guessed wrong suffer losses. In short, the market tends to distribute income in proportion to the contribution each person makes to the process of production.

The distributional function of the market is a source of great controversy, much of it over the normative question of whether the distribution of income in a market economy is *fair*. Not surprisingly, the answer depends largely on what is meant by *fairness*. To those for whom fairness is the observation of market justice, the distribution of income in a market economy does appear equitable. People receive what they earn from their own labor and from the voluntary exchange of property with others. All that is required for fairness, in this view, is that the contracts and exchanges be voluntary so they will work out to the mutual benefit of buyers and sellers.

To those who view fairness in terms of distributive justice, the distribution of income in the market economy is not inherently fair. Because skills, talents, and resource ownership are not distributed equally among people, the market does not distribute income equally either.

Is Distribution Separable?   The controversy over the distributive function of markets also raises an important question of positive economics: can the function of distributing income be separated from the functions of transmitting information and providing incentives? Answers differ to this question as well.

One answer is a flat no — the distributional function cannot be separated from the others. The reasoning behind this answer begins with the observation that there are only two ways to alter the distribution of income produced by the market — either to take from some people part of what they earn in order to give it to others, or to manipulate prices so that some people earn more and some earn less than they otherwise would have earned. The first alternative interferes with incentives if people know that part of what they earn will not be theirs to keep, their incentive to put their resources to best use will be correspondingly diminished. The second alternative interferes with the transmission of information through the price system if prices are manipulated for the purpose of affecting income distribution, they cannot at the same time carry accurate signals regarding the relative scarcity of resources.

Despite the apparent reasonableness of this argument, not everyone accepts it on a practical level. It may be true, critics say, that attempts to redistribute income always carry the danger of distorting incentives or sending false signals regarding scarcity; but in practice, the distortions can be held to an insignificant level. Many think, for example, that people will not work much less or invest their capital much differently if they are subject to income taxes than if they are not. To take another kind of example, if rents on urban housing are held down to make housing more accessible to the poor, the distortion of the incentive to build such housing can be offset with other regulations or subsidies.

IMPERFECTIONS IN THE MARKET SYSTEM

Are markets perfect? Economists from Adam Smith to Milton Friedman sometimes get so enthusiastic about the principles according to which markets operate that they forget to point out that in the real world these principles operate only as tendencies. Imperfections in the market economy stem from a number of sources. By far the most important is the fact that although the price system *cheapens* the process of transmitting information to a large degree, it does not make information *free*.

Even after the price system has done its best, there is a level of ignorance that cannot be reduced. Producers and consumers remain at least partly ignorant of what is happening in other places and substantially ignorant of what is likely to happen in the future. They may conceal their preferences for strategic reasons when dealing with others and at the same time remain ignorant of the preferences of others. A modern industrial market economy is worlds ahead of the bazaar at Sefrou in terms of the quality of information available; but as long as information is less than perfect, mistakes will be made.

Part 3 of this book focuses on a wide range of market imperfections and notes their impact on efficiency and equality in an economy like ours. It must be stressed here that our markets are indeed far from perfect. In product markets, monopoly firms use their **monopoly power**—their power to raise prices without losing customers—to charge higher prices than consumers would otherwise have to pay. In those industries in which only a few firms control most of the production, prices may be "fixed" by agreement among the firms. New competitors may be kept out of the market by market agreements that favor the existing firms, or by substantial but temporary price reductions that make it difficult for a new firm to gain a foothold in the industry. In the labor market, professionals may restrict the entry of new competitors by setting high admission standards, and unions may succeed in negotiating contracts that make it difficult for management to replace incompetent workers with new ones. In the financial markets, relatively few banks dominate the industry, with the result that lending rates appear to be the same from one bank to another. In agriculture, marketing boards have virtually destroyed competition in the selling of a wide range of agricultural products.

Monopoly power A seller's power to raise the price of a product without losing all, or nearly all, customers.

Such imperfections are both the result of, and the cause of, government intervention in the marketplace. Where the market seems to be destructive of peoples' livelihood, as in agriculture, the government intervenes to alter the market in favor of the producer. In other markets the government may enter in order to increase competition so that the consumer will be favored. Such government actions are discussed more fully in Chapter 4.

CONCLUSIONS

This chapter has developed the notions of opportunity cost, the production possibility frontier, and comparative advantage, to demonstrate that societies can benefit from specialization and trade.

Trade also requires markets. This chapter has given just a few examples of how markets perform their functions of transmitting information, providing incentives, and distributing income. In later chapters we will examine more closely why markets do not always perform well, and what can be done to improve their performance.

SUMMARY

1. The production possibility frontier illustrates the fact that every economy operates under conditions of scarcity, and that increased production of one good, in the absence of increases or improvements in the factors of production, can only be obtained at the expense of other goods. Such a trade-off between goods reflects the opportunity cost of producing them.

2. If one trading area is able to produce a good at lower cost, in terms of its factor inputs, than another trading area, it is said to have an absolute advantage. If a trading area is able to produce a good at lower opportunity cost, in terms of foregone goods, than another trading area, it is said to have a comparative advantage.

3. A trading area can utilize its resources more efficiently if it engages in specialization, based on the principle of comparative advantage. Such specialization can take place both within countries, between different regions, and on the international level, between different nations. The benefits of the division of labor are not restricted by political boundaries.

4. Markets play a crucial role in coordinating the division of labor in the market economy. This role includes performance of three basic functions: transmitting information, providing incentives, and distributing income.

5. In an advanced industrial market economy, the price system functions as a mechanism for broadcasting information about opportunity costs and the relative scarcity of resources. Rising relative prices signal increasing scarcity; falling relative prices signal increasing abundance.

6. Knowledge of the best use of resources is a necessary but not sufficient condition for efficient coordination of economic activity. In addition to knowing the uses to which resources should be put, the people controlling those resources must have incentives to devote them to their known best use. Consumers, resource owners, and entrepreneurs all have incentives to heed the information that comes to them through the price system, because doing so increases their satisfaction, income, and profit.

7. As a by-product of their function in providing incentives, markets perform the further function of distributing income and wealth. People who possess skills and talents or who own resources that are scarce and highly valued get richly rewarded for putting the resources to their best use. People whose talents or resources are less scarce or of poor quality get less well rewarded even if they use what they have wisely.

8. Despite their acknowledged effectiveness in coordinating the division of labor, markets are neither necessarily fair nor always perfectly efficient. There is considerable monopoly power in most markets today, posing major problems for consumers and governments.

DISCUSSION QUESTIONS

1. Suppose you learned that Vladimir Horowitz, the great pianist, was also an amazingly proficient typist. Knowing this, would it surprise you to learn also that he hired a secretary to type his correspondence, even though he could do the job better and faster himself? What does this situation have to do with comparative advantage?

2. Turn to Exhibit 2.3. Suppose that new, high-yield grains were introduced in the Maritimes, so that the number of labor hours needed to grow a ton of grain there were cut from 4 hours to 2 hours. What would happen to trade between the Maritimes and the Prairies? Would it still pay for Maritimers to buy their grain from the Prairies? If the labor hours per ton of grain in the Maritimes fell all the way to 1, what would happen to the pattern of trade?

3. In your opinion, do the wages or salaries of various occupations have much influence on people's decisions about whether to go to college and what to major in? Justify your answer by explaining what it has to do with the functions of markets in transmitting information, providing incentives, and distributing income.

4. If you were the manager of a division of a major automobile manufacturer and you noticed that the price of steel had been going up relative to the prices of other materials used in the manufacturing of automobiles, how would you react? What would you do and have others do to make adjustments? How would you expect your competitors to react? Explain.

5. Even in an advanced industrial economy such as Canada's, not all transactions take place in accordance with uniform, published prices. What sorts of transactions do you know of that are still subject to bargaining between buyer and seller? Why do you think they are carried out by means of bargaining rather than by fixed prices?

CHAPTER 3
SUPPLY AND DEMAND — THE BASICS

WHAT YOU WILL LEARN IN THIS CHAPTER
Everyday experience teaches that, other things being equal, the quantity of a good that buyers are willing to purchase tends to increase as the price of the good decreases. Similarly, it teaches that the quantity of a good suppliers are willing to sell tends to increase as the price increases. This chapter will show how these commonsense ideas form the basis for supply and demand analysis — one of the most useful analytical tools in all of economics. It will show how terms such as shortage *and* surplus *can be given a precise meaning and will introduce the concept of market equilibrium. These new concepts will then be applied to practical economic problems.*

FOR REVIEW
Here are some important terms and concepts that will be put to use in this chapter. If you do not understand them, review them before proceeding.
• *Working with graphs (Appendix to Chapter 1)*
• *Opportunity cost (Chapter 2)*

The number of markets in the Canadian economy is as large as the number of different kinds of goods and services produced — and that is very large. Despite the great diversity of markets, though, there are some economic principles so powerful that they are useful in understanding all of them. The principles of supply and demand fit into this category.

The fundamental ideas of supply and demand have long been known to practical merchants and traders. For as long as there have been markets, sellers have realized that one way to encourage people to buy more of their product is to offer it at a lower price, and buyers have known that one way to get more of the goods they want is to offer to pay more for them. Only in the last hundred years, though, have economists made systematic use of the principles of supply and demand as the central basis of their science. In the English-speaking world, Alfred Marshall deserves much of the credit for showing how useful the ideas of supply and demand can be. This chapter — and the corresponding chapters in all modern textbooks — is little more than a rewrite of the principles he taught in his own famous *Principles of Economics*.

Alfred Marshall (1842–1924)

Alfred Marshall was born in London in 1842, the son of a Bank of England cashier. His father hoped that he would enter the ministry, but young Marshall had other ideas. He turned down a theological scholarship at Oxford to study mathematics instead. He received an M.A. in mathematics from Cambridge in 1865.

While at Cambridge, he joined a philosophical discussion group. There, he became interested in promoting the wide development of the human mind. He was soon told, however, that harsh economic reality would prevent his ideas from being carried out. Britain's productive resources, it was said, could never allow the mass of the people sufficient leisure for education. This disillusioning episode appears to have first turned Marshall's attention to economics.

At the time, British economics was dominated by the so-called classical school. Marshall had great respect for the classical writers. Initially, he saw his own work as simply using his mathematical training to strengthen and systematize the classical system. It was not long, however, before he was breaking new ground and developing a system of his own. By 1890, when he brought out his famous *Principles of Economics*, he had laid the foundation of what is now called the neoclassical school.

Attempting to explain the essence of his approach, Marshall included this passage in the second edition of his *Principles*:

In spite of a great variety in detail, nearly all the chief problems of economics agree in that they have a kernel of the same kind. This kernel is an inquiry as to the balancing of two opposed classes of motives, the one consisting of desires to acquire certain new goods, and thus satisfy wants; while the other consists of desires to avoid certain efforts or retain certain immediate enjoyment.... In other words, it is an inquiry into the balancing of the forces of demand and supply.

Marshall's influence on economics, at least in the English-speaking world, was enormous. His *Principles* was the leading text for decades, and the modern student can still learn from reading it. As a professor at Cambridge, he taught a great many of the next generation of leading economists. Today the neoclassical school he founded continues to dominate the profession. It has received many challenges but so far has weathered them all.

THE LAW OF DEMAND

Law of demand The law that the quantity of a good demanded by buyers tends to increase as the price of the good decreases and tends to decrease as the price increases, other things being equal.

The analysis begins with the **law of demand**, which says simply that, in the market for any good, the quantity of that good demanded by buyers tends to increase as the price of the good decreases and tends to decrease as the price increases, other things being equal. This law corresponds so closely to what common sense tells us about the way markets work that we could simply state it without further elaboration. But a few additional comments will ensure that it is properly understood.

Effective Demand

Effective demand The quantity of a good that purchasers are willing and able to buy at a particular price.

First, what is meant by *quantity demanded*? It is important to understand that the quantity demanded at a given price means the **effective demand** — the quantity purchasers are willing and able to buy at that price. The effective demand at a particular price may be different from the quantity consumers want or need. I may *want* a new Jaguar XJ-6; but given my limited financial resources, I am not willing actually to offer to buy such a car at its current price of $20,000. My want does not count as part of the quantity demanded in the market for Jaguars. Similarly, I might *need* corrective dental surgery to avoid premature loss of my teeth, but I might be very poor. If I were unable to pay, and no other person or agency were willing to pay, my need would not be counted as part of the quantity demanded in the market for dental services.

Other Things Being Equal

Second, why is the phrase *other things being equal* attached to the law of demand? The reason is that a change in the price of a product is not the only thing that affects the quantity of that product demanded. If people's incomes go up, they are likely to increase the quantities they demand of a great many goods, even if prices do not change. If people's basic tastes and preferences change, the quantities of things they buy will change. If their expectations about future prices or their own future incomes change, they may change their spending patterns even before those price and income changes actually take place.

Above all, in the law of demand, the "other things being equal" condition indicates that the prices of other goods remain unchanged. What really counts in determining the quantity demanded of some good is its price *relative* to the prices of other goods. If the price of gasoline goes up and consumers' incomes and the prices of all other goods go up by the same proportion, the law of demand does not suggest any change in the quantity of gasoline demanded. But if the price of gasoline goes up 10 percent while the price of everything else goes up 20 percent, an increase can be expected in the quantity of gasoline demanded, because its relative price has fallen.

Why?

Now that the meaning of the law of demand is clear, we can ask why it works. Three explanations are worth considering.

First, when the price of a good falls while the prices of other goods remain unchanged, we are likely to substitute some of that good for other things. For example, if the price of fish falls while the price of meat remains the same, we are likely to put fish on the menu a few of the times when we would have used meat had the price of fish not changed.

Second, when the price of a good changes, other things being equal, our effective purchasing power changes even though our income measured in money terms does not. For example, if the price of clothing rises while nothing else changes, we will feel poorer, very much as if a few dollars a year had been trimmed from our paycheque or allowance. Feeling poorer, it is likely that we will buy a bit less of many things, including clothing.

Third — and this reason is not quite distinct from the other two — when the price of a good falls, new buyers who did not use a product at all before are drawn into the market. There was a time, for example, when tape recorders were playthings for the rich or technical tools for businesses. Today, they can be bought very cheaply. Rich people are not buying ten or twenty tape recorders apiece at the lower prices, but sales have gone up ten- or twentyfold because many people are buying them who never had entered that market at all before.

Exceptions to the Law

Are there exceptions to the law of demand? Are there cases in which an increase in the price of a good causes people to use more of it? Theoretically, such exceptions are possible, although in practice they are quite rare. One kind of exception can occur if the change in the price of a good has such a strong impact on effective purchasing power that it causes a radical change in people's whole pattern of consumption. Imagine a family that lives in Manitoba and habitually spends January each year vacationing in Florida. One year, the price of home heating fuel jumps dramatically. The family reacts by turning down the thermostat a little, but the fuel bills for September through December still go up so much that the family cannot afford to take its Florida vacation in January. Yet, staying at home, even though it is cheaper than going to Florida, requires the family to burn more fuel than during the previous winters, when it left the house unheated for that month. The total effect of the rise in fuel prices is therefore an *increase* in the consumption of the product.

Perhaps other rare kinds of exceptions to the law of demand are also possible. The point is, though, that we have to think so hard to come up with examples that we end up being more convinced than ever of the validity of the law.

Demand Schedules and Curves

The law of demand, like so many other economic ideas, can usefully be illustrated with numerical tables and graphs. Suppose, for example, that we want to study the operation of the law of demand in the market for wheat. One way to express the relationship between the price of wheat and the quantity of wheat demanded by all buyers in the market is in the form of a table like that given in Exhibit 3.1a.

From the first line of the table, we learn that when the price of wheat is

(b) Demand curve

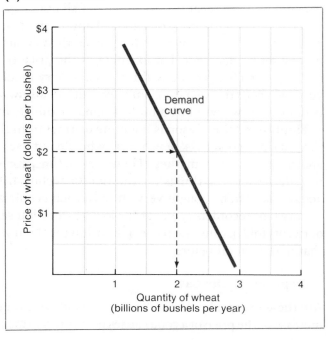

Exhibit 3.1

A demand schedule and a demand curve for wheat
Both the demand schedule and the demand curve show the quantity of wheat demanded at various possible prices. Both show, for example, that when the price is $2 per bushel, the quantity is 2 billion bushels per year.

(a) Demand schedule

Price of Wheat (dollars per bushel)	Quantity of Wheat Demanded (billions of bushels per year)
$3.20	1.4
3.00	1.5
2.80	1.6
2.60	1.7
2.40	1.8
2.20	1.9
2.00	**2.0**
1.80	2.1
1.60	2.2
1.40	2.3
1.20	2.4
1.00	2.5
.80	2.6

$3.20, the quantity demanded per year will be 1.4 billion bushels. Reading further, we see that as the price decreases, the quantity demanded increases. At $3 per bushel, buyers are willing and able to purchase 1.5 billion bushels per year; at $2.80, the quantity demanded is 1.6 billion bushels. The complete table is called the **demand schedule** for wheat.

The information given by the demand schedule can be expressed just as easily in graphical form. This is done in Exhibit 3.1b. The diagonal line of the graph is called the **demand curve** for wheat. Suppose that we want to use the demand curve to determine what quantity will be demanded when the price is $2 per bushel. Beginning at $2 on the vertical axis, we follow across as shown by the arrow until we reach the demand curve. We then go down from that point to the horizontal axis, where we read off the answer—2 billion bushels per year. This, of course, is the same answer given in the tabular demand schedule.

Demand schedule A table showing the quantity of a good demanded at various prices.

Demand curve A graphical representation of the relationship between the price of a good and the quantity of it demanded.

Movements along the Demand Curve

To repeat what has been said before, the demand curve shows how the quantity demanded changes in response to a change in price, *other things being equal*. When a change in the quantity of wheat demanded occurs as a result of a change in the price of wheat, acting alone, that change is represented graphically as a movement along the demand curve for wheat. If something other than the price of wheat changes, a different graphical representation is required.

Consider Exhibit 3.2. The demand curve labeled D_1 is the same as that shown in Exhibit 3.1. It is based on certain assumptions about household income, the prices of other goods, and buyers' expectations about future changes in price. Given those assumptions, the quantity demanded at a

Exhibit 3.2
A shift in the demand curve for wheat
The effect of a change in the price of wheat, other things being equal, is represented by a movement along the demand curve for wheat, as from Point A to Point B along Demand Curve D_1. The effect of a change in something other than a change in the price of wheat (say a change in household income) must be represented by a shift in the entire demand curve, as from the position D_1 to the position D_2, and a movement from Point A on the old demand curve to Point C on the new one.

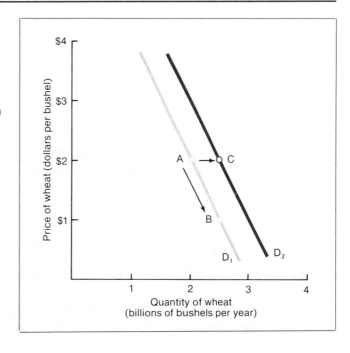

price of $2 per bushel will be 2 billion bushels per year, as at Point A on Demand Curve D$_1$. A fall in the price from $2 per bushel to $1 per bushel, other things being equal, will cause the quantity demanded to increase to 2.5 billion bushels per year. This change in price is represented by a movement along Demand Curve D$_1$ from Point A to Point B.

Shifts in the Demand Curve Return now to Point A. Suppose that the price does not change but that something else changes — say, household income rises. A sufficiently large increase in household income could cause consumers to demand an additional half billion bushels per year, even without a change in the price of wheat. This change is represented by a movement from Point A to Point C in the diagram — a movement *off* Demand Curve D$_1$ rather than along it. With household income established at its new, higher level, changes in *price* would now cause movements up or down along the new demand curve, D$_2$, which passes through Point C and lies everywhere to the right of the old demand curve, D$_1$. The new demand curve indicates that, whatever the price of wheat, the quantity demanded, given the new, higher level of household income, will be larger than it would have been at the same price, given the old level of income.

A similar story could have been told if the prices of other goods or buyers' expectations, rather than income, had changed. The general point to be established is this: when the demand for some good changes for a reason *other* than a change in the price of the product itself, the change is represented graphically by a *shift* in the entire demand curve to a new position.

It is a rather widely established convention among economists to refer to a shift in a demand curve as a *change in demand*. The phrase *change in quantity demanded* refers to a movement along a given demand curve.

Normal and Inferior Goods Economists use some special terms in discussing the sources of shifts in demand curves. Changes in income are one source of such shifts. When a rise in buyers' incomes causes the demand curve for a good to shift to the right (as happened in Exhibit 3.2), the good is called a **normal good**. People tend to reduce their consumption of some goods when their incomes go up. Such goods, called **inferior goods**, are those goods for which there are more desirable but also more costly substitutes. Hamburger and intercity bus travel are examples. An increase in buyers' incomes causes the demand curve for an inferior good to shift to the left.

Substitutes and Complements The position of the demand curve for a good may also be affected by changes in the prices of other, closely related goods. For example, salads can be made from lettuce or from spinach. An increase in the price of lettuce is likely to cause not only a decrease in the quantity of lettuce demanded (represented graphically by a movement up and to the left along the lettuce demand curve) but also an increase in the demand for spinach (represented graphically by a shift to the right of the entire spinach demand curve). When an increase in the price of one good causes an increase in the demand for another good, those two goods are said to be **substitutes** for each other. Photographic film and flashbulbs tend to be used together. If the price of film were to rise, we would expect not only a

Normal good A good for which an increase in the income of buyers causes a rightward shift in the demand curve.

Inferior good A good for which an increase in the income of buyers causes a leftward shift in the demand curve.

Substitutes A pair of goods for which an increase in the price of one causes an increase in the demand for the other, other things being equal.

decrease in the quantity of film sold but a decrease in the demand for flashbulbs also. The effect of the change in the price of film is represented graphically as a movement along the film demand curve and as a leftward shift of the flashbulb demand curve. When an increase in the price of one good causes a decrease in the demand for another good, the two goods are said to be **complements**.

Complements A pair of goods for which an increase in the price of one causes a decrease in the demand for the other, other things being equal.

SUPPLY

The next step in the analysis of markets will be to examine the relationship between the price of a good and the quantity of it that suppliers are willing and able to provide for sale. Everyday experience suggests that, in order to induce sellers to increase the quantity of a good supplied, it is necessary, other things being equal, to offer them a higher price. When this is true, the supply curve for the good in question slopes upward. Exhibit 3.3 shows a **supply schedule** and a corresponding upward sloping **supply curve** for wheat.[1]

Why exactly is the supply curve for wheat expected to slope upward? There are a number of possible reasons, any or all of which may operate in a particular case. For one thing, a higher price gives farmers a greater incentive to devote more of their time and energy to wheat production. In

Supply schedule A table showing the quantity of a good supplied at various prices.

Supply curve A graphical representation of the relationship between the price of a good and the quantity of it supplied.

[1] Exceptions to the rule that supply curves slope upward are not so rare as exceptions to the rule that demand curves slope downward. A few examples of negatively sloped supply curves will occur later in this book. For the present, however, we will stick to upward sloping curves.

Exhibit 3.3

A supply schedule and supply curve for wheat

Both the supply curve and supply schedule for wheat show the quantity of wheat supplied at various prices. An increase in the price of wheat induces farmers to supply a greater quantity of it. This is partly because they have an incentive to devote more time and energy to the crop, partly because they substitute wheat for other crops grown previously, and partly because new resources (and even new farmers) may be drawn into wheat production.

(a) Supply schedule

Price of Wheat (dollars per bushel)	Quantity of Wheat Supplied (billions of bushels per year)
$3.20	2.6
3.00	2.5
2.80	2.4
2.60	2.3
2.40	2.2
2.20	2.1
2.00	2.0
1.80	1.9
1.60	1.8
1.40	1.7
1.20	1.6
1.00	1.5
.80	1.4

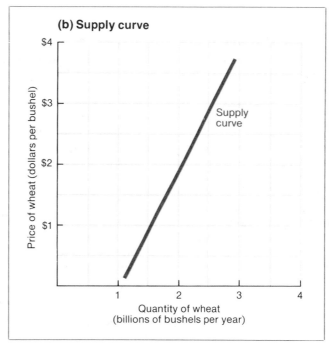

addition, it may induce them to substitute wheat for other crops they had been producing. Finally, the higher price may make it possible to attract resources into wheat farming from other lines of production, perhaps even leading to the establishment of new farms. Chapters 22 and 23 will discuss in some detail the assumptions that underlie the upward sloping supply curve. For now, these commonsense observations will suffice.

Shifts in Supply Curves

As in the case of demand, changes in the quantity supplied of a good, represented by movements along a given supply curve, are distinguished from changes in the supply of a good, represented by shifts in the supply curve. A change in the quantity supplied comes about as the result of a change in the price of the good, other things being equal. A shift in the supply curve requires a change in some other factor affecting supply.

One thing that can produce a change in the supply of a good is a change in production technology. If new technology permits more output to be produced from the same quantity of inputs, the supply curve will shift to the right. A second factor that can cause a change in supply is a change in the price of inputs used to produce a good. If input prices go up, for example, suppliers will probably want a higher price than before in order to offer the same quantity of output for sale. This effect is represented by a leftward shift in the supply curve. Finally, the supply curve for one good can be shifted as the result of a change in the price of another good, other things being equal. For example, a rise in the price of soybeans might well cause the supply curve for wheat to shift to the left, as farmers pull land out of wheat production and plant it in the newly profitable soybeans. Some examples of shifting supply curves will be given later in this chapter.

THE INTERACTION OF SUPPLY AND DEMAND

Market Equilibrium

Chapter 2 showed how the market transmits information in the form of prices to the people who are potential buyers and sellers of any good. Taking the price of the good into account, together with the other knowledge they possess, these buyers and sellers form plans. Each one decides to enter the market and buy or sell a certain number of units of the good.

Commonly, large numbers of buyers and sellers formulate their market plans independently of one another. When buyers and sellers of some particular good actually meet and engage in the process of exchange, some of them may find it impossible to carry out their plans. Perhaps the total quantity of planned purchases will exceed the total quantity of planned sales at the expected price. In this case, some of the would-be buyers will find their plans frustrated and will have to modify them. Perhaps, instead, planned sales will exceed planned purchases. Then, some would-be sellers will be unable to sell all they had expected to and will have to change their plans.

Sometimes no one will be disappointed. Given the information that market prices have conveyed, the total quantity of the good that buyers plan to purchase may exactly equal the quantity that suppliers plan to sell.

The separately formulated plans of all market participants may turn out to mesh exactly when tested in the marketplace, and no one will have frustrated expectations or be forced to modify plans. When this happens, the market is said to be in **equilibrium**.

If we have supply and demand schedules for a market, we can describe more exactly the conditions under which that market will be in equilibrium. Take the market for wheat as an example. In Exhibit 3.4, Columns 1 to 3 give the supply and demand schedules. Reading down Column 2, we see how much wheat producers will plan to sell at each price. Reading down Column 3, we see how much wheat buyers will plan to purchase at each price. Comparing the two, it does not take long to discover that only when the price is $2 do the separately formulated plans of buyers and sellers exactly mesh. Thus $2 per bushel is the price at which this market is in equilibrium. If all buyers and sellers make their market plans in the expectation that the price will be $2, none of them will be disappointed, and none will have to change plans.

Market equilibrium A condition in which the separately formulated plans of buyers and sellers of some good exactly mesh when tested in the marketplace, so that the quantity supplied is exactly equal to the quantity demanded at the prevailing price.

Shortages

What if, for some reason, buyers and sellers expect the market price to be something different from $2? Suppose, for example, that a price of $1 per bushel somehow becomes established in the market. Column 2 of Exhibit 3.4 tells us that, at this price, producers will plan to supply wheat to the market at the rate of 1.5 billion bushels per year. Column 3 tells us that

Exhibit 3.4

Supply and demand in the market for wheat

When the quantity of a product demanded exceeds the quantity supplied, there is an excess quantity demanded, or shortage, of the product. A shortage puts upward pressure on the price of the product. When the quantity supplied exceeds the quantity demanded, there is an excess quantity supplied, or surplus, of the product. A surplus puts downward pressure on the price. Only when the price of wheat here is $2 per bushel is there no shortage or surplus and no upward or downward pressure on price. At $2 the market is in equilibrium.

Price per Bushel (1)	Quantity Supplied (billions of bushels) (2)	Quantity Demanded (billions of bushels) (3)	Shortage (billions of bushels) (4)	Surplus (billions of bushels) (5)	Direction of Pressure on Price (6)
$3.20	2.6	1.4	—	1.2	Downward
3.00	2.5	1.5	—	1.0	Downward
2.80	2.4	1.6	—	0.8	Downward
2.60	2.3	1.7	—	0.6	Downward
2.40	2.2	1.8	—	0.4	Downward
2.20	2.1	1.9	—	0.2	Downward
2.00	2.0	2.0	—	—	Equilibrium
1.80	1.9	2.1	0.2	—	Upward
1.60	1.8	2.2	0.4	—	Upward
1.40	1.7	2.3	0.6	—	Upward
1.20	1.6	2.4	0.8	—	Upward
1.00	1.5	2.5	1.0	—	Upward
.80	1.4	2.6	1.2	—	Upward

buyers will plan to purchase at a rate of 2.5 billion bushels per year. When the quantity demanded exceeds the quantity supplied, the difference between the two is called an **excess quantity demanded** or, more simply, a **shortage**.[2] In the case of wheat, the shortage (shown in Column 4 of the exhibit) is 1 billion bushels per year when the price is $1 per bushel.

In most markets, the first sign of a shortage is the depletion of inventories of the product available for sale. If inventories run out entirely, or if the market is for a good or service that cannot be stored in inventory at all, a queue of potential buyers may form. Under such circumstances, either sellers take the initiative to raise prices or buyers take the initiative to offer higher prices in the hope of getting part of the available quantity. In either event, the shortage puts upward pressure on price.

As the price of the product rises, producers begin to plan to sell more and buyers begin to plan to purchase less. The higher the price, the smaller the shortage. When the price of wheat in Exhibit 3.4 reaches $2 per bushel, the shortage is entirely eliminated. With its elimination, there is no further upward pressure on prices. The market is in equilibrium.

Surpluses

Suppose that, for some reason, the price of wheat becomes established at a level higher than the equilibrium price, say at $3 a bushel. At this price, according to Exhibit 3.4, producers will plan to sell 2.5 billion bushels per year, but buyers will plan to purchase only 1.5 billion bushels. When the quantity supplied exceeds the quantity demanded, there is an **excess quantity supplied** or a **surplus**. As Column 5 of the exhibit shows, the surplus of wheat is 1 billion bushels per year when the price is $3 a bushel.

When there is a surplus of the product, some producers will be disappointed, since they will not be able to make all their planned sales at the expected price. Inventories of unsold goods will begin to accumulate. Although the details may vary from market to market, the generalization can be made that a surplus puts downward pressure on the product price. Exhibit 3.4 shows that as the price falls, the quantity supplied decreases and the quantity demanded increases. Gradually, the surplus is eliminated until, when the price reaches $2 per bushel, the market returns to equilibrium.

Graphical Presentation

A graphical presentation of the material just covered will help reinforce the points made. Exhibit 3.5 shows both the demand curve (taken from Exhibit 3.1) and the supply curve (taken from Exhibit 3.3) for wheat. With both curves on the same diagram, the quantity demanded and the quantity supplied at any price can be directly compared. The distance from the vertical axis to the demand curve measures the quantity demanded, and the

Excess quantity demanded The amount by which the quantity of a good demanded exceeds the quantity supplied when the price of the good is below the equilibrium level.

Shortage As used in economics, an excess quantity demanded.

Excess quantity supplied The amount by which the quantity of a good supplied exceeds the quantity demanded when the price of the good is above the equilibrium level.

Surplus As used in economics, an excess quantity supplied.

---

[2] We introduce two equivalent terms—*shortage* and *excess quantity demanded*—in order to make it clear that economists use the term *shortage* in a somewhat narrower sense than it is used in everyday speech. In this book, the word *shortage* will be used most of the time when it is clear that the economic meaning is intended. But sometimes, to avoid possible ambiguity, the more precise term *excess quantity demanded* will be used instead. The same considerations apply to the terms *surplus* and *excess quantity supplied*.

Exhibit 3.5

Supply and demand in the market for wheat

In this diagram, a surplus or shortage is indicated by the horizontal distance between the supply and demand curves. A surplus puts downward pressure on price, and a shortage puts upward pressure on it, as indicated by the arrows following the supply and demand curves. The market is in equilibrium at the point where the supply and demand curves intersect. Compare this diagram with the table in Exhibit 3.4.

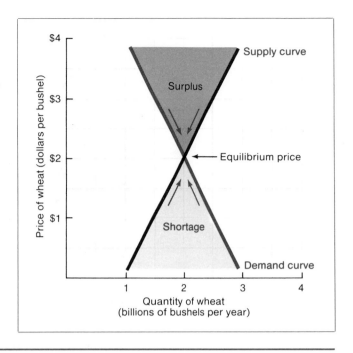

distance from the vertical axis to the supply curve measures the quantity supplied. It follows that the horizontal gap between the two curves measures the surplus or shortage at any price.

As we saw when working through the numerical example for this market, a surplus tends to put downward pressure on the price, and a shortage tends to put upward pressure on it. These pressures result from the actions of frustrated buyers and sellers, who must change their plans when they find they cannot buy or sell the quantities they had intended at the price they had expected. The pressures are indicated by the arrows pointing along the supply and demand curves toward equilibrium.

There is only one price where neither upward nor downward pressure is in force—the price of $2 per bushel, the point where the supply and demand curves intersect. There is neither shortage nor surplus at that point. The quantity that buyers plan to purchase exactly equals the quantity that suppliers plan to sell. Both can carry out their plans exactly as intended, and the market is in equilibrium.

Changing Economic Conditions

When underlying economic conditions change, supply and demand curves can shift to new positions. These shifts upset the plans of buyers and sellers, who may have adjusted to some previous market equilibrium, and they bring about changes in prices and quantities. The following example describes an episode that is typical of the way markets work every day. Particular attention should be paid to the distinction between the kinds of changes that cause shifts in supply or demand curves and the kinds that cause movements along curves.

Case 3.1
Supply and Demand in the British Columbia Lumber Industry

This reprinted newspaper article illustrates how the forces of supply and demand changed the price of B.C. lumber in a short period of time in the summer of 1977:

A U.S. home building boom has increased lumber prices in the B.C. market from 15 to 20 percent in the past two-and-a-half months, and local builders fear prices will continue to climb.

Since U.S. builders are the Canadian lumber industry's biggest customers, accounting for half of its sales, they tend to set prices for the Canadian market as well. U.S. housing starts are expected to peak in the last quarter of 1977 at an annual rate of 1.93 million units.

The exchange rate, giving U.S. buyers a better deal for their dollar, hasn't helped any as far as Canadian buyers are concerned.

"The mills are booked two months solid," said Paul Pannozzo, a lumber purchaser for the Lumberland retail chain. He said what happens then is that buyers are forced to bid higher prices in order to snatch enough material for their needs, before it's sold down south.

Pannozzo predicted that "unless California slows down on home-building," B.C. prices could go up another $20 per thousand board feet by 1978. He said there could be a drop in November when cold weather sets in, but prices are likely to jump again in January.

As an example of the recent price jumps, Bob Swannell, general marketing manager for lumber at MacMillan Bloedel Ltd., noted that Western white spruce 2x4s, considered something of a price indicator in the trade, were selling at $190 per thousand board feet on July 29 but had jumped to $209 as of Friday.

He agreed that it's the U.S housing boom causing the rapid price hikes here and noted that unlike Canada, the U.S. is building a large number of single-family houses which consume a high percentage of framing lumber, pushing up lumber consumption.

This year, said Swannel, the U.S. is likely to exceed its record year of 1972 for single-family dwelling starts.

What has happened, he said, is that the U.S. boom came at the same time the B.C. forest industry had let production drop somewhat. With inventory down and demand increasing, prices inevitably started rising.

In addition, he said, the demand came at a time of production drop-offs due to summer holidays and fire closures, especially in Washington and Oregon.

Source: Pat Johnson, "Price of Lumber Zooms," *Vancouver Province*, August 13, 1977. Reprinted in *Dateline Canada*, ed. Peter Kennedy and Gary Dorosh (Scarborough, Ont.: Prentice-Hall, 1978), p.3.

(a) Quantity of white spruce (thousand board feet)

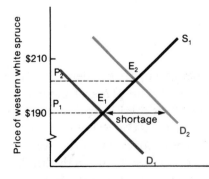

(b) Quantity of white spruce (thousand board feet)

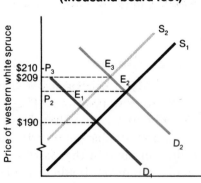

Exhibit 3.6
The effects of changing economic conditions on the price of white spruce (B.C. lumber) between July 29 and August 13, 1977
Part a shows the effects of a demand shift resulting from increased demand by U.S. home builders. The demand curve is shifted to the right from D_1 to D_2. The resulting shortage of lumber drives the price up from P_1 to P_2. Part b shows the effects of a reduction in lumber supply because of production drops by the B.C. lumber industry. Now the supply curve shifts too, from S_1 to S_2. Together, the shift of both curves caused the price of white spruce lumber (2x4s) to rise from $190 per thousand board feet (P_1) to $209 ($P_3$) in the two-week period.

As the article indicates, the price of one particular type of lumber, white spruce 2x4s, rose from $190 per thousand board feet to $209 in a two-week period. This was the result of changes in demand and supply conditions.

On the demand side, a major factor in the price rise was the home-building boom in the United States. The increased U.S. demand for Canadian lumber was also due to the declining value of the Canadian dollar. This is a good illustration of how our exports increase when the value of our dollar decreases, and it also shows why our prices may rise at the same time.

Exhibit 3.6a gives a graphic representation of growing U.S. demands on Canadian lumber. The immediate result is shown as a rightward shift in the demand curve, from its initial position D_1 to a new position D_2. Before this shift occurred, the market equilibrium price was $190 ($P_1$). After the shift there was a shortage of white spruce 2x4s as long as the price remained at its previous level. The shortage caused the market price to be bid up. As the price rose, suppliers moved up and to the right along the supply curve S_1. When the price had risen to P_2, the shortage was eliminated, and if no further changes in economic conditions had occurred, P_2 would have been the new equilibrium price.

Other economic conditions did not remain unchanged, however. At the same time the demand shift occurred, conditions were also changing on the supply side of the market. The B.C. forest industry had let production drop, partly due to summer layoffs and fire closures. We can represent the effect of these supply-side changes as an upward shift of the supply curve, from its original position S_1 to a new position S_2, as shown in Exhibit 3.6b. With the supply curve shifting at the same time as the demand curve shifted, a rise in price from P_1 to P_2 was no longer sufficient to eliminate the entire shortage of lumber. Instead, the price rose all the way to P_3 ($209). In comparison to the equilibrium shown in Part a of the exhibit, we can see that the shift in the supply curve requires a movement of consumers along their new demand curve D_2, until equilibrium is finally reached at the point where S_2 and D_2 intersect. The simultaneous shifts in the supply and demand curves reinforced one another and caused the rise in the price of lumber to be much sharper than it would have been had only one of the changes occurred

Markets in Disequilibrium

We have seen that when a market is not in equilibrium, an excess quantity demanded or excess quantity supplied will put upward or downward pressure on the price. If the price is free to respond to this pressure, a new equilibrium will be established at a higher or lower price. Sometimes, though, market prices are not free to fluctuate. The forces of supply and demand must then work themselves out in some other way, as the following example shows.

Case 3.2
The Gasoline Shortage of 1979

In the spring of 1979, a significant gasoline shortage struck California, partly due to the cutting of supplies from Iran. Because there was no immediate alternative source to which to turn, the supply curve for gasoline could be considered almost vertical, as shown in Exhibit 3.7.

This exhibit shows that a sufficiently high price ($1.60 per gallon as the graph is drawn, but this is only a guess) would have put the gasoline market in equilibrium. However, government price controls in force at the time kept the price from rising much above $.80 per gallon. There was a substantial excess quantity demanded that, instead of making itself visible in terms of rising prices, made itself visible in the form of long lines at gas stations.

People who waited in line for gasoline had lots of time to think, and anyone who had studied a little economics could have figured out that the forces of supply and demand were still at work in a roundabout way. There were opportunity costs of waiting in line. Some people actually missed work. Others sacrificed valuable leisure hours. As the lines grew, the opportunity cost of waiting in them grew also, until at some point the *total* cost of gasoline—the money cost plus the opportunity cost of waiting—was at least roughly equal to the price of $1.60 to which gasoline would have risen without controls. At that point, the lines stopped growing longer, and a sort of rough-and-ready equilibrium was established.

Who benefited from the fact that long lines, rather than high prices, were used to ration scarce gas among users? Who was harmed? Consumers in general did not gain, because what they saved in money, they lost in time. But some consumers—those for whom the opportunity cost of time spent in line was low—were hurt less severely than they would have been by a price rise, whereas those for whom time was particularly precious were hurt more.

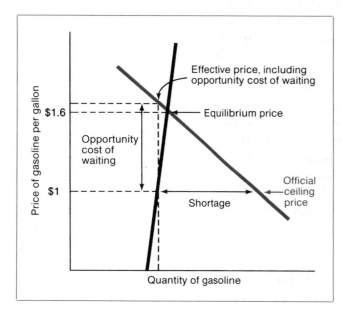

Exhibit 3.7
The gasoline shortage of 1979
During the gasoline shortage of 1979, U.S. government price controls prevented gasoline prices from rising to the equilibrium level, here estimated as $1.60 per gallon. Instead of causing the price to rise, the shortage of gasoline caused long lines to form at gas stations, until the opportunity cost of waiting in line became great enough roughly to fill the gap between the official ceiling price and the true equilibrium price.

CONCLUSIONS

This completes the presentation of the basics of supply and demand analysis. The chapter will conclude with a few remarks that relate supply and demand to the role of markets as a mechanism for utilizing knowledge and that concern the scope of applicability of supply and demand analysis.

Information and Equilibrium

There is a simple connection between the idea of equilibrium and the idea of the market as a mechanism for distributing information. The connection is found in the fact that the market can be in equilibrium when, and only when, it has entirely completed its job of distributing information among buyers and sellers.

It is easy to see why this it true. First, if buyers and sellers have incomplete knowledge of prices and of other economic conditions, it is unlikely that their separately formulated market plans will exactly mesh. It may be that both buyers and sellers expect the price tomorrow to be higher (or lower) than it actually will be. It may be that buyers have one idea about what the price will be and sellers another. Whatever the case, someone is bound to be disappointed, and disappointed plans are the stuff of which disequilibrium is made.

On the other hand, if both buyers and sellers have complete and accurate knowledge of both present and future prices and market conditions, how can their plans fail to mesh? No one will plan to sell knowing that there will be no one to buy. With perfect information, people will formulate only such market plans as they know can be carried out on the expected terms, and that is what *equilibrium* means.

Saying that markets are in equilibrium only when all buyers and sellers have perfect information leads to a conclusion that may seem strange. The conclusion is that, in the real world, we can hardly ever expect to find a market in equilibrium! To paraphrase a famous saying, all people know something some of the time, and some people know a great deal all of the time, but everybody does not know everything all of the time. In real markets, prices are always being pushed this way or that by changes in underlying economic conditions. Some people learn of these changes right away, and the buying and selling they do telegraphs that information, via the price system, to others. But the market telegraph does not work with the speed of light. Before everyone who is directly or indirectly interested in what goes on in a particular market learns of some change, other changes have occurred. The whirling stream of human knowledge never quite catches up with an even more fluid reality.

Applicability

The fact that markets are never really in equilibrium is, in a sense, a limitation on the applicability of supply and demand analysis. There are other limitations too. As Part 3 of this book will show, supply and demand analysis applies in its pure form only to markets where the number of buyers and sellers is very large and where the products offered by one seller differ very little from those offered by another. Some real world markets fit the conditions fairly well. The markets for agricultural products such as wheat are an example. But the markets for many other products do not look exactly like the idealized markets of economic theory.

For now, though, there is no need to be overly concerned with differences between the real and the ideal. The theory of supply and demand may not *exactly* fit any market at any particular moment in time; yet, in a general sense, thinking in terms of supply and demand can give extremely useful insights into the way almost all markets work. The usefulness of these tools will be proved in application as we work through this book. Fine points can be left for more advanced courses.

SUMMARY

1. The law of demand says that the quantity of a good demanded by buyers tends to change in a direction opposite to any change in price, other things being equal. By *quantity demanded*, economists mean effective demand, as distinguished from wants or needs not backed up by willingness and ability to buy. By *other things being equal*, they have in mind such things as buyers' incomes, the prices of other goods, and buyers' expectations about future price changes.

2. A change in the quantity of a good demanded that results solely from a change in the price of that good is represented graphically as a movement along a demand curve. When something other than its price changes (for example, buyers' incomes, the prices of substitutes or complements, or buyers' expectations), the result is a change in demand, represented graphically as a shift of the entire demand curve.

3. A supply curve shows the relationship between the price of a good and the quantity of it supplied, other things being equal. Unless there is some particular reason to do otherwise, economists usually draw supply curves with upward slopes. A change in the price of a good produces a change in the quantity supplied, shown by a movement along a supply curve. A change in some other factor—technology, input prices, prices of other goods—produces a change in supply, shown by a shift of the supply curve.

4. Market equilibrium is a condition in which the separately formulated plans of buyers and sellers exactly mesh, so that the quantity supplied is equal to the quantity demanded. If the price of a product is too high for equilibrium, there will be a surplus of the good, which, in turn, will tend to push the price down. If the price is below the equilibrium, there will be a shortage, which will tend to drive the price up. Equilibrium is possible only when the market has completely carried out its job of distributing information among buyers and sellers.

DISCUSSION QUESTIONS

1. The *law of demand* states that there is an inverse relationship between the price of a good and the quantity that people will be willing and able to pay for. How is this "law" like the law of gravity? How is it different? Explain.

2. Illustrate the supply of McDonald's hamburgers to an individual consumer. What is the slope of the supply curve?

3. Suppose there were a drought on the Prairies, where the nation's wheat is grown. What would be the impact of the drought on the demand and supply of wheat? What would happen to the price of wheat? Why? How would this be likely to affect the individual consumers of products containing wheat?

4. If you drop a marble into a bowl, it will eventually come to rest at the bottom. You can then say that the marble is at equilibrium at the bottom of the bowl. What is meant by *equilibrium*? In what ways is equilibrium in a market similar to the equilibrium of the marble? In what ways is it different?

5. If you were a wholesaler and you could see sooner than your competitors when the demand curve for the product you deal in was about to shift to the right, how could you use this advance knowledge to make money? Would you be benefiting anyone besides yourself in getting rid of the disequilibrium? Explain.

6. Suppose you read the following news item in the daily paper: "Frost in Brazil has caused a severe shortage of coffee, which has driven the price well above normal levels. The shortage is expected to persist for several years, until new coffee bushes can be planted and reach maturity." Do you think the writer is using the word *shortage* in the same sense that it has been used in this chapter? Explain.

7. Suppose that the opportunity cost of time spent waiting in line to buy gasoline were uniformly $5 per hour for all consumers. Would imposing price controls on gasoline to deal with a sudden decrease in supply then benefit anyone at all? Would it make anyone worse off than if the price were simply allowed to rise to a higher equilibrium level? Should the owners of gas stations and oil companies be counted as "anyone" in answering this question?

SUGGESTIONS FOR FURTHER READING

Breit, William, and Ransom, Roger L. *The Academic Scribblers*. New York: Holt, Rinehart and Winston, 1971, Chapter 3.
An essay on Alfred Marshall. The preceding two chapters provide useful background.

Marshall, Alfred. *Principles of Economics*. Various editions.
First published in 1891, this book served as the definitive treatise on economics in the English-speaking world for generations. It remains remarkably accessible to browsing, even by the beginning student. For a start, look up Marshall's treatment of the determinants of demand or his discussion (and dismissal) of cases of apparently upward sloping demand curves.

C H A P T E R 4

THE ROLE OF GOVERNMENT IN THE ECONOMY

WHAT YOU WILL LEARN IN THIS CHAPTER

Not all economic decisions in the Canadian economy are made in the marketplace; many are made in government at the federal, provincial, and municipal levels. From the time of Confederation, governments have played an important role in the development of the Canadian economy. This chapter provides an overview of the role of government in the economy — what distinguishes government from other actors in the economy and what the major functions of government are. It also provides an overview of how federal, provincial, and municipal governments raise taxes and what each level of government spends money on. Finally it explains how to apply supply and demand theory to help determine the real economic burden of taxation.

FOR REVIEW

Here are some important terms and concepts that will be put to use in this chapter. If you do not understand them, review them before proceeding.
- *Markets and their function (Chapter 2)*
- *Supply and demand analysis (Chapter 3)*

The forces of supply and demand, acting through markets, affect every significant economic decision in the Canadian economy. Nonetheless, Canada is not a pure market economy. There are other economic forces as well that affect how resources are used. By far the most important of the nonmarket forces is that of government.

As an actor on the economic stage, government differs in a number of important ways from other actors. Three characteristics in particular distinguish it from the individuals and firms constituting the market sector.

First, government can legitimately use force in economic affairs. In the private sector, firms and individuals are limited by law and custom to peaceable means of production and exchange that require the voluntary consent of everyone involved. Governments, on the other hand, are able to employ force, coercion, and involuntary expropriation in pursuit of their economic goals. When the government taxes incomes, regulates prices, conscripts soldiers, or outlaws gambling, it does not require the immediate, explicit consent of the individuals taxed, regulated, conscripted, or outlawed. Although in a democracy these uses of government power are supposed to rest, at least indirectly, on the consent of the voters, they are binding on minorities and nonvoters as well. Without the use or threat of force, government could do very few of the things it does.

A second characteristic setting governments apart from other economic agents is the fact that the great bulk of goods and services produced by governments are provided to users without charge. In most cases, people do not have to pay directly for defense services, highway use, education, or police protection. Instead, they pay for these things indirectly, through taxes. In only a few cases do the taxes paid vary according to the quantity of public service consumed. The fact that governments do not charge users directly for most of their services has important implications for measuring the total contribution of government to the national product and for measuring the degree of efficiency with which government services are utilized. More on this will appear in later chapters.

A third way governments differ from other economic agents is in how they arrive at economic decisions. The system of voting and bargaining by which public decisions are made is much more complex and hard to analyze than the decision processes of private business firms and consumers. As a result, economists have not gotten as far in formulating simple rules or theories to explain resource allocation in the public sector. In the past, economists traditionally treated government decisions as givens for purposes of economic analysis and did not try to explain why one government decision rather than another was made at a particular time. In recent years, though, some progress has been made in formulating an economic theory of "public choice" to parallel the theory of private choice with which economists have traditionally worked.

Despite the peculiarities of government, market forces of supply and demand do make themselves felt to a degree even within the public sector of the economy. The principal reason is that governments have to purchase most of the inputs they require on the open market. The federal Department of Justice cannot hire a new clerk unless it pays at least the wage determined by supply and demand for workers with the required skills. The city of Montreal cannot buy police cars unless it pays something pretty close to what private individuals would pay for the same vehicles. The necessity of purchasing inputs at market prices makes government aware of the relative cost of various programs and helps constrain total public spending.

Of course, particular government agencies sometimes ignore the messages the market sends to them via the price system. Corrupt bidding practices, for example, result in government purchases from politically favored firms at higher than market prices. In such instances, the degree of market influence on government is less than usual.

GOVERNMENT AND THE CANADIAN ECONOMY

How Government Became Involved in the Canadian Economy

In order to understand the important role that governments play in the Canadian economy it is necessary to recognize the special pressures that resulted in the creation of Canada. Confederation was a response to both political and economic forces, and successive Canadian governments were required to use both political and economic means to strengthen the new nation.

It was noted in Chapter 1 that the rapid penetration of the Canadian hinterland, accompanied by the exploitation of staple products, produced a far-flung economic network that was oriented toward foreign trade, was exposed to an aggressive economic and political system in the south, and was heavily dependent on a well-developed transportation and communication network. By the mid-nineteenth century there were strong regional economies in the Maritimes and in Central Canada, but it was far from clear whether, and how, these economies would affiliate with each other and how they should relate to the countries with which they did most of their trading.

Until the 1840s Central Canada and the Maritimes benefited immensely from their connections with Great Britain, because the latter applied preferential tariffs on most of their exports. However, in the 1840s a free trade movement in Great Britain resulted in the repeal of the Corn Laws and the Navigation Acts, forcing Central Canada and the Maritimes to compete with other countries in the British market. They found that they could not compete effectively in products like timber and, feeling abandoned by Great Britain, turned increasingly to the American market. For twelve years, beginning in 1854, virtually free trade took place with the U.S. under the terms of the Reciprocity Treaty. However, in 1866, after the conclusion of the American Civil War, the northern states decided to impose protective tariffs against Canadian goods. These events provided a powerful stimulus to the creation of a new east-west economic and political union. Another stimulus was the political deadlock that had developed between the French and English factions in the central Canadian legislative assembly, and a third was the threat posed by American interests who wished to encroach on the Canadian prairies. Political tensions between Canada's two principal language groups, and the threat of domination by a powerful southern neighbor, gave the impetus to Confederation in 1867, and they remain the major reasons why some Canadians wish to maintain that Confederation and why others question its viability.

The Confederation looked westward, and Manitoba and British Columbia were added to it in 1871 and 1873, respectively, with the promise of a national railway system. The federal government thereby committed itself to a huge public investment project. The governments of Central and Eastern Canada had subsidized railway construction in the 1850s and 1860s by guarantees of bonded debt. Such guarantees had proved to be crippling financial burdens, so when the transcontinental railway system was first proposed in the early 1870s the federal government decided to assist by means of cash and land grants. The Liberal government was prepared to build a government railway in stages, keeping pace with the advance of settlement, but the Conservative government of John A. Macdonald opted for a full-scale transcontinental system utilizing private enterprise and government grants.

In 1880 a group of private investors took up the government offer, and with $25 million in government cash grants and 25 million acres of free land, they proceeded to build the Canadian Pacific Railway—a feat that has become one of the few legends in Canadian history.

Government-supported railway construction was part of a Conservative government development program which has been called the National Policy.[1] In addition to railway subsidies it included the establishment of protective tariffs in 1878, a cheap land policy in the west, and the vigorous promotion of immigration. Tariff protection encouraged new industries in Central Canada and immigration to Western Canada provided greater markets for those industries and a good supply of foodstuffs. The movements of goods and immigrants helped to ensure the profitability of at least some of the railways that were built.

Government and business cooperated so closely in this development policy that the question can be raised whether private business interests used government to promote their own ends or whether government used business to achieve its purposes. Consequently, the distinction between the state and private enterprise in Canada often seems artificial.

It is certainly true that over the years governments at all levels have continued to play an extremely important role in the Canadian economy. According to Vernon Fowke, the programs initiated by the National Policy in 1878 had more or less run out by the early twentieth century, but beginning in the Depression of the 1930s and continuing through World War II to the present, a new "National Policy" can be said to have been set in motion, consisting of a program of public welfare, agricultural assistance, and fiscal and monetary management. In the process, public corporations like the CNR, CBC, and Petrocan were created to provide a government presence in industries which are privately owned in the United States.

A large part of the remainder of this book will be devoted to exploring the interactions between government and the private market economy. This chapter will provide some background material about what governments do and how their activities are paid for. First, however, we will look at the constitutional framework within which the various levels of government are required to operate in Canada.

The Distribution of Government Powers in Canada

One of the main purposes of a national constitution is to reconcile the conflicting demands of various regional interests with each other and with the interests of the nation as a whole, by creating different levels of government and by assigning specific jurisdictions to each. Canada's constitution, the British North America Act, also sought to do this. However, no completely satisfactory way was found to assign specific functions to the different levels of government, and government action in the economic sphere has been made more difficult by disputes over divisions of power. The B.N.A. Act gave the most far-reaching powers to the federal Parlia-

---

[1] This policy was examined most thoroughly by Professor Vernon C. Fowke of the University of Saskatchewan in his book, *The National Policy and the Wheat Economy* (Toronto: University of Toronto Press, 1957).

ment. The aim, as we have seen, was to produce a strong nation which would withstand its southern rival and avoid the type of civil war that had just occurred there.

Section 91 listed twenty-nine specific matters that belonged in the federal sphere, including the regulation of trade and commerce, taxation, the postal service, defense, banking and currency, and transportation and communication systems that serve two or more provinces. Later amendments gave to the federal government jurisdiction over unemployment insurance and the old age pension (the latter concurrently with the provinces). Most important, the federal government was assigned residual powers (powers not explicitly granted to the other levels of governments) and the general power to engage in any work deemed to be for the advantage of Canada.

In Section 92, the provincial legislatures were given general powers over local concerns and were assigned sixteen specific matters, including the power of direct taxation,² jurisdiction over municipal institutions, and most importantly, all property and civil rights in the province. Section 93 placed education under their jurisdiction.

Agriculture and immigration were assigned to both the federal and provincial governments in Section 95, with the federal government taking precedence in case of a conflict.

The federal government was intentionally placed in a much stronger financial position than the provincial governments. It could levy all kinds of taxes, while the provincial governments were restricted to direct taxes (for example, income and property taxes), which were quite unimportant at the time of Confederation.

During the Great Depression of the 1930s, provincial and municipal governments found it impossible to cope with the social and economic problems that came under their jurisdiction. The Report of the Royal Commission on Dominion-Provincial Relations (the Rowell-Sirois Report) in 1940 called for the redistribution of some tax revenues from the federal to the provincial governments. The latter in turn were urged to transfer more of their revenue to the municipalities.

The Growth of Government Expenditures

Exhibit 4.1 gives an indication of how government has grown over time. The chart shows what has happened to federal, provincial, and municipal **government purchases of goods and services** since 1947. Government purchases of goods and services (or **government purchases**, for short) include all the finished products purchased by government (everything from submarines to typewriter ribbons) plus the cost of hiring the services of all government employees (everyone from the prime minister to the courthouse janitor). These purchases are shown as a percentage of gross national product (GNP), a measure of the economy's total output of goods and services. By this measure, government has clearly grown over time. Before

Government purchases of goods and services (government purchases) Expenditures made by federal, provincial, and municipal governments to purchase goods from private firms and to hire the services of government employees.

---

² A direct tax is a tax applied to the person who is intended to pay it. An indirect tax may be shifted from the person to whom it is applied to another person. For example, the excise tax on cigarettes is an indirect tax because it is applied to the manufacturer but is actually added to the price of cigarettes and eventually paid for by the consumer.

Exhibit 4.1
Government current expenditures on goods and services as a percentage of GNP, 1947–1979
The percentage of total government purchases in GNP has grown substantially over time. Before the Depression of the 1930s, government purchases averaged less than 10 percent of GNP. Now, however, government expenditures have grown to a peacetime average of about 20 percent of GNP.

Source: Department of Finance, *Economic Review*, April 1980, p.160.

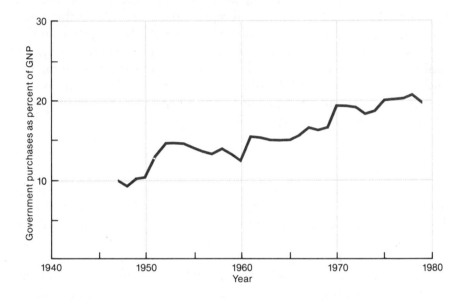

World War I, government purchases averaged less than 10 percent of GNP. They followed a steady trend upward from about 1947 until 1970. During the 1970s total government purchases appear to have leveled off at about 20 percent of GNP. Government purchases have followed almost precisely the same trend, and reached the same levels, in the United States.

Exhibit 4.2 provides a different kind of comparison. This graph gives data for several countries on total government expenditures, including transfer payments as well as government purchases. **Transfer payments** are all payments made by government to individuals that are not in return for goods or services currently supplied. They include such things as family allowance benefits, welfare payments, and unemployment compensation. Using total expenditures rather than government purchases as a measure makes the public sector look somewhat larger. Government purchases plus transfer payments now equal about a third of GNP in Canada. In comparison with the advanced industrial countries of Western Europe, however, the public sector in Canada is not a particularly large percentage of GNP. In Sweden, a country with roughly the same level of per capita income as Canada, government expenditures are equal to nearly two-thirds of GNP; and in Norway and the Netherlands, government expenditures are equal to more than half of GNP.

Transfer payments All payments made by government to individuals that are not made in return for goods or services currently supplied. Social security benefits, welfare payments, and unemployment compensation are major forms of transfer payments.

Exhibit 4.2
Total government expenditures as a percentage of GNP for selected countries
The data in this graph refer to total expenditures of central and local government units, including both government purchases of goods and services and transfer payments. By this measure, the size of government relative to the rest of the economy is larger than when only government purchases are taken into account. Note that although government expenditures in Canada are growing, they are still considerably lower in relation to the size of the economy than for the other countries shown, except for the United States.

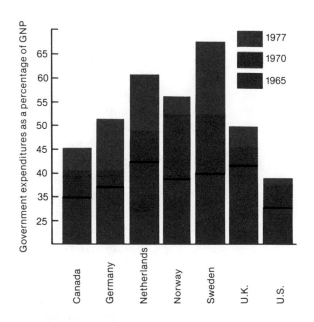

Source: Data from Theodore Geiger, *Welfare and Efficiency: Their Interactions in Western Europe and Implications for International Economic Relations* (Washington, D.C.: National Planning Association, 1979), Table 1-1. Used by permission. Note that the 1977 percentage for the Netherlands is actually based on 1976 data. Also, Department of Finance, *Economic Review*, April 1980, pp. 125, 183.

It should be noted, however, that these measurements of government activity in Canada do not include the expenditures of a wide variety of government-owned enterprises, such as provincial hydro utilities, or crown corporations (such as Air Canada, CN Rail, and Polysar Corporation). If their activities were included the figures for Canada would be higher.

The Functions of Government

Governments use the third to two-thirds of GNP that passes through their hands to perform a wide variety of functions. These functions can be classified under five general headings: provision of public goods, transfer of income, economic stabilization, regulation of private businesses, and administration of justice.

Provision of Public Goods The first function of government is to provide what economists call **public goods**—goods or services having the properties that (1) they cannot be provided to one citizen without being supplied also to that citizen's neighbors, and (2) once provided for one citizen, the cost of providing them to others is zero. Perhaps the best example of a public good is national defense. One citizen cannot very well be protected against foreign invasion or nuclear holocaust without having the protection "spill over" on neighbors. Also, it costs no more to protect a single resident of a given area than to protect an entire city.

Public goods are traditionally provided by government because their

Public goods Goods or services having the properties that (1) they cannot be provided to one citizen without being supplied also to that person's neighbors, and (2) once they are provided for one citizen, the cost of providing them to others is zero.

special properties make it hard for private business to market them profitably. Imagine what would happen if someone tried to set up a commercially operated ballistic missile defense system. If you subscribed, I would have no reason to subscribe too and would instead play the "free rider," relying on the spillover effect for my protection. But you would not subscribe, hoping that I would, so that you could be the free rider. The missile defense company would soon go bankrupt.

Transfer of Income The second function of government consists of making transfers of income and wealth from one citizen to another. Income or wealth is usually taken from citizens by means of taxation; but sometimes, as in the case of jury duty, it is taken by conscription of services. Benefits are distributed either in the form of direct cash payments or in the form of the free or below-cost provision of goods and services. Among the more familiar types of cash transfers are family allowance payments, welfare benefits, and unemployment compensation. Goods and services used for transfers include public education, public broadcasting (the CBC), public housing, fire protection, and medical care. They are provided at low or zero cost on the basis of political decisions rather than at market prices on the basis of ability to pay.

The federal government first became actively involved in the social welfare field during the 1930s, but the courts declared that these matters were under the jurisdiction of the provinces. In the post-World War II period this problem was solved by means of joint federal-provincial programs. By the 1960s the federal government was sharing the costs of provincial hospitalization and medical care programs, welfare assistance (under the Canada Assistance Plan), and post-secondary education in addition to its own programs of family allowances, Canada Pension Plan, Unemployment Insurance, and a wide range of other services. Quebec has now withdrawn from these shared-cost programs and the method of financing has been changed, from one in which the federal government paid 50 percent of approved expenditures to one in which the federal government transfers blocs of funds which grow at about the rate of growth of the economy as a whole, rather than the more rapid growth rate of medical and educational services characteristic of the last decade.

From the viewpoint of economic theory, the subsidized services used as vehicles for income transfers are different from the true public goods discussed earlier. They are consumed individually by selected citizens and do not share the two special properties of public goods.

In Canada, governments also provide a range of public utility services for which the user must pay either the full cost or a substantial part of it. These include provincial hydro utilities, national transportation (Air Canada and Canadian National Railways), provincial telephone systems, liquor outlets, and others. Government participation in such industries, in addition to government medical care and hospitalization programs, distinguishes our mixed-enterprise system from that in the United States.

Economic Stabilization Stabilization is a third economic function of government. Particularly since World War II, governments have tried to control the rates of economic growth, inflation, unemployment, and the balance of payments. The particular fiscal and monetary policies by which they have tried to do this are referred to as **stabilization policies**. These are discussed in detail in Part 2 of this book.

Income redistribution is also an aspect of stabilization policy, but it has not been the prime focus of fiscal and monetary policy. Income disparities in Canada are partly the result of regional disparities, which are the object of special government strategies described in the following paragraphs. Variations in income also result from peculiar characteristics of labor and product markets. Policies designed to correct imbalances produced by such markets are discussed in Part 4.

The Economic Council of Canada pointed out in its first *Annual Review* of 1964 that "Ever since Confederation the notion of 'balanced regional development' has been an implicit, if not explicit, objective of national policy." The Council was itself directed by Parliament "to study how national economic policies can best foster the balanced development of all areas of Canada."[3]

Stabilization policy An effort by government to control the level of national income and the related conditions of inflation, unemployment, and the balance of payments.

---

[3] Economic Council of Canada *Living Together: A Study of Regional Disparities* (Ottawa: Minister of Supply and Services, 1977), p. 3.

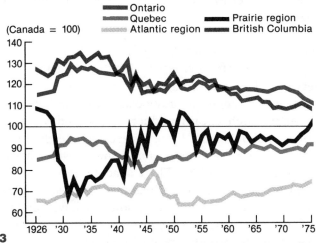

Exhibit 4.3
Index of personal income per capita, Canada, by region, 1926–1975

Source: Economic Council of Canada, *Living Together: A Study of Regional Disparities* (Ottawa: Minister of Supply and Services, 1977), p. 35.

As Exhibit 4.3 indicates, there are wide income disparities in Canada, reflecting the unequal distribution of natural resources, markets, transportation systems, and other important economic conditions. Ontario and British Columbia have had income levels considerably above average, while Quebec and the Atlantic region have fared worse than average. The Prairie region has had extremely erratic income behavior, but per capita income on the whole has been close to average.

Exhibit 4.3 also shows that the disparities among regions have been declining, especially since the mid-1950s. This is at least partly due to government programs. Quebec and the Atlantic region have received a large proportion of transfer payments since the early 1970s, coinciding with the revisions to the Unemployment Insurance Act of 1971. In 1969 the Department of Regional Economic Expansion (DREE) was established by the federal government to stimulate output in the least-advantaged areas of the country. The program has consisted of direct financial assistance to the private sector, manpower programs, and the provision of better infrastructure (for example, roads, water and sewer systems) for business. Between 1969 and 1975 almost one-half billion dollars was spent by DREE, with Quebec receiving just over 33 percent and the Atlantic region over 45 percent of the total.

In addition to such special projects the federal government has entered into an Equilization Payments arrangement with the provinces. The amount of money a province receives for health, education, and other public services is tied to a formula that takes into account both the expenditure needs of the province and its sources of revenue. Such revenue-equalization grants form a large proportion of the transfers now paid by the federal government to the provinces. Under the current formula, the provinces of Alberta, British Columbia, and Ontario do not receive equalization payments. Economists differ in their opinions about the effectiveness of these programs, but there is no denying that a substantial part of federal government activity consists of trying to overcome regional disparities.

Regulation of Private Businesses A fourth major function of government is the regulation of private businesses. Regulatory control is exercised through a network of specialized agencies and takes a variety of specific forms. Some agencies, such as provincial milk marketing boards, set maximum prices at which certain products can be sold, whereas others set minimum prices. The Food and Drug Directorates of the Department of Health and Welfare exercise considerable control over what can be produced by the firms they regulate. The Canadian Transport Commission sets basic operating conditions for airlines and railways. Regulatory boards have come to influence a wide range of economic behavior and regulation is a subject of widespread research and controversy. Chapter 29 will examine some major issues in the economics of regulation.

Administration of Justice The fifth major function of government is the administration of justice. Usually, the police and courts are not thought of as part of the economic area of government; but their activities do, in fact, have important economic consequences.

Consider what happens, for example, when a judge makes a decision in a case involving an unsafe product, a breach of contract, or an automobile accident. The decision has an immediate effect on resource allocation in the particular case, because one party must pay damages to the other or make some other form of compensation. More importantly, other people will observe the outcome of the decision and, as a result, may change the way they do things. If the courts say that buyers can collect damages from the makers of unsafe products, firms are likely to design their products differently. If certain standards are set for liability in automobile accidents, car makers, road builders, and insurance companies will take notice.

One further area of economic policy combines the judicial and regulatory functions of government: the field of anticombines policy and the control of monopoly. Chapter 28 in Part 3 of this book will take up the problem of public policy toward monopoly.

Overlapping Functions

The classification of government activities by function helps provide a theoretical understanding of the role of government in the economy, but it does not correspond very well to any breakdown of government activities by program or agency. Particular programs and agencies often perform a number of different functions at the same time. For example, the main business of the Department of National Defence appears to be the provision of a public good—national defense—but it performs other functions as well. In wartime it may perform a transfer function by shifting part of the cost of wars from the general taxpayer to young males via conscription. In peacetime it may provide an instrument of economic stabilization through the way it administers its substantial budget for the purchase of goods and services.

A full picture of the role of government, then, comes from looking at a breakdown of its activities not only by function but also by levels, agencies, and programs.

Public Expenditures by Type of Program

Exhibit 4.4a shows the pattern of federal government expenditures in 1979. The biggest single category was health and welfare, which includes unemployment compensation, social assistance (welfare), pension benefits, and shared cost of medical care and hospitalization.

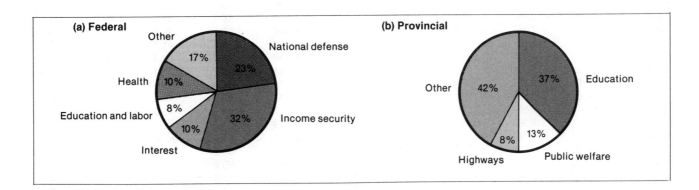

Exhibit 4.4
Patterns of government expenditure: federal versus provincial
This exhibit shows the pattern of government expenditure at the federal and provincial levels. The federal government bears the major burden of expenditures for national defense and income security, whereas education is by far the largest category of expenditure at the provincial level.

Sources: Department of Finance, *Economic Review*, April 1980, p. 237, and Statistics Canada, *Provincial Government Finance Revenue Expenditure (Estimates) 1978* (November 1979), pp. 10–11.

Exhibit 4.4b shows the pattern of provincial expenditure. Here, health and welfare combined are also the biggest item, with education also absorbing a large share.

To complete the picture, some idea of the relationship between the federal government on the one hand and provincial and municipal governments on the other is needed. Exhibit 4.5 shows that this relationship has been changing. Column g indicates that the federal share of total government outlays, before transfer payments, fell from a high of 65.1 percent in 1952 to a low of 49.3 percent in 1970. The federal share is shown in better perspective in column i, which takes into account the transfers made by the federal government to provincial and municipal governments. These transfers are actually spent by provincial and municipal authorities and

Exhibit 4.5

Allocation of expenditures by levels of government before and after transfer payments, 1950–1978

Years	Before transfer payments			After transfer payments			Before transfer payments		After transfer payments	
	(a) Total federal expenditures	(b) Total provincial-municipal expenditures	(c) Federal transfers to provinces and municipalities	(d) Total federal expenditures	(e) Total provincial-municipal expenditures	(f) Total government expenditures	(g) Federal share	(h) Provincial-municipal share	(i) Federal share	(j) Provincial-municipal share
				(a)−(c)	(b)+(c)	(d)+(e)	(a)÷(f)	(b)÷(f)	(d)÷(f)	(e)÷(f)
	(Millions of dollars)									
1950	$ 2,322	$ 1,758	$ 203	$ 2,119	$ 1,961	$ 4,080	56.9	43.1	51.9	48.1
1951	3,142	2,085	207	2,935	2,292	5,227	60.1	39.9	56.2	43.8
1952	4,297	2,308	173	4,124	2,481	6,605	65.1	34.9	62.4	37.6
1953	4,412	2,400	166	4,246	2,566	6,812	64.8	35.2	62.3	37.7
1954	4,390	2,701	166	4,224	2,867	7,091	61.9	38.1	59.6	40.4
1955	4,543	2,955	187	4,356	3,142	7,498	60.6	39.4	58.1	41.9
1956	4,813	3,411	198	4,615	3,609	8,224	58.5	41.5	56.1	43.9
1957	5,205	3,701	304	4,901	4,005	8,906	58.4	41.6	55.0	45.0
1958	5,930	4,016	417	5,513	4,433	9,946	59.6	40.4	55.4	44.6
1959	6,210	4,437	612	5,598	5,049	10,647	58.3	41.7	52.6	47.4
1960	6,457	4,923	705	5,752	5,628	11,380	56.7	43.3	50.5	49.5
1961	6,883	5,251	822	6,061	6,073	12,134	56.7	43.3	50.0	50.0
1962	7,406	5,729	1,054	6,352	6,783	13,135	56.4	43.6	48.4	51.6
1963	7,609	6,222	1,169	6,440	7,391	13,831	55.0	45.0	46.6	53.4
1964	8,010	6,807	1,252	6,758	8,059	14,817	54.1	45.9	45.6	54.4
1965	8,551	7,962	1,431	7,120	9,393	16,513	51.8	48.2	43.1	56.9
1966	9,753	9,239	1,664	8,089	10,903	18,992	51.4	48.6	42.6	57.4
1967	10,990	10,751	1,992	8,998	12,743	21,741	50.5	49.5	41.4	58.6
1968	12,229	12,116	2,372	9,857	14,488	24,345	50.2	49.8	40.5	59.5
1969	13,469	13,583	2,726	10,743	16,309	27,052	49.8	50.2	39.7	60.3
1970	15,262	15,685	3,397	11,865	19,082	30,947	49.3	50.7	38.3	61.7
1971	17,386	17,477	4,323	13,063	21,800	34,863	49.9	50.1	37.5	62.5
1972	20,126	19,329	4,558	15,568	23,887	39,455	51.0	49.0	39.5	60.5
1973	22,422	22,049	4,807	17,615	26,856	44,471	50.4	49.6	39.6	60.4
1974	28,869	26,453	6,165	22,704	32,618	55,322	52.2	47.8	41.0	59.0
1975	35,478	31,879	7,660	27,818	39,539	67,357	52.7	47.3	41.3	58.7
1976	38,753	36,837	8,510	30,243	45,347	75,590	51.3	48.7	40.0	60.0
1977	43,778	40,823	9,961	33,817	50,784	84,601	51.7	48.3	40.0	60.0
1978	48,854	45,313	10,859	37,995	56,172	94,167	51.9	48.1	40.3	59.7

Source: Department of Finance, *Economic Review*, April 1979, p. 201.

should be included in their expenditures. When this is done (in columns i and j) the share of federal expenditures is seen to have been below 50 percent ever since 1961. Federal expenditures are now around 40 percent of the total and provincial-municipal expenditures are around 60 percent. This reflects the growing importance of health and welfare expenditures.

WHO PAYS FOR GOVERNMENT?

In recent years, people have become increasingly conscious of the costs as well as the benefits of a large, economically active public sector. In one sense, this is nothing new; people have grumbled about taxes ever since taxes were first invented. Nonetheless, in the late 1970s, citizens began to do more than grumble. In the United States, voters forced governments in several states to impose legal limits on state spending or taxes. In Canada, the revolt was not so dramatic, but several changes in government policy may have been due to growing citizen concern over taxes.

What Kinds of Taxes?

We can begin by looking at the kinds of taxes that federal, provincial and municipal governments use to raise revenue. Exhibit 4.6 gives the breakdowns. On the federal side, individual income taxes, which include social insurance contributions, are the largest revenue-raising item. Sales and excise taxes form the second largest source of revenue, followed by taxes on corporate profits.

Provincial governments rely heavily on personal income taxes (collected by the federal government but belonging to the provincial government), sales taxes, and transfers from the federal government. Municipalities depend almost entirely on property taxes and transfers from provincial governments (some of which come, in turn, from the federal government). Total taxes, like total government expenditures, amount to about 40 percent of GNP.

The Problem of Tax Incidence

Exhibit 4.6 shows the kinds of taxes paid to support various levels of government but not who really pays them. Economists refer to the question of who actually bears the burden of taxation as the problem of *tax incidence*. This problem is not at all an easy one to solve. It is not enough just to look up the tax records of federal, provincial, and municipal governments. That would reveal only who had handed over the tax money to the authorities, not who actually bore the economic burden of the taxes. What makes tax incidence a difficult problem is the fact that the party who is obligated by law to pay the tax can often shift the burden of it to someone else.

An Illustration of Tax Incidence For a simple example, suppose a law is passed that requires all retailers to make a tax payment of $.50 to the government for each pack of cigarettes they sell. Who will bear the economic burden of this tax? A simple supply and demand analysis will provide the answer.

shapes of the supply and demand curves really are for the goods and services that are taxed.

Overall Tax Incidence Taxes can be classified in terms of their incidence as progressive or regressive. A **progressive tax** takes a larger percentage of income from people whose incomes are high, and a **regressive tax** takes a larger percentage of income from people whose incomes are low. A **proportional tax** takes a constant percentage of income from all people. One of the most interesting questions about the economics of taxation is whether the overall effect of federal, provincial, and municipal taxes is progressive, regressive, or somewhere in between.

Progressive tax A tax that takes a larger percentage of income from people whose income is high.

Regressive tax A tax that takes a larger percentage of income from people whose income is low.

Proportional tax A tax that takes a constant percentage of income from people of all income levels.

Exhibit 4.7
The effects of a $.50 per pack sales tax on cigarettes
Before the sales tax is imposed, the equilibrium price for cigarettes is $1 per pack. The $.50 per pack sales tax can be treated as the sellers' added cost of doing business. It pushes the supply curve up by $.50, as shown. After the shift in the supply curve, the price paid by buyers rises to $1.25 per pack, and the price received by sellers falls to $.75. Thus, when the slopes of the supply and demand curves are equal, as shown in this exhibit, half the burden of the tax falls on sellers, and half is shifted to buyers.

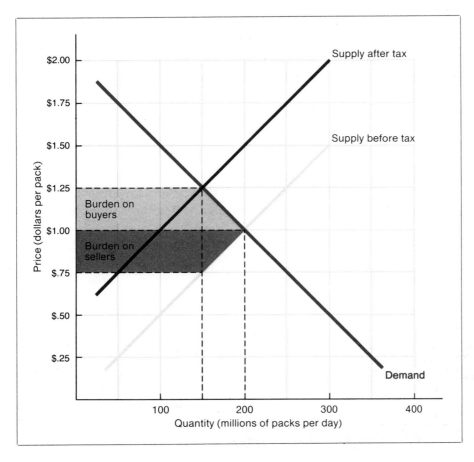

Fraser Institute An independent economic and social research organization with headquarters in Vancouver. It is firmly committed to the study and preservation of a competitive market system.

A study of the real tax burden of Canadian families was published by the **Fraser Institute** of Vancouver in 1979. Exhibit 4.8 is based on data from that study, showing how different types of taxes affect families at different levels of income. Three examples of annual income for 1978 — $10,000, $20,000, and $30,000 were chosen to represent low, middle, and high-income families respectively (average family income in Canada was about $20,000). Exhibit 4.8 shows that between the lowest and highest classes all types of taxes were progressive. The overall tax burden increased from 36.9 percent for low-income families to 59.8 percent for high-income families. However, between the lower and middle-income families the picture is quite different. Income taxes were clearly progressive, but property taxes were regressive and the other taxes were almost proportional. This mixture of progressive, regressive, and proportional taxes results in a total tax burden that is only slightly progressive in this range of income.

However, this picture is somewhat misleading. To appreciate what the real tax burden is, something has to be known about the benefits that different income levels receive from government transfer payments. The **net incidence of taxation** can be defined as the difference between the amount paid to governments and the amount received from them, calculated as a percentage of income.

Net incidence of taxation The difference between the amount paid to government in taxes and the amount received from government, calculated as a percentage of income.

According to Fraser Institute estimates, families in the lowest third of the income scale paid net taxes of $-475 million in 1978, or -1.9 percent of total taxes paid. In other words, they received more from government than they paid. Families in the average income third paid net taxes of $7,021 million or 27.9 percent of total taxes, while families in the highest income third paid net taxes of $18,638 million, or 74.0 percent of total taxes.

It should be noted that these figures are based only on measurable benefits and payments. The argument is sometimes advanced that wealthy people receive sizeable benefits from government in the form of business grants, government-financed training programs, highways, and numerous other types of benefits that cannot be measured. This should be kept in mind in evaluating the above figures.

CONCLUSIONS

This chapter has explained something of the services government performs and something of who bears the costs of providing these services. But one

Exhibit 4.8
Incidence of selected taxes,
(selected taxes as percentage of cash income)

Cash Income	Income Tax as Percent of Income	Sales Tax as Percent of Income	Liquor, Tobacco, Other Excise Taxes as Percent of Income	Social Security, Pension, Medical and Hospital Taxes as Percent of Income	Property Taxes as Percent of Income	Total Taxes as Percent of Income
$10,000	8.0%	5.3	1.8	4.3	4.8	36.9
$20,000	15.7	5.5	1.9	6.0	1.5	37.3
$30,000	20.2	7.5	2.6	5.5	6.5	59.8

Source: Michael Walker and Sally Pipes, eds., *Tax Facts* (Vancouver, B.C.: The Fraser Institute, 1979), pp. 39–41.

major question not asked is *how well* the vast machinery of government does its job. This important question involves both normative and positive economics. The normative element comes in deciding what goals the government ought to pursue and the positive element in measuring how closely it meets those goals. This question of *how well* is one to which we shall return repeatedly throughout the book.

Readers who proceed immediately to Part 2 of this book will begin to learn the analytical tools needed to determine how well the government performs its function of economic stabilization. This is one of the most important applications of economics, and in some respects it is one of the most controversial. The high rates of inflation and unemployment that the Canadian economy has experienced in the 1970s have given rise to some important new theories and important new doubts about how well the government has been doing its job.

Readers who go from here directly to Part 3 will soon encounter other parts of the question of how well government does its job. Part 3 begins with a more detailed look at the tools of supply and demand analysis and the theory of prices and markets that stands behind it. This theory is then applied to evaluating government performance in the areas of agricultural policy, policy toward monopoly, the production of public goods, and the regulation of private business.

SUMMARY

1. Canadian economic development has been shaped and supported by deliberate government policies, called the "National Policy" by economists like Vernon C. Fowke. This has included subsidies to business, protective tariffs, a cheap land policy, and the promotion of immigration. In recent decades, such policies have been supplemented by programs of public welfare and fiscal and monetary management.

2. Governments in Canada have had their jurisdictions defined by the British North America Act. The different levels of government have been forced to resolve their respective revenue and expenditure difficulties by frequent negotiations and various types of cost-sharing arrangements.

3. Five major economic functions of government are the provision of public goods, the transfer of income, the stabilization of the economy, the regulation of private businesses, and the administration of justice.

4. The determination of the incidence of various kinds of taxes is a difficult problem of applied economics. The burden of many taxes can be shifted from those who bear the legal obligation of paying them to other parties. When all kinds of shifting are taken into account, it appears that the combined federal, provincial, and municipal tax systems are neither progressive nor regressive overall.

DISCUSSION QUESTIONS

1. What would happen to Canadian society if we did away with the federal government? In which cases could provincial and municipal governments fill in? In which cases would they be unable to do so?

2. List the major goods and services provided by the government at different levels. Then determine the extent to which these goods are public goods. Which level of government tends to supply the most public goods? Which one the least? (Can you determine which?)
3. How can a government respond to changes in the relative prices of the goods and services it buys and provides for its constituents? How is it subject to the same forces as a business? How not?
4. Would you prefer living where income taxes are progressive or regressive? Why?
5. When a tax is imposed on cigarettes, the price paid by consumers goes up and the price received by sellers goes down. The government benefits by the amount of the difference on each pack sold. There is also a second effect of the tax: fewer packs are sold. Who benefits and who is hurt by the second effect? Does the fact that cigarettes are harmful to people influence your answer? What if they were good for people?

SUGGESTIONS FOR FURTHER READING

Fowke, Vernon C. *The National Policy and the Wheat Economy*. Toronto: University of Toronto Press, 1957.
Describes the continuation into the twentieth century, through a series of new government policies, of the national policy begun in the nineteenth century.

Aitkin, Hugh G.J., ed. *The State and Economic Growth*, pp. 79–114. New York: Social Science Research Council, 1959. Reprinted in *Approaches to Canadian Economic History*, edited by W.T. Easterbrook and M.H. Watkins, pp. 183–221. Toronto: Macmillan, 1978.
Describes the important role played by government in Canadian economic development, particularly in containment of U.S. expansion.

NATIONAL INCOME, INFLATION, AND UNEMPLOYMENT

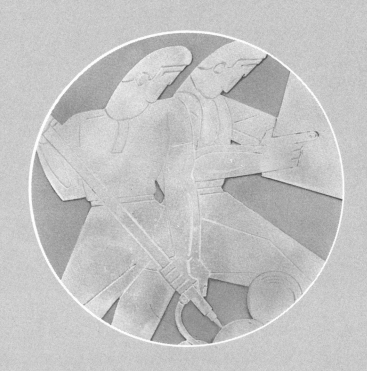

C H A P T E R 5

THE CIRCULAR FLOW OF INCOME AND PRODUCT

WHAT YOU WILL LEARN IN THIS CHAPTER

This chapter will describe how the circular flow of income and product sends goods from firms to households and factor services from households to firms. At the same time, it will show how payments for these goods and services flow in the opposite direction through the economy. The idea of the circular flow will be used in two ways. First, it will give a framework for a set of important definitions and equalities. Second, it will show how the concepts of supply, demand, and equilibrium can be applied in a macroeconomic context.

FOR REVIEW

Here are some important terms and concepts that will be put to use in this chapter. If you do not understand them, review them before proceeding.
- *Factors of production (Chapter 1)*
- *Equilibrium (Chapter 3)*
- *Government purchases and transfer payments (Chapter 4)*

This chapter begins putting together a theory that will explain unemployment, inflation, and economic growth and that will offer a framework for thinking about economic stabilization policy. These subjects make up the branch of economics known as **macroeconomics**. The prefix *macro* comes from the Greek work meaning "big"; but although inflation, unemployment, and economic growth are big issues in the sense of being important, that is not the reason for using the term *macroeconomics*. Instead, the term is applied because this branch of economics works primarily with **aggregate** economic data — any data that are grand totals for the economy as a whole. Macroeconomics is thus distinguished from **microeconomics** (*micro* meaning "small"), which studies individual prices, the behavior of individual firms and households, and so on.

Because it will take several chapters to complete the study of macroeconomics, it is necessary to have a clear idea of the lay of the land before beginning. The best way to get an overview of the relationships among the

Macroeconomics The branch of economics devoted to the study of unemployment, inflation, economic growth, and stabilization policy.

Aggregate A term used in economics to describe any quantity that is a grand total for the whole economy.

Microeconomics The branch of economics devoted to the study of the behavior of individual households and firms and to the determination of the relative prices of individual goods and services.

Circular flow of income and product The flow of goods from firms to households and factor services from households to firms, counterbalanced by the flow of expenditures from households to firms and factor payments from firms to households.

major economic aggregates is to represent them in terms of a **circular flow of income and product.** The rest of this chapter, then, will be devoted to the circular flow.

THE STRUCTURE OF THE CIRCULAR FLOW

A Simple Economy

To see the circular flow in its most basic form, begin by imagining an economy made up only of households and business firms — an economy with no public sector at all. To make things simpler still, assume that households live entirely from hand to mouth, spending all of their income on consumer goods as soon as that income is received. Similarly, assume that firms sell their entire output to consumers as soon as it is produced.

The circular flow of income and product for this ultra-simple economy is shown in Exhibit 5.1. The diagram is drawn with physical goods and

---

Exhibit 5.1

The circular flow in a simple economy

In this simple economy, households spend all their income on consumer goods as soon as they receive it, and firms sell all their output to households as soon as they produce it. Physical goods and factor services flow clockwise, while corresponding money payments flow counterclockwise.

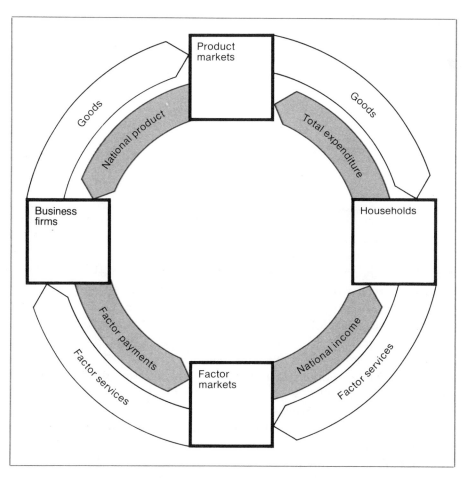

services flowing clockwise and the corresponding money payments flowing counterclockwise.

Two sets of markets link households to firms in this economy. Product markets, which appear at the top of the diagram, are markets where households purchase goods and services—bread, television sets, houses, dry cleaning services, entertainment—for their own direct consumption. Factor markets, which appear at the bottom of the diagram, are the markets in which households sell to firms the **factors of production** they use in making the things sold in product markets.

In return for the natural resources, labor, and capital that they buy from households, firms make **factor payments** in the form of rents, wages, salaries, and interest payments. As a matter of accounting convention, when firms use land, labor, or capital that they themselves own, they are counted as "purchasing" those factors from the households that own the firms, even though no money changes hands and no explicit factor payment is made. For purposes of macroeconomic analysis, profits are thus considered an implicit factor payment from firms to the households that own them.[1]

Factors of production The basic elements of natural resources, labor, and capital used in the production of all goods.

Factor payments The payments with which firms purchase factors of production (natural resources, labor, and capital).

Stocks and Flows

Having said this much, let's pause for a moment to concentrate on a word used several times already. Economists call all of the things shown in Exhibit 5.1 **flows** because they are processes that occur continuously through time. Flows are measured in units per time period—for example, in dollars per year, gallons per minute, or tons per month. Measurements of flows are measurements of rates at which things are happening.

The technical language of economics distinguishes carefully between flows and stocks. A **stock** is an accumulated quantity of something existing at a particular time. (The word *stock* in this general sense has nothing to do with the stock market kind of stocks that are bought and sold on Wall Street.)

For an illustration of the difference between stocks and flows, we can think of a bathtub filling. When we talk about how fast the water is running, we are talking about a *flow*, measured in gallons per minute. When we talk about how much water is in the tub at a given moment, we are talking about a *stock*, measured only in gallons. Similarly, in the world of economics, we might talk about the rate of housing construction in Toronto, Ontario, in terms of new units per month (the flow) as distinct from the actual number of houses in Toronto as of January 1, 1980 (the stock).

Flows Processes occurring continuously through time, measured in units per time period.

Stocks Accumulated quantities existing at a particular time, measured in terms of simple units.

National Income and Product

Two of the flows in Exhibit 5.1 deserve special attention and have special names. The first is **national income**—the total of all wages, rents, interest payments, and profits received by households. National income is shown

National income The total of all incomes, including wages, rents, interest payments, and profits received by households.

---

[1] For certain purposes of microeconomics, profits are not considered factor payments.

National product The total value of all goods and services supplied in the economy.

in the diagram as an arrow aimed at the box representing households. The second important flow is **national product** — a measure of the total value of the goods and services produced. In the diagram, national product is shown as an arrow passing from the box representing product markets to the box representing firms.

In this economy, national income and national product are equal, simply because of the way they are defined.[2] This equality can be verified in either of two ways. First, consider household expenditures as a link between national income and national product. Households are assumed to spend all of their income on consumer goods as soon as they receive it, and firms are assumed to sell all of their output to consumers as soon as it is produced. The payments made by buyers must equal the payments received by sellers, so national product must equal national income.

Alternatively, consider factor payments as a link between national income and national product. When firms receive money for goods they sell, they use part of it to pay the workers, natural resource owners, and others who contributed factors of production to make the goods. Anything left over is profit. Factor payments, including profits, account for all the money received by firms, so total factor payments must be equal to national product. Factor payments also account for all of the income received by households, so total factor payments must be equal to national income. It again follows that national income and national product must be equal.

Saving and Investment

The circular flow shown in Exhibit 5.1 is so simple that not very much of interest can be said about it. To build a theory that will be useful for understanding the real-world economy, a few complications must be introduced.

The first change will be to drop the requirement that households immediately spend all of their income to purchase consumer goods and to permit them instead to save part of what they earn. The rate of saving by households, under this assumption, is simply the difference between national income and household consumption expenditures.

Fixed investment Purchases by firms of newly produced capital goods, such as production machinery, newly built structures, and office equipment.

Inventory investment Changes in the stocks of finished products and raw materials that firms keep on hand. If stocks are increasing, inventory investment is positive; if they are decreasing, it is negative.

The second change will be to drop the requirement that firms immediately sell all of their output to consumers. Instead, they will be permitted to sell some products to other firms and to let some accumulate in inventory before selling them to anyone. When firms buy newly produced capital goods (for example, production machinery, newly built structures, or office equipment) from other firms, they are said to engage in **fixed investment**. When firms increase the stock of finished products or raw materials that they keep on hand, they are said to engage in **inventory investment**. The rate of inventory investment can be less than zero in periods when firms are

---

[2] Chapter 6 will show that the equality between national income and product does not hold precisely as these concepts are actually measured by the official statisticians of the Canadian government. It would be pointless, though, to let this statistical detail complicate all theoretical discussions. Everywhere in this chapter, and everywhere from Chapter 7 onward, the necessary simplifying assumptions are made so that national income and product *are* equal.

decreasing their stocks of goods or raw materials on hand. The sum of fixed investment and inventory investment will be called simply **investment**.

Investment The sum of fixed investment and inventory investment.

Circular Flow with Saving and Investment Exhibit 5.2 shows how the circular flow of income and expenditure looks when saving and investment are added. (The clockwise arrows showing the flows of goods and services have been omitted to simplify the diagram). There are now two pathways along which expenditures can travel on their way from households to product markets. Some household income is used for consumption expenditure and reaches product markets directly. Other household income is diverted to saving, which supplies a source of funds for firms to use in making investment expenditures; this income reaches product markets indirectly.

Exhibit 5.2

The circular flow with saving and investment

When saving and investment are added to the circular flow, there are two pathways by which expenditures can travel on their way from households to product markets. Some income is spent directly on consumer goods. The rest is saved and passes to firms via financial markets. The firms then use the investment expenditures in the product markets.

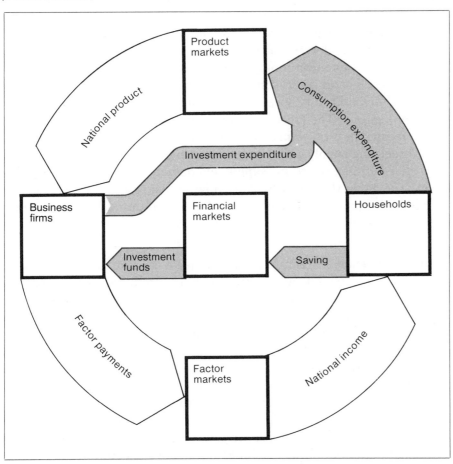

On the way from households to firms, the flow of saving passes through a set of financial markets. These markets include a great variety of financial institutions—chartered banks, trust and loan companies, credit unions and caisses populaires, the stock and bond markets, insurance companies, and other institutions that act as intermediaries between households that save and firms that make investment expenditures. Households supply funds to these financial markets. Firms can then borrow from financial markets to obtain the funds they need to make investment expenditures. (Chapter 11 will discuss the operation of financial markets in detail.)

Equilibrium and Disequilibrium in the Circular Flow   Adding saving and investment to the circular flow raises an entirely new issue: can total expenditure still be counted on to provide an equalizing link between national income and national product? There are now two entirely different sets of people making expenditure decisions. Households decide how much to spend on consumption, and firms decide how much to spend on investment. How can we be sure that when these two kinds of expenditures are added together, the total will just equal the total value of all goods produced? A new way of applying supply and demand analysis will help find the answers.

Aggregate Supply and Demand

Aggregate supply The total value of all goods and services supplied in the economy; identical to national product.

Aggregate demand The total value of all planned expenditures of all buyers in the economy.

The term **aggregate supply** refers to the grand total of all goods supplied by all firms in the entire economy. There is already another term for the same thing: national product. *Aggregate supply* and *national product* are two names for the total value of goods and services supplied by all firms. Following the same terminology, **aggregate demand** can be used to mean the grand total of all goods demanded for the whole economy. In defining *aggregate demand* this way, though, care must be taken in the way "demand" is used. The precise way of defining *aggregate demand* is to say that it means the total *planned* expenditures of all buyers in the economy.

In discussing supply and demand for individual goods or services, the step after defining the terms *supply* and *demand* was to explain equilibrium. The same thing can be done now by using aggregate supply and aggregate demand to explain the ideas of equilibrium and disequilibrium in the circular flow.

A Numerical Example   A numerical example will make the point. Imagine an economy in which only three goods are produced: apples, milling machines, and radios. The various firms in this economy have plans to produce apples at a rate of $30,000 worth per year, milling machines at a rate of $40,000 worth per year, and radios at a rate of $30,000 worth per year. All firms are busy carrying out their plans. The result is a flow of output at a rate of $100,000 per year. This flow, which can be called either *national product* or *aggregate supply*, is detailed in lines 1 to 4 of Exhibit 5.3.

While producers are busy carrying out their plans, buyers make plans too. Consumers plan to buy apples at a rate of $25,000 worth per year and radios at a rate of $30,000 worth per year. Also, the firms that make radios are planning to buy milling machines at a rate of $35,000 worth per year in order to increase their radio-producing capacity for the future. No one is planning either to increase or to decrease the stocks of finished products held in inventory, so planned inventory investment is zero. All these buying plans are expressed in lines 5 to 11 of Exhibit 5.3. The total of all planned expenditures (consumption plus planned investment) is listed in line 11 as aggregate demand.

Comparing line 1 with line 11, *it is obvious that the plans of producers and the plans of buyers do not mesh*. Aggregate supply is not equal to aggregate demand. There is nothing very surprising about the situation. After all, there have been no direct consultations among the various buyers and sellers when plans have been made. Each has acted on the basis of whatever knowledge has been available from the price system, plus private judgments about future trends or changes. As a result, things are not working out for everyone according to plan. The apples, radios, and milling machines are all being produced, but not all of them are being sold. After buyers have bought all they plan to, $5,000 worth of apples are left over, as are $5,000 worth of milling machines. These products cannot simply vanish into thin air. The firms that made them are putting them into inventory, even though they had not planned to do so, in the hope of selling them at some time in the future. The result is an *unplanned* inventory investment of $10,000, as shown in lines 12 to 14 of Exhibit 5.3.

Exhibit 5.3

A numerical example of the circular flow for a simple economy

National product must always be equal to total expenditure, even when the circular flow is not in equilibrium. In the example shown here, national product (aggregate supply) exceeds total planned expenditure (aggregate demand), so unplanned inventory investment makes up the difference.

Output Resulting from Producers' Plans			
1 Total national product (aggregate supply)			$100,000
2 Apples	$30,000		
3 Radios	30,000		
4 Milling machines	40,000		
Expenditures Resulting from Buyers' Plans			
5 Total consumption expenditure		$55,000	
6 Apples	$25,000		
7 Radios	30,000		
8 Total planned investment expenditure		35,000	
9 Fixed investment	35,000		
10 Planned inventory investment	0		
11 Total planned expenditure (aggregate demand)			$90,000
Other Expenditure			
12 Total unplanned inventory investment			10,000
13 Unsold apples	5,000		
14 Unsold milling machines	5,000		
Summary			
15 Total national product			$100,000
16 Total national expenditure			100,000
17 Planned	$90,000		
18 Unplanned	10,000		

An Important Equality When aggregate buying plans do not mesh with aggregate productions plans, the circular flow is said to be in *disequilibrium*. Aggregate supply and aggregate demand are not equal; national product and total planned expenditure are not equal. One crucial equality does hold, though. National product is still equal to total expenditure *when both planned and unplanned expenditures are taken into account.* The reason is that goods that are produced and not sold *must* be added to inventories, whether firms planned to put them there or not. As long as unplanned inventory investment is counted as part of total expenditure — and it is — total expenditure is by definition equal to national product. In equation form:

$$\text{National product} = \text{Total planned expenditure} + \text{Unplanned inventory investment} = \text{Total expenditure.}$$

Another way to write exactly the same thing is:

$$\text{Aggregate supply} = \text{Aggregate demand} + \text{Unplanned inventory investment.}$$

Reactions to Disequilibrium In the numerical example outlined in Exhibit 5.3, aggregate demand fell short of aggregate supply. Because buyers' and sellers' plans failed to mesh, there was an unplanned accumulation of inventories. Firms would not want this unplanned rise in inventories to go on and on. In order to stop it, they would reduce their rate of output, or lower prices in order to stimulate sales, or both. These reactions would amount to a reduction in aggregate supply. The size of the circular flow would begin to shrink as the number of dollars received by firms for their products and the number of dollars paid out to workers fell.

At another time, aggregate demand might exceed aggregate supply. With total planned expenditures greater than national product, unplanned inventory depletion would take place. Firms would react in a way opposite to their reaction to an excess of aggregate supply over aggregate demand. Either they would increase output to rebuild inventories, or they would take advantage of the high level of demand to raise prices, or both. Whichever they did, the size of the circular flow would grow as incomes and expenditures rose.

Finally, it is entirely possible that when the plans of buyers and sellers were tested in the market, they would turn out to mesh. In that case, with production and planned expenditure equal, no unplanned inventory investment would occur, and no corrections would be necessary. The circular flow would be in equilibrium.

Income and Expenditure

Nothing has yet been said about national income. Go back for a moment to the situation in Exhibit 5.3. Firms are shown to be producing $100,000 worth of goods a year. To produce those goods they must make factor payments (including profits, if any) of $100,000 to households, which means that national income is also $100,000. The households receiving this income plan to buy consumer goods at a rate of $55,000 per year, which means that they plan to save at a rate of $45,000 per year. (Remember that saving plus consumption exhausts income in this simple economy.)

These household saving plans do not mesh with firms' investment plans, as shown in line 8 of Exhibit 5.3 As things actually have turned out, though, the firms have invested more than they had planned to. The actual total of their investment, including unplanned inventory investment, is exactly equal to saving. It must be. Once again, goods cannot vanish into thin air after they are produced, and unplanned inventory investment acts as the balancing item.

The Place of Government in the Circular Flow

When government enters the circular flow of income, expenditure, and product, things become slightly more complicated. Exhibit 5.4 shows how

---

Exhibit 5.4

The circular flow with government included

With government added to the circular flow of income and product, there are two new channels along which funds can flow from households to product markets. Some income is diverted to government in the form of net taxes and then used to finance government purchases. Alternatively, if the government runs a budget deficit, it may borrow from the public via financial markets and use the borrowed funds to finance its expenditures. If the government runs a budget surplus, the flow of funds along this pathway may be reversed, in which case the arrow from government to financial markets will point in the opposite direction from that shown.

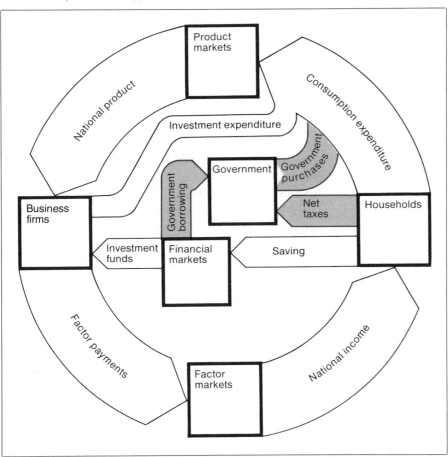

Net taxes Total tax revenues collected by government at all levels minus total transfer payments disbursed.

Deficit In referring to government budgets, an excess of government purchases over net taxes.

Surplus In referring to government budgets, an excess of net taxes over government purchases.

the circular flow looks when government is added. Two new pathways along which expenditures can flow from households to the product markets are opened up.

First, governments take in revenue from taxes they levy on households. Some of that revenue, as shown in Chapter 4, is immediately returned to households in the form of transfer payments. The difference between what governments take in as tax revenue and what they pay out as transfer payments is called **net taxes**. Funds thus flow from households to government as net taxes and then from government to product markets as government purchases.

Second, if government purchases of goods and services exceed net taxes, the government may need to borrow from the public through financial markets. In this case, the government budget is said to be in **deficit**. When the government runs a deficit, funds flow from households to financial markets as saving, then from financial markets to the government as government borrowing, and finally from government to the product markets as government purchases.

Sometimes, the government budget is in **surplus** rather than deficit. In that case, government's borrowing from the public is less than its repayment of past debts. The net flow of funds between government and financial markets is the reverse of what is shown in Exhibit 5.4.

Adding the Foreign Sector

The final step in constructing the circular flow of income and product is to add the foreign sector, as in Exhibit 5.5. This exhibit shows that some of the expenditures made by consumers, firms, and governments do not flow to domestic product markets but instead flow to foreign economies to pay for imports of goods and services. These expenditures are shown by the arrow labeled *imports* in the exhibit. At the same time, some expenditures on domestically produced goods and services are made by foreigners. These are shown in the exhibit by the arrow labeled *exports*, which passes from the foreign economy sector to domestic product markets.

Remember that the arrows in Exhibit 5.5 all represent flows of funds, not flows of physical goods and services. The import arrow thus shows the flow of funds out of the Canadian economy to pay for imported goods and services, and the export arrow shows the flow of funds into the Canadian economy in payment for exports of goods and services. If imports exceed exports, the Canadian economy is said to run a foreign deficit. This deficit must be paid for by borrowing from foreigners, hence the arrow labeled *loans from foreigners to finance trade deficit*, which points from foreign economies to the domestic financial markets. If instead Canadian exports exceed imports, Canada is said to run a foreign trade surplus. In this case (not shown), foreign buyers of Canadian goods have to pay for them by borrowing funds in Canadian financial markets, and the direction of the arrow is reversed.

Leakages and Injections The first section of this chapter described a highly simplified economy in which households spent all their income on consumption goods, so that all expenditures flowed directly from households to domestic product markets. As financial markets, government, and foreign economies were added, however, it was shown that in the real

Exhibit 5.5
The circular flow with government and the foreign sector

This exhibit adds a foreign sector to the circular flow with government that was shown in Exhibit 5.4. Some consumption, investment, and government purchases are for goods produced abroad; this is shown as the triple arrow pointing toward the imports. Some purchases of domestically produced goods and services are made by foreigners; these are shown as the arrow labeled *exports* running from the foreign sector to domestic product markets. If imports exceed exports, the excess imports must be paid for by borrowing from abroad; this is shown by the arrow labeled *loans from foreigners to finance trade deficit*. If exports instead exceed imports, there is a foreign trade surplus, and the direction of that arrow is reversed. Note that all the arrows in this exhibit represent flows of funds, not of physical goods and services. That is why the exports arrow points into the domestic economy and the imports arrow points away from it.

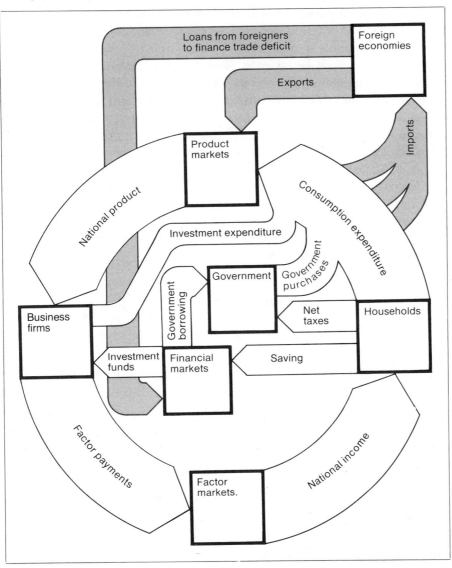

Injections The part of total expenditures that does not originate from domestic households — that is, investment, government purchases, and exports.

Leakages The part of national income not devoted to consumption (saving plus net taxes) plus domestic expenditures on foreign-made goods (imports).

world, three kinds of purchases of goods and services do not originate directly in domestic households: investment (purchases of capital goods and goods for inventory by domestic business firms), government purchases, and exports (purchases of domestic goods and services by foreigners). From now on, these three kinds of purchases will be referred to collectively as **injections** into the circular flow of goods and services.

Offsetting these injections are imports (expenditures of households, business firms, and units of government on goods produced abroad), plus saving and taxes (the use of household income for purposes other than the direct purchase of goods and services). From now on, saving, net taxes, and imports will be referred to collectively as **leakages** from the circular flow.

The Equality of National Income and National Product Another numerical example will show that adding the government and foreign sectors, with their associated injections and leakages, to the economy does not disturb the fundamental equality between national income and national product on which the circular flow is based. Exhibit 5.6 shows an economy in which consumption is $70,000, investment is $22,000, government purchases are $10,000, and exports are $8,000. Of the consumption, investment, and government purchases shown, $10,000 is spent on imported goods, which cannot be counted as part of the national product of the country represented in the exhibit. National product is thus shown as the total of consumption, investment, and government purchases, plus expenditures on domestic goods by foreigners (exports), minus that part of consumption, investment, and government purchases not spent on domestic goods and services (imports). As Exhibit 5.6 is constructed, the total comes to $100,000.

The production of $100,000 of national product generates $100,000 in factor payments for domestic households. As the second table in Exhibit 5.6 shows, this amount is divided among consumption ($70,000), saving ($25,000), and net taxes ($5,000). Introducing the term **net exports** to represent exports minus imports, the relationships shown in Exhibit 5.6 can be written in equation form as:

Net exports Total exports minus total imports.

$$\text{National product} = \text{Consumption} + \text{Investment} + \text{Government purchases} + \text{Net exports}$$

$$= \text{Consumption} + \text{Saving} + \text{Net taxes}$$

$$= \text{National income.}$$

The Equality of Leakages and Injections It follows from the relationship between national income and national product that total injections must equal total leakages. Beginning with the equation shown above, consumption can be subtracted from both sides, and imports can be added to both sides. The result is:

$$\text{Investment} + \text{Government purchases} + \text{Exports} = \text{Saving} + \text{Net taxes} + \text{Imports}$$

or

$$\text{Total injections} = \text{Total leakages.}$$

Exhibit 5.6
The equality of national income and product
This numerical example shows that the equality of national income and product is maintained when the government and foreign sectors, with their associated injections and leakages, are added to the economy. National product is a measure of the goods and services produced in the domestic economy. To arrive at its total, we add consumption, investment, and government purchases of all kinds, plus foreign purchases of domestically produced goods (exports), and we subtract the portion of consumption, investment, and government purchases devoted to foreign-made goods (imports). Using the term *net exports* to stand for exports minus imports, we could say that national product equals consumption plus investment plus government purchases plus net exports. This is equal to national income, which is divided among consumption, saving, and net taxes — as shown in the second part of the table.

Consumption	$ 70,000
Plus investment	22,000
Plus government purchases	10,000
Plus exports	8,000
Less imports	−10,000
Equals national product	$100,000
Consumption	$ 70,000
Plus saving	25,000
Plus net taxes	5,000
Equals national income	$100,000

Note that this relationship holds even though, in the numerical example of Exhibit 5.6, no individual pair of items on the leakages and injections list exactly matches up. In that example, saving exceeds investment by $3,000, imports exceed exports by $2,000, and net taxes fall short of government purchases by $5,000. The reason total injections must always equal total leakages is that injections include unplanned inventory investment as a balancing item. Suppose, for example, that beginning from the position shown in Exhibit 5.6, government purchases suddenly rise by $5,000, while planned expenditures by households, firms, and foreigners remain constant. The additional purchases made by government cannot come out of thin air; unless or until production of goods and services increases, they must come out of inventory. Total investment, including unplanned inventory disinvestment, thus falls by $5,000 to compensate for the rise in government purchases.

Or suppose, again beginning from the situation shown in Exhibit 5.6, that foreigners suddenly decide to buy $2,000 less of Canadian goods. Exports will fall, but the $2,000 worth of goods that otherwise would have been exported will accumulate as unplanned inventories of Canadian firms, once again maintaining the required equality.

CONCLUSIONS

This chapter has served two basic purposes. One purpose has been to establish certain key equalities among items in the circular flow of income and product. The two most important of these equalities are the equality of national income and national product and the equality of injections and leakages. The equalities hold by definition, because they are based on the concept of total investment—which includes both planned and unplanned investment.

The other purpose the chapter has served has been to introduce the concepts of equilibrium and disequilibrium in the circular flow. These concepts depend crucially on the distinction between planned and unplanned investments, which are lumped together in defining the basic equalities. To be specific, the circular flow is said to be in equilibrium when, and only when, the plans of buyers and sellers exactly mesh, so that no unplanned inventory accumulation or depletion takes place. If buyers do not demand as much as firms supply, the excess products go into inventory, whether or not firms had planned to put them there. To correct any unplanned inventory accumulation, firms must cut output or reduce prices to boost sales. Either action causes the circular flow to shrink— when this flow is measured in terms of dollars spent on products or earned in incomes. If buyers demand more than firms currently produce, goods come out of inventory, even if firms had not planned to run their inventories down. This unplanned inventory depletion causes firms to raise prices or increase output, either of which causes the volume of the circular flow to grow.

SUMMARY

1. Two of the most important elements of the circular flow are national income and national product. These two elements are linked on one side by factor payments and on the other by total expenditures. National income and national product are equal.

2. Saving and investment can be added to the circular flow without disturbing the equality between national product and total expenditure. If total *planned* expenditure is not exactly equal to national product, unplanned inventory investment (positive or negative) will make up the difference between the two.

3. *Aggregate supply* is another term for national product and *aggregate demand* another term for total planned expenditure. When aggregate supply is equal to aggregate demand, unplanned inventory investment is zero, and the circular flow is said to be in equilibrium. When aggregate supply and demand are not equal, unplanned inventory investment (positive or negative) must take place. The circular flow is then said to be in disequilibrium.

4. Adding government and a foreign sector to the circular flow of income and product does not disturb the basic equalities of the circular flow. Total injections (investment plus government purchases plus exports) must equal total leakages (saving plus net taxes plus imports). National product (consumption plus investment plus government purchases plus net exports) must equal national income (consumption plus saving plus net taxes).

DISCUSSION QUESTIONS

1. Contrast the flow of money you put into your bank account each payday with the stock of money indicated by the balance in your passbook. How are the flow and stock related? Why is one referred to as a *flow* and the other as a *stock*?

2. In the real world, who are the savers and who are the investors? Provide examples of when a person can be both a saver and an investor. Describe situations where someone is a saver but not an investor, then an investor but not a saver.

3. In what sense is the owner of a grocery store chain "investing" when the store's inventories increase? How is this similar to investment in new display freezers for the stores? How is it different?

4. Because savers and investors are not always the same people, why is it that after-the-fact savings must always equal investment? Or must they? Is this relationship true in the real world or only under certain restrictive assumptions? Explain.

5. Suppose you bought a dollar's worth of gasoline. Trace through the route this dollar might take; in fact, trace several routes it might take to go through the whole circular flow.

6. Use the circular flow diagram to analyze each of the following:
   a. The interest rate falls, and businesses borrow more money and do more investing.
   b. People decide to work less; they prefer more time off to watch ball games or take up some other leisuretime activity.
   c. Governments in the economy raise their taxes.
   d. Business firms decide to lower their inventories, so they lay off 10 percent of their work force.
   e. The government increases its flow of both taxes and government spending.

7. How would the circular flow model change if there were no money in the system—that is, if all exchanges had to be barter exchanges?

8. How do unemployed workers fit into the circular flow diagram? What flows are connected to them?

C H A P T E R 6

NATIONAL INCOME, NATIONAL PRODUCT, AND THE BALANCE OF PAYMENTS ACCOUNTS

WHAT YOU WILL LEARN IN THIS CHAPTER

This chapter will explain how the various elements of the circular flow of income and product can be measured. It will describe the methods used by government statisticians to measure both nominal national product and nominal national income and show why these flows, as officially measured, correspond only approximately to the theoretical concepts in the last chapter. The chapter will explain how changes in the price level can be measured by means of price indexes, and it will introduce several specific price indexes in common use. Finally, it will explain Canada's international balance of payments.

FOR REVIEW

Here are some important terms and concepts that will be put to use in this chapter. If you do not understand them, review them before proceeding.
- *Government purchases (Chapter 4)*
- *Transfer payments (Chapter 4)*
- *Basic equalities of the circular flow (Chapter 5)*
- *The circular flow and the foreign sector (Chapter 5)*

The last chapter cut the circular flow of income and product into convenient pieces and gave the pieces names like *national income, investment,* and *saving.* These concepts are basic to macroeconomic theory. Because they are so important, it is useful to know how they can be measured, so the theory can be compared to what happens in the real world. This chapter will take a brief tour through some of the basics of national income accounting. The chapter is divided into two parts, corresponding to the important distinction between nominal and real measures of national income and product and their component parts. **Nominal values**, discussed in the first part, are measurements that are made in terms of the actual market prices at which goods are sold. **Real values**, discussed in the second part, are measurements that are adjusted for inflation — for changes in the price level over time.

Nominal values
Measurements of economic values made in terms of actual market prices at which goods are sold.

Real values Measurements of economic values that include adjustments for changes in prices between one year and another.

MEASURING NOMINAL NATIONAL INCOME AND PRODUCT

Gross National Product

Gross national product (GNP) The dollar value at current market prices of all final goods and services produced annually by the nation's economy.

Final goods and services Goods and services sold directly for household consumption, business investment, or government purchase. Excludes intermediate goods sold for use as inputs in the production of other goods.

Gross national expenditure A measurement of aggregate economic activity arrived at by adding together the nominal expenditure of all economic units on newly produced final goods and services.

Of all economic statistics, perhaps the most widely publicized is the measure of an economy's level of total production called the **gross national product (GNP)**. This statistic represents the dollar value at current market prices (the nominal value) of all final goods and services produced annually by the nation's economy. **Final goods and services** are goods and services sold directly for household consumption, business investment, government purchase, or export. Intermediate goods, such as the flour used to bake bread at commercial bakeries, are not counted in GNP. To count both the value of the flour at its market price (an intermediate good) and the value of the bread at its market price (a final good) would be to count the flour twice, because the value of the flour is included in the price of the bread.

In principle, GNP could be measured directly by constructing a table that shows the quantity of each final good and service produced—massages, apples, submarines, housing units, and all the rest—multiplying these quantities by the prices at which they were sold, and adding the resulting column of figures. But that is not what national income accountants actually do. Instead, they take a shortcut based on the equality of national product and total expenditure. In practice, GNP is measured by summing the nominal expenditures of all economic units on domestically produced final goods and services. This way of measuring aggregate economic activity may be called the expenditure approach to GNP. The result in Canada is officially known as **gross national expenditure** (GNE). Exhibit 6.1 provides an illustration of how it works, using actual 1979 data for the Canadian economy.

Personal consumption expenditure		$150.8
Durable goods	$22.6	
Semidurable goods	19.0	
Nondurable goods	47.1	
Services	62.2	
Plus: gross fixed capital formation (investment)		63.8
Machinery and equipment	21.0	
Residential construction	13.9	
Nonresidential construction	24.3	
Changes in inventories	4.6	
Plus: government expenditure on goods and services		51.8
Plus: net exports of goods and services		−5.6
Exports	76.4	
Less imports	82.1	
Plus: residual error of estimate		−0.3
Equals gross national expenditure		$260.5

Exhibit 6.1

Nominal gross national expenditure 1979 (billions of dollars)

Gross national product can be measured by the expenditure approach, in which case—in Canada—it is officially called gross national expenditure (GNE). This means adding together the values of expenditures on newly produced goods and services by all economic units to get a measure of aggregate economic activity.

Source: Statistics Canada, *National Income and Expenditure Accounts,* Fourth Quarter 1979 and preliminary Annual, pp. 4-5, 11.

Consumption Consumption expenditures by households and unattached persons fall into four categories: durable goods, semidurable goods, nondurable goods, and services. In principle, goods that do not wear out entirely in one year—such as automobiles, furniture, and household appliances—are considered durable, and goods that are possibly used up in a shorter period of time, but not instantaneously—such as clothing, books, and magazines—are considered semidurable. Goods used up almost immediately—such as soap, food, and gasoline—are considered nondurable. (In practice, the classifications are often arbitrary.) The remaining item, services, includes things that are not embodied in any physical object when sold, such as haircuts, legal advice, and education. No distinction is made between services that are durable and those that are nondurable in their effects.

Both the goods and the services components of consumption contain items that are produced but that do not actually pass through the marketplace on their way to consumers. One such item is an estimate of the food produced and directly consumed on farms. Another is an estimate of the rental value of owner occupied homes. (Rental payments on tenant occupied housing are included automatically.)

Investment The item called *gross fixed capital formation* is the sum of all firms' purchases of newly produced capital goods (fixed investment by both government and private business firms) plus changes in business inventories. Fixed investment, in turn, is broken down into the durable equipment of producers: such as machine tools, trucks, and office equipment; and new construction: including both business structures and residential housing.

When thinking about investment, keep in mind the phrase *newly produced capital goods*. The businessperson who buys a used machine is not engaging in an investment expenditure, according to the national income accountants' definition. The machine was already counted in some previous year. Also, people who speak of making investments in land or corporate bonds are not using the word *investment* in the national income accountants' sense. Real estate and securities are not capital goods. In fact, they are not even part of the more general category, goods and services, with which the measure of GNE is concerned.

Government Purchases The contribution that government makes to GNE at the federal, provincial, and municipal levels presents a special problem for national income accountants. Ideally, this contribution should be measured in terms of the value of the services that government produces—education, national defense, police protection, and all the rest. However, since very few government services are actually sold to consumers and businesses, there are no market prices in terms of which to value them. Instead, national income accountants use government purchases of goods and services to approximate the contribution of government to GNE.

Government purchases of goods and services, as explained in Chapter 4, include the wages and salaries of all civilian and military personnel hired by government plus the purchase of all the buildings, computers, assault rifles, paper clips, and so on used by those employees. Presumably, all the government workers using all that equipment produce an output at least as valuable as the same inputs could have produced in the private sector. In any event, that is the assumption that justifies inclusion of government purchases in GNE. Note that government transfer payments are not included, since they do not represent expenditures made to purchase newly produced goods or current services.

Net Exports The final item in GNE is net exports—the difference between the nominal value of goods and services exported abroad and the nominal value of goods and services imported from abroad. Exported goods must be added in because they are products produced in Canada, even though they are bought elsewhere. Imports must be subtracted because some of the expenditures on consumer goods, investment goods, and government purchases that have already been added in were purchases of goods made abroad; and these goods should not be counted as part of national product.

Net National Income

Income approach A method of estimating aggregate economic activity by adding together the incomes earned by all households.

Net national income Total income received by a nation's productive factors, including wages and salaries, interest and rent, corporate taxes before profits, and income of unincorporated enterprises. It is also equal to GNP − capital consumption allowances and indirect business taxes.

The chapter will turn now to a different way of measuring what goes on in the circular flow: the income approach to national income accounting. As the name implies, the **income approach** measures the overall nominal rate of the circular flow by adding up all the different kinds of income earned by households. This is done as shown in Exhibit 6.2. The various incomes add up to what is known as **net national income** (or simply national income; see definition in Chapter 5). The categories of income used by national income accountants differ somewhat from the theoretical classification of incomes into wages, rent, interest, and profit; and they deserve some explanation.

The category *wages and other labor income* includes not only wages and salaries but two other items as well. The first is employer contributions for social insurance (Chapter 4 argued that the economic burden of these taxes was borne by employees even though employers actually made the payments.) The second is other labor income, which includes various fringe benefits received by employees, and rental income.

Wages and other labor income		$145.8
Corporation profits	$34.7	
Less: dividends paid to nonresidents	−2.7	32.0
Interest and miscellaneous investment income		18.6
Net income of farm and nonfarm unincorporated business, including rent		15.0
Inventory valuation adjustment		−6.4
Net national income (NNI) at factor cost		$205.0

Exhibit 6.2
Nominal net national income (NNI), 1979 (billions of dollars)
National income is officially estimated by the income approach. This means adding together the values of all income earned by households. Note that some items of income, such as the portion of corporate profits that goes to pay corporate profits taxes, are counted as "earned" by households even though households never actually receive the income.

Source: Statistics Canada, *National Income and Expenditure Accounts*, Fourth Quarter 1979 and preliminary Annual, p. 3.

The category *corporate profits* includes all income earned by the owners (that is, the shareholders) of corporations, whether the owners actually receive that income or not. Dividends are the part of that income that the owners actually receive. Another part goes to pay the taxes on corporate profits, and a third part, "undistributed corporate profits," is retained by the corporations to use for investment purposes. Dividends paid to nonresidents do not form part of income received by Canadians, and are therefore deducted.

The category *interest income* excludes interest paid by government on the public debt, which is considered a transfer payment. Miscellaneous investment income includes profits or losses of government business enterprises.

The category *net income of farm and unincorporated business* is a grab-bag including all income earned by farmers, small unincorporated businesses, and self-employed professionals. No attempt is made to sort out what parts of this income ought theoretically to be classified as wages, interest, or profit. Rental income is the income of persons acting as landlords.

The final item, *inventory valuation adjustment*, refers to the artificial increase in value of inventories resulting from price increases. An appropriate deduction is made for this.

The Relationship among GNE, GNP, and NNI

In the simplified economy of Chapter 5, national product and national income were defined in such a way that they were exactly equal. In the real world, things do not work out quite so neatly. Some adjustments must be made so that GNP, which equals GNE, also "fits" net national income (NNI). These adjustments are shown in Exhibit 6.3.

For one thing, net and gross national expenditure must be distinguished from each other — a distinction that is not made in elementary theoretical discussions. What makes gross national expenditure "gross"? It is the fact that gross fixed capital formation is not a measure of the actual change in capital assets and business inventories for a particular year. In the process of production, existing buildings and equipment wear out or lose their value through obsolescence. As a result, the actual increase in the stock of capital goods and business inventories each year, which might be called *net* fixed capital formation, is less than gross fixed capital formation. Although depreciation and obsolescence are difficult to measure accurately, national income accountants make an approximation called the **capital consumption allowance**. Gross investment minus the capital consumption allowance equals net investment. The investment expenditures made to replace worn-out or obsolete equipment are counted as part of the business expenses of firms, so they do not show up either in corporate profits or in proprietors' income. The first step in going from GNP to national income, then, is to subtract the capital consumption allowance.

Capital consumption allowance The amount by which a nation's capital goods, including buildings and equipment, are estimated to wear down (depreciate) in a given year.

Next, an adjustment must be made to reflect the fact that some of the money firms receive from sales of their product is not "earned" by the owners of the firms. Instead, it is taken directly by government in payment of so-called *indirect business taxes*, which include sales taxes, excise taxes,

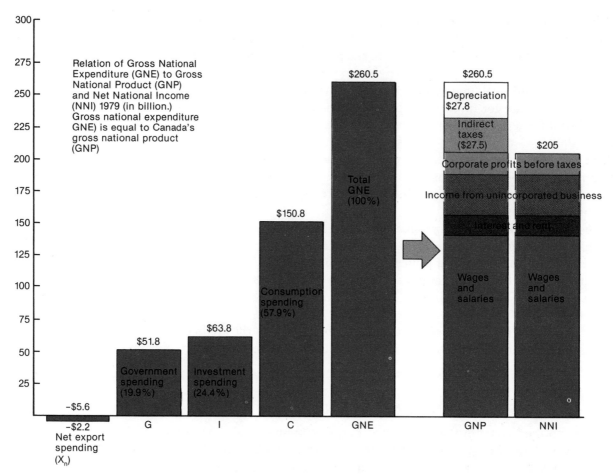

Exhibit 6.3

Relation of gross national expenditure (GNE) to gross national product (GNP) and net national income (NNI), 1979 (billions of dollars)

Gross national expenditure (GNE) is equal to Canada's gross national product (GNP). In the simple world of elementary economic theory, national product (GNP) and net national income (NNI) are equal by definition. In the real world, certain adjustments must be made to get GNP and NNI to "fit." First depreciation, the capital consumption allowance, is subtracted from GNP. Then indirect business taxes are subtracted to get NNI.

Source: Statistics Canada, *National Income and Expenditure Accounts*, Fourth Quarter 1979 and preliminary Annual.

and business property taxes paid to federal, provincial, and municipal governments. These taxes are treated differently from the corporate tax, which is considered to be money earned by owners and then taken by government out of corporate profits. Indirect business taxes are included in the prices of goods and services, so they count as part of gross national product, but they are not included in income, so they must be subtracted when going from GNP to national income, as shown in Exhibit 6.3.

Exhibit 6.3 can also be understood in another way. In its complete form, it illustrates the two different ways of measuring national product. Approached from the left side, expenditures on final goods and services are totalled to arrive at a measure of national output (GNE). Approached from the right side, the incomes generated by current output are totalled to approximate the value of national output (GNP). Such incomes do not include indirect business taxes and depreciation allowances. These, items, however, are added into the price that businesspeople charge for their output and must therefore be added to NNI to make it equal to the value of national output (GNP).

A technical difficulty is caused by the fact that output estimated by the expenditure approach, and output measured by the income approach, use an entirely different set of data. Inevitably, no matter how carefully the work is done, there are some errors and omissions, so that the two sets of figures do not quite fit. The difference between GNE, measured by the expenditure approach, and GNP, measured by the income approach, is called the *residual error of estimate*. The discrepancy has no statistical significance; it is simply a "fudge factor" that makes things balance (see Exhibit 6.1).

Personal Income Net national income, as mentioned several times, is a measure of income earned by households, whether or not those households ever actually get their hands on the income. For some purposes, it is more important to measure what households actually receive than what they earn. The total income actually received by households is called **personal income**.

Exhibit 6.4 shows the steps required to transform net national income into personal income. First, two items that are earned by households but not received by them are subtracted. These items are corporate profits taxes and undistributed corporate profits. Next, transfer payments — payments received by households although not earned by them — are added. The result is personal income.

One further income measure is shown at the bottom of Exhibit 6.4: **personal disposable income** (or **disposable income** for short). This income is what households have left of their personal income after they pay personal taxes of various kinds to federal, provincial, and municipal governments, including transfer payments to government, such as pension and unemployment insurance contributions.

Personal income The total of all income, including transfer payments, actually received by households before payment of personal income taxes and other transfer payments to government.

Personal disposable income (disposable income) Personal income minus personal taxes.

Exhibit 6.4
Net national income and personal income, 1979 (in billions)
Net national income is a measure of all income earned by households, while personal income is a measure of the income they actually receive. To go from national income to personal income, subtract corporate profits taxes and undistributed corporate profits; then add transfer payments. If personal taxes and transfer payments to government are subtracted from this figure, the result is personal disposable income.

Net national income	$205.0
Less corporate profits taxes	−10.3
Less undistributed corporate profits	−18.6
Plus transfer payments[a]	34.8
Equals personal income	$210.9
Less personal taxes and transfer payments to government	−38.7
Equals personal disposable income	$172.2

[a] Includes government and consumer interest payments and business transfer payments

Source: Statistics Canada, *National Income and Expenditure Accounts*, Fourth Quarter 1979 and preliminary Annual.

This completes the discussion of the nominal side of national income accounting. The next section turns to the problem of making adjustments for changing prices.

MEASURING REAL INCOME AND PRICES

Measuring Real GNP (or GNE)

The investigation of real income and prices will begin with a look at an economy much simpler than that of Canada. This will permit the presentation of the essentials in the clearest possible way before getting into practical details.

Exhibit 6.5 shows nominal GNP accounts in two different years for a simple economy in which only three goods are produced: movies, apples, and shirts. It indicates that nominal GNP grew from $400 in 1972 to $1,000 in 1980. But how are these figures to be interpreted? Do they mean that people really had more of the things they wanted in 1980 than in 1972? More exactly, do they mean that people had 2.5 times as much? These questions require careful answers.

A line-by-line comparison of the two years in Exhibit 6.5 shows that the figures on nominal income do not tell the whole story. The problem is that prices went up sharply between 1972 and 1980. Movies cost twice as much as they used to, apples three times as much, and shirts half again as much. So how much more was really produced in the second year than in the first?

We can try looking directly at the quantities of individual goods and services produced. But if we do so, we get conflicting indications: twice as many movies and shirts were produced in 1980 as in 1972 but only half as many apples. Instead, we can approach the matter in another way, by asking how much the total value of output would have changed from 1972 to 1980 *if prices had not changed*.

This approach to the problem gives the results shown in Exhibit 6.6. There, we see that the 1980 output of 100 movies, 500 apples, and 20 shirts, which had a value of $1,000 in terms of the prices at which the goods and services were actually sold, would have had a value of only $500 in terms of the prices that prevailed in 1972. The $500 figure is a measure of *real* GNP for 1980, and it is this measure that we should compare with the 1972 GNP of $400 if we want to know what really happened to physical production in the economy between the two years. Much of the apparent growth of the

1972	Quantity	Price	Value
Movies	50	$ 2.00	$ 100
Apples	1,000	.20	200
Shirts	10	10.00	100
1972 nominal GNP			$ 400
1980			
Movies	100	$ 4.00	$ 400
Apples	500	.60	300
Shirts	20	15.00	300
1980 nominal GNP			$1,000

Exhibit 6.5

Nominal GNP in selected years for a simple economy
In this simple economy, in which only three goods are produced, nominal national income grew from $400 in 1972 to $1,000 in 1980. Prices also went up in that time, though, so people did not really have 2.5 times as much of these things in 1980.

economy is seen to have been due to higher prices. Thus, instead of having 250 percent more in 1980 than in 1972 (an increase from $400 to $1,000), the people in this simple economy had only about 25 percent more (an increase from $400 to $500).

Price Indexes

In the example covered in Exhibits 6.5 and 6.6, while 1980 nominal GNP rose to a level of $1,000 from a $400 base in 1972, real GNP in 1980 rose only to $500.

The ratio of 1980 nominal GNP to 1980 real GNP provides one possible measure of the rate of price increase between the two years: the reason for the discrepancy between 1980 nominal and real GNP is that the price level doubled between the two years. This measure of the rate of price increase is actually used for some purpose by Canadian national income accountants. The ratio of current year nominal GNP to current year real GNP is the **GNE implicit price deflator** (so called because GNP is measured by the expenditure approach) — known by most economists simply as the **GNE deflator**. It is, in effect, a **weighted average** reflecting changes in the prices of all of the various goods and services of which GNP is composed:

$$\text{GNE deflator} = \frac{\text{Current year output valued at current year prices}}{\text{Current year output valued at base year prices}} \times 100.$$

The GNE deflator is too broad a measure of price change for some purposes, however. To supplement it, Statistics Canada publishes another price index each month, which is a weighted average of the prices of more narrowly defined selections of goods and services.

This index is known as the **consumer price index (CPI)**. It differs from the implicit deflator both in the products that are included and in the way the index is constructed. The consumer price index measures the average prices of all major categories of goods and services purchased by urban wage earners and clerical workers whose family income in 1967 ranged from $4,000 to $12,000. A "representative market basket" has been chosen by studies of actual expenditures by such individuals. The prices of almost 400 different goods and services are currently included in this index. At the time this book is being written, the CPI used 1971 as the base year.

GNE implicit price deflator (GNE deflator) A measure of the price level equal to the ratio of current nominal GNP to current real GNP times 100.

Weighted average An average that gives appropriate weights to products in proportion to their relative importance in the total basket of goods purchased.

Consumer price index (CPI) A price index based on a "representative market basket" of almost 400 goods and services purchased by urban wage earners and clerical workers. This index is calculated using base year quantities.

Exhibit 6.6

Nominal and real GNP in 1980 for a simple economy

This exhibit shows how the numbers from Exhibit 6.5 can be adjusted to take changing prices into account. The 1980 quantities are multiplied by 1972 prices to get the value of 1980 GNP as it would have been had prices not changed. The total of 1980 quantities valued at 1972 prices is called the real GNP for 1980.

	1980 Quantity	1980 Price	Value at 1980 Price	1972 Price	Value of 1980 Output at 1972 Price
Movies	100	$ 4.00	$ 400	$ 2.00	$200
Apples	500	.60	300	.20	100
Shirts	20	15.00	300	10.00	200
Totals		1980 nominal GNP = $1,000		1980 real GNP = $500	

Exhibit 6.7

Calculation of consumer price index for a simplified economy

The consumer price index is the base year market basket of goods valued at current year prices divided by the base year market basket of goods valued at base year prices, multiplied by 100. This exhibit shows how a CPI can be calculated using the data for the simplified economy first given in Exhibit 6.5 The 1972 output cost $400 at the prices at which it was actually sold. If it had been sold at 1980 prices, it would have cost $950. The CPI for 1980 is thus 237.5.

Good	1972 Quantity	1972 Price	Value of 1972 Quantity at 1972 Price	1980 Price	Value of 1972 Quantity at 1980 Price
Movies	50	$ 2.00	$100	$ 4.00	$200
Apples	1,000	.20	200	.60	600
Shirts	10	10.00	100	15.00	150
Totals			$400		$950

$$\text{CPI} = \frac{\$950}{\$400} \times 100 = 237.5$$

Statistics Canada, which constructs the index, changes the base year once a decade or so.

The consumer price index is constructed by using base year quantities rather than current year quantities. The index number is the formula:

$$\text{Price index} = \frac{\text{Value of base year quantities at current year prices}}{\text{Value of base year quantities at base year prices}}.$$

Using base year quantities rather than current year quantities provides an important practical advantage. It means that in order to recalculate the index it is necessary to collect new data only on prices, which are easily available, and not on quantities, which are not quite so readily measured. Consequently, Statistics Canada is able to issue up-to-date computations of the consumer price index every month, before data on the GNE implicit price deflator are issued.

Comparing the CPI and the GNE Deflator Exhibit 6.7 shows how the consumer price index can be calculated using the data for the simplified economy first displayed in Exhibit 6.5. Notice that the value of the CPI, 237.5, differs from the value of the GNE deflator, 200, calculated from exactly the same underlying data. Which, if either, of the two price indexes is the true measure of change in the price level between the two years?

The reply is that neither the CPI nor the GNE deflator is **the** correct measure of change in the price level. Instead, each is the answer to a different question. The GNE deflator is the answer to the question: how much more did the 1980 output cost at the prices at which it was actually sold than it would have cost if it had been sold at 1972 prices instead? The CPI, in contrast, is the answer to the question: how much more would the 1972 output have cost if it had been sold at 1980 prices instead of at its actual 1972 prices?

Careful inspection of Exhibit 6.5 shows why the answers to the two questions are not the same. In 1972, lots of apples and not very many shirts

Exhibit 6.8

Consumer price index and weekly earnings, 1961 – 1978

Part a of this exhibit shows what has happened to the consumer price index for the Canadian economy since 1961. Note that the CPI uses 1971 as a base year. Part b shows a typical application of the CPI — the adjustment of nominal weekly earnings by changes in the cost of living.

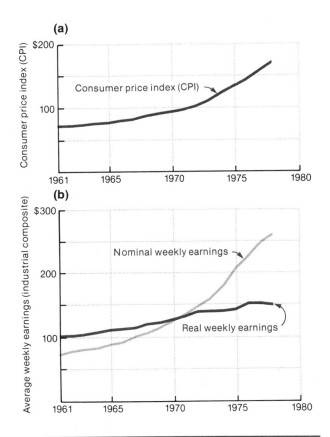

Source: Department of Finance, *Economic Review*, April 1980, pp. 211, 215.

were produced in comparison to the outputs of 1980. Yet, between the two years, the price of apples increased 300 percent while the price of shirts increased only 150 percent. Because the CPI uses base year quantities, it gives heavy weight to apples, which experienced the greatest price increase, and not much weight to shirts, which experienced only a modest price increase. In contrast, the GNE deflator uses current year quantities, thereby downplaying the importance of apples and emphasizing that of shirts.

In general, if there is a tendency for the quantities consumed of goods whose prices increase relatively slowly to grow more rapidly than the quantities consumed of goods whose prices increase relatively rapidly, the CPI will indicate more rapid inflation than will the GNE deflator. There is a slight tendency for this to be true in the Canadian economy, although the discrepancy between the two measures of inflation is not nearly so great as in the simplified numerical example.

Exhibit 6.8a shows what has happened to the CPI since 1961. Note that Statistics Canada uses 1971 as the base year for the CPI. Exhibit 6.8b shows a typical use to which the CPI can be put — namely, adjusting average weekly earnings in nonagricultural industries for changes in the cost of living. Each year's figure for real earnings is equal to that year's nominal earnings divided by the consumer price index, then multiplied by 100. Real and nominal earnings thus cross in 1971, the base year used for the CPI.

Biases in Price Indexes It was noted earlier that changes in the relative quantities of goods produced may tend to make the consumer price index increase more rapidly than the GNE deflator. For this reason, the CPI is sometimes said to have an *upward bias*.

There is, however, a much more troublesome source of upward bias that affects all price indexes, regardless of the formulas on which they are based. This bias has its origin in quality changes rather than quantity changes. It would be highly misleading, for example, to say that the price of a new automobile increased by 300 percent between 1958 and 1978 if the 1978 car was more durable, got better gas mileage, and was significantly safer than its predecessor of a generation ago. National income accountants try to adjust the price changes of important classes of goods, such as automobiles, for changes in quality; but the adjustments are of necessity subjective, and they are widely criticized as inadequate.

BALANCE OF PAYMENTS

Exhibit 6.1 indicated that exports and imports are important elements in Canada's gross national expenditure. In the years 1970–79 Canada exported an average of 25 percent of its GNP annually, while it imported about 27 percent. In other words, we depend upon foreigners to buy about 25 percent of the goods and services we produce, and we depend upon them for about 27 percent of the goods and services that we consume. Such imports are part of our consumption, investment, and government expenditures. Separate accounts, called **balance of payments** accounts, are kept of these international transactions, as well as of other important transactions that we carry on with other countries.

Balance of payments
A record of all economic transactions between Canada and other countries in a given year. The balance is in surplus when receipts in the current and capital account exceed total payments to foreigners. It is in deficit when such receipts are less than total payments.

In the balance of payments accounts, Canada's international receipts and payments are broken down into three categories: (1) transactions in goods and services produced in the current year, summarized in what is called the *current account*; (2) transactions in short- and long-term securities and bonds, summarized in the *capital account*; (3) changes in official holdings of reserves, recorded as a *net change in official reserve account*.

Exhibit 6.9 illustrates the relationship among these accounts for the year 1979. In that year Canada ran a current account deficit of $5,019 million. In merchandise trade, Canada, as it usually does, exported considerably more than it imported, so that it had a sizable surplus on this part of the current account (line 3). However, as is also quite customary, it had a deficit in its service transactions (line 14) large enough to more than offset the surplus in merchandise trade. The service sector includes travel — in which Canada normally has a deficit — and receipts and payments for interest and dividend transactions. Canada normally pays much more to foreigners in the form of interest and dividends than it receives from them, indicating that foreigners have invested much more in the Canadian economy than Canadians have invested abroad. Net transfers are private and government transfer payments in the form of pension payouts, inheritances, and migrant transfers which produced an additional deficit of $620 million.

It is important to note that imports and exports (lines 1 and 2) include trade in both merchandise goods and services, but not transfers. Therefore the overall export-import balance (or net exports, as recorded in Exhibit 6.1)

NATIONAL INCOME, INFLATION, AND UNEMPLOYMENT

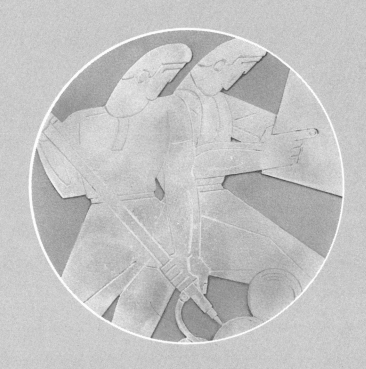

C H A P T E R 5

THE CIRCULAR FLOW OF INCOME AND PRODUCT

WHAT YOU WILL LEARN IN THIS CHAPTER

This chapter will describe how the circular flow of income and product sends goods from firms to households and factor services from households to firms. At the same time, it will show how payments for these goods and services flow in the opposite direction through the economy. The idea of the circular flow will be used in two ways. First, it will give a framework for a set of important definitions and equalities. Second, it will show how the concepts of supply, demand, and equilibrium can be applied in a macroeconomic context.

FOR REVIEW

Here are some important terms and concepts that will be put to use in this chapter. If you do not understand them, review them before proceeding.
- *Factors of production (Chapter 1)*
- *Equilibrium (Chapter 3)*
- *Government purchases and transfer payments (Chapter 4)*

This chapter begins putting together a theory that will explain unemployment, inflation, and economic growth and that will offer a framework for thinking about economic stabilization policy. These subjects make up the branch of economics known as **macroeconomics**. The prefix *macro* comes from the Greek work meaning "big"; but although inflation, unemployment, and economic growth are big issues in the sense of being important, that is not the reason for using the term *macroeconomics*. Instead, the term is applied because this branch of economics works primarily with **aggregate** economic data—any data that are grand totals for the economy as a whole. Macroeconomics is thus distinguished from **microeconomics** (*micro* meaning "small"), which studies individual prices, the behavior of individual firms and households, and so on.

Because it will take several chapters to complete the study of macroeconomics, it is necessary to have a clear idea of the lay of the land before beginning. The best way to get an overview of the relationships among the

Macroeconomics The branch of economics devoted to the study of unemployment, inflation, economic growth, and stabilization policy.

Aggregate A term used in economics to describe any quantity that is a grand total for the whole economy.

Microeconomics The branch of economics devoted to the study of the behavior of individual households and firms and to the determination of the relative prices of individual goods and services.

Circular flow of income and product The flow of goods from firms to households and factor services from households to firms, counterbalanced by the flow of expenditures from households to firms and factor payments from firms to households.

major economic aggregates is to represent them in terms of a **circular flow of income and product.** The rest of this chapter, then, will be devoted to the circular flow.

THE STRUCTURE OF THE CIRCULAR FLOW

A Simple Economy

To see the circular flow in its most basic form, begin by imagining an economy made up only of households and business firms — an economy with no public sector at all. To make things simpler still, assume that households live entirely from hand to mouth, spending all of their income on consumer goods as soon as that income is received. Similarly, assume that firms sell their entire output to consumers as soon as it is produced.

The circular flow of income and product for this ultra-simple economy is shown in Exhibit 5.1. The diagram is drawn with physical goods and

Exhibit 5.1

The circular flow in a simple economy

In this simple economy, households spend all their income on consumer goods as soon as they receive it, and firms sell all their output to households as soon as they produce it. Physical goods and factor services flow clockwise, while corresponding money payments flow counterclockwise.

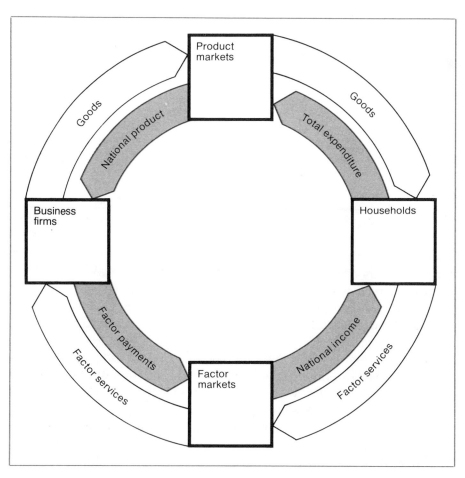

services flowing clockwise and the corresponding money payments flowing counterclockwise.

Two sets of markets link households to firms in this economy. Product markets, which appear at the top of the diagram, are markets where households purchase goods and services — bread, television sets, houses, dry cleaning services, entertainment — for their own direct consumption. Factor markets, which appear at the bottom of the diagram, are the markets in which households sell to firms the **factors of production** they use in making the things sold in product markets.

In return for the natural resources, labor, and capital that they buy from households, firms make **factor payments** in the form of rents, wages, salaries, and interest payments. As a matter of accounting convention, when firms use land, labor, or capital that they themselves own, they are counted as "purchasing" those factors from the households that own the firms, even though no money changes hands and no explicit factor payment is made. For purposes of macroeconomic analysis, profits are thus considered an implicit factor payment from firms to the households that own them.[1]

> **Factors of production** The basic elements of natural resources, labor, and capital used in the production of all goods.

> **Factor payments** The payments with which firms purchase factors of production (natural resources, labor, and capital).

Stocks and Flows

Having said this much, let's pause for a moment to concentrate on a word used several times already. Economists call all of the things shown in Exhibit 5.1 **flows** because they are processes that occur continuously through time. Flows are measured in units per time period — for example, in dollars per year, gallons per minute, or tons per month. Measurements of flows are measurements of rates at which things are happening.

The technical language of economics distinguishes carefully between flows and stocks. A **stock** is an accumulated quantity of something existing at a particular time. (The word *stock* in this general sense has nothing to do with the stock market kind of stocks that are bought and sold on Wall Street.)

For an illustration of the difference between stocks and flows, we can think of a bathtub filling. When we talk about how fast the water is running, we are talking about a *flow*, measured in gallons per minute. When we talk about how much water is in the tub at a given moment, we are talking about a *stock*, measured only in gallons. Similarly, in the world of economics, we might talk about the rate of housing construction in Toronto, Ontario, in terms of new units per month (the flow) as distinct from the actual number of houses in Toronto as of January 1, 1980 (the stock).

> **Flows** Processes occurring continuously through time, measured in units per time period.

> **Stocks** Accumulated quantities existing at a particular time, measured in terms of simple units.

National Income and Product

Two of the flows in Exhibit 5.1 deserve special attention and have special names. The first is **national income** — the total of all wages, rents, interest payments, and profits received by households. National income is shown

> **National income** The total of all incomes, including wages, rents, interest payments, and profits received by households.

---

[1] For certain purposes of microeconomics, profits are not considered factor payments.

National product The total value of all goods and services supplied in the economy.

in the diagram as an arrow aimed at the box representing households. The second important flow is **national product** — a measure of the total value of the goods and services produced. In the diagram, national product is shown as an arrow passing from the box representing product markets to the box representing firms.

In this economy, national income and national product are equal, simply because of the way they are defined.[2] This equality can be verified in either of two ways. First, consider household expenditures as a link between national income and national product. Households are assumed to spend all of their income on consumer goods as soon as they receive it, and firms are assumed to sell all of their output to consumers as soon as it is produced. The payments made by buyers must equal the payments received by sellers, so national product must equal national income.

Alternatively, consider factor payments as a link between national income and national product. When firms receive money for goods they sell, they use part of it to pay the workers, natural resource owners, and others who contributed factors of production to make the goods. Anything left over is profit. Factor payments, including profits, account for all the money received by firms, so total factor payments must be equal to national product. Factor payments also account for all of the income received by households, so total factor payments must be equal to national income. It again follows that national income and national product must be equal.

Saving and Investment

The circular flow shown in Exhibit 5.1 is so simple that not very much of interest can be said about it. To build a theory that will be useful for understanding the real-world economy, a few complications must be introduced.

The first change will be to drop the requirement that households immediately spend all of their income to purchase consumer goods and to permit them instead to save part of what they earn. The rate of saving by households, under this assumption, is simply the difference between national income and household consumption expenditures.

Fixed investment Purchases by firms of newly produced capital goods, such as production machinery, newly built structures, and office equipment.

Inventory investment Changes in the stocks of finished products and raw materials that firms keep on hand. If stocks are increasing, inventory investment is positive; if they are decreasing, it is negative.

The second change will be to drop the requirement that firms immediately sell all of their output to consumers. Instead, they will be permitted to sell some products to other firms and to let some accumulate in inventory before selling them to anyone. When firms buy newly produced capital goods (for example, production machinery, newly built structures, or office equipment) from other firms, they are said to engage in **fixed investment**. When firms increase the stock of finished products or raw materials that they keep on hand, they are said to engage in **inventory investment**. The rate of inventory investment can be less than zero in periods when firms are

---

[2] Chapter 6 will show that the equality between national income and product does not hold precisely as these concepts are actually measured by the official statisticians of the Canadian government. It would be pointless, though, to let this statistical detail complicate all theoretical discussions. Everywhere in this chapter, and everywhere from Chapter 7 onward, the necessary simplifying assumptions are made so that national income and product *are* equal.

decreasing their stocks of goods or raw materials on hand. The sum of fixed investment and inventory investment will be called simply **investment**.

Circular Flow with Saving and Investment Exhibit 5.2 shows how the circular flow of income and expenditure looks when saving and investment are added. (The clockwise arrows showing the flows of goods and services have been omitted to simplify the diagram). There are now two pathways along which expenditures can travel on their way from households to product markets. Some household income is used for consumption expenditure and reaches product markets directly. Other household income is diverted to saving, which supplies a source of funds for firms to use in making investment expenditures; this income reaches product markets indirectly.

Investment The sum of fixed investment and inventory investment.

Exhibit 5.2

The circular flow with saving and investment

When saving and investment are added to the circular flow, there are two pathways by which expenditures can travel on their way from households to product markets. Some income is spent directly on consumer goods. The rest is saved and passes to firms via financial markets. The firms then use the investment expenditures in the product markets.

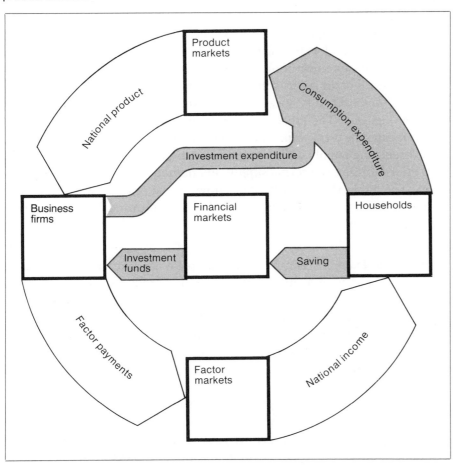

On the way from households to firms, the flow of saving passes through a set of financial markets. These markets include a great variety of financial institutions — chartered banks, trust and loan companies, credit unions and caisses populaires, the stock and bond markets, insurance companies, and other institutions that act as intermediaries between households that save and firms that make investment expenditures. Households supply funds to these financial markets. Firms can then borrow from financial markets to obtain the funds they need to make investment expenditures. (Chapter 11 will discuss the operation of financial markets in detail.)

Equilibrium and Disequilibrium in the Circular Flow   Adding saving and investment to the circular flow raises an entirely new issue: can total expenditure still be counted on to provide an equalizing link between national income and national product? There are now two entirely different sets of people making expenditure decisions. Households decide how much to spend on consumption, and firms decide how much to spend on investment. How can we be sure that when these two kinds of expenditures are added together, the total will just equal the total value of all goods produced? A new way of applying supply and demand analysis will help find the answers.

Aggregate Supply and Demand

Aggregate supply The total value of all goods and services supplied in the economy; identical to national product.

The term **aggregate supply** refers to the grand total of all goods supplied by all firms in the entire economy. There is already another term for the same thing: national product. *Aggregate supply* and *national product* are two names for the total value of goods and services supplied by all firms. Following the same terminology, **aggregate demand** can be used to mean the grand total of all goods demanded for the whole economy. In defining *aggregate demand* this way, though, care must be taken in the way "demand" is used. The precise way of defining *aggregate demand* is to say that it means the total *planned* expenditures of all buyers in the economy.

Aggregate demand The total value of all planned expenditures of all buyers in the economy.

In discussing supply and demand for individual goods or services, the step after defining the terms *supply* and *demand* was to explain equilibrium. The same thing can be done now by using aggregate supply and aggregate demand to explain the ideas of equilibrium and disequilibrium in the circular flow.

A Numerical Example   A numerical example will make the point. Imagine an economy in which only three goods are produced: apples, milling machines, and radios. The various firms in this economy have plans to produce apples at a rate of $30,000 worth per year, milling machines at a rate of $40,000 worth per year, and radios at a rate of $30,000 worth per year. All firms are busy carrying out their plans. The result is a flow of output at a rate of $100,000 per year. This flow, which can be called either *national product* or *aggregate supply*, is detailed in lines 1 to 4 of Exhibit 5.3.

While producers are busy carrying out their plans, buyers make plans too. Consumers plan to buy apples at a rate of $25,000 worth per year and radios at a rate of $30,000 worth per year. Also, the firms that make radios are planning to buy milling machines at a rate of $35,000 worth per year in order to increase their radio-producing capacity for the future. No one is planning either to increase or to decrease the stocks of finished products held in inventory, so planned inventory investment is zero. All these buying plans are expressed in lines 5 to 11 of Exhibit 5.3. The total of all planned expenditures (consumption plus planned investment) is listed in line 11 as aggregate demand.

Comparing line 1 with line 11, *it is obvious that the plans of producers and the plans of buyers do not mesh*. Aggregate supply is not equal to aggregate demand. There is nothing very surprising about the situation. After all, there have been no direct consultations among the various buyers and sellers when plans have been made. Each has acted on the basis of whatever knowledge has been available from the price system, plus private judgments about future trends or changes. As a result, things are not working out for everyone according to plan. The apples, radios, and milling machines are all being produced, but not all of them are being sold. After buyers have bought all they plan to, $5,000 worth of apples are left over, as are $5,000 worth of milling machines. These products cannot simply vanish into thin air. The firms that made them are putting them into inventory, even though they had not planned to do so, in the hope of selling them at some time in the future. The result is an *unplanned* inventory investment of $10,000, as shown in lines 12 to 14 of Exhibit 5.3.

Exhibit 5.3

A numerical example of the circular flow for a simple economy

National product must always be equal to total expenditure, even when the circular flow is not in equilibrium. In the example shown here, national product (aggregate supply) exceeds total planned expenditure (aggregate demand), so unplanned inventory investment makes up the difference.

Output Resulting from Producers' Plans			
1 Total national product (aggregate supply)			$100,000
2 Apples	$30,000		
3 Radios	30,000		
4 Milling machines	40,000		
Expenditures Resulting from Buyers' Plans			
5 Total consumption expenditure		$55,000	
6 Apples	$25,000		
7 Radios	30,000		
8 Total planned investment expenditure		35,000	
9 Fixed investment	35,000		
10 Planned inventory investment	0		
11 Total planned expenditure (aggregate demand)			$90,000
Other Expenditure			
12 Total unplanned inventory investment			10,000
13 Unsold apples	5,000		
14 Unsold milling machines	5,000		
Summary			
15 Total national product			$100,000
16 Total national expenditure			100,000
17 Planned	$90,000		
18 Unplanned	10,000		

An Important Equality When aggregate buying plans do not mesh with aggregate productions plans, the circular flow is said to be in *disequilibrium*. Aggregate supply and aggregate demand are not equal; national product and total planned expenditure are not equal. One crucial equality does hold, though. National product is still equal to total expenditure *when both planned and unplanned expenditures are taken into account*. The reason is that goods that are produced and not sold *must* be added to inventories, whether firms planned to put them there or not. As long as unplanned inventory investment is counted as part of total expenditure — and it is — total expenditure is by definition equal to national product. In equation form:

$$\begin{matrix} \text{National} \\ \text{product} \end{matrix} = \begin{matrix} \text{Total} \\ \text{planned} \\ \text{expenditure} \end{matrix} + \begin{matrix} \text{Unplanned} \\ \text{inventory} \\ \text{investment} \end{matrix} = \begin{matrix} \text{Total} \\ \text{expenditure.} \end{matrix}$$

Another way to write exactly the same thing is:

$$\begin{matrix} \text{Aggregate} \\ \text{supply} \end{matrix} = \begin{matrix} \text{Aggregate} \\ \text{demand} \end{matrix} + \begin{matrix} \text{Unplanned} \\ \text{inventory} \\ \text{investment.} \end{matrix}$$

Reactions to Disequilibrium In the numerical example outlined in Exhibit 5.3, aggregate demand fell short of aggregate supply. Because buyers' and sellers' plans failed to mesh, there was an unplanned accumulation of inventories. Firms would not want this unplanned rise in inventories to go on and on. In order to stop it, they would reduce their rate of output, or lower prices in order to stimulate sales, or both. These reactions would amount to a reduction in aggregate supply. The size of the circular flow would begin to shrink as the number of dollars received by firms for their products and the number of dollars paid out to workers fell.

At another time, aggregate demand might exceed aggregate supply. With total planned expenditures greater than national product, unplanned inventory depletion would take place. Firms would react in a way opposite to their reaction to an excess of aggregate supply over aggregate demand. Either they would increase output to rebuild inventories, or they would take advantage of the high level of demand to raise prices, or both. Whichever they did, the size of the circular flow would grow as incomes and expenditures rose.

Finally, it is entirely possible that when the plans of buyers and sellers were tested in the market, they would turn out to mesh. In that case, with production and planned expenditure equal, no unplanned inventory investment would occur, and no corrections would be necessary. The circular flow would be in equilibrium.

Income and Expenditure

Nothing has yet been said about national income. Go back for a moment to the situation in Exhibit 5.3. Firms are shown to be producing $100,000 worth of goods a year. To produce those goods they must make factor payments (including profits, if any) of $100,000 to households, which means that national income is also $100,000. The households receiving this income plan to buy consumer goods at a rate of $55,000 per year, which means that they plan to save at a rate of $45,000 per year. (Remember that saving plus consumption exhausts income in this simple economy.)

These household saving plans do not mesh with firms' investment plans, as shown in line 8 of Exhibit 5.3 As things actually have turned out, though, the firms have invested more than they had planned to. The actual total of their investment, including unplanned inventory investment, is exactly equal to saving. It must be. Once again, goods cannot vanish into thin air after they are produced, and unplanned inventory investment acts as the balancing item.

The Place of Government in the Circular Flow

When government enters the circular flow of income, expenditure, and product, things become slightly more complicated. Exhibit 5.4 shows how

---

Exhibit 5.4

The circular flow with government included

With government added to the circular flow of income and product, there are two new channels along which funds can flow from households to product markets. Some income is diverted to government in the form of net taxes and then used to finance government purchases. Alternatively, if the government runs a budget deficit, it may borrow from the public via financial markets and use the borrowed funds to finance its expenditures. If the government runs a budget surplus, the flow of funds along this pathway may be reversed, in which case the arrow from government to financial markets will point in the opposite direction from that shown.

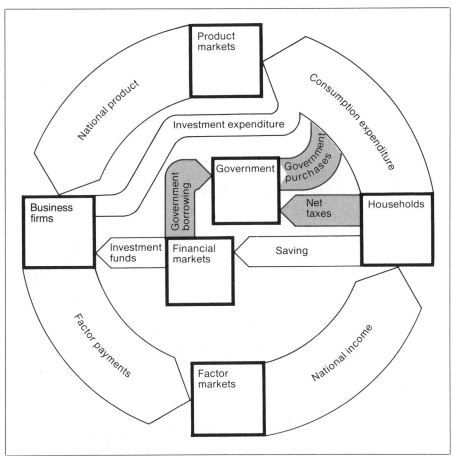

the circular flow looks when government is added. Two new pathways along which expenditures can flow from households to the product markets are opened up.

First, governments take in revenue from taxes they levy on households. Some of that revenue, as shown in Chapter 4, is immediately returned to households in the form of transfer payments. The difference between what governments take in as tax revenue and what they pay out as transfer payments is called **net taxes**. Funds thus flow from households to government as net taxes and then from government to product markets as government purchases.

Second, if government purchases of goods and services exceed net taxes, the government may need to borrow from the public through financial markets. In this case, the government budget is said to be in **deficit**. When the government runs a deficit, funds flow from households to financial markets as saving, then from financial markets to the government as government borrowing, and finally from government to the product markets as government purchases.

Sometimes, the government budget is in **surplus** rather than deficit. In that case, government's borrowing from the public is less than its repayment of past debts. The net flow of funds between government and financial markets is the reverse of what is shown in Exhibit 5.4.

Adding the Foreign Sector

The final step in constructing the circular flow of income and product is to add the foreign sector, as in Exhibit 5.5. This exhibit shows that some of the expenditures made by consumers, firms, and governments do not flow to domestic product markets but instead flow to foreign economies to pay for imports of goods and services. These expenditures are shown by the arrow labeled *imports* in the exhibit. At the same time, some expenditures on domestically produced goods and services are made by foreigners. These are shown in the exhibit by the arrow labeled *exports*, which passes from the foreign economy sector to domestic product markets.

Remember that the arrows in Exhibit 5.5 all represent flows of funds, not flows of physical goods and services. The import arrow thus shows the flow of funds out of the Canadian economy to pay for imported goods and services, and the export arrow shows the flow of funds into the Canadian economy in payment for exports of goods and services. If imports exceed exports, the Canadian economy is said to run a foreign deficit. This deficit must be paid for by borrowing from foreigners, hence the arrow labeled *loans from foreigners to finance trade deficit*, which points from foreign economies to the domestic financial markets. If instead Canadian exports exceed imports, Canada is said to run a foreign trade surplus. In this case (not shown), foreign buyers of Canadian goods have to pay for them by borrowing funds in Canadian financial markets, and the direction of the arrow is reversed.

Leakages and Injections The first section of this chapter described a highly simplified economy in which households spent all their income on

Net taxes Total tax revenues collected by government at all levels minus total transfer payments disbursed.

Deficit In referring to government budgets, an excess of government purchases over net taxes.

Surplus In referring to government budgets, an excess of net taxes over government purchases.

consumption goods, so that all expenditures flowed directly from households to domestic product markets. As financial markets, government, and foreign economies were added, however, it was shown that in the real

Exhibit 5.5
The circular flow with government and the foreign sector

This exhibit adds a foreign sector to the circular flow with government that was shown in Exhibit 5.4. Some consumption, investment, and government purchases are for goods produced abroad; this is shown as the triple arrow pointing toward the imports. Some purchases of domestically produced goods and services are made by foreigners; these are shown as the arrow labeled *exports* running from the foreign sector to domestic product markets. If imports exceed exports, the excess imports must be paid for by borrowing from abroad; this is shown by the arrow labeled *loans from foreigners to finance trade deficit*. If exports instead exceed imports, there is a foreign trade surplus, and the direction of that arrow is reversed. Note that all the arrows in this exhibit represent flows of funds, not of physical goods and services. That is why the exports arrow points into the domestic economy and the imports arrow points away from it.

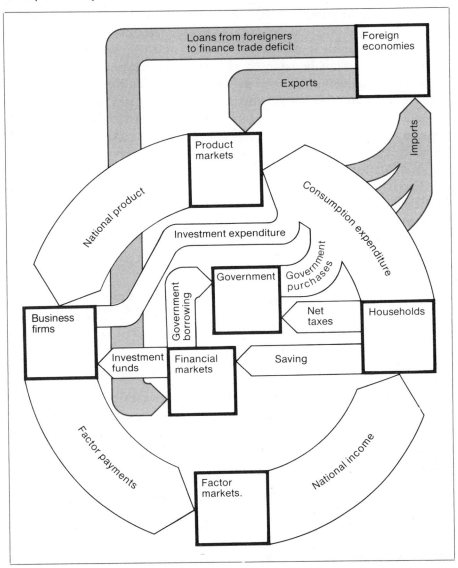

Injections The part of total expenditures that does not originate from domestic households — that is, investment, government purchases, and exports.

Leakages The part of national income not devoted to consumption (saving plus net taxes) plus domestic expenditures on foreign-made goods (imports).

Net exports Total exports minus total imports.

world, three kinds of purchases of goods and services do not originate directly in domestic households: investment (purchases of capital goods and goods for inventory by domestic business firms), government purchases, and exports (purchases of domestic goods and services by foreigners). From now on, these three kinds of purchases will be referred to collectively as **injections** into the circular flow of goods and services.

Offsetting these injections are imports (expenditures of households, business firms, and units of government on goods produced abroad), plus saving and taxes (the use of household income for purposes other than the direct purchase of goods and services). From now on, saving, net taxes, and imports will be referred to collectively as **leakages** from the circular flow.

The Equality of National Income and National Product Another numerical example will show that adding the government and foreign sectors, with their associated injections and leakages, to the economy does not disturb the fundamental equality between national income and national product on which the circular flow is based. Exhibit 5.6 shows an economy in which consumption is $70,000, investment is $22,000, government purchases are $10,000, and exports are $8,000. Of the consumption, investment, and government purchases shown, $10,000 is spent on imported goods, which cannot be counted as part of the national product of the country represented in the exhibit. National product is thus shown as the total of consumption, investment, and government purchases, plus expenditures on domestic goods by foreigners (exports), minus that part of consumption, investment, and government purchases not spent on domestic goods and services (imports). As Exhibit 5.6 is constructed, the total comes to $100,000.

The production of $100,000 of national product generates $100,000 in factor payments for domestic households. As the second table in Exhibit 5.6 shows, this amount is divided among consumption ($70,000), saving ($25,000), and net taxes ($5,000). Introducing the term **net exports** to represent exports minus imports, the relationships shown in Exhibit 5.6 can be written in equation form as:

$$\text{National product} = \text{Consumption} + \text{Investment} + \text{Government purchases} + \text{Net exports}$$

$$= \text{Consumption} + \text{Saving} + \text{Net taxes}$$

$$= \text{National income}.$$

The Equality of Leakages and Injections It follows from the relationship between national income and national product that total injections must equal total leakages. Beginning with the equation shown above, consumption can be subtracted from both sides, and imports can be added to both sides. The result is:

$$\text{Investment} + \text{Government purchases} + \text{Exports} = \text{Saving} + \text{Net taxes} + \text{Imports}$$

or

$$\text{Total injections} = \text{Total leakages}.$$

Exhibit 5.6

The equality of national income and product

This numerical example shows that the equality of national income and product is maintained when the government and foreign sectors, with their associated injections and leakages, are added to the economy. National product is a measure of the goods and services produced in the domestic economy. To arrive at its total, we add consumption, investment, and government purchases of all kinds, plus foreign purchases of domestically produced goods (exports), and we subtract the portion of consumption, investment, and government purchases devoted to foreign-made goods (imports). Using the term *net exports* to stand for exports minus imports, we could say that national product equals consumption plus investment plus government purchases plus net exports. This is equal to national income, which is divided among consumption, saving, and net taxes — as shown in the second part of the table.

Consumption	$ 70,000
Plus investment	22,000
Plus government purchases	10,000
Plus exports	8,000
Less imports	−10,000
Equals national product	$100,000
Consumption	$ 70,000
Plus saving	25,000
Plus net taxes	5,000
Equals national income	$100,000

Note that this relationship holds even though, in the numerical example of Exhibit 5.6, no individual pair of items on the leakages and injections list exactly matches up. In that example, saving exceeds investment by $3,000, imports exceed exports by $2,000, and net taxes fall short of government purchases by $5,000. The reason total injections must always equal total leakages is that injections include unplanned inventory investment as a balancing item. Suppose, for example, that beginning from the position shown in Exhibit 5.6, government purchases suddenly rise by $5,000, while planned expenditures by households, firms, and foreigners remain constant. The additional purchases made by government cannot come out of thin air; unless or until production of goods and services increases, they must come out of inventory. Total investment, including unplanned inventory disinvestment, thus falls by $5,000 to compensate for the rise in government purchases.

Or suppose, again beginning from the situation shown in Exhibit 5.6, that foreigners suddenly decide to buy $2,000 less of Canadian goods. Exports will fall, but the $2,000 worth of goods that otherwise would have been exported will accumulate as unplanned inventories of Canadian firms, once again maintaining the required equality.

CONCLUSIONS

This chapter has served two basic purposes. One purpose has been to establish certain key equalities among items in the circular flow of income and product. The two most important of these equalities are the equality of national income and national product and the equality of injections and leakages. The equalities hold by definition, because they are based on the concept of total investment—which includes both planned and unplanned investment.

The other purpose the chapter has served has been to introduce the concepts of equilibrium and disequilibrium in the circular flow. These concepts depend crucially on the distinction between planned and unplanned investments, which are lumped together in defining the basic equalities. To be specific, the circular flow is said to be in equilibrium when, and only when, the plans of buyers and sellers exactly mesh, so that no unplanned inventory accumulation or depletion takes place. If buyers do not demand as much as firms supply, the excess products go into inventory, whether or not firms had planned to put them there. To correct any unplanned inventory accumulation, firms must cut output or reduce prices to boost sales. Either action causes the circular flow to shrink—when this flow is measured in terms of dollars spent on products or earned in incomes. If buyers demand more than firms currently produce, goods come out of inventory, even if firms had not planned to run their inventories down. This unplanned inventory depletion causes firms to raise prices or increase output, either of which causes the volume of the circular flow to grow.

SUMMARY

1. Two of the most important elements of the circular flow are national income and national product. These two elements are linked on one side by factor payments and on the other by total expenditures. National income and national product are equal.

2. Saving and investment can be added to the circular flow without disturbing the equality between national product and total expenditure. If total *planned* expenditure is not exactly equal to national product, unplanned inventory investment (positive or negative) will make up the difference between the two.

3. *Aggregate supply* is another term for national product and *aggregate demand* another term for total planned expenditure. When aggregate supply is equal to aggregate demand, unplanned inventory investment is zero, and the circular flow is said to be in equilibrium. When aggregate supply and demand are not equal, unplanned inventory investment (positive or negative) must take place. The circular flow is then said to be in disequilibrium.

4. Adding government and a foreign sector to the circular flow of income and product does not disturb the basic equalities of the circular flow. Total injections (investment plus government purchases plus exports) must equal total leakages (saving plus net taxes plus imports). National product (consumption plus investment plus government purchases plus net exports) must equal national income (consumption plus saving plus net taxes).

DISCUSSION QUESTIONS

1. Contrast the flow of money you put into your bank account each payday with the stock of money indicated by the balance in your passbook. How are the flow and stock related? Why is one referred to as a *flow* and the other as a *stock*?

2. In the real world, who are the savers and who are the investors? Provide examples of when a person can be both a saver and an investor. Describe situations where someone is a saver but not an investor, then an investor but not a saver.

3. In what sense is the owner of a grocery store chain "investing" when the store's inventories increase? How is this similar to investment in new display freezers for the stores? How is it different?

4. Because savers and investors are not always the same people, why is it that after-the-fact savings must always equal investment? Or must they? Is this relationship true in the real world or only under certain restrictive assumptions? Explain.

5. Suppose you bought a dollar's worth of gasoline. Trace through the route this dollar might take; in fact, trace several routes it might take to go through the whole circular flow.

6. Use the circular flow diagram to analyze each of the following:
   a. The interest rate falls, and businesses borrow more money and do more investing.
   b. People decide to work less; they prefer more time off to watch ball games or take up some other leisuretime activity.
   c. Governments in the economy raise their taxes.
   d. Business firms decide to lower their inventories, so they lay off 10 percent of their work force.
   e. The government increases its flow of both taxes and government spending.

7. How would the circular flow model change if there were no money in the system — that is, if all exchanges had to be barter exchanges?

8. How do unemployed workers fit into the circular flow diagram? What flows are connected to them?

CHAPTER 6

NATIONAL INCOME, NATIONAL PRODUCT, AND THE BALANCE OF PAYMENTS ACCOUNTS

WHAT YOU WILL LEARN IN THIS CHAPTER

This chapter will explain how the various elements of the circular flow of income and product can be measured. It will describe the methods used by government statisticians to measure both nominal national product and nominal national income and show why these flows, as officially measured, correspond only approximately to the theoretical concepts in the last chapter. The chapter will explain how changes in the price level can be measured by means of price indexes, and it will introduce several specific price indexes in common use. Finally, it will explain Canada's international balance of payments.

FOR REVIEW

Here are some important terms and concepts that will be put to use in this chapter. If you do not understand them, review them before proceeding.
- *Government purchases (Chapter 4)*
- *Transfer payments (Chapter 4)*
- *Basic equalities of the circular flow (Chapter 5)*
- *The circular flow and the foreign sector (Chapter 5)*

The last chapter cut the circular flow of income and product into convenient pieces and gave the pieces names like *national income, investment,* and *saving.* These concepts are basic to macroeconomic theory. Because they are so important, it is useful to know how they can be measured, so the theory can be compared to what happens in the real world. This chapter will take a brief tour through some of the basics of national income accounting. The chapter is divided into two parts, corresponding to the important distinction between nominal and real measures of national income and product and their component parts. **Nominal values**, discussed in the first part, are measurements that are made in terms of the actual market prices at which goods are sold. **Real values**, discussed in the second part, are measurements that are adjusted for inflation — for changes in the price level over time.

Nominal values
Measurements of economic values made in terms of actual market prices at which goods are sold.

Real values Measurements of economic values that include adjustments for changes in prices between one year and another.

MEASURING NOMINAL NATIONAL INCOME AND PRODUCT

Gross National Product

Gross national product (GNP) The dollar value at current market prices of all final goods and services produced annually by the nation's economy.

Final goods and services Goods and services sold directly for household consumption, business investment, or government purchase. Excludes intermediate goods sold for use as inputs in the production of other goods.

Gross national expenditure A measurement of aggregate economic activity arrived at by adding together the nominal expenditure of all economic units on newly produced final goods and services.

Of all economic statistics, perhaps the most widely publicized is the measure of an economy's level of total production called the **gross national product (GNP)**. This statistic represents the dollar value at current market prices (the nominal value) of all final goods and services produced annually by the nation's economy. **Final goods and services** are goods and services sold directly for household consumption, business investment, government purchase, or export. Intermediate goods, such as the flour used to bake bread at commercial bakeries, are not counted in GNP. To count both the value of the flour at its market price (an intermediate good) and the value of the bread at its market price (a final good) would be to count the flour twice, because the value of the flour is included in the price of the bread.

In principle, GNP could be measured directly by constructing a table that shows the quantity of each final good and service produced — massages, apples, submarines, housing units, and all the rest — multiplying these quantities by the prices at which they were sold, and adding the resulting column of figures. But that is not what national income accountants actually do. Instead, they take a shortcut based on the equality of national product and total expenditure. In practice, GNP is measured by summing the nominal expenditures of all economic units on domestically produced final goods and services. This way of measuring aggregate economic activity may be called the expenditure approach to GNP. The result in Canada is officially known as **gross national expenditure** (GNE). Exhibit 6.1 provides an illustration of how it works, using actual 1979 data for the Canadian economy.

Personal consumption expenditure		$150.8
Durable goods	$22.6	
Semidurable goods	19.0	
Nondurable goods	47.1	
Services	62.2	
Plus: gross fixed capital formation (investment)		63.8
Machinery and equipment	21.0	
Residential construction	13.9	
Nonresidential construction	24.3	
Changes in inventories	4.6	
Plus: government expenditure on goods and services		51.8
Plus: net exports of goods and services		−5.6
Exports	76.4	
Less imports	82.1	
Plus: residual error of estimate		−0.3
Equals gross national expenditure		$260.5

Exhibit 6.1

Nominal gross national expenditure 1979 (billions of dollars)

Gross national product can be measured by the expenditure approach, in which case — in Canada — it is officially called gross national expenditure (GNE). This means adding together the values of expenditures on newly produced goods and services by all economic units to get a measure of aggregate economic activity.

Source: Statistics Canada, *National Income and Expenditure Accounts,* Fourth Quarter 1979 and preliminary Annual, pp. 4-5, 11.

Consumption Consumption expenditures by households and unattached persons fall into four categories: durable goods, semidurable goods, nondurable goods, and services. In principle, goods that do not wear out entirely in one year—such as automobiles, furniture, and household appliances—are considered durable, and goods that are possibly used up in a shorter period of time, but not instantaneously—such as clothing, books, and magazines—are considered semidurable. Goods used up almost immediately—such as soap, food, and gasoline—are considered nondurable. (In practice, the classifications are often arbitrary.) The remaining item, services, includes things that are not embodied in any physical object when sold, such as haircuts, legal advice, and education. No distinction is made between services that are durable and those that are nondurable in their effects.

Both the goods and the services components of consumption contain items that are produced but that do not actually pass through the marketplace on their way to consumers. One such item is an estimate of the food produced and directly consumed on farms. Another is an estimate of the rental value of owner occupied homes. (Rental payments on tenant occupied housing are included automatically.)

Investment The item called *gross fixed capital formation* is the sum of all firms' purchases of newly produced capital goods (fixed investment by both government and private business firms) plus changes in business inventories. Fixed investment, in turn, is broken down into the durable equipment of producers: such as machine tools, trucks, and office equipment; and new construction: including both business structures and residential housing.

When thinking about investment, keep in mind the phrase *newly produced capital goods*. The businessperson who buys a used machine is not engaging in an investment expenditure, according to the national income accountants' definition. The machine was already counted in some previous year. Also, people who speak of making investments in land or corporate bonds are not using the word *investment* in the national income accountants' sense. Real estate and securities are not capital goods. In fact, they are not even part of the more general category, goods and services, with which the measure of GNE is concerned.

Government Purchases The contribution that government makes to GNE at the federal, provincial, and municipal levels presents a special problem for national income accountants. Ideally, this contribution should be measured in terms of the value of the services that government produces— education, national defense, police protection, and all the rest. However, since very few government services are actually sold to consumers and businesses, there are no market prices in terms of which to value them. Instead, national income accountants use government purchases of goods and services to approximate the contribution of government to GNE.

Government purchases of goods and services, as explained in Chapter 4, include the wages and salaries of all civilian and military personnel hired by government plus the purchase of all the buildings, computers, assault rifles, paper clips, and so on used by those employees. Presumably, all the government workers using all that equipment produce an output at least as valuable as the same inputs could have produced in the private sector. In any event, that is the assumption that justifies inclusion of government purchases in GNE. Note that government transfer payments are not included, since they do not represent expenditures made to purchase newly produced goods or current services.

Net Exports The final item in GNE is net exports — the difference between the nominal value of goods and services exported abroad and the nominal value of goods and services imported from abroad. Exported goods must be added in because they are products produced in Canada, even though they are bought elsewhere. Imports must be subtracted because some of the expenditures on consumer goods, investment goods, and government purchases that have already been added in were purchases of goods made abroad; and these goods should not be counted as part of national product.

Net National Income

Income approach A method of estimating aggregate economic activity by adding together the incomes earned by all households.

Net national income Total income received by a nation's productive factors, including wages and salaries, interest and rent, corporate taxes before profits, and income of unincorporated enterprises. It is also equal to GNP − capital consumption allowances and indirect business taxes.

The chapter will turn now to a different way of measuring what goes on in the circular flow: the income approach to national income accounting. As the name implies, the **income approach** measures the overall nominal rate of the circular flow by adding up all the different kinds of income earned by households. This is done as shown in Exhibit 6.2. The various incomes add up to what is known as **net national income** (or simply national income; see definition in Chapter 5). The categories of income used by national income accountants differ somewhat from the theoretical classification of incomes into wages, rent, interest, and profit; and they deserve some explanation.

The category *wages and other labor income* includes not only wages and salaries but two other items as well. The first is employer contributions for social insurance (Chapter 4 argued that the economic burden of these taxes was borne by employees even though employers actually made the payments.) The second is other labor income, which includes various fringe benefits received by employees, and rental income.

Wages and other labor income		$145.8
Corporation profits	$34.7	
Less: dividends paid to nonresidents	−2.7	32.0
Interest and miscellaneous investment income		18.6
Net income of farm and nonfarm unincorporated business, including rent		15.0
Inventory valuation adjustment		−6.4
Net national income (NNI) at factor cost		$205.0

Exhibit 6.2

Nominal net national income (NNI), 1979 (billions of dollars)

National income is officially estimated by the income approach. This means adding together the values of all income earned by households. Note that some items of income, such as the portion of corporate profits that goes to pay corporate profits taxes, are counted as "earned" by households even though households never actually receive the income.

Source: Statistics Canada, *National Income and Expenditure Accounts*, Fourth Quarter 1979 and preliminary Annual, p. 3.

The category *corporate profits* includes all income earned by the owners (that is, the shareholders) of corporations, whether the owners actually receive that income or not. Dividends are the part of that income that the owners actually receive. Another part goes to pay the taxes on corporate profits, and a third part, "undistributed corporate profits," is retained by the corporations to use for investment purposes. Dividends paid to nonresidents do not form part of income received by Canadians, and are therefore deducted.

The category *interest income* excludes interest paid by government on the public debt, which is considered a transfer payment. Miscellaneous investment income includes profits or losses of government business enterprises.

The category *net income of farm and unincorporated business* is a grab-bag including all income earned by farmers, small unincorporated businesses, and self-employed professionals. No attempt is made to sort out what parts of this income ought theoretically to be classified as wages, interest, or profit. Rental income is the income of persons acting as landlords.

The final item, *inventory valuation adjustment*, refers to the artificial increase in value of inventories resulting from price increases. An appropriate deduction is made for this.

The Relationship among GNE, GNP, and NNI

In the simplified economy of Chapter 5, national product and national income were defined in such a way that they were exactly equal. In the real world, things do not work out quite so neatly. Some adjustments must be made so that GNP, which equals GNE, also "fits" net national income (NNI). These adjustments are shown in Exhibit 6.3.

For one thing, net and gross national expenditure must be distinguished from each other—a distinction that is not made in elementary theoretical discussions. What makes gross national expenditure "gross"? It is the fact that gross fixed capital formation is not a measure of the actual change in capital assets and business inventories for a particular year. In the process of production, existing buildings and equipment wear out or lose their value through obsolescence. As a result, the actual increase in the stock of capital goods and business inventories each year, which might be called *net* fixed capital formation, is less than gross fixed capital formation. Although depreciation and obsolescence are difficult to measure accurately, national income accountants make an approximation called the **capital consumption allowance**. Gross investment minus the capital consumption allowance equals net investment. The investment expenditures made to replace worn-out or obsolete equipment are counted as part of the business expenses of firms, so they do not show up either in corporate profits or in proprietors' income. The first step in going from GNP to national income, then, is to subtract the capital consumption allowance.

Next, an adjustment must be made to reflect the fact that some of the money firms receive from sales of their product is not "earned" by the owners of the firms. Instead, it is taken directly by government in payment of so-called *indirect business taxes*, which include sales taxes, excise taxes,

Capital consumption allowance The amount by which a nation's capital goods, including buildings and equipment, are estimated to wear down (depreciate) in a given year.

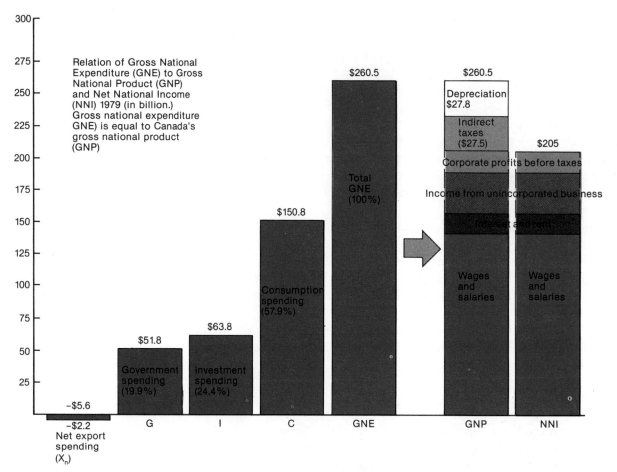

Relation of Gross National Expenditure (GNE) to Gross National Product (GNP) and Net National Income (NNI) 1979 (in billion.) Gross national expenditure GNE) is equal to Canada's gross national product (GNP)

Exhibit 6.3

Relation of gross national expenditure (GNE) to gross national product (GNP) and net national income (NNI), 1979 (billions of dollars)

Gross national expenditure (GNE) is equal to Canada's gross national product (GNP). In the simple world of elementary economic theory, national product (GNP) and net national income (NNI) are equal by definition. In the real world, certain adjustments must be made to get GNP and NNI to "fit." First depreciation, the capital consumption allowance, is subtracted from GNP. Then indirect business taxes are subtracted to get NNI.

Source: Statistics Canada, *National Income and Expenditure Accounts*, Fourth Quarter 1979 and preliminary Annual.

and business property taxes paid to federal, provincial, and municipal governments. These taxes are treated differently from the corporate tax, which is considered to be money earned by owners and then taken by government out of corporate profits. Indirect business taxes are included in the prices of goods and services, so they count as part of gross national product, but they are not included in income, so they must be subtracted when going from GNP to national income, as shown in Exhibit 6.3.

Exhibit 6.3 can also be understood in another way. In its complete form, it illustrates the two different ways of measuring national product. Approached from the left side, expenditures on final goods and services are totalled to arrive at a measure of national output (GNE). Approached from the right side, the incomes generated by current output are totalled to approximate the value of national output (GNP). Such incomes do not include indirect business taxes and depreciation allowances. These, items, however, are added into the price that businesspeople charge for their output and must therefore be added to NNI to make it equal to the value of national output (GNP).

A technical difficulty is caused by the fact that output estimated by the expenditure approach, and output measured by the income approach, use an entirely different set of data. Inevitably, no matter how carefully the work is done, there are some errors and omissions, so that the two sets of figures do not quite fit. The difference between GNE, measured by the expenditure approach, and GNP, measured by the income approach, is called the *residual error of estimate*. The discrepancy has no statistical significance; it is simply a "fudge factor" that makes things balance (see Exhibit 6.1).

Personal Income Net national income, as mentioned several times, is a measure of income earned by households, whether or not those households ever actually get their hands on the income. For some purposes, it is more important to measure what households actually receive than what they earn. The total income actually received by households is called **personal income**.

Exhibit 6.4 shows the steps required to transform net national income into personal income. First, two items that are earned by households but not received by them are subtracted. These items are corporate profits taxes and undistributed corporate profits. Next, transfer payments — payments received by households although not earned by them — are added. The result is personal income.

One further income measure is shown at the bottom of Exhibit 6.4: **personal disposable income** (or **disposable income** for short). This income is what households have left of their personal income after they pay personal taxes of various kinds to federal, provincial, and municipal governments, including transfer payments to government, such as pension and unemployment insurance contributions.

Personal income The total of all income, including transfer payments, actually received by households before payment of personal income taxes and other transfer payments to government.

Personal disposable income (disposable income) Personal income minus personal taxes.

Exhibit 6.4
Net national income and personal income, 1979 (in billions)
Net national income is a measure of all income earned by households, while personal income is a measure of the income they actually receive. To go from national income to personal income, subtract corporate profits taxes and undistributed corporate profits; then add transfer payments. If personal taxes and transfer payments to government are subtracted from this figure, the result is personal disposable income.

Net national income	$205.0
Less corporate profits taxes	−10.3
Less undistributed corporate profits	−18.6
Plus transfer payments[a]	34.8
Equals personal income	$210.9
Less personal taxes and transfer payments to government	−38.7
Equals personal disposable income	$172.2

[a] Includes government and consumer interest payments and business transfer payments

Source: Statistics Canada, *National Income and Expenditure Accounts*, Fourth Quarter 1979 and preliminary Annual.

This completes the discussion of the nominal side of national income accounting. The next section turns to the problem of making adjustments for changing prices.

MEASURING REAL INCOME AND PRICES

Measuring Real GNP (or GNE)

The investigation of real income and prices will begin with a look at an economy much simpler than that of Canada. This will permit the presentation of the essentials in the clearest possible way before getting into practical details.

Exhibit 6.5 shows nominal GNP accounts in two different years for a simple economy in which only three goods are produced: movies, apples, and shirts. It indicates that nominal GNP grew from $400 in 1972 to $1,000 in 1980. But how are these figures to be interpreted? Do they mean that people really had more of the things they wanted in 1980 than in 1972? More exactly, do they mean that people had 2.5 times as much? These questions require careful answers.

A line-by-line comparison of the two years in Exhibit 6.5 shows that the figures on nominal income do not tell the whole story. The problem is that prices went up sharply between 1972 and 1980. Movies cost twice as much as they used to, apples three times as much, and shirts half again as much. So how much more was really produced in the second year than in the first?

We can try looking directly at the quantities of individual goods and services produced. But if we do so, we get conflicting indications: twice as many movies and shirts were produced in 1980 as in 1972 but only half as many apples. Instead, we can approach the matter in another way, by asking how much the total value of output would have changed from 1972 to 1980 *if prices had not changed.*

This approach to the problem gives the results shown in Exhibit 6.6. There, we see that the 1980 output of 100 movies, 500 apples, and 20 shirts, which had a value of $1,000 in terms of the prices at which the goods and services were actually sold, would have had a value of only $500 in terms of the prices that prevailed in 1972. The $500 figure is a measure of *real* GNP for 1980, and it is this measure that we should compare with the 1972 GNP of $400 if we want to know what really happened to physical production in the economy between the two years. Much of the apparent growth of the

1972	Quantity	Price	Value
Movies	50	$ 2.00	$ 100
Apples	1,000	.20	200
Shirts	10	10.00	100
1972 nominal GNP			$ 400
1980			
Movies	100	$ 4.00	$ 400
Apples	500	.60	300
Shirts	20	15.00	300
1980 nominal GNP			$1,000

Exhibit 6.5

Nominal GNP in selected years for a simple economy
In this simple economy, in which only three goods are produced, nominal national income grew from $400 in 1972 to $1,000 in 1980. Prices also went up in that time, though, so people did not really have 2.5 times as much of these things in 1980.

economy is seen to have been due to higher prices. Thus, instead of having 250 percent more in 1980 than in 1972 (an increase from $400 to $1,000), the people in this simple economy had only about 25 percent more (an increase from $400 to $500).

Price Indexes

In the example covered in Exhibits 6.5 and 6.6, while 1980 nominal GNP rose to a level of $1,000 from a $400 base in 1972, real GNP in 1980 rose only to $500.

The ratio of 1980 nominal GNP to 1980 real GNP provides one possible measure of the rate of price increase between the two years: the reason for the discrepancy between 1980 nominal and real GNP is that the price level doubled between the two years. This measure of the rate of price increase is actually used for some purpose by Canadian national income accountants. The ratio of current year nominal GNP to current year real GNP is the **GNE implicit price deflator** (so called because GNP is measured by the expenditure approach) — known by most economists simply as the **GNE deflator**. It is, in effect, a **weighted average** reflecting changes in the prices of all of the various goods and services of which GNP is composed:

$$\text{GNE deflator} = \frac{\text{Current year output valued at current year prices}}{\text{Current year output valued at base year prices}} \times 100.$$

The GNE deflator is too broad a measure of price change for some purposes, however. To supplement it, Statistics Canada publishes another price index each month, which is a weighted average of the prices of more narrowly defined selections of goods and services.

This index is known as the **consumer price index (CPI)**. It differs from the implicit deflator both in the products that are included and in the way the index is constructed. The consumer price index measures the average prices of all major categories of goods and services purchased by urban wage earners and clerical workers whose family income in 1967 ranged from $4,000 to $12,000. A "representative market basket" has been chosen by studies of actual expenditures by such individuals. The prices of almost 400 different goods and services are currently included in this index. At the time this book is being written, the CPI used 1971 as the base year.

GNE implicit price deflator (GNE deflator) A measure of the price level equal to the ratio of current nominal GNP to current real GNP times 100.

Weighted average An average that gives appropriate weights to products in proportion to their relative importance in the total basket of goods purchased.

Consumer price index (CPI) A price index based on a "representative market basket" of almost 400 goods and services purchased by urban wage earners and clerical workers. This index is calculated using base year quantities.

Exhibit 6.6
Nominal and real GNP in 1980 for a simple economy
This exhibit shows how the numbers from Exhibit 6.5 can be adjusted to take changing prices into account. The 1980 quantities are multiplied by 1972 prices to get the value of 1980 GNP as it would have been had prices not changed. The total of 1980 quantities valued at 1972 prices is called the real GNP for 1980.

	1980 Quantity	1980 Price	Value at 1980 Price	1972 Price	Value of 1980 Output at 1972 Price
Movies	100	$ 4.00	$ 400	$ 2.00	$200
Apples	500	.60	300	.20	100
Shirts	20	15.00	300	10.00	200
Totals		1980 nominal GNP = $1,000		1980 real GNP = $500	

Exhibit 6.7

Calculation of consumer price index for a simplified economy

The consumer price index is the base year market basket of goods valued at current year prices divided by the base year market basket of goods valued at base year prices, multiplied by 100. This exhibit shows how a CPI can be calculated using the data for the simplified economy first given in Exhibit 6.5 The 1972 output cost $400 at the prices at which it was actually sold. If it had been sold at 1980 prices, it would have cost $950. The CPI for 1980 is thus 237.5.

Good	1972 Quantity	1972 Price	Value of 1972 Quantity at 1972 Price	1980 Price	Value of 1972 Quantity at 1980 Price
Movies	50	$ 2.00	$100	$ 4.00	$200
Apples	1,000	.20	200	.60	600
Shirts	10	10.00	100	15.00	150
Totals			$400		$950

$$\text{CPI} = \frac{\$950}{\$400} \times 100 = 237.5$$

Statistics Canada, which constructs the index, changes the base year once a decade or so.

The consumer price index is constructed by using base year quantities rather than current year quantities. The index number is the formula:

$$\text{Price index} = \frac{\text{Value of base year quantities at current year prices}}{\text{Value of base year quantities at base year prices}}.$$

Using base year quantities rather than current year quantities provides an important practical advantage. It means that in order to recalculate the index it is necessary to collect new data only on prices, which are easily available, and not on quantities, which are not quite so readily measured. Consequently, Statistics Canada is able to issue up-to-date computations of the consumer price index every month, before data on the GNE implicit price deflator are issued.

Comparing the CPI and the GNE Deflator Exhibit 6.7 shows how the consumer price index can be calculated using the data for the simplified economy first displayed in Exhibit 6.5. Notice that the value of the CPI, 237.5, differs from the value of the GNE deflator, 200, calculated from exactly the same underlying data. Which, if either, of the two price indexes is the true measure of change in the price level between the two years?

The reply is that neither the CPI nor the GNE deflator is **the** correct measure of change in the price level. Instead, each is the answer to a different question. The GNE deflator is the answer to the question: how much more did the 1980 output cost at the prices at which it was actually sold than it would have cost if it had been sold at 1972 prices instead? The CPI, in contrast, is the answer to the question: how much more would the 1972 output have cost if it had been sold at 1980 prices instead of at its actual 1972 prices?

Careful inspection of Exhibit 6.5 shows why the answers to the two questions are not the same. In 1972, lots of apples and not very many shirts

Exhibit 6.8

Consumer price index and weekly earnings, 1961 – 1978

Part a of this exhibit shows what has happened to the consumer price index for the Canadian economy since 1961. Note that the CPI uses 1971 as a base year. Part b shows a typical application of the CPI — the adjustment of nominal weekly earnings by changes in the cost of living.

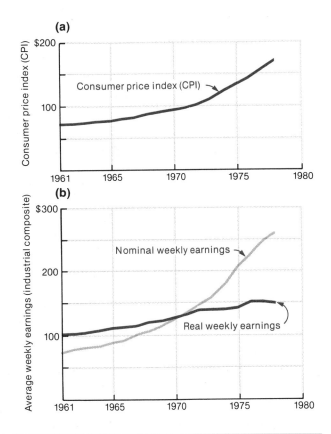

(a)

Consumer price index (CPI)

(b)

Nominal weekly earnings

Real weekly earnings

Source: Department of Finance, *Economic Review*, April 1980, pp. 211, 215.

were produced in comparison to the outputs of 1980. Yet, between the two years, the price of apples increased 300 percent while the price of shirts increased only 150 percent. Because the CPI uses base year quantities, it gives heavy weight to apples, which experienced the greatest price increase, and not much weight to shirts, which experienced only a modest price increase. In contrast, the GNE deflator uses current year quantities, thereby downplaying the importance of apples and emphasizing that of shirts.

In general, if there is a tendency for the quantities consumed of goods whose prices increase relatively slowly to grow more rapidly than the quantities consumed of goods whose prices increase relatively rapidly, the CPI will indicate more rapid inflation than will the GNE deflator. There is a slight tendency for this to be true in the Canadian economy, although the discrepancy between the two measures of inflation is not nearly so great as in the simplified numerical example.

Exhibit 6.8a shows what has happened to the CPI since 1961. Note that Statistics Canada uses 1971 as the base year for the CPI. Exhibit 6.8b shows a typical use to which the CPI can be put — namely, adjusting average weekly earnings in nonagricultural industries for changes in the cost of living. Each year's figure for real earnings is equal to that year's nominal earnings divided by the consumer price index, then multiplied by 100. Real and nominal earnings thus cross in 1971, the base year used for the CPI.

Biases in Price Indexes It was noted earlier that changes in the relative quantities of goods produced may tend to make the consumer price index increase more rapidly than the GNE deflator. For this reason, the CPI is sometimes said to have an *upward bias*.

There is, however, a much more troublesome source of upward bias that affects all price indexes, regardless of the formulas on which they are based. This bias has its origin in quality changes rather than quantity changes. It would be highly misleading, for example, to say that the price of a new automobile increased by 300 percent between 1958 and 1978 if the 1978 car was more durable, got better gas mileage, and was significantly safer than its predecessor of a generation ago. National income accountants try to adjust the price changes of important classes of goods, such as automobiles, for changes in quality; but the adjustments are of necessity subjective, and they are widely criticized as inadequate.

BALANCE OF PAYMENTS

Exhibit 6.1 indicated that exports and imports are important elements in Canada's gross national expenditure. In the years 1970–79 Canada exported an average of 25 percent of its GNP annually, while it imported about 27 percent. In other words, we depend upon foreigners to buy about 25 percent of the goods and services we produce, and we depend upon them for about 27 percent of the goods and services that we consume. Such imports are part of our consumption, investment, and government expenditures. Separate accounts, called **balance of payments** accounts, are kept of these international transactions, as well as of other important transactions that we carry on with other countries.

Balance of payments
A record of all economic transactions between Canada and other countries in a given year. The balance is in surplus when receipts in the current and capital account exceed total payments to foreigners. It is in deficit when such receipts are less than total payments.

In the balance of payments accounts, Canada's international receipts and payments are broken down into three categories: (1) transactions in goods and services produced in the current year, summarized in what is called the *current account*; (2) transactions in short- and long-term securities and bonds, summarized in the *capital account*; (3) changes in official holdings of reserves, recorded as a *net change in official reserve account*.

Exhibit 6.9 illustrates the relationship among these accounts for the year 1979. In that year Canada ran a current account deficit of $5,019 million. In merchandise trade, Canada, as it usually does, exported considerably more than it imported, so that it had a sizable surplus on this part of the current account (line 3). However, as is also quite customary, it had a deficit in its service transactions (line 14) large enough to more than offset the surplus in merchandise trade. The service sector includes travel — in which Canada normally has a deficit — and receipts and payments for interest and dividend transactions. Canada normally pays much more to foreigners in the form of interest and dividends than it receives from them, indicating that foreigners have invested much more in the Canadian economy than Canadians have invested abroad. Net transfers are private and government transfer payments in the form of pension payouts, inheritances, and migrant transfers which produced an additional deficit of $620 million.

It is important to note that imports and exports (lines 1 and 2) include trade in both merchandise goods and services, but not transfers. Therefore the overall export-import balance (or net exports, as recorded in Exhibit 6.1)

Exhibit 6.9
Canadian balance of international payments, 1979 (millions of dollars)

This exhibit shows in simplified form the actual Canadian balance of payments for 1979. In merchandise trade, Canada had a surplus of $3,985 million (line 3). However, in service transactions, it had a negative balance of $9,624 million (line 14), caused largely by negative balances in travel and in the payment and receipt of interest and dividends. Net exports (= exports of goods and services) was therefore $5,639 million (line 15). Adding a negative balance in transfers of $620 million produces a current account deficit of $5,019 million (line 17).

The current account deficit was more than balanced by a capital surplus of $11,121 million (line 31). This was the result of large sales of Canadian stocks and bonds to foreigners, (line 19) and increases in short-term bank deposits abroad (line 27). The result was a current *and* capital account balance of $6,102 million (line 32). After allowing for errors and omissions and the allocation of special drawing rights, Canada's official foreign reserves increased by $1,919 million (line 35).

(a) Current account

1. Merchandise exports		$65,163	
2. Merchandise imports		61,178	
3. Merchandise balance			$3,985
4. Service receipts		11,249	
5. travel	$2,866		
6. interest & dividends	1,039		
7. freight & shipping	3,072		
8. other	4,274		
9. Service payments		− 20,873	
10. travel	$3,963		
11. interest & dividends	6,248		
12. freight & shipping	2,973		
13. other	7,689		
14. Services balance			− 9,624
15. Balance of goods and services (net exports)			− 5,639
16. Net transfers			− 620
17. Current account balance			−$5,019

(b) Capital account

a. Capital movements in long-term form:

Capital inflows:	
18. Direct investment in Canada	$ 735
19. Portfolio investment in Canada	5,973
20. Other (government loans and credits)	1,993
21. Total long-term capital inflows	$8,701
Capital outflows:	
22. Direct investment abroad	− 1,855
23. Portfolio investment abroad	− 2,307
24. Other	− 1,329
25. Total long-term capital outflows	− 5,491
26. Balance on long-term capital movements	$3,210

b. Capital movements in short-term form:

Capital inflows:	
27. Resident holdings of short-term funds abroad	4,472
28. Nonresident holdings of Canadian currency	1,244
29. Other short-term capital transactions	2,195
30. Balance of short-term capital movements	7,911
31. Total net capital balance	11,121

c. Net change in official holdings of foreign exchange and reserves:

32. Current and capital account balance	$6,102
33. Errors and omissions	− 4,402
34. Allocation of special drawing rights	219
35. Changes in official reserves	− 1,919
36. Overall net balance of international payments	0

Source: Statistics Canada, *Canadian Statistical Review*, March 1980, p. 32.

is equal to exports of goods and services minus imports of goods and services, or about −$5.6 billion for 1979.

Canada's deficit on the current account (line 17) was more than offset by a net capital inflow of $11,121 million, recorded as a net capital balance (line 31). Foreigners bought $8,701 million of new long-term[1] Canadian securities or physical assets in 1979 (line 21), encouraged by the maintenance of higher interest rates in Canada than in the United States and elsewhere, and by good investment opportunities in such Canadian resource industries as oil. Such purchases provided us with some of the necessary foreign exchange needed to pay for our current account deficit, but at the expense of creating more foreign debt. Canadians invested $5,491 million in new long-term securities and assets abroad (line 25), resulting in a $3,210 million balance in long-term capital movements (line 26). In addition, Canada had an increase of $7,911 million in short-term capital (line 30), largely because of increased bank balances abroad.

The surplus on capital account was large enough to create a combined current and capital account balance of $6,102 million (line 32). To this net capital inflow was added $219 million in special drawing rights by the International Monetary Fund.

"Errors and omissions" of $4,402 (line 33) is a balancing figure. We know that the current and capital account balance, added to the allocation of special drawing rights (lines 32 & 34) gave Canada a potential increase in foreign reserves of $6,321 million. However, it is also known that reserves increased by only $1,919 million (line 35). Therefore, Canadians *must* have lent $4,402 million to foreigners that is not accounted for.

The increase in official reserves of $1,919 million (line 35) is called a balance of payments surplus. (A decrease in reserves would be a balance of payments deficit.) It is preceded by a minus sign to indicate how the potential increase in reserves (lines 32 and 34) was actually "used up." By adding up all sources and uses of foreign currency in this way, the balance of payments (line 36) is always equal to zero. Receipts equal payments. However, economists focus on balances within this statement that are not equal to zero. Particularly important are the current account balance (line 17), the capital account balance (line 31), and what is sometimes called the *overall balance* — the current and capital account balance combined (line 32). This, apart from errors and omissions, tells us how our holdings of foreign reserves will change.

CONCLUSIONS

We have now looked in some detail at the ways nominal and real GNP are measured and how the main elements of the balance of payments are calculated. In conclusion, it will be well to give some idea of the limitations of GNP measurements. Several points need to be made in this connection.

---

[1] Long-term securities refers to obligations such as bonds that have a maturity of one year or more; short-term capital involves obligations with a maturity of less than one year. Direct investment refers to the acquisition of physical assets such as buildings, land, or machinery; portfolio investment involves purchase of bonds and common stocks not sufficient to gain control of an enterprise.

First, much economic activity is not included in GNP at all. There are whole industries — gambling, bootlegging, narcotics, prostitution — whose multi-billion-dollar sales go unreported because they are illegal. Some legal economic activity also goes unreported for purposes of tax evasion. Other market activity — such as babysitting and casual yard work — goes unreported because it is too scattered to keep track of, even though the total sums involved may be quite large. The size of the underground market economy is surely large — perhaps as much as 10 percent of reported GNP. Even this does not count the enormous amount of nonmarket economic activity that takes place, including such highly valuable services as unpaid housekeeping and child care.

Second, even if real GNP did accurately measure the level of market and nonmarket economic activity, it would still not be a very good measure of welfare or human satisfaction. For example, the way income is distributed may affect the level of satisfaction. The level of real GNP per capita does not directly reflect the number of families in poverty or the relative income status of upper- and lower-income groups.

Third, fewer and fewer labor hours per worker are devoted to producing real GNP as the years go by. It is plausible to think that more leisure will cause satisfaction to rise. Leisure is evidently a scarce economic good valued by workers. However, the substantial increase in the leisure of the Canadian worker in this century is not explicitly reflected in GNP calculations.

Fourth, real GNP is a measure only of currently produced goods and services. Satisfaction also comes from durable consumer goods produced in the past that are still providing services. Surely, the larger the present stock of consumer durables, the higher is satisfaction.

Fifth, the market prices at which goods are sold do not accurately reflect costs or benefits affecting third parties not directly involved in the exchange. For example, environmental pollution caused by productive activities detracts from welfare. Pollution adversely affects people who are neither buyers nor sellers of the goods whose production created it. Like several of the nonmarket goods discussed above that affect satisfaction, pollution is not entered into GNP calculations. Unlike those goods, however, pollution is a "bad" — an output with a negative value. Annual additions to the amount of pollution should, in principle, be subtracted from GNP; but practical problems make this adjustment impossible.[2]

Sixth, an increase in output does not necessarily imply an increase in welfare, even if none of the problems yet mentioned is there. An unseasonably cold winter, for example, or an epidemic of infectious disease could cause the purchases of heating fuel or medical services to rise dramatically. Yet the resulting increases in real GNP would hardly represent an increase in satisfaction! Wartime defense expenditures provide another example of the lack of direct correspondence between output and welfare. We could argue that in principle these kinds of expenditures are for the maintenance

---

[2] The best one can probably do is to subtract from GNP the total expenditures made solely to abate or prevent pollution. Even after such cleanup expenditures, however, enough pollution remains to adversely affect welfare.

of the stock of human beings and should be treated just like investment expenditures that offset depreciation of the capital stock; that is, they should be subtracted from real GNP to get real new output. Putting this idea into practice, however, would be difficult.

Finally, many aspects of human welfare are not related at all to the flow of economic goods and services or to the economic satisfaction obtained from them. Everyone would agree that people do not live by bread alone, but obtaining agreement about exactly what else is important would not be easy. How important are unspoiled natural areas, unalienating work, loving human contact, social justice, income equality, economic growth, and freedom? These are normative questions that each person must answer individually. The economist could never hope to lump these social and economic conditions into an objective measure of social welfare.

For all these reasons, then, real GNP should never be interpreted as a measure of social welfare. Still, it is not completely worthless. It provides a roughly accurate picture of the economy's annual production of final goods and services, which, of course, is all that it was ever intended to do. As will be seen, it is valuable for several purposes even given its limitations.

SUMMARY

1. Official measurements of national product are made using the expenditure approach. Gross national expenditure (GNE) is obtained by adding together the values of all expenditures on newly produced goods and services.

2. National income is officially estimated by the income approach, which means adding together the values of all income earned by households. In the real world, certain adjustments must be made to get GNE and national income to fit, even though for elementary theoretical purposes, the two are considered equal. The difference between GNE and net national income is equal to the capital consumption allowance plus indirect business taxes plus the residual error of estimate.

3. Net national income measures all income earned by households, while personal income measures all the income they actually receive. To go from national income to personal income means subtracting corporate profits taxes, and undistributed corporate profits, then adding transfer payments. If personal taxes are subtracted from personal income, the result is personal disposable income.

4. Measurements of aggregate economic activity can be made in real terms in order to adjust for changes in prices. Real GNP or GNE means the total value of current year quantities of output evaluated in terms of the prices of some base year. The GNE deflator is the ratio of current year nominal GNE to current year real GNE.

5. Real GNE does not attempt to be a measure of welfare or satisfaction; it is only a measure of the output of goods and services. It does not do even that job perfectly because of sampling error, omitted items, and biases in price indexes. It is important to remember that a great many things contribute to overall human welfare that are not in any way measured by GNE.

6. Balance of payment accounts record the important international transactions in which Canada is involved. These transactions are broken down into three categories: (a) transactions in goods and services produced in the current year (summarized in the current account); (b) transactions in securities and bonds (summarized in the capital account); (c) changes in official holdings of reserves, recorded as a net change in the official reserve account.

DISCUSSION QUESTIONS

1. In 1971, the base year for the consumer price index, average earnings of construction workers were $188.27 per week. By 1978, earnings in construction had reached $390.33 per week, but the CPI stood at 175.2. What were real earnings in 1978, stated in 1971 dollars?
2. If all parents in Canada traded off child care services with their neighbors, received a wage for doing their neighbors' work, and hence did none of their own child care, what would happen to GNP as measured by national income accountants? Who, if anyone, would be better off with a situation where everyone got paid? Explain.
3. Do you think transfer payments should be included in the measure of GNP? Explain.
4. In 1933, net fixed business investment was equal to about −$300 million. How could this have been possible?
5. A firm gets rid of its inventory of $10,000 worth of shoes by having a sale to the public. What happens to GNP in this case? What happens to each of its components?
6. If the government increased the unemployment insurance deduction, what would happen to GNP, net national income, and personal disposable income?
7. Determine whether each of the following expenditures of an individual's own earnings is consumption, saving, investment, or something else:
   a. Purchase of a new home.
   b. Purchase of a new automobile for cash.
   c. Payment of a monthly installment on a loan.
   d. Purchase of an item of clothing for $4 plus $.20 sales tax.
   e. Purchase of common stock.
   f. Giving the individual's children a weekly allowance.
   g. Payment of tuition for additional education.
   h. A tip at a restaurant.
8. The following table shows output and prices for a simple economy in 1967 and 1977. Use the data to calculate both the CPI and the GNP deflator for 1977, using 1967 as the base year.

	1967 Quantity	1967 Price	1977 Quantity	1977 Price
Cars	1,000	$ 2,500	2,000	$ 4,000
Houses	100	20,000	150	40,000
Hospital services (total days of care)	500	100	550	250

9. How would an increase in imports of $5 billion affect net exports and gross national expenditure as recorded in Exhibit 6.1? (Be careful here. Recall that imports are included in consumption, investment, and government expenditures.) How would such an increase change the current account deficit recorded in Exhibit 6.10?

C H A P T E R 7

THE GOALS OF STABILIZATION POLICY AND THE PERFORMANCE OF THE CANADIAN ECONOMY

WHAT YOU WILL LEARN IN THIS CHAPTER

The four major goals of stabilization policy are full employment, price stability, growth of real output, and balance of payments stability. This chapter reviews the past performance of the economy in terms of each of these goals, and concludes with a discussion of important interrelationships among them.

FOR REVIEW

Here are some important terms and concepts that will be put to use in this chapter. If you do not understand them, review them before proceeding.
* *Production possibility frontier (Chapter 2)*
* *Marginal tax rate (Chapter 4)*
* *Stocks and flows (Chapter 5)*
* *National income and product (Chapters 5 and 6)*
* *Price indexes including the GNE deflator (Chapter 6)*
* *Balance of payments account (Chapter 6)*

Economic stabilization policy, one of the major functions of government listed in Chapter 4, can be broken down into the pursuit of four more specific policy goals: full employment, price stability, growth of real output, and balance of payments stability.

FULL EMPLOYMENT

Definition and Performance

The goal of maintaining full employment has a simple meaning for most Canadians: ensuring the availability of jobs for people who seek them. This simple idea is what the federal government appears to have had in mind when it declared in the **White Paper on Employment and Income of 1945** that it had unequivocally adopted a high and stable level of employment and income as a major aim of government policy.

The White Paper of 1945
Committed the federal government to the maintenance of stable, full-employment economic growth.

Exhibit 7.1

Unemployment in Canada since 1950

The Economic Council of Canada originally set a 3.5 percent unemployment rate target for the Canadian economy. In the 1970s this target was increased to 4.5 percent and then to 6 percent. In fact, however, unemployment rates below 4.5 percent have been achieved in only nine of the past thirty years.

Source: M.C. Urquhart and K.A.H. Buckley, *Historical Statistics of Canada* (Toronto: Macmillan, 1965), and Department of Finance, *Economic Review*, April 1980.

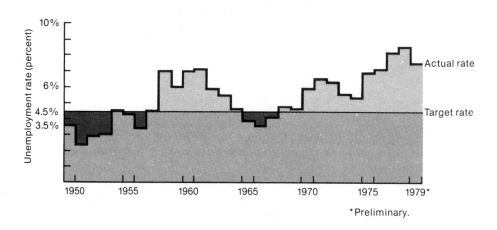

* Preliminary.

Over the years, however, pursuing the goal of full employment has become less a matter of this general principle, and more a numbers game. The particular number that is now the focus of employment policy is the unemployment rate, as measured by Statistics Canada and published in a monthly bulletin, *The Labour Force*. To calculate this rate, each month Statistics Canada first surveys about 55,000 Canadian households to determine how many Canadians are members of the **labor force**. The labor force is made up of those persons 15 years and over who at the time of the survey were either *employed* (which means, among other things, that they were working at least one hour per week as paid employees) or *unemployed* (actively but unsuccessfully looking for work). The **unemployment rate** is the percentage of people in the labor force who are actively looking for employment but who are not currently employed. Persons under 15, adults not actively seeking employment, military personnel, and certain institutionalized persons are counted as outside the labor force, and thus as neither employed nor unemployed.[1]

Clearly, the goal of "jobs for people who want jobs" implies that the officially measured unemployment rate should be kept low. But how low is low? Because of the way the unemployment rate is defined, a zero unemployment rate is impossible. The reason is that even when the economy is performing as smoothly and efficiently as possible, there are a certain

Labor force All members of the noninstitutionalized civilian population over the age of 15 who are either officially employed or looking for employment.

Unemployment rate Percentage of the labor force who are actively looking for employment but who are not employed.

---

[1] Additional details concerning the definition and measurement of the labor force and the unemployment rate will be introduced in Chapter 15.

number of people who have voluntarily quit their jobs to look for better ones, or who have entered the labor force for the first time and have not yet found a job. The process of job search, through which workers are matched to the jobs best suited for them, takes time. During the search process, such workers are counted as unemployed, even though their unemployment is voluntary and not a source of hardship. Some economists feel that current social welfare programs make it rational behavior for some people to declare themselves unemployed even when jobs are available and that the generous provisions of the Unemployment Insurance Act of 1971 may have increased this type of "voluntary" unemployment.

The White Paper of 1945 did not specify a particular employment target, and subsequent governments have been equally loathe to be precise. However, the White Paper stated that "in setting as its aim a high and stable level of employment and income, the Government is not selecting a lower target than 'full employment'"![2] The Economic Council of Canada has tried to define the percentage of unemployment that is consistent with such **full employment**. It originally chose an "acceptable" unemployment rate of 3.5 percent; by 1972 the target rate had been increased to 4.5 percent and in 1979 to 6 percent.

At the First Ministers' Conferences in February and November 1978, the federal government set a 5.5 percent unemployment rate for the early 1980s. A recent Bank of Canada report maintains that the rate of unemployment consistent with full employment is currently as high as 7 percent.[3]

Full employment The greatest possible utilization of the labor force consistent with price stability and allowing for unavoidable unemployment of workers between jobs.

Distribution of the Burden of Unemployment

The burdens of unemployment, and hence the potential benefits of a full employment policy, are unevenly distributed over the population. In February 1979, for example, the unemployment rate for Canada was 8.8 percent. However, the rate for young people, aged 15–24, was 15.6 percent while for those 25 years and over it was only 6.5 percent. For married males the rate was only 5.4 percent, while for married females it was 8.95 percent. For males in general the rate was 8.4 percent, while for females it was 9.4 percent.

Although higher education is no longer considered an absolute guarantee against unemployment, persons with a university degree had an unemployment rate of only 3.0 percent, while those with only a high school certificate had a rate of 11.4 percent.

The unemployment rate also varied considerably from one region of the country to another. It ranged from a high of 18.8 percent in Newfoundland to a low of 4.9 percent in Alberta. The provinces of Alberta, Saskatchewan, Manitoba, and Ontario had unemployment rates below the national average, while for all the other provinces the rate was above the national average.

The person least likely to be unemployed in Canada, therefore, may be a married male with a university degree living in Alberta. The person most

---

[2] Canadian Trade Committee, *Canadian Economic Policy since the War*, 1966, p. 136.
[3] Daryl L. Merret, *The Process of Wage Determination: A Survey of Some Recent Work*, Bank of Canada Technical Report 19, December 1979.

likely to be unemployed is a young, unmarried individual with little formal schooling living in Newfoundland. The monthly labor force surveys of Statistics Canada do not provide such fine detail, but they report, for February 1979, an unemployment rate of 38.4 percent for males aged 15–19 in Newfoundland, and a rate of only 2.3 percent for males aged 45 years and over in Alberta.

Because of such extreme variations by region, sex, age, education, and marital status (not to mention race and other factors that are normally not included in the surveys), it is extremely difficult to deal with unemployment through national economic policies. This point should be kept in mind when appropriate economic policies are discussed in Chapters 14 to 17.

PRICE STABILITY

Definition and Performance

In addition to setting unemployment targets, the Economic Council of Canada has suggested goals for price increases in the economy. In its First Annual Review of 1964 the council defined reasonable price stability as a maximum increase of 2 percent per year in the gross national expenditure price deflator. This seemed to be a reasonable objective in the light of the experience of the 1950s, but it turned out to be quite unrealistic for the 1960s and 1970s. In the 1960s the average rate of price increase was 3.2 percent per year. The council, therefore, in its Ninth Annual Review of 1972, increased the maximum price target to 3.0 percent for the period 1973 to 1975. This goal also proved to be elusive: the GNE deflator rose by 8.4 percent in 1973, by 13.8 percent in 1974, and by 9.7 percent in 1975. Exhibit 7.2, which measures Canada's experience with inflation by means of the Consumer Price Index, rather than by the GNE deflator (the two generally move in very similar ways), shows clearly how poor our performance has been when measured against these unofficial targets. This was especially the case in the 1970s.

After consumer prices rose by 10.9 percent in 1974 and were rising by about 11 percent in 1975, the federal government decided, in October of 1975, to control prices by setting up an Anti-Inflation Board. This board was given the power to limit wages and profits, and its stated objective was to use these indirect measures to hold price increases down to 10 percent in 1978, 8 percent in 1976, 6 percent in 1977, and 4 percent in 1978.

Even such drastic action failed to achieve the government's objectives. As Exhibit 7.2 indicates, consumer prices increased by 10.8 percent in 1975. The annual increase was limited to 7.5 percent in 1976, but instead of falling to 6 percent in 1977, the inflation rate rose to 8 percent, and in 1978 consumer prices increased by 9.0 percent instead of by 4 percent. In 1979 they rose by 9.1 percent. In view of this performance the federal government target of a 3.5 percent inflation rate for the 1980s, as announced in November 1978, seems very ambitious indeed. The Economic Council of Canada admitted as much, by noting in 1978 that it was highly unlikely that the inflation rate would fall below 6 percent before 1982. In 1978 the Anti-Inflation Board was replaced with a price commission that had no power to enforce price targets.

Exhibit 7.2
Inflation in Canada since 1950
The Economic Council of Canada set an inflation-rate target for Canada in 1964 of 2 percent. In 1972 the target was raised to 3 percent, and by the late 1970s it was acknowledged that rates of less than 6 percent were highly unlikely in the near future. The Exhibit shows how the actual inflation rate has exceeded the successive targets.

Source: M.C. Urquhart and K.A.H. Buckley, *Historical Statistics of Canada* (Toronto: Macmillan, 1965), and Department of Finance, *Economic Review*, April 1980.

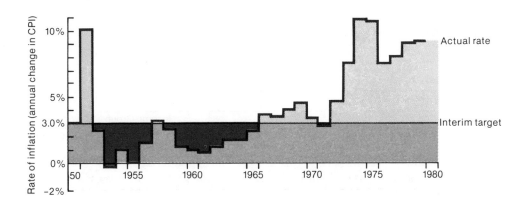

A careful comparison of Exhibits 7.1 and 7.2 reveals an even more distressing feature of our recent macroeconomic record. Until 1968, inflation and unemployment tended to alternate. Only in one year, 1957, was there both unemployment of more than 4.5 percent and inflation of more than 3 percent. Since 1968, however, both goals have been exceeded in every year, with the exception of 1971.

Who Gains and Who Loses from Inflation?

As in the case of unemployment, the burdens of inflation and the potential benefits of a policy of price stability are not distributed equally among different groups in the population. Various income groups fare very differently in times of inflation. Determining exactly who gains and who loses from inflation, however, is by no means an easy problem. A study by the Economic Council of Canada has tried to identify those Canadian households that lose and benefit most. Exhibit 7.3 provides a picture of what likely happened to various types of households during the inflationary period 1969–75. Prices increased by 47 percent over those seven years.

Somewhat surprisingly, the poorest group fared best in terms of income increases, largely because they depended heavily on social security benefits, which were raised substantially. Middle-aged and middle-income people also fared well, because their income was derived largely from wages and salaries, which increased more rapidly than the inflation rate. Wealthier people fared less well, because of the poor performance of the stock market and the erosion of real value of income derived from assets such as bonds.

These results, however, must be balanced by the erosion of purchasing power that occurred through rising prices, particularly for utilities and food, which weigh heavily in the consumer purchases of the poor. When this is taken into account, all classes appear to have fared about equally. Their expenditures increased by 48.6 percent (for the lowest income group) to 45.8 percent (for the highest income group).

Exhibit 7.3

Estimated impact of inflation on the relative positions of householders by age and income group, 1969–75

Source: Economic Council of Canada, *Thirteenth Annual Review*, p. 22.

	Age Group in 1969						Income Group			
	Under 25	25–34	35–44	45–54	55–64	65 and over	Less than $4,000	$4,000– 7,999	$8,000– 14,900	$15,000 and over
Increase in income (percent)	n.a.	70.4	67.4	65.5	n.a.	n.a.	107.1	74.5	69.3	54.2
Increase or decrease in value of net assets (percent)	21.1	14.5	4.4	7.2	−10.8	−11.6	−10.8	5.1	10.9	−10.0

One way to make a more detailed examination of the distributional effects of inflation is to look separately at its effects on wage and salary income, transfer payments, interest income, and wealth.

Wage and Salary Income Because wages and salaries rise roughly in step with prices, real income from these sources is among the areas least affected by inflation. For example, between 1971 and the end of 1978, while the consumer price index rose from its base of 100 to a level of 175.2, average earnings in manufacturing rose from $3.28 per hour to $6.82 per hour, more than keeping pace. In a number of industries, wages are **indexed** — adjusted automatically for changes in the cost of living through escalator clauses. Not all wage and salary earners are equally well protected from inflation. As the inflation rate rose in 1973–74, workers organized in labor unions in larger enterprises were able to increase their wages slightly more than the average. However, some unions were tied into long-run contracts that made it difficult for them to adjust their wages to rising prices. Workers in the forestry, mining, transport, and financial sectors were able to get wage increases larger than the price increases, while those in manufacturing, commercial, and service sectors experienced a reduction in real wages.[4] It should also be noted that food prices have risen much more rapidly in recent years than other prices, so that poor families who spend a larger proportion of their income on food than other families have suffered more from inflation. Between February 1978 and February 1979, food prices rose by 16.1 percent, while nonfood prices rose by only 6.8 percent.

Indexing The practice of automatically adjusting wages, salaries, or other payments to compensate for changes in the price level.

[4] Economic Council of Canada, Thirteenth Annual Review: *The Inflation Dilemma*, 1976, pp. 25, 27.

Transfer Payments Over the last decade, total transfer payments have increased much more rapidly than the rate of inflation. Much of the increase, however, can be attributed to changes in social policy not directly related to inflation one way or the other. The relevant question is not whether transfer payments to individuals have increased in real terms but whether they have increased as much as they would have if price stability had been maintained.

There is no way of answering this question with certainty. In many cases, however, recipients of transfer payments appear at least as well protected against inflation as wage and salary earners. One major reason is the indexing of social welfare benefits, which now automatically keep pace with rising prices.

For example, between 1965 and 1975, while prices increased by 47 percent, and the average working family increased its income by slightly more than 70 percent, retired persons dependent completely on public old-age security pensions enjoyed an 85 percent increase in benefits. Persons receiving benefits from private pension plans generally did not receive increases. As a result, the real value of their pensions fell to less than half between 1969 and 1979. In addition to substantial increases in government transfer payments, an increasing proportion of all transfers is now being paid in kind (that is, in the form of free or subsidized housing, medical care, and so forth) rather than in cash. Although the spread of in-kind transfers may not consciously have been intended to protect the poor from inflation, it has had that effect.

Interest Income—Debtors versus Creditors What does inflation do to the real income of creditors, who receive interest income from bonds, mortgages, and the like, and to the real income of debtors, who pay this interest? Although the effects are somewhat more complex than for wage income or transfer payments, they are worth looking at in some detail.

The Traditional View The traditional view of the matter is that inflation injures creditors and aids debtors. Suppose, for example, that I borrow $100 from you today, promising to repay $105 next year. If there is no inflation during the year, I get use of the funds for the year, and you get a $5 increase in your purchasing power. But suppose that during the year the price level goes up 10 percent. In that case, I get the use of the funds for the year, and what is more, I get to pay you back in depreciated dollars. The $105 I give you next year will buy you only as much then as $95 will today. Your real income is negative. I, the debtor, am benefited by inflation; you, the creditor, are hurt.

Expected and Unexpected Inflation It is now recognized, however, that this traditional view of the effects of inflation on debtors and creditors is seriously incomplete, in that it does not distinguish between *unexpected* and *expected* inflation. The example just given implicitly assumes that neither I, the debtor, nor you, the creditor expected any inflation at the time the loan was made. Suppose instead that we both had expected a 10 percent increase in the price level between the time the loan was made and the time it was repaid. You would not then have loaned me the $100 in return for a promise to repay just $105 at the end of the year. Instead, you would have insisted on a repayment of something like $115: $10 to compensate you for the decline in the purchasing power of the $100 principal plus the $5 you originally wanted as real return for relinquishing use of the funds for a year. I, in turn, would have agreed to those terms, expecting that $115 in the next year's depreciated dollars would be no more than the equivalent, in terms of real purchasing power, of the $105 I would have been willing to repay in a noninflationary world. In real terms, then, correctly anticipated inflation is neutral between debtor and creditor.

Nominal versus Real Interest Rates The example just given shows why it is necessary in an inflationary world to distinguish three separate interest rate concepts. The first, the **nominal rate of interest**, means the rate of interest measured in the ordinary way in current dollars. The second, the **expected real rate of interest**, means the nominal rate of interest minus the expected rate of inflation. And the third, the **realized real rate of interest**, means the nominal rate of interest minus the actual rate of inflation.

If no inflation is expected and none actually occurs, all three rates of interest are equal. If inflation does occur and is accurately anticipated, the expected and realized real rates of interest are equal, and both are less than the nominal rate. In the example given above, for instance, an accurately anticipated rate of inflation of 10 percent transformed a 15 percent nominal rate of interest into a 5 percent expected and realized real rate of interest.

If inflation does occur and is not accurately expected, the expected and realized real rates of interest will differ from one another. To extend the example, suppose that you had loaned me the $100 in question at a 15 percent nominal rate in the expectation of a 10 percent rate of inflation but that the actual rate of inflation turned out to be 12 percent. Instead of earning your expected real rate of interest of 5 percent (the 15 percent nominal rate minus 10 percent expected inflation), you would actually have earned a realized rate of interest of only 3 percent (the 15 percent nominal rate minus 12 percent actual inflation).

The distinction between nominal and real rates of interest can be used to express precisely the distributional effects of inflation as between debtors and creditors. Accurately expected inflation is neutral between creditors and debtors, because the parties will fully adjust the nominal rate of interest they agree on to take the expected inflation into account. If the actual rate of inflation exceeds the expected rate, debtors will gain at the expense of creditors, because the realized real rate of interest will fall below the expected real rate. If the actual rate of inflation falls short of the expected rate, creditors will gain at the expense of debtors, because the realized real rate will exceed the expected real rate. Note that the traditional view of inflation fits into these generalizations as a special case that applies when the expected rate of inflation is zero.

Inflation and Wealth A complete picture of the distributional effects of inflation must consider not only its effects on flows of income to individuals but also its effects on the same individuals' stocks of wealth. The effects of inflation on wealth very much depend on the form in which that wealth is held.

Nominal rate of interest The rate of interest measured in the ordinary way, without adjustment for inflation.

Expected rate of interest The nominal rate of interest minus the expected rate of inflation.

Realized real rate of interest The nominal rate of interest minus the actual rate of inflation.

The one group of the population that most clearly benefited from the inflation of the 1970s consisted of those people who had most of their personal wealth tied up in their own homes. In fact, most such people actually benefited in two ways. First, the market value of their houses, at least in most areas of the country, not only kept pace with inflation but outstripped it. Second, many homeowners had long-term, low-interest mortgages negotiated during the 1950s and 1960s. The unexpected increase in inflation during the 1970s benefited them as debtors, allowing them to pay off their mortgages in depreciated dollars.

People who held their wealth in common stocks, on the other hand, fared very poorly during the inflationary 1970s. This came as a major surprise. For generations, investment advisers had regarded it as dogma that corporate stocks were a sound hedge against inflation. Their reasoning was simple and persuasive. A share of common stock represents a share of ownership of the firm that issues it. If prices double, the firm's costs of doing business will double, but so should its revenues, the prices of the things it sells, the value of its plant and equipment, its profits, its dividends, and so on. The market price of the stocks should thus also be expected to double, leaving the stockholder no worse off as a result of the inflation.

Somewhere toward the end of the 1960s, however, something went wrong. Inflation accelerated, but the stock market failed to respond. The reasons are complex and not yet fully understood, but the facts are clear. By the end of the 1970s, stock prices were fluctuating around an average level no higher in nominal terms than what they had reached in the mid-1960s. People who had kept their money in the stock market, on the average, lost more than half their real wealth.

Effects of Inflation on Business and Government

As Exhibit 7.4 illustrates, during the rapid inflation of 1972–74 Canadian corporations were able to increase both their before- and after-tax profits by much more than the rate of inflation, and at a considerably faster pace than workers were able to increase their wages and salaries. Apparently business firms were able to react more swiftly than workers to the opportunities

Exhibit 7.4
Percentage change in corporation profits
(and average weekly wages and salaries)

	1972	1973	1974	1975
Corporate profits percentage change before taxes	24.4	42.8	28.5	1.8
Corporate profits percentage change after taxes	28.9	50.2	24.5	−4.6
Percentage change in average weekly wages and salaries	8.4	7.5	11.0	14.2

Source: Canadian Imperial Bank of Commerce, *Commercial Letter*, No. 4, 1977, p. 5.

[5] These observations are based on Glenn P. Jenkins, *Inflation: Its Financial Impact on Business in Canada* (Ottawa: Economic Council of Canada, 1977).

presented by increased demand in the economy. Since profit levels had been low for a few years before 1972, the 1972 increase might be seen as an overdue return to normal profit rates, but the sharp increases in 1973 and 1974 indicate that many business firms were put into an unusually favorable profit position by rising inflation.

As a recent study has shown, however, much of this increased profit was due to the effect of inflation on the valuation of inventories.[5] In the initial phases of inflation, firms realize extra profits through higher markups on goods held in inventory. Those goods were produced with low material and labor costs. They will have to be replaced, however, with goods that embody higher-cost material and labor inputs. Because accountants are required by tax laws to value inventory at the original cost and not at replacement cost, an artificially high profit rate, due to inventory appreciation, will result. For example, assume that a firm has 1,000 units of goods in inventory at the beginning of a year, for which it paid $2.00 per unit in the previous year. Because of inflation, it sells these goods during the course of the year for $2.20, earning a unit profit of $.20 and total profits of $200. This is the profit that it must report to the tax authorities. However, the firm replaces its inventory during the year at a unit cost of $2.20, so that its actual inventory costs during the year are $2,200, and the difference between sales revenue for that year and actual costs incurred is zero. If the firm had been permitted to count the value of its inventory at current replacement costs, no profits due to inventory appreciation would have been reported, and the firm would not have had to pay taxes on such profits. About 20 percent of the profits reported by corporations in 1977 and 1974 were due to inventory appreciation. It is estimated that in those two years, because of inflated profit figures, corporations paid between $2.5 billion and $3.0 billion more in taxes than they would have if they had been permitted to use replacement cost to calculate the value of their inventories.

In addition, profit taxes were increased because inflation reduces the real value of capital cost allowances. With inflation, the replacement costs of capital assets rise, but corporations are allowed to depreciate their assets only at a fixed percentage of original costs. The amount of depreciation that corporations could write off against their profits would increase if they could revalue their capital on the basis of replacement costs. It is estimated that corporations paid more than $1 billion in increased taxes in 1973 and 1974 because of this effect of inflation.

However, despite such accounting problems, it is obvious that corporation profits benefited immensely from the early phases of inflation, in 1972–74, as seen by their rapidly rising after-tax profits. By 1975, the picture had changed somewhat. High profit levels were maintained, but profits before taxes increased by only 1.8 percent, while profits after taxes declined by 4.6 percent. At the same time, wages and salaries were finally adjusting to high inflation rates, increasing by 14.2 percent in 1975. It was at this juncture of stable or declining profits and rapidly increasing worker income, that the government, in October 1975, imposed income controls. It has seemed to labor union leaders, and some economists, that the government timed its actions at the most convenient time for business — when prospects for further profit increases were dim — and at a bad time for labor — when renegotiated contracts were just beginning to catch up to the high inflation of the previous few years.

The various levels of government are also affected by inflation. Our federal and provincial governments benefit directly from inflation, because the progressive personal and corporate income taxes which they levy rise steadily with inflation-induced income and profit increases. Since 1974, personal income taxes have been indexed against inflationary effects so that most — though not all — of the bias has been removed from that particular tax, although at the time of writing, the federal government is investigating the removal of this concession. Even with indexing, government revenues increase more rapidly than normal in times of inflation. Like all debtors, governments also gain during inflation from a decline in real interest rates. It has been estimated that the federal government gained more than $3 billion dollars in the years 1973–75 through declines, caused by inflation, in the real burden of their debt.[6] Governments must also, of course, pay more in wages and salaries and other costs during inflationary periods, but they are net beneficiaries from inflation.

It will be important to keep these distributional effects of inflation in mind in succeeding chapters as various theories of inflation and proposed anti-inflationary policies are discussed. For the moment, though, attention can be turned to the third major goal of macroeconomic policy — economic growth.

ECONOMIC GROWTH

Growth of Potential GNP

Economic growth means the growth of opportunities to satisfy economic wants. At any one time, economic opportunities are limited. Labor, natural resources, and capital are scarce. Their scarcity, together with the state of technological knowledge, limits production possibilities. Not all the useful goods and services desired can be produced at once.

As time passes, though, the range of possibilities expands. Capital accumulates, and new resources are found. New methods of production make it possible to get more output from each unit of input. People still will not be able to have everything at once, but they can have more things at once than before.

Growth and the Production Possibility Frontier The production possibility frontier, first introduced in Chapter 2, provides a convenient graphical method of representing economic growth. Exhibit 7.5 shows production possibility frontiers for an economy producing only two goods, which will be called "guns" and "butter." In any single year, total output is constrained by the production possibility frontier. Over time, however, as new resources become available and as technology improves, the frontier expands outward. Exhibit 7.5 shows four successive production possibility frontiers, each permitting a greater potential real output.

---

[6] Economic Council of Canada, *Thirteenth Annual Review*, p. 71.

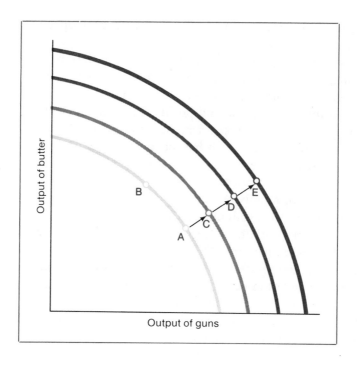

Exhibit 7.5
The process of economic growth
Economic growth can be represented as an outward expansion of the production possibility frontier. In any one year, getting more "guns" means giving up some "butter," as in a movement from B to A. Over time, however, growth could give more of both guns and butter, as in a movement from A to C, D, and E.

Actual versus Potential Real Output In practice, real output may not actually expand exactly in step with the outward shift in the production possibility frontier. Remember that, in any given year, the economy may operate inside the production possibility frontier if resources are not fully employed. Economists use the term **potential real GNP** (or **potential real output**) to indicate the level of real output that the economy could achieve if resources were fully employed. If factors of production are not fully employed actual output is said to lag behind potential output.

It has been calculated that between 1973 and 1978 output in Canada could have grown by 4.2 percent annually, whereas it actually grew at an annual rate of 4.0 percent.[7]

> **Potential real GNP (potential real output)** The level of real GNP that the economy could, in principle, produce if resources were fully employed.

The Growth Record

Economic growth is measured in terms of real gross national product. Although real GNP is not a perfect measure of our ability to satisfy wants, or even of output, it is the best measure we have. Exhibit 7.6 shows the growth of per capita real GNP in Canada from 1948 to 1978. This growth rate is impressive in the length of time over which it has been maintained,

---

[7] Economic Council of Canada, *Sixteenth Annual Review: Two Cheers for the Eighties*, 1979, p. 15.

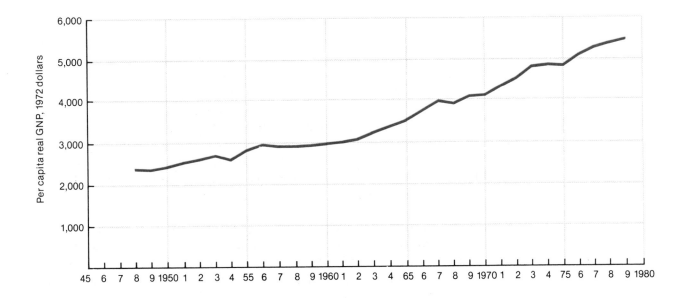

Exhibit 7.6

Growth of per capita real GNP in Canada, 1948–1978

Real gross national product per capita in Canada has grown steadily over the post-World War II period.

Source: Department of Finance, *Economic Review*, April 1980, pp. 156, 162.

and average annual rates of growth compare favorably with those of the other advanced economies. Per capita real GNP increased by 132 percent in the 32 year period. Exhibit 7.7 shows that Canadian economic growth in the 1970s has been relatively good by comparison with that of many other countries. The only country listed that had a better growth rate than Canada over the whole period 1970–1979 was Japan.

Exhibit 7.7

Principal indicators of international economic activity, 1970–1979

	1970	1971	1972	1973	1974	1975	1976	1977	1978	1979	Average 1970–1979
Real GNP/GDP Seven major countries				(Percent change)							
Canada	2.5	6.9	6.1	7.5	3.6	1.2	5.4	2.4	3.4	2.9	4.2
United States	−0.3	3.0	5.7	5.5	−1.4	−1.3	5.9	5.3	4.4	2.3	2.9
Japan	11.8	5.2	9.4	9.9	−0.3	1.5	6.5	5.4	6.0	6.1	6.1
France	5.7	5.4	5.9	5.4	3.2	0.2	4.9	2.8	3.3	3.4	4.0
Germany	5.9	3.4	3.6	4.9	0.3	−1.8	5.3	3.5	4.3	4.4	3.3
Italy	5.0	1.6	3.1	6.9	4.2	4.7	5.9	2.0	2.6	4.5	4.1
United Kingdom	2.3	2.8	2.4	8.0	−1.5	−1.0	3.7	1.3	3.3	0.8	1.9
Total	2.7	3.8	5.6	6.3	−0.1	−0.5	5.4	4.0	4.2	3.4	3.4
Total OECD	3.1	3.8	5.5	6.3	0.5	−0.4	5.2	3.7	3.9	3.4	3.5

Source: Department of Finance, *Economic Review*, April 1980, p. 8.

Is Economic Growth Really Desirable?

For many years, everyone thought economic growth was a good thing. The only debates about growth took place between people who thought that the present pace was good enough and those who wanted government action to increase the growth rate. Now things are different.

Today, the people who are satisfied with the record of growth and those who would like to step up the pace have been forced into a defensive alliance. On the other side are two groups. One is made up of people who think that further economic growth is impossible or will soon be so. The other is made up of those who think that further growth may be possible but who do not want it. The matter is important enough to make it worth giving at least an outline of the main issues here.

Questioning the Desirability of Growth Look first at the argument that further economic growth is not desirable whether or not it is possible. The heart of this argument is the perfectly valid proposition that GNP is not a measure of human welfare. The trouble, it is said, is that growth of GNP can be offset by a decline in the quality of life. These fears can be expressed in the form of a parable.

Imagine a peaceful little country with a per capita GNP of $100. All the GNP is produced by the women, who work the fields in the morning and gossip in the afternoon. The men do nothing but sit around and play cards and drink tea all day. Suppose now that an enterprising foreign company sets up a soap factory and puts all of the men to work. Each man can make $40 worth of soap per year. Previously there was no market for soap in this pastoral nation, but now the soap factory's boilers belch black coal smoke that soils everyone's curtains. The entire output of the soap factory is sold to local housewives, who now spend all their afternoons at the laundromat.

What has happened to the GNP of this country? As any economist will explain, it has gone up by 20 percent to $120 per capita. Farm output has not fallen, and industrial production of $20 per capita has been added. But what has happened to the level of well-being of the people of this country? They have no more to eat than before, their curtains wear out faster than before, and they are working four times as hard as before. They are, say, about one-quarter as well off as before.

Many people believe that this parable applies to the Canadian economy. They are worried not only about pollution but about values that they think will be lost as growth continues. Rapid economic growth makes skills, and hence people, obsolete before their working lives are over. Economic growth crowds out green places and covers them with asphalt. It replaces the community life of the town with the anonymity of the city. Growth is thus said to make life less worth living in ways for which more cars and microwave ovens do not fully compensate.

Separating the Issues How valid is this "quality of life" argument? Are people really becoming worse off year by year, or is that claim just romanticism? It cannot be denied that economic growth is a *potential* threat to the quality of life. As it stands, though, the argument is misleading because it confuses two issues. One issue has to do with the size of gross national product and the other with its composition.

Exhibit 7.8
Pollution and economic growth

In any single year, there is a trade-off between cars and clean air. More cars make the air dirtier, whereas having fewer cars makes cleaner air possible. As the production possibility frontier moves outward, the choice can be made between two kinds of growth. Many new dirty cars can be made (moving from A to B), if that is what people want. Alternatively, fewer cars can be produced, and more can be spent on each car to make it run cleaner (moving from A to C instead).

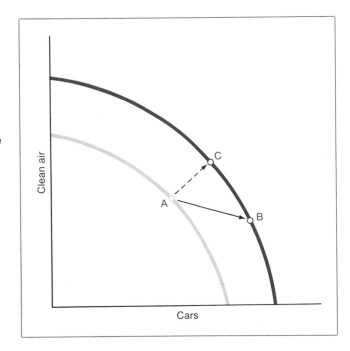

In Exhibit 7.8, the production possibility frontier is used to help separate the two issues. The diagram shows an economy in which the two goods produced are called "clean air" and "cars" rather than "guns" and "butter." In any single year, there is a trade-off between the two goods. More cars make the air dirtier; making fewer cars (or spending more money on each car to make them run cleaner) means having better air.

As technology improves and more capital is accumulated, the production possibility frontier shifts outward. If the actual growth path of the economy is from Point A to Point B, people will complain that the quality of life has

John Stuart Mill was in every respect one of the most brilliant and remarkable figures of the nineteenth century. Eldest son of the prominent economist and philosopher, James Mill, John Stuart lived an extraordinary childhood. He began his study of classical Greek at the age of three. By eight, he was reading Plato's dialogues in the original and teaching Latin to the younger members of the Mill family. His education in economics began at thirteen, under his father's tutorship, with a study of Adam Smith's work and the other classics.

This unusual upbringing was bound to produce a strong reaction sooner or later. In his early twenties, Mill went through a spiritual crisis that led him to reject many of his father's ideas. About that time, he met Harriet Taylor and began a long association with her. (Years later, after her husband's death, they were married.) Her ideas on feminism and socialism powerfully influenced Mill's thinking.

Mill published his *Principles of Political Economy* in 1848. This work is seen today as the high-water mark of the classical school, founded by Adam Smith three generations before. As a textbook and authority on economic questions, Mill's *Principles* stood unchallenged until Alfred Marshall transformed "political economy" into "economics" at the end of the century.

Mill's *Principles* is by no means limited to the narrowly technical side of economics. Mill always faced squarely the broad social implications of economic theory wherever

John Stuart Mill (1806–1873)

Mill published his *Principles of Political Economy* in 1848. This work is seen today as the high-water mark of the classical school, founded by Adam Smith three generations before. As a textbook and authority on economic questions, Mill's *Principles* stood unchallenged until Alfred Marshall transformed "political economy" into "economics" at the end of the century.

Mill's *Principles* is by no means limited to the narrowly technical side of economics. Mill always faced squarely the broad social implications of economic theory wherever they arose. For example, like other economists of the classical school, he believed there were not-too-distant limits to the process of economic growth. "At the end of the progressive state," he wrote, "lies the stationary state. All progress in wealth is but a postponement of this and all advance is an approach to it." Mill was not content, however, simply to describe the mechanics of growth and the technical properties of the stationary state. He wondered what a world without progress would be like. His conclusions so clearly address the concerns of our own age that they are worth quoting at length:

I cannot...regard the stationary state of capital and wealth with the unaffected aversion so generally manifested towards it by political economists of the old school. I am inclined to believe that it would be, on the whole, a very considerable improvement on our present condition. I confess I am not charmed with the ideal of life held out by those who think that the normal state of human beings is that of struggling to get on; that the trampling, crushing, elbowing, and treading on each other's heels, which form the existing type of social life, are the most desirable lot of human kind, or anything but the disagreeable symptoms of one of the phases of our industrial progress....

If the earth must lose that great portion of its pleasantries which it owes to things that the unlimited increase of wealth and population would extirpate from it, for the mere purpose of enabling it to support a larger, but not a better or happier population, I sincerely hope, for the sake of posterity, that they will be content to be stationary long before necessity compels them to.

It should be noted that the choice made may affect the size of output. For example, to force a move from point B to point C may cause a shift in the curve.

Pollution is a serious problem. It cannot be brushed aside. Still, it is wrong to blame pollution on economic growth. To stop growth in order to stop pollution would be to throw the baby out with the bath water. Controlling pollution requires policies to encourage the correct composition of national product, not to control its size. Chapter 19 will take a look at a number of such policies.

Questioning the Possibility of Growth There is little point in arguing about the direction of growth if resources are being depleted so rapidly that no future growth will be possible. So is growth still possible? A look at the sources of past economic growth may help answer this question.

Refer to Exhibit 7.9, which presents Economic Council of Canada figures on the sources of Canadian economic growth over the period 1950–73. The major source of growth in the past is not of a nature likely to be adversely affected by possible depletion of natural resources in the future. Changes in the quality of the factors of production and the efficiency of their use (factor productivity), which together account for some 35 percent of all growth, use up relatively few natural resources. The category "Labor" takes into account the effects of population growth, which is unlikely to be as rapid in the future as in the past. But although this will slow the growth of total real income, it will not affect the rate of growth of real income per capita.

Although depletion of natural resources may impede the accumulation of capital in some forms, not all capital accumulation takes the form of such resource-intensive items as steel mills and nuclear power plants. Many recent technological developments, in fact, are resource saving. Industry, for example, is learning how to build factories that are somewhat more expensive to construct initially but that require less energy to operate once they are in place. And the trend in the important field of electronics has been to put increasingly more powerful capital devices into smaller and smaller physical packages.

It would appear, then, that most arguments about the impossibility of future economic growth rest on the fallacy of thinking of growth in purely physical terms. To be sure, if economic growth meant nothing other than endlessly piling up duplicates of the gas-guzzling cars and smoke-belching factories of the past, people might someday come up against a blank wall. But exactly because certain important natural resources are gradually being depleted, that is not the direction in which growth will proceed. Instead, it will proceed in the direction of developing new generations of capital goods and consumer goods that do their job better with fewer physical inputs and more inputs of technology and human ingenuity.

Exhibit 7.9
Sources of Canadian economic growth
This table shows the relative importance of various sources of economic growth in Canada in the period 1950–73, and as projected by the Economic Council of Canada for the period 1980–85. The role of factors of production (labor and capital) in the growth of national output is calculated by weighting the increase in employment and capital stock by their respective shares in national income. Whatever is not accounted for in actual growth by this method is attributed to change in the quality of production or changes in factor productivity due to advances in knowledge, technology, and education.

	Relative contribution of factors of production (in percent) to GNP			
	1950–62	1964–69	1966–73	Projected 1980–85
Labor	32	48	50	44
Capital	27	20	20	29
Factor productivity	41	34	30	27
Net national income	100	100	100	100

Source: Economic Council of Canada, *Twelfth Annual Review*, pp. 44–45.

The Distributional Effects of Economic Growth

A brief explanation of distributional effects will complete the discussion of economic growth. In the long run, the distributional effects of growth in Canada appear to have been largely neutral. Workers, resource owners, and recipients of interest and profits appear each to be getting about the same sized slice of the national income pie as a century ago. As the economy has grown, the benefits have been shared by rich and poor alike.

In the context of stabilization policy, however, it is important also to consider the relatively short-term effects of economic growth. In the short run, changes in the year-to-year rate of real economic growth are closely linked to changes in employment. The faster the economy grows, other things being equal, the more jobs are created and the more rapidly the unemployment rate is reduced. In the short run, then, economic growth appears to provide the greatest benefits for those most disadvantaged by high rates of unemployment.

Besides lowering the overall unemployment rate, economic growth has the additional benefit of making it easier for people to upgrade their jobs and improve their economic circumstances. As one prominent civil rights leader in the U.S. has put it: "A limited-growth policy tends to freeze people to whatever rung of the ladder they happen to be on. That's OK if you're a highly educated 28-year-old making $50,000 per year as a presidential adviser. It's utter disaster if you're unskilled, out of work, and living in a ghetto." [8]

BALANCE OF PAYMENTS STABILITY

A fourth goal of Canadian stabilization policy is to maintain a strong balance of payments position and to avoid extreme fluctuations in the value of the Canadian dollar. As will be noted in Chapter 8, between 1958 and 1979 Canada experienced a positive balance in its net exports in only two years. This chronic negative balance in the current account forces Canada — if it wishes to stabilize its exchange rate — to maintain interest rates that are higher than those of its major trading partners, particularly the United States. This is necessary in order to attract foreign currency into the country through the purchase of Canadian bonds. Failing large new inflows of foreign capital, the Bank of Canada must use its reserves of foreign currency to bolster the value of the Canadian dollar. If the country wishes to maintain a high level of such reserves *and* a stable exchange rate, then high interest rates appear to be inevitable. Such interest rates, however, may interfere with Canadian domestic policy. During high rates of inflation and unemployment it would seem highly desirable to have low rates of interest to stimulate investment demand and to decrease the cost of borrowing. Weaknesses in our balance of payments make it extremely difficult to pursue such a rational policy.

In recent years, it has not been found possible to maintain a stable relationship between the Canadian dollar and other world currencies. Exhibit 7.10 indicates how the values of many other currencies have risen against the Canadian dollar in the 1970s. The deutschmark, for example, has increased in value by more than 100 percent (its value was 220 in 1979 versus a value of 100 assigned to it in Exhibit 7.10a in 1971). Germans used to have to pay about four marks for the Canadian dollar; now they pay less than two.

Because of our close relationship to the United States, and our heavy dependence on trade and capital flows with the United States, we naturally are most concerned about the value of the Canadian dollar in relation to the U.S. dollar. Exhibit 7.10a indicates that the U.S. dollar was slightly above

---

[8] Margaret Bush Wilson, chairman of the National Association for the Advancement of Colored People, quoted in "Review and Outlook: The NAACP Turns a Corner," *Wall Street Journal,* January 12, 1978, p. 12.

par with the Canadian dollar from about 1962 to 1970. It then fell below **par** from 1970 to 1976. Since late 1976 the value of the U.S. dollar has risen above par, and the value of the Canadian dollar has correspondingly depreciated by about 15 percent against the U.S. dollar.

Such fluctuations are not at all unusual in Canadian-American history. After World War I, the value of the Canadian dollar fell briefly to a low of $.82 U.S., rising back to par by the mid-1920s. In the early 1930s the dollar fell again, to $.80 U.S., returning to par before World War II.

Par The point at which one unit of a currency is traded for exactly one unit of another currency.

Exhibit 7.10

The behavior of Canada's exchange rate and Bank rate

Part a gives each currency a value of 100 in 1971 and then shows how the values of other currencies have risen, holding the value of the Canadian currency steady at 100. Part b illustrates the way in which the Bank of Canada has moved its Bank rate up in accordance with changes in the U.S. discount rate, to maintain a differential between interest rates in Canada and the U.S., so as to create a capital account surplus, offsetting our current account deficits.

Source: *The Financial Post*, April 7, 1979, p. 35, and July 28, 1979, p. 3.

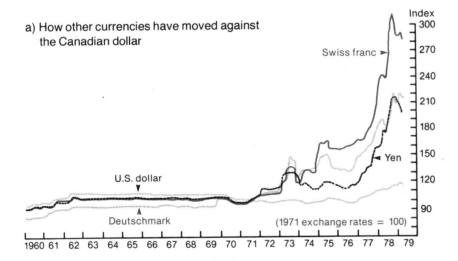

a) How other currencies have moved against the Canadian dollar

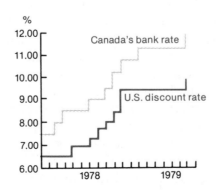

b) Canada's Bank rate in relation to the U.S. discount rate

Fluctuations of this type are due to current and capital account surpluses or deficits and differences in interest rates, discussed more fully in Chapter 15. They are also due to different experiences with inflation. Such forces determine the strength of demand by Canadians for U.S. dollars and the strength of demand by Americans for Canadian dollars. During much of the postwar period, the Canadian dollar has been allowed to float within limits, so that the value has been set largely through demand and supply forces.

Canada's balance of payments position vis-à-vis the U.S. can be summarized briefly. We almost always have a deficit in our current account with the United States. This is largely due to the interest and dividends on investments in Canada that we pay to American investors. These investors want to be paid in U.S. dollars, so companies in Canada paying interest and dividends to them must purchase U.S. dollars in the foreign exchange market. Doing so pushes up the value of the U.S. dollar. Therefore, our heavy dependence on American investment has created a perennial problem for us, by saddling us with heavy debt payments that push down the value of our dollar. In order to stabilize the value of the dollar around par, we have tried to lure more investment into Canada by keeping our interest rates above those prevailing in the United States. Because of our higher interest rates, Americans are induced to buy our securities in preference to their own. It is operations of this kind that have counterbalanced the negative impact on the value of our dollar caused by the normal deficits in our current account.

In 1976, several factors coincided to bring about a substantial decline in the value of our dollar. First, we allowed our interest rates to approach those of the United States, so that fewer Canadian bond issues were sold in the United States. There was therefore little counterpressure to the normal downward pressure on the dollar. Second, our inflation rate had been allowed to rise above that of the United States, so that we had additional problems in our current account. Third, the victory of the Parti Québecois in the province of Quebec, which threatened the unity of the country, probably led to some speculative action against the dollar by people anticipating a diminution of Canadian resources as a result of Quebec's secession.

By 1979, the value of the Canadian dollar had stabilized at about $.85 U.S. The Bank of Canada tried to use interest rate policy and special intervention with reserve funds to prevent the value of the dollar from falling lower than that. Exhibit 7.10b illustrates the way in which our interest rates have been maintained at a level at least 1 percent above those of the United States. When the Federal Reserve Bank of the United States pushes U.S. interest rates up, ours follow. In the early part of 1980 this brought about an increase in the Bank of Canada rate to its highest level ever, more than 16 percent. The move to this high, unpopular rate prompted the Bank to allow the Bank rate to *float* — that is, to move in accordance with the market rate of short-term government bonds.

One of the main concerns of the Bank of Canada, and of the federal government, seems to be to prevent the value of the Canadian dollar from falling too far below the value of the American dollar. High interest rates, and purchases of Canadian dollars in the foreign exchange market by the

Bank of Canada, using its reserves of American dollars, help to accomplish this. Such action, as noted previously, can seriously deplete Canada's reserves. In addition, high interest rates threaten to throw the domestic economy into both recession and inflation. The fear of letting the value of the dollar fall further seems to be largely political. Canadians seem to be of the opinion that there is something wrong with the country if our dollar is not at par with the U.S. dollar. Politicians must give heed to such notions, and prevent the value of the dollar from falling. There is also an inflationary factor. The declining value of our dollar forces up the effective price of the goods that we buy abroad. However, in the long run, such effects are minimized, and the positive impact on exports (because our goods are cheaper to others) is a major compensation for problems caused by declines in the value of our dollar.

Basically, if we allowed the value of our dollar to float freely, it should settle down to a value that approximates the difference between the price levels of the two countries. U.S. prices are between 10 and 15 percent lower than Canadian prices, reflecting the U.S. advantage in productivity, so that the value of our dollar should be about 10 to 15 percent below that of the U.S.

CONCLUSIONS

We have described four goals of economic stabilization policy, reviewed the past performance of the Canadian economy in terms of each goal, and discussed the likely effects of achieving or failing to achieve each goal. These goals will be used in following chapters to develop a theory of macroeconomics that will explain past performance and, it is hoped, provide some guidance as to the policies that might improve future performance.

Even when stripped of unnecessary complexities, the theory to be introduced is too large to be bitten off and digested in a single piece. It will be necessary to take things one at a time. It would be convenient to break the whole into four separate bodies of theory, one explaining changes in unemployment, a second explaining changes in the price level, a third explaining changes in real output, and a fourth explaining changes in the balance of payments and in the exchange rate. Unfortunately, that is impossible; the four goals are too closely interrelated. Any policy affecting the performance of a single goal can normally be expected to have effects on the others as well. Instead of organizing the discussion in terms of the four policy goals, it will be organized in terms of the now-familiar distinction between *nominal* and *real* values.

There will first be a discussion of what determines the size and composition of nominal national income and product and an evaluation of various policies that can control nominal aggregate demand. This discussion, in turn, will be divided into two sections. Chapters 8 to 10 will be devoted to matters relating to government spending and taxation policy and their impact on nominal national product. The effects on the foreign trade sector of the economy will also be noted. Chapters 11 to 14 will be devoted to the banking system and monetary policy.

Second, when it is understood what determines nominal national income and product, including net exports, attention will be turned to what determines how changes in nominal national income and product are resolved into changes in employment and real output on the one hand, and changes in the price level on the other. In doing this, we will rely on a simple and important relationship between nominal and real values: *the rate of growth of nominal national income and product is always equal to the rate of change of real national income and product plus the rate of inflation*. Suppose, for example, that in one year nominal GNP increases by 10 percent from $200 billion to $220 billion. This can mean that prices have not changed at all and that 10 percent more real goods and services have been produced, that real output has not changed but that there has been 10 percent inflation, that there has been 5 percent real growth and 5 percent inflation, or that there has been any other combination of a rate of growth of real output and a rate of inflation adding up to the 10 percent growth in nominal GNP. Chapters 16 to 17 will be devoted to explaining why any given change in nominal national income and product is split up in one way rather than another and to a discussion of policies through which the split can be manipulated in the hope of achieving simultaneous full employment, price stability, and balanced growth. Chapter 15 will discuss the implications of such policies for Canada's foreign trade sector.

SUMMARY

1. The general policy of economic stabilization, which means simply the avoidance of harmful fluctuations in economic activity, can be broken down into the pursuit of four more specific policy goals: maintaining full employment, maintaining price stability, maintaining steady growth of real national income, and maintaining stability in the balance of payments and the exchange rate.
2. The White Paper of 1945 committed the Canadian government to pursuing a policy of full employment, by which it meant a job for everyone who wanted a job. Subsequent government statements and Economic Council of Canada reports have proposed numerical targets for unemployment, of from 3.5 to 6.0 percent of the civilian labor force. Other studies suggest an even higher target rate would be realistic. Such low levels of unemployment have rarely been achieved in Canada in the last 30 years.
3. The Economic Council of Canada has also proposed numerical goals for inflation of 2 to 3 percent per year changes in the consumer price index. This goal was achieved through most of the 1950s and early 1960s, but during the late 1960s and the 1970s, inflation exceeded this goal in every year except one (1971). Recent studies of the distributional impact of inflation suggest that the burden of inflation rests more heavily on older people and on households with relatively high incomes than on younger people and households with low and moderate incomes. Both business and government benefit from inflation, although business profits may be exaggerated by the distorting effects of inflation on the values of inventory.

4. The Canadian economy has had a long-sustained record of economic growth that compares favorably with that of many other developed countries, and has brought per capita real income to very high levels. In recent years, a controversy has developed over whether rapid economic growth will be possible, or even desirable, in the future. The controversy raises both environmental and distributional concerns.

5. Canada has a chronic problem in its balance of payments because of persistent, and growing, deficits in its current account. High interest rates and the spending of foreign reserves have been used to keep the value of the Canadian dollar from depreciating too rapidly or too far. Such interest rate policies, however, may have contributed to the high rates of inflation and unemployment that were experienced in Canada in the 1970s.

DISCUSSION QUESTIONS

1. It is sometimes suggested that the proper goal for employment policy would be a zero level of *involuntary* employment. How might one distinguish between voluntary and involuntary unemployment? What measurement problems might arise in distinguishing the two? Give this matter some general thought now; we will return to it in more detail in Chapter 14.

2. Go to your library and locate recent issues of *The Labour Force* and the *Canadian Statistical Review*, published monthly by Statistics Canada (Catalogue Nos. 71-001 and CSI-003). In each you will find a statistical section that will give you data with which you can update Exhibits 7.1 and 7.2. What progress, if any, is being made toward achievment of the goals of the full employment and price stability? Do you think it will be possible to reach our goals by the mid-1980s?

3. Locate a copy of a good financial newspaper, such as the *Financial Post* or the *Financial Times*, and find out the current interest rates on bonds. Compare these to the current rate of inflation as measured in terms of the Consumer Price Index. What is the real rate of interest? What does this exercise suggest to you about the current state of inflationary expectations?

4. Make a list of some of the costs and some of the benefits that past economic growth has brought to your particular area or community. Has there been too much or too little economic growth there, in your opinion? Do you think future economic growth in your area or community will bring benefits that outweigh costs? Why or why not?

5. What might be possible benefits and costs in allowing the value of the Canadian dollar to fall freely, perhaps below $.80 U.S.?

SUGGESTIONS FOR FURTHER READING

Beckerman, Wilfred, *In Defense of Economic Growth*. London: Jonathan Cape, 1974.
A reply to the Meadows et al. doomsday book listed below.

Meadows, Dennis L., et al. *The Limits to Growth*. Washington, D.C.: Potomac Associates, 1972.
A report on a highly controversial and widely debated computer simulation study purporting to show sharp limits to economic growth in the relatively near future.

Mill, John Stuart. *Principles of Political Economy*. 1871 ed.
Excerpts available in Pelican Books edition of 1970 and many other editions. Book VI, "Of the Stationary State," contains Mill's views on the limits to growth.

C H A P T E R 8
THE DETERMINANTS OF PLANNED EXPENDITURE

WHAT YOU WILL LEARN IN THIS CHAPTER

British economist John Maynard Keynes made aggregate demand a key element of his economic theory. This chapter will follow his approach by looking at the determinants of each of the major components of aggregate demand. The first component, consumption expenditure, depends to a substantial extent on the level of national income. The second, planned investment expenditure, depends on the expected real rate of interest and on business expectations concerning the profitability of investment projects. Government purchases and exports are determined by forces outside the scope of elementary economic theory and will be treated as "givens" for the sake of further analysis. Imports are a part of consumption expenditures, investment expenditures, and government purchases. Since they play an important role in our consumption expenditures, it is assumed that they depend at least partly on the level of national income.

FOR REVIEW

Here are some important terms and concepts that will be put to use in this chapter. If you do not understand them, review them before proceeding.

- *Aggregate demand (Chapter 5)*
- *Planned and unplanned investment (Chapter 5)*
- *Relationships among gross national product, national income, personal income, and disposable income (Chapter 6)*
- *The balance of payments (Chapter 6, Chapter 7)*
- *Real and nominal interest rates (Chapter 7)*

Chapter 5 introduced the circular flow and the ideas of aggregate supply and demand. Chapter 6 showed how national income accountants go about measuring the elements of the circular flow, including consumption, investment, government purchases, and net exports. Chapter 7 set forth a number of goals and reviewed recent macroeconomic experience in terms of those goals. Now it is time to put all these preliminary concepts and definitions to work and to begin developing a theory—one that will explain why national income and product are at one level rather than another in any particular year, and why they have their ups and downs over time.

Some Simplifications

In economics, theory building always begins by making some simplifications in order to concentrate on essentials. One simplification that will be used throughout this discussion of macroeconomic theory is the elimination of indirect business taxes, the capital consumption allowance, and the residual error of estimate. Getting rid of these elements of the national income accounts makes things much easier. Gross national product and national income once again become equal by definition, as they were in the simplified circular flow diagrams of Chapter 5.

A second simplification that will be used throughout the following chapters is the omission of undistributed corporate profits. With neither indirect business taxes nor undistributed corporate profits, personal income will be equal to national income minus net taxes. (The term *net taxes*, as in Chapter 5, means all taxes — personal income tax, transfers to government, and corporate profits tax — minus all transfer payments by government.)

A third simplification will be the concentration for the time being on *nominal* values of national income, consumption, and so on — primarily a matter of taking one thing at a time. Chapters 8 to 15 will be explaining why nominal income is, say $200 billion rather than some other value in a certain year. Then, Chapters 16 to 17 will turn to the question of why changes in nominal income sometimes take the form of changes in prices rather than in real output.

In these early chapters, where the discussion is entirely in terms of nominal values, the term *nominal* will not be repeated every time consumption, investment, income, or whatever is mentioned. Keep in mind, though, that nominal values are meant in every case unless real values are explicitly specified.

**John Maynard Keynes
(1883–1946)**

John Maynard Keynes was born into economics. His father, John Neville Keynes, was a lecturer in economics and logic at Cambridge University. John Maynard began his own studies at Cambridge with an emphasis on mathematics and philosophy. His abilities soon so impressed Alfred Marshall, however, that the distinguished teacher urged him to concentrate on economics. In 1908, after Keynes had finished his studies and done a brief stint in the civil service, Marshall offered him a lectureship in economics at Cambridge, which he accepted.

Keynes is remembered above all for his *General Theory of Employment, Interest, and Money*, published in 1936, although that was by no means his first important work. Keynes's reputation as the outstanding economist of his generation lay in the departure from classical and neoclassical theory he made there. It is hardly necessary to say much about the substance of the *General Theory* in these paragraphs, because they are extensively discussed in every modern textbook on economics. It will be enough to note that its major features are a theory boldly drawn in terms of broad macroeconomic aggregates and a policy position tending toward activism and interventionism.

Keynes was no "narrow" economist. He was an honored member not only of the British academic upper class but also of Britain's highest financial, political, diplomatic, administrative, and even artistic circles. He was intimately involved with the colorful "Bloomsbury set" of London's literary-Bohemian world. He was a friend of Virginia Woolf, E. M. Forster, and Lytton Strachey; and in 1925, he married ballerina Lydia Lopokovia. He was a dazzling success at whatever he turned his hand to, from mountain climbing to financial speculation. As a speculator, he made an enormous fortune for himself, and as bursar of Kings College, he turned an endowment of £30,000 into one of £380,000.

In even the briefest discussion of Keynes, it would be unforgivable not to give his most famous quotation. Writing in the *General Theory*, he pronounced that

the ideas of economists and political philosophers, both when they are right and when they are wrong, are more powerful than is commonly understood. Indeed the world is ruled by little else. Practical men, who believe themselves to be quite exempt from any intellectual influences, are usually the slaves of some defunct economist. Madmen in authority, who hear voices in the air, are distilling their frenzy from some academic scribbler of a few years back. . . . There are not many who are influenced by new theories after they are twenty-five or thirty years of age, so that the ideas which civil servants and politicians and even agitators apply to current events are not likely to be the newest.

Was Keynes issuing a warning here? Whether or not he had any such thing in mind, his words, forty years later, have become one of the great ironies in the history of economic ideas.

Keynes had a profound and direct impact on economic policymaking in Canada. A number of Canadian economists worked with or studied under him, before and during World War II. One of them, W. A. Mackintosh, who during the war was Director General of Economic Research in the Department of Reconstruction and Supply in the Canadian government, and later became Principal of Queen's University, wrote a government White Paper on Employment and Income in 1945 that was based on Keynesian ideas. Mackintosh said of that document: "Though the battle over Keynesianism had been pretty well conceded, I had some interest in seeing how far some of the elements of Keynesianism could be presented as the most ordinary of common sense." As was noted in Chapter 7, the White Paper was one of the first commitments by any government to a high employment policy.

Keynes

One further note is in order at the beginning of the discussion of macroeconomic theory—the introduction of the British economist, John Maynard Keynes, whose writings have strongly influenced macroeconomic thought since the 1930s. Although many of Keynes's particular conclusions have been challenged by contemporary economists, the fact that these challenges occur within his basic theoretical framework attests to his lasting influence. Keynes's ideas underlie all of modern macroeconomic theory as well as the contents of this book, even in places where they are not specifically acknowledged.

Keynes made the concept of **aggregate demand** a key element of his theory. He taught that macroeconomic analysis should begin by asking what determines each of the separate types of planned expenditure that make up aggregate demand: consumption, planned investment expenditure, government purchases, and net exports. This chapter will follow his plan by discussing each of these areas in turn.

Aggregate demand Total planned expenditure for an economy, consisting of consumption, planned investment, government purchases, and net exports.

CONSUMPTION

The Consumption Schedule

Keynes began his theory of consumption expenditure from the observation that each year, consumers spend most, but not all, their disposable personal income on personal consumption. This tendency is as clearly observable for the postwar Canadian economy as it was in Keynes's day. As Exhibit 8.1

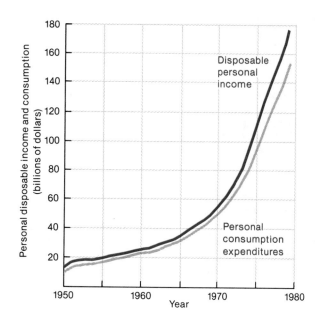

Exhibit 8.1

Disposable personal income and personal consumption expenditures in the Canadian economy, 1950-1978

As this exhibit shows, Canadian consumers each year spend most, but not all, of their disposable personal income on personal consumption. The percentage of disposable personal income devoted to consumption has remained roughly constant over the period shown.

Sources: Statistics Canada, *National Income and Expenditure Accounts*, Vol. 1, Annual Estimates, 1926–1974, No. 13-531, and Vol. 2, Quarterly Estimates, 1947–1974, No. 13-533; and Department of Finance, *Economic Review*, April 1980.

shows, nominal disposable income in Canada grew from $13.3 billion in 1950 to $155.7 billion in 1978. Each year, consumers spent somewhat over 85 percent of their disposable income on personal consumption.

Reasoning on the basis of this observation, Keynes hypothesized a theoretical relationship between disposable personal income and personal consumption somewhat like the one displayed in Exhibit 8.2. This exhibit shows how consumption changes in response to changes in disposable income — not for the actual Canadian economy but rather for a simplified economy in which consumers each year devote exactly $.75 out of each $1 of added disposable income to consumption. The relationship shown in Exhibit 8.2 is known as a **consumption schedule**.

Consumption schedule A graphical or numerical representation of how nominal consumption expenditure varies as nominal income varies, other things being equal.

Autonomous Consumption Note that the consumption schedule in Exhibit 8.2 includes a constant term. Even when aggregate disposable income is zero, aggregate consumption expenditure is equal to $100. The constant term in the consumption schedule is often referred to as **autonomous consumption**.

Autonomous consumption The level of consumption shown by a consumption schedule for a zero disposable income level.

Taken literally, the $100 level of autonomous consumption would indicate that aggregate consumption expenditures would be $100 even if aggregate disposable income were zero. In reality, of course, aggregate disposable income never falls to zero. Individual households, however, may temporarily experience zero disposable income; and when they do, they do not cut consumption expenditures to zero. Instead, they borrow or draw on past savings to maintain some minimal level of consumption. To that extent, the concept of autonomous consumption is rooted in actual consumer behavior.

Exhibit 8.2

The consumption schedule

The table and graph both show a simple numerical example of the relationship between disposable income and consumption. The level of autonomous consumption is shown on the graph by the height of the intersection of the consumption schedule with the vertical axis. The slope of the consumption schedule is equal to the marginal propensity to consume.

(a)

Nominal Disposable Income (1)	Nominal Consumption Expenditure (2)	Change in Income (3)	Change in Consumption (4)	Marginal Propensity to Consume (5)
$ 0	$ 100			
100	175	$100	$75	0.75
200	250	100	75	0.75
300	325	100	75	0.75
400	400	100	75	0.75
500	475	100	75	0.75
600	550	100	75	0.75
700	625	100	75	0.75
800	700	100	75	0.75
900	775	100	75	0.75
1,000	850	100	75	0.75
1,100	925	100	75	0.75
1,200	1,000	100	75	0.75

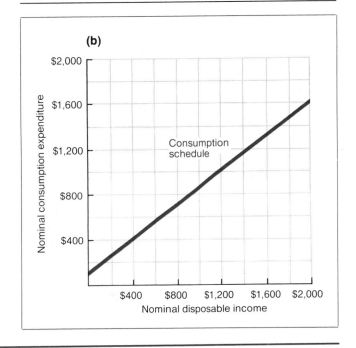

(b)

Consumption schedule

Nominal consumption expenditure / Nominal disposable income

Marginal Propensity to Consume Look now at Columns 1 to 4 of Exhibit 8.2a. The numbers in these columns show that whenever household income increases, some of the additional income is devoted to consumption above and beyond autonomous consumption. The fraction of each added dollar of disposable income that goes to added consumption is called the **marginal propensity to consume**.

For example, a $100 increase in disposable income, from $500 to $600, raises consumption by $75 from $475 to $550. Similarly, a $100 decrease in disposable income from $500 to $400 would cause consumption to fall by $75, from $475 to $400. The value of the marginal propensity to consume for this numerical example is thus 0.75 (75 divided by 100).

In geometric terms, the marginal propensity to consume is equal to the slope of the consumption schedule. In Exhibit 8.2b, a horizontal movement of $100 in disposable income corresponds to a vertical movement of $75

Marginal propensity to consume The fraction of each added dollar of disposable income that goes to added consumption. Algebraically it can be written: $MPC = \frac{\Delta C}{\Delta DI}$, where MPC is the marginal propensity to consume, C is consumption, and DI is personal disposable income.

in planned consumption. The slope of the consumption schedule is thus 75 divided by 100 equals 0.75, the same as the marginal propensity to consume.

Saving Schedule

Saving schedule A graphical or numerical representation of how nominal saving varies as nominal disposable income varies, other things being equal.

Once we know the level of consumption corresponding to each level of disposable income, we can easily calculate the level of saving that corresponds to each level of disposable income. The relationship between saving and income, called the **saving schedule**, is given in numerical form in Exhibit 8.3a. The numbers in this table are calculated simply by subtracting consumption from disposable income.

The saving schedule is shown in geometric form in Exhibit 8.3b. This figure can be constructed simply by plotting the numbers from Column 3 of the table. The saving schedule can also be derived directly from the consumption schedule, which is Exhibit 8.3c. The level of saving corresponding to each level of disposable income is equal to the vertical distance between the consumption schedule and the 45 degree reference line.

Dissaving Negative saving—the difference between disposable income and consumption expenditure when consumption exceeds disposable income.

In the numerical example, a **dissaving**—negative saving—of $100 occurs when disposable income is zero. Saving at a zero disposable income is the negative of autonomous consumption. At the $400 level of disposable income there is a breakeven point at which neither saving nor dissaving occurs. Below that point, consumption exceeds disposable income; and above it, consumption falls short of disposable income.

Marginal propensity to save The fraction of each added dollar of disposable income that is not consumed. Algebraically, it can be written:

$$MPS = \frac{\Delta S}{\Delta DI},$$

where MPS is the marginal propensity to save, S is saving, and DI is personal disposable income.

The **marginal propensity to save** is the fraction of each additional dollar of disposable income that is not consumed. Because all disposable income is, by definition, either saved or consumed, it follows that the marginal propensity to save (MPS) is equal to 1 minus the marginal propensity to consume (MPC):

$$MPS = 1 - MPC.$$

In geometric terms, the marginal propensity to save is equal to the slope of the saving schedule, which is 0.25 in Exhibit 8.3.

Short Run versus Long Run

In practice, the marginal propensities to consume and save depend on, among other things, the time horizon under discussion. Over long historical periods, aggregate consumption expenditures have risen by about $.90 for each $1 increase in aggregate disposable income. In the short run, however, people tend to change their consumption by somewhat less than $.90 out of each $1 change in income that they perceive as being only temporary. A household accustomed to a yearly disposable income of $15,000 would tend to economize somewhat on its consumption if its income dropped, in one exceptional year, to $12,000. But as long as it expected better times to return, it would tend to spend more in that year than if it expected the decline in income to be permanent.

Because this book focuses primarily on short-run problems of economic stabilization policy, the numerical examples in this and the following chapters employ a marginal propensity to consume of 0.75, which is lower

(a)

Nominal Disposable Income (1)	Nominal Consumption (2)	Nominal Saving (3)
$ 0	$ 100	−$100
100	175	−75
200	250	−50
300	325	−25
400	400	0
500	475	25
600	550	50
700	625	75
800	700	100
900	775	125
1,000	850	150
1,100	925	175
1,200	1,000	200
1,300	1,075	225
1,400	1,150	250
1,500	1,225	275
1,600	1,300	300
1,700	1,375	325
1,800	1,450	350
1,900	1,525	375
2,000	1,600	400

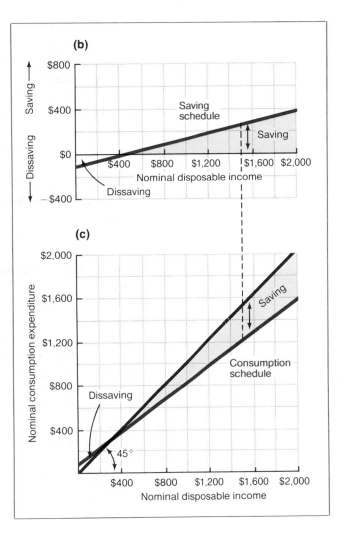

Exhibit 8.3
The saving schedule
The saving schedule shows the relationship between saving and income. In the table (Part a), saving is found by subtracting consumption from disposable income. In Part b of the exhibit, the saving schedule is given in graphical form. It could be constructed directly from the numbers in Column 3 of the table or from the consumption schedule shown in Part c.

than the long-run marginal propensity to consume of about 0.9. No claim is made that 0.75 is exactly the value of the marginal propensity to consume for the Canadian economy, but for the short run it is probably realistic.

Shifts in the Consumption Schedule

In working with the consumption schedule (as in many areas of economics) it is important to distinguish between movements along the schedule and shifts in the whole schedule. The consumption schedule represents the relationship between nominal consumption expenditures and nominal disposable income, other things being equal. A change in consumption brought about by a change in nominal disposable income, then, is represented by a movement *along* the schedule. A change in consumption brought about by a change in something other than nominal disposable income is represented by a *shift* in the schedule. Among the possible causes of shifts, the following are particularly important: changes in wealth, changes in expectations, changes in the price level, and changes in the rate of inflation.

Changes in Wealth　The consumption decisions that a household makes are influenced not only by its current flow of income but also by its accumulated stock of wealth. Other things being equal, a household with a monthly income of $1,000 and $100,000 in the bank can be expected to spend more freely than a household living on the same monthly income and having few, if any, financial reserves. What is true for individual households is also true for the economy as a whole. Any increase in the aggregate wealth of all households, then, can be expected to produce an upward shift in the consumption schedule—that is, more consumption spending at each given level of disposable income. For example, many people hold a substantial part of their wealth in the form of corporate stocks. A rise in the average value of those stocks would increase the aggregate wealth of stockholders and would tend to produce an upward shift in the consumption schedule. A decline in aggregate wealth, other things being equal, would tend to reduce consumption and shift the consumption schedule downward.

Changes in Expectations　People's consumption decisions depend not only on their current income but also on their expectations regarding their future income. Other things being equal, an increase in the expected future nominal income tends to increase present consumption expenditure, even before the increase in income is actually realized. This effect is represented by an upward shift in the consumption schedule. Similarly, a decrease in expected future income tends to depress current consumption spending. For example, if consumers feared a coming recession, in which many of them would lose their jobs and hence their sources of income, they might cut back on their consumption expenditures even before the expected decline in income actually occurred. This would be represented by a downward shift in the consumption schedule.

Changes in the Price Level　All changes in nominal disposable income are represented as movements along the consumption schedule, whether they refer to changes in real disposable income with the price level constant, changes in the price level with real income constant, or some mix of the two. It is worth enquiring, however, whether a change in the price level might cause a shift in the consumption schedule as well. Two possibilities are worth considering.

First, it seems reasonable to assume that a single, permanent change in the price level, once consumers fully adjust to it, will produce a proportional change in autonomous consumption—the point at which the consumption schedule intercepts the vertical axis. Think of real autonomous consumption as the level of consumption that consumers would maintain in the hypothetical event that real aggregate disposable income fell to zero. If the price level doubles, the nominal value of autonomous consumption will also have to double in order to keep the real value of autonomous consumption constant. This implies that an increase in the price level will tend to shift the nominal consumption schedule upward.

A second effect of changes in the price level, however, tends to offset the first effect. The second effect results from the fact that many of the forms in which people hold their wealth—bank deposits, private and government bonds, life insurance, private pension rights, and so on — have values that are fixed in nominal terms. An increase in the price level thus decreases the real value of household wealth. If the price level doubles, a savings account or life insurance annuity or other savings instrument ends up with only half the purchasing power it had before. By itself, therefore, the effect of an increase in the price level on real wealth tends to cause the consumption schedule to shift downward.

In practice, it is not known which of these two effects acts more strongly on short-run consumption decisions. To simplify the discussion, this and the following chapters will assume that the two effects exactly offset one another. They will thus treat the nominal consumption schedule as not shifting either up or down in response to a single, permanent change in the price level.

Changes in the Rate of Inflation The preceding section discussed the effects of a single, permanent price level change to which consumers are fully able to adjust. Equally, if not more, important as a determinant of consumer spending are changes in the rate of inflation — that is, variations in the rate of change of the price level. Once again, two different consumer reactions to changes in the rate of inflation must be distinguished.

First, consumers tend to view increases in the rate of inflation as a sign of hard times to come. They may not expect their nominal wages and salaries to keep up with inflation, or they may expect government to fight the inflation with policies that increase unemployment and that may therefore cost them their jobs. To the extent that consumers treat inflation as a sign of hard times to come, an increase in the rate of inflation tends to depress consumer spending, thereby shifting the consumption schedule downward.

However, an increase in the rate of inflation can also have the opposite effect. When consumers see the rate edging up, they may decide to buy before prices go up still more. This anticipatory buying tends to increase consumer spending, which shifts the consumption schedule upward.

There is no way to be certain which of the two effects of inflation on consumer spending will predominate. There are indications, however, that a major shift in consumer reactions to inflation occurred during the 1970s. In the past, the "hard times" effect apparently predominated, and consumers reduced their expenditures when inflation accelerated. Today, however, the anticipatory buying effect seems to be the stronger of the two, so that news of accelerating inflation tends to stimulate, rather than depress, consumer spending.

Adjusting for Taxes

Up to this point, consumption has been discussed only in relation to disposable income. But the consumption schedule can also be adjusted for taxes and expressed in terms of national income rather than disposable income. (These chapters assume that there are no indirect business taxes or undistributed corporate profits, which means that national income is considered equal to disposable personal income plus net taxes.)

In adjustment of the consumption schedule for taxes, two separate cases

Lump sum taxes Taxes that do not vary as income varies.

will be considered. In the first case, illustrated by Exhibit 8.4, all taxes and transfers are of the **lump sum** form — that is, they do not change as income changes. Columns 3 and 4 of the table give the familiar consumption schedule in terms of disposable income, while Columns 1 and 4 show the relationship between national income and consumption expenditure.

In the second case, illustrated by Exhibit 8.5, the government employs a personal income tax. Here, the amount of tax collected does change as the level of national income changes. In construction of the table, the assumption has been that everyone pays a straight 20 percent income tax, regardless of the amount of earnings. (The actual income tax is much more complicated, of course.) Again, Columns 3 and 4 give the consumption schedule in terms of disposable income, and Columns 1 and 4 give the schedule in terms of national income.

Compare the two cases. With lump sum taxes, an additional $1 of national income results in an additional $.75 of consumption expenditure and an additional $.25 in saving. With an income tax, the additional $1 of national income results in an additional $.60 of consumption, an additional $.20 of saving, and an additional $.20 of net taxes. One might say that, in the second case, there are two different marginal propensities to consume. The propensity to consume out of national income (0.6) is lower than the propensity to consume out of disposable income (0.75).

The Canadian government does make heavy use of the personal income tax, so the second of the two cases considered here is the more realistic. On the other hand, lump sum taxes simplify the job of theory building. In the chapters that follow, the simplifying assumption of lump sum taxes will be used whenever possible. When it is important for questions of policy, though, the effects of an income tax will also be discussed.

Exhibit 8.4
National income and consumption with lump sum taxes

Lump sum taxes are taxes that do not change when the level of income changes. This table shows how the consumption schedule can be expressed in terms of either disposable income (Columns 3 and 4) or national income (Columns 1 and 4) for an economy where all taxes are of the lump sum variety. In the simple economy on which the table is based, there are no undistributed corporate profits or indirect business taxes, so national income is equal to disposable income plus net taxes.

Nominal National Income (1)	Nominal Lump Sum Taxes (2)	Nominal Disposable Income (3)	Nominal Consumption Expenditure (4)	Nominal Saving (5)
$ 100	$100	$ 0	$100	−$100
200	100	100	175	−75
300	100	200	250	−50
400	100	300	325	−25
500	100	400	400	0
600	100	500	475	25
700	100	600	550	50
800	100	700	625	75
900	100	800	700	100
1,000	100	900	775	125
1,100	100	1,000	850	150
1,200	100	1,100	925	175

Exhibit 8.5
National income and consumption with a 20 percent proportional income tax
With an income tax, net taxes rise as income increases. Each additional $1 of national income results in an additional $.60 of consumption, an additional $.20 of saving, and an additional $.20 of net taxes. Three-quarters of each added $1 of *disposable* income goes to consumption, but only 60 percent of each added $1 of *national* income goes to consumption.

Nominal National Income (1)	Nominal Net Taxes (2)	Nominal Disposable Income (3)	Nominal Consumption Expenditure (4)	Nominal Saving (5)
$ 100	$ 20	$ 80	$160	−$80
200	40	160	220	−60
300	60	240	280	−40
400	80	320	340	−20
500	100	400	400	0
600	120	480	460	20
700	140	560	520	40
800	160	640	580	60
900	180	720	640	80
1,000	200	800	700	100
1,100	220	880	760	120
1,200	240	960	820	140

The Stability of the Consumption Schedule

So many things can produce shifts in the consumption schedule that its usefulness can be questioned. What good does it do to draw a relationship between consumption expenditure and disposable income, other things being equal, if the "other things" change so frequently?

There is some validity to this criticism. Short-run predictions of changes in consumer spending have not always proved accurate, even when forecasters have taken precautions to correct for changes in wealth, expectations, and inflation. The concern in this book, however, is not with practical forecasting techniques but rather with establishing a general theoretical understanding of important macroeconomic relationships. For present purposes, then, the consumption schedule will be treated as a reasonably stable relationship between nominal consumption expenditures and nominal disposable income. Shifts in the schedule will be introduced only when strictly necessary.

PLANNED INVESTMENT EXPENDITURE

After consumption, the second major component of aggregate demand is planned investment expenditure. Planned investment, as discussed earlier, includes both fixed investment and planned inventory investment. Total investment, as measured in the national income accounts, includes planned investment plus unplanned inventory investment. Our immediate interest is in what determines aggregate demand, so unplanned inventory investment will be ignored for the moment.

Determinants of Planned Investment

The rate of planned investment expenditure depends on two things: the expected real rate of return on investment and the expected real rate of interest. The **expected real rate of return** is the real net annual improvement in a business firm's cost or revenue that it expects to obtain by making an investment; it is expressed as a percentage of the sum invested. The expected real rate of interest is the expected real cost to the firm of borrowing funds from outside sources or the expected real opportunity cost to the firm of using its own funds. A simple example will show how these two factors enter into the decision to invest.

Expected real rate of return The annual real net improvement in a firm's cost or revenue that it expects to obtain by making an investment; it is expressed as a percentage of the sum invested.

Suppose you are the manager of a small factory. You are worried about the rising cost of energy, so you hire a consultant who is a specialist in energy conservation. The consultant tells you that if you insulate the roof of your warehouse, you will save $1,200 per year in heating and cooling costs. The insulation will cost $10,000 to install and, once installed, will last forever. How do you decide whether to undertake this investment project?

First, you calculate the rate of return on the investment. A saving of $1,200 per year means a saving of $.12 per year for each $1 invested to install the insulation, so the rate of return is 12 percent per year. Next, you find out what the interest rate on a $10,000 loan will be. You call your banker, who says that the money is available at a nominal rate of 10 percent per year. (Neither you nor your banker expects any inflation, so that rate is also the expected real rate of interest.) You will have to pay $1,000 per year in interest charges. Even after paying the interest, you will have $200 in pure profit left from your $1,200 saving in energy costs. The investment is worthwhile, so you go ahead with it.

Perhaps you do not need to borrow money to make the investment. Instead, your firm has $10,000 or more in uncommitted cash balances left over from last year's profits. In that case, the interest rate you must use for your investment decision is the real rate those funds are now earning for you. Suppose that your uncommitted cash is invested in Canadian government bonds that pay an expected real rate of 10 percent per year. Taking $10,000 out of bonds has an opportunity cost to you of $1,000 per year in forgone interest payments, but the $1,200 saving in energy costs will more than make up for that. You still decide to put in the insulation.

This very simple example provides the basis for an important generalization. A firm will find it profitable to undertake an investment project if, and only if, the expected real rate of return on that project is higher than the expected real rate of interest. If the rate of return is equal to the rate of interest, the project will just break even, and it will be a matter of indifference whether or not it is undertaken. If the rate of interest exceeds the rate of return, the project will involve a loss and should therefore not be undertaken.

Planned Investment Schedule

The analysis of the determinants of planned investment suggests a general relationship between the expected real rate of interest and the rate of planned investment for the economy as a whole. The lower the expected real rate of interest, the greater the number of profitable investment projects. Other things being equal, then, the rate of planned investment will be higher the lower the expected real rate of interest. This relationship between interest and planned investment is shown graphically in the form of a **planned investment schedule** in Exhibit 8.6.

Movements along the Planned Investment Schedule Anything that causes a change in the expected real rate of interest, other things being equal, will produce a movement along the planned investment schedule. In Chapter 7, the expected real rate of interest was defined as the nominal rate of interest minus the expected rate of inflation. This definition suggests two possible causes of movements along the planned investment schedule.

First, an increase in the nominal rate of interest, with the expected rate of inflation held constant, would increase the expected real rate of interest. This would produce a movement up and to the left along the planned investment schedule. Similarly, a decrease in the nominal rate of interest, with the expected rate of inflation held constant, would produce a movement down and to the right along the planned investment schedule.

Second, an increase in the expected rate of inflation, with the nominal rate of interest held constant, would reduce the expected real rate of interest. This would produce a movement down and to the right along the planned investment schedule. Similarly, a decrease in the expected rate of inflation, with the nominal rate of interest held constant, would produce a movement up and to the left along the planned investment schedule.

Shifts in the Planned Investment Schedule A change in planned investment expenditure resulting from any cause other than a change in the expected real rate of interest is properly represented by a shift in the planned investment schedule. Such a shift can occur as the result of any factor affecting the expected real rate of return on investment projects — hence the willingness of business to undertake any given investment project at any given expected real rate of interest. A variety of factors can affect the expected real rate of return. For example, changes in technology might introduce attractive investment opportunities, such as computerization of production or accounting operations, that did not exist before. Or changes in the prices of inputs — for example, an increase in energy prices — might increase the attractiveness of investment projects, such as the roof insulation in the example just given, that previously would not

Planned investment schedule A graphical representation of how the rate of planned investment for the economy as a whole varies as the expected real rate of interest varies, other things being equal.

Exhibit 8.6
The planned investment schedule
The planned investment schedule shows how planned investment expenditure varies as the expected real rate of interest varies, other things being equal. The downward slope of the schedule indicates that decreases in the expected real rate of interest tend to cause increases in planned investment expenditure.

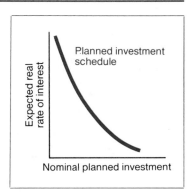

have been considered worthwhile. Or improved expectations of the growth in demand for real output would encourage investment in increasing the capacity to supply that output. All these things would tend to cause the planned investment schedule to shift to the right, as shown in Exhibit 8.7.

Certain other kinds of developments would tend to discourage investment, shifting the planned investment schedule to the left. Pessimistic expectations about the growth of real demand would be one such factor. Another might be the introduction of government regulations limiting the price for which output could be sold, increasing production costs, or otherwise reducing the expected real rate of return on investment.

The Stability of Planned Investment

Because the rate of planned investment depends so heavily on expectations, and because expectations can sometimes change quickly, planned investment expenditure can vary considerably from year to year. As Exhibit 8.8a shows, there have been times in Canadian economic history when investment has undergone wide swings over short periods.

Inventory investment is a particularly unstable component of total investment expenditure, as Exhibit 8.8b shows. Unfortunately, it is impossible to distinguish statistically between year-to-year changes in *planned* inventory investment and year-to-year changes in *unplanned* inventory investment. As the theory developed in the following chapters will make clear, changes in planned inventory investment can be considered a *cause* of instability for the economy as a whole, while changes in unplanned inventory investment can be considered a *consequence* of disequilibrium originating elsewhere in the economy. Exhibit 8.8b lumps together planned and unplanned inventory investment.

OTHER TYPES OF EXPENDITURE

Government Purchases

A third major component of aggregate demand, after consumption and planned investment, is government purchases of goods and services. As noted in Chapter 4, such purchases by the various levels of government in Canada have been growing more rapidly than national output, to the point where they now account for slightly more than 20 percent of the gross

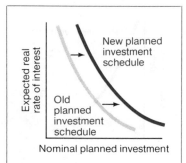

Exhibit 8.7

A shift in the planned investment schedule

A change in the expected real rate of interest, other things being equal, causes a movement along the planned investment schedule. A change in either the nominal rate of interest or the expected rate of inflation could cause such a change in the expected real rate of interest. Changes in other factors affecting planned investment cause shifts in the planned investment schedule. The shift shown here could be caused, for example, by an increase in business optimism or the appearance of a new technological development that makes investment more attractive at any given rate of interest.

Exhibit 8.8

Investment expenditures in the Canadian economy, 1929–1978

Investment expenditure in the Canadian economy has often changed sharply from year to year. The changes shown here were caused partly by changes in interest rates and partly by changes in expected rates of return. The inventory component of total investment expenditure is particularly unstable. The data on inventory investment shown here lump together planned and unplanned inventory expenditure.

(a) Gross private domestic investment

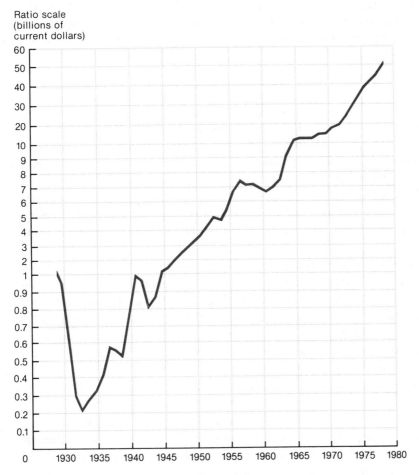

(b) Change in business inventories

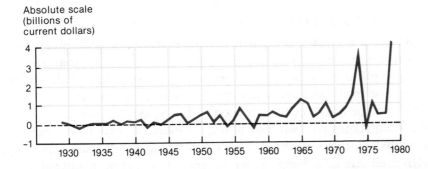

Source: Statistics Canada, *National Income and Expenditure Accounts* (Annual), Catalogue No. 13–201, 1979.

national product. In several of the years since 1969, they have exceeded the amount spent by business enterprises on investment.

Despite the importance of government purchases, their level is traditionally considered, in macroeconomic analysis, to be determined by political decision processes that are "outside" the economic system. In adhering to that tradition here, we do not mean to pretend that the legislators and executives who make spending decisions at various levels of government are uninfluenced by economic considerations such as the level of national income or the rate of unemployment. Our later analysis of fiscal policy will show that they are guided very much by such considerations. However, the relationships, whatever they are, between government spending and unemployment and national income, are too indirect and complex to be put into a simple theory.

Net Exports

Net exports are the fourth and final component of aggregate demand. As defined in Chapter 6, net exports represent the difference between the value of goods and services exported to foreigners and the value of goods and services imported from foreign countries. As noted previously, foreign trade is extremely important to the Canadian economy, accounting for about 25 percent of Canada's GNP annually. It is important, therefore, to understand some of the factors that determine the levels of our imports and exports.

Before we examine these factors, however, it should be noted that it is the *difference* between exports and imports (*net* exports) that determines the impact that the foreign market will have on the Canadian economy. Net exports are normally only 1 or 2 percent of Canadian GNP, but that small size may understate their importance as a source of disturbances in aggregate demand, because net exports can be very volatile. For example, from 1970 to 1975, net exports fell from   + $.953 billion to   − $5.137 billion, a total swing equivalent to about 3.5 percent of GNP (see Exhibit 8.9).

A comprehensive picture of the balance of payments accounts was presented in Chapter 6. Here we content ourselves with a brief examination of how export and import expenditures are determined so that their role in aggregate demand can be understood.

The Determinants of Net Exports

Imports are a part of total consumption, investment, and government expenditures. As such, they are the result of the same forces that underlie those expenditures: income, prices, interest rates, and a multitude of other factors. The major determinants are generally assumed to be national income and the prices of foreign goods relative to the prices of domestic goods. As incomes rise, we tend to import more cameras from Japan and more stylish clothes from Paris. The cost of foreign goods is affected by the foreign exchange rate. Suppose, for example, that a certain golf ball costs $2.20 in Canada in Canadian currency and only $2.00 in the United States in U.S. currency. If the two currencies exchange at a ratio of 1:1 Canadians

Exhibit 8.9
Canadian net exports and gross national product (billions of current dollars)

Year (1)	Gross National Product (2)	Exports (3)	Imports (4)	Net Exports (5)
1958	$ 34.777	$ 6.329	$ 7.321	−$ .992
1959	36.846	6.674	8.028	−1.354
1960	38.359	7.004	8.092	−1.088
1961	39.646	7.624	8.480	−.856
1962	42.927	8.234	9.045	−.811
1963	45.978	9.068	9.561	−.493
1964	50.280	10.503	10.913	−.410
1965	55.364	11.182	12.341	−1.159
1966	61.828	13.045	14.259	−1.214
1967	66.409	14.663	15.234	−.571
1968	72.586	16.719	17.010	−.291
1969	79.815	18.761	19.821	−1.060
1970	85.685	21.167	20.214	.953
1971	93.462	22.187	22.019	.168
1972	103.952	24.502	25.251	−.749
1973	120.438	30.684	31.003	−.319
1974	140.880	38.488	40.675	−2.187
1975	165.428	40.452	45.589	−5.137
1976	191.492	45.685	49.997	−4.312
1977	210.132	52.716	57.232	−4.516
1978	231.835	61.913	67.174	−5.261
1979	260.533	76.412	82.051	−5.639

Source: Department of Finance, *Economic Review*, April 1980 and previous years.

will be inclined to import that golf ball from the United States, because they can do so for only $2.00 in Canadian currency. However, if the value of the U.S. dollar rises relative to the Canadian dollar so that it costs $1.10 in Canadian dollars to purchase $1.00 U.S., Canadians will be forced to spend $2.20 in Canadian currency to purchase the two U.S. dollars required to pay for the golf ball in the United States. This will make it just as expensive to purchase the ball in the United States as in Canada, even though the price of the ball in the U.S. is still only $2.00 in U.S. currency.

Therefore, changes in prices and in the exchange rate can affect imports. Usually these are assumed to be constant in order to relate imports to another important variable: disposable income (DI). We will assume in this text that imports, like consumption, consist of an autonomous element (M_a) *and* an element that is related to disposable income through what we shall call the *marginal propensity to import* (MPM). This indicates the fraction of each added dollar of disposable income that goes to added imports. In the short run this MPM has been found to be as high as .49.[1]

In our model, where the only difference between disposable income and national income is a lump-sum tax (T), the marginal propensity

Marginal propensity to import The fraction of each added dollar of disposable income (DI) that goes to added imports.

$$MPM = \frac{\Delta M}{\Delta DI}$$

In our model of the economy, where the only difference between disposable income and national income is a lump-sum tax, the marginal propensity to import out of disposable income will be the same as the marginal propensity to import out of national income. For purposes of analysis we will often express MPM in terms of national income, i.e.

$$MPM = \frac{\Delta M}{\Delta Y}, \text{ where}$$

Y = national income.

[1] T. R. Robinson, "Canadian Imports and Economic Stability" *Canadian Journal of Economics* 1 (May 1968), p. 421. In another study Robinson indicates that a longer run MPM is about half as large ("Foreign Trade and Economic Stability," *Studies of the Royal Commission on Taxation*, No. 5 (Ottawa, 1967), p. 175).

Exhibit 8.10
Hypothetical export, import, and net export schedules

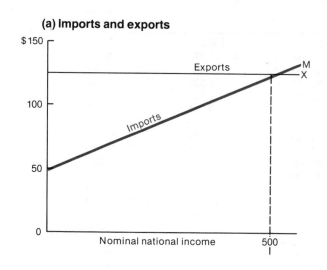

(a) Imports and exports

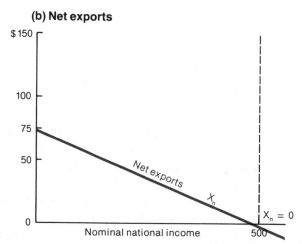

(b) Net exports

to import out of disposable income will be the same as the marginal propensity to import out of national income. Assume, for example, that imports $(M) = M_a + m(DI)$, where m is an abbreviation for the marginal propensity to import (MPM). If $M_a = \$65$ and $m = 0.15$, then (1) $M = \$65 + 0.15\ DI$. Now, in our model, disposable income = national income minus taxes, or $DI = Y - T$. Equation (1) can then be rewritten as follows: $M = M_a + m(Y - T)$. If we add a tax of $100 to the other money values, $M = \$65 + 0.15\ (Y - \$100)$, or $M = \$65 + 0.15\ Y - \$15$. This simplifies to: (2) $M = \$50 + 0.15\ Y$. The two equations show that the marginal propensity to import (m) is the same for both DI and Y. What changes is the value of M_a. When disposable income is used as a basis, $M_a = \$65$. When national income is used M_a is reduced to $50. This occurs because disposable income is less than national income at every level of national income. A given level of imports will then be a larger proportion of disposable income than of national income, even though imports will *change* at the same rate in relation to *changes* in national income and disposable income. For example, if imports = \$80, national income = \$200, and disposable income = \$100, it is consistent with the data to say either that M = \$65 + 0.15 DI or M = \$50 + 0.15 Y. For purposes of equilibrium analysis, in which values are expressed in terms of national income, it is useful to relate changes in imports to changes in national income. This is what will be done in this and the next few chapters. However, in Chapter 10, where brief consideration will be given to the impact of changes in taxes on national income, it will prove helpful to express the import function in terms of disposable income, since tax changes affect expenditures in the economy through changes in disposable income.

Having clarified some of the terms to be used, something more specific must be said about the export and import functions that will be utilized in the following analysis. Exports are related primarily to the income of other countries and to relative prices. They are therefore treated similarly to government purchases: as a very important demand component that is connected to forces "outside" the system. A "constant" value is therefore assigned to exports. It is assumed in Exhibit 8.10a that exports (X) equal \$125 at each level of nominal national income, while imports (M) are \$50 plus 0.15 of national income (that is, the MPM is 0.15). If exports and imports behave in this way, then at a level of national income of \$500 exports would equal imports (both would equal \$125). Note carefully that at levels of income below \$500 exports would be larger than imports; that is, net exports would be positive. At levels of income higher than \$500 imports would be greater than exports, and net exports would be negative. Recall that *net exports* equal exports minus imports, or X − M. Since, in this hypothetical example, exports = \$125 and imports = \$50 + 0.15 national income, net exports (X − M) = \$125 − (\$50 + 0.15 national income) or \$75 − 0.15 national income. If income were zero, exports would be \$125 and imports would be \$50; therefore, net exports would be \$75. This situation is illustrated in Exhibit 8.10b. As national income increases, exports remain the same but imports increase, so that net exports fall with rising income. At an income level of \$500, net exports become zero (at the point where exports=imports in Exhibit 8.10a), and, at income levels higher than \$500, net exports will be negative, meaning that imports will be greater than exports.

This hypothetical example corresponds to the type of export and import behavior that a country like Canada can expect. As the level of income in Canada rises, imports may be stimulated more than exports, resulting in a growing deficit in the export-import balance.

CONCLUSIONS

The objective in this chapter has been to look at the determinants of each kind of planned expenditure in order to understand how aggregate demand as a whole is determined. The chapter has shown that consumption depends on disposable income, that planned investment depends on the expected real interest rate (among other things), that government spending depends on the political process, and that net exports depend on income, in addition to many other things. Now these relationships can be pulled together and applied — in a new chapter.

SUMMARY

1. Following the tradition of Keynesian economics, the theory building begins by looking at what determines each separate component of aggregate demand—consumption, planned investment, government purchases, and net exports.

2. The consumption schedule shows that as nominal disposable income increases, nominal consumption expenditure also increases—but not by as much as the increase in income. The fraction of each added dollar of income that is devoted to consumption is called the marginal propensity to consume. The part of disposable income that is not consumed is saved. The marginal propensity to save is equal to 1 minus the marginal propensity to consume.

3. Planned investment expenditure depends on the expected real rate of interest and the expected real rate of return on investment projects. The planned investment schedule represents the way planned investment varies as the expected real rate of interest varies, other things being equal. Other kinds of changes that affect the expected real rate of return on investment are represented graphically as shifts in the planned investment schedule.

4. For purposes of elementary theory, we consider government purchases to be determined by forces not directly related to national income. It is assumed that the export component of net exports is determined by forces that exist outside the Canadian economy, but that the import component is related to our national income. Imports rise with income so that net exports (which equal exports minus imports) decline with income. They may become negative at high levels of income.

DISCUSSION QUESTIONS

1. Autonomous consumption is the level of consumption that would occur if national income were zero. Since national income will never be zero, why do we talk about autonomous consumption? In other words, what does it really mean? And how does it affect the consumption schedule? What word or expression might you use in place of *autonomous* when talking about autonomous consumption?

2. Since saving and consumption are related, is there an autonomous saving that can be related to autonomous consumption? How would you find this "autonomous saving"?

3. Suppose you unexpectedly won $1,000 in a lottery. How much of the winnings would you devote to current consumption, and how much would you save? Do you think you would spend as large a fraction of the one-time lottery prize as you would of a $1,000 increase in your annual income that you expected to be permanent? Would it surprise you to learn that some economic studies have indicated that, on the average, the fraction of windfalls spent on current consumption is less than the overall marginal propensity to consume? Explain.

4. Have you ever consciously engaged in anticipatory buying, fearing that if you did not buy some item now, its price would only be higher later? Did your fears prove justified? Would you have been better off in preparing for the coming inflation by increasing your rate of saving, thereby building a pool of funds to help you through the hard times that inflation might bring? Explain.

5. Turn back to the example of investment in roof insulation given earlier in the chapter. Assume the same facts as before, including a 10 percent nominal interest rate, with one exception: assume that you expect a 5 percent rate of

inflation over the indefinite future, with the prices of all goods and services rising at exactly the same rate. Will that make the investment more attractive or less attractive than under the assumption of price stability? Explain.

6. Explain carefully why it is assumed that net exports will decline as national income increases.

THE MULTIPLIER THEORY OF NATIONAL INCOME DETERMINATION

WHAT YOU WILL LEARN IN THIS CHAPTER

Chapter 8 discussed the determinants of each of the major components of aggregate demand — consumption, planned investment, government purchases, and net exports. This chapter takes the next step in theory building by showing how knowledge of these determinants makes it possible to discover the level of nominal national income for which the circular flow is in equilibrium. Any shifts in the components of aggregate demand will be shown to result in changes in the equilibrium level of nominal national income.

FOR REVIEW

Here are some important terms and concepts that will be put to use in this chapter. If you do not understand them, review them before proceeding.
- *Aggregate supply and demand (Chapter 5)*
- *Equilibrium and disequilibrium in the circular flow (Chapter 5)*
- *Injections and leakages (Chapter 5)*
- *Consumption, saving, investment, and import and export schedules (Chapter 8)*

Chapter 5 showed that the circular flow could be in equilibrium only when aggregate demand was equal to aggregate supply — that is, only when total planned expenditures were equal to total national product. If planned expenditures exceeded national product, buyers' attempts to purchase more than was currently being produced would lead to unplanned decreases in business inventories. Business firms would react to these decreases by increasing output or by raising prices, thereby causing the level of the circular flow — as measured in nominal terms — to increase. If planned expenditures fell short of national product, business inventories would accumulate at a rate faster than planned, and firms would react by cutting production or lowering prices so the nominal level of the circular flow would drop.

These are the ideas on which the Keynesian theory of national income determination is based. All that need be done now is to add a bit more precision by making use of the detailed analysis of planned expenditure developed in the last chapter.

THE AGGREGATE DEMAND AND SUPPLY SCHEDULES

Aggregate Demand Schedule

Aggregate nominal demand schedule A graph showing the relationship between aggregate nominal demand (the nominal value of total planned expenditure) and nominal national income.

The first step in constructing a theory of nominal income determination is to prepare an **aggregate nominal demand schedule** — a schedule that shows what the nominal level of total planned expenditure will be for each possible level of nominal national income. Exhibit 9.1 indicates how such a schedule can be built up from the separate consumption, investment, government purchase, and net export components discussed in the previous chapter.

(a)

Nominal National Income (1)	Nominal Consumption Expenditure (2)	Nominal Planned Investment (3)	Nominal Government Purchases (4)	Nominal Exports (5)	Nominal Imports (6)	Nominal Net Exports (7)	Nominal Total Planned Expenditure (Aggregate Demand) (8)
$ 100	$ 100	$110	$150	$125	$ 65	+$60	$ 420
200	175	110	150	125	80	+ 45	480
300	250	110	150	125	95	+ 30	540
400	325	110	150	125	110	+ 15	600
500	400	110	150	125	125	0	660
600	475	110	150	125	140	− 15	720
700	550	110	150	125	155	− 30	780
800	625	110	150	125	170	− 45	840
900	700	110	150	125	185	− 60	900
1,000	775	110	150	125	200	− 75	960
1,100	850	110	150	125	215	− 90	1,020
1,200	925	110	150	125	230	−105	1,080
1,300	1,000	110	150	125	245	−120	1,140
1,400	1,075	110	150	125	260	−135	1,200
1,500	1,150	110	150	125	275	−150	1,200
1,600	1,225	110	150	125	290	−165	1,320

(b)

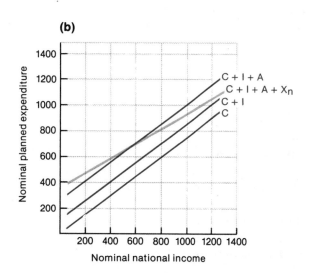

Exhibit 9.1

Construction of the aggregate nominal demand curve

Aggregate nominal demand is the nominal value of all planned expenditures. This exhibit shows how an aggregate nominal demand schedule can be built up from the separate components of consumption, planned investment, government purchases, and net exports. In the simplified economy represented in this exhibit, consumption and imports are the only elements of expenditure that vary as nominal national income varies (net exports vary because of imports). The slope of the aggregate demand schedule is thus equal to the marginal propensity to consume (0.75) minus the marginal propensity to import (0.15), that is, 0.6.

Look first at the tabular form of the aggregate nominal demand schedule in Exhibit 9.1a. The consumption schedule in Column 2 is based on an assumed marginal propensity to consume of 0.75, an autonomous consumption of $100, and lump sum net taxes of $100. Interest rates and business conditions are assumed to yield the $110 of planned investment expenditure shown in Column 3. This component of expenditure is assumed not to vary as nominal income varies. Nominal government purchases (Column 4) are also assumed not to vary.

Exports, imports, and net exports (Columns 5-7) are assumed to vary as described in Exhibit 8.10. Aggregate nominal demand (Column 8) is equal to the sum of consumption, planned investment, government purchases, and net exports.

The procedure for constructing the graphical form of the aggregate nominal demand schedule, shown in Exhibit 9.1b, is as follows: first, a set of axes is drawn with nominal national income on the horizontal and nominal planned expenditure on the vertical. Next, the consumption schedule is drawn in—adjusted for taxes so that it is stated in terms of national income (as given in Column 2 of the table). This schedule is labeled C in Exhibit 9.1b.

Then, planned investment expenditure is added. Given the shape and position of the planned investment schedule and the rate of interest, planned investment is fixed and does not change as national income changes. A line, labeled C + I, is thus drawn parallel to the consumption schedule, separated from it by a distance equal to the level of planned investment.

The next component of aggregate demand to be added is government purchases, which are assumed to be constant at $150. Adding this component gives a new line, labeled C + I + G.

Net exports are assumed in this exhibit to have a value of $75 − .15 national income. When national income is zero, X_n (net exports) adds $75 to aggregate expenditure. Thereafter the gap between C + I + G + X_n and C + I + G declines as X_n declines. When national income is $500, X_n is zero and C + I + G + X_n = C + I + G. At higher levels of income, where X_n is negative, C + I + G + X_n actually lies below C + I + G. (The declining X_n function is illustrated in Exhibit 8.10b.)

Aggregate Supply Schedule

Chapter 5 introduced the term *aggregate nominal supply* to refer to the total nominal value of goods and services produced by the economy. The term, it was pointed out, is a synonym for *nominal national product*. Making use of this relationship of aggregate nominal supply and nominal national product allows an **aggregate nominal supply schedule** to be introduced to show the level of nominal national product associated with each level of nominal national income.

In this simplified economy, there are no indirect business taxes, capital consumption allowances, or statistical discrepancies. As a result national product is, by definition, equal to national income. This means that the aggregate supply schedule is extremely easy to draw. Because the level of nominal national product associated with any given level of nominal

Aggregate nominal supply schedule A graph showing the relationship between aggregate nominal supply (nominal national product) and nominal national income. The schedule has the form of a 45 degree line passing through the origin.

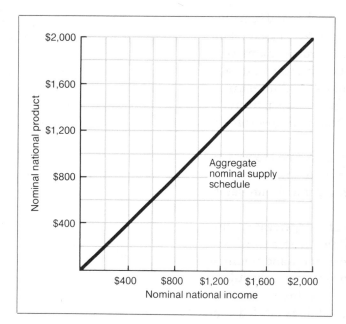

Exhibit 9.2
The aggregate nominal supply curve
Aggregate nominal supply is another term for *nominal national product*. Given the simplifying assumptions used in these chapters (no indirect business taxes, capital consumption allowances, or statistical discrepancies) nominal national product and nominal national income are, by definition, equal. The aggregate nominal supply curve, which shows the relationship between aggregate nominal supply and nominal national income, is thus a 45 degree line passing through the origin, as shown here.

national income is equal to that level of nominal national income, the aggregate supply schedule is simply a straight 45 degree line (see Exhibit 9.2). It can easily be checked that each point on the schedule is equally far from the horizontal axis (national income) and the vertical axis (national product).

FINDING THE EQUILIBRIUM LEVEL OF NOMINAL NATIONAL INCOME

The Keynesian Cross

Taken together, the aggregate nominal supply and demand schedules make it possible to determine the equilibrium level of nominal national income. Drawing the aggregate nominal supply and demand schedules together on the same diagram, as in Exhibit 9.3, gives a figure that economists call the **Keynesian cross**. A diagram much like this was used by early followers of Keynes to show how the equilibrium level of national income is determined.

From Chapter 5, we know that the circular flow will be in equilibrium only when total planned expenditure (aggregate demand) is equal to national product (aggregate supply). The point of intersection of the two schedules that comprise the Keynesian cross shows exactly which level of national income permits aggregate supply and demand to be equal. That point, which corresponds to a nominal national income of $900 in Exhibit 9.3, is the equilibrium point (E).

It is easy to see that no other level of nominal national income can represent equilibrium in the circular flow. If national income were lower than the equilibrium level, say $600, planned expenditure (aggregate demand) would exceed national product (aggregate supply). There would be unplanned depletion of business inventories equal to the vertical distance

Keynesian cross A figure formed by the intersection of the aggregate nominal demand and aggregate nominal supply schedules.

Exhibit 9.3
Using the Keynesian cross to determine equilibrium national income
The aggregate nominal supply and demand schedules drawn on one diagram form a figure called the Keynesian cross. This figure provides a simple way to determine the equilibrium level of nominal national income, given the assumptions concerning planned expenditure on which the aggregate demand curve is based. Any national income higher than the equilibrium level would result in excess aggregate supply, unplanned inventory accumulation, and downward pressure on nominal national income. Any national income below the equilibrium level would result in excess aggregate demand, unplanned inventory depletion, and upward pressure on nominal national income.

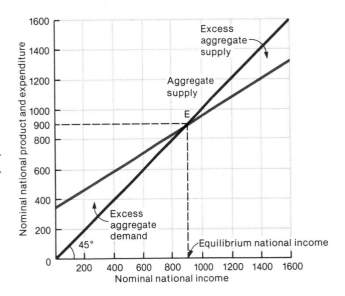

between the aggregate demand schedule and the aggregate supply schedule, as shown in Exhibit 9.3. Firms would try to restore inventories to their planned levels by increasing production and/or prices. That increase would in turn cause nominal national income to rise until equilibrium was reached.

If, on the other hand, nominal national income were to be higher than the equilibrium level, say $1,200, then planned expenditures would fall short of national product. The unsold goods would go to unplanned inventory investment equal to the gap between the aggregate demand schedule and the aggregate supply schedule. Business firms would react to the unplanned buildup in inventories by cutting production and/or prices. The cutback would cause nominal national income to fall until equilibrium was restored.

A Numerical Example

The same story is told in Exhibit 9.4, which gives numerical values for nominal national income, planned expenditure, and other variables that correspond to the Keynesian cross diagram of Exhibit 9.3. The table confirms that $900 is the only level of national income that allows equilibrium in the circular flow. Column 5 shows that national income tends to move toward equilibrium whenever it is at any level other than $900.

Leakage-Injection Approach

The leakage-injection approach to determining the equilibrium level of nominal national income is an alternative method for arriving at the same conclusion reached with the aid of the Keynesian cross. It uses the saving schedule rather than the consumption schedule as its starting point.

Exhibit 9.4

Finding equilibrium nominal national income: a numerical example

This exhibit gives a numerical example of the determination of equilibrium nominal national income, based on the same assumptions that underlie Exhibit 9.3. At every level of nominal national income except the equilibrium level, aggregate supply either falls short of aggregate demand, causing unplanned inventory depletion, or exceeds aggregate demand, causing unplanned inventory accumulation. Unplanned inventory depletion stimulates firms to raise output or prices or both, causing nominal national income to increase; unplanned inventory accumulation causes firms to cut output or prices or both, causing nominal national income to decrease.

Nominal National Income	Nominal Planned Expenditure (Aggregate Demand)	Nominal National Product (Aggregate Supply)	Unplanned Inventory Change	Tendency of Change in National Income
$ 100	$ 420	$ 100	−$320	Increase
200	480	200	−280	Increase
300	540	300	−240	Increase
400	600	400	−200	Increase
500	660	500	−160	Increase
600	720	600	−120	Increase
700	780	700	− 80	Increase
800	840	800	− 40	Increase
900	900	900	0	No change
1,000	960	1,000	+ 40	Decrease
1,100	1,020	1,100	+ 80	Decrease
1,200	1,080	1,200	+120	Decrease
1,300	1,140	1,300	+160	Decrease
1,400	1,200	1,400	+200	Decrease
1,500	1,260	1,500	+240	Decrease
1,600	1,320	1,600	+280	Decrease

Exhibit 9.5 illustrates the use of this approach. Columns 2 to 5 of Part a show how national income is divided into consumption, saving, net taxes, and imports. Saving, net taxes, and imports are all leakages from the circular flow. In Part b, a diagonal line is drawn to show how total leakages vary as national income varies. The slope of the line representing total leakages is equal to the marginal propensity to save (0.25) plus the marginal propensity to import (0.15).

Columns 7 to 9 of Part a show planned injections: planned investment, government purchases, and exports. Under the simplifying assumptions adopted earlier, none of these is assumed to vary as nominal national income varies. The planned injections line in Part b is thus perfectly horizontal. These injections represent planned expenditures on final goods and services that do not originate in domestic households.

The point in Part b where the injections and leakages schedules cross denotes the equilibrium level of nominal national income. At that point, planned injections are equal to total leakages. Under the saving approach, then, nominal national income is in equilibrium when, and only when, saving plus net taxes plus imports are equal to planned investment plus government purchases plus exports.

A careful comparison of Exhibits 9.5 and 9.3 reveals that the gap between the leakage and injection schedules at any level of nominal national income is exactly equal to the gap between the aggregate nominal demand and supply schedules at the same level of nominal national income.

(a)

Nominal National Income (1)	Consumption (2)	Saving (3)	Net Taxes (4)	Imports (5)	Total Leakages (6)	Planned Investment (7)	Government Purchases (8)	Exports (9)	Total Planned Injections (10)
$ 100	$ 100	−$100	$100	$ 65	$ 65	$110	$150	$125	$385
200	175	−75	100	80	105	110	150	125	385
300	250	−50	100	95	145	110	150	125	385
400	325	−25	100	110	185	110	150	125	385
500	400	0	100	125	225	110	150	125	385
600	475	25	100	140	265	110	150	125	385
700	550	50	100	155	305	110	150	125	385
800	625	75	100	170	345	110	150	125	385
900	700	100	100	185	385	110	150	125	385
1,000	775	125	100	200	425	110	150	125	385
1,100	850	150	100	215	465	110	150	125	385
1,200	925	175	100	230	505	110	150	125	385
1,300	1,000	200	100	245	545	110	150	125	385
1,400	1,075	225	100	260	585	110	150	125	385
1,500	1,150	250	100	275	625	110	150	125	385

Exhibit 9.5
The injection-leakage approach to national income determination
This exhibit shows how the equilibrium level of nominal national income can be determined by finding the point where planned injections to the circular flow (planned investment plus government purchases plus exports) are equal to total leakages from the circular flow (saving plus net taxes plus imports).

(b)

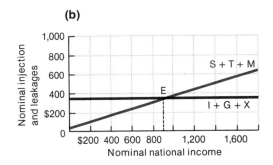

CHANGES IN NOMINAL NATIONAL INCOME AND THE MULTIPLIER EFFECT

Expenditure Changes

A great many economic factors can affect the level of planned expenditure. The aggregate demand schedule singles out the effects of changes in national income on planned expenditure. The effects of these changes are represented by movements along a given aggregate demand schedule.

Other factors also influence planned expenditure. Changes in consumer expectations, in wealth, or in the rate of inflation cause the level of autonomous consumption to vary. Changes in the expected real rate of interest or the expected real return on investment projects cause the level of planned investment to vary. Changes in policy cause the government purchases component of planned expenditure to vary, and changes in the world economy affect the volume of net exports. All the changes in planned expenditure that arise from reasons other than changes in national income must be represented by shifts in the aggregate demand schedule.

Consider Exhibit 9.6, which shows the effects of a $100 increase in planned expenditure at all levels of income. For the moment, it does not

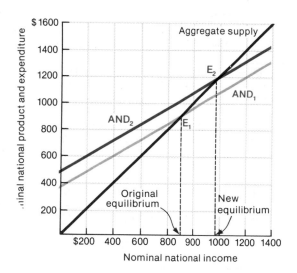

Exhibit 9.6
The multiplier effect of a shift in the aggregate demand schedule
A shift in the aggregate nominal demand schedule produces a more than equal change in equilibrium nominal national income. This is known as the multiplier effect. Here, a $100 upward shift in the aggregate nominal demand schedule produces a $250 increase in equilibrium nominal national income. The ratio of the change in equilibrium income to the original shift in demand, known as the multiplier, thus has a value of 2.5 in this example.

matter whether this increase originates in the consumption, investment, government purchases, or net export component of aggregate demand. The effect in any case is to shift the aggregate nominal demand schedule upward by $100, from the position AND_1 to the position AND_2.

The Multiplier Effect

What happens to the equilibrium level of national income when the planned expenditure schedule shifts upward by $100? The immediate effect is that planned expenditure exceeds national product, so that inventories start to be depleted. Firms react to this unplanned inventory depletion by increasing output and/or prices. Nominal national income rises to its new equilibrium level of $1,150.

Notice what has happened: a $100 upward shift in the aggregate demand schedule has induced a $250 increase in equilibrium nominal income. This ability of a given shift in aggregate demand to create a larger increase in equilibrium national income is the famous **multiplier effect**, a central pillar of Keynesian macroeconomics.

Multiplier effect The ability of a $1 shift in the aggregate nominal demand schedule to induce a change of more than $1 in the equilibrium level of nominal national income.

Round by Round   One way to view the multiplier effect is to imagine the effects of the initial upward shift in aggregate demand percolating down through the economy "round by round." Suppose that the original shift is caused by a $100 per year increase in the rate of autonomous consumption expenditure on domestic goods and services. When autonomous consumption expenditures increase, it is likely that part of the increase will be spent on foreign goods and services. The result will be both increased imports and increased expenditures on domestic goods and services. We have chosen here to focus only on the net increase in consumption expenditure devoted to domestic goods and services. This means, in terms of Exhibit 9.1b, that the consumption function will shift upwards by

In 1970, the Swedish Academy of Sciences awarded its Nobel Memorial Prize in Economics to MIT Professor Paul Samuelson. In doing so, the academy announced that "Professor Samuelson's extensive production, covering nearly all areas of economic theory, is characterized by an outstanding ability to derive important new theorems and to find new applications for existing ones. By his contributions, Samuelson has done more than any other contemporary economist to raise the level of scientific analysis in economic theory." The multiplier theory of national income determination is just one of dozens that has been refined, restated, and sharpened by Samuelson's penetrating mind.

Samuelson began his task of raising the level of scientific analysis in economic theory early in his career. His doctoral dissertation at Harvard, written when he was just twenty-six, was boldly entitled *Foundations of Economic Analysis*. (Contrast this with the narrow, ultraspecialized topics of most dissertations!) Published in 1947, the *Foundations* immediately became — and to a great extent remains — the definitive statement in modern mathematical dress of much of neoclassical economics.

In the nineteenth century, leading economists had seen their major theoretical statements go on to become textbooks to future generations. Alas, Samuelson's *Foundations* could not serve that purpose. One must already be well educated in economics and mathematics even to read it. Something had to be done to bring the advances in economic theory made during the 1930s and 1940s into the college classroom. Samuelson solved the problem with his famous *Economics*. That book was based on the simple assumption that beginning students did not need to be taught a different *kind* of economics than the kind economists wrote in their own professional journals. What they needed was a lucid, step-by-step presentation. The formula was so successful that Samuelson's *Economics* sold millions of copies as it went through a total of eleven editions.

On policy issues Samuelson ranks as a liberal and an activist. He derides the laissez-faire market economy as a "system of coercion by dollar votes." Unlike many like-minded colleagues, however, Samuelson did not move to Washington during the Kennedy-Johnson years. He was called on frequently for his opinions and advice, but he resisted service on the Council of Economic Advisers. Although much sought as a lecturer and writer of popular articles, Samuelson remains fundamentally an economist's economist. "In the long run," he has said, "the economic scholar works for the only coin worth having — our own applause."

Paul Anthony Samuelson (1915–   )

this net amount and there will be no downward shift in the net export function (because nothing explicit has been said about the change in imports). Therefore, the aggregate demand function shifts upward by $100. In response to the $100 increase in demand, business firms raise their prices and/or output enough to cause a $100 increase in nominal national product. The increase in national product results in $100 of additional nominal income for some people in the form of higher profits, wages, rents, or interest payments. All of what has happened so far can be called the first-round effect of the shift in aggregate demand for domestic goods.

Another way of handling this would be to focus on the *gross* change in autonomous consumption and to specify the proportion of such a change spent on imports. For example, assume that gross autonomous consumption increases by $125, of which $25 is spent on imports. In terms of Exhibit 9.1b, the consumption function (C) would shift upwards by $125, the net export function would decline by $25 (because autonomous imports have increased by $25) and the net result would again be a $100 upward shift in the aggregate demand function $(C + I + G + X_n)$.

Because, for reasons of simplicity, we have chosen not to specify the proportion of autonomous expenditures allocated to imports, the changes in autonomous expenditures considered here with the multiplier analysis are always net of imports. That is, the initial change in autonomous expenditures always refers to a change in expenditures on domestic goods and services only.

The second round consists of tracing the effects of the $100 in new income generated by the first round. Given an assumed marginal propensity to consume of 0.75 and a marginal propensity to import of 0.15, the people who receive this income will spend $75 of it on consumer goods and services, of which $15 will be spent on imports. The net effect is to increase the aggregate demand for domestic goods and services by $60. This spending will cause firms to step up output by $60 more and generate $60 in new factor payments and income.

Exhibit 9.7
The multiplier effect, round by round
This exhibit shows the round-by-round multiplier effects of an initial $100 upward shift in the aggregate nominal demand schedule for domestic goods and services. Each increase in aggregate nominal demand for domestic output produces an equal increase in nominal national income. Each $1 increase in nominal national income in turn produces $.75 of new consumer demand, in which is included a $.15 increase in expenditures on imports. This means that each $1 increase in national income produces $.60 of new demand on domestic goods and services. In total, the infinite series of rounds produces a $250 increase in aggregate nominal demand for domestic output and nominal national income. In comparing this exhibit with Exhibit 9.6, note that the original $100 increase in aggregate demand corresponds to the upward shift in the aggregate demand schedule, whereas the subsequent increases in aggregate demand for domestic goods and services correspond to movements along the new schedule.

Round	Increase in Total Aggregate Demand	Increase in Imports	Increase in Aggregate Demand for Domestic Goods and Services	Increase in National Income
1	$100.00	$ 0	$100.00	$100.00
2	75.00	15.00	60.00	60.00
3	45.00	9.00	36.00	36.00
4	27.00	5.40	21.60	21.60
5	16.20	3.24	12.96	12.96
6	9.72	1.94	7.78	7.78
7	5.84	1.17	4.67	4.67
8	3.50	.70	2.80	2.80
All later rounds	5.24	1.05	4.19	4.19
Totals	$287.50	$37.50	$250.00	$250.00

In the third round, three-quarters of the $60, or $45, is spent, of which $9 is spent on imports. This means that the aggregate demand for domestic goods and services increases by $36. Nominal income will go up by the same amount. In the fourth round, total aggregate demand will increase by $27 (= 0.75 × $36), $5.40 of which will go to imports (= 0.15 × $36). Therefore, the aggregate demand for domestic goods and services will rise by $21.60. This will continue until the increments become too small to worry about. When all the increments to income induced by the original $100 upward shift in the aggregate nominal demand function for domestic goods and services are added together, the total is:

$100 + $60 + $36 + $21.60 + $12.96... = $250,

just as expected. This round-by-round version of the multiplier effect is summarized in Exhibit 9.7.

The Multiplier Exhibit 9.7 shows quite clearly that as income increases in response to the original upward shift in the aggregate demand schedule, national income "catches up" with planned expenditure. For each $1 increase in nominal national income there is an equivalent increase in output, but expenditure on domestic output increases by only a fraction of a dollar. The fraction is equal to the marginal propensity to consume minus the marginal propensity to import. At the new equilibrium, the difference between planned expenditure on domestic goods and services and national income is eliminated.

The ratio of the induced increase in national income to the original increase in planned expenditure on domestic output is called the **multiplier**.[1] The value of the multiplier depends on the fraction of each added dollar of income that goes to added planned expenditure on domestically produced goods and service. More precisely, the multiplier is given by the formula:

$$\text{Multiplier} = \frac{1}{1 - (\text{MPC}_D)}, \text{ where } \text{MPC}_D = \text{MPC} - \text{MPM}.[2]$$

MPC stands for the marginal propensity to consume, MPM for the marginal propensity to import, and MPC_D for the marginal propensity to consume domestic output. Applying the figures used previously, the multiplier, is

$$\frac{1}{1 - (.75 - .15)} = \frac{1}{.4} = 2.5.$$

As the formula for the multiplier indicates, the value of the multiplier is related to that portion of any change in income that is spent on domestic goods and service. This equals MPC minus MPM.

Multiplier The ratio of an induced change in the equilibrium level of national income to an initial change in planned expenditure. For an economy in which imports play an important role, the value of the multiplier is given by the formula

$$\text{Multiplier} = \frac{1}{1 - (\text{MPC} - \text{MPM})}$$

or $\frac{1}{1 - \text{MPC}_D}$.

MPC_D is the marginal propensity to consume domestic output.

$$\text{MPC}_D = \frac{\Delta C}{\Delta DI} - \frac{\Delta M}{\Delta D1}.$$

---

[1] An algebraic derivation of the multiplier formula is given in the Appendix to Chapter 10.

[2] If the foreign market were not so important to Canada, one could ignore the effect of income on imports and derive a simpler multiplier using only the MPC. This simpler multiplier, used in many American texts, $= \frac{1}{1 - \text{MPC}}$. If MPC is 0.75 and MPM is 0.15 note that our multiplier will equal 2.5, while the simpler multiplier will equal 4. In other words, introducing import leakages reduces the multiplier. The "Buy Canadian" campaigns that are occasionally promoted on billboards are prompted by the desire to lessen the leakage of spending from the Canadian economy.

Alternatively, the multiplier can be related to that portion of any change in income that is not spent on domestic output. This is equal to the marginal propensity to save (MPS) *plus* the marginal propensity to import (MPM).

Therefore, an alternative formula for the multiplier is:

$$\text{Multiplier} = \frac{1}{\text{MPS} + \text{MPM}}.$$

Using previous figures

$$\text{the multiplier} = \frac{1}{.25 + .15} = 2.5.$$

Whichever way we write the formula, the multiplier is larger, the larger the propensity to consume and the smaller the marginal propensity to import; and it is smaller, the larger the marginal propensity to save and the larger the marginal propensity to import.

CONCLUSIONS

The multiplier effect plays a central role in Keynesian economic theory and economic policy analysis. The central implication of the multiplier is that even small changes in planned expenditure will have magnified effects on the national economy. Early Keynesian economists saw the instability of planned expenditure, magnified by the multiplier effect, as an explanation for the cycle of boom and bust that had plagued capitalist economies since the nineteenth century. They also saw in the multiplier effect the key to a new policy for economic stabilization. This part of their analysis is important enough that a separate chapter is devoted to it.

SUMMARY

1. For a given aggregate demand schedule, the circular flow can be in equilibrium at only one level of nominal national income. The equilibrium condition is achieved when planned expenditure on domestic output and national product must be equal. If planned expenditure exceeds national product, there will be unplanned depletion of inventories and upward pressure on income. If national product exceeds planned expenditure, there will be unplanned accumulation of inventories and downward pressure on national income.

2. The injection-leakage approach to the determination of the equilibrium level of nominal national income shows that equilibrium can occur only when planned injections (planned investment plus government purchases plus exports) are equal to total leakages (saving plus net taxes plus imports). In equation form:

   $$S + T + M = I + G + X.$$

3. A shift in the aggregate demand schedule changes the equilibrium level of nominal national income. According to the multiplier effect, the induced change in equilibrium nominal national income will be larger than the initial shift in planned expenditure. The ratio of the change in income to the shift in planned expenditure is known as the multiplier.

DISCUSSION QUESTIONS

1. It is possible to analyze the determinants of national income and product with either the circular flow or the Keynesian cross. Which do you prefer? Why? Does each contribute some insights of its own? Explain.

2. Explain the "round-by-round" effect of the multiplier by using the circular flow model.

3. If you expected a depression in the near future, would it be to your advantage to save in order to prepare for it? What would happen if we all tried to save a larger fraction of our income than usual to prepare for an expected depression?

4. If planned saving exceeds planned investment, will gross national product increase or decrease? Suppose you know the government's budget is exactly in balance. Now can you answer the question? What else, if anything, do you need to know?

5. What would be the size of the multiplier if the marginal propensity to consume were 0.5, 0.75, and 0.8 and the marginal propensity to import in each case were 0.25?

6. In what ways are the Keynesian cross and the supply and demand diagram of previous chapters similar, and in what ways are they different?

7. What changes in the economy would force a movement along the aggregate demand curve? What changes would result in a shift of the curve?

8. Suppose that consumers suddenly increase their marginal propensity to consume from 0.70 to 0.80 while the marginal propensity to import is and remains 0.1. What effect will the increase have on the aggregate demand curve? Trace the impact of this change using the Keynesian cross diagram.

C H A P T E R **10**

FISCAL POLICY AND THE MULTIPLIER THEORY

WHAT YOU WILL LEARN IN THIS CHAPTER

This chapter applies the multiplier theory of national income determination to some important practical problems of economic stabilization policy. It shows how taxes and government purchases can be adjusted in an attempt to achieve a level of nominal national income judged compatible with the goals of full employment, price stability, real economic growth, and balance of payments stability. In addition to discussing the use of discretionary changes in taxes and government purchases for stabilization purposes, the chapter also looks briefly at certain built-in automatic stabilizers contained in the economy. The chapter ends with a review of the long-standing controversy about the economic burden of the national debt.

FOR REVIEW

Here are some important terms and concepts that will be put to use in this chapter. If you do not understand them, review them before proceeding.

- *Nominal values for gross national product and net national income (Chapter 6)*
- *Goals of stabilization policy (Chapter 7)*
- *Multiplier theory (Chapter 9)*

The multiplier theory, introduced in the previous chapter, shows how shifts in aggregate demand cause changes in the equilibrium level of national income. This chapter applies the theory to shifts in aggregate demand produced by changes in the levels of net taxes or government purchases. The control of aggregate demand through these changes is known as **fiscal policy**.

In this chapter, as in the last two, the discussion continues in nominal terms. This is quite natural, in that government budgets are ordinarily cast in nominal terms. However, it should be kept in mind that manipulating the level of nominal national income is only an intermediate policy goal. The ultimate policy goals of full employment, price stability, the growth of real output, and stability in the foreign trade sector are affected only indirectly by changes in the nominal level of national income.

Fiscal policy The collective term for the policies that determine the levels of government purchases and net taxes.

These changes can take the form of changes in either real output (with accompanying changes in employment) or the price level — or some combination of the two. When fiscal policy is used to stimulate aggregate demand and drive up the level of nominal national income, policy makers naturally hope that all or most of the expansion will take the form of job-creating increases in real output. Part of the expansion of nominal income, however, may also take the form of unwanted inflation and unwanted increases in imports. Similarly, when fiscal policy is used to moderate aggregate demand and slow the growth of nominal income, it is hoped that most of the slowdown will take the form of a reduction in the rate of inflation. However, some of it may also take the form of a slowdown in real economic growth, possibly accompanied by a rise in unemployment.

It will be several chapters yet before we have assembled all the pieces of macroeconomic theory needed to determine exactly what part of a change in nominal income will take the form of changes in real output and what part will take the form of changes in the price level. For the time being, we should keep in mind that the manipulation of nominal aggregate demand is a powerful but imperfect means of achieving full employment, price stability, real economic growth, and balance of payments stability.

FISCAL POLICY IN ACTION

The Target Level of Nominal National Income

We turn now to the matter of applying fiscal policy, once it has been decided what level of nominal national income is most likely to promote the goals of full employment, price stability, economic growth and a healthy foreign-trade sector. That level of income, whatever it is, can be referred to as the **target level of nominal national income** (or the **income target** for short).

Target level of nominal national income (income target) The level of nominal national income judged by policy makers to be most nearly compatible with the goals of full employment, price stability, real economic growth, and balance of payments stability.

If, at any time, the equilibrium level of nominal national income is equal to the target level, no active fiscal policy is called for. To see fiscal policy in action, we need to look at the more interesting cases in which equilibrium nominal income either falls short of or exceeds the income target.

A Contractionary Gap Consider the case shown in Exhibit 10.1. As the aggregate supply and demand curves are drawn, they determine an equilibrium level of nominal national income of $900. Suppose policy makers consider $900 too low and set their target instead at $1,200. With the planned expenditure schedule shown, $1,200 cannot be the equilibrium level of income, because planned expenditures will fall short of national product by $120 if income is at the target level. At the income level of $1,200 planned expenditure will be only $1,080.

Contractionary gap The difference between planned expenditures and national product at the target level of national income when aggregate supply exceeds aggregate demand at that level.

Whenever planned expenditure is less than national product at the target level of income, there is a **contractionary gap**. The size of the gap represents the rate of unplanned inventory accumulation that will take place at the target level of income with the given aggregate demand schedule. Geometrically, the gap is measured by the vertical distance between the aggregate demand and supply schedules at the target level of national income. The word *contractionary* refers to the fact that unplanned inventory accumula-

Exhibit 10.1

A contractionary gap

A contractionary gap is said to occur whenever planned expenditure (aggregate demand) is less than national product (aggregate supply) at the target level of national income. Under this condition, the equilibrium level of nominal national income is below the target level. If national income were at the target level, unplanned inventory accumulation would put downward pressure on the level of income and cause it to contract.

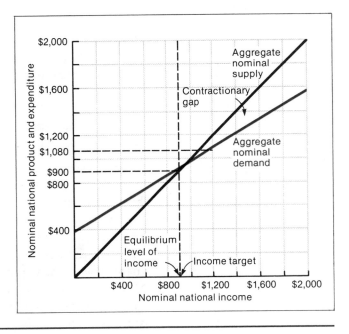

tion tends to cause the level of nominal national income to fall if income is at the target level.

An Expansionary Gap Alternatively, the equilibrium level of nominal national income may be higher than the target level. Such a case is shown in Exhibit 10.2, where the aggregate demand schedule is $280 higher than the one shown in Exhibit 10.1. Now planned expenditures will exceed national income at the target level of national income. Instead of unplanned inventory accumulation and a contractionary gap at the target income, there is unplanned inventory depletion and an **expansionary gap**.

Expansionary gap The difference between planned expenditures and national product at the target level of national income when aggregate demand exceeds aggregate supply at that level.

Exhibit 10.2

An expansionary gap

An expansionary gap is said to occur whenever planned expenditure (aggregate demand) is greater than national product (aggregate supply) at the target level of national income. Under this condition, the equilibrium level of nominal national income is above the target level. If national income were at the target level, unplanned inventory depletion would put upward pressure on the level of income and cause the circular flow to expand.

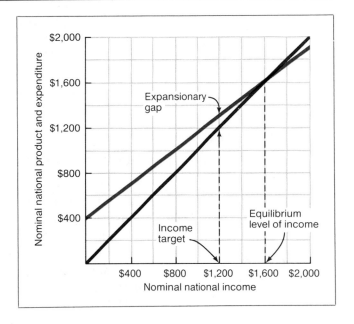

When such a gap exists, nominal national income is again not in equilibrium at the target level. If national income were to be at the target level, unplanned inventory depletion would cause the circular flow, measured in nominal terms, to expand.

Filling a Contractionary or Expansionary Gap

When there is an expansionary or contractionary gap in the economy, fiscal policy can be used to fill it. In the case of a contractionary gap, consumption, planned investment, government purchases, and net exports combined are not great enough to equal national income at the target level. Policy makers can try to fill the gap directly by increasing government purchases or indirectly by stimulating consumption through reduced taxes. In the case of an expansionary gap, consumption, planned investment, government purchases, and net exports are together so great that they exceed national income at the target level. Policy makers then try to eliminate the gap by cutting government purchases or discouraging consumption with a tax increase.

Injection-Leakage Approach Chapter 9 introduced the injection-leakage approach as an alternative way of determining the equilibrium level of national income. This approach sheds additional light on the process of eliminating expansionary and contractionary gaps. According to the approach, in equilibrium, saving plus net taxes plus imports must equal planned investment plus government purchases plus exports.

When there is a contractionary gap, leakages exceed planned injections at the target level of nominal income. Unless fiscal policy intervenes, the difference is taken up by unplanned inventory investment, which holds nominal national income below the target level. Fiscal policy can close the gap by adding to injections with government purchases or by reducing leakages through a cut in net taxes.

When there is an expansionary gap, saving plus net taxes plus imports fall short of planned investment plus government purchases plus exports at the target level of nominal national income. Fiscal policy can bring the two into balance either by increasing leakages in the form of taxes or by reducing injections in the form of government purchases.

In outline, this is how fiscal policy works. Now we turn to an examination of the details of multiplier theory.

Government Purchases Policy

We begin with a simple case in which the government fills a contractionary gap by increasing government purchases. In Exhibit 10.3a, initial conditions are represented by the aggregate nominal demand curve AND_1. The consumption schedule on which this curve is based assumes a marginal propensity to consume of 0.75, autonomous consumption of $100, and lump sum taxes of $100. Interest rates and business conditions generate $110 of planned investment expenditure, and government purchases are $150. Net exports are 75 –0.15 of national income. The result is an initial equilibrium nominal national income of $900. There is a contractionary gap of $120, measured vertically at the target level of national income.

Policy makers want to fill the contractionary gap, and one way to do so is by increasing government purchases. To illustrate: suppose policy makers authorize spending an extra $120 to accelerate the completion of a stretch of interprovincial highway. If the policy is to work, this added spending must be paid for, not by increased taxes, but instead by borrowing from the public. The consequences of the increased spending can be considered from three viewpoints: round by round, aggregate supply and demand, and injection-leakage.

Round by Round First, we can take a round-by-round approach. Spending $120 on the highway project creates $120 in new income for the construction workers, which raises total national income in the first round from $900 to $1,020. Given a marginal propensity to consume of 0.75, the workers save one-quarter of their new income and spend the rest ($90) on, say, clothing. Because 15 percent of the increased income ($18) is spent on clothing produced outside the country, the increased expenditure generates $72 of new income for domestic clothing workers and retailers, which raises total income to $1,092 in the second round. In the third round, clothing workers spend three-quarters of their new income on something else, including 15 percent on imports, which adds $43.20 more to the stream of income and expenditure. As further rounds progress, the target level of $1,200 national income is approached more and more closely.

Aggregate Supply and Demand Approach Instead of taking the round-by-round approach, we can refer to Exhibit 10.3a, which shows the effects of the increased government purchases in terms of the Keynesian cross. The decision to spend $120 on the highway project shifts the aggregate demand schedule upward by $120 to the position labeled AND_2. At the initial level of national income, $900, planned expenditures exceed national income and hence national product by $120. This added demand initially causes inventories to decline unexpectedly. In response, firms either step up output or raise prices or both, which sends nominal national income and product upward. The unplanned depletion of inventories is not eliminated entirely until the new equilibrium level of nominal national income is reached — at the point where the new aggregate demand schedule intersects the aggregate supply schedule. This new equilibrium occurs at the target income of $1,200.

Injection-Leakage Approach Finally, we can consider the effects of increased government purchases in terms of the injection-leakage approach. In Exhibit 10.3b, increased government purchases shift the injection schedule upward by $120, from $(I + G + X)_1$ to $(I + G + X)_2$. At the $900 income level, planned investment, government purchases, and exports add up to more than total leakages, so that inventories are unexpectedly depleted and incomes begin to rise. With a marginal propensity to save of 0.25, $.25 in new saving results from each $1 of added income. By the time national income reaches $1,200, saving has increased by $75 and imports

Exhibit 10.3

Use of fiscal policy to fill a contractionary gap

This exhibit illustrates the use of fiscal policy to fill a contractionary gap and move equilibrium nominal national income to the target level. Part a illustrates this process with the Keynesian cross and Part b with the injection-leakage approach. In both cases, a $120 increase in government purchases results in a $300 increase in equilibrium nominal national income.

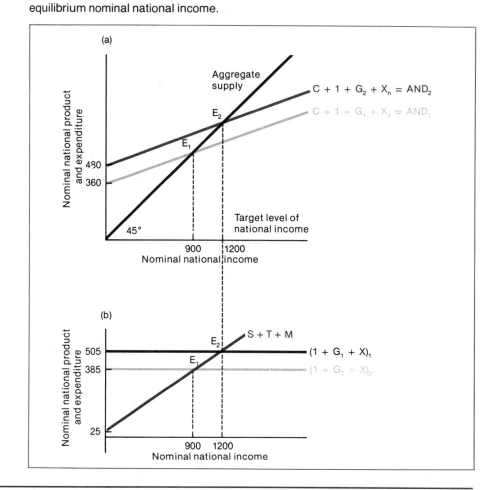

by $45 (so that leakages have increased by $120) and equilibrium is restored.

The Multiplier Whichever approach we use, we come to the same conclusion: when government purchases are increased while taxes, planned investment, the net exports schedule, and the consumption schedule remain unchanged, equilibrium nominal national income changes by an amount equal to the change in government purchases times the multiplier. In this case, where the change in government purchases is $120 and the multiplier is 2.5, the change in equilibrium income is:

$2.5 \times \$120 = \$300$ (note: the multiplier =

$$\frac{1}{1-MPC_D} = \frac{1}{1-(0.75-0.15)} = \frac{1}{0.4} = 2.5).$$

This can also be written as follows:

$$\text{Change in national income} = \frac{1}{1-\text{MPC}_D} \times \text{Change in government purchases.}$$

$$\$300 = 2.5 \times \$120.$$

Net Tax Policy

Instead of stimulating aggregate demand by increasing government purchases or moderating it by cutting purchases, fiscal policy authorities can instead manipulate demand by raising or lowering net taxes. Net tax policy is potentially as capable of filling a contractionary or expansionary gap as government purchase policy, but the chain of effects through which it operates is sufficiently different to warrant a separate discussion.

Net Taxes and Consumption Expenditure The major difference between the two types of fiscal policy is that changes in government purchases are themselves changes in aggregate demand, whereas changes in net taxes operate on aggregate demand only indirectly—through changes in consumption expenditures. The immediate effect of a $1 tax cut is a $1 increase in the part of national income left to households as disposable income. The effect of this change on aggregate demand—on domestic goods and services—depends on the marginal propensity to consume and the marginal propensity to import. If the marginal propensity to consume is 0.75, and the marginal propensity to import is 0.15, as assumed in the recent examples, a $1 tax cut produces a $.75 increase in consumption expenditure, other things being equal, and a $.15 increase in imports or a $.60 increase in expenditure on domestic goods and services.[1]

Geometrically, this initial effect of a tax cut appears as an upward shift in the aggregate nominal demand schedule. With a marginal propensity to consume of 0.75 and a marginal propensity to import of 0.15, each $1 cut in taxes shifts the demand schedule up by $.60. (A $1 increase in net taxes would cut $1 from disposable income, which in turn would shift the aggregate demand schedule downward by $.60.) Once the aggregate demand schedule has shifted, the multiplier process takes over. The $.60 in new first-round expenditure on domestic goods and services stimulated by each $1 cut in net taxes becomes someone's second-round income. Sixty percent of this second-round income is spent on further domestic output, which generates third-round income, and so on. Equilibrium is reestablished only when the economy has moved along the new, higher aggregate nominal demand curve to the point where it intersects the aggregate nominal supply curve.

The Net Tax Multiplier The change in equilibrium nominal national income produced by a change in taxes is equal to the multiplier times the

---

[1] The tax cut changes disposable income, not national income. Because we have chosen to relate imports to national income and not to disposable income, the increase in disposable income does not result in increased imports. It follows, therefore, that the initial increase in expenditures of $75 will be spent entirely on domestic output. This expenditure will increase national income, which will result in increased imports in subsequent rounds.

amount of the shift in the aggregate demand curve produced by the tax change. This shift is opposite in direction to the tax change (up for a tax cut, down for a tax increase) and equal in magnitude to the amount of the tax change times the marginal propensity to consume minus the marginal propensity to import. With a marginal propensity to consume of 0.75 and a marginal propensity to import of 0.15 the multiplier has a value of 2.5. A $1 tax cut shifts the aggregate demand curve up by $.60. Multiplying this by 2.5 gives an increase in equilibrium nominal national income of $1.50. Similarly, a $1 tax increase shifts the aggregate demand curve down by $.60, which produces a $1.50 fall in equilibrium nominal national income.

Net tax multiplier A multiplier showing how much equilibrium nominal national income will change in response to a change in net taxes. The formula for the net tax multiplier is
$$-\frac{(MPC-MPM)}{MPS+MPM} \text{ or } \frac{-MPC_D}{1-MPC_D}$$

This analysis of the effects of a change in taxes can be used to define the **net tax multiplier** — the change in equilibrium nominal national income resulting from a $1 change in net taxes. The net tax multiplier is negative because a change in net taxes causes an opposite shift in the aggregate demand curve. It is also smaller than the previous multiplier, because the size of the shift in the aggregate demand curve produced by each $1 change in disposable income is equal only to $1 times the marginal propensity to consume minus the marginal propensity to import. Using MPC to represent the marginal propensity to consume, MPS to represent the marginal propensity to save, MPM to represent the marginal propensity to import, and MPC_D to represent the marginal propensity to consume domestic output $(MPC-MPM)$, the formula is:

$$\text{Net tax multiplier} = -\frac{(MPC-MPM)}{MPS+MPM}, \text{ or } -\frac{(MPC-MPM)}{1-MPC-MPM}, \text{ or } \frac{-MPC_D}{1-MPC_D}$$

If MPC = 0.75, MPM = 0.15, the MPC_D = 0.6 and the net tax multiplier is:

$$\frac{-0.6}{1-0.6} = -\frac{0.6}{0.4} = -1.5$$

The complete algebraic derivation of the net tax multiplier is given in the Appendix to Chapter 10.

Taxes and Transfers   A final comment on net tax policy: the term *net taxes*, as explained earlier, means taxes collected by government minus transfer payments. The net tax multiplier thus applies to changes in transfer payments as well as to changes in taxes paid. A $1 increase in transfer payments is a $1 decrease in net taxes, and a $1 decrease in transfer payments is a $1 increase in net taxes. With a marginal propensity to consume of 0.75 and a marginal propensity to import of 0.15, a $1 increase in transfer payments can be expected to produce a $1.50 increase in equilibrium nominal national income. This is the result of applying the net tax multiplier of 1.5 to the change in net taxes of −$1.

The Multipliers Compared

Two multipliers have now been introduced. With a marginal propensity to consume of 0.75 and a marginal propensity to import of 0.15, and hence a marginal propensity to consume domestic output of 0.6, there is a multiplier related to changes in expenditures of 2.5 and a net tax multiplier of 1.5. If the marginal propensity to consume were 0.9 and the marginal propensity to import remained at 0.15, the expenditure multiplier would be 4 and the net tax multiplier would be 3.

However, these multipliers should be interpreted with caution. A change in government spending is the most powerful tool of fiscal policy, in the sense that it takes advantage of the full value of the multiplier. That power does not mean, though, that a change in government spending is necessarily the best way to eliminate an expansionary or contractionary gap. Any of the two policies can be as effective as the other, so long as a big enough change in taxes or transfer payments is used. It is time now to look beyond the multiplier at some other topics in fiscal policy.

DISCRETIONARY FISCAL POLICY AND AUTOMATIC STABILIZERS

Discretionary Policy

Up to this point, it has been assumed that policy makers are free to adjust taxes and government purchases as they please, for no other purpose than to manipulate aggregate nominal demand. Policy actions of this type are known as **discretionary fiscal policy**. The following two case studies illustrate this type of fiscal policy.

Discretionary fiscal policy
Changes in the levels of taxes, transfers, or government purchases made for the specific purpose of economic stabilization.

Case 10.1
The Kennedy Tax Cut

Probably the most famous example of discretionary fiscal policy was the Kennedy tax cut in the United States. John F. Kennedy assumed the office of president in January 1961 in the middle of a recession. He had been elected on a promise to "get the country moving again," and he brought to Washington a group of economic advisers firmly committed to the active use of fiscal policy.

At first, the emphasis of the new administration was primarily on the spending side of fiscal policy. The president issued orders aimed at stepping up federal expenditures by speeding highway fund allocations and accelerating procurement activities. He also submitted a package of new spending proposals to Congress.

By the next year, the economy seemed to be making considerable progress. Presidential advisers thought that the administration's national income target, aimed high enough to ensure full employment, would be achieved by the end of 1963. But contrary to these forecasts, the expansion slowed. By June 1962, the president decided to use more stimulus. On June 7, 1962, he announced that he favored a tax cut of some $10 billion.

Kennedy's tax cut proposal did not get quick treatment from Congress. Long delays resulted from congressional demands to couple the tax cut to reforms in the tax structure and changes in expenditure policy. As it turned out, Kennedy did not live to see his great tax cut enacted. But in February 1964, his successor, Lyndon Johnson, finally signed the Kennedy tax cut into law. This tax cut is now considered a famous test case of fiscal policy. The U.S. economy entered an expansion phase following the tax cut, leading Keynesian economists to hail the policy as a good demonstration of the validity of Keynesian theory. However, monetarists pointed out that the tax cut was accompanied by an expansionary monetary policy. Who could say which policy had made a greater impact on economic growth? The debate goes on.

Kennedy's tax cut, conceived during a recession, was clearly meant to fill a contractionary gap, raising output and employment. The next example concerns a Canadian proposal to use discretionary fiscal policy to deal with a contractionary gap.

Case 10.2
The Turner Tax Concessions

In May 1972, Canada's Minister of Finance, John Turner, announced tax concessions for manufacturing and processing firms. Beginning in 1973, such firms would receive tax reductions based on the portion of their income devoted to investment. Though the economy was not in a slump, the unemployment rate was rising and it was felt by the government that more investment was needed in the 1970s to assure a high rate of growth for the Canadian economy.

In 1975, after the tax concessions had been in effect for almost three years, the government undertook a study to assess the impact of the tax reductions on industrial investment. The report claimed that the reductions were responsible for $2.5 billion of new investment, some 73,000 new jobs, and $4.8 billion in increased sales. A multiplier effect was also claimed, with about $1.2 billion new investment in the second round. It was conceded that the government lost over $1 billion in tax revenue as a result of the tax reductions, but much of this was regained through increased tax revenues resulting from the alleged growth in output. Businessmen surveyed, however, were not so sure that the government's fiscal strategy was primarily responsible for the growth in investment, output, and employment. Only 32 percent indicated that they had been favorably influenced by the tax reductions. It is finally impossible, of course, to know what would have been done in the absence of special government tax measures. The minister pointed out that in the year before the measures came into effect, real investment had declined by 2.1 percent. In contrast to this, in 1973 and 1974, investment increased annually at an average rate of 20 percent. It seems reasonable to assume that at least part of that increase was due to fiscal policy, but there is no way of knowing how much.

Automatic Stabilizers

Although discretionary fiscal policy is what makes the headlines, not all fiscal policy is of a discretionary nature. Some policy changes occur automatically, without any positive action taken by Parliament or the federal cabinet. Although ignored in the simplified examples up to this point, where lump sum taxes were assumed, these automatic changes are quite important in practice. For example, many kinds of taxes — including corporate and personal income taxes, payroll taxes, and sales taxes — automatically increase as the level of nominal national income increases. Also, many kinds of transfer payments tend to decrease as nominal national income increases. Unemployment benefits are a case in point.

Automatic stabilizers
Changes in taxes, transfers, and government purchases that occur automatically as nominal GNP rises or falls.

Because these nondiscretionary changes in taxes and transfer payments tend to have a contractionary influence when the economy is expanding and an expansionary influence when it is contracting, they are called **automatic stabilizers**. In effect, these stabilizers reduce the value of the simple multiplier for the economy. Because of them, the economy is less sensitive than it otherwise would be to unexpected changes in planned investment, government purchases, autonomous consumption expenditure, and net exports.

Automatic stabilizers are not by themselves enough to guarantee full employment and price stability. They do, however, provide a useful supplement to discretionary fiscal policies.

FISCAL POLICY AND THE BALANCE OF PAYMENTS

If the government uses fiscal policy to stimulate the economy by increasing government expenditures (and perhaps simultaneously increasing transfer payments or decreasing taxes), it may manage to increase national income and decrease unemployment, but at the expense of increasing the current account deficit. Imports will likely increase with national income, but there is no guarantee that exports will increase as well, or by as much. To pay for the increased imports, it may be necessary to increase the inflow of capital, which in turn may require higher interest rates in Canada. Such higher rates may discourage private investment, thus counteracting increased government expenditure.

The initial increase in imports could be halted in the long run by allowing the value of the Canadian dollar to decline. This would happen almost automatically as Canadians demanded more foreign currency to pay for the increased imports, though the process could take some time and other factors would also play a role in determining the value of the dollar. It is important to note here, however, that government fiscal policies will have an impact on Canada's foreign trade as well as on its domestic economy, and the desired goals for one market may conflict with desired goals for the other.

FISCAL POLICY AND THE NATIONAL DEBT

This chapter so far has drawn a very symmetrical picture of fiscal policy. If the economy is in a slump, the government cuts taxes or increases expenditures; the resulting deficit acts as an injection of new demand into the circular flow, and national income and product are boosted toward their target level. If the economy is overheated, with inflation and tight job markets, spending is cut or taxes are raised; enough of this results in a surplus, which withdraws demand from the circular flow and cools off the economy.

In the 30 years from 1950 to 1979 inclusive, the federal government of Canada has varied surpluses and deficits in a remarkably even way: it has had surpluses in 14 years and deficits in 16. All levels of government together have had surpluses in 16 years and deficits in 14. There are critics of government policy, however, who have been disturbed by the size of government deficits in recent years and are worried about the increase in government debt.

After running a surplus of more than $1 billion in 1974, the federal government incurred a deficit of more than $3 billion in each of the years 1975 and 1976. In 1977 the deficit soared to $7.4 billion. In 1978 it increased to $11.4 billion. It is small wonder that Prime Minister Trudeau, while running for office in 1979, announced that his government, if reelected, would adhere as closely as possible to a balanced budget.

In the late 1970s, political support began to grow in both the United States and Canada for stricter limits on discretionary fiscal policy. Constitutional amendments were proposed in the United States to force governments to restrain spending and keep their budgets in balance. Little attention has been given in Canada to such legal or constitutional restraints, but both provincial and federal governments sense a growing public desire for what is sometimes called "fiscal responsibility." Do these political developments represent the last gasp of an economic conservatism that dates back to pre-Keynesian times, or do they instead represent a justified disenchantment with the results of several decades of deficit spending? The debate is likely to continue for years to come, so it is worthwhile to look at the economic arguments advanced by each side.

In Defense of Deficit Spending

In the opinion of fiscal activists, the important thing is to provide the right amount of stimulus or restraint each year, in order to move toward the goals of full employment, price stability, economic growth, and balance of payments stability. If this requires running budget deficits more often than surpluses, then so be it. There is no reason to make controlling the size of the national debt a separate, fifth goal of policy. No one is hurt if the national debt grows, so nothing should be sacrificed in order to keep it small. Four arguments underlie this position:

Trend of the National Debt The first argument given for not being concerned with the size of the national debt is that the trend of the debt, in relation to gross national product, has been steadily down, not up. If ever the national debt was a burden, it was at the end of World War II. In 1946, the government of Canada debt stood at an all-time high of 135 percent of GNP. By the mid-1970s, it had been reduced to less than 25 percent of the GNP.[2]

The Power of Taxation A second argument for not being concerned with the size of the national debt is that the federal government never need worry about bankruptcy, no matter how large its debt becomes. The federal debt is backed by the federal power of taxation, which is enormous. As long as the power of taxation exists, people will continue to lend the government money to refinance the debt as it becomes due, confident that they will be repaid on time, in full, and with interest.

We Owe It to Ourselves The third argument is that the size of the national debt is not a matter of serious concern because it is a debt that the Canadian people owe largely to themselves. It is a mere bookkeeping entry that can be cleared by shuffling funds from one account to another with no net drain on the real resources of the country. From the point of view of the circular flow, interest payments on the national debt are only transfer payments.

Can't Build Today's Houses with Tomorrow's Bricks Finally, it is said that there is no reason to be concerned that the national debt will put an unfair burden on future generations. Even if those in authority want to do so, the argument goes, today's houses cannot be built with tomorrow's bricks. Real

---

[2] In 1816, during the course of England's industrial revolution, the national debt was more than twice the size of the gross national product. Source: Arthur Redford, *The Economic History of England, 1760–1860* (London: Longmans, 1960), p. 103.

goods and services, that is to say, cannot be transferred from the future to the present. No matter how government spending is financed today, annual real income consists in the real goods and services we produce—no more and no less. The same has been true at every time in the past and will be true at every time in the future.

Beware False Comparisons Taken together, these arguments add up to a warning not to make false comparisons between the national debt and the debts of individual families or private firms. Individuals and private firms can go bankrupt if their debts get larger than their ability to repay. Repayments of private debts (unless they are debts to people within the same family or firm) are not mere bookkeeping entries but instead are real flows of purchasing power from those within to outsiders. Thus private debts do represent a real burden on the future consumption or investment capacity of the unit that incurs them. But none of these things, it is said, hold true for the national debt.

Reservations about Deficit Spending

Although acknowledging that the four arguments for deficit spending are valid as far as they go, modern fiscal conservatives nonetheless have grave reservations about the wisdom of unlimited deficit spending and limitless growth of the national debt. They raise four points of their own.

Reversal of the Trend First, although recognizing the downward postwar trend of the national debt in relation to GNP, they are alarmed by the apparent break with the trend that occurred in the late 1970s. Although the debt had by then fallen to a postwar low in relation to GNP, the size of the deficit itself—which measures the rate at which new debt is accumulated—reached a postwar high. Over the four years 1975–1978, the average federal deficit was more than 3 percent of GNP, compared with an average of less than 1 percent over the previous twenty-five years. Furthermore, although the debt had fallen to a relatively low level, interest rates had risen to historic highs, so that the proportion of GNP needed to service the debt was as high in the 1970s as at the end of World War II.

Limits to Taxation Second, those people who are concerned about the size of the national debt are skeptical of assurances that taxes can be raised without limit to repay debts. There are the examples of cities like New York and Cleveland, which have already found their taxing power insufficient to repay past debts on schedule. Cities in Canada have not reached the same crisis stage, but they too are severely pinched by a narrow tax base and growing demands for services. The federal government does have one power that makes it more able to meet debt payments than provincial and municipal governments, but it is not the power of unlimited taxation. Instead, it is the power to create money. This power, discussed in coming chapters, does indeed guarantee that the federal government need never default on its debts; but in the long run, use of this power can impart an inflationary bias to stabilization policy.

Rising Foreign Share of the Debt Third, fiscal conservatives reject the notion that national debt payments have no economic impact because they are mere costless transfers from one group of people to another. For one thing, because of administrative costs and the disincentive effect of taxes, no transfer is truly costless. Each dollar in debt repayment imposes an opportunity cost of more than a dollar on someone.

On a more practical level, it is no longer as true as it once was that the national debt is something citizens owe to themselves. Between 1966 and 1976, the share of the federal government debt held by other countries increased from about 4 percent to nearly 6 percent. In 1978 the federal government increased the outstanding amount of government securities held by Canadians by $8.2 billion, while it increased the amount held by foreigners by $2.3 billion.

Possible Burdens on Future Generations Fourth, critics of excessive deficit spending are not convinced that borrowing to finance government spending imposes no burden on future generations. True, it is literally impossible to build today's houses with tomorrow's bricks. But future generations can be burdened with the necessity of exporting some of those future bricks to pay off borrowing from abroad. In addition, heavy government borrowing today may indirectly cause real national product to be lower in the future than it otherwise would have been. The reason is that the government and private firms must compete in financial markets for the same pool of funds created by savers. At some point, government borrowing may begin to crowd out the private investment on which future economic growth depends. (More on this subject will appear in later chapters.)

To summarize, modern fiscal conservatives are willing to accept the arguments used in defense of deficit spending by fiscal policy activits, but only up to a point. The national debt—at least that part of it held by people within Canada—is indeed not strictly comparable to private debts. The federal government is admittedly not in danger of literal bankruptcy. Nonetheless, there is a danger that excessive short-run reliance on deficit spending as a means of promoting full employment may in the long run threaten the ability of the economy to achieve price stability and real economic growth.

CONCLUSIONS

The discussion of stabilization policy has now been carried about as far as it can be on the basis of the multiplier theory alone. Already, the discussion of the controversy over the national debt has had occasion to mention money and the federal government's power to control its supply. Monetary policy is, in fact, the second side of stabilization policy, and it is as important as fiscal policy. The next three chapters will discuss the banking system and monetary policy. Then, Chapter 14 will take a fresh look at what this chapter has explained and will discuss the interactions between monetary policy and fiscal policy.

SUMMARY

1. If the equilibrium level of nominal national income is different from the target level, there is a gap between total planned expenditure and national product measured at the target level of income. If the equilibrium level of income is lower than policy makers want it to be, a contractionary gap is said to exist. If the equilibrium level of nominal income is too high, the gap is said to be expansionary.

2. One way to fill a contractionary gap is by increasing government purchases without increasing net taxes. When such purchases are increased while net taxes, planned investment, the consumption schedule and the net export schedule remain unchanged, equilibrium nominal national income changes by an amount equal to the change in government purchases times the multiplier.

3. A contractionary gap can also be filled by cutting net taxes without changing government purchases. When net taxes are changed while government purchases, planned investment, autonomous consumption, autonomous net exports, the marginal propensity to consume, and the marginal propensity to import remain unchanged, equilibrium nominal national income changes in the direction opposite to the change in taxes by an amount equal to the change in net taxes times the net tax multiplier.

4. Changes in taxes, transfers, or the level of government purchases made for the specific purpose of achieving the goal of economic stabilization are called discretionary fiscal policy. In addition to discretionary fiscal policy, other changes in taxes, transfers, and even government purchases occur automatically as the level of national product varies. Examples are changes in income taxes and unemployment benefits. These are called automatic stabilizers.

5. Fiscal policy will also affect the balance of payments. The pursuit of domestic objectives may conflict with the goal of balance of payments stability.

6. At least since the 1930s, there has been a running controversy between fiscal conservatives, who would like to see the federal government balance its budget at least most of the time, and fiscal activists, who think that persistent deficit spending is no real cause for worry. The issue centers largely on whether the national debt (and the repayment of it) imposes a real burden, present or future, on the economy. The fiscal activists have succeeded in establishing that naive fears of national bankruptcy are based on misleading analogies between private debt and the national debt. But fiscal conservatives counter that in the long run, excessive government borrowing and indebtedness can pose a threat to economic growth and price stability.

DISCUSSION QUESTIONS

1. Is the target level of national income always the level of national income at which there will be equilibrium?
2. Should the major tool of fiscal policy be changes in government spending or changes in taxation? Justify your position.
3. Use the circular flow to trace the effect of government spending in closing a contractionary gap.

4. What importance does the size of the marginal propensity to consume and the marginal propensity to import have for the effectiveness of fiscal policy in closing both inflationary and deflationary gaps?

5. Explain why a given change in government spending has a greater impact on the economy than does the same change in taxation.

6. If there were a contractionary gap, would there be some advantage to simply paying workers to dig ditches and then fill them in? Under what circumstances would this policy be beneficial?

7. Who pays the cost and who receives the benefits of (a) increased government spending and (b) increased taxes? Does your answer to this question differ now from what it would have been just after you read Chapter 4?

8. Do you think that there is an expansionary gap in the economy right now (as you are taking this course)? A contractionary gap? How can you tell? What is the government doing about the gap if there is one?

9. Evaluate the following possible rule for the conduct of fiscal policy: set the level of government purchases by looking at the actual economic merit of spending projects without considering macroeconomic effects. Then, if the resulting budget does not provide the right amount of macroeconomic stimulus, aim for the target level of national income by adjusting net taxes upward or downward as required. Is this rule compatible with active use of discretionary fiscal policy?

10. Would a rule requiring the federal government to balance its budget every year completely preclude the use of discretionary fiscal policy for stabilization purposes? Explain. Would a rule requiring the budget to be balanced on average each five years be a reasonable way of compromising the concerns of fiscal activists and conservatives?

APPENDIX TO CHAPTER 10
AN ALGEBRAIC APPROACH TO INCOME DETERMINATION AND THE MULTIPLIER

All the theoretical propositions illustrated with graphs and numerical examples in the last three chapters can also be expressed in terms of elementary algebra. Begin with the consumption schedule. Using a for the constant term in the schedule (autonomous consumption), b for the marginal propensity to consume, C for nominal consumption expenditure, T for net taxes, Y for nominal national income, and M for imports, Ma for autonomous imports, and m for the marginal propensity to import, the consumption schedule and the import schedule can be written:

$$C = a + b(Y - T);$$
$$M = Ma + m(Y - T).$$ **10A.1**

Note that the expression $(Y - T)$ that appears in the right-hand side of this expression represents nominal disposable income.

With the consumption schedule as a basis, the aggregate nominal demand (AND) schedule is put together by adding planned investment (I), government purchases (G), and exports (X) and subtracting imports (M). This gives:

$$AND = C + I + G + X - M.$$ **10A.2**

Substituting in Equation 10A.1:

$$AND = a + b(Y - T) + I + G + X - Ma - m(Y - T)$$ **10A.3**

It is convenient to rewrite this equation by grouping the constant terms, so that it becomes:

$$AND = (a - bT + mT + I + G + X - Ma) + bY - mY$$ **10A.4**

The term in parentheses in Equation 10A.4 represents the constant term, or vertical intercept, of the aggregate nominal demand schedule; and b, the marginal propensity to consume, minus m, represents its slope.

This equation can now be used to determine the equilibrium level of nominal national income. The theory set forth in Chapter 9 showed that for the economy to be in equilibrium, national income must be equal to planned expenditure, so that there is no unplanned inventory accumulation or depletion. This equilibrium condition can be written:

$$Y = AND. \qquad\qquad \textbf{10A.5}$$

Substituting Equation 10A.4 into Equation 10A.5, the equilibrium condition becomes:

$$Y = [a - bT + I + G + X - (Ma - mT)] + bY - mY \qquad\qquad \textbf{10A.6}$$

Solving Equation 10A.6 for Y then gives this formula for the equilibrium value of nominal national income:

$$Y^* = \frac{1}{1 - b_d}[a - bT + I + G + X - (Ma - mT)],$$

where b_d is the marginal propensity to consume domestic output which equals $b - m$. \qquad **10A.7**

The asterisk after the Y in this formula is a reminder that the equation holds only for the equilibrium value of nominal national income.

Equation 10A.7 can now be applied to solve a number of problems.

Problem 1 Use Equation 10A.7 to derive the formulas for the multiplier and the net tax multiplier.

Solution The multiplier was defined in Chapter 9 as the ratio of an induced change in the equilibrium level of nominal national income to an initial shift in the aggregate nominal demand schedule for domestic output. In algebraic terms, a shift in the aggregate nominal demand schedule means an increase or decrease in the intercept term $[a - bT + I + G + X - (Ma - mT)]$. For ease in notation, let A represent this intercept term:

$$A = [a - bT + I + G + X - (Ma - mT)]. \qquad\qquad \textbf{10A.8}$$

Equation 10A.7 then becomes:

$$Y^* = \frac{1}{1 - b_d}A. \qquad\qquad \textbf{10A.9}$$

Suppose now that this constant term changes from an initial value of A_0 to a new value, A_1, thereby producing a shift in the aggregate nominal demand schedule of $A_1 - A_0$. This increases the equilibrium value of nominal national income from

$$Y_0^* = \frac{1}{1 - b_d}A_0$$

to a new value of

$$Y_1^* = \frac{1}{1 - b_d}A_1.$$

The multiplier, as the ratio of the change in equilibrium income to the shift in the aggregate nominal demand schedule, can now be calculated as follows:

$$\text{Multiplier} = \frac{Y_1^* - Y_0^*}{A_1 - A_0}$$

$$= \frac{(A_1 - A_0)/(1 - b_d)}{A_1 - A_0} = \frac{1}{1 - b_d}$$

This is exactly the result given in Chapter 9, except that b is used in place of MPC to represent the marginal propensity to consume domestic output.

Once this multiplier is established, finding the net tax multiplier is easy. Suppose that net taxes change by an amount ΔT. From Equation 10A.8, it is apparent that the resulting shift in the aggregate nominal demand schedule will be $\Delta A = -b\Delta T - m\Delta T$. The change in equilibrium income can be found by applying the multiplier to the shift in the aggregate demand curve, which gives:

$$\Delta Y^* = \frac{1}{1 - b_d}\Delta A = -b + m\frac{1}{1 - b_d}\Delta T \text{ or } -b + m\ \frac{1}{1 - b_d}\Delta T.$$

Simplifying the last expression on the right:

$$\Delta Y^* = \frac{-b + m}{1 - b_d}\Delta T, \text{ or } \Delta Y = -\frac{b_d}{1 - b_d}\Delta T.$$

The net tax multiplier is thus equal to $-\dfrac{b_d}{1 - b_d}$ or $-\dfrac{MPC_D}{1 - MPC_D}$ as given in the text.

Problem 2 Suppose that $a = 100$, $b = 0.75$, $T = 100$, $I = 110$, $G = 150$, $X = 125$, and $M = 65 + 0.15(Y - T)$. What is the equilibrium value of aggregate nominal demand?

Note: $b - m = 0.75 - 0.15 = 0.6$.

Solution Simply substitute the various values into Equation 10A.7. This gives:

$$Y^* = \frac{1}{(1 - 0.6)}[100 - 0.75(100) + 110 + 125 + 125 - (-65 - 15)]$$

$$= 2.5(360)$$

$$= \$900.$$

Compare this result with Exhibits 9.3 and 9.4, which provide graphical and numerical solutions to the same problem.

Problem 3 Suppose that, initially, all variables and constants have the values given in Problem 2 but that the government adopts a target value for nominal national income of $1,200. Assuming no change in taxes, how much will government purchases have to be in order to reach the income target?

Solution Substitute the known values for a, b, T, I, X, and M into Equation 10A.7, leaving G as the unknown. Use the target income of $1,200 in place of Y^*. This gives:

$$1,200 = 2.5[100 - 0.75(100) + 110 + 150 - 75 + G].$$

Solve for G as follows:

$$1,200 = 525 + 2.5G$$

$$2.5\,G = 675$$

$$G = 270.$$

C H A P T E R 11

CHARTERED BANKS AND OTHER FINANCIAL INTERMEDIARIES

WHAT YOU WILL LEARN IN THIS CHAPTER

This chapter provides an introduction to the financial sector of the economy. It explains how banks, thrift institutions, insurance companies, pension funds, and securities markets operate as financial intermediaries to channel funds from savers to investors. Because banks will play a particularly important role in the subsequent analysis, the balance sheets of Canadian chartered banks are discussed here in some detail. The chapter also introduces the Bank of Canada, which plays an important role in regulating the Canadian banking system and in conducting monetary policy.

FOR REVIEW

Here are some important terms and concepts that will be put to use in this chapter. If you do not understand them, review them before proceeding.
- *Circular flow of income and product (Chapter 5)*
- *Nominal and real interest rates (Chapter 7)*

This chapter is the first of four devoted to the financial sector of the Canadian economy. This sector consists of a set of markets that provide the monetary and financial arrangements necessary to facilitate the production and distribution of real goods and personal services.

Financial Intermediaries The chapter focuses on the important institutions in the financial sector that are know as **financial intermediaries** because of their role in channeling funds from savers to investors. Financial intermediaries include chartered banks, credit unions and caisses populaires, insurance companies, securities markets, and a number of other institutions. They are a necessary part of the economy because the needs of individual lenders and individual borrowers do not necessarily match in terms of quantity of funds, time horizons, or attitudes toward risk.

The job of financial intermediaries is to reconcile the diverse interests of lenders and borrowers. For example, intermediaries can pool the funds of

Financial intermediary Any financial institution that performs the function of channeling funds from savers to investors.

many small savers and use the proceeds to make large loans. They can tap the steady stream of funds flowing through the chequing accounts of households and firms (funds that remain in these accounts for only a few days or weeks at a time) and use them as a basis for extending long-term loans. And, as will be shown, they can reconcile the needs of people who want to borrow in order to undertake somewhat risky investments with the needs of people who want to find relatively risk-free uses for their savings.

Financial Intermediaries in the Circular Flow   Exhibit 11.1 shows the place of financial intermediaries in the circular flow of income and product. This exhibit is similar to Exhibit 5.4, except that it has additional arrows to show flows both into and out of the markets in which financial intermediaries operate. The large arrow from households to financial markets

Exhibit 11.1
The circular flow with financial intermediaries
This diagram of the circular flow of income and product features the role of the financial intermediaries that operate in the economy's financial markets. Their role is to channel funds from savers to investors. Households are net savers, as shown by the large arrow; but they also do some borrowing. Businesses are net borrowers, but they also do some saving. Units of government run deficits (borrow) in larger amounts than they run surpluses (save).

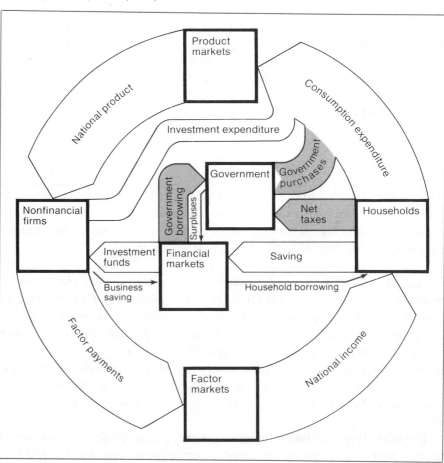

indicates that households are net lenders; but, as the small arrow from credit markets to households indicates, they do some borrowing. Non-financial business firms, on the other hand, are net borrowers, although they do provide loanable funds to financial markets in lesser amounts than their borrowings, as shown by the smaller arrow. Similarly, the government sector is on the average a net borrower, because government budget deficits tend to be larger than surpluses. However, the units of government that do run budget surpluses are a source of funds to financial markets.

Now that the general introduction to the function of financial intermediaries has been given, the chapter will consider the various major classes of intermediaries one by one. It will begin with chartered banks.

CHARTERED BANKS

Chartered banks are financial intermediaries that accept a wide variety of deposits from firms and households and in turn make loans to the public in a wide variety of forms. They are, in many respects, the most important and least specialized of financial intermediaries. In Canada the name "bank" can be used only by institutions that obtain a special charter from Parliament and operate under the Bank Act (a requirement that may be dropped when the Bank Act is revised). This makes them subject to control by the Bank of Canada. It also gives them the right to accept deposits for chequing purposes and to transfer such cheques from one bank to another through clearing houses maintained by the Canadian Payments Association.

The best way to get an idea of how chartered banks operate is to look at their total balance sheet. This will make it clear just where the funds handled by banks come from and where they go.

A Balance Sheet for Chartered Banks

Exhibit 11.2 shows the consolidated balance sheet of Canada's chartered banks as of December 31, 1979. Like all balance sheets, this one is divided into two columns. The left-hand column lists all the banks' *assets* — all the things to which the banks hold legal claim. The right-hand column shows the banks' *liabilities* — all the claims held against the banks by outsiders — and their *net worth* — the difference between assets and liabilities. Net worth represents claims against the banks' assets by the owners of the banks. It includes shareholders' equity and reserves for losses.

Because of the way the terms are defined, the right-hand and left-hand columns exactly balance — hence the *balance sheet*. For all balance sheets, whether of banks or of any other financial unit or aggregate, it must always be true that

Assets = Liabilities + Net worth.

The balance sheet shows that most of the assets held by banks are financial claims against others. These claims are mostly loans granted to individuals and businesses, and securities issued by business and federal, provincial, and municipal governments. On the liability side of the balance sheet, the biggest items are demand and notice deposits, which are claims

Exhibit 11.2

Consolidated balance sheet of chartered banks, December 31, 1979 (in billions of dollars)

This table shows the consolidated balance sheet for all the Canadian chartered banks. Listed as assets are all the things that the banks own. Liabilities are all claims against the banks' assets held by individual firms or institutions other than the banks' owners. The banks' net worth is obtained by subtracting liabilities from assets.

Assets		Liabilities and Net Worth	
Bank of Canada reserve deposits and notes	6.5	Canadian demand deposits	22.3
Mortgages	18.1	Canadian savings or notice deposits	98.3
Loans to Canadians	84.8	Deposits held by foreigners	85.0
Loans to foreigners	38.4		
Canadian securities	18.2	Other liabilities	16.4
Foreign securities	5.8	Total liabilities	222.0
Deposits with foreign banks	35.2	Net worth	7.2
Other assets	22.2		
Total assets	229.2	Total liabilities plus net worth	229.2

Source: *Bank of Canada Review*, February 1980, p. S32–S34, S45.

against the bank owned by depositors. The net worth figure represents what would be left to the owners of the bank if they were to sell all their assets and pay off all their liabilities at "book" values.

Reserves

Reserves (of chartered banks) Money held by chartered banks as cash or non-interest-bearing deposits with the Bank of Canada.

The **reserves** item on the asset side of the balance sheet deserves some further explanation. Historically, the reason that banks hold some of their assets in the form of reserves is that at any moment depositors may want to withdraw their money from the bank, either by writing a cheque to someone who will deposit it in another bank, or by walking up to the teller's window and asking for currency. In the Canadian banking system today, the quantity of reserves that banks hold is not left up to the judgment of individual bankers. Instead, the Bank Act sets certain reserve requirements for chartered banks. These take the form of fixed percentages of deposits that banks must hold as reserves. These percentages are called **required reserve ratios**. They vary according to the type and size of deposits, and are set down in the Bank Act, which is reviewed every ten years. The rates set at the time of the last review, in 1967, are 12 percent for demand deposits and 4 percent for notice deposits. The Bank Act Review of 1977 was delayed several years because of strong reactions by various financial institutions to suggested amendments. The new act is expected to be in place by 1981.

Required reserve ratios Legally required minimum quantities of reserves, expressed as ratios of reserves to various types of deposits.

THE BANK OF CANADA

Canada's central bank is a child of the Depression. In 1933 the federal government responded to growing demands for better monetary leadership in typical Canadian fashion, by appointing a Royal Commission to investigate the situation and make recommendations to the government. The commission made its report that same year and recommended the establishment of a central bank for Canada. Early in 1934, in remarkably quick fashion, Parliament acted on these recommendations and passed the Bank of Canada Act, thereby establishing a central bank for Canada.

Initially all shares of the Bank of Canada were sold to the public, making it a private bank. The first governor, Graham Towers, and the directors of the Bank were appointed by the government, but provision was made for future election of the directors by the private shareholders. However, political pressure developed to make the Bank more subject to government control. Therefore, in 1936, the federal government acquired 51 percent of the Bank's shares, and in 1938 it bought the rest. The Bank of Canada thereby became a true government bank.

Structure of the Bank of Canada

The structure of the Bank of Canada is quite simple. The Bank is managed at the top by a Board of Directors, consisting of the governor, the senior deputy governor, and twelve directors. The deputy minister of finance is also on the board as a non-voting member. The directors are appointed for three-year terms by the minister of finance, with the approval of the federal cabinet. Unlike the Federal Reserve System in the United States, the Bank of Canada does not have formal regional divisions, but the directors on the board are usually chosen on a regional basis, and periodical meetings are held across the country. In addition, the bank has branch offices in all major Canadian cities.

The governor and senior deputy governor are appointed by the board of directors, with cabinet approval, to seven-year terms. An executive committee, consisting of the governor, senior deputy minister, and two directors selected by the board, plus the nonvoting deputy minister of finance, is the real power within the Bank and meets weekly to implement board policy. The full board is called together at least eight times a year to review and ratify policy.

From its establishment in 1934 to the present day, the Bank of Canada has had only four governors. The first governor was Graham F. Towers, a native of Montreal and an economist and accountant by training. He served longer than any other governor, from 1934 to 1954, and developed for the Bank of Canada a worldwide reputation for monetary responsibility and imaginative direction. International recognition of his work led to his appointment as alternate governor of the International Monetary Fund from 1946 to 1954. In the post-World War II period, Towers followed an expansionary policy and maintained low interest rates in order to stimulate investment. He was criticized in the early 1950s for not fighting growing signs of inflation with a more restrictive policy, but he remained primarily concerned with the possibility of recession.

His successor, James Coyne, a lawyer and a native of Winnipeg, was criticized in the late 1950s for following a much more restrictive course at a time when the government and many economists felt that the economy needed some stimulation. The Minister of Finance, Donald Fleming, asked Coyne to change course, and when Coyne refused the minister asked for his resignation. Coyne refused to resign, whereupon the government initiated action in Parliament to declare his office vacant. After an appearance before the Senate and before being evicted by the government, Coyne did resign, on July 13, 1961.

Graham F. Towers (1897–1975)

James Coyne (1910–   )

Louis Rasminsky (1908–   )

Gerald K. Bouey (1920–   )

James Coyne was succeeded by the third governor, Louis Rasminsky, an economist from Montreal. Upon taking the office, he publicly declared that, while the Bank of Canada has the responsibility for monetary policy, if the government disapproves of this policy and asks the Bank to change it, the governor of the Bank is faced with only one choice: he must either change his mind and follow the government's advice, or resign.

When the Bank Act was revised in 1967, it provided for closer and more continuous consultation between the minister of finance and the governor of the Bank of Canada and clarified the steps to be taken in case of a disagreement.

The fourth and current governor, Gerald K. Bouey, an economist from Saskatchewan, took over from Louis Rasminsky in 1973. About the time that Governor Bouey assumed his duties, Canada came to be plagued by unusually high rates of inflation *and* unemployment. The years since 1973 have been marked by a vigorous debate among economists and government advisers about which of these problems poses the greater danger to the Canadian economy. The Economic Council of Canada has often given more weight to the unemployment problem and has urged the government to take steps to stimulate the economy. The governor of the Bank of Canada, obviously in harmony with the various ministers of finance, has placed greater stress on the inflation problem and, in the last few years of the decade particularly, has attempted to follow a fairly restrictive monetary policy.

The Bank of Canada is expected to formulate and execute monetary policy for Canada, and it is designed to be fairly free from political interference. When it attempts, for example, to control inflation by cutting down on the amount of money that people have to spend, it may run into considerable opposition from members of the public. The government will then be pressured into changing the Bank's policy. It obviously wouldn't do for the Bank to give in to such pressure whenever it develops. The governors of the Bank of Canada have tried to maintain a certain tradition of independence, especially the second governor, James Coyne, who refused to follow government policy and was eventually forced to resign (see the profile of the governors).

The government, of course, as the sole shareholder of the Bank, and as the body that is responsible for overall economic policy, has ultimate control over the Bank. There is regular, close consultation between the minister of finance and the governor, and in case of serious disagreement, it is clearly the minister who holds the upper hand. Some argue that the Bank should be a mere arm of government, a division of the Treasury, since the elected representatives of the government are answerable to the people and should formulate all economic policy for the country. Despite this view, it has been considered advisable to give the Bank as much independence as possible.

The work of the Bank is carried out through several departments, including Securities (to handle open-market operations), Research, and International Transactions. Through its nationwide network of offices and its role as the ultimate clearing agency, the Bank not only manages to regulate monetary operations in the country, but it is one of the few government agencies that regularly produces a surplus on its operations.

The chartered banks are required to submit regular reports on their operations to the minister of finance and the Bank of Canada. Their most closely watched duty is to keep reserve deposits with the Bank of Canada. The importance of reserve deposits will be discussed in more detail in Chapter 12.

THE BANKING SYSTEM

The Canadian banking system consists (in early 1980) of eleven chartered banks. It resembles the British system and is very different from the banking system of the United States, which has 15,000 separate banks. Amalgamation of banks, and the creation of a branch system such as ours, has been discouraged in the United States. The power of large branch banks is feared, and the objective has been to make the banks serve the needs of industry in local communities. In Canada we have only a few banks with about 7,500 branches. The emphasis has been on consolidation and safety. Managers are moved around frequently to prevent a local branch from losing its objectivity in advancing loans to local business. Credit unions and other financial institutions have often taken advantage of this situation by providing the kind of local service that small banks in the U.S. provide.

The chartered banks of Canada play an extremely important role in the economy, and they have done so with admirable success. There has not been a bank failure since 1923. The kind of bank crisis described in Arthur Hailey's novel *The Money Changers*, in which an individual bank is brought close to bankruptcy when depositors panic and withdraw their money, could hardly occur in this country. No branch bank would be left on its own to weather a run on its deposits.

Exhibit 11.3 illustrates the large assets built up by some of the banks, and their relative positions. The top five banks hold about 90 percent of the assets and play a major role in determining economic activity in the country. The combined assets of all the banks in November 1978 were $184.9 billion, or about 80 percent of Canada's gross national product.

Exhibit 11.3
Assets of the chartered banks, 1979

Bank	Millions of Dollars	Percentage of Total
Royal Bank of Canada	$51,722	23.5%
Canadian Imperial Bank of Commerce	45,995	20.9
Bank of Montreal	38,180	17.3
Bank of Nova Scotia	34,869	15.8
Toronto Dominion Bank	28,209	12.8
National Bank of Canada	15,475	7.0
Mercantile Bank of Canada	3,109	1.4
Bank of British Columbia	2,000	0.9
Others	500[a]	0.4

[a] Figure approximate.

Source: *The Financial Post 500: The 1980 Ranking of Canada's 500 Largest Companies* (June 14, 1980), p. 96.

NONBANK FINANCIAL INTERMEDIARIES

Banks are by no means the only financial institutions active in the economy. Many other institutions—including trust and mortgage-loan companies, credit unions and caisses populaires, and consumer loan companies—perform some, although not all, of the same functions that banks do. In particular, these institutions function as go-betweens for savers with funds to lend and investors with the need to borrow. For this reason they are considered financial intermediaries, as are banks.

Exhibit 11.4 illustrates the important role played by some of these intermediaries, as well as the chartered banks, in providing loans and mortgages to private persons. (The chartered banks extend many other forms of credit in addition to those listed here, including more than $34 billion dollars in business loans in 1978. Life insurance companies also provide funds to business and to other institutions through the purchase of securities.)

The various financial intermediaries can be classified into several groups: near-banks, contractual savings institutions, and securities markets.

Near-Banks

Near-banks Institutions that accept deposits on which cheques can be written but that are not chartered banks and not subject to direct Bank of Canada control.

The most familiar financial intermediaries, after the chartered banks, are the so-called **near-banks**. They include trust and mortgage-loan companies, credit unions, caisses populaires, and the Quebec savings banks. These institutions accept deposits on which cheques can be written, but they are currently not subject to reserve requirements with the Bank of Canada. With some exceptions, they are subject to provincial regulations. In recent years, credit unions alone have accounted for personal or consumer loans to Canadians equal to more than 25 percent of the loans issued by chartered banks.

Contractual Savings Institutions

Contractual savings institutions Financial intermediaries such as insurance companies and pension funds, to which individuals and groups commit savings on a long-term, contractual basis.

Contractual savings institutions are financial intermediaries such as insurance companies and pension funds, to which individuals and groups commit savings on a long-term, contractual basis. More savings are committed to such institutions annually than to the near banks. Since the important role played by these institutions is not always clearly understood, a further description of some of their functions is in order.

Exhibit 11.4
Selected loans of major financial institutions, 1978 (end of period)

	Millions of Dollars	
Types of Institutions	Consumer Loans	Mortgage Loans
Chartered banks	$21,575	$15,162
Credit unions and caisses populaires	5,490	11,429
Trust and mortgage companies	650	28,954
Sales finance and consumer loans corporations	3,073	–
Life insurance companies	1,367	1,024

Source: *Bank of Canada Review*, December 1979, pp. 538, 578, 580, 590. Data for 16 life insurance companies only.

The Insurance Industry The insurance industry is really two industries. One part of the business of an insurance company is selling protection against risk. The other is operating as a financial intermediary.

Risk Protection Insurance companies sell protection against risk on the principle that although exposure to risk is inherently unpredictable for any single individual, it is highly predictable for large numbers of individuals. No family, for example, can be certain that its house will not burn down during the coming year. An insurance company, however, can predict quite accurately, on the basis of past experience, that (say) one in every thousand houses in a given type of neighborhood will burn down each year. Knowing this, it can sell insurance. Each family pays a premium each year equal to a thousandth of the value of its house, and the pool of funds thus collected is used to compensate the unlucky one family in a thousand whose house burns down.

Today, one can buy insurance against risks of almost any kind. Fire insurance, automobile accident insurance, and health insurance are the most common types. All of them protect the buyer against losses that might never occur but that would be very costly if they did.

Life insurance is a very important kind of insurance. Superficially, it differs somewhat from the other kinds of insurance mentioned in that the risk it appears to insure against—death—is something certain to befall everyone. On closer examination, however, it turns out that what life insurance really does is protect the buyer against the risk of *premature* death. Although everyone can be certain of dying sometime, death during any single year is a risk, not a certainty—much like the risk of having a house burn down.

Pensions and annuities are closely related to life insurance. They are arrangements under which a person pays in a premium each year up to a given age, say sixty-five years, and then receives a fixed sum each year until death. In a sense, pensions and annuities insure people against the risk that they will live too long. Pension premiums and benefits are based on participants' average life expectancy at retirement. Those who die sooner than expected will, in a sense, not get their money's worth out of the program. But those who live longer than expected will receive payments totaling more than the value of the premiums they paid in.

Insurance Companies as Financial Intermediaries This picture of what insurance companies do is, of course, an extremely simplified one. If the companies actually paid out benefits as rapidly as they took in premiums, they would not be able to cover administrative expenses, let alone make a profit. In part, insurance companies allow for administrative expenses and profit by charging premiums that are somewhat higher than the level dictated by the exact probability of risk. (In the earlier example, this would mean collecting from each purchaser of a fire insurance policy somewhat more than a thousandth of the value of the insured home.) But insurance companies and pension funds have another important source of income as well—namely their operations as financial intermediaries.

Insurance companies are able to operate as financial intermediaries because all insurance involves an element of saving. This results because premiums are collected before benefits are paid out, which generates in the meantime a pool of funds controlled by the insurance company. In the case of life insurance and pension funds, the lag between receipt of premiums and payment of benefits is often particularly long, which gives these companies billions of dollars to put to work in financial markets. The assets of life insurance companies alone are nearly as large as the assets of thrift institutions.

These vast quantities of funds are put to work principally through the purchase of securities such as corporate stocks and bonds. Insurance companies and pension funds also often buy commercial mortgages and sometimes invest directly in real estate. Certain types of life insurance policies also permit policyholders to take out personal loans from these companies at advantageous interest rates.

Securities Markets as Financial Intermediaries

The chapter has frequently mentioned government and corporate securities — bills, bonds, stocks, mortgage notes, and the like — without mentioning a further important class of financial intermediaries — the markets in which such securities are bought and sold. These institutions too play an important role in channeling savings from households to business and government borrowers. Conceptually, the securities markets can be divided into two classes — primary and secondary.

Primary Markets Primary securities markets are those in which new borrowing takes place. Suppose, for example, General Motors wants to build a new assembly plant or testing facility. It might finance the project with a bank loan, but it has an alternative that is often more attractive: it can sell newly issued bonds or stocks to the public. Bonds are a promise to repay a fixed nominal amount at a later date, with periodic interest payments to be made in the meantime. Stocks represent a share in the ownership of the firm, including the right to receive part of future profits in the form of dividends.

A corporation seeking to raise money through the sale of stocks or bonds does not normally approach individual households directly. Instead, it uses the services of brokers and underwriters — specialists in putting individuals and firms with funds to loan in touch with companies wishing to sell newly issued bonds and stocks. Brokers and underwriters thus act as financial intermediaries. Since the purchaser of the new securities may itself be a bank, savings institution, or insurance company, the funds involved may pass through a chain of two or more financial intermediaries on their way from the original saver to the ultimate borrower.

Secondary Markets When most people think of securities markets, however, it is not these primary markets that they have in mind. Instead, they think of highly publicized institutions such as the New York Stock Exchange or Toronto Stock Exchange. These exchanges are *secondary* markets; they stand in relation to the primary markets discussed above exactly as used car dealers stand in relation to new car dealers. The sellers in secondary security markets are typically not themselves issuers but instead are savers or financial institutions who own and now wish to sell stocks or bonds issued by firms or government units at some time in the past.

Strictly speaking, then, secondary security markets are not financial intermediaries. Rather than channeling money from savers to investors, they permit savers to exchange "used" securities for money or money for securities. Indirectly, however, these markets are very important to the operation of the economy's system of financial intermediaries. They give households, banks, thrift institutions, insurance companies, pension funds, and all the rest a much-needed flexibility in their financial operations.

A corporation makes a long-term financial commitment when it uses a new bond or share of stock, but the buyer need not make an equally long-term commitment. Because the secondary market with its network of brokers is always there, the buyer can resell the security tomorrow, obtaining cash to spend on goods, services, or some different kind of asset.

CONCLUSIONS

This chapter has wandered rather far from macroeconomic policy — but for a reason. Chartered banks and other financial intermediaries play a crucial role in regulating the circular flow of income and product, which is what macroeconomic policy seeks to stabilize. The focus here has been on their functions in channeling funds from savers to investors. The next chapter will look at the function of banks as creators of money and at the Bank of Canada as the regulator of the money supply.

SUMMARY

1. Financial intermediaries are institutions that channel funds from savers to investors. They are a necessary part of the circular flow of income and product because the needs of individual lenders and borrowers do not necessarily match in terms of quantity of funds, length of commitment, and degree of risk.
2. Chartered banks are the least specialized and most important class of financial intermediary. They accept demand deposits, savings deposits, and time deposits from households and firms and earn income by making loans and purchasing securities. Banking practices are regulated by the Bank Act and by federal and provincial regulatory bodies. One of the most important Bank Act regulations is that chartered banks must maintain reserves with the Bank of Canada.
3. A number of nonbank financial intermediaries also operate in the Canadian economy. They include savings institutions, insurance companies, and organized securities markets. Each plays an important role in channeling funds from savers to investors.

DISCUSSION QUESTIONS

1. Do you have a chequing or savings account in a local chartered bank? If so, go to that bank (and if not, go to any convenient chartered bank) and ask for a copy of

its most recent balance sheet. Compare the balance sheet for your bank with the consolidated chartered bank balance sheet shown in Exhibit 11.2.

2. Go to your library and look at a recent issue of the *Bank of Canada Review*. Use the data in the section of tables at the back of the issue to update the chartered bank balance sheet shown in Exhibit 11.2. Also examine the detailed breakdowns of loans, securities, and so on into particular subcategories.

3. Do you maintain an account at a local trust company or credit union? If so, see if you can obtain a copy of that institution's balance sheet. (If not, obtain the balance sheet of any convenient savings institution.) Compare it to the balance sheet for the chartered bank that you obtained for Question 1.

4. What kinds of insurance do you carry: health insurance? auto insurance? life insurance? If it is convenient, call your insurance agent and ask for a copy of your insurance company's balance sheet. What kinds of assets and liabilities does it hold? Compare this balance sheet to that of a chartered bank.

5. Go to your library and find a recent copy of the business section of the *Globe and Mail*. Look carefully through the ads and the columns and tables relating to stock and bond markets. Which items refer to secondary markets? (Hint: the Dow-Jones Industrial Average is one such item. It is an average of industrial stock prices on the New York Stock Exchange, which is a secondary market.) Which items refer to primary markets? (Hint: look for individual advertisements mentioning the sale of new stocks or bonds, or look for daily or weekly columns discussing new issues in the stock and bond markets.)

SUGGESTIONS FOR FURTHER READING

Boreham, Gordon F., et al. *Money and Banking: Analysis and Policy in a Canadian Context*. 2nd ed. Toronto: Holt, Rinehart and Winston, 1979.
A comprehensive description of Canada's banking system and banking policy.

C H A P T E R 12

THE SUPPLY OF MONEY

WHAT YOU WILL LEARN IN THIS CHAPTER

This chapter is about money—what it is, how it is created by the banking system, and how the Bank of Canada controls the quantity of it in circulation. The first section examines the thorny problem of how to define and measure the stock of money in the economy. The next, through a series of examples based on a simplified banking system, shows how chartered banks create money on the basis of reserves supplied by the Bank of Canada. The final section discusses the policies used by the Bank of Canada to control the money supply and shows why these policies are not always completely reliable.

FOR REVIEW

Here are some important terms and concepts that will be put to use in this chapter. If you do not understand them, review them before proceeding.
- *Assets, liabilities, and balance sheets (Chapter 11)*
- *Currency, demand deposits, and notice (term and savings) deposits (Chapter 11)*
- *Chartered banks and other financial intermediaries (Chapter 11)*
- *The Bank of Canada (Chapter 11)*

Chapter 11 emphasized the role of banks and savings institutions as financial intermediaries. In that capacity, they play a crucial role in channeling investment funds from savers to investors, thereby lowering transaction costs and facilitating the circular flow of income and product. The chapter also introduced the Bank of Canada, concentrating on its regulation of banks in their role as financial intermediaries. But there is much more to be said about the role of banks and the Bank of Canada in the economy. In fact, the most important function of these institutions is one that has not been mentioned yet.

To be specific, nothing has yet been said about the role of banks and the Bank of Canada in the creation of money. In fact, no formal definition of *money* has been given. This chapter will fill the gap by explaining what money is, where it comes from, and how its supply is controlled by the Bank of Canada. The next two chapters will then return to the theory of national income determination, showing how monetary policy is used side by side with fiscal policy in pursuit of the goals of economic stabilization.

MONEY AND ITS FUNCTIONS

Money Anything that serves as a unit of account, a medium of exchange, and a store of purchasing power.

Money can best be defined in terms of what it does. It serves as a means of payment, a store of purchasing power, and a unit of account. Its physical form is of secondary importance; gold, beaver skins, paper currency, and electronic bookkeeping records have all been found serviceable at various times and places because each has served these three central functions.

Means of Payment As a means of payment, money keeps transaction costs low and makes it possible to avoid the inconvenience of barter. Because it performs this function, we do not have to find out what the dentist wants for dinner before we get our teeth fixed. Instead of taking a dozen eggs or a side of bacon with us, we take money; and the dentist stops off at the supermarket on the way home to pick up whatever looks good.

Store of Purchasing Power As a store of purchasing power, money makes it possible to arrange economic activities conveniently through time. Income and expenditures thus need not be synchronized exactly. Instead, a stock of money can be kept on hand to dip into if expenditures run ahead of income or to add to if income runs ahead of expenditures.

Unit of Account Finally, and perhaps most importantly, as a unit of account, money makes it possible to measure and record economic stocks and flows in consistent terms. Movies, apples, and shirts cannot be added together to get gross national product; but dollars' worth of movies, dollars' worth of apples, and dollars' worth of shirts can be added up to get GNP measured in dollars.

Money as a Liquid Asset

Economists refer to all the things of value that people own as assets. A typical household's assets might include a house, a car, other personal possessions, maybe a few stocks or bonds, and, of course, some money. All assets serve to one degree or another as stores of purchasing power, because they can be sold and the proceeds can be used to buy something else.

Money, however, has two important properties that no other asset has to the same degree. First, money itself can be used as a means of payment without first having to be exchanged for something else. Second, it never experiences a gain or loss in nominal value. The nominal value of a house or a bond or a share of corporate stock can go up or down for any number of reasons, but the nominal value of a dollar is always a dollar. The constancy of the nominal value of money is a consequence of the fact that money is itself the unit of account in terms of which nominal values are defined.

Liquid Description of an asset that can be used as a means of payment or easily converted to a means of payment without risk of gain or loss in nominal value.

Because it can be used directly as a means of payment, and because its nominal value never changes, money is said to be **liquid**. No other asset is as liquid as money, although some assets can be exchanged for money quickly and easily, with little danger of a change in their nominal value, and are thus fairly liquid.

MEASURING THE QUANTITY OF MONEY

For the purpose of economic policy, it is important to know not only what money is but also how much money there is in the economy at any time. In all modern economies, the quantity of money in circulation is controlled by government.

Types of Money

In modern economies, there are two things that perform all three of the basic functions of money: currency and demand deposits. By **currency** we mean coins and paper money. **Demand deposits** are the accounts in chartered banks that we commonly call chequing accounts. By conventional definition, money is held only by households and firms other than banks. No currency or demand deposits that belong to the Bank of Canada or chartered banks are included in the definition of money. When we speak of the economy's stock of money in this book, this is what we mean: the total currency outside banks plus the public's holdings of demand deposits in chartered banks. This total is generally called M_1.

Some other assets closely resemble money. Of these, the most important are **notice deposits** in chartered banks. By notice deposits we mean term and savings deposits. Some economists think that when we total up the economy's money stock we should add these in too. When this is done, the total is called M_2. Exhibit 12.1 shows us the total amount of each component of the money stock for Canada, according to recent data.

Currency outside Banks

Since 1945, the Bank of Canada has been solely responsible for issuing the nation's currency. Prior to 1945, this privilege was shared with the chartered banks. Before the establishment of the Bank of Canada in 1934, the federal government and the chartered banks were in charge of currency issues.

Paper money and coins are no longer backed by any intrinsically valuable commodity. The Bank of Canada will not give anything in exchange for a

Currency Coins and paper money.

Demand deposits Deposits at chartered banks that permit the depositor to make payments to others by writing a cheque against the deposit. Demand deposits are what we commonly call chequing accounts.

M_1 The money supply defined as currency plus demand deposits in chartered banks.

Notice deposits Interest-paying accounts at chartered banks agaist which it is not ordinarily possible to write cheques.

M_2 The money supply defined as M_1 plus notice (savings and term) deposits at chartered banks.

Exhibit 12.1
Components of money and near-money, January 1980 (billions of current dollars)
Money takes several forms in the Canadian economy. Currency held by the public, and private demand deposits, fully perform all three of the major functions of money. Together they are called M_1. Savings, term, and notice deposits act as stores of value but generally not as means of payment. Such "near-money" plus M_1 is called M_2.

Type	Amount in circulation
Currency outside banks	$9.1
Demand deposits	14.8
Money supply M_1	23.9
Non-personal term, notice, and personal savings deposits	67.0
Money supply M_2	90.9

Source: *Bank of Canada Review*, February 1980, p. S44.

$10 bill other than $10 in paper money and/or coins—another promise to pay. Until the beginning of World War II, the Bank of Canada supported the currency with gold. It was required to hold the equivalent of 25 percent of its note and deposit liabilities in gold. This provision was suspended during the war, because the money supply had to be increased substantially to support the war effort. The requirement was abolished in 1967. We now have a currency whose value is based entirely on the public's faith in its ability to exchange it for all kinds of goods and services.

Demand Deposits

Demand deposits are bookkeeping entries of chartered banks. They represent obligations of these banks to their depositiors. As shown in Exhibit 12.1, demand deposits account for some 62 percent of the money supply (M_1), but this figure actually understates their importance. Demand deposits turn out to be used to conduct some 90 percent of the dollar volume of all transactions in the economy. Although demand deposits are issued by chartered banks, there are limits on the volume of such deposits that banks can create. We shall discuss these limits shortly.

Near-Money

Near-money Assets that are less than perfectly liquid but still liquid enough to be reasonably good substitutes for money.

Currency, demand deposits, and savings deposits are only three of a great many kinds of assets held by households and firms. Some of the other assets are sufficiently liquid that they are known as **near-money**. It should be noted that savings deposits at nonbank financial institutions, such as credit unions and trust companies, hardly differ from savings deposits in chartered banks. Securities such as government bonds, commerical paper, and treasury bills are also very liquid.

Credit and Credit Cards

In their efforts to make transactions ever more convenient for their customers, bankers have succeeded in blurring not only the distinction between money and near-money but also the distinction between money and credit. A case in point is the "plastic money" that almost everyone carries around in purses and billfolds these days—Master Charge cards, Visa cards, and all the rest. But money and credit cards are different things, and it is important to understand why.

What distinguishes a credit card both from money and from near-money is that it is not a store of purchasing power. Instead, it is just a document that makes it easy for its holder to obtain a loan. When you go into a store, present your credit card, and walk out with a can of tennis balls, you have not yet paid for your purchase. What you have done, instead, is borrow money from the bank that issued the credit card. Simultaneously, you have instructed the bank to turn over the proceeds of the loan to the merchant. Later, the bank will send money to the merchant, thus paying for the tennis balls; and later still, you will send money to the bank to pay off the balance on your credit card account.

Although credit cards are not a form of money, a discussion of them is not entirely out of place here. The reason is that credit cards allow households to *economize* on the use of money. If people use credit cards, they do not have to keep as much cash in their billfolds or as large a balance in their chequing accounts as they otherwise would. In this strictly limited sense, it is not altogether wrong to think of credit cards as "plastic money."

THE CREATION OF MONEY BY THE BANKING SYSTEM

The chapter has so far discussed in some detail the problem of how the quantity of money is to be measured. It turns now to the important matter of how the quantity of money is controlled by the Bank of Canada.

Although currency is issued directly by the Bank of Canada, demand deposits — the most important component of the money supply, however measured — are issued by chartered banks. The Bank of Canada's control over the money supply is thus inherently indirect, and it is exercised primarily through its powers to establish reserve requirements and to determine the outstanding amount of member bank reserves. To understand how this control works, we must first understand how money, in the form of demand deposits, is created by the chartered banking system.

A Simplified Banking System

To keep things simple, we will take a vacation from certain complexities of real-world financial markets in this section. Once the major principles governing the supply of money are made clear, we will reintroduce some of the complexities in a discussion of monetary policy.

Our simplified banking system is comprised of just ten banks, all of which are identical in every respect. The liabilities of these banks consist entirely of demand deposits, which are also the only form of money in the system. There is no currency, and the banks have zero net worth. On the other side of the banks' balance sheets, only three kinds of assets are found. The first is reserves, which consist entirely of non-interest-bearing deposits with the Bank of Canada. In addition to reserves, the banks hold two kinds of interest-bearing assets — loans and government securities.

Regulation and Required Reserves The banks in our simple system are subject to regulation by an equally simplified version of the Bank of Canada. The only assets of this simplified Bank of Canada are Canadian government securities, and the only liabilities are bank reserve deposits. All bank demand deposits are subject to a uniform **required reserve ratio** of 10 percent. This means that they are required to hold ten cents in reserves for each dollar of deposits.

Required reserve ratio The fraction of each type of deposit that the Bank of Canada requires chartered banks to hold in the form of non-interest-bearing assets.

Balance Sheet Equilibrium Like any other firms, our simplified banks want to earn the maximum possible profit for their shareholders. The source of their income is interest earned on securities and loans. To maximize profits, then, they want to expand their loans and security holdings to the greatest extent possible. Given the choice between holding assets in the form of non-interest-bearing reserves or interest-bearing loans and securities, they choose loans and securities. They thus tend to expand their loans and securities to the greatest extent they can without violating

Excess reserves Reserves held by chartered banks in excess of required reserves.

their required reserve ratio. In doing so, they try to avoid holding any **excess reserves** — reserves in excess of the required amount. A bank that has expanded loans and security holdings to the maximum extent possible is said to have its balance sheet in equilibrium.

Balance Sheets To further set the stage for our discussion of the banking system's creation of money, we can fill in some numbers in the balance sheets of our simplified chartered banks and of the simplified Bank of Canada. Each of the ten chartered banks will start from the following equilibrium balance sheet position:

Representative Chartered Bank Balance Sheet

Assets			Liabilities	
Reserves:		$10,000	Demand deposits	$100,000
Required	$10,000			
Excess	0			
Loans		45,000		
Securities		45,000		
Total assets		$100,000	Total liabilities	$100,000

The simplified Bank of Canada will begin with a balance sheet that looks like this:

Simplified Bank of Canada Balance Sheet

Assets		Liabilities	
Canadian government securities	$100,000	Chartered bank reserve deposits	$100,000

The Process of Deposit Creation The stage is now set in such a way as to give the Bank of Canada control of the quantity of reserves at chartered banks. This in turn makes it possible for the Bank of Canada to control the quantity of money supplied by the banking system in the form of demand deposits. Suppose, for example, that the Bank of Canada decides to increase the quantity of money available to the economy. Here is how it might typically proceed.

Open market operation A purchase of securities from the public or a sale of securities to the public made by the Bank of Canada for the purpose of altering the quantity of reserves available to chartered banks.

An Open Market Purchase Injecting New Reserves The easiest way for the Bank of Canada to set in motion an expansion of demand deposits is through an **open market operation** — an open market purchase in this case. To be specific, suppose the Bank of Canada's securities department decides to buy $10,000 in securities from a member of the public.

The Bank of Canada pays for these securities with a cheque — a special cheque drawn on itself, not on one of the chartered banks. The seller of the securities deposits this special Bank of Canada cheque in his or her local chartered bank account. To keep track of things, we will call this bank the Alberta Bank. That bank in turn deposits the cheque in its account with the Bank of Canada, at which point the objective of injecting $10,000 of reserves into the system has been accomplished. After all this has taken place, the balance sheets of the Bank of Canada and the Alberta Bank now look like this:

The Bank of Canada

Assets		Liabilities	
Canadian government bonds	$110,000 (+10,000)a	Chartered bank reserve deposits	$110,000 (+10,000)

aHere and in subsequent balance sheets, changes are shown in brackets.

Alberta Bank

Assets			Liabilities	
Reserves at Bank of Canada		$20,000 (+10,000)	Demand deposits	$110,000 (+10,000)
Required	$11,000 (+1,000)			
Excess	9,000 (+9,000)			
Loans		45,000		
Securities		45,000		
Total assets		$110,000 (+10,000)	Total liabilities	$110,000 (+10,000)

Notice how the $10,000 in new reserves at the Alberta Bank is distributed between required reserves and excess reserves. Deposits have gone up by $10,000, which means that the bank must hold $1,000 more in required reserves. The other $9,000 is not required to be held as reserves, so it is listed as excess reserves. The bank is no longer in equilibrium; it can increase its income by putting those reserves to work. What happens when it does is the subject of the next section.

Making a New Loan Suppose that the Alberta Bank decides to put its $9,000 to work by making a new loan of $9,000. It does this simply by crediting $9,000 to the chequing account of the borrower, James Anderson. At the moment the loan is completed, the balance sheet of the bank will look like this:

Alberta Bank

Assets			Liabilities	
Reserves		$20,000	Demand deposits	$119,000 (+9,000)
Required	$11,900 (+900)			
Excess	8,100 (−900)			
Loans		54,000 (+9,000)		
Securities		45,000		
Total assets		$119,000 (+9,000)	Total liabilities	$119,000 (+9,000)

The bank now has $9,000 in new assets (loans) matched by $9,000 in new liabilities (the increase in the borrower's demand deposits). Required reserves have increased sufficiently to maintain a level of 10 percent of deposits. The bank still has excess reserves of $8,100, but it does not make further new loans, because it knows that the situation is only temporary. Anderson did not borrow $9,000 just to leave it sitting idle in his chequing account; he borrowed it to buy a car.

Chequing Away the Proceeds of the Loan Anderson pays for the car by writing a cheque on his account in the Alberta Bank. The dealer from whom he buys the car — Joyce Barnard — has her account at the Brandon Bank.

When Barnard deposits Anderson's Alberta Bank cheque in her Brandon account, the Brandon Bank sends it to the Bank of Canada for collection. The Bank of Canada credits $9,000 to Brandon's reserve account and debits (subtracts) $9,000 from Alberta's reserve account. Then it puts the cheque itself (the actual piece of paper) in the mail so that the Alberta Bank can eventually forward it to Anderson for his personal records. When all these transactions have taken place, the balance sheets of the two banks look like this:

Alberta Bank

Assets			Liabilities	
Reserves		$11,000 (−9,000)	Demand deposits	$110,000 (−9,000)
Required	$11,000 (−900)			
Excess	0 (−8,100)			
Loans		54,000		
Securities		45,000		
Total assets		$110,000 (−9,000)	Total liabilities	$110,000 (−9,000)

Brandon Bank

Assets			Liabilities	
Reserves		$19,000 (+9,000)	Demand deposits	$109,000 (+9,000)
Required	$10,900 (+900)			
Excess	8,100 (+8,100)			
Loans		45,000		
Securities		45,000		
Total assets		$109,000 (+9,000)	Total liabilities	$109,000 (+9,000)

No further changes take place in the Bank of Canada's balance sheet totals.

Now we can see why the Alberta Bank could not loan out more than its initial $9,000 of excess reserves. It knew that the new $9,000 deposit it created by the loan was not likely to stay there for long. As soon as the cheque cleared, Alberta lost $9,000 in total reserves. Its required reserves went down by only $900 (10 percent of the amount of the loss in deposits), so the $8,100 of the excess reserves that Alberta had immediately after making the loan was needed to make up the difference.

Buying Securities When all transactions were completed, the Alberta Bank ended up with $10,000 more in deposits and $10,000 more in assets.

But that is not the end of the story. The $8,100 in excess reserves that the bank lost did not disappear from the banking system. The Brandon Bank's excess reserves rose by exactly the same amount that Alberta's fell. Brandon gained $9,000 in deposits and $9,000 in reserves, of which only $900 were required reserves. The remaining $8,100 became excess reserves for Brandon.

Although the Alberta Bank has now returned to a state of balance sheet equilibrium, the Brandon Bank is out of equilibrium. To increase its earning assets to the maximum, it must put its excess reserves to work. It could, like Alberta, make a new loan, but it decides instead to buy $8,100 in securities. It purchases these securities from a private dealer and pays for them by writing a cheque on its own account. The seller then deposits the cheque in the Cornwall Bank. This time we omit Brandon's intermediate balance sheet showing the situation after the securities are bought but before the cheque is cleared. After the cheque has been cleared through the Bank of Canada, here is what Brandon's and Cornwall's balance sheets look like:

Brandon Bank

Assets			Liabilities	
Reserves		$10,900 (−8,100)	Demand deposits	$109,000
Required	$10,900 (no change)			
Excess	0 (−8,100)			
Loans		45,000		
Securities		53,100 (+8,100)		
Total assets		$109,000	Total liabilities	$109,000

Cornwall Bank

Assets			Liabilities	
Reserves		$18,100 (+8,100)	Demand deposits	$108,100 (+8,100)
Required	$10,810 (+810)			
Excess	7,290 (+7,290)			
Loans		45,000		
Securities		45,000		
Total assets		$108,100 (+8,100)	Total liabilities	$108,100 (+8,100)

The Multiple Expansion of Deposits We really do not have to trace much farther the effects of the Bank of Canada's initial injection of $10,000 of new reserves into the chartered banking system. A clear pattern is beginning to emerge. Bank A received a deposit of $10,000, of which it set aside 10 percent as required reserves and used the remainder to finance a loan of $9,000. Bank B received a deposit of $9,000, of which it set aside 10 percent as required reserves and used the remainder to finance securities purchases of $8,100. Bank C received a deposit of $8,100, of which it put aside $810 as required reserves. It used the remaining $7,290 to finance either loans or securities purchases. (The examples above show that it makes no difference which.) Each bank makes new loans and/or securities purchases equal to 90 percent of the deposit it receives, thereby generating new deposits for the next bank in line. Total new deposits generated by the initial injection of $10,000 of new reserves is thus equal to the sum of the infinite series $10,000 + $9,000 + $8,100 + $7,290 + $6,561 + $5,905 + . . . = $100,000. The whole process is referred to as the multiple expansion of deposits by the chartered banking system.

A Shortcut Just to check what we have learned, we can go back to the beginning and look at the effects of the injection of new reserves, using a shortcut method based on the consolidated balance sheet for all ten member banks. The initial purchase by the Bank of Canada of $10,000 in securities from a member of the public puts $10,000 in new reserves into the banking system. The first bank to get those reserves does not hold on to all of them; it holds only the required portion (10 percent) and passes the remainder on to some other bank. Another 10 percent of these reserves come to rest as required reserves in the second bank, another 10 percent of the remainder in the third, and so on.

The multiple expansion of deposits continues in this way until all reserves have eventually come to rest as required reserves in one bank or another. But no matter how often the reserves are passed from hand to hand, the total increase in the quantity of reserves in the banking system remains $10,000. Total deposits have to rise by enough to convert all of the initial $10,000 of excess reserves into required reserves. With a 10 percent required reserve ratio, this takes $100,000 in new deposits. In the eventual equilibrium position, the consolidated balance sheet for the ten identical member banks looks like this:

**Consolidated Balance Sheet of All Chartered Banks
(Final Position)**

Assets			Liabilities	
Reserves		$110,000 (+10,000)	Demand deposits	$1,100,000 (+100,000)
Required	$110,000 (+10,000)			
Excess	0			
Loans and securities		990,000 (+90,000)		
Total assets		$1,100,000 (+100,000)	Total liabilities	$1,100,000 (+100,000)

Contraction of the Money Supply

If the Bank of Canada withdraws reserves from the simplified banking system, the whole process works in reverse. Suppose, for example, that the Bank of Canada begins by selling $1,000 in securities to a member of the public. The seller pays for the securities with a cheque drawn on the Dalhousie Bank. Dalhousie loses $1,000 in deposits and $1,000 in reserves. That leaves it $900 short of required reserves, as the following balance sheet shows (assuming the same initial balance sheet for the Dalhousie Bank as for all the banks in the previous examples):

Dalhousie Bank

Assets			Liabilities	
Reserves		$9,000	Demand deposits	$99,000
		(−1,000)		(−1,000)
Required	$9,900			
	(−100)			
Excess	−900			
Securities		45,000		
Loans		45,000		
Total assets		$99,000	Total liabilities	$99,000
		(−1,000)		(−1,000)

In order to meet its legal reserve requirements, the Dalhousie Bank must somehow obtain $900 in new reserves. One obvious way to do this is to sell $900 in securities. When someone writes a cheque to pay for these securities, another bank, say the Edmonton Bank, loses $900 in deposits and $900 in reserves, leaving it with an $810 shortfall from required reserves. Edmonton in turn sells securities to meet its requirements, and the operation of the multiple contraction process continues until it causes a total loss of $10,000 in deposits.

The Money Multiplier

We will conclude our analysis of the simplified banking system by drawing an important generalization from both the expansionary and contractionary examples just given: in every case, the ultimate change in total demand deposits (and hence in the total money supply) in the simplified chartered banking system must be equal to the initial change in reserves divided by the required reserve ratio. The ratio of the change in the money supply to the initial change in reserves can be called the **money multiplier** for the banking system. (More precisely, it can be called the demand-deposits-to-total-reserves multiplier.)

In the simplified banking system, the formula for the money multiplier is:

$$\text{Money multiplier} = \frac{1}{\text{Required reserve ratio}}$$

With the required reserve ratio of 0.10 used in the examples, the money multiplier is 10. Hence the $10,000 injection of new reserves results in a $100,000 expansion of the money supply, and a $1,000 withdrawal of reserves results in a $10,000 contraction. Hence,

Change in the money supply = money multiplier × change in reserves.
$100,000   =   10   × $10,000.

Money multiplier The ratio of the quantity of money to the total reserves in a banking system. Various money multipliers can be defined, depending on the definition of money used. In the simplified banking system, the formula for the money multiplier is:

$$\text{Money multiplier} = \frac{1}{\text{Required reserve ratio}}$$

INSTRUMENTS AND PROBLEMS OF MONETARY POLICY

We turn now from the simplified banking system to the real world. On the surface, everything looks similar. Demand deposits still make up the most important part of the money supply, although not all of it. The Bank of Canada still has the power to control bank reserves and to impose reserve requirements. And changes in the total reserves of the banking system still result in multiple expansions or contractions of the money supply.

On closer examination, however, the actual banking system of Canada differs from that of the simplified economy in a number of details, which, taken together, crucially affect both the methods and the success of the Bank of Canada in controlling the nation's money supply.

THE INSTRUMENTS OF MONETARY POLICY

The Bank of Canada uses five major instruments to orchestrate its monetary policy. These are *open market operations* (sales and purchases of government securities in the open market), *moral suasion* (attempts by the Bank of Canada to persuade the chartered banks to follow a certain policy), *draw downs* and *redeposits* (transfers of government deposits between the Bank of Canada and the chartered banks), changes in the *Bank rate* (the interest rate paid by chartered banks to borrow reserve funds from the Bank of Canada), and changes in the *required reserve ratios* for chartered banks.

Open market operations have already been illustrated for the simplified banking system. By the purchase and sale of securities, the Bank of Canada can inject new reserves directly into the banking system or withdraw reserves from it. Something more must be said about the other methods used by the Bank of Canada.

Moral Suasion

Because the number of chartered banks in Canada is so small, the Bank of Canada can easily contact their presidents to obtain their support in implementing a certain policy. This may be done through general discussion or special directives. The Bank of Canada might request that the chartered banks, for example, tighten up on their loans or raise their interest rates. Because of its legal supervisory powers, the Bank of Canada has considerable clout when it engages in such **moral suasion**.

> **Moral suasion** Direct attempts by the Bank of Canada to influence the practices of the chartered banks.

Draw Downs and Redeposits

The federal government has substantial deposits with the Bank of Canada and the chartered banks. With the permission of the minister of finance, the Bank of Canada can transfer government deposits from itself to the chartered banks, thereby increasing the reserves of the banks, or it can reduce those reserves in support of a tight money policy by transferring government deposits from the chartered banks to the Bank of Canada. These **draw downs** and **redeposits** have become one of the most important short-term techniques used by the Bank of Canada in implementing monetary policy.

> **Draw downs and redeposits** Transfer of government deposits between the Bank of Canada and the chartered banks.

The Bank Rate

Another policy instrument that the Bank of Canada can use is the **Bank rate**, or discount rate as it is called in the United States. A rise in the Bank rate, other things being equal, has the effect of discouraging chartered banks from borrowing to augment their reserves. A decline in the Bank rate has the opposite effect.

> **Bank rate** The interest rate paid by chartered banks to borrow reserve funds from the Bank of Canada. Acts as a signal as to desired changes in interest rates charged by chartered banks.

Actually, the chartered banks in Canada rarely borrow from the Bank of Canada to augment their reserves. They can call in loans or sell assets in the market to satisfy the reserve requirements. Changes in the Bank rate act more as a signal to the chartered banks, telling them whether the Bank of Canada would like them to raise or lower their own interest rates. Most market interest rates, including the "prime rate" that chartered banks charge their best customers, tend to follow the Bank rate. In the late 1950s and again in 1980 the Bank of Canada allowed this rate to "float" in relation to the interest rate on short-term government bonds. Since the rate on such bonds is itself affected by the Bank's open market operations, interest rates were still subject to Bank of Canada influence.

Changes in Required Reserve Ratios

The fifth instrument of monetary policy, changing required reserve ratios, is more powerful in the United States than in Canada. In Canada the rates for so-called cash or primary reserves are set when the Bank Act is reviewed. The Bank of Canada actually lost its right to vary primary reserve ratios when the Bank Act was amended in 1967. Instead, it was given the right to establish secondary reserve requirements for the chartered banks, and to vary these requirements. Chartered banks can now be required to hold up to 12 percent of their total Canadian deposits in the form of such liquid, interest-bearing assets as short-term Treasury bills and day-to-day loans. These are the secondary reserves. The Bank of Canada has, since 1967, varied the secondary reserve ratio from 5 to 9 percent.

PRACTICAL PROBLEMS OF MONETARY POLICY

The Bank of Canada has relied on the major tools of monetary policy described in the preceding section to control the growth of the money supply for many years, but only relatively recently has it begun to publicize its monetary growth targets in advance.

During the rapid inflation of 1975, the Governor of the Bank of Canada, Gerald Bouey, followed the example of other central bankers and announced annual growth targets for M_1, the most immediately spendable money. High growth rates in the money supply were linked in the minds of many economists with the rapidly increasing inflation. The target growth rate in the money supply for the first few years was set at 10 percent to 15 percent annually. By the end of 1979 this target had been reduced to a 5 percent to 9 percent annual growth rate.

Despite the variety of policy instruments available, and despite the announced targets, monetary policy in practice is a far more imprecise affair than in the simplified economy described earlier in this chapter. The real world is full of many problems and pitfalls not yet mentioned. As a result, the Bank of Canada, even with the best of intentions, has had only mixed success in meeting the monetary policy objectives it has set for itself.

Variations in Money Multipliers

The key to control over the money supply in the simplified banking system was a fixed money multiplier, equal to the reciprocal of the required reserve ratio on demand deposits. In the real world, the closest equivalent to this multiplier is the so-called M_1-to-total reserves multiplier (the M_1 multiplier, for short). As the name implies, this multiplier is the ratio of M_1 to total reserves of the chartered banking system. It is more complicated and subject to more variation than the money multiplier of our simple banking system.

Structure of Reserve Requirements One major reason for the greater complexity of this real-world money multiplier is that required reserve ratios vary from one kind of deposit to another. Some reserves must be used to support savings deposits that are not counted as part of M_1. Other things being equal, the greater the ratio of savings and time deposits to demand deposits at banks, the lower the M_1 multiplier.

Near-Banks A second major reason for variations in the M_1 multiplier is the existence of near-banks such as trust companies and credit unions. They offer savings and term deposits that compete with those offered by chartered banks, but their deposits are not considered part of the money supply. Hence shifts in deposits among banks and near-banks are also a source of variability in the money multiplier.

Excess Reserves Yet a third reason for variability in the M_1 multiplier is the fact that real-world banks, unlike those in the simplified banking system, cannot always keep their excess reserves exactly at zero. Banks sometimes find it hard to keep up with unexpected deposit flows resulting in excess reserves. Such excess reserves, while only a small amount on average, do show some variation over time.

Currency The Bank of Canada allows chartered banks to count currency on hand (so-called vault cash) as reserves, which means that when individuals or firms withdraw money from their banks in the form of currency, they drain total reserves from the banking system. When this happens, a multiple contraction of the money supply takes place unless the Bank of Canada offsets the shift with an injection of new reserves.

In addition, currency is a form of money that is not a liability of the banking system and thus is not itself subject to reserve requirements. Even if the Bank of Canada maintains the level of reserves, the larger the fraction of their money balances people choose to hold as currency, the larger the M_1 multiplier.

CONCLUSIONS

This chapter has examined in some detail a few questions concerning the supply of money: how the money supply can be measured, how money is created by the banking system, and how the Bank of Canada attempts to exercise control over the money supply. Now it is time to return to a theme sounded briefly at the beginning of the chapter—the relationship between monetary policy and the goals of full employment, price stability, economic growth, and balance of payment stability. It is the importance of money to these goals of stabilization policy, after all, that justifies the attention to technicalities in this chapter.

The next chapter will turn from the supply side of the money market to the demand side. Chapter 14 will examine the effect of variations in money demand and supply on nominal national income and product. Chapters 15 to 17 will show how monetary and fiscal policy together affect the success or failure of stabilization policy as a whole.

SUMMARY

1. Money is defined in terms of what it does. As a unit of account, it allows us to keep accounts and measure aggregate economic magnitudes. As a means of payment, it allows us to escape the inconvenience of barter. And as a store of purchasing power, it helps us arrange our economic activities in an orderly way through time.

2. One traditional definition of money, M_1, includes currency plus demand deposits at chartered banks. Another definition, M_2, adds notice (term and savings) deposits at banks to this total. In addition to the money included in M_1 and M_2, there are other highly liquid assets, such as deposits at savings and loan associations, short-term government securities, credit union shares, money market mutual fund shares, and repurchase agreements. Recent innovations in banking practices have made it necessary to rethink the traditional definitions of money.

3. In a simplified banking system, an injection of new reserves sets off a multiple expansion of deposits and the money supply. Each bank receiving new reserves makes loans or buys securities equal to its excess reserves. In that way, it passes along part of the reserves to the next bank in line. The process continues until deposits have risen enough to convert all the new reserves into required reserves. The ratio of money to reserves is known as the money multiplier.

4. In the actual Canadian banking system, the Bank of Canada has available five main instruments of monetary policy: open market operations (buying and selling securities on the open market), changes in required reserve ratios, changes in the discount rate (the rate charged to chartered banks for loans of reserves), moral suasion (efforts by the Bank of Canada to get the chartered banks to follow a proposed policy), and draw downs and redeposits (transfers of government deposits between the Bank of Canada and the chartered banks).

5. The Bank of Canada's instruments of monetary policy do not give it precise control of the money supply. A major reason is that the money multiplier can change for reasons not under direct control of the Bank of Canada. Shifts of funds from one type of bank to another, from banks to near-banks, from one type of deposit to another within banks, and from deposits to currency can all affect the money multiplier. So can changes in banks' excess reserves. In addition, shifts of funds from chartered bank deposits to currency can alter the total reserves available to the banking system.

DISCUSSION QUESTIONS

1. List the functions that money performs in the economy, and illustrate them with examples of how you yourself have used money for each purpose. Have you ever used something other than money for any of the three purposes?

2. Do you have an account at any bank or other financial institution? If so, is your account part of M_1? Of M_2?

3. Is it possible that with increased use of credit cards we will eventually do away with currency and demand deposits? Explain. Would we be doing away with money if this did occur?

4. Go to your library and look in any back issue of the *Bank of Canada Review*. Where the recent banking data are reported, find the current values for currency, demand deposits, and time deposits at chartered banks. Use these values to update Exhibit 12.1. Next, examine the data given for M_1 and M_2 and the definitions of these quantities. Is the Bank of Canada still using traditional definitions, or has it modified them?

5. Using the same starting position given in the text for the simplified banking system, work through the multiple expansion (or contraction) process for the following policy actions:

   a. An injection of $5,000 in new reserves via an open market purchase.

   b. A withdrawal of $500 in new reserves via an open market sale.

   c. A selective reduction in the required reserve ratio for the Alberta Bank only — from 10 percent to 8 percent. (Assume that once the expansion process gets underway, no one ever deposits new reserves in the Alberta bank but uses only the other nine banks.)

   d. A general reduction in the required reserve ratio for all banks from 10 percent to 8 percent.

6. Go to your library and obtain copies of the *Globe and Mail* business section or the *Financial Post*. Usually, these papers contain short news items or columns reporting weekly changes in the money supply, which the Bank of Canada has announced. What is happening to the money supply? What comments do the papers make regarding Bank of Canada policy? Are any comparisons of actual and target money growth given?

C H A P T E R 13

THE DEMAND FOR MONEY AND THE MONEY MARKET

WHAT YOU WILL LEARN IN THIS CHAPTER

This chapter discusses the determinants of the quantity of money that people wish to hold at any given time — that is, people's demand for money. People value money for its liquidity, but because money normally earns no interest, the nominal rate of interest represents an opportunity cost of holding it. The relationship between the demand for money and the rate of interest can be used to draw a demand schedule for money. This schedule can be combined with the supply of money to show how equilibrium is established in the money market.

FOR REVIEW

Here are some important terms and concepts that will be put to use in this chapter. If you do not understand them, review them before proceeding.
* *Nominal and real interest rates (Chapter 7)*
* *Liquidity (Chapter 12)*
* *Control of the money supply by the Bank of Canada (Chapter 12)*

Chapter 12 defined money, discussed the various things that serve as money and near-monies in the Canadian economy, and explained how the supply of money is determined. This chapter turns first to the determination of the demand for money and then to the interaction of the supply and demand for money in the money market. It will lay the groundwork for the discussion of the interaction of monetary and fiscal policy in Chapter 14.

THE DEMAND FOR MONEY

Portfolio Balance

In discussing the demand for money, as in dealing with other subjects in economics, it is important to distinguish between stocks and flows. The demand for money is the demand for a stock. The question is not one of how much money people would like to spend per day or month — that would be a flow of money — but rather of how large a share of their total wealth people would at any time like to hold in the form of money, as opposed to other forms such as securities, real estate, and consumer durables.

Portfolio balance The idea that people try to maintain a balance among the various kinds of assets they own — including money, consumer durables, stocks, and bonds — shifting from one kind of asset to another as economic conditions change.

Economists find it useful to talk about the demand for money in terms of the concept of **portfolio balance**. A *portfolio* is simply the collection of assets of all kinds that a person owns. Balancing the portfolio means adjusting the proportions of currency, chequing account funds, savings deposits, securities, real estate, and so on to best suit the interests of the portfolio holder.

Liquidity and the Demand for Money

The reason people want to hold at least part of their portfolio in the form of money is that money is liquid. As Chapter 12 explained, liquidity means that money can be used directly as a means of payment and that holding it involves no risk of gain or loss of nominal value. These two aspects of liquidity provide the motives for holding at least part of any portfolio in the form of money.

Transactions motive A motive for holding money arising from the convenience of using it as a means of payment for day-to-day transactions.

The Transactions and Precautionary Motives The most familiar reason for holding money is that it is a quick and convenient way to purchase things. With money on hand, it is not necessary to borrow or to sell some less liquid asset every time a purchase is made. This reason is often called the **transactions motive** for holding money. Generally speaking, people's demand for money for transactions purposes is expected to increase as their nominal incomes increase, other things being equal.

In addition to holding enough money to take care of normal weekly or monthly purchases between paycheques, people may also want to keep some highly liquid reserves on hand for emergency use or to take advantage of unexpected opportunities. Some writers distinguish this from the transactions motive for holding money by calling it the **precautionary motive**. Both the transactions and the precautionary motives arise primarily from the use of money as a means of payment.

Precautionary motive A motive for holding money arising from its usefulness as a reserve of liquid funds for use in emergencies or in taking advantage of unexpected opportunities.

The Speculative Motive In addition to serving as a means of payment, money also protects its holder against any possible loss of nominal value. If portfolio holders have reason to think there may be a decline in the market price of other assets they might hold — such as stocks, bonds, or real estate — it will pay them to hold money instead, at least temporarily. If the expected drop in the nominal value of the other assets does materialize, they will have avoided a possible capital loss. If no further declines are expected, they can purchase the other assets at a bargain price.

Speculative motive A motive for holding money arising from its fixed nominal value, when the nominal value of alternative assets is expected to decline.

Keynes called this the **speculative motive** for holding money, because people holding money for this reason are speculating that the price of other assets will fall. The term has stuck, despite the fact that, in practice, it is difficult to compartmentalize the demand for money into transactions, precautionary, and speculative components.

The Opportunity Cost of Holding Money Offsetting the advantages of holding money — its usefulness as a means of payment and its fixed nominal value — is a major disadvantage. To hold money, one forgoes the opportunity to earn interest. When it is narrowly defined to include only currency and chartered bank demand deposits, money pays no interest at all.

Even when it is more broadly defined to include some interest-earning accounts on which cheques can be written, the interest paid on transaction-type deposits is less than that available on nonmonetary assets.

The proper measure of the opportunity cost of holding money is the nominal rate of interest that could be earned on other assets. As Chapter 7 showed, the nominal rate of interest is equal to the expected real rate of interest plus the expected rate of inflation. Normally, the nominal rate of interest exceeds the expected rate of inflation. Holders of interest-bearing assets thus expect to earn a real return even after allowing for the expected decline in the purchasing power of their funds. Using the nominal rate of interest to represent the opportunity cost of holding money, then, reflects both the lost opportunity to earn a real return and the lost opportunity for protection from expected inflation.

The Demand for Money in a Two-Asset Economy

In order to bring out more clearly some of the essential features of the demand for money, it will be useful to introduce a simplified economy in which there are only two financial assets available to portfolio holders. These assets are money (in the narrow sense of non-interest-bearing currency and demand deposit balances) and long-term bonds.

The Price of Bonds and the Rate of Interest A short digression on the subject of bonds is needed at this point. Bonds are simply IOUs of firms and units of government. They have been mentioned several times without explanation of one of their important features — the relationship between the price of a bond and the rate of interest.

In Canada, long-term corporate bonds are often issued in denominations of $1,000. The issuing firm promises to pay the bondholder a certain sum per year for a certain number of years (usually twenty to thirty years) until maturity and, upon maturity, to repay the initial $1,000. The annual sum the bondholder receives until maturity is set according to the nominal rate of interest prevailing at the time the bond is issued. If the interest rate is 8 percent, the annual payment on a $1,000 bond will be $80; if the interest rate is 10 percent, the payment will be $100; and so on.

As Chapter 11 showed, there are active secondary markets in which bonds of this type can be bought and sold. The original purchaser need not hold the bond until maturity. There is no guarantee, however, that the bond can be sold in the secondary market "at par" — that is, at its original purchase price of $1,000. Instead, the price at which the bond can be resold depends on what has happened to the interest rate between the date of issue and the date of resale.

To illustrate: suppose a certain firm issues a twenty-five-year bond at a time when the nominal interest rate on such bonds is 10 percent, agreeing to pay $100 per year for twenty-five years plus $1,000 on maturity. The original purchase price is $1,000. A year later, the original buyer wants to sell the bond; but in the meantime, the nominal interest rate has gone up to 12.5 percent. That means brand new $1,000 bonds are scaled to pay $125 per year to their purchasers, so no one is willing to buy last year's bond with the $100 payment unless its price is cut to approximately $800—since $100 is 12.5 percent of $800. The original buyer of the bond with the $100 annual payment suffers a capital loss of $200 in selling the bond.

If, instead, the interest rate had fallen, say to 5 percent, new bonds would be paying only $50 per year. In that case, the old bond carrying a $100 annual payment could be sold at a premium in the secondary market—for roughly $2,000, in fact.

Actually, there is a little bit more to calculating how much a bond is worth on the secondary market, because we have not taken into account the fact that all bonds are worth the same $1,000 amount at maturity regardless of the annual payment the bondholder receives in the meantime. That is why the prices in the above examples are stated as approximations. However, as long as we stick to long-term bonds for which the date of maturity lies in the rather distant future, the price of the bond is determined almost entirely by the interaction of the size of the annual payment and the nomimal interest rate. In any event, the important thing to remember is this: *a rise in the nominal rate of interest depresses the price of bonds in the secondary market, and a fall in the nominal rate of interest raises the price of bonds in the secondary market.*

Portfolio Balance in the Simple Economy The quantity of money demanded by the inhabitants of the simplified economy depends on how they decide to balance their portfolios between money and bonds. Two factors can be expected to influence their decision.

First, the higher the nominal income in the simplified economy, the greater the desired quantity of money. The reason is the transactions motive. People's purchases increase when their income increases, so their demand for money also increases.

Second, the higher the nominal rate of interest, the lower the desired quantity of money. There are two reasons for this. One is that a high nominal rate of interest means a high opportunity cost to holding money; holders of money could be earning a high income by holding bonds instead. Second, relative to what has been experienced in the past and what is expected in the future, the higher the rate of interest, the lower the price of bonds. If the price of bonds is perceived as low, people will be inclined to hold more bonds relative to money in the hope that their price will go up and they can be resold for capital gain. Conversely, if the interest rate is low, the price of bonds will be high and people are likely to be reluctant to hold them for fear the price will drop and they will be stuck with a capital loss. In this situation, people will be inclined to hold more of their portfolio in money. The speculative motive for holding money is thus seen to influence people's decisions regarding the balance of their portfolios between bonds and money.

Money demand schedule A schedule showing the quantity of money that people desire to hold in their portfolios given various values for the nominal interest rate and the level of nominal income.

A Money Demand Schedule The quantity of money demanded, then, increases as the nominal interest rate falls and as nominal income increases. The relationship among the amount of money demanded, the interest rate, and the level of nominal income that prevails in a given economy in a given period is known as that economy's **money demand schedule**. Exhibit 13.1 shows what the schedule might look like for the

(a)

Nominal Interest Rate (Percent)	Level of Nominal National Income					
	$200	$400	$600	$800	$1,000	$1,200
2	$120	$240	$360	$480	$600	$720
4	60	120	180	240	300	360
6	40	80	120	160	200	240
8	30	60	90	120	150	180
10	24	48	72	96	120	144
12	20	40	60	80	100	120
14	17	34	51	68	85	102
16	15	30	45	60	75	90

Exhibit 13.1

Money demand schedule for a hypothetical economy

The table and diagram show how the quantity of money demanded varies as the nominal interest rate and the level of nominal income vary in a simplified economy like the one used in these numerical examples. The entries in the body of the table show the quantity of money demanded at the nominal interest rate corresponding to the row and the nominal income corresponding to the column. Each column of the table can be graphed to get a money demand curve like that shown in Part b of the exhibit. The curve MD_1 assumes income to be fixed at $600. A rise in income to $1,200 would shift the money demand curve to the position MD_2.

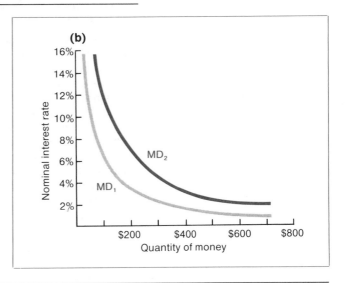

simplified economy. The entries in Exhibit 13.1a give the quantity of money demanded when the interest rate is that indicated at the left-hand border of the table and the level of nominal national income is that shown at the top of the table. For example, when the interest rate is 10 percent per year and the level of nominal national income is $600, the quantity of money demanded is $72.

Exhibit 13.1b gives the money demand schedule in graphical form. At any given level of income, the relationship between the quantity of money demanded and the interest rate can be shown by a downward-sloping curve that looks much like an ordinary demand curve. For example, the curve labeled MD_1 shows the way money demand varies as the interest rate varies when income is $600. This curve is drawn from the data in the $600 column of the table in Part a. A change in the level of income would produce a shift in the money demand curve. For example, if income were to increase to $1,200, the money demand curve would shift to the position labeled MD_2 in the figure. The data given in the last column of the table indicate that when income doubles, the quantity of money demanded at any particular level of the interest rate doubles.

Income Velocity As Exhibit 13.1 is constructed, the ratio of money demanded to nominal income is constant for all levels of income, given a particular rate of interest. For example, when the nominal interest rate is 6 percent, money demand is $1 for each $5 of nominal income. When the interest rate rises to 12 percent, $1 of money is demanded for each $10 of income, and so on.

Sometimes, instead of speaking in terms of the ratio of money demanded to nominal income, economists use its reciprocal. The ratio of nominal income to money demanded is known as the **income velocity of money**. It measures the rate at which money circulates — that is, the number of times each year that the money stock turns over in carrying out transactions involving final goods and services.

Income velocity of money (velocity) The ratio of nominal income to the quantity of money.

Case 13.1
The Demand for Money, Velocity, and Nominal Interest Rates in the Canadian Economy

Exhibit 13.2a presents the relationship between the demand for money (M_1) as a fraction of nominal GNP and the nominal rate of interest on three-month Treasury bills. Exhibit 13.2b shows the relationship between the income velocity of money and this interest rate. Because the income velocity of money is measured here as the ratio of nominal GNP to M_1 (the reciprocal of the ratio shown on the horizontal axis in Exhibit 13.2a), the two parts of the figure are mirror images of one another, showing the same relationship from two points of view.

The relationships shown are much as would be expected. As nominal interest rates have risen over the last thirty years, the demand for money as a fraction of GNP has fallen, and the income velocity of money has risen. In 1979 nominal interest rates jumped sharply to new high levels, partly because of growing inflation in the United States. The rates began to fall in mid-1980.

Exhibit 13.2
Velocity and interest rates in the Canadian economy, 1963–1978

Part a of this exhibit traces the relationship between the demand for money (M_1) as a fraction of GNP and the nominal rate of interest on three-month Treasury bills from 1963 to 1978. Part b shows the relationship between the income velocity of money (measured at the ratio of GNP to M_1) and the same interest rate. The two graphs are mirror images — alternative ways of looking at the same underlying relationship.

Source: Department of Finance, *Economic Review*, April 1980, pp. 263, 268, and previous years.

(a)

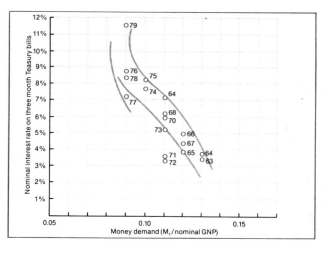

(b)

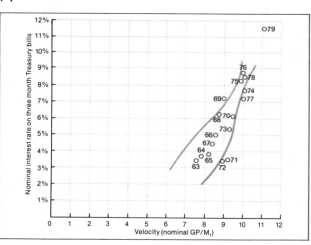

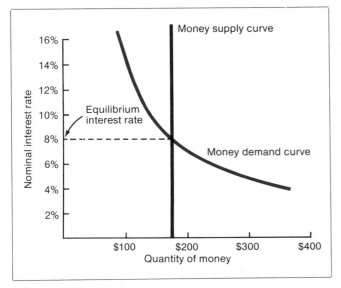

Exhibit 13.3
Equilibrium in the money market
The money demand curve in this diagram is based on the data given in Exhibit 13.1, and it uses an assumed nominal national income of $1,200. The money supply curve assumes a quantity of money supplied of $180. The equilibrium nominal interest rate is 8 percent. At any higher interest rate, an excess quantity of money supplied would put downward pressure on the interest rate. If the interest rate were below equilibrium, there would be an excess quantity of money demanded and upward pressure. Both money supply and money demand are measured in stock terms.

EQUILIBRIUM AND DISEQUILIBRIUM IN THE MONEY MARKET

Now that both the supply and the demand for money have been analyzed, the next step will be to put the two together and investigate the nature of equilibrium and disequilibrium in the money market. Exhibit 13.3 shows the basic diagram that will be used to do this. It contains a downward-sloping demand curve for money (taken from Exhibit 13.1) and a money supply curve; and it uses an assumed national income of $1,200. The money supply curve is simply a vertical line; it reflects an assumption that in the simple economy the money supply is determined solely by Bank of Canada policy and is not directly affected by changes in economic conditions. As Exhibit 13.3 is drawn, the quantity of money supplied is assumed to be $180.

It is important to remember that both the demand for money and the supply of money are measured in terms of stocks, not flows. The supply represents the stock in existence at a given time, and the demand represents the stock that people desire to hold in their portfolios under given conditions.

Equilibrium

It is apparent from the diagram that there is only one nominal rate of interest, 8 percent, at which the stock of money that people want to hold is equal to the stock of money supplied by the banking system in accordance with Bank of Canada policy. At any higher rate of interest, there would be an excess quantity of money supplied.

Reactions to an Excess Supply of Money At an interest rate of 12 precent, for example, the excess quantity supplied would be $60. This quantity reflects the fact that people do not want to hold as much money in their portfolios as the Bank of Canada has caused the banking system to put into circulation.

Individual asset holders react to an excess quantity of money supplied by using their excess money to buy other assets. Given the high interest rate, they are particularly attracted to the idea of replacing some of the money in their portfolios with bonds. However, although some individual asset holders can successfully reduce the quantity of money in their portfolios by buying bonds, not all asset holders can do so at once. Every time someone takes money out of his or her portfolio to buy a bond from someone else, that money ends up in the portfolio of the seller.

No matter how much money is churned around from portfolio to portfolio in pursuit of bonds, every cent of the fixed stock of money supplied by the banking system has to be in someone's portfolio at each moment. What occurs as a result of all this churning is not a fall in the money stock but a rise in the price of bonds. This rise in bond prices means a fall in the nominal rate of interest on bonds. As the interest rate falls, the excess quantity of money supplied is reduced, not because the extra money disappears but because the amount of money that people desire to keep in their portfolios rises until it catches up with the quantity of money supplied. Soon the nominal interest rate reaches its equilibrium level, and the excess demand is entirely eliminated.

Reactions to an Excess Demand for Money If the interest rate were for some reason below the equilibrium level, there would be an excess quantity of money demanded, and a process opposite to that just described would occur. People would want to sell bonds in order to get the greater quantity of money they would prefer to hold at the low interest rate. This would not increase the total supply of money available in the system, but it would depress the price of bonds — which in turn would raise the interest rate until equilibrium were restored.

Equilibrium in the money market thus associates one and only one nominal interest rate with a given quantity of money and a given nominal income. The reactions to excess supply and demand just discussed play a critical role in the adjustment of the money market to two important types of disturbances, as will now be shown.

Effects of a Change in Money Supply

The first step will be to examine the effects of an increase in the money supply resulting from an open market purchase of securities from the public by the Bank of Canada. Suppose that initially the money supply is $180, as shown by the money curve MS_1 in Exhibit 13.4. A nominal national income of $1,200 gives the money demand curve MD. The equilibrium interest rate is 8 percent, and the money multiplier is 9.0.

Imagine that the Bank of Canada makes an open market purchase of $20 worth of government securities, paying for them with one of its own cheques. The immediate effect of this purchase is to increase the money supply by $20 and to raise bond prices slightly and lower the rate of interest slightly.

If this were the end of the story, the money supply curve would be put in the position indicated as MS_2, and the market would be put in a new equilibrium at the intersection of that curve with the money demand

Exhibit 13.4

Effects of an increase in the money supply

Initially, a money supply of $180 puts the money supply curve in the position MS_1. An open market purchase of $20 by the Bank of Canada has the immediate effect of moving the money supply curve to MS_2. That is not the end of the story, however. With a money multiplier of 9.0, the money supply reaches $360 ($MS_3$) before the deposit expansion process works itself out completely. The new equilibrium nominal interest rate is 4 percent.

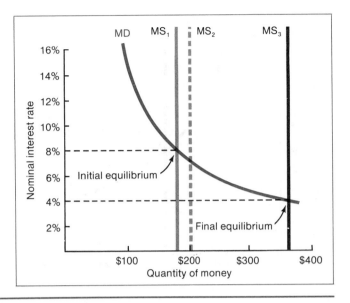

curve. But this is not the end of the story. As soon as the original Bank of Canada cheque is deposited in the bond seller's bank, the total reserves of the banking system go up by $20 to a new level of $40. This sets off the process of deposit expansion described in Chapter 12, and by the time the reserves-to-money multiplier has worked itself out, the money supply will reach $360. This will shift the money supply curve all the way to the position MS_3.

New Equilibrium Now there will be a large excess quantity of money supplied. Asset holders will not desire to hold the new money at the old interest rate and will try to reduce their money holdings. It is likely that some excess money balances will be spent on physical assets, including consumer durables, and it is certain that some will be spent on bonds. As before, the actions of portfolio holders will bid up bond prices and lower interest rates. When the interest rate falls low enough (to 4 percent as this example is constructed), the demand for money will rise sufficiently to reestablish equilibrium. In the new equilibrium, total money balances outstanding will be larger than initially, and the nominal interest rate will be lower.

Effects of an Increase in Income

In looking at the money market effects of an increase in the money supply, we assumed that nominal income remained unchanged throughout. Now we will look at the effects of a change in nominal income, assuming that the money supply will remain fixed. This will complete the groundwork for the next chapter, where the two types of changes will be considered in combination.

A Shift in the Money Demand Curve Exhibit 13.5 sets the scene for exploring the effects of a change in nominal income. Suppose that initially the economy is in equilibrium with a money supply (MS) of $180, a nominal income ($MD_1$) of $600, and an interest rate of 4 percent. At this

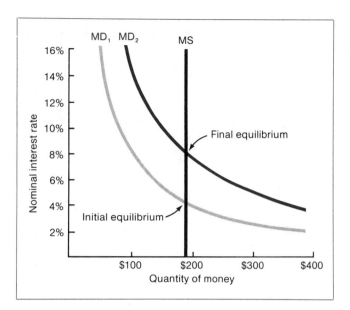

Exhibit 13.5

Effects of an increase in national income

Initially, a nominal income of $600 puts the money demand curve at MD$_1$. The equilibrium nominal interest rate is 4 percent with the money supply at $180. If an increase in nominal income to $1,200 shifts the money demand curve to MD$_2$, the interest rate will have to rise to 8 percent to restore equilibrium.

interest rate, the desired quantity of money holdings is $180, just equal to the money supply — as of course it must be in equilibrium.

Now suppose that for some reason nominal income rises to $1,200. The increase in income causes the money demand curve to shift to the new position, MD$_2$. With the money supply still at $180, this means a very substantial excess quantity of money demanded. To meet the increased demand for money, portfolio holders will have to sell some of their earning assets, especially bonds. This will depress the price of bonds and raise the nominal interest rate.

As the nominal interest rate rises, the desired ratio of money to income falls, since the higher interest rate raises the implicit cost of holding money balances. When the nominal interest rate rises high enough, the desired quantity of money will fall to $180, entirely eliminating the excess quantity of money demanded. This will happen at an interest rate of 8 percent for the current example. Therefore, the new equilibrium rate of interest is 8 percent.

CONCLUSIONS

This completes the initial discussion of the supply and demand for money. The important next step — to apply this theory to the problem of national income determination — is the aim of the next chapter. That chapter will show how the inclusion of the money market in the analysis of national income determination leads to some important modifications of the multiplier theory and sets the stage for the discussion of inflation and unemployment.

SUMMARY

1. The collection of various assets a person owns (money, real estate, consumer durables, bonds, stocks, or whatever) is called a portfolio.

Portfolio holders try to maintain a balance among the various kinds of assets they own, shifting from one to another as economic conditions change. As nominal income rises, people tend to want more money in their portfolios to satisfy their transactions demand. As the nominal rate of interest rises, people tend to want less money in their portfolios, because the opportunity cost of holding money increases and because their speculative demand for money decreases.

2. A downward-sloping money demand curve can be drawn to indicate, in graphical form, how the quantity of money demanded changes as the interest rate changes, given some level of nominal income. An increase in the level of nominal income shifts this curve to the right, and a decrease shifts it to the left.

3. If the money supply is assumed to be fully controlled by Bank of Canada policy, the money supply curve can be represented by a vertical line. Together, the money supply and money demand curves associate one and only one nominal rate of interest with each quantity of money supplied and each level of nominal income. With nominal income unchanged, an increase in the money supply must be followed by a fall in the nominal rate of interest, other things being equal. With the money supply unchanged, an increase in nominal income causes the nominal rate of interest to rise, other things being equal.

DISCUSSION QUESTIONS

1. List the items that you might consider part of your portfolio. Is your portfolio basically similar to the one discussed in the text? In what ways is it similar? In what ways is it different?

2. Which is most important in determining your own demand for money—the transactions motive, the precautionary motive, or the speculative motive? Explain.

3. If the interest rate paid on savings deposits were increased, would you change your portfolio? Would you invest more or less in a savings account? Explain.

4. What is the average balance in your chequebook during a typical month? How much currency do you carry on a typical day? The sum of these two figures will give the quantity of money demanded. In order to get a point on your demand for money schedule, a price is needed. What price should be used?

5. Evaluate the following statement: It is at best a mere metaphor, and at worst seriously misleading, to speak of the money "market." Money cannot be bought and sold; it is just the means of payment we use in buying and selling everything else. Since it cannot be bought and sold, it cannot have a true market.

6. Do you know what the interest rate is on three-month Treasury bills at the time you are reading this chapter? Try to find out.

SUGGESTIONS FOR FURTHER READING

Boreham, Gordon F., with Shapiro, Eli, Solomon, Ezra, and White, William. *Money and Banking: Analysis and Policy in a Canadian Context*, 2nd ed. Toronto: Holt, Rinehart and Winston, 1979.
Chapters 10 and 18 parallel the discussion of this chapter but offer additional details.

THE INTERACTION OF MONEY AND THE MULTIPLIER

WHAT YOU WILL LEARN IN THIS CHAPTER

This chapter ties together the analysis of fiscal and monetary policy given in previous chapters. First, it shows how the two policies interact to establish simultaneous equilibrium in the money market and the circular flow. Next, it shows how the effects of fiscal policy actions are modified when monetary reactions to fiscal policy are taken into account. Finally, after discussing the basic tools of fiscal and monetary policy analysis, the chapter introduces some important controversies concerning the relative importance and effectiveness of fiscal and monetary policy.

FOR REVIEW

Here are some important terms and concepts that will be put to use in this chapter. If you do not understand them, review them before proceeding.
- *Real and nominal interest rates (Chapter 7)*
- *Fiscal policy (Chapter 10)*
- *Supply of money (Chapter 12)*
- *Demand for money (Chapter 13)*

This chapter ties together the multiplier analysis of Chapters 8 to 10 with the analysis of the financial sector presented in Chapters 11 to 13. In doing so, it makes a transition from what economists call partial equilibrium analysis to what they call general equilibrium analysis.

The difference between the two lies in the role played by the "other things being equal" assumption. In **partial equilibrium analysis**, it is said that if Event X occurs, the effect on Market Y will be Z, provided that the equilibrium of other markets is not disturbed. In **general equilibrium analysis**, in contrast, it is said that if Event X occurs, the effect on Market Y will be Z, provided that other markets also adjust fully to the event in question.

So far, the multiplier theory and the theory of money have been examined only from the partial equilibrium point of view. Chapter 10, for example, analyzed the effect of a change in fiscal policy on the equilibrium level of the circular flow without considering the possible effects that the change might have on the demand for money, on the nominal interest rate,

Partial equilibrium analysis
An approach to the study of markets along the lines of: if Event X occurs, the effect on Market Y will be Z, provided that the equilibrium of other markets is not disturbed.

General equilibrium analysis An approach to the study of markets along the lines of: if Event X occurs, the effect on Market Y will be Z, provided that other markets also adjust fully to the event in question.

and on the level of planned investment. Similarly, Chapter 13 looked at the effect a change in the money supply would have on the equilibrium nominal interest rate without considering the possible effect of such an act of monetary policy on the level of nominal national income or the position of the money demand curve.

This chapter will also look at fiscal and monetary policy, but now using the general equilibrium approach. After delineating some basic principles, it will turn to important controversies surrounding the relative strength and effectiveness of monetary and fiscal policy.

THE INTERACTION OF MONEY AND NATIONAL INCOME

The Conditions for General Equilibrium

The chapter begins by showing what the economy looks like when the circular flow and the money market are simultaneously in equilibrium. Consider Exhibit 14.1, which shows two main channels of interaction (represented by large arrows) between money and the level of nominal national income. Each of these channels requires some comment.

Nominal Income and Money Demand The first interaction runs from the level of nominal national income, as determined by aggregate supply and demand, to the position of the money demand curve. As shown in the last chapter, the quantity of money demanded depends both on the nominal rate of interest and on the level of national income. A change in the nominal interest rate produces a movement along a given money demand curve, whereas a change in nominal national income produces a shift in the money demand curve. In order to put the money demand curve in its proper position, then, it is necessary to know the equilibrium level of nominal national income.

Nominal Interest, Real Interest, and Investment The second channel of interaction runs from the money market to the aggregate demand schedule by way of the effect of interest rates on the level of planned investment. Low interest rates encourage investment; and investment, in turn, is an important component of aggregate nominal demand. It is necessary to be careful in analyzing this interaction, because supply and demand in the money market are brought into equilibrium by the *nominal* rate of interest, whereas the level of planned investment expenditure is determined by the *expected real* rate of interest. This is no problem so long as the expected rate of inflation is zero, because with no inflation expected, the nominal rate of interest and the expected real rate of interest are equal. Such a case is shown in Exhibit 14.1. The first part of this chapter will assume zero expected inflation. Later, however, the chapter will consider the important case where inflationary expectations are not zero, so that the nominal and expected real rates of interest diverge.

Finding the Equilibrium Values The money market and the circular flow can be in equilibrium simultaneously only if a certain pair of values for the interest rate and nominal national income prevail. Let the required level of nominal national income be Y and the required interest rate be r. (The r

Exhibit 14.1

A general equilibrium view of national income determination

The money market and the circular flow can both be in equilibrium at once only if a certain pair of values for the interest rate and nominal income prevail. The large arrows in this figure show how the interest rate and nominal national income interact. The equilibrium interest rate helps determine the position of the aggregate demand curve through its effect on planned investment spending. The level of nominal national income helps determine the interest rate through its effect on the position of the money demand curve.

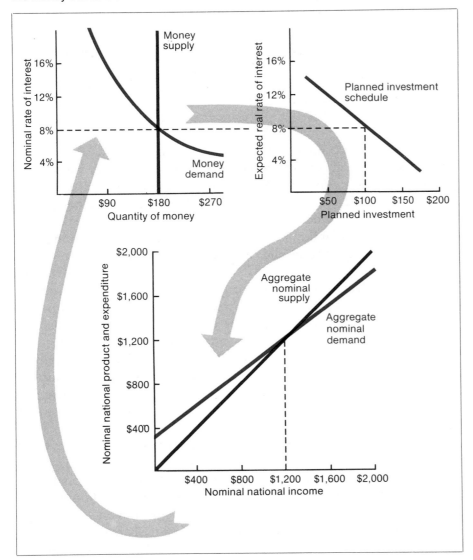

stands for both the nominal and the expected real rate of interest, which are equal under the present assumption of zero expected inflation.) Then the value of r must be just right to induce the level of planned investment needed to put equilibrium nominal national income exactly at the level Y, and the value of Y must be just right to put the money demand curve in the position needed to keep the equilibrium interest rate at r.

As Exhibit 14.1 is drawn, an interest rate of 8 percent and a nominal national income of $1,200 are called for. The aggregate demand schedule is drawn on the assumptions that autonomous consumption is $100, the marginal propensity to consume is 0.75, government purchases are $280, net exports are $75−0.15 national income, and net taxes are $100. Planned investment must therefore be $100 in order for equilibrium nominal national income to be $1,200. A check of the planned investment schedule reveals that an interest rate of 8 percent is just what is needed to encourage that amount of planned investment.

Turning to the money market, where a money supply of $180 is assumed, the money demand curve must be in exactly the position indicated in Exhibit 14.1 for the equilibrium rate of interest to be 8 percent. This position, which corresponds to a nominal national income of $1,200 verifies that r = 8 percent and Y = $1,200 are an equilibrium pair for the interest rate and nominal national income.

The Equilibrium Is Unique For any given set of assumptions about autonomous consumption, the marginal propensity to consume, government purchases, net taxes, net exports, the money supply, and the position of the planned investment schedule, there is just one pair of values for the interest rate and nominal national income that permits both the money market and the circular flow to be in equilibrium. Thus, equilibrium values of nominal national income and the interest rate are unique.

To see this, assume momentarily that one of the values is different, and then show that this does not permit both markets to be in equilibrium. Suppose, for example, that the interest rate were only 4 percent, while all underlying economic conditions were the same as before. The planned investment schedule in Exhibit 14.1 shows that a 4 percent interest rate would cause planned investment to rise to $150. With planned expenditure $50 higher than before, equilibrium nominal national income would rise by $125 to $1,325 under the impact of the multiplier effect. Thus an interest rate of 4 percent requires an equilibrium nominal national income of $1,325.

The money market part of Exhibit 14.1 shows that 4 percent cannot be the equilibrium rate of interest when the money demand curve is in the position shown and the money supply is $180. The money demand curve would have to shift to the left to make 4 percent the equilibrium rate of interest. But an increase in nominal national income from $1,200 to $1,325 would shift the curve not to the left but to the right. There is no way that 4 percent can be an equilibrium rate of interest when the level of nominal national income is $1,325, given the assumed money supply. There is also no way that the equilibrium level of nominal national income can be anything but $1,325 when the rate of interest is 4 percent. Given the assumed underlying economic conditions, it is necessary to conclude that when the interest rate is 4 percent, there is no value of nominal national income that permits both the money market and the circular flow to be in equilibrium.

The same reasoning could be repeated for any value of r other than 8 percent and any value of Y other than $1,200. This pair of equilibrium values for nominal national income and interest rate is unique.

A Revised Look at the Effects of Fiscal Policy

Chapter 10 discussed the effects of two kinds of changes in fiscal policy: changes in government purchases and changes in net taxes. Each of these kinds of fiscal policy must now be reconsidered from the point of view of general equilibrium analysis. For purposes of comparison with what follows, recall the conclusion reached in Chapter 10 about the effects of a change in government purchases: when government purchases are increased while taxes, planned investment, the consumption schedule, and the net export schedule remain unchanged, equilibrium nominal national income will change by an amount equal to the change in government purchases times the multiplier.

Effects of a Change in Government Purchases Beginning with government purchases, assume that the economy is initially in equilibrium with interest rate r and nominal national income Y. Then assume that fiscal policy makers decide to increase government purchases of domestic goods and services by $100, with no accompanying change in taxes. Consider the effects of this fiscal policy as they work their way through the economy.

The first effect of the increase in government purchases is to shift the aggregate demand schedule upward by $100. Planned expenditure now exceeds national product at the initial income level. This causes unplanned depletion of inventories, to which business firms respond by increasing output and/or raising prices. The level of nominal national income begins to rise.

Money Market Effect As nominal national income rises, the change in fiscal policy begins to affect the money market. The increase in nominal national income causes the money demand curve to shift rightward. In Exhibit 14.2 this is shown as a shift from the initial position of the money demand curve, MD_1, toward a new position, MD_2. The money demand curve shifts because when incomes rise, people tend to want more money in their portfolios. Because the money supply does not increase, people's attempts to get more money by selling bonds simply drives down the price of bonds and drives up the rate of interest. Altogether, then, the effect on the money market of the increase in government purchases is to push up the rate of interest

The Crowding Out Effect Attention can now be shifted from the money market to the planned investment schedule, also shown in Exhibit 14.2. Increased money demand has driven up the nominal rate of interest. With zero inflation expected, as assumed, the expected real interest rate rises in step with the nominal rate. Firms find it more costly to undertake fixed investment projects and to increase inventories of raw materials or finished goods. They therefore reduce their planned investment expenditures, shown by a movement upward and to the left along the planned investment schedule. This decrease in planned investment expenditures, as an indirect effect of an increase in government purchases, is called the **crowding out effect**. The amount of investment crowded out is labeled ΔI in the exhibit.

Crowding out effect The tendency of expansionary fiscal policy to cause a drop in private planned investment expenditure as a result of a rise in the interest rate.

Exhibit 14.2

The crowding out effect

An increase in government purchases causes nominal national income to rise via the multiplier effect. The increase in income shifts the money demand curve from its initial position, MD_1, to the new position, MD_2. The equilibrium interest rate rises from r_1 to r_2. An amount of private investment equal to ΔI is "crowded out."

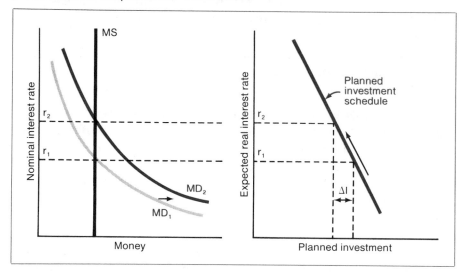

Exhibit 14.3 shows what happens in terms of aggregate supply and demand. The original position of the aggregate demand curve is shown as AND_1. Considered in isolation, the increase in government spending would have pushed the schedule all the way up to the position AND_2. When the crowding out effect is taken into account, though, it is apparent that the upward shift in aggregate demand is less than the amount of increase in government purchases. If ΔG stands for the increase in government purchases and ΔI for the amount of investment crowded out, the upward shift is reduced to $\Delta G - \Delta I$. This puts the final position of the aggregate demand curve at AND_3.

Looking at Exhibits 14.2 and 14.3 together, now, notice that both income and the interest rate have changed. The new equilibrium interest rate, r_2, and the new equilibrium nominal national income, Y_2, are higher than they were to begin with. Government purchases and private consumption are higher than initially, but private investment is lower.

Crowding Out and the Multiplier Because an increase in government purchases crowds out some private investment, nominal national income does not rise by the full amount of the multiplier times the increase in government purchases. This fact does not, however, directly contradict the conclusion reached in Chapter 10 and repeated above. The trouble is that the earlier conclusion, which was based on partial equilibrium analysis, included the assumption that planned investment would not change when nominal national income changed. The general equilibrium approach

Exhibit 14.3

The crowding out effect in terms of aggregate supply and demand

Here the crowding out effect is shown from the perspective of aggregate supply and demand. Taken by itself, the increase in government purchases (ΔG) would have pushed the aggregate demand curve from AND$_1$ to AND$_2$. The crowding out effect chops ΔI off private investment, however, so the actual shift is only from AND$_1$ to AND$_3$, a distance equal to $\Delta G - \Delta I$.

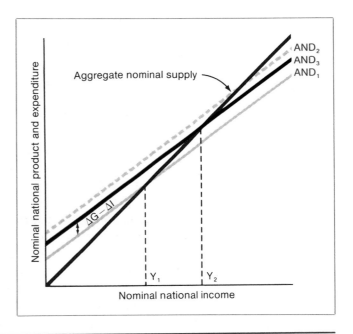

taken here shows that that assumption is invalid. This makes it necessary to modify the way the multiplier theory is applied to the analysis of fiscal policy. The multiplier must now be applied not just to the change in government purchases but rather to the change in government purchases minus the induced change in private planned investment expenditure.

The new way of applying the multiplier theory to the analysis of fiscal policy can be put in the form of a simple equation. Using the symbol ΔY to represent the change in nominal national income resulting from a change in government purchases, ΔG, and using $(1/1 - MPC_D)$ to stand for the multiplier:

$$\Delta Y = \frac{1}{1 - MPC_D}(\Delta G - \Delta I).$$

Other Fiscal Policies The crowding out effect applies to other types of fiscal policy as well as to changes in government purchases. When taxes are lowered, or when the level of government purchases is increased while the budget is kept in balance, nominal national income rises. This pushes interest rates up and crowds out some investment. The result is that the overall effectiveness of these fiscal policies is somewhat less than would be predicted by the simple applications of the tax multiplier.

It must also be remembered that when taxes are raised or government purchases lowered, as might be done to eliminate an expansionary gap from the economy, the crowding out effect works in reverse. The contractionary impact of fiscal policy is somewhat diminished, because as incomes fall, the demand for money and the interest rate fall too. These effects stimulate new planned investment expenditure, somewhat offsetting the downward shift in the aggregate demand schedule that the contractionary policy produces.

A Revised Look at the Effects of Monetary Policy

Chapter 13 described the effects of a change in the money supply from a partial equilibrium point of view, taking into account only what happens in the money market. This section will reconsider the effects of changes in the money supply in a general equilibrium context, taking into account the interaction of money and the multiplier theory of income determination.

An Open Market Purchase To be specific, suppose that the Bank of Canada initiates an expansion of the money supply through an open market purchase of bonds. It will not be necessary to give separate consideration to the expansion of the money supply by the use of other instruments of monetary policy because the effects are very little different from those of an open market operation.

Chapters 12 and 13 analyzed initial effects of the open market purchase. The open market purchase creates an increase in chartered bank reserves, and banks are induced to begin the process of deposit expansion. When the expansion is complete, the money supply will have increased by an amount equal to the expansion in the reserves times the money multiplier. This is indicated in Exhibit 14.4 by the shift in the money supply curve from the position MS_1 to the position MS_2.

As the money supply expands, people find that they have more money than they want to hold in their portfolios at the original rate of interest. They attempt to reduce these holdings by buying other assets, including

---

Exhibit 14.4

Money market and investment effects of an increase in the money supply
An increase in the money supply shifts the money supply curve from MS_1 to MS_2. The immediate effect of this shift is a movement down along the money demand curve, MD_1, toward its intersection with the new money supply curve. The interest rate then falls and planned investment expenditure rises, which stimulates nominal national income through the multiplier effect. The rise in income in turn shifts the money demand schedule to a new position, MD_2, which cuts short the fall in the interest rate — and a new equilibrium is established.

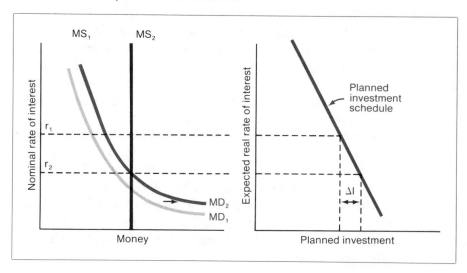

Exhibit 14.5
The effect of an increase in the money supply on aggregate demand and nominal national income
An increase in planned investment spending, caused by an increase in the money supply, shifts the aggregate demand curve upward. The amount of the shift is equal to the change in investment, ∆I. A new equilibrium is established, with nominal national income increasing from Y_1 to Y_2.

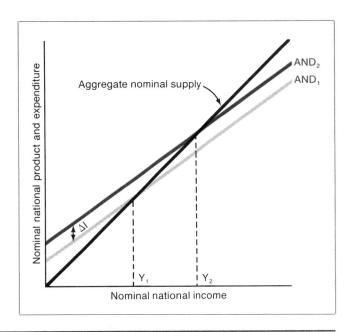

bonds. This tends to push the price of bonds up and the interest rate down. In the diagram, the process is represented by a movement along the original money demand curve, MD_1, toward its intersection with the new money supply curve, MS_2.

Income and Expenditure Effect   As the interest rate begins to fall, business executives are encouraged to increase their level of planned investment, which is indicated by a movement down and to the right along their planned investment schedule. The increase in investment expenditure shifts the aggregate nominal demand schedule upward, as shown in Exhibit 14.5. Planned expenditure now temporarily exceeds nominal national income; and by the familiar multiplier process, nominal national income begins to increase.

As this income increases, the money market is once again affected. Now the money demand curve begins to shift to the right, moving toward the position marked MD_2 in Exhibit 14.4. This shift cuts off the fall in the interest rate, and a new equilibrium interest rate is established where MD_1 and MS_2 intersect.

Once this interest rate is established, planned investment stops expanding. The aggregate nominal demand schedule comes to rest at a new equilibrium position, AND_2, as shown in Exhibit 14.5. That means the new equilibrium level of nominal national income will be higher than it was before the increase in the money supply.

In short, general equilibrium analysis shows that an increase in the money supply will result in new equilibrium values for both the interest rate and nominal national income. With zero inflationary expectations, as assumed, both the nominal interest rate and the expected real interest rate will be lower than before the monetary expansion took place, and the level of nominal national income will be higher.

Accommodating Monetary Policy

Now that the separate effects of fiscal and monetary policy have been described, it is not difficult to envision how the two policies might be used in combination. Although not every possible combination of policies will be discussed here, one case is important enough to deserve at least a brief mention: the case of accommodating monetary policy.

Accommodating monetary policy A policy under which the Bank of Canada expands the money supply in an attempt to keep interest rates from rising when the government sells bonds to cover a budget deficit.

The Bank of Canada is said to pursue an **accommodating monetary policy** when, in the face of expansionary fiscal policy, it expands the money supply in an attempt to keep interest rates stable. To see why the Bank might want to do this, consider what happens when the government increases its purchases without raising taxes in order to stimulate aggregate demand. It must finance the deficit by selling bonds to the public. This depresses the price of bonds, thereby raising the nominal interest rate. The increase in the interest rate is unwelcome — for two reasons. First, with unchanged inflationary expectations, it raises the expected real rate of interest and crowds out some private investment. This partially negates the intended stimulative effect of the increased government purchases. Second, it makes it more expensive for the government to raise the money needed to finance the deficit. By making open market purchases of bonds at the same time the government is selling new bonds to finance the deficit, the Bank of Canada keeps the interest rate from rising, thereby "accommodating" the government.

But, of course, by feeding new reserves to the banking system, the Bank of Canada's actions cause the money supply to expand. In effect, the combined actions of the Bank of Canada and the government mean that the government is paying for its purchases with newly created money.

To understand accommodating monetary policy more fully, refer back to Exhibit 14.2, which described the crowding out effect. Increased government purchases increased interest rates from r to r_2, by increasing the demand for money from MD_1 to MD_2. Higher interest rates lowered planned investments. By engaging in accommodating monetary policy, through the purchase of bonds in the open market, the Bank of Canada causes the money supply curve to shift to the right. This lowers interest rates and increases planned investment.

In times gone by, governments did not always bother with such niceties as bonds and open market purchases when they wanted to spend more than they collected in taxes. Instead, they just cranked up their presses and printed new currency. In remembrance of this ancient custom, economic journalists to this day sometimes refer to the combination of deficit spending and accommodating monetary policy as "deficit finance via the printing press."

CONTROVERSIES OVER MONETARY POLICY

The analysis of the interactions of monetary and fiscal policy just worked through may appear to be perfectly straightforward and perhaps not particularly exciting. Yet some of the major economic controversies of the twentieth century revolve around the ideas presented in the preceding pages. Taking things in historical sequence, the so-called Keynesian-monetarist controversy will be the first one looked at.

The Keynesian-Monetarist Controversy

Keynes's general theory of employment, interest, and money was intended to be "general" in the sense that it would take into account both monetary and fiscal influences on the economy.[1] However, in the first years after the publication of Keynes's book, it was not the general theory as a whole that dominated the thinking of the economics profession. Instead, some followers of Keynes tended to place one-sided emphasis on planned expenditure and to downplay the role of money in the economy. Early followers of Keynes interpreted the experience of the Great Depression as justifying the view that "money doesn't matter." They attributed the fact that monetary policy had failed to prevent both the 41 percent decline in nominal income and the increase in the unemployment rate to 19 percent of the labor force that occurred in Canada between 1929 and 1933 not to poor conduct of monetary policy but to its ineffectiveness. The fact that the Great Depression did not end until World War II had brought on a massive increase in government spending appeared to support this view.

After the war, many of the early Keynesians forecasted a new depression and economic stagnation. They thought that private investment opportunities would dry up with the disappearance of wartime government spending. Experience proved them wrong. Canada, the United States, and the countries of Western Europe experienced rapid postwar recovery. Central banks in most of the major economies pursued "easy" monetary policies during these years, and inflation was a more widespread problem than depression. Those countries that succeeded in controlling inflation did so only by orthodox monetary policies. Economists began to wonder if perhaps money mattered after all and began to look once again at the general theory as a whole.

The Monetarists The reaction against the one-sided theories of the early Keynesians received major support during the 1950s and 1960s from a group of economists working under the intellectual leadership of Milton Friedman of the University of Chicago. Friedman's empirical research led him to think that monetary policy had had a much greater influence on the course of economic events than the Keynesians were willing to admit. It appeared to be possible to explain even the Great Depression in this way. Because of the emphasis they gave to monetary phenomena, Friedman and his followers became known as **monetarists**.

The economics profession did not immediately become converted to monetarism. In fact, the 1960s were in some respects the heyday of Keynesian policy, as such prominent Keynesians as Walter Heller, James Tobin, and Gardner Ackley left their academic posts to join the Council of Economic Advisers under American Presidents Kennedy and Johnson. Nonetheless, the ideas of the monetarists proved influential in persuading the Keynesians to return to the idea of a general theory in which monetary and fiscal policy played co-equal roles.

Monetarists Economists who believe that movements in the money supply are the primary causes of ups and downs in business activity.

[1] John Maynard Keynes, *The General Theory of Employment, Interest, and Money* (New York: Harcourt, Brace, & World, 1936).

Milton Friedman (1912–   )

In October 1976, Milton Friedman received the Nobel Memorial Prize in economics, becoming the sixth American to win or share in that prize. Few were surprised. The main surprise was that this most original and influential of economists had had to wait in line so long! The explanation is that Friedman has built his career outside the economics establishment — built it, in fact, by challenging virtually every major establishment doctrine.

Friedman was born in New York in 1912, the son of immigrant garment workers. His hard-working parents sent him across the river to Rutgers University in New Jersey, where Friedman came under the influence of Arthur Burns, then a young assistant professor. From Burns, Friedman learned the importance of empirical work in economics. Statistical testing of all theory and policy prescriptions became a key characteristic of Friedman's later work. From Rutgers, Friedman went to the University of Chicago for an M.A. and then east again to Columbia University, where he got his Ph.D. in 1946. With his degree in hand, he returned to Chicago to teach. There, he became the leading member of the "Chicago School," which provides the main intellectual counterweight to the Eastern Establishment in U.S. economics today.

If one were to single out the theme that underlies all of Friedman's work, it would be his conviction that the market economy works — and works best when left alone. This can be seen in his best-known work, *A Monetary History of the United States*. Written with Anna Schwartz, the work challenges two major tenets of orthodox Keynesian economics: first, the idea that the market economy is inherently unstable without the guiding hand of government, and second, that monetary policy had been tried and found useless as a cure for the Great Depression. Friedman and Schwartz found both beliefs to be the opposite of the truth. "The Great Depression," Friedman later wrote, "far from being a sign of the inherent instability of the private enterprise system, is a testament to how much harm can be done by mistakes on the part of a few men when they wield vast power over the monetary system of the country."

Friedman strongly favors a hands-off policy by governments in almost every area, not just in monetary matters. The trouble, in his view, is not that government is evil by nature but rather that so many policies end up having the opposite of their intended effects. "The social reformers who seek through politics to do nothing but serve the public interest invariably end up serving some private interest that was no part of their intention to serve. They are led by an invisible hand to serve a private interest." Transport regulation, the income tax, public education, agricultural subsidies, and housing programs are among the many policy areas where Friedman believes the government has done more harm than good and where a free competitive market would do better.

Today, Friedman continues to take on new challenges. He promotes his ideas before congressional committees, in professional journals, in his *Newsweek* column, and in face-to-face debate with his colleagues. Economics has never had a more respected heretic.

In Canada, economists like David Laidler, Thomas Courchene, and Michael Parkin of the University of Western Ontario, and Jack Carr of the University of Toronto, among others, are providing a monetarist critique of Canadian economic policy. A number of them are graduates of the University of Chicago.[2] A famous Canadian economist, the late Harry G. Johnson, took an eclectic, Keynesian-Monetarist approach to the analysis of economic change. Many economists similarly elude classification into a single school of thought.

[2] Students are sometimes surprised to discover how the ideas of their professors can apparently be traced back to the schools in which they studied. The influence of Friedman and the so-called "Chicago School" can now be traced through two generations in Canada. As mentioned, a number of monetarists at the University of Western Ontario received their training at Chicago. In turn, one of the more vocal young monetarists, Michael Walker, chief economist of the Fraser Institute in Vancouver, studied economics at Western.

One of the world's most famous interpreters of macroeconomics, until his death in May 1977, at the age of 53, was Harry G. Johnson. Johnson was born in Toronto and, after studying economics at the University of Toronto and Cambridge University, he taught economics for several years in Canada. After completing his Ph.D. at Harvard University in 1958 he became Professor of Economics at the University of Chicago. For a number of years, from 1966 to 1973, he was also Professor of Economics at the London School of Economics, jetting back and forth across the Atlantic to teach and advise students at both universities. At the time of his death he was professor at the University of Geneva as well as at Chicago.

Johnson was a prodigious worker and a prolific writer. One colleague observed that "he seemed to be intellectually 'all Muscle.' Physically too he gave an impression of tremendous power under easy self-control. He was broad, thick-chested, inclined towards a solid plumpness."[4] During his brief career, he published hundreds of articles on economics and more than a dozen books, dealing largely with the interpretation and application of Keynesian theory.

Harry G. Johnson (1923–1977)

Though most of Johnson's career was spent outside of Canada, he retained a lively interest in the Canadian economy, as evidenced by several of his major books (for example, *The Canadian Quandary* and *Canada in a Changing World Economy*) and the numerous lectures that he gave in this country. Just a year before his death he gave the Harold Innis Lecture at the meetings of the Canadian Economics Association, on the topic: "Keynes's General Theory: Revolution or War of Independence?" In keeping with his previous work, he argued in this lecture that Keynes had produced some new and interesting ideas for economists to follow but that they did not amount to a revolution in economic thought. Johnson felt that pre-Keynesian ideas still had considerable validity, as shown by, among others, his colleague at the University of Chicago, Milton Friedman. Johnson felt that Keynes's view had been too short-run. For example, not enough attention was given in Keynes's work on the multiplier process to the shocks and adjustments that affect that process over time. However, Johnson thought that Keynes had revitalized the study of economics and had provided it with helpful new tools and directions.

As a result of his cosmopolitan experience and outlook, Johnson was very critical of Canadian nationalism. He firmly believed in the benefits of free trade and competition and decried the defeatist, defensive attitude that he detected among many Canadians. He was frequently invited to lecture in less-developed countries, and there too he was outspoken in his criticism of centralized direction of the economy and the extreme nationalism of some of those countries. He will be remembered by most of his students and readers as one of the clearest interpreters of macroeconomics since Keynes.

Monetarist ideas are making an impact on government and Bank of Canada policy. Courchene, who had earlier criticized the Bank of Canada for contributing to the inflation of the early 1970s, noted with delight in 1976 that "the Bank of Canada has embraced the tenets of the monetarist approach to stabilization policy."[3]

Monetarism versus Keynesianism: Unresolved Issues Today, the theoretical gap between monetarism and Keynesian economics has been narrowed but not altogether eliminated. The analysis presented in the first part of this chapter can be used as a framework for discussing some of the important unresolved issues, including the following:

1. What is the relative importance of monetary and fiscal policy in determining nominal national income?

---

[3] Thomas J. Courchene, *Monetarism and Controls: The Inflation Fighters* (Montreal: C. D. Howe Research Institute, 1976), p. 1.

[4] Edward Shils, "Harry Johnson, Memoir," *Encounter*, November 1977, p. 87.

2. How are the effects of monetary policy actions transmitted through the economy?
3. To what extent is monetary policy a determinant of the rate of inflation, in both the long run and the short run?
4. What kind of monetary and fiscal policies are best suited to achieve the goals of economic stabilization?

The first two of these issues will be discussed in the remainder of this chapter. The third and fourth will be left for Chapters 15 to 18.

How Large a Crowding Out Effect? The debate over the relative importance of monetary and fiscal policy as determinants of nominal national income is, to a considerable extent, a debate over the importance of the crowding out effect. Exhibit 14.6 shows why. Suppose that the money demand curve has the shape shown by MD_1, indicating that the demand for money is not very sensitive to changes in the interest rate. If this is the case, the portfolio adjustments required when the money demand curve shifts relative to the money supply curve (as when nominal income changes) or when the money supply curve shifts relative to the money demand curve (as in the conduct of monetary policy) will bring about large changes in the rate of interest. Suppose that at the same time the planned investment schedule is relatively flat, like the curve I_1, so that a change in the rate of interest will induce a large change in planned investment expenditure.

Taken together, the curves MD_1 and I_1 tend to give the sort of results expected by monetarists. An expansion of government purchases leads to a large increase in the rate of interest, a large drop in private investment spending, and hence a large crowding out effect. Also, an increase in the money supply leads to a large decline in the rate of interest and a large increase in investment spending. Therefore, given curves of these shapes, fiscal policy tends to be relatively ineffective and monetary policy relatively effective.

On the other hand, if the money demand curve has the shape MD_2 and the planned investment schedule the shape I_2, the situation is reversed. Fiscal policy will have relatively little impact on interest rates; and interest rates, in turn, will have relatively little impact on private investment. Changes in taxes or government purchases will then operate on aggregate nominal demand without much hindrance from the crowding out effect. At the same time, the economy will become much less sensitive to changes in the money supply. The world will behave more like a Keynesian would expect it to.

The Transmission Mechanism In addition to disagreeing about the size of the crowding out effect, monetarists and Keynesians continue to disagree about the nature of the mechanism by which the effects of monetary policy are transmitted through the economy.

Keynesians tend to emphasize the chain of causation running from changes in monetary policy to changes in interest rates to changes in planned investment spending. This is the transmission mechanism emphasized so far in the chapter. Keynesians also suggest that there may be a secondary chain of causation running from a decrease in interest rates to

Exhibit 14.6
Alternative views of monetary and fiscal policy effectiveness.
If the money demand curve has a shape like MD_1, while the planned investment
schedule is shaped like I_1, monetary policy will tend to be more effective than fiscal
policy. A change in the money supply will have a big impact on planned expenditure,
while fiscal policy will be severely hampered by the crowding out effect. On the other
hand, a money demand schedule like MD_2, with a planned investment schedule like
I_2, will give the advantage to fiscal policy. Changes in the money supply will have little
impact on investment spending, and the crowding out effect will be small.

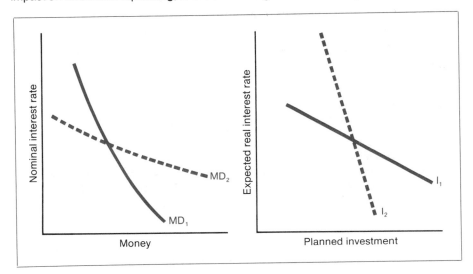

an increase in stock prices and, hence, via an increase in wealth, to an
increase in consumer spending.

Monetarists, without disagreeing that interest rates and planned investment play an important role in transmitting the effects of monetary policy,
tend to emphasize that changes in the money supply affect the economy in
many other ways as well. In particular, they point out that it can be very
misleading to think in terms of a world in which money and bonds and
perhaps stocks are the only assets that people hold in their portfolios—
however convenient such a two- or three-asset economy may be as an
expositional device for writers of textbooks.

Instead, when the Bank of Canada injects new money into the
economy—more money than people initially want to hold—those who
first receive the new money are likely to try to rebalance their portfolios by
purchasing a broad variety of assets. These assets might include not only
bonds of various types and maturities as well as stocks, but also productive
capital equipment, housing, and even consumer durables. Increased
demand for all these assets tends to drive their prices up, which in turn
stimulates construction firms to build more houses, corporations to issue
new stock and purchase new capital equipment, and durable goods makers
to increase production to replace depleted inventories. The effects of
expansionary monetary policy are thus transmitted through a great variety
of channels, including some that are not adequately reflected in market
interest rates, to many parts of the economy. The implication is that
monetary policy may thus be more effective than the traditional Keynesian
transmission mechanism would imply.

Evidence Not surprisingly, a number of attempts have been made to bring empirical evidence to bear on the Keynesian-monetarist controversy. These efforts have succeeded in narrowing, although not entirely closing, the gap between the two schools of thought. The following case studies represent two of a number of possible approaches to evaluating the relative importance of fiscal and monetary policy as determinants of nominal national income. One approach, discussed in Case 14.1, is to look at critical policy episodes when monetary and fiscal policy move in opposite directions. Unfortunately, this happens too infrequently to provide conclusive answers. The alternative approach, discussed in Case 14.2, is to sort out monetary from fiscal influences in periods when the two policies have worked in the same direction.

Case 14.1
Two Critical Episodes in American Economic Policy

During the 1960s, there were two important episodes in the U.S. in which monetary and fiscal policy moved in opposite directions. Both have been interpreted as favoring the monetarist position in regard to the relative power of fiscal and monetary policy.

The first episode occurred in the second half of 1966. In that year, the Federal Reserve (the American equivalent of the Bank of Canada) became worried about possible overheating of the economy and suddenly cut the growth of the money supply from 6.4 percent per year to zero. During the same period, the federal budget swung from surplus to deficit. President Johnson, who did not believe in the need for restraint, was angered by the Fed's policy. He called William McChesney Martin, then the Federal Reserve Board chairman, down to the LBJ Ranch for consultation. Martin flew down but remained unpersuaded. Champions of the Fed's independence from political control have picturesquely dubbed this episode "the Fed's finest hour." The outcome of the finest hour was the mini-recession of early 1967, which apparently indicated that the restrictive monetary policy outweighed the effect of the rising federal deficit.

The second episode also occurred during the Johnson administration, but this time the lineup of forces was reversed. In mid-1968, Congress, at the request of the administration, passed a 10 percent income tax surcharge to cool off the economy. The surcharge swung the federal budget very sharply from a strong deficit position to a strong surplus position. This time, the Federal Reserve feared "fiscal overkill" and continued through the end of 1968 to maintain a very rapid rate of monetary expansion. The outcome of the episode was that the tax surcharge failed to have its intended restraining effect on the economy. The growth of nominal GNP did not decline. This too is cited by monetarists as a demonstration of the relative importance of monetary policy.

Case 14.2
A Monetarist vs. Keynesian Analysis of the 1974 Inflation

In Chapter 7, we noted the double-digit inflation (10.9 percent) that Canada experienced in 1974. The causes of this inflation will be examined in greater detail in chapters 15 and 16. However, it can be observed here that the controversy between monetarists and Keynesian fiscal theorists is reflected in their differing interpretations of what caused the inflation of 1974. Those who follow the ideas of Keynes argue that prices rose because of increased demand for our goods and services, and because of rising costs such as wages and profits. All these things happened. But monetarists argue that such demand and cost factors could not have caused higher prices if the Bank of Canada had not allowed the money supply to increase. It takes more money to increase prices in general. Therefore it is the monetary authorities who control the process of inflation.

This is the viewpoint, for example, of Thomas Courchene, who maintains that "money is at the root of all inflation.... Inflation is always and everywhere a monetary phenomenon."[5] He notes that in 1974, in one quarter alone, M_1, the narrowly defined money supply, increased by 20 percent. Though spending and cost pressures had increased, it was the rapid expansion of the money supply that made the inflation possible.

To some extent the debate on this issue boils down to a question of immediate versus primary cause. When someone shoots another person, the immediate cause is the firing of the pistol. It is possible to argue that the particular murder would not have occurred in that particular way if a gun had not been made available to the murderer. To apply the analogy to the inflation process, the gun is the money supply, and its availability enables a person with inflationary intent to increase purchases, which causes prices to rise. This is the immediate cause that monetarists focus on.

Keynesians tend to look for the primary cause. Given that murderers need weapons, the primary question is: what conditions brought about the murderer's intent to kill? To apply it to inflation, given that spenders need money, what brought about the increased spending pressure? It is from this difference in focus that some of the controversy between monetarists and Keynesians stems.

Inflationary Expectations and the Effects of Monetary Policy

As the debate between monetarists and Keynesians continues, other controversies that do not always exactly parallel this older one have developed. Take, for example, the issue of the effects of monetary policy in a world of nonzero inflationary expectations. The analysis of these effects involves elements about which there is fairly broad agreement among economists, but at the same time it serves to illustrate some new areas of controversy.

Inserting a Wedge Up to this point, to simplify the analysis, it was assumed that the expected rate of inflation in the economy was zero. This simplification conveniently made the nominal interest rate equal to the expected real interest rate, but it clearly came at some cost in terms of realism. In what follows, it will be worth sketching at least roughly the way the theory can be modified to take inflationary expectations into account.

Turn first to Exhibit 14.7. This exhibit shows how the expected rate of inflation can be represented as a wedge between the nominal rate of interest, which appears on the vertical axis of the money market diagram, and the expected real rate of interest, which appears on the vertical axis of the planned investment curve. The figure is drawn on the assumption of a 5 percent per year expected rate of inflation. That brings an 8 percent nominal interest rate down to a 3 percent expected real rate. A lower expected rate of inflation would insert a thinner wedge between the two rates and a higher expected rate of inflation a fatter one.

How Large a Wedge? It would be simple enough to modify Exhibits 14.1, 14.3, 14.4, and 14.6 to take into account any given level of inflationary expectations. To do so, it would be necessary only to add a wedge of the

---

[5] Thomas Courchene, *Money, Inflation, and the Bank of Canada* (Montreal: C. D. Howe Research Institute, 1976), p. 263.

Exhibit 14.7
Inflationary expectations and interest rates
If the expected rate of inflation is not zero (zero was assumed earlier in this chapter), the nominal interest rate will differ from the expected real interest rate by an amount equal to the expected rate of inflation. The expected rate of inflation can thus be pictured as a "wedge" between the nominal interest rate, appearing on the vertical axis of the money market diagram, and the expected real rate of interest, appearing on the vertical axis of the planned investment diagram.

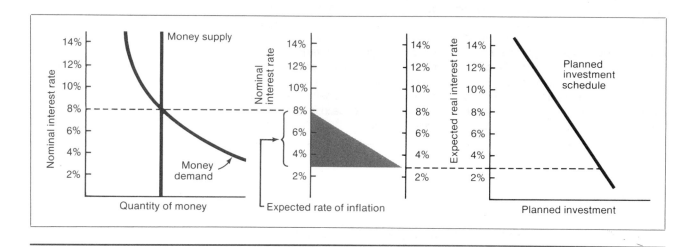

kind shown in Exhibit 14.7. But how large a wedge? That is to say, what determines the expected rate of inflation at any one time? Economists are not altogether in agreement as to the answer.

Adaptive Expectations   One hypothesis is that people form their expectations of future inflation primarily on the basis of the rate of inflation experienced in the immediate past. If inflation is rapid, people expect rapid inflation to continue, if prices are stable, they expect continued price stability. This is known as the **adaptive expectations** hypothesis, because it says that people's expectations about inflation adapt fairly quickly to what has recently happened to the price level.

Adaptive expectations
Expectations about the rate of inflation or other future economic events formed primarily on the basis of experience in the recent past.

Rational Expectations   Clearly, the adaptive expectations hypothesis makes a lot of sense, in that all it really says is that people tend to learn from experience. Some economists argue, however, that this hypothesis may be too restrictive. In forming their expectations about inflation, these economists say, people may not look only at the past rates of inflation that reflect the outcome of past economic policy. They may look also at policies presently being pursued or likely soon to be introduced and may try to judge the effects of these policies on the price level. Their judgments about the future effects of current and future policies are then combined with their lessons of past experience to form expectations about the future rate of inflation.

Rational expectations
Expectations about the rate of inflation or other future economic events based on a rational weighing of all available evidence, including evidence on the probable effects of present and future economic policy.

This view of how expectations are formed has come to be known as the **rational expectations** hypothesis, because it emphasizes the rational sifting and weighing of all available indications of how the price level might move in the future.

Monetary Policy, Expectations, and Interest Rates The fact that inflationary expectations change in response to changing economic conditions and policies makes it necessary to modify the analysis of the effects of monetary policy on interest rates. Under the simplifying assumption of zero inflationary expectations used earlier in the chapter, expansionary monetary policy led to a new equilibrium in which both nominal and real interest rates were lower. In the real world, however, things are not always so simple.

Long-Term Effect Imagine for example, that the economy is initially in an equilibrium with zero inflationary expectations and the nominal and real rates of interest both at 4 percent. Suppose that the Bank of Canada then undertakes a sustained, rapid expansion of the money supply, stimulating the growth of nominal GNP. Some of this growth will presumably take the form of growth of real output; but in the present case, suppose that nominal GNP grows too rapidly for real GNP to keep up. The difference between the growth of nominal and real GNP must be made up by inflation.

Initially, no inflation is anticipated; but as inflation continues, it comes to be expected. This drives a wedge between the nominal rate of interest and the expected real rate of interest. If inflation is rapid enough and continues long enough, the wedge will grow large enough to begin pushing up the nominal rate of interest. If, say, everyone comes to expect 6 percent per year inflation as the long-term norm, the initially assumed 4 percent nominal rate of interest surely cannot be maintained. The nominal rate would in principle rise to 10 percent, enough to restore the expected real rate to its original 4 percent. The conclusion, then, is that if the money supply is continuously expanded sufficiently to produce sustained inflation, the long-term effect will be to raise, not lower, nominal interest rates.

Short-Term Effects As a long-term proposition, this conclusion is now widely accepted. The short-term effects of monetary policy on interest rates are less settled, however, and depend in part on whether one emphasizes adaptive or rational expectations.

With purely adaptive expectations, the short-term effects of monetary expansion might well be exactly as represented earlier in this chapter: both the nominal and real interest rates would be depressed. Only later, after the actual rate of inflation accelerated, would more rapidly rising prices begin to be reflected in expectations and in a higher nominal rate.

Rational expectations, however, introduce new possible short-term effects of policy changes. For example, the Bank of Canada has recently undertaken to announce its plans for monetary expansion up to a year in advance. If it were possible to predict exactly the effects on the rate of inflation of the Bank's policy, borrowers and lenders would begin to take that amount of inflation into account from the day the announcement was made. If the announcement implied a higher than previously expected rate of inflation, nominal interest rates would jump upward immediately, even before the announced policy was put into effect. With full adjustment of the nominal rate, the expected real rate of interest might not change at all.

In practice, perfect forecasting of inflation is not possible. "Bank of Canada watchers" try to guess the significance of every speech made by the governor of the Bank, and every week's data on the monetary aggregates. More often than not, however, these watchers cannot even agree among themselves. The short-run effects of monetary policy remain difficult to forecast.

CONCLUSIONS

In tying together fiscal and monetary policy, this chapter has rounded out the discussion of the determination of nominal national income and product. As the discussion of monetary policy and inflationary expectations made clear, it is time now to turn to the question of how the growth of nominal income is split up between inflation and the growth of real income. Only when we have thoroughly investigated that question will we be able to make a judgment as to what fiscal and monetary policy can and cannot hope to accomplish in promoting full employment, price stability, economic growth, and balance of payments stability.

SUMMARY

1. Analysis of the interaction between money and the multiplier requires moving from partial equilibrium analysis to general equilibrium analysis. What happens in the money market affects aggregate demand because any change in the interest rate changes planned investment expenditure. What happens to aggregate demand affects the money market, because movements in nominal national income shift the money demand curve.

2. The money market and the circular flow can both be in equilibrium at once only if a certain pair of values for the interest rate and nominal income prevail. With the money supply, autonomous consumption, the marginal propensity to consume, net taxes, net exports, and the position of the planned investment schedule given, the equilibrium values for nominal national income and the interest rate are unique.

3. An increase in government purchases has a somewhat weaker impact on the equilibrium level of nominal national income than a simple application of the multiplier theory predicts. The reason is that any growth in nominal income shifts the money demand curve to the right and pushes up the interest rate. This in turn crowds out some private investment, partially offsetting the increase in government purchases.

4. If the expected rate of inflation is assumed not to change, an increase in the money supply has the initial effect of depressing the nominal and the expected real rate. This stimulates planned investment, and aggregate demand increases. As nominal national income rises, the money demand schedule shifts to the right, limiting but not completely cancelling out the fall in the interest rate. In the new equilibrium position, the interest rate will be lower and the level of nominal national income higher than before the monetary expansion.

5. Keynesian and monetarist economists have long debated the relative effectiveness of monetary and fiscal policy and the transmission mechanisms through which they influence the economy. The inflationary experience of the 1970s has added new elements of controversy—for

example, over the role played by inflationary expectations in determining the effects of monetary policy.

DISCUSSION QUESTIONS

1. Suppose that you wanted to study the effect of a variation in rainfall on the prices of three agricultural products: corn, soybeans, and hogs. Do you think a general equilibrium approach or a partial equilibrium approach would give you more insight into the problem? Explain.
2. Use the theory presented in this chapter to trace the effects of a tax increase. What happens to national income, the interest rate, investment, consumption, and net exports?
3. Use the theory presented in this chapter to trace the effects of an increase in required reserve ratios on demand deposits. What happens to national income, the interest rate, investment, consumption, and net exports?
4. Suppose there is a contractionary gap in the economy. For the sake of discussion, assume that the government can with equal ease bring national income up to its target level by using expansionary monetary policy or by increasing government purchases. Suppose that the government also has a long-term goal of promoting rapid economic growth. Can you think of any reason for the government to use one policy rather than the other? Explain.
5. Would you say that the governor of the Bank of Canada is one of the most powerful people in Canada? Would your opinion have been the same before you read this chapter? Before you started this course?
6. Suppose that the Bank of Canada decided on a policy of pegging the nominal interest rate at some level, r, by smoothly expanding or contracting the money supply. (This policy could be represented graphically by drawing a horizontal rather than a vertical money supply curve.) Assume zero inflationary expectations. How would the policy affect the effectiveness of fiscal policy? What would happen to the crowding out effect? (Bonus question: Suppose the Bank attempted to peg the nominal interest rate in the face of rising inflationary expectations. What do you think would happen?)

APPENDIX TO CHAPTER 14
THE ELEMENTARY ALGEBRA
OF MONEY AND
INCOME DETERMINATION

This appendix is a continuation of the Appendix to Chapter 10, which developed a simple algebraic version of the multiplier theory. It adds no new theory to what has been presented in the body of Chapter 14. Nonetheless, readers who feel comfortable with elementary algebra may find the approach presented here useful in consolidating their understanding of the general theory of nominal income determination. Throughout this appendix, the real rate of inflation is assumed to be zero, as in the first part of the chapter.

AGGREGATE DEMAND

The basis equation for aggregate nominal demand or planned expenditure is:

$$AND = C + I + G + X - M. \qquad \textbf{14A.1}$$

In the Appendix to Chapter 10, the C in this equation was replaced with a consumption schedule, which was written as:

$$C = a + b(Y - T),$$ **14.A2a**

and imports with a schedule written as:

$$M = Ma + m(Y),$$ **14A.2b**

where a and b were constants representing autonomous consumption and the marginal propensity to consume, $Y - T$ stood for nominal disposable income, Ma was autonomous imports, and m was the marginal propensity to import. Now, I in Equation 14A.1 will also be replaced with a simple planned investment schedule:

$$I = c + dr,$$ **14A.3**

where I stands for planned investment and r for the interest rate, and where c and d are constants. The constant d, which is the reciprocal of the slope of the planned investment schedule, will have a negative value, because planned investment increases as the rate of interest falls.

Putting together Equations 14A.1, 14A.2a and b, and 14A.3, the following general expression for the aggregate demand schedule is arrived at:

$$AND = a + c + b(Y - T) + dr + G + X - Ma - mY.$$ **14A.4**

MONEY DEMAND

For a general equilibrium analysis of nominal income determination, a money demand schedule is also needed. The one used in Chapters 11 and 12 gave a money demand curve in the shape of a rectangular hyperbola. (Exhibit 12.2, for example, is based on the formula MD = 1.2Y/r.) To retain this kind of money demand schedule would involve the use of quadratic equations and would unnecessarily complicate the arithmetic, so it is replaced with a linearized money demand schedule written as:

$$MD = e + fY + gr,$$ **14A.5**

where MD stands for the quantity of money demanded, r for the interest rate, and Y for income and where $e, f,$ and g are constants. The constant g is the reciprocal of the slope of the money demand schedule. It is negative because money demand decreases when the interest rate rises.

The reader is cautioned that this linear formulation of the money demand function has certain drawbacks. One is that, except for a certain central range of the variables, algebraic solution of the equilibrium equations (to be presented below) may produce negative values for income or the interest rate. Such negative values have no reasonable economic meaning. Care will be taken to keep within the safe range of values in the examples.

NUMERICAL VALUES

The constants in these equations can be replaced with representative numerical values to show how the algebraic formulations of planned expenditures and money demand can be put to work. Using $a = 100, b = 0.75, c = 210, d = -500, e = 80, f = 0.2, m = 0.15,$ and $g = -400$, Equations 14A.4 and 14A.5 can be rewritten as:

$$AND = 310 + 0.75(Y - T) - 0.15Y - 500r + G + X - Ma$$ **14A.6**

and

$$MD = 80 + 0.2Y - 400r.$$ **14A.7**

EQUILIBRIUM CONDITIONS

As shown in the text of Chapter 12, the economy as a whole can be in equilibrium only when both the money market and the circular flow are in equilibrium. Money market equilibrium requires that money supply equal money demand, and equilibrium in the circular flow requires that national product be equal to planned expenditure. These equilibrium conditions can be written as:

$$MS = MD \qquad \text{14A.8}$$

for the money market, where MS stands for the money supply, and

$$Y = AND \qquad \text{14A.9}$$

for the circular flow.

Substituting Equations 14A.6 and 14A.7 into Equations 14A.8 and 14A.9:

$$MS = 80 + 0.2Y - 400r \qquad \text{14A.10}$$

and

$$Y = 310 + 0.75(Y - T) - 0.15Y - 500r + G + X - Ma, \qquad \text{14.A11}$$

which simplifies to:

$$Y = 775 - 1.875T + 2.5(G + X - Ma) - 1250r. \qquad \text{14A.12}$$

Equilibrium in the economy is possible only for pairs of values for r and Y that simultaneously satisfy Equations 14A.10 and 14A.12.

POLICY VARIABLES

Besides r and Y, there are five variables in Equations 14A.10 and 14A.12 for which numerical values have not yet been specified. Two of these values are X (exports) and M (imports). The problems that follow assume that exports (X) are autonomous, while imports (M) are partly autonomous (Ma) and partly related to national income (mY). The remaining three variables are G (government purchases), T (net taxes), and MS (the money supply). These are collectively referred to as policy variables, because they stand for the elements of the economy that are under the direct control of the government. The following problems will show how the manipulation of these variables can be used by policy makers in their attempts to hit their economic targets.

Problem 1: Government policy makers set their policy variables at the values G = 125, T = 80, MS = 300, Ma = 50, and X = 245. Apply Equations 14A.10 and 14A.12 to determine the equilibrium values of r and Y.
Solution: Equation 14A.10 becomes:

$$300 = 80 + 0.2Y - 400r,$$

and Equation 14A.12 becomes:

$$Y = 775 - 150 + 800 - 1250r.$$

Simplifying and setting the equations equal to zero:

$$220 - 0.2Y + 400r = 0$$

$$1425 - Y - 1250r = 0.$$

The usual methods for solution of simultaneous equations give the pair of values r = 0.10 and Y = 1,300 as the equilibrium levels for interest rate and national income.

Problem 2: Using the solution to Problem 1 as a starting point, assume that the authorities want to raise the equilibrium level of national income to a target level of $1,400, using monetary policy alone. How much will the money supply have to be increased to accomplish this objective?

Solution: Substitute Y = $1,400, G = 125, T = 80, X = 245, and Ma = 50 into Equation 14A.12 in order to find the required equilibrium value for r.

The substitution gives:

$$1400 = 775 - 150 + 800 - 1250r,$$

which simplifies to:

$$25 - 1250r = 0.$$

The solution to this last equation is r = 0.02.

Next, substitute the equilibrium values Y = 1,400 and r = 0.02 into Equation 14A.10 in order to determine the money supply necessary to give a 0.02 rate of interest when national income is $1,400. This gives:

$$MS = 80 + 0.2(1400) - 400(0.02) = 352.$$

The solution to the problem, then, is that the money supply must be increased by $52—from $300 to $352—in order to raise national income to $1,400.

Problem 3: Using the solution to Problem 1 as a starting point, show that an increase of $26 in government purchases will be more effective in raising the equilibrium level of national income if the Bank of Canada pursues an accommodating monetary policy than if it leaves the money supply unchanged.

Solution: An accommodating monetary policy is one that expands the money supply enough to keep the interest rate unchanged—in this case, equal to 0.10. Substitute the values T = 80, G = 151, Ma = 50, X = 245, and r = 0.10 into Equation 14A.12 to get the new value that equilibrium national income will reach if accommodating monetary policy is pursued. Without going into details, the new equilibrium Y with accommodating monetary policy is $1,365. (Further substitution of Y = $1,365 and r = 0.10 into Equation 14A.10 shows that the money supply would have to be increased to $313 to achieve this result.)

Without accommodating monetary policy, the new values of Y and r are found by going through the same steps outlined in the solution to Problem 1, using G = 151. Again without going into details, the solution turns out to be Y = $1,340 and r = 0.12. Substitution of the new, higher value of the interest rate into the investment schedule (I = 210 − 500r) shows that $10 of the original $160 in private planned investment is crowded out by the $26 increase in government purchases. This accounts for the lower equilibrium value of Y when accommodating monetary policy is not used.

THE INTERACTION OF THE FOREIGN SECTOR AND THE MULTIPLIER

WHAT YOU WILL LEARN IN THIS CHAPTER

This chapter completes the general equilibrium analysis introduced in Chapter 14 by integrating the foreign sector into the multiplier process. First, the determination of exchange rates is examined briefly. An explanation of balance of payments equilibrium follows. Equilibrium in the foreign sector is related to equilibrium in the money market and in the circular flow, and to monetary and fiscal policy. The effects of fixed and floating exchange rates are also examined. The last part of the chapter discusses the functioning of the international monetary sector and concludes with a brief summary of Canada's current problems.

FOR REVIEW

Here are some important terms and concepts that will be put to use in this chapter. If you do not understand them, review them before proceeding.
* *Supply and demand (Chapter 3)*
* *Balance of payments accounts (Chapter 6)*
* *Net exports (Chapter 8)*
* *Net exports in the multiplier process (Chapter 9)*
* *Integration of the money market and the circular flow (Chapter 14)*

Several important elements associated with Canada's participation in international trade and finance have been discussed in previous chapters. The bases for both domestic and international trade were examined in Chapter 2. The various sources of international receipts and payments, and the method used to record them, were examined in Chapter 6, in connection with Canada's national income accounts. The exact meaning of "net exports" was explained in Chapter 6, and "balance of payments equilibrium" will be defined later in this chapter.

The macro model of the Canadian economy developed in Chapter 8 included net exports as one of the important components of planned expenditure. The multiplier formula of Chapter 9 incorporated the leakage effect of imports, and it was shown how such leakages change the impact of fiscal and monetary policies. Thus, throughout the preceding analysis, Canada has been treated as an open economy, heavily dependent on trade with other countries.

However, foreign trade is just one aspect of Canada's international transactions. Exports and imports form the current account component of Canada's balance of payments, but, as Chapter 6 indicated, the balance of payments also consists of capital flows, recorded in the capital account, and changes in reserves of foreign currency. A deficit or surplus in one account must be offset by surpluses or deficits in the other accounts.

The balancing process is affected by fiscal and monetary policy and in turn determines the effectiveness of such policies. A main concern of this chapter is to extend the general equilibrium approach of Chapter 14, in order to show how fiscal and monetary policy interact with the foreign sector, and how this in turn influences conditions in the money market and in the circular flow.

THE THEORY OF EXCHANGE RATE DETERMINATION

How supply and demand determine the short-run value of the Canadian dollar

One of the most popular topics of conversation among Canadians (next to the weather) is the fluctuating value of the Canadian dollar. Why was our dollar worth more than the American dollar for many years prior to 1976, and why has it become less valuable in the last few years? The supply and demand analysis described in Chapter 3 helps to explain this.

At any given time, there is a demand for our dollar by foreigners who wish to buy from us. Those Canadians from whom foreigners make their purchases want to be paid in Canadian dollars. Foreign purchasers must go to the foreign exchange market to obtain Canadian dollars for their transactions. This results in a demand for Canadian dollars in the foreign exchange market. On the other hand, each time a Canadian purchases goods or services from abroad, he must exchange Canadian dollars in the foreign exchange market for the currency of the country where the purchase is made. This results in a supply of Canadian dollars in the foreign exchange market, and a corresponding demand for other currencies. The value of our dollar is determined through such demand and supply forces.

Foreign exchange market
The complex of institutions through which the currency of one country may be exchanged for that of another.

The term **foreign exchange market** refers to the whole complex of institutions, including banks, specialized foreign exchange dealers, and official government agencies through which the currency of one country may be exchanged for that of another.

All kinds of goods and services are exchanged between countries, as was noted in Chapter 6. Payments on *current account* consist of payments for imports of goods and services, including payment of interest and dividends to foreigners for past loans and investments. For the moment, assume that no other transactions occur between the citizens of the various countries of the world.

Suppose, for example, that an American clothing importer wants to buy a shipment of parkas from Canada. The importer plans to finance the purchase with U.S. dollars held in a New York bank account. However, the parka manufacturer wants to be paid in Canadian dollars, which can be used to meet payrolls and buy materials in Canada. The American bank sells the necessary quantity of U.S. dollars on the foreign exchange market, receiving Canadian dollars in return. These are then forwarded to the Canadian manufacturer to pay for the parkas.

THE SUPPLY AND DEMAND FOR FOREIGN EXCHANGE

Meanwhile, thousands of other Canadians and Americans are also buying and selling dollars for their own purposes. The overall activity in the foreign exchange market, like that in any other market, can be characterized in terms of supply and demand curves, such as those shown in Exhibit 15.1. This market has been drawn so that it shows the supply and demand for Canadian dollars, with the price (that is, the exchange rate) shown in terms of U.S. dollars per Canadian dollar. But it could equally well have been drawn to show the supply and demand for U.S. dollars with the price in Canadian dollars per U.S. dollar.

Look first at the demand curve for Canadian dollars that appears in this market. The shape and position of the demand curve for Canadian dollars depends on how American demand for Canadian goods varies as the exchange rate varies, other things being equal. It is easy to see that the demand curve will normally be downward sloping. Suppose, for example, that parkas sell in Canada for $50. At an exchange rate of 1 U.S. dollar per Canadian dollar, American consumers would have to pay $50 U.S. They might buy a total of, say, 200,000 parkas per year, thus generating a demand for 10 million Canadian dollars in the foreign exchange market. If the exchange rate were to fall to 0.8 U.S. dollars per Canadian dollar while the parka price remained unchanged, American consumers would be able to buy parkas more cheaply for U.S. dollars. At that lower price, they would presumably buy a greater quantity, say, 510,000 parkas. The demand for Canadian dollars on the foreign exchange market would thus increase to $25.5 million.

The supply curve for dollars in Exhibit 15.1 (S_1) is drawn with an upward slope, indicating that more Canadian dollars will be supplied to the foreign exchange market as the price of Canadian dollars, in terms of U.S. dollars, rises. This will be the case whenever Canadian demand for American goods increases so much when the value of the Canadian dollar rises that more Canadian dollars are actually spent and supplied to Americans. Suppose, for example, that a certain model American-built motor home has a price of $20,000 U.S. At an exchange rate of 1 U.S. dollar per Canadian dollar, the motor home would sell for $20,000 in Canada (forgetting about shipping costs and other charges). If, say, 5,000 of the motor homes per year were sold at that price, Canada would have to supply 100 million Canadian dollars to the foreign exchange market in order to get the 100 million U.S. dollars needed to pay the American manufacturer. Suppose next that the exchange rate rose to 1.25 U.S. dollars per Canadian dollar, so that Canadian buyers could get the motor home for just 16,000 Canadian dollars. If the quantity imported rose to 7,500 per year as a result of the increase in the value of the Canadian dollar, Canadians would supply 120 million Canadian dollars to the exchange markets.

Exhibit 15.1

Equilibrium between demand and supply in the foreign exchange market

The demand curve for Canadian dollars (D) indicates that Americans will desire a greater quantity of Canadian dollars as the cost per U.S. dollar declines. The quantity supplied (S_1) increases at higher exchange rates.

When only current account transactions are taken into account, the process by which equilibrium is maintained in the foreign exchange market is very simple. Suppose that a sudden increased preference of Canadians for travel in the United States shifts the supply curve for Canadian dollars to the right, from S_1 to S_2. This creates an excess supply of dollars and puts downward pressure on the exchange rate. As the exchange rate falls, Americans are induced to spend more on Canadian goods, and Canadians to spend less on American goods. The exchange rate reaches a new equilibrium at 0.8 U.S. dollars per Canadian dollar.

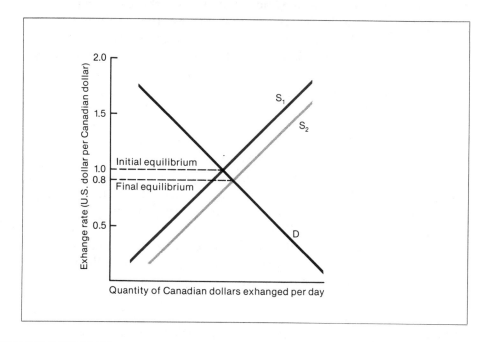

Exhibit 15.1 also helps to illustrate how exchange rates can change as a result of shifts in demand and supply. As that Exhibit is drawn, the foreign exchange market is initially in equilibrium at an exchange rate of 1 U.S. dollar per Canadian dollar. Suppose then that some change in Canadian spending habits occurs. Canadians might decide to travel more in the United States, and pay more to Americans in the form of interest and dividends. This could increase the supply of Canadian dollars in the foreign exchange market, at the existing exchange rate. This is shown in Exhibit 15.1 as a shift in the Canadian dollar supply curve from S_1 to S_2. The shift in the supply curve initially creates an excess supply of Canadian dollars, which tends to depress the exchange rate. As the exchange rate falls, Canadian goods become cheaper for Americans to buy, encouraging an increase in the quantity demanded of Canadian dollars. This is represented by a movement down along the demand curve in Exhibit 15.1. At the same time, American goods become more expensive for Canadian buyers, some-what decreasing the quantity of Canadian dollars supplied. This appears as a downward movement along the new Canadian dollar supply curve. As the

figure is drawn, the supply and demand for Canadian dollars comes into equilibrium again at an exchange rate of 0.8 U.S. dollars per Canadian dollar.

In the terminology of foreign exchange markets, the Canadian dollar is said to **depreciate** when its price falls in terms of foreign currency, as in the example above. Seen from the American point of view, a fall in the price of the Canadian dollar in terms of U.S. dollars is equivalent to a rise in the price of the U.S. dollar in terms of Canadian dollars. The American dollar, then, can be said to have **appreciated** against the Canadian dollar.

Depreciation and appreciation of the exchange rate The Canadian dollar is said to depreciate when its price falls in terms of foreign currency, and to appreciate when its price rises in terms of foreign currency.

The Capital Account

Current account transactions are not the only ones that take place between residents of different countries. We must also consider international lending and borrowing, and international sales and purchases of assets. A Canadian company might, for example, obtain a short-term loan from a Milwaukee bank to finance the purchase of a shipload of beer for import to Canada. The Ontario government might get a long-term loan from Citibank of New York to help finance construction of a hydroelectric project. A Canadian millionaire might open an account in a Swiss bank. Or an oil-rich Middle Easterner might purchase Saskatchewan farmland or shares in a Canadian corporation.

All of these transactions and others like them are called transactions on *capital account*. Purchases of Canadian assets by foreigners and borrowing by Canadians from foreigners create a flow of Canadian dollars into Canada, and are thus called *capital inflows*. Purchases of foreign assets by Canadians or loans by Canadians to foreigners create a flow of Canadian dollars away from Canada, and are thus called *capital outflows*.

Foreign Exchange Markets with Current and Capital Accounts

When only current account transactions were considered, equilibrium in foreign exchange markets required that every dollar's worth of goods or services imported be paid for by a dollar's worth of goods or services exported. Once capital account transactions are introduced, however, this need no longer be the case. Imports of goods or services can now be paid for either by exports, or by capital inflows; that is, by borrowing from foreigners or selling assets to foreigners. Similarly, a country can export more goods and services than it imports, so long as it provides its trading partners with the means to do so, by making loans to them or buying assets from them.

Consider the hypothetical case shown in Exhibit 15.2. In the year for which these accounts are drawn, Canada is shown as importing more in goods and services than it exports, and running a current account deficit of $5 billion. (In the table, all flows of dollars away from Canada are shown with a minus sign and all flows of dollars toward Canada are shown with a plus sign.) At the same time, however, borrowing from foreigners plus sales of Canadian assets to foreigners (capital inflows) exceed loans to foreigners plus purchases of foreign assets (capital outflows) by $5 billion. Canada thus has a $5 billion capital account surplus that exactly balances the current account deficit.

Exports (including travel by foreigners in Canada and receipt by Canadians of interest and dividends from abroad)		+$62
Imports (including payments by Canadians for travel abroad and for interest and dividends to foreigners)		−$67
Transfers		0
Current account deficit		−$5
Sales of Canadian assets to foreigners and borrowing from foreigners	+$7	
Purchases of foreign assets and loans to foreigners	−$2	
Capital account surplus		+$5

Exhibit 15.2

Hypothetical balance of payments accounts, current and capital accounts only (billions of Canadian dollars)

In a world where the only international transactions are those taking place on current and capital account, any current account deficit must be balanced by a capital account surplus, and vice versa. In this hypothetical example, Canada is shown importing more than it exports, thus running a current account deficit. This is financed by a capital inflow; that is, by borrowing from abroad or by sales of assets to foreigners. Note that all outflows of dollars are listed with a minus sign and all inflows with a plus sign.

It is not necessary to draw a new set of foreign exchange supply and demand curves to take both current and capital transactions into account. There is still just one supply curve of Canadian dollars, one demand curve for Canadian dollars, and one exchange rate for the Canadian dollar in terms of any other currency, such as the U.S. dollar. However, there are now additional sources of shifts in the supply and demand curves, such as a rise in Canadian interest rates. One immediate effect of this would be to make Canadian securities more attractive than before to foreign buyers. Their increased demand for Canadian dollars with which to buy these securities would show up as a rightward shift in the demand for Canadian dollars in the foreign exchange market. That would tend to cause the Canadian dollar to appreciate against the U.S. dollar. As will be discussed later in this chapter, the Bank of Canada might deliberately cause interest rates in Canada to be higher than those in the U.S., in order to get the demand curve for the Canadian dollar to shift to the right. The exchange rate would then rise above 0.8 U.S. dollars per Canadian dollar. It is shifts in the type of international transactions just described that explain, through demand and supply analysis, how the value of our dollar changes in the short run.

The Official Reserve Account

One important category of international transactions has yet to be explained: the sales and purchases of foreign currency reserves held by the Bank of Canada and the corresponding central banks of other countries. As Chapter 6 indicated, these sales and purchases are not included in the current account because they are not made to pay for imports or exports or to make unilateral transfers. They are not included in the capital account, because they are not necessarily made for investment purposes. Often, sales and purchases of foreign currency reserves by central banks are made instead to offset an excess supply or demand of dollars or other currencies, thereby preventing or moderating exchange rate fluctuations that would otherwise take place. These sales and purchases are referred to as transactions on the **official reserve account.**

Official reserve account The account whose transactions include purchases and sales of reserves of foreign currency by central banks.

An example of how official reserve transactions might affect exchange rates appears in Exhibit 15.3. This diagram begins with the same scenario as

Exhibit 15.3

Official intervention in the foreign exchange market

This exhibit begins with the same scenario shown in Exhibit 15.1. Starting from an exchange rate of one U.S. dollar per Canadian dollar at the intersection of D_1 and S_1, an increase in transfers from Canada shifts the Canadian dollar supply curve to the right, to S_2. That shift creates a surplus of Canadian dollars and puts downward pressure on the exchange rate. To prevent the exchange rate from falling, the Canadian or U.S. government begins official reserve purchases of dollars. These purchases shift the demand curve for dollars to the right, to D_2, until the demand curve intersects the new supply curve at the old exchange rate.

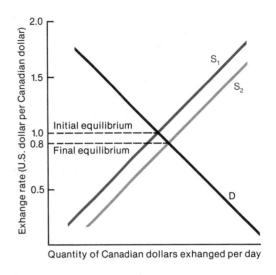

Quantity of Canadian dollars exchanged per day

did Exhibit 15.1: initially, the market is in equilibrium at an exchange rate of 1 U.S. dollar per Canadian dollar. This is shown by the intersection of D_1 and S_1. Next an increase in Canadian transfer payments causes a rightward shift in the dollar supply curve to S_2, which creates an excess supply of Canadian dollars at the original exchange rate. Normally, this would cause the Canadian dollar to depreciate against the U.S. dollar. Instead of permitting the exchange rate to fall, however, the Bank of Canada could decide to use some of the U.S. dollars it holds as part of its foreign currency reserves to purchase the surplus Canadian dollars. Alternatively, the U.S. Federal Reserve might sell U.S. dollars in order to build up its reserves of Canadian dollars, or both central banks might act together, coordinating their efforts. In any event, the transactions would show up on the exchange market diagram as a rightward shift in the demand curve for Canadian dollars. As Exhibit 15.3 is drawn, sufficient official reserve purchases of Canadian dollars are made to shift the demand curve all the way to Position D_2. The entire excess supply of Canadian dollars is thus soaked up, and the exchange rate does not change.

So far, only the mechanics of exchange rate determination have been discussed; exchange rates, like other prices, are determined by supply and demand. The next step is to look beyond the supply and demand curves for a theory explaining why, at any particular time, the curves intersect at one exchange rate rather than another. Once that step has been taken, the next section will discuss the conditions for equilibrium in both the domestic and foreign sectors of the economy. This will then be followed by an examination of how and why governments use interest rate policies and reserve transactions to intervene in foreign exchange markets.

THE LONG RUN: PURCHASING POWER PARITY

Purchasing power parity theory (of exchange rates)
The theory holding that the price of a unit of Currency A in terms of Currency B will, in the long run, tend to be equal to the ratio of the price level in Country B to the price level in Country A.

The leading theory of exchange rate determination in the long run is the so-called **purchasing power parity theory**. According to this theory, the price of a unit of Currency A in terms of Currency B (that is, the exchange rate) will, in the long run, tend to equal the ratio of the price level in Country B to the price level in Country A.

In a world where all goods and services were traded internationally, with no transportation costs or other barriers to trade, the purchasing power parity theory would presumably hold exactly. Suppose, for example, that the Canadian and German domestic price levels are such that $100 will buy exactly twice as large a market basket of goods in Canada as can be bought for 100 marks in Germany. The purchasing power parity theory will then imply that the exchange rate must be 2 marks per dollar. If a dollar could be exchanged for more than 2 marks, Canadian consumers would all try to turn in their dollars and do their shopping in Germany. Their attempt to do so would immediately drive the price of the dollar back down to 2 marks. Similarly, if a dollar could be purchased for less than 2 marks, Germans would try to turn in all their marks for dollars and shop in Canada. This would quickly push the price of the dollar up to 2 marks. In such a world, in fact, the expressions "100 dollars" and "200 marks" would simply be different names given in Germany and Canada to equal-sized lumps of abstract purchasing power.

In practice, exchange rates do not always reflect purchasing power parities exactly. According to a study by economist Irving B. Kravis, for example, in 1978, $1 in the United States had as much purchasing power as 3.12 marks in Germany, even though the official exchange rate was 2.08 marks per dollar.[1] The difference can be explained in part by the fact that purchasing power parities reflect the prices of all goods and services, while exchange rates tend to reflect the value of goods and services traded internationally. For example, Kravis estimated that a dollar in the U.S. would buy 3.8 times as much telephone service as a mark would buy in Germany—but telephone calls are not an internationally traded service.

Also, deviations of exchange values from present purchasing power parities may reflect future expectations as much as current realities. For example, if participants in foreign exchange markets come to expect Canadian inflation in the future consistently to average higher in relation to German inflation than they thought in the past, they may shift out of dollar denominated assets into mark denominated assets. These capital account transactions can depress the value of the dollar even before enough actual inflation takes place to justify the new exchange rate in terms of purchasing power parities. Similarly, if participants in foreign exchange markets judge that future real economic growth will cause the demand for a country's exports to increase more rapidly than its demand for imports, the present exchange rate for its currency may be bid up in anticipation of the expected future improvement in its current account balance.

With the necessary reservations, as noted, the purchasing power parity theory can be thought of as determining exchange rates in the long run.

---

[1] Based on unpublished research by Kravis, reported by Alfred Malabre, Jr., "Despite the Dollar's Decline, U.S. Retains Top Living Standards," *Wall Street Journal*, May 1, 1979, p. 48.

THE INTERACTION OF MONEY, NATIONAL INCOME, AND THE BALANCE OF PAYMENTS

The Conditions for General Equilibrium

It was shown in Chapter 14 that the money market and the circular flow can be in equilibrium only if there is a perfect matching of interest rates and nominal national income. Exhibit 14.1 illustrated a general equilibrium situation for the money market and the circular flow. No consideration, however, was given to equilibrium in the balance of payments.

It was observed in Chapter 6 that, in a purely accounting sense, the balance of payments will always be shown to be in equilibrium, because in principle the sum of the current, capital, and reserve accounts will always be exactly zero. However, economists define a **balance of payments equilibrium** as a situation in which there are no changes in reserves. That is, the balance of payments is considered to be in equilibrium when the capital account exactly balances the current account. This means that any loss of foreign currency required to pay for a deficit on the current account is matched by a net capital inflow of the same amount, while a surplus in the current account will be utilized to finance net capital outflows. If such balancing occurs, there will be no loss or build-up of foreign currency reserves.

Balance of payments equilibrium A situation in which transactions in the capital account exactly match transactions in the current account, so that there is no loss or build-up of foreign currency reserves.

As we have seen (Chapter 6), Canada persistently runs a deficit on its current account. An equilibrium in Canada's balance of payments can be said to exist only when capital inflows exceed capital outflows by the amount of the current account deficit. (When capital inflows do exceed capital outflows it is defined as a positive *net* capital inflow.) This kind of equilibrium might be considered a minimal objective. Even more desirable would be a balance or near-balance in the current account itself, with exports equaling imports, easing the pressure to increase inflows of foreign capital to help to pay for a current account deficit. However, the minimal objective will be considered here.

To have a balance of payments equilibrium, negative net exports (deficit on current account) must be matched by positive net capital inflows (surplus on capital account), or positive net exports must be matched by negative net capital inflows.

Net exports, as shown in Exhibit 8.10b, have a positive autonomous element. However, because imports increase with nominal national income, and exports are assumed not to increase, net exports decline as nominal national income increases. The current account, therefore, becomes negative at high levels of income.

We can again make use of the net export function illustrated in Exhibit 8.10b and in Exhibit 15.4c. Exports are assumed to be $125 regardless of income, and imports are $50 plus 0.15 of nominal national income. Net exports (exports minus imports) are equal to $75 − 0.15 national income. At an income level of $500 net exports would be zero, and at levels of income above $500 they become negative.

To have a minimal equilibrium in the balance of payments, net exports must be matched by capital flows. Capital flows are related primarily to interest rates. The higher our interest rates are compared to those of other countries (for example, the United States), the more inclined Canadians will be to borrow in those countries and the less inclined foreigners will be to borrow in Canada. What is important is not the absolute level of our interest rates but the differential between our rates and those of other countries. However, it will be assumed here that as our rates go up the differential increases. Net capital inflows will then be related positively to the rate of interest.

It follows from these assumptions that at a specific level of nominal national income, which produces a particular level of net exports, it will require one particular rate of interest to create capital flows that exactly match the net exports. Therefore, equilibrium in the foreign market requires a matching of interest rates and nominal national income, just as a matching of interest rates and national income was required to create equilibrium simultaneously in the money market and in the circular flow. In fact, as we shall see, general equilibrium in an economy requires that the money market, the circular flow, and the balance of payments all be brought into equilibrium simultaneously by a unique combination of interest rates and nominal national income.

General Equilibrium Including the Foreign Market

The nature of such a general equilibrium, and its necessity, was illustrated in Exhibit 14.1. An interest rate of 8 percent caused the demand for money to be equal to the supply of money. Simultaneously that interest rate resulted in investment spending of $100, which, together with the other spending flows in the economy, was consistent with a nominal national income of $1,200. Therefore, that interest rate, in combination with that particular level of nominal national income, created equilibrium in both the money market and the circular flow.

However, nothing was said in that illustration about equilibrium in the foreign market — that is, in the balance of payments. For that reason it was not really correct to call it a situation of *general* equilibrium.

Exhibit 14.1 told us what was happening to net exports. At a nominal national income of $1,200 they were −$105. Were they matched by a corresponding inflow of capital? We don't know, because up to that point no capital flow function had been developed. This gap must now be filled.

The requirements for simultaneous equilibrium in the circular flow and in the balance of payments are illustrated in Exhibit 15.4. It is assumed that an interest rate of 8 percent has been established in the money market, based on the first diagram in Exhibit 14.1. A hypothetical net capital inflow function is shown in Exhibit 15.4a. At low rates of interest, below 4 percent, it is assumed that net capital inflows would be negative. More capital would leave the country in order to take advantage of higher interest rates elsewhere, than would enter the country, resulting in net capital outflows (or a negative net capital inflow). At rates of interest above 4 percent, capital inflows would begin to exceed capital outflows. At 8 percent interest, it is assumed that net capital inflows would equal $105.[2]

---

[2] The net capital inflow function utilized here is expressed by the equation F = −$105 + 2625 (r), where F = the net capital inflow, $105 is the autonomous net capital inflow, and the number 2625 expresses the rate at which F will change in relation to interest rates (r). E.g., if r = .08, F = −$105 + 2625 (0.8) = −$105 + $210 = +$105.

Exhibit 15.4

A general equilibrium view of the circular flow and the foreign market

Demand and supply forces in the money market (not shown here) have created an interest rate of 8 percent. This interest rate generates a net capital inflow of $105 (15.4a). This is exactly sufficient to pay for the $105 deficit on the current account shown in 15.4c. The latter resulted from a nominal national income of $1,200, which in turn was caused partly by a level of investment of $100. That level of investment was due to the 8 percent rate of interest, as illustrated in 15.4b. A different rate of interest would have led to a net capital inflow and a nominal national income level such that the current and capital accounts would not have been equal. A unique combination of interest and income is required for equilibrium in the foreign sector.

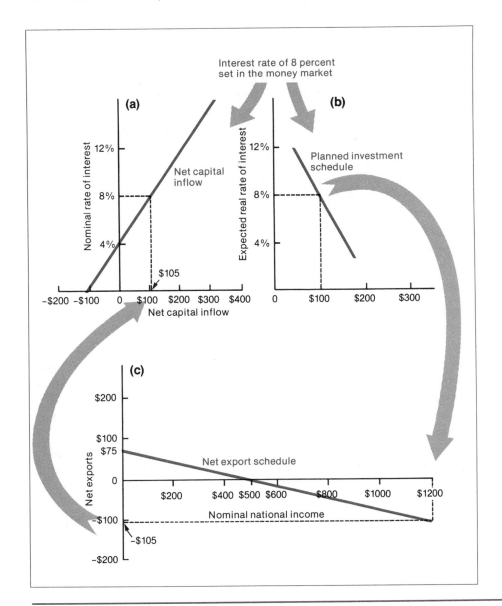

At the same time, at a rate of interest of 8 percent, investment would equal $100, as illustrated in Exhibit 15.4b. This, together with the other expenditure flows noted previously, would result in an equilibrium level of nominal national income of $1,200 (Exhibit 15.4c). Exhibit 15.4c also shows that an income of $1,200 produces net exports of −$105. These net exports are exactly matched by the net capital inflows which the 8 percent rate of interest produced.

We thus have the following simultaneous equilibrium conditions:

1. In the money market, supply and demand forces have been brought into equilibrium at a rate of interest of 8 percent. Given those forces, only that rate of interest will produce equilibrium.

2. In the circular flow, the 8 percent rate of interest helps to create expenditure flows (through the investment function), which produce an equilibrium level of nominal national income of $1,200. Given a rate of interest of 8 percent, no income level other than $1,200 will produce an equivalent level of planned expenditures. Therefore, the circular flow is uniquely in equilibrium at a rate of interest of 8 percent and a nominal national income of $1,200.

3. In the foreign market, the 8 percent rate of interest creates a net capital inflow of $105. Simultaneously, the nominal national income of $1,200 results in a current account deficit of $105. Equilibrium in the foreign market, therefore, results from a perfect matching of interest rates and nominal national income.

The important result is this: a unique combination of a particular rate of interest and a particular level of income is required to produce a general equilibrium for the economy. Government policy may be able to establish interest rates and income levels that achieve equilibrium in two markets but not in all three. Failure to achieve equilibrium in one may frustrate policies designed to maintain equilibrium in the others.

The Difficulty of Achieving General Equilibrium

To understand the difficulty of achieving an equilibrium situation, assume that the government decides to increase nominal national income, because there is too much unemployment when national income is $1,200. Suppose that the Bank of Canada increases the money supply in order to reduce interest rates to 4 percent. This lower rate of interest would increase investment to $150, and—as noted in Chapter 14—the nominal national income would eventually increase by $125, to a new level of $1,325. Before, when only the circular flow and the money market were considered, the economy was judged to be in general equilibrium at the new interest rate and the new level of income. However, note now what happens to equilibrium in the foreign market. At a rate of interest of 4 percent, net capital inflows will fall to zero, while simultaneously, at the income level of $1,325, net exports will decline to −$113.75 ($75−0.15($1,325)). The current account deficit has grown larger as a result of the monetary policy, but at the same time the net capital inflow required to pay for the deficit has diminished. The balance of payments is in serious disequilibrium, and reserves of foreign currency will have to be drawn down in order to pay for the current account deficit.

If fiscal policy, without accommodating monetary policy, were used to increase national income, the effects on the balance of payments would not be as clear cut. The rise in income would increase the current account deficit, but higher interest rates would simultaneously increase net capital inflows. It is highly unlikely that the current and capital accounts would change by the same amount (one down, the other up), so that the end result would probably be either a small overall surplus or a small deficit.

What is likely to happen in an economy in which the foreign market is in serious disequilibrium, perhaps because of a monetary policy designed to lower interest rates and increase income? The result will depend largely on whether the exchange rate is fixed or whether it is allowed to change because of the pressures created by changed interest rates and income.

Government Policy with Fixed and Flexible Exchange Rates

If the exchange rate is fixed, and the interest rate remains at 4 percent, the deficit in the balance of payments will not be self-correcting. However, the Bank of Canada will have to use up its reserves of foreign currency to pay for the imbalance. In the process of selling foreign currency to private dealers who need the foreign currency to pay for the deficit, the Bank will receive cheques in Canadian currency from those dealers, which will reduce deposits of the chartered banks. This will reduce the money supply, thereby increasing interest rates once again and lowering the level of income. Unless the Bank of Canada counterbalances such reductions in the money supply with new infusions of money, the economy will revert to its old equilibrium level. The result is that the monetary policy designed to increase the level of income and reduce the level of unemployment has been completely stymied. Monetary policy, therefore, may be made ineffectual by fixed exchange rates.

Very different results are possible with flexible exchange rates. When the money supply is increased, and the current account deficit increases while net capital inflows diminish, the value of the Canadian dollar will decline. This will happen because the *supply* of Canadian currency in the foreign exchange market will *increase* (as Canadians react to lower interest rates and higher incomes by exchanging more Canadian dollars for foreign currency, in order to purchase more bonds and goods and services from foreigners), and the *demand* for Canadian dollars will *decrease* (as foreigners react to our lower interest rates by buying fewer bonds from us). The decline in the value of our dollar should reduce the current account deficit. Foreigners will find our goods and services cheaper than before, while Canadians will find that foreign goods and services have become more expensive.

In terms of Exhibit 15.4, the net export schedule in Exhibit 15.4c will shift to the right, because at a given level of income more will now be exported and less imported. In fact, it can be assumed that the value of the Canadian dollar will keep dropping until net exports and net capital inflows are equal (meaning that the net export schedule in Exhibit 15.4c shifts so far to the right that net exports equal zero at an income level of $1,325). The foreign market then will have achieved a new equilibrium, at interest rates of 4 percent and the target income level of $1,325. With flexible exchange rates, policy makers have some hope of moving the economy in the desired direction.

Flexible exchange rates may appear to make fiscal policy more potent than our previous examples of the multiplier effect (in Chapter 10) indicated. Partly because of import leakages, the multiplier in our example was only 2.5 for an increase in government expenditures. However, if the government uses an expansionary fiscal policy to increase income, the increased deficit on the current account resulting from higher imports may result in a depreciation of our currency. This will decrease imports and increase exports, thereby increasing the demand forces and the level of income. Yet, higher interest rates will accompany this increased demand, in the absence of increases in the money supply, and the higher rates will attract more foreign capital, driving the exchange rate back up. The net result of flexible exchange rates may actually be less effective fiscal policy but more effective monetary policy.

Exchange Rate Policy

In general, flexible exchange rates are favored by most economists because they eliminate imbalances in the foreign sector that might result from monetary and fiscal policy, so that domestic stabilization policies can be pursued without too much worry about repercussions in the balance of payments.

However, the real world is one in which other considerations also play an important role, so that fixed or semifixed exchange rates are more often the rule than the exception. In the 1950s (until 1961) Canada allowed its exchange rate to fluctuate freely; in the 1960s it operated with fixed exchange rates, and in the 1970s rates were semi-flexible, being controlled partly by special purchases and sales of foreign currency by the Bank of Canada.

The Case for and against Fixed Rates

Real Effects of Currency Disturbances The first point made by proponents of fixed rates is that variations in exchange rates have significant real effects on the economy. When a country's currency appreciates, its expert industries find it harder to compete in world markets. At the same time, industries that face import competition find it difficult to compete in domestic markets. When a country's currency depreciates, in contrast, export and import-competing industries boom, but industries that rely on imported energy or raw materials suffer. If the appreciation or depreciation in question reflects fundamental long-term changes in patterns of world trade, these adjustments in import and export industries may be necessary and desirable. But it is argued that short-term random, cyclical, or speculative changes in exchange rates should not be allowed to disturb the domestic economy. After all, labor and other factors of production cannot make costless moves from sector to sector at a moment's notice.

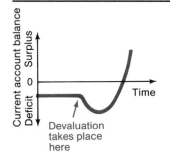

Exhibit 15.5

The J-curve effect

The so-called J-curve effect occurs because a devaluation may initially worsen a country's balance of payments on its current account before eventually improving it. Here, the country has been experiencing a moderate current account deficit for some time. At the point shown, it devalues its currency. At first, the current account drops farther into deficit, but eventually it rises into surplus, following the J-shaped path shown.

The J-curve Effect A second reason frequently advanced for fixing exchange rates is that, in the short run, the depreciation of a country's currency may worsen rather than improve its balance of payments on current account. This is known as the J-curve effect, and is illustrated in Exhibit 15.5. When a country's currency first depreciates, few additional export sales are made immediately, and importers do not or cannot immediately reduce the quantity of goods they purchase. At the lower exchange rates, however, importers do have to offer greater quantities of the domestic currency in order to obtain the foreign currency they need to buy the unchanged physical quantity of imports. The current account balance thus moves toward deficit, putting further downward pressure on the exchange rate. Eventually, the lower exchange rate attracts new export buyers and encourages importers to find domestic substitutes. Supporters of fixed rates emphasize possible negative short-term effects of flexible rates. Supporters of flexible rates can argue that, in the long run, such rates do produce favorable results. Something like this appears to have happened after Canada's dollar fell sharply in value toward the end of 1976. It took some time — as Chapter 17 will discuss — before the foreign market benefited from the exchange rate depreciation.

Inflationary Effects A third argument in favor of fixed exchange rates is based on the relationship between exchange rate variations and inflation. Countries experiencing relatively rapid inflation can expect their currencies to depreciate — in accordance with the purchasing power parity theory. However, the causation may also run the other way; a currency depreciation may cause domestic cost-push inflation. This occurs in part directly, because the prices of imported goods and raw materials rise, and in part indirectly, because domestic import-competing industries feel free to raise their prices when the prices of imports rise.

Under the proper conditions, a vicious cycle that runs something like this can be touched off: inflation in, say, Canada causes the dollar to depreciate. Depreciation brings a round of cost-push inflation. International asset holders see the worsening inflation and react by pulling their funds out of Canadian banks and securities, thereby creating a capital account deficit. Especially if the J-curve effect of the depreciation is creating a current account deficit at the same time, the value of the dollar can plunge out of control in the absence of official intervention.

Meanwhile, a less inflationary country, say Switzerland, enters a "virtuous" cycle that is the mirror image of the vicious cycle described for Canada. Currency appreciation lowers import prices, further dampening inflation. International investors rush to put their funds in the ultra-safe Swiss franc, thereby creating a capital account surplus that causes further appreciation. But while the banks of Zurich grow fat, Swiss watchmakers find themselves increasingly priced out of the world market on which their livelihood depends.

The way to prevent such runaway vicious-virtuous cycles, it is said, is to prevent exchange rate fluctuations in the first place. Rather than letting differential rates of inflation disturb exchange markets, countries should use the time gained by exchange rate intervention to undertake domestic policies to control inflation.

The real world, however, has dealt with exchange rates in its own way, and it is time to turn from theory to a review of the postwar history of the international monetary system.

Bretton Woods

After World War II, the major trading nations of the world met under United Nations auspices at Bretton Woods, New Hampshire, to forge a new world monetary system of the fixed rate variety. The Bretton Woods conference also set up the International Monetary Fund (IMF), with headquarters in Washington, D.C., to administer the system. The rules of the international monetary game as it was played under the Bretton Woods system are presented here.

It was not quite an ideal fixed rate system. Instead, it featured what might best be called an "adjustable peg." Par values for each currency were established in terms of the U.S. dollar. Exchange rates were pegged at the par values; thus they were allowed to fluctuate under the influence of supply and demand within a narrow range of 2.25 percent above par to 2.25 percent below par. (The limits were only 1 percent until December 1971.) When the value of a currency rose to the upper limit or fell to the lower one, the government of the country in question was obligated under IMF rules to intervene and prevent further movement. A government faced with an excess demand for its currency at the limit rate had to sell enough of its own currency in exchange for dollars to soak up the excess demand. A government faced with an excess supply of its currency had to buy it in exchange for dollars if necessary to keep its price from slipping below the limit.

Although governments were supposed to intervene in exchange markets to counteract temporary distrubances, they had another option if they felt the disturbances reflected fundamental long-term changes. In the face of such changes, they could adjust the peg—change the par values of their currencies. This could be done in either of two slightly different ways. One way was to declare immediately a new par value above or below the initial value. The other was to float the currency temporarily, letting it find a new equilibrium value under the influence of supply and demand without government intervention. A new par value would later be fixed at the market determined rate when things seemed to have settled down. (A few countries, notably Canada, let their currencies float for years at a time in the postwar period. This, however, was considered to be a violation of at least the spirit, if not the letter, of IMF rules.)

Problems of the Bretton Woods System

Resisting Adjustment Under the Bretton Woods system, a country whose currency fell to the lower limit of the permissible range either was supposed to let automatic monetary policy do its job until the imbalance was corrected or was supposed to adjust the peg, make a new start at a new par value, and try to keep serious imbalances from arising again in the future. Unfortunately, governments often did neither when faced with downward pressure on their currencies. Fearing unemployment and high interest rates, they short-circuited the monetary adjustment mechanism. And, concerned about possible sectoral effects, they resisted downward adjustment of their par value. In desperate attempts to prop up their currencies, they engaged in all sorts of trade restrictions. They imposed tariffs and quotas to try to improve current account balances, and they slapped on foreign exchange controls to prevent free international movements of capital, all in the hope of improving the capital account. But these mechanisms usually did little more than postpone the day of reckoning.

Crises Because adjustments were seldom fully automatic, the system was crisis-prone. Governments often resisted making small adjustments when the adjustments would have been only slightly painful. Instead, they waited for pressures to build up, and these pressures eventually tore the system apart.

Here is the scenario for the kind of international monetary crisis that repeatedly occurred under the Bretton Woods rules. Some country, say the United Kingdom, runs a persistent balance of payments deficit. A chronic excess supply of British pounds sterling appears on the world's exchange markets. The British government is forced to support the pound. It resists monetary restraint. Gradually, dollar reserves are run dangerously low, and the British government is forced to borrow from the IMF or the U.S. Treasury. It may try imposing exchange controls or other trade restrictions, but its efforts are met with threats of retaliation and domestic political resistence. It becomes harder and harder to keep the pound from breaking through the floor.

Speculation At this point speculation enters the picture. Speculators are active all the time in international currency markets. Under the Bretton Wood rules, if I were a speculator, my game would work like this; suppose the pound is floating between its upper limit of $2.45 and its lower limit of $2.35, changing a bit from day to day. If I buy 100,000 pounds today at $2.40, and tomorrow the vagaries of supply and demand carry the rate up to $2.41, I can change them back into dollars and pocket a clear profit of $1,000. The problem is that in normal times no one can be sure whether the pound is on its way up or on its way down. I might just as easily lose $1,000. Heads I win, tails I lose. Speculators are professional risk takers who perform a number of useful economic functions. In normal times, though, they do not play a very big role in the international payments picture.

But back to the scenario of the British government hanging desperately on the brink of a forced devaluation. At this point, I am faced with the kind of situation speculators are always looking for but are rarely lucky enough to find: the situation where heads I win, tails I break even. The question is: will the pound hold at $2.35, or will it be devalued? Suppose I sell all the pounds I can get my hands on, borrowing them if necessary. If the pound is devalued to $2.10 tomorrow, I can buy pounds back to pay off the loans and make a huge profit. If the British government somehow muddles through, and the pound holds, I lose practically nothing. At the very worst, the pound will rise a cent or two off its floor and I will have to pay a few days' or weeks' interest on the loans.

The final scene in the sterling crisis is set when speculators start to pour hundreds of millions of pounds into the foreign exchange markets. The excess supply of sterling becomes overwhelming, and the last straw forcing an actual devaluation is the speculative pressure occurring in anticipation of the devaluation.

The End of the Bretton Woods System

In early 1973, an especially severe crisis occurred, involving the U.S. dollar, the German mark, and the Japanese yen. In response to this crisis, the major trading nations took the bold step of abandoning the adjustable peg and allowing their currencies to float relative to each other. The relative values of the yen, the dollar, and the mark were allowed to find their own levels under the influence of supply and demand.

The international monetary system that emerged from the crisis of 1973 is still a mixed system. It contains a number of features that do not conform exactly to a pure floating rate system. Although it is much more flexible than the adjustable peg, two important restrictions must be kept in mind.

First, not every currency floats against every other currency. Rather, the system is one in which major blocks of currencies float against one another. A number of Western European countries have attempted to peg their currencies against one another in an arrangement known as the European Monetary Union. Countries with strong trading ties to the United States have pegged their currencies to the dollar. Those with strong ties to Britain have pegged theirs to the pound. Movements between blocks have been substantial, though. Because increased flexibility has been introduced, several currencies have swung by as much as 20 to 30 percent. Occasionally there have been swings of 2 or 3 percent in a single day.

Second, governments have not taken a strictly hands-off attitude toward exchange rates. Instead, they have frequently intervened in foreign exchange markets to damp what they perceive to be temporary or unjustified fluctuations in exchange rates. This intervention is, however, not guided by any specific rules, as under the Bretton Woods agreements. The present mixture of floating rates and sporadic intervention is often referred to as a "dirty float."

The following case study illustrates the present international monetary system in action. The problems it describes highlight a number of the features of the system that have just been discussed in theoretical terms.

Case 15.1
The Relationship between High Interest Rates and the Foreign Market

The following are excerpts from a statement prepared for the appearance of Gerald Bouey, Governor of the Bank of Canada, before the Commons Finance Committee.

For some time now, the Bank of Canada has been trying to improve prospects for the functioning of the Canadian economy in the years ahead by following a monetary policy directed towards resisting any acceleration of inflation and encouraging its gradual reduction.

Canada's external payments deficit on current account has been widening again this year and now appears to be running at a rate of around $7 billion a year. Among the major industrial countries, this is the largest current account deficit in relation to GNP and it may even be the largest in absolute terms.

This is both disappointing and worrying in view of the fact that we have already had a large downward adjustment in the external value of our currency. That decline in our exchange rate has reestablished our competitive position in the world.

However, in many of our export and import-competing industries, business has increased to the point where they are now operating at, or close to, existing capacity and thus have no further scope at present to exploit their new opportunities. Efforts by these industries to increase their productive capacity are underway but this will take time. Until these increases in productive capacity are achieved, we shall not be in a position to reap the full benefits of our improved competitive position.

In the meantime, the current account deficit must be financed one way or another. If it is to be financed without a further significant depreciation of the Canadian dollar, interest rates must be high enough in Canada to attract an adequate inflow of funds into this country and to discourage capital outflows.

Source: *The Globe and Mail*, October 26, 1979.

Case Study 15.1 provides excerpts from a statement presented to the House of Commons Finance Committee by the Governor of the Bank of Canada, Gerald Bouey, in the fall of 1979. It outlines some of the basic problems that Canada faces in the international sphere.

The second paragraph of the statement highlights the serious disequilibrium in Canada's balance of payments. The current account deficit was running at an annual rate of $7 billion in 1979. The governor noted that a downward adjustment of the exchange rate might be one way of reducing the deficit, but he dismissed this strategy for two reasons. First, the dollar had already declined substantially in value (by more than 15 percent between late 1976 and 1979) but this had failed to halt the increase in the deficit. He obviously doubted that further declines would reverse the trend. Further, exporting industries were in a poor position to take advantage of a lower-priced dollar because, in the governor's opinion, they were already operating at close to capacity. However, since the current account deficit had to be financed in some way, there was only one soluton left: allowing interest rates to increase in order to attract more foreign capital to pay for the current account deficit.

It is important to note several controversial and disputable observations in this statement, to which the previous discussion in this chapter should alert us. First, the governor was concerned about inflation and justified a tight money policy and high interest rates as anti-inflationary measures. High interest rates, as we have seen, may counteract inflation by dampening investment demand, but they may also contribute to cost-push inflation by increasing the cost of borrowing. Second, it was assumed, in the governor's statement that the export sector was operating at close to capacity. Nothing was said, however, about the 7.5 percent unemployment rate in the country. It is clear that unemployment was seen neither as a problem, which should possibly be tackled with a more expansionary monetary policy and lower interest rates, nor as an opportunity to enlist more workers in the export industries to take advantage of still lower exchange rates.

Third, the long-run consequences of still larger capital inflows were not considered. One of the main reasons for the large deficit on current account in Canada has been the large payments made to foreigners in the form of interest and dividends for debts created by previous capital inflows. New capital inflows will increase the current account deficit in the future. We are paying for our long-run obligations by incurring further debt, which does not seem to be a satisfactory way of solving our problems.

What, then, is the solution? It is not clear that a further decline in the value of the dollar would have been as ineffective as the governor suggested. Canada was just passing through the J-curve effect after the initial devaluation, so that past experience was not necessarily a good guide to the future. Further, as already noted, there may have been unused capacity in the economy. However, further devaluations of the dollar would undoubtedly have been unpopular, and that may indeed be one of the main reasons why they were rejected.

A decline of the dollar below 80 cents U.S. would be extremely upsetting to many Canadians. However, such a devaluation might just reverse the deficit trend in the current account, and free us from the creation of further debt in the capital account. As our theory of exchange rate determination showed, the long-run value of the Canadian dollar in terms of the U.S. dollar should settle at a ratio equal to the ratios of their purchasing power. Therefore, though there might be a decline of our dollar to below 80 cents U.S. in the short run, (in the absence of higher interest rates) in the long run it should move in a range between $.85 and $.90 U.S.

To solve our problems in the international sector will not be easy, but the pain of short-run currency devaluations may be better than the long-run pain of increasing deficits and high interest rates.

CONCLUSIONS

As the international economy enters the 1980s, the world of Bretton Woods fades more and more into history. The academic debates over fixed versus floating rates that characterized the fifties and sixties have been overtaken by events. At present, it is clear that the dirty float is here to stay for quite a while. Critics of free floating exchange rates argue that such rates have been tried and found wanting. Supporters of such rates counter that they haven't been tried enough, especially recently, to know whether they could do the job.

What Canada has currently is a dirty float, in which our dollar is allowed to move up and down as long as it stays somewhere above $.80 U.S. The Bank of Canada intervenes in the foreign exchange markets to prevent the dollar from falling too drastically. We may not know for some time whether truly flexible rates would solve some of our serious economic problems.

SUMMARY

1. The many kinds of international transactions that take place in the world economy can conveniently be classified into three "accounts." The first is the current account, which comprises imports and exports of goods and services and unilateral transfers. The second is the capital account, which includes all international borrowing and lending and all international purchases and sales of assets for investment purposes. The third is the official reserve account, which is made up of central bank purchases and sales of foreign currency reserves. Because all international transactions are included in one account or another, the sum of

the surpluses or deficits on these three accounts must always be zero (except for unavoidable statistical discrepancies).

2. Despite the inevitable zero balance for all the accounts, an imbalance or disequilibrium in the balance of payments can be said to exist whenever deficits or surpluses in the current account are not matched by equal surpluses or deficits in the capital account. Such an imbalance will require the use of foreign currency reserves, and under a system of floating exchange rates will be reflected in exchange rate fluctuations.

   A unique combination of interest rates and nominal national income is required to produce equilibrium in the foreign sector. General equilibrium can be said to exist only when the money market, the circular flow, and the foreign market are all in equilibrium. Under fixed exchange rates, monetary policy will create disequilibrium in the foreign sector which will negate the effectiveness of such policies.

3. The mechanics of exchange-rate determination can be explained by means of supply and demand analysis. In the long run, international exchange rates tend to reflect, at least approximately, changes in the purchasing power parity of various national currencies.

4. From 1944 to 1973, the international monetary system operated under a system of fixed exchange rates. Many observers of the international economy continue to favor such a system. They argue (a) that it shields the domestic economy from international financial disturbances, (b) that under flexible rates, depreciation of a currency does not necessarily improve the current account balance in the short run, and (c) that a depreciating exchange rate can cause as well as be caused by inflation, thereby creating the danger of a vicious-virtuous cycle.

5. Advocates of floating rates dispute each of these arguments and contend that fixed rate proponents exaggerate the inherent instability of the international economy. They see the unwillingness of governments to play by the rules of the game as a fatal flaw in all fixed rate systems.

DISCUSSION QUESTION

1. Using Exhibit 15.4 as your model for analysis, assume that the government increases its expenditures on goods and services by $100 and that the multiplier is 2.5. Also assume that the Bank of Canada "accommodates" the new fiscal policy by increasing the money supply to prevent interest rates from rising, so that interest rates remain at 8 percent.
   a. By how much would the nominal national income increase?
   b. Would the foreign sector be in equilibrium at the new level of income? Explain precisely what would happen to the current and capital accounts.
   c. If the Bank of Canada refuses to allow the exchange rate to fall, what would it have to do to interest rates to correct any imbalances that might exist? How does this compare with recent Bank of Canada policy in Canada?
   d. How would any imbalances be solved through flexible exchange rates?

UNEMPLOYMENT AND INFLATION: SOME TRADITIONAL ANSWERS

WHAT YOU WILL LEARN IN THIS CHAPTER

This chapter and the next are devoted to inflation and unemployment. This chapter introduces four traditional theories that attempt to explain how a given change in nominal national income and product affects employment, the price level, and real output. The theories are the quantity theory, the Keynesian theory, the Phillips curve theory, and the cost-push theory. None of them is in itself complete, but each contains an important element of truth.

FOR REVIEW

Here are some important terms and concepts that will be put to use in this chapter. If you do not understand them, review them before proceeding.
- *Goals of stabilization policy (Chapter 7)*
- *Theory of nominal income determination (Chapters 8 to 15)*

Chapter 7 introduced full employment, price stability, economic growth, and balance of payments equilibrium as the major goals of macroeconomic policy. The eight chapters since then, however, have been concerned only indirectly with these policy goals. They have been devoted primarily to the question of what determines the level of *nominal* national income and product. Fiscal and monetary policies, the two main weapons in the government's macroeconomic policy arsenal, have been portrayed as determining nominal income and product instead of acting directly on employment, prices, growth, and balance of payments equilibrium.

This chapter will discuss how a given change in the level of nominal national income and product is translated into specific effects on employment, prices, and real output. As pointed out earlier, the percentage rate of change in nominal GNP must always be equal, by definition, to the percentage rate of change in real GNP plus the percentage rate of inflation. If fiscal and monetary policy combine to bring about a nominal GNP growth rate of, say, 10 percent per year, it clearly makes a great deal of difference whether the rate is 8 percent real growth and 2 percent inflation or 2 percent real growth and 8 percent inflation.

The chapter starts by reviewing some traditional theories of the relationships among real and nominal income, inflation, and unemployment. Although none of these traditional theories is in itself sufficient to explain the complex macroeconomic events of the 1970s, each contains valid pieces. Chapter 17 will show how these pieces can be fitted together to provide a comprehensive understanding of recent macroeconomic experience.

THE QUANTITY THEORY

The Income Velocity of Money

The first of the four traditional theories — the quantity theory — is also the oldest. It begins with the observation that as the circular flow of income and product churns around during the year, any given dollar, whether a dollar bill or a dollar's worth of demand deposits, is used again and again to conduct first one person's business and then another's. Chapter 13 introduced the *income velocity of money* — the average number of times each dollar is used for income generating purposes during a year. The income velocity of money is given by the formula:

$$V = \frac{Y}{M_1},$$

where V stands for velocity, Y for nominal national income, and M_1 for the quantity of money (defined traditionally to include currency and chartered bank demand deposits).

This formula can be rewritten by breaking down nominal national income into the product of two separate elements — real income (y) and the price level (P), which gives:

$$V = \frac{Py}{M_1}.$$

The equation can be further rewritten to isolate the element of price on the left-hand side, giving:

$$P = \frac{M_1 V}{y}.$$

The Quantity Theory Itself

So far, no theory has been stated. All that has been done is to rewrite the definition of velocity. To turn the definition into a theory, two additional assumptions must be made. One is that the income velocity of money is at least approximately constant and is determined by customary and institutional factors. It was noted in Chapter 13 that the velocity has increased slightly in the past few decades, but because it is determined by institutional factors, such as the number of times people receive their pay each month (practices which do not change radically), it remains fairly constant. The other is that the level of real income is determined entirely by "real" factors such as population, technology, productivity, and capital stock. With both assumptions in place, the relationship $P = M_1 V/y$ says that in a country with some predetermined level of real income, the price level is proportional to the quantity of money in circulation. It also follows that a given rate of growth of the money supply, with real income constant, will result in an equal rate of inflation.

Does It Work? Does the quantity theory of prices work — in the sense of providing a valid basis for scientific predictions about the relationship between prices and money? It appears that at least one prediction based on the theory is borne out by a surprisingly broad range of examples. The prediction is that if an economy is exposed to a sustained, rapid increase in its money supply, the result will be sustained, rapid inflation. The following case study suggests how widely this generalization applies.

Case 16.1
The Quantity Theory and the Collapse of the Cowrie System in West Africa

As early as the eighth century, the economic system of West Africa passed beyond the stage of primitive barter and became monetarized. The monetary unit was the cowrie shell. These shells were portable, easily identified, difficult to counterfeit, and scarce — which made them suitable as a medium of exchange, a store of value, and a unit of account. As an eighteenth century Dutch writer reported:

What we call money being arbitrary, and its nature and value depending on tacit convention betwixt men, these shells, in several parts of Asia and Africa, are accounted current money, with a value assigned to them. This is established by a reciprocal consent, and those who are pleased to show a contempt of them do not reflect that shells are as fit for a common standard of pecuniary value as either gold or silver.[1]

But cowries were not everywhere as scarce as in West Africa. As commerce with Europe began to develop, English, Dutch, Portuguese, and French traders began to import them into the region from Europe and the Orient. For a time, the increase in the quantity of cowries apparently did not exceed what was needed to finance an expanding real volume of trade; but after about 1850, things got out of hand. Between 1850 and 1892, the price of an ox rose from 9,000 cowries to 60,000 and the price of kola nuts from 2,000 cowries to 50,000. At such price levels, cowries became impractical as a unit of currency; too many hours of labor would be required simply to count them. The cowrie system collapsed. Even today, however, cowries are reported in use as currency for small transactions in very rural areas in West Africa.

Source: Based on Okonwo A. Nwani, "The Quantity Theory in the Early Monetary System of West Africa, with Particular Emphasis on Nigeria, 1850–1895," *Journal of Political Economy* 83 (February 1975), pp. 185–193. © 1975 by the University of Chicago. Used by permission.

Hyperinflation The example of the cowrie currency is only one of hundreds of similar episodes in world history. In this century, probably the most infamous inflation was that which occurred in Germany after World War I. Between 1919 and 1923, the quantity of money in circulation increased by a multiple of nearly 10 billion. This increase in the money supply, aided by an increase in velocity, pushed the price level up by a factor of more than 10 billion. At the height of the inflation, it was said to have taken a larger basket to carry one's money to the store than to carry one's groceries home. Very rapid and sustained inflation of this sort is called **hyperinflation**.

Hyperinflation Very rapid and sustained inflation.

[1] *A Voyage to the Island of Ceylon by a Dutch Gentleman* (London, 1754), as quoted in Okonwo A. Nwani, "The Quantity Theory in the Early Monetary System of West Africa, with Particular Emphasis on Nigeria, 1850–1895," *Journal of Political Economy* 83 (February 1975), p. 186.

Quantity Theory in the Short Run The quantity theory of prices is recognized as the leading theory of hyperinflation. For the purposes of short-term stabilization policy with which this book is primarily concerned, however, the quantity theory in its crude form is inexact at best.

One problem is that velocity is not really a constant. As shown in Chapter 13, it tends to vary in the same direction as changes in interest rates. Interest rates, in turn, are affected by both monetary and fiscal policy. This does not necessarily negate the monetarist proposition that the money supply is the major factor determining the level of nominal national product, provided that the changes in velocity are minor and reasonably predictable. But velocity sometimes changes unpredictably, which significantly complicates the use of the quantity theory for short-term forecasting.

Furthermore, even granting the monetarist view of the relationship between money and nominal national product, there remains the problem of how a given change in nominal national product will be split up between changes in prices and changes in real output. In the long run, changes in real output tend to be dominated by such factors as population growth, capital formation, and technological change, which are reasonably predictable. But in the short run, changes in real output depend strongly on changes in the unemployment rate. Thus another reason that the quantity theory of prices cannot be used for short-run purposes is that it does not provide a theory relating short-run changes in employment and real output to short-run changes in nominal national product.

These matters will be raised again in the next three chapters. For the moment, however, it is enough to conclude that the crude quantity theory contains a part of the key to the inflation-unemployment puzzle, but only a part. Another theory is presented now.

UNEMPLOYMENT, INFLATION, AND THE KEYNESIAN CROSS

Keynesian Theory

During the first two postwar decades, when periods of high unemployment alternated with periods of inflation, most economics textbooks featured a theory of unemployment and inflation that was based on simple Keynesian multiplier analysis. For want of a better term, this theory can be called the "crude Keynesian theory."

Exhibit 16.1 contains a Keynesian cross diagram of the familiar kind. Notice, though, that one significant change has been made. A point on the horizontal axis has been labeled "full employment national income." That label replaces the indication of a "target" level of national income that some of the earlier diagrams contained.

To get a theory of unemployment and inflation from this diagram, we can reason as follows: first, suppose that consumption, planned investment, government spending and net exports are just sufficient to put the aggregate demand schedule at the level of AND_1. In this position, it intersects the aggregate nominal supply schedule exactly at the "full employment" level of nominal national income. By assumption, when equilibrium

Exhibit 16.1
Inflation and the Keynesian cross

The crude Keynesian theory of inflation is based on this Keynesian cross diagram and some additional assumptions. When the aggregate demand curve is in position AND₁, it is assumed that real GNP will be sufficient to keep everyone employed. If the aggregate demand curve shifts to AND₂, it is assumed that the resulting fall in nominal GNP will take the form of reduced real output and increased unemployment. If the aggregate demand curve shifts to AND₃, it is assumed that all of the subsequent increase in nominal GNP will take the form of a price increase.

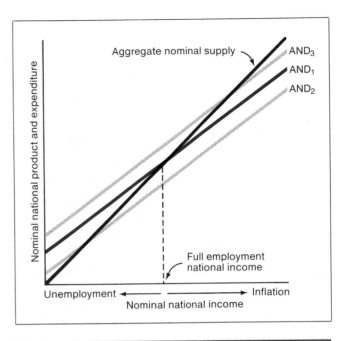

nominal national income is at this level, just enough goods will be demanded to keep everyone who wants a job busy. (To put it less casually, just enough goods will be demanded to keep all but 5 to 6 percent of the labor force at work, as measured by official statistics.)

Contraction of Nominal Demand Causes Unemployment Next, suppose that because of an error in policy or some unexpected change in private consumption, planned investment, or net exports the aggregate demand schedule slips to the level marked AND₂. This move creates a contractionary gap. Applying the multiplier theory, one can predict that this downward shift in planned expenditure will be followed by a downward movement of nominal national income. Now, one more crucial assumption is added. The assumption is that in the short run, at least, all or most of the downward movement of nominal national income below the full employment level will take the form of a fall in real income and product, and not much, if any, will take the form of a decline in prices. Because the lower level of real output requires fewer workers to produce it, the economy will experience a period of relatively high unemployment and price stability.

Expansion of Nominal Demand Causes Inflation Finally, assume that for one reason or another the aggregate nominal demand schedule shifts upward, reaching the position labeled AND₃ in Exhibit 16.1. This high level of planned expenditure produces an expansionary gap. In accordance with the multiplier theory, nominal national income rises. Remember, though, that everyone, or almost everyone, who wants a job now has one, although people not previously in the labor force, such as teenagers and housewives, may be drawn into the labor force by an expanding market. It is not physically possible to squeeze more than a little extra real output from the economy above the full employment level. The rise in nominal national income that the multiplier theory requires can take place only in the form of an increase in the price level. As a result, the expansionary gap brings on a period of lower unemployment and inflation of the general price level. Because the inflation is caused by demand forces it is often called "demand-pull inflation."

Does It Work?

Like the crude quantity theory, the crude Keynesian theory has considerable intuitive appeal if applied in the proper time and place. In particular, the theory provides a fairly plausible reading of the record of inflation and unemployment in Canada in the 1950s and 1960s. Nonetheless, it cannot be judged entirely satisfactory for several reasons.

First, proponents of this theory have always had difficulty explaining why downward movements in nominal national income affect real output so much more strongly than they affect prices, at least in the short run. A number of hypotheses have been advanced by various authors, but none of them has ever been universally accepted. Also, it has sometimes been difficult to rationalize the various hypotheses in terms of microeconomic theory.

Second, where expansionary gaps are involved, the crude Keynesian theory tells us at most how much prices will rise but not how fast. Because inflation is by nature a matter of speed of change in the price level, the theory is thus seriously incomplete. The same criticism can be applied to the quantity theory.

Finally, the crude Keynesian theory by itself is unable to explain how high (and even rising) unemployment can occur simultaneously with high (and even rising) rates of inflation. For this reason, the theory has lost some of its intuitive appeal as an explanation of unemployment and inflation in the 1970s, though when supplemented by other analytical tools it is still a useful basis for understanding some of our current problems.

THE PHILLIPS CURVE

Early Empirical Work

Economists place a strong emphasis on empirical work — work based on real-world data — as well as on abstract theorizing. Sometimes a single empirical study can suggest a whole new direction for a theory to take. A well-known research paper by British economist A.W.H. Phillips, outlined in the following case study, had such an impact.

Case 16.2
A. W. H. Phillips and the Phillips Curve

In 1958, A. W. H. Phillips published the results of some attempts he had made to test the simple hypothesis that wage rates tend to rise faster when unemployment is low than when it is high. The data he had available covered a very long period in the economic history of Great Britain, stretching from 1861 to 1957. The statistical evidence he assembled seemed to support the idea that the rate of change in money wages can be explained by the level of unemployment.

Phillips presented his results in a series of charts, one of which is reproduced here as Exhibit 16.2. This diagram contains a curve that represents the average relationship between unemployment and the rate of change of wages during the period 1861 to 1913. The points scattered near the curve show wage and unemployment data for the years 1948 to 1957. The fit of the modern years in Phillips's study to the curve calculated on much earlier data is remarkably close.

Source: A. W. H. Phillips, "The Relationship between Unemployment and the Rate of Change of Money Wage Rates in the United Kingdom, 1861–1957," *Economica* New Series 25 (November 1958), pp. 283–299.

Since the publication of Phillips's article, curves like the one in Exhibit 16.2 have come to be called **Phillips curves**. In recent years, the term *Phillips curve* has been broadened to include similar curves drawn on diagrams where the vertical axis measures the rate of change of prices (that is, the rate of inflation) instead of the rate of change of wages. Recent data for Canada will be presented in a Phillips curve framework in Chapter 17.

Phillips curve A curve showing the relationship between the rate of inflation and the level of unemployment. Inflation, usually placed on the vertical axis of such a figure, can be measured in terms of either the rate of change in wages or the rate of change in a price index.

Interpreting the Phillips Curve

Like the crude quantity theory and the crude Keynesian theory already examined, the intuitively appealing concept of the Phillips curve is open to serious misinterpretation when applied to economic policy. One tempting but misleading interpretation is to regard the curve as a menu of alternatives from which policy makers can choose a preferred compromise between the evils of inflation and unemployment.

The Phillips Curve as a Menu Suppose, for example, that the minister of finance was presented with data that suggested the Phillips curve shown in Exhibit 16.3. It can easily be imagined that if the administration were an NDP one, strongly influenced by union labor or sympathetic to the plight of the unemployed, it might pursue expansionary policies and aim for a

Exhibit 16.2

One of A. W. H. Phillips's original Phillips curves for the British economy

In 1958, A. W. H. Phillips published an influential paper that looked at the relationship between unemployment and the rate of change in wages over a long period in Great Britain. He found that data from the period 1948 to 1957 fit rather closely a curve based on data from the period 1861 to 1913, as shown here. Curves like this have since come to be called *Phillips curves*.

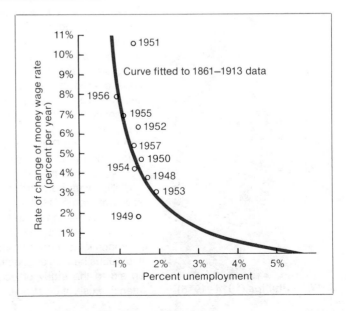

Source: A. W. H. Phillips, "The Relationship between Unemployment and the Rate of Change of Money Wage Rates in the United Kingdom, 1861–1957." *Economica* New series 25 (November 1958), pp. 283–299. Reprinted by permission.

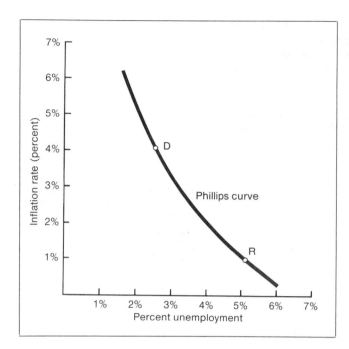

Exhibit 16.3
The Phillips curve as a policy menu
The Phillips curve is sometimes misleadingly interpreted as a policy menu offering a fixed trade-off between inflation and unemployment. If the curve for the Canadian economy had the shape shown here, it could be imagined that New Democrats would want to choose a point like D, where low unemployment would be "bought" at the price of high inflation, while Liberals or Conservatives might prefer a point like R. Unfortunately for this interpretation, the Phillips curve is not stable. Policies designed to produce movements along it can cause it to shift to a new position.

point high up and to the left, such as the point marked D in the figure. In contrast, a Conservative or Liberal cabinet, dominated by conservative businesspeople and bankers, might aim for a point such as R, near the intersection of the Phillips curve and the horizontal axis.

Shifts in the Phillips Curve The trouble with interpreting the Phillips curve as a policy menu is that it may not stand still while the diners enjoy

A. W. H. Phillips (1914–1975)

A. W. H. Phillips was an economist whose reputation was based largely on a single paper published on the right topic at the right time. In the late 1950s, the relationship between inflation and unemployment ranked as the major unsolved problem of macroeconomic theory. The curves that Phillips drew in his famous article in *Economica* suggested a simple, stable relationship between inflation and unemployment. Phillips's paper offered little by way of a theoretical explanation of the relationship, but his curves became the peg on which all future discussion of the problem was hung. Almost immediately, every article on inflation and unemployment became a discussion of what was the shape of the Phillips curve, what point on the Phillips curve was best as a policy target, how the Phillips curve could be shifted, and so on. Today, the term is so well established that Phillips's name enjoys a sort of immortality even though his own interpretation of the famous curve has fallen into disrepute.

Phillips was born in New Zealand, but he made London his base for most of his academic career. He taught at the London School of Economics during the 1950s and 1960s until moving to the Australian National University in 1967. Phillips was originally trained in electrical engineering, and this training seems to have influenced his approach to economic problems, which has been characterized as "scientistic." In the mid-1950s he was suggesting the use of an "electric analog machine or simulator" as an aid to the study of economic dynamics. This idea perhaps foreshadowed the intensive use of electronic computers in contemporary economic research.

their meal. As the 1960s progressed, economists in Canada began to notice that inflation-unemployment points for recent years did not fit the Phillips curves they had plotted using data from the 1950s. It became common to speak of an upward drift in the Phillips curve. The menu seemed to be getting less appetizing as time went by. If the upward drift had been entirely spontaneous, policy makers could simply have been told to make the best of disappointing circumstances and still choose the point they liked best from the new, higher Phillips curve. However, to the extent that the shifts in the Phillips curve have been caused by the particular policies chosen to move the economy along a supposedly fixed curve, the idea of the Phillips curve as a policy menu needs to be reevaluated altogether.

The next section explores further the way in which the choice of particular inflation and unemployment goals determines the position and rate of drift of the Phillips curve. Modern theories of inflation that economists are now developing do have a place for the Phillips curve, but the place is not quite the one that early interpreters had in mind.

UNEMPLOYMENT, JOB SEARCH, AND THE PHILLIPS CURVE

In Chapter 7, the unemployment rate was defined as the ratio of two groups (or "stocks") of workers — those officially counted as unemployed to those officially counted in the civilian labor force. Changes in the unemployment rate thus occur as the result of flows into and out of the underlying stocks.

Additions to the stock of the unemployed occur whenever people enter the labor force and are unable to find work or when they leave a job and begin immediately to look for a new one. (If they don't look for a new one they are not considered part of the labor force and are no longer counted among the unemployed.)

The Duration of Unemployment

The length of time that people are out of work will affect the unemployment rate. An economy in which each worker was out of work for about three weeks of each year would have an unemployment rate of about 6 percent (6 percent of the working weeks are lost). An economy in which each worker was out of work for about five weeks would have an unemployment rate of about 10 percent.

There is a tendency, therefore, for the unemployment rate to move closely together with the average duration of unemployment. For this reason, much recent work on the theory of unemployment has focused closely on the process of job search as a key to the average duration of unemployment and hence to the measured unemployment rate. There are many variations of the job search theory of unemployment and new ideas are still being put forth and tested. Just a brief outline of some basic assumptions and approaches is given here.

Economists usually assume that when people are looking for work they will not automatically take the first job offered. A search is made for the best wages and working conditions.

The Reservation Wage

Reservation wage The wage (adjusted for nonmonetary advantages and disadvantages of a job) below which a person will not accept a job offer.

There is a limit, however, to the length of time people will search for a job when jobs are available. That limit can be expressed in terms of a reservation wage. A person's **reservation wage** is the wage (adjusted for nonmonetary advantages of the job, as always) below which he or she will not accept an offer. A person who has a reservation wage of $150 per week, for example, will reject any offer of $149 a week or less and take any job that offers $150 a week or more.

People's reservation wages tend to decline the longer their job search continues. There are at least two reasons for this. First, the people may initially be very optimistic, overestimating their own worth in the eyes of potential employers, and then gradually become more realistic as the hoped-for top-level offers do not materialize. Second, even if unemployment insurance is available, long periods without work tend to cut into people's savings, and financial pressure to get back to work increases. Empirical studies confirm the idea that reservation wages decline as the job search period lengthens.

Determining the Duration of Unemployment

The idea of repeated sampling to find the best job offer plus the idea of a declining reservation wage offers a simple theory of the duration of unemployment. Exhibit 16.4 gives a graphical presentation of the theory. An upward-sloping curve is drawn in the diagram to show that, on the average, a worker can find a better job offer by spending more time in the job search. A downward-sloping curve is drawn to show how the worker's reservation wage falls as time goes on. The two curves come together the first time the worker gets a job offer that meets that worker's reservation wage. This takes five weeks on the average as the figure is drawn. The worker takes the job, and the period of unemployment is at an end.

Two things should be stressed about this figure. First, the curves express averages for workers of similar skills and experience. Individual workers may, simply by good luck, find offers meeting their reservation wage on the

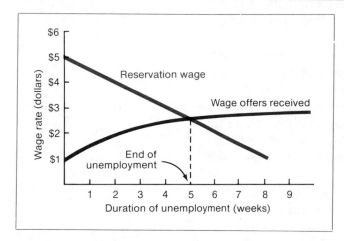

Exhibit 16.4

Determination of the average duration of unemployment

The longer people search for jobs, the better, on the average, will be the best wage offers they uncover. At the same time, the longer they search, the lower their reservation wages tend to fall. In this exhibit, the duration of unemployment is determined by the intersection of the reservation wage curve and the wage offer curve. It indicates the point at which people first receive job offers that meet their reservation wage.

first or second try. Others, less lucky, may have to look longer than average before they find something they will accept. Second, the positions of the curves, and hence the average length of the job search, may be very different for workers at different skill levels. In particular, for many types of unskilled workers, wage offers received are likely to be very low. At the same time, hope for something better, even if unrealistic, keeps the reservation wage from falling very rapidly. This can stretch out the period of unemployment to many months.

Job Search and Inflation

The job search theory just outlined, simple though it is, provides many useful insights into what happens to unemployment when economic conditions change. For example, if the number of job seekers increases while other things (including the number of job openings) remain unchanged, there will be more competition for the available jobs. Each unemployed person will, on the average, have to search longer before finding an acceptable job that some other worker has not found first. The average duration of unemployment and the unemployment rate will thus rise. On the other hand, if the number of job openings increases while other things (including the number of job seekers) remain unchanged, it will be easier for the average worker to find an acceptable job. The duration of unemployment and the unemployment rate will fall. Variations such as these in the number of job openings and the number of job seekers play an important role in causing ups and downs in the unemployment rate from month to month and year to year.

The job search theory also proves very helpful in understanding the effects of inflation on unemployment. Because these effects will play a central role in the discussion of the dynamics of inflation in the next chapter, it will be worthwhile to look at them in some detail here.

The Effect of Unexpected Inflation From earlier discussions of financial markets, we are already familiar with the notion that unexpected inflation can produce effects that are quite different from those produced by expected inflation. This is as true in the case of job markets as it is in the case of financial markets. We begin by looking at the effects of unexpected inflation on the process of job search.

Imagine an economy in which neither prices nor wages have been changing in the recent past and in which neither is expected to change in the immediate future. Suppose that under these initial conditions, the average duration of unemployment is five weeks and the measured unemployment rate is 5 percent. Suddenly, out of the blue, all prices and nominal wages begin to rise. What will happen?

Look at things from the point of view of the unemployed job seekers. By assumption, they do not expect prices to go up. It does not occur to them that during the period they work at their new jobs, it will cost them more to live than before. Also by assumption, they do not know that wages in general have gone up, so they do not immediately reconsider their own estimates of their value to potential employers. Unexpected inflation thus has no initial effect on their reservation wages. What does happen is that before they have searched very long, they get nominal wage offers that look pretty good. Operating on their own, with incomplete information, job seekers are likely to consider such high wage offers to be isolated pieces of good luck. They will quickly accept the jobs.

No individual job seeker realizes, of course, that many other job seekers are also experiencing "good luck" and taking under five weeks, on the average, to find jobs. The decrease in the average duration of the job search shows up as a drop in the measured unemployment rate. The conclusion is that unexpected inflation causes unemployment to fall.

The Effects of Expected Inflation It will not take too long, of course, for workers to catch on to what is happening. Unexpected inflation then becomes expected inflation. The effects of expected inflation are quite different.

Expected inflation, unlike unexpected inflation, does cause reservation wages to rise. If wages and prices begin rising by, say, 5 percent per year, and job seekers know it, it is easy to see what they will do. Expecting prices to be higher than before, they will reestimate the level of the nominal wage they will need to keep up with the cost of living. Also, expecting wages to be higher than before, they will know that the first high nominal wage offer they get is not an isolated bit of good luck but part of a general trend. They will not need to grab at that job because later offers may be even better. Such expectations are often set by unions that have asked for and received higher wages. Their success becomes a model for other unions.

In fact, if inflation is fully expected by all workers and employers, it will have no real impact on the labor market. Workers will know that by waiting they will get better nominal wage offers but that the cost of living will be going up just as fast as the wage offers. Employers will know that the higher nominal wages they have to pay each year will be entirely offset by the prices they will get for the products they sell. No one will be any better off or any worse off than if neither prices nor wages changed at all. Job seekers will behave no differently than they would if prices and wages were stable.

The Effects of False Expectations There is a third case to consider—that in which people falsely expect prices to rise when in fact they are remaining stable. If wages and prices stopped rising but workers still expected them to go up by 5 percent a year, the search for jobs would become more difficult. People would raise their reservation wages, thinking that they needed the extra money to cover a higher cost of living. They would expect average nominal wage offers to rise also, but these offers would not rise. The workers, operating in isolation from one another, might well think that they were just having uncommonly bad luck. For a while, at least, they would keep looking for jobs that met their expectations. Eventually, they would either really get lucky and find one or become discouraged and lower their reservation wages to realistic levels. Meanwhile, though, the average duration of their job search would have risen, and so would the measured unemployment rate.

The Natural Rate of Unemployment   Some important generalizations can be drawn from the preceding discussion of the effects of inflation on job search and unemployment. First, job search theory suggests that a higher rate of inflation than workers expect tends to shorten the average duration of unemployment and lower the unemployment rate. If the actual rate of inflation is lower than expected, in contrast, the duration of unemployment lengthens and the unemployment rate rises. In the middle lie all cases where the expected and actual rates of inflation are just equal. The middle ground includes the special case where the actual and expected rates of inflation are zero — that is, the case of price stability.

The case of fully anticipated inflation, when the price level changes neither more nor less rapidly than it is expected to, provides an important benchmark for economic policy. To emphasize its importance, a special term will be used to refer to the rate of unemployment that prevails when the actual rate of inflation equals the expected rate of inflation. That rate is called the **natural rate of unemployment**. It is natural not in the sense that it is a god-given constant beyond the influence of economic policy. Instead, it is natural in the sense that it is the rate of unemployment that prevails when everyone knows what is going on and no one is fooled. Because it is the rate of unemployment that prevails when everyone has accurate knowledge of market conditions, it can also be called the equilibrium rate of unemployment. The term *natural rate*, however, is too well-established to abandon.

Natural rate of unemployment The rate of unemployment that would prevail if the expected rate of inflation were equal to the actual rate of inflation.

The Phillips Curve and the Natural Rate of Unemployment

The Phillips curve was introduced earlier to represent the trade-off between inflation and unemployment. The curve contained an element of truth, but it seemed to shift over time. The job search theory of unemployment now offers an explanation of why the Phillips curve can shift from one year to another.

Consider Exhibit 16.5, in which three Phillips curves are sketched. Each curve represents the short-run trade-off between unemployment and inflation for a given expected rate of inflation. On each curve, unemployment is at the natural rate (here assumed to be 5 percent) when the actual and expected rates of inflation are equal.

If people expect the rate of inflation to be 2 percent, but in fact inflation accelerates to 3.5 percent, the economy will move up and to the left along the middle Phillips curve, from Point A to Point B. If people expect the rate of inflation to be 4 percent, but in fact it slows to 3.5 percent, the economy will move down and to the right along the top Phillips curve, from Point C to Point D.

Suppose that the economy had experienced a long period of price stability, so that the actual and expected inflation rates were both zero. In that case, the bottom Phillips curve would provide a short-run menu from which policy makers might choose. They might, for example, get unemployment down to 3 percent if they were willing to tolerate a bit of inflation, moving from Point E to Point F.

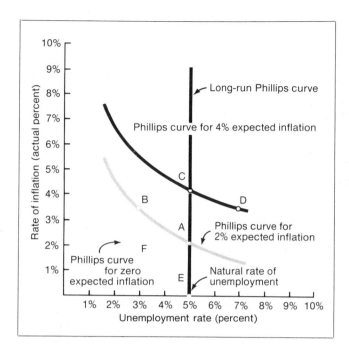

Exhibit 16.5
Expected inflation and the shifting Phillips curve
The position of the Phillips curve depends on the rate of expected inflation and the rate of unemployment depends on the relationship between the expected rate of inflation and the actual rate. With expected inflation at 2 percent for example, an acceleration of actual inflation to 3.5 percent would lower the unemployment rate, moving the economy from Point A to Point B. Unemployment is at the natural rate whenever actual and expected inflation are equal. Because expectations eventually catch up to any sustained rate of inflation, the long-run Phillips curve is vertical at the natural rate of unemployment.

Shifts in the Phillips Curve They could do that only in the short run, however. After a while, people would notice that prices were going up. They would begin to expect them to continue to do so. As soon as that happened, the Phillips curve would begin to shift upward, and the policy menu would suddenly begin to look less appetizing. At any point in time, the position of the Phillips curve thus depends on the expected rate of inflation. Notice that each Phillips curve in Exhibit 16.5 passes through the point corresponding to the natural rate of unemployment and the expected rate of inflation. It will be noted in Chapter 17 that such shifts have been occurring in Canada.

The Phillips Curve in the Long Run Once it is understood how the Phillips curve shifts in response to changing inflationary expectations, it becomes apparent that Phillips curves of the usual kind are essentially short-run phenomena. Movements along a given Phillips curve can take place only so long as the actual rate of inflation changes while the expected rate of inflation remains unchanged. In the long run, however, any given rate of inflation, if maintained over a period of time, will come to be expected. Economists do not all agree about the mechanisms through which people adjust their expectations of inflation or about the speed of those adjustments, but they do agree that adjustments eventually take place. In the long run, then, the unemployment rate will tend to return to its natural rate as soon as the adjustment of expectations to the actual rate of inflation is complete. This tendency is represented in Exhibit 16.5 by a long-run Phillips curve that is perfectly vertical. In the long run, there is no trade-off between inflation and unemployment.

THE COST-PUSH THEORY

Demand-Pull Inflation

All three of the theories looked at so far share the common element that inflation is touched off by a rise in aggregate demand. In the quantity theory, the excessive aggregate demand results from an injection of new money into the economy. In the Keynesian theory, it is represented by a shift in the aggregate demand schedule to a position high enough to produce an expansionary gap. And according to the Phillips curve analysis, inflation does not become serious until demand has risen enough to produce a shortage of labor. Because all these theories single out a rise in aggregate demand as the initial cause of a rise in the price level, they are collectively referred to as **demand-pull theories of inflation**.

Demand-pull inflation Inflation that is initially touched off by an increase in aggregate demand.

Cost-Push Inflation

In the course of the 1950s and 1960s, economists began to realize that serious inflation could occur even when there was considerable slack in overall demand and a substantial level of unemployment. None of the demand-pull theories adequately explained this possibility, and it became increasingly popular to speak of a new kind of inflation, called **cost-push inflation**.

Cost-push inflation Inflation that is initially touched off by a spontaneous rise in wages, profit margins, commodity prices, or other elements of cost during a period of slack aggregate demand.

The Wage-Price Linkage The most commonly heard version of the cost-push theory runs something like this. Suppose that, initially, the economy is enjoying a period of relative price stability and moderate, but not unusually low, unemployment. Then it comes time for some powerful labor union in an important basic industry (say the steel industry) to renegotiate its contract with employers. Through aggressive bargaining and perhaps the threat or actual occurrence of a strike, the union wins a very generous raise for all its members.

Suppose the rise in wages is so high that it cannot be fully offset by increases in output per labor hour. If so, the cost of making a ton of steel goes up. Citing the increase in cost as justification, the steel companies raise their prices. Steel is used to make cars, refrigerators, apartment buildings, and hundreds of other things, so costs rise in all these other industries. The makers of the goods using steel all raise their prices, again citing the rise in costs as justification. The increase in the price of steel has now become a general increase in the price level.

As other union contracts expire, the bargaining becomes tougher and tougher. For one thing, the leaders of the auto workers, coal miners, postal workers, and so on have put their reputations on the line with their rank-and-file union members, who expect them to do as well as the steel-workers did. On top of that, union negotiators are now able to point to the rise in the cost of living as additional justification for giving their workers a fat wage package. The cost-push mechanism is now in full swing, and the initial spark has touched off an inflationary wage-price spiral.

Adherents of the cost-push theory of inflation point out that, over time, the average price level tends to move together with unit labor costs—that is, with the average cost of labor per unit of output. This is particularly true when volatile food and energy prices are excluded. Because unit labor cost is just average wages divided by output per worker, cost-push theorists stress that upward pressure on wages tends to cause upward pressure on prices, assuming that productivity remains constant.

Other Versions of the Cost-Push Theory   Another version of the cost-push theory holds that the process need not start with a rise in wages. Other powerful economic interests may touch off the first spark. For example, it is often suggested that some large, highly concentrated industry like the automobile industry may initiate the cycle by unilaterally raising its prices simply to increase profits, even though there is no justification for the increase in terms of rising costs or rising demand. The resulting inflation is then called **profit-push inflation** to distinguish it from the **wage-push inflation** of the first scenario.

Finally, the cost-push cycle may be touched off by a rise in the price of important basic commodities, such as oil. The initial source of commodity price rises may lie altogether outside the Canadian economy. It may involve such uncontrollable elements as Arab politics. Nonetheless, once underway, commodity price increases can spread throughout the economy by the cost-push mechanism, producing **commodity inflation**.

Does It Make Sense?

Does the cost-push theory of inflation make sense? The answer is that, like the other theories examined, it contains an element of truth; but that element is subject to strict qualifications. These qualifications are worth reviewing in detail.

The Cost-Push Illusion   The first qualification is the distinction between genuine cost-push inflation on the one hand and the **cost-push illusion** on the other. Because of the cost-push illusion, ordinary demand-pull inflation may look like cost-push inflation to those who are actually caught up in it. Milton Friedman uses a vivid example to illustrate the illusion. His story is based on a much longer parable told by A. A. Alchian and W. R. Allen.

Case 16.3
The Cost-Push Illusion

Let us suppose that, in a country in which everything else is fine, all of a sudden there is a great craze for increasing the consumption of meat, and all the housewives rush to the butchers to buy meat. The butchers are delighted to sell them the meat. They do not mark up the prices at all; they just sell out all the meat they have, but they place additional orders with the wholesalers. The wholesalers are delighted to sell the meat. They clean out their inventories. They go back to the packing houses. The packing houses ship out their meat. The price is the same but the packing houses send orders to their buyers at the cattle market: "Buy more beef!" There is only a fixed amount of cattle available. And so the only thing that happens is that in the process of each packer trying to buy more beef, he bids up the price. Then a notice goes from the packer to the wholesaler. "We are very sorry, but due to an increase in our costs we are required to increase the price." A notice goes from the wholesaler to the retailer. And the retailer finally says to the customer when she comes in to complain

---

Profit-push inflation A variety of cost-push inflation in which a spontaneous increase in profit margins is the initial source of price increases.

Wage-push inflation A variety of cost-push inflation in which a spontaneous increase in nominal wage rates is the initial source of price increases.

Commodity inflation A variety of cost-push inflation in which a spontaneous increase in commodity prices is the initial source of general price increases.

Cost-push illusion The phenomenon that demand-pull inflation often looks like cost-push inflation to those caught up in it, because inventories cushion the immediate impact of demand on prices at each link in the chain of distribution from producers to retailers.

that the beef has gone up: "I'm terrible sorry, but my costs have gone up." He's right. But what started the increase in costs all the way up and down the line? It was the housewife rushing in to buy the meat.

Source: Based on Milton Friedman, *Unemployment versus Inflation*? Institute for Economic Affairs Occasional Paper No. 44 (London: Institute for Economic Affairs, 1975), pp. 34–35. Originally appeared in Armen A. Alchian and William R. Allen, *University Economics: Elements of Inquiry*, 3rd ed. (Belmont, Calif.: Wadsworth, 1972). Used by permission.

The point of this example is that what is true for individuals is not necessarily true for the economy as a whole. Each person may raise prices only reluctantly and only when placed under severe pressure by a rise in wages and costs. But where does the pressure come from? It comes from an increase in demand, according to the critics of the cost-push theory of inflation.

What keeps the true cause of inflation from being evident to everyone is the existence of inventories at each link in the chain from producer to consumer. The initial impact of an increase in demand is a decline in inventories, first at the retail level, then at the wholesale level, then at the factory level, and so on. As businesspeople at each link in the chain increase their orders to replenish stocks, the process eventually reaches someone who cannot respond by pulling goods out of the inventories of the next person in line. This person may be the packer who has to buy beef at auction, the importer who has to bid for raw materials on world commodity markets, or the employer who can find new workers only by bidding them away from other jobs. Sooner or later, the rise in demand encounters the inescapable fact of the scarcity of resources, and then a price rise starts getting passed back up the chain of distribution.

The Direction of Causation   A second qualification to the cost-push theory is also related to the question of the direction of causation. As mentioned above, the price level tends, over time, to move closely together with unit labor costs. Yet this does not necessarily mean that changes in wages are causing changes in prices. The wages employers are willing to pay workers are closely related to the value, at current market prices, of the output produced per hour by those workers. Even if the physical quantity of output produced per hour does not increase, an increase in the price of that output can provide a basis for raising wages. Thus wages rising to keep up with price increases, which themselves were caused by increases in demand, could produce the observed close relationship between the price level and unit labor costs.

Monopoly Power

A third qualification to the cost-push theory of inflation hinges on the concept of monopoly power. Economists say that a firm has *monopoly power* whenever it is able to raise the price of its product without losing all, or nearly all, its customers to competitors. Applied to the labor market, a union can be said to have monopoly power if it is able to obtain a substantial increase in the wages of its members without a serious loss of jobs to nonunion workers.

Most accounts of cost-push inflation depend on monopoly power to set the cost-price spiral in motion. Clearly, a union or a firm would not make the initial push in wages or prices if it did not think it could gain an advantage by doing so. Without monopoly power, making such a push would result only in a loss of jobs or sales to competitors. About the only exception to the rule that cost-push inflation has to begin in a relatively monopolistic part of the economy is commodity inflation set in motion by bad weather, which in turn leads to rising prices in the agricultural sector.

According to a well-established proposition of microeconomic theory, other things being equal, prices (or wages) will be higher in a market where sellers have substantial monopoly power than in a market where there is a high degree of competition.[2] For any given degree of monopoly power, though, there will be a level beyond which prices cannot profitably be raised. In nontechnical language, this is a matter of charging all that the market will bear. Once the profit-maximizing equilibrium price (or workers' welfare-maximizing wage) is reached, the price (or wages) in a monopolistic market, although high, will stop rising.

Here, then, is the confusion that must be avoided. Monopoly power can cause high prices and wages, but there is no reason to expect it to cause steadily rising prices and wages. If follows that a firm or labor union with firmly established monopoly power is no more likely suddenly to push its prices or wages above the prevailing equilibrium level than one that operates in a fully competitive manner. Only a sudden increase in the degree of a firm's or union's monopoly power could cause the sudden increase in prices or wages needed to touch off the mechanism of cost-push inflation. No evidence has been found of any substantial increase in the monopoly power of either business or labor that could account for the acceleration of inflation over the last fifteen years.

Relative Prices   Even if a sudden increase in monopoly power as a source of cost-push inflation could be identified, one more qualification would still be needed. Assume for the sake of discussion that some major union (make it the steelworkers again) wins a sudden large increase in wages. The increase is caused by the election of a new union leader, who is determined to bargain much more aggressively than the old one. The question is why this should cause a general increase in prices and wages, rather than just an increase in steel prices and steelworkers' wages relative to those in other sectors of the economy. That is, why will the increased prices and wages in the steel industry not be offset by lower prices and wages elsewhere?

Think of it this way. When the price of steel goes up, either the quantity of steel sold will be reduced, or the buyers of steel will have to spend more than before to buy the unchanged quantity. Very probably both will happen. If the quantity of steel produced falls, some steelworkers will be laid off. They will have to hunt for work elsewhere, and the presence of these new job seekers will tend to depress wages outside the steel industry. If buyers of steel spend more to purchase steel, they will have less left over to purchase other things. The demand for and prices of other goods will thus tend to

---

[2] The issue of monopoly power is discussed at length in Chapter 24.

fall. Instead of a general wage price spiral, then, all the economy will experience is a shift in relative prices. The price of steel will go up, and the prices of other things will go down. As measured by a general price index, no significant inflation will occur.

This argument suggests that in order to have true cost-push inflation, something must prevent the smooth adjustment of relative prices and wages. Suppose that prices and wages in other sectors did not fall when steel prices and wages went up. Other sectors of the economy would not be able to absorb the newly laid off steelworkers, so they would have to stay home and draw unemployment. Real output would drop, and unemployment would rise. Price indexes would go up because steel prices would be higher and no other prices would be lower.

Cost-Push Summary All these qualifications together greatly narrow the range of circumstances in which the cost-push theory of inflation can be made to work. First, all those cases of demand-pull inflation that masquerade as cost-push inflation as a result of the cost-push illusion or as a result of wages rising to catch up with previous price movements must be eliminated. Second, there must be some factor or combination of factors that touches off the wage-price spiral. A rise in international commodity prices might be sufficient, but the simple presence of monopoly power is not by itself enough. Third, there must be some reason for inflexibility of wages and prices in all sectors of the economy, so that wage and price increases in one sector are not simply offset by wage and price declines elsewhere. These qualifications do not entirely undermine the validity of the cost-push theory, but they do indicate that we have quite a bit more work to do before we know how to apply it properly.

CONCLUSIONS

Each of the four traditional theories of inflation and unemployment presented in this chapter has something to recommend it. Each seems to fit the facts in some particular time or place. None is a completely general theory of inflation and unemployment, however. The theories are like the separate pieces of a puzzle not yet put together.

Putting together the unemployment-inflation puzzle is perhaps the most important single job for economists today. The job is by no means finished, but little by little the outlines of a picture are beginning to emerge. Perhaps the most fascinating feature of the emerging picture is that it appears to have room for all the pieces. As the modern theories of unemployment and inflation are developed in the next chapter, it will be found that, properly qualified and interpreted, none of the four theories of this chapter directly contradicts any other. Taken together, there is reason to hope that they form a theory that can help policy makers guide the economy back toward full employment and price stability.

SUMMARY

1. The crude quantity theory of prices has a very long tradition in economic thought. It is based on the assumption that the velocity of money

is a constant, so that prices are proportional to the money supply when real output is given. This theory appears to work fairly well during episodes of hyperinflation; but for practical short-run applications, a more sophisticated theory of velocity and real output is needed.

2. The crude Keynesian theory of inflation and unemployment is based on the usual Keynesian nominal income determination theory, plus a few other assumptions. One assumption is that there is a particular level of nominal income associated with full employment. A second assumption is that below this level, movements in nominal income take the form only of movements in employment and real output, with prices unchanged. A third assumption is that above the full employment level, movements in nominal income take the form of pure price movements. The crude Keynesian theory does not allow for the possibility that high rates of inflation and unemployment may occur at the same time.

3. A Phillips curve shows the relationship between inflation rates and unemployment rates for an economy. If the Phillips curve were stable, it would provide a "menu" from which policy makers could choose according to their tastes. However, the curve is not stable. It turns out that its position is partly determined by the very policies that government authorities pursue when they try to choose a particular point on the curve.

4. The idea of cost-push inflation was introduced to explain how prices could rise when there was substantial slack in employment and aggregate demand. According to the theory, inflation can be touched off by spontaneous increases in profits, prices, or wages. In applying the cost-push theory, it is very important to distinguish between genuine cost-push inflation and the cost-push illusion.

DISCUSSION QUESTIONS

1. Milton Friedman writes, "Long-continued inflation is always and everywhere a monetary phenomenon that arises from a more rapid expansion in the quantity of money than in total output."[3] Why does he add the qualifying phrase *long-continued*? Can short-term inflation have other sources?

2. The crude Keynesian theory implies a sharply kinked, L-shaped Phillips curve. Explain why.

3. Some people maintain that unemployment is a painful human tragedy while inflation is just a matter of dollars chasing dollars. What sort of choice would such a person make if faced with a Phillips curve "menu" (assuming, for the sake of discussion, that the menu were a stable one)? Do you think that inflation, like unemployment, also affects people? If inflation is not "about people" but only "about dollars," why is it studied in an economics course?

4. Assume that in a country where everything else is fine, there is suddenly an outbreak of hoof and mouth disease that sharply decreases the supply of beef cattle. Would the resulting rise in the price of beef be true cost-push inflation? Trace this kind of inflation through the marketing chain for beef. At what points would it look different from demand-pull inflation? At what points would it be hard to tell the difference?

[3] Milton Friedman, *Monetary Correction*, Institute for Economic Affairs Occasional Paper No. 41 (London: Institute for Economic Affairs, 1974), p. 10.

C H A P T E R *17*

THE DYNAMICS OF
INFLATION

WHAT YOU WILL LEARN IN THIS CHAPTER

This chapter explores the dynamic interaction between inflation and unemployment. It shows how persistently expansionary monetary and fiscal policy can hold unemployment below the natural rate for an extended period of time, but only at the expense of accelerating inflation. It also shows why, when the policy brakes are applied after a period of accelerating inflation, the economy may temporarily experience the worst of both worlds — a high rate of inflation together with rising unemployment. The theory of inflationary dynamics developed here will be applied to the interpretation of recent macroeconomic experience in Canada.

FOR REVIEW

Here are some important terms and concepts that will be put to use in this chapter. If you do not understand them, review them before proceeding.
* *Real and nominal values and the price curve (Chapter 6)*
* *Theory of nominal income determination (Chapters 8 to 15)*
* *Adaptive and rational expectations (Chapter 14)*
* *The Phillips curve (Chapter 16)*

The subject of inflation has entered the discussion at many points in the last several chapters. Controlling inflation has been presented as a major goal of economic policy. The effects of inflation on financial markets and the job search process have been examined in some detail. What has not yet been done in any systematic way, however, is to explain what determines the rate of inflation itself. What determines which part of a given growth rate of nominal GNP will take the form of real output growth and which part the form of inflation? Why did the average annual rate of inflation take such a big jump in the 1970s in comparison with all previous peacetime experience? And once the genie of inflation is out of the bottle, why is it so difficult to get it back in?

The suspicion that these questions have been put off because economists just do not know the answers is in a sense correct. Rapid peacetime inflation is only a little over ten years old in this economy, and explaining the phenomenon has required some very serious rethinking of previous economic theory.

What is more, it is not only economists who have needed time to adjust their thinking to chronic inflation. Consumers, business managers, and government decision makers have been adjusting too. People have now come to view inflation as the norm rather than the exception. Expecting inflation, they plan to protect themselves from it. The reactions of the economy to expected inflation are thus very different from its initial reaction to unexpected inflation. This has been a complicating factor in the search for an adequate theory.

Nonetheless, the fact that economists may not yet know all the answers is no reason to avoid giving a progress report. Despite disagreements on details, virtually all modern theories of inflation contain certain elements in common. In an introductory treatment such as this, it will be enough to concentrate on these common elements and leave the details to be worked out as time goes by.

THE EFFECTS OF ACCELERATING INFLATION

The fundamental insight on which modern theories of inflation are based is that it is not so much the rate of inflation itself as changes in it that affect employment and real output. This insight will be put to work first by an examination of the case of accelerating inflation. The examination will make use of four building blocks for a theory of inflation.

Building Blocks for a Theory of Inflation

The first building block is the theory of nominal income determination developed in Chapters 8 through 14; this theory explains the effects of monetary and fiscal policy on nominal income, national income, and product.

Second, at all times, the rate of growth of nominal national product must be equal to the growth rate of real output plus the rate of inflation. With this rule and with a given rate of change of nominal national product, the job of a theory of inflation becomes simply that of determining how the given rate of change in nominal national income will be split up between change in real output and change in prices. Will a 10 percent increase in nominal GNP come out as a 3 percent gain in real output and 7 percent inflation? As no inflation and a 10 percent gain in real output? As 12 percent inflation and a 2 percent drop in real output? The outcome must lie somewhere along this spectrum of possibilities.

The third building block is the relationship between the rate of growth of real output and changes in the unemployment rate. According to **Okun's law**, named after its discoverer, the late American economist Arthur Okun, the unemployment rate will remain unchanged in any year in which actual real output grows at the same rate as potential real output. At present, the growth rate of potential real output appears to be approximately 3 percent per year. Deviations from this long-run trend are associated with changes in the unemployment rate. More specifically, for each three percentage points by which real economic growth exceeds (or falls short of) the long-run trend in any year, the unemployment rate will tend to fall (or rise) by 1 percentage point. Conversely, for every 1 percent change in the unemploy-

Okun's law Each 1 percent increase (decrease) in unemployment results in a 3 percent decrease (increase) in real economic growth. Or, conversely, each 3 percent increase (decrease) in real economic growth results in a 1 percent decrease (increase) in unemployment.

ment rate, the real growth rate of the GNP will change by 3 percent.[1] The growth of Canada's "potential" output is now around 3 percent per year, based on a normal unemployment rate of about 5 percent. **Potential output growth** is the average growth that can be expected each year as a result of changes in population, changes in labor force participation (the percentage of those in the employable age who want to be part of the labor force), and changes in labor productivity.

Potential output growth
The average growth that can be expected each year as a result of changes in population, in labor force participation, and in labor productivity.

The fourth and final building block is the Phillips curve, which was developed in Chapter 16 in terms of a job search theory of unemployment. The Phillips curve links the unemployment rate to the difference between the expected and actual rates of inflation.

With these building blocks at hand, we turn now to an analysis of accelerating inflation.

Expansionary Policy from a Standing Start

Exhibit 17.1 shows a short-run Phillips curve representing a "standing start" equilibrium position for the economy. A standing start means that:
1. The unemployment rate is equal to the natural rate of unemployment (assumed to be 5 percent) and has not changed during the current year.
2. There is currently no inflation and no expected inflation.
3. The current growth rate of nominal national product is 3 percent per year, just equal to the 3 percent rate of growth of potential real GNP resulting from changes in productivity and in the size of the labor force.

As shown in Chapter 16, all short-run Phillips curves pass through a point corresponding to the natural rate of unemployment and the expected rate of inflation. In this case, the Phillips curve is one in which the expected rate of inflation is zero and the natural rate of unemployment 5 percent, so the Phillips curve passes through Point A in Exhibit 17.1.

Assume that the government takes fiscal or monetary policy action sufficient to increase the growth rate of nominal output from its initial 3 percent per year to 10 percent per year. As aggregate nominal demand increases in response to the policy stimulus, a familiar train of events gets underway. Expenditures increase, and firms unexpectedly find their inventories falling. Some respond by stepping up output, others by raising prices, and still others by doing a little of both.

Effects on the Labor Market Soon the effects of the expansionary policy begin to be felt in the labor market. The firms that are stePping up their output, attempt to recruit new workers. Some offer higher nominal wages, knowing that the rising level of demand will let them recoup these wages in higher prices and expanded sales volume. Job seekers consider themselves luckier, on the average, in finding good offers. They are not expecting any inflation, so they have not raised their reservation wages. The average duration of unemployment drops, and the economy begins to move away from Point A — up and to the left along the short-run Phillips curve.

---

[1] Results similar to those traced by Okun in the U.S. have been obtained for Canada. See Economic Council of Canada, *Performance and Potential: Mid-1950s to Mid-1970s*, 1970, p.18.

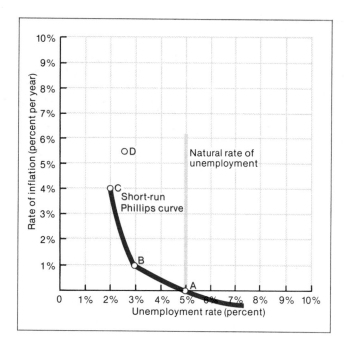

Exhibit 17.1

The effects of expansionary policy from a standing start

This exhibit shows the effects of expansionary monetary or fiscal policy beginning from a standing start position at Point A. Initially, the actual and expected rates of inflation are assumed to be zero, and both real and nominal output are assumed to be growing just at the 3 percent trend rate of growth of potential real GNP. Expansionary policy is then assumed to accelerate the rate of growth of nominal output to 10 percent per year. This moves the economy up and to the left along the short-run Phillips curve to Point B. Total real growth is 9 percent, including 3 percent growth of potential output plus 6 percent growth associated with the drop in unemployment. Adding 1 percent inflation makes a total of 10 percent. Further attempts to increase expenditure will result in smaller declines in unemployment and larger increases in inflation, represented by movement to points C and D.

How Far along the Phillips Curve? How far along the Phillips curve will the economy move in response to this initial dose of expansionary policy? To answer this question, two of the building blocks listed at the beginning of this section must be called on. The first is the rule that the growth rate of nominal output must equal the sum of the growth of real output and the rate of inflation. And the second is Okun's law, which explains that the decline in unemployment as the economy moves to the left along the Phillips curve will be accompanied by an increase in the growth rate of real output.

In the present example, a 10 percent growth rate of nominal national income is assumed. Since the growth rate will equal the sum of the growth rate of real output and the rate of inflation, it is necessary, first of all, to have an idea of how real growth is likely to change. For example, if the real growth rate is 5 percent, inflation will be 5 percent; if the real growth rate is 6 percent, inflation will be only 4 percent. What will hapPen to the real growth rate? First, it is likely to go up by at least 3 percent, because of the annual rate of growth of potential GNP, which happens to be about 3 percent. Additional increases in real growth depend on the decline in the unemployment rate that accompanies the increase in expenditures. According to Okun's law, if the unemployment rate falls by 1 percent, real growth should increase by 3 percent.

Therefore, as the result of government efforts to increase nominal GNP by 10 percent, the economy will move up and to the left along the Phillips curve until that entire 10 percent nominal growth rate is accounted for by the sum of three items: (1) the 3 percent annual rate of growth of potential real GNP; (2) the additional growth of real GNP associated, according to Okun's law, with the decline in the unemployment rate; and (3) the rate of inflation. As Exhibit 17.1 is drawn, this accounting requires the economy to move to Point B, where the unemployment rate has fallen from 5 percent to 3 percent and the rate of inflation has risen from 0 to 1 percent. At Point B, the assumed 10 percent growth rate of nominal national product is split up as follows: 3 percent is accounted for by the long-run growth trend of potential real GNP; another 6 percent is converted to real growth by the two percentage point drop in the unemployment rate (three percentage points are added to real growth for each one point drop in unemployment, according to Okun's law); the remaining 1 percent takes the form of inflation, as shown.

Repeated Applications of Expansionary Policy

We now have a simple but powerful set of tools for judging the effects of macroeconomic policy. Chapters 8 through 15 showed how fiscal and monetary policy affect nominal national income and product and the balance of payments. Now the Phillips curve, assisted by Okun's law, shows how any given growth rate of nominal output will be split up between changes in real output and changes in the price level. These tools will be applied now to determining the effects of repeated application of expansionary monetary and fiscal policy.

The Deteriorating Trade-off In the example just given, acceleration of the growth rate of nominal output to 10 percent from a standing start produced a two percentage point drop in the unemployment rate at the cost of just 1 percent inflation. Policy makers would have every reason to be very pleased with those results. They would be so pleased, in fact, that they would surely want to try another dose of the same medicine. In the second year, unfortunately, a further 10 percent expansion of nominal GNP would not be split up so favorably between inflationary and real output effects — for two reasons.

First of all, to keep real output growing at the same 9 percent rate as in the first year, it is not enough just to keep unemployment at a low level. Instead, a further drop in the unemployment rate is required. Yet the farther to the left the economy moves along the Phillips curve, the steeper the curve gets — which means that a bigger shot of unexpected inflation is needed to give each additional percentage point reduction in unemployment.

This is illustrated in Exhibit 17.1 as a movement from Point B to Point C along the Phillips curve. Another 10 percent expansion of nominal GNP results in a decrease of 1 percent in the unemployment rate. Real output will grow by 6 percent (3 percent due to increases in potential output and 3 percent attributable to the 1 percent drop in unemployment). The remaining 4 percent increase in nominal GNP will take the form of inflation.

What is more, in the second year of expansionary policy, the government no longer has the advantage of a standing start. People have experienced some inflation, although mild, and some of them may be alert enough to realize that continued expansionary policy will bring more. Once people come to expect inflation, the short-run Phillips curve begins to shift upward. That too makes the inflation-unemployment trade-off less attractive than in the first year.

This is illustrated in Exhibit 17.1 by an actual move of the economy from Point B on the original Phillips curve to Point D, which is on a higher curve. Because of the previous inflation (1 percent at Point B), workers will increase their reservation wage, leading to a smaller decrease in unemployment than assumed in the original Phillips curve. Therefore, unemployment drops by only .5 percent, real output increases by only 4.5 percent, and inflation increases by 5.5 percent.

Continuous Acceleration It follows, then, that although a second year of expansionary policy is likely to produce some further gain in both employment and real output, the cost in terms of inflation will be higher than before. In subsequent years, the trade-off will become less favorable still. Soon it will not be enough just to repeat the original policy of 10 percent growth of nominal output. Nominal output will have to expand faster and faster just to keep unemployment from rising.

Assume that in the third year nominal GNP again increases by 10 percent. In the previous two years, the anticipated inflation rate always turned out to be less than the actual rate. For the first year, workers had expected inflation to be zero, but it was actually 1 percent. In the second year, based on the first year's experience, they may have anticipated that the rate would again be 1 Percent, but it turned out to be 5.5 percent. In the third year, they will probably demand wage increases exceeding 5.5 percent. Employers may be able to pay such increases only if they are able to raise prices by, say, at least 8.5 percent. However, if nominal GNP increases by only 10 percent and if the unemployment rate does not change, real output will increase by 3 percent and inflation will increase by only 7 percent. Employers may be forced to lay off workers, perhaps increasing the unemployment rate by .5 percent (back to a rate of 3 percent). Then real output will increase by only 1.5 percent (+ 3 percent because of the increase in potential output, and −1.5 percent because of the increase in unemployment). Prices will then be able to rise by 8.5 percent, compensating the employers for their increased costs of production.

If government policy makers now decide that they don't want to have a further increase in the unemployment rate, they may have to increase nominal GNP each year by an increasing percentage. For example, an inflation rate of 9 percent may be required in the fourth year to employ all the workers currently employed at a higher level of wages. With a normal 3 percent increase in real output, this would require an increase of 12 percent in nominal GNP. Because of rising prices, even higher wages would need to be paid in the fifth year, requiring still higher prices and even larger increases in the rate of growth of nominal GNP. The economy will then have reached the situation shown in Exhibit 17.2. Each year, the growth rate of nominal output has to be stepped up just to keep even with the upward drift of the short-run Phillips curve and ever-accelerating inflation.

A Generalization All this information can be put in the form of an important generalization: To keep unemployment below the natural rate for a sustained period requires a continuous acceleration of inflation. A case study will show the principle in action.

Exhibit 17.2
The effects of prolonged acceleration

To keep unemployment below the natural rate for a sustained period requires a continuous acceleration of the rate of inflation. The actual rate of inflation must always be higher than the expected rate. Here, as rising inflationary expectations push the Phillips curves up from P_1 to P_4, an accelerating growth of nominal output holds the economy to the path marked by Points A, B, C, and D in successive years.

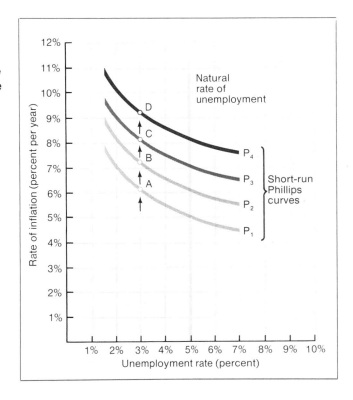

Case 17.1
Acceleration in the Pearson Era

In 1958–61, the Canadian economy was in a very depressed state. There was virtually no growth in real GNP and unemployment averaged 7 percent. Despite this, the government and the Bank of Canada followed restrictive policies. Interest rates were kept high, and the small deficit that the government incurred was due not to expansionary fiscal measures but to lower tax revenues resulting from the recession. In the last few years of the Diefenbaker government, from mid-1961 until the defeat of the government in 1963, the government reversed some of its policies, and the Bank of Canada, under a new governor, Louis Rasminsky, began to follow a more expansionary policy. The expansion that began in 1961 was reinforced during the Pearson era (1963–68) and continued almost unabated until the end of 1969. This has been called the longest period of expansion in Canadian peacetime history. Exhibit 17.3 shows the unemployment-inflation record for the economy up to the end of the Pearson era. The pattern is very much one that our theory would lead us to expect. Expansionary policy at first produced substantial gains in employment with little inflation penalty. However, between 1962 and 1966, with the exception of 1964, each successive reduction in unemployment was accompanied by a bigger jump in prices.

In 1967, unemployment began to increase, and in 1968 there was a further increase in unemployment, accompanied by a further increase in prices. A new phenomenon, inflationary recession, or *stagflation*, began to occur. It too can be explained by means of our theory.

INFLATIONARY RECESSION AND THE STOP-GO CYCLE

In theory, there is no limit to the number of years that unemployment can be held below its natural rate by continued acceleration. In practice,

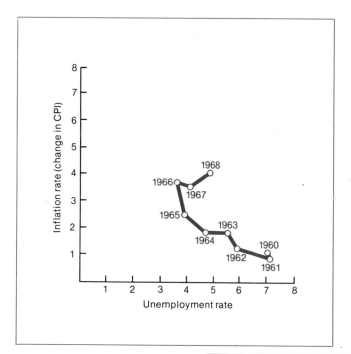

Exhibit 17.3
The Pearson acceleration
During the Pearson administration, 1963–68, the economy expanded rapidly. Growing demand accompanied by inflation pulled unemployment below the "natural" rate and kept it there for several years in a row..

Source: Department of Finance, *Economic Review*, April 1980, pp.202, 216.

though, political pressures eventually build up to do something about inflation. The most obvious thing to do is to put on the monetary and fiscal brakes and decelerate the growth of aggregate demand in nominal terms. It is not necessary that nominal aggregate demand actually fall — just that its rate of growth be reduced.

The Effects of Deceleration

As might be expected, the effects of such a deceleration are much like the initial effects of expansion, taken in reverse. As deceleration begins, aggregate demand does not grow as fast as firms have foreseen when making their production, Pricing, and inventory plans. The result is unplanned inventory accumulation. As stocks of unsold goods pile up, some firms react by cutting prices (or at least raising them less than they had planned), while others cut back production.

The production cutbacks mean fewer job openings. They also mean that the firms still taking on workers are able to get the Personnel they want without offering wages as high as they would otherwise have had to. Remember, though, that the deceleration is at first unexpected. Workers who have become used to low unemployment and rapid inflation initially continue to have high reservation wages as they set out to look for jobs. At first, they do not realize that conditions in the labor market as a whole have changed. Each attributes his or her difficulty in finding a job to individual bad luck. The average duration of the job search lengthens, and the unemployment rate rises.

A word should be said about the unionized sector of the labor market. Inflationary expectations play an important role in labor-management

Exhibit 17.4
Inflationary recession
This exhibit, which begins where Exhibit 17.2 left off, shows how an inflationary recession is produced when the rate of growth of nominal national output is cut back after a prolonged period of accelerating inflation. In the episode shown, the rate of growth of nominal national product is cut back from 12 percent per year to 6 percent per year, while inflationary expectations, still adjusting to accelerating inflation, carry the short-run Phillips curve up from P_4 to P_5. As a result, the economy moves from Point D to Point E. Unemployment rises, and real output falls; but inflation initially continues unabated. A second year of 6 percent growth of nominal national output would result in a further increase in unemployment, but the rate of inflation would begin to decline as the short-run Phillips curve stopped shifting upward. This would move the economy to Point F.

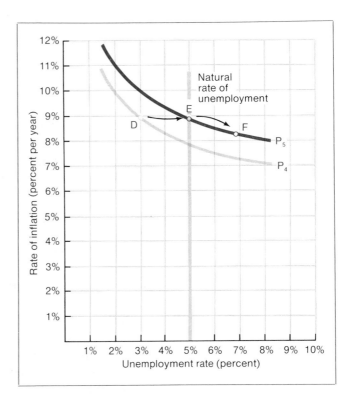

negotiations. If, as deceleration begins, both parties expect prices to continue rising as before, they are likely to agree on nominal wage increases that fully reflect that expectation. To the extent that nominal wages in unionized industries continue to rise rapidly, however, job openings in these industries become even scarcer than they otherwise would be, as demand falls off. High wage settlements in unionized industries thus make the job search prospects of the unemployed that much more difficult.

Inflationary Recession   What happens next can be called an **inflationary recession**. Unemployment goes up, real output goes down, and prices continue to rise, perhaps even faster, temporarily, than before.

Exhibit 17.4 gives a graphical interpretation. This diagram starts where Exhibit 17.2 left off, at the end of a period of accelerating inflation. The economy is initially assumed to be at Point D. Policy makers have raised the growth rate of nominal output to 12 percent. With unemployment steady, the economy experiences 9 percent inflation after allowing for the annual 3 percent growth of potential real GNP. This actual 9 percent rate of inflation continues to run ahead of the 8 percent expected rate of inflation on which Phillips curve P_4 is based.

Then the brakes are applied. To be specific, assume that contractionary fiscal and monetary policy is used to cut the growth rate of nominal output to 6 percent. Inflationary expectations, however, are still moving up. Last year, people expected an inflation rate of only 8 percent, but they experienced 9 percent. This year, they presumably expect the 9 percent to continue, shifting the economy onto short-run Phillips curve P_5.

Inflationary recession A period of rising unemployment during which the rate of inflation remains high or even continues to rise.

With the economy on Phillips curve P_5, inflation would have to accelerate to 10 percent to keep unemployment from rising. The reduced growth rate of nominal output does not permit that much inflation, however. Unemployment begins to rise, and the economy moves to the right toward Point E. By the time it gets there, unemployment has risen two percentage points. The growth rate of real output drops to −3 percent. (This represents a 3 percent growth of potential GNP minus 6 percent attributable—according to Okun's law—to the two percentage point rise in unemployment.) At Point E, then, the 6 percent growth rate of nominal GNP is split up into 9 percent inflation and −3 percent real growth.

Cost-Push Inflation During an inflationary recession, cost-push inflation becomes important. Chapter 16 showed that two conditions must be met for true cost-push inflation (as distinct from the cost-push illusion) to occur:

1. Some force that will touch off a rise in wages or prices when demand is not rising must be present.
2. Something must prevent prices and wages in competitive markets from falling when prices or wages in more monopolistic markets rise.

During inflationary recession, exactly the conditions required are present. In highly concentrated and highly unionized industries, inflationary expectations cause wages and prices to keep rising, even when demand begins to slow down. These wage and price increases mean fewer jobs in the sectors affected. Falling wages in nonunionized sectors cannot be counted on to take up the slack in employment. Any decline in wage offers that

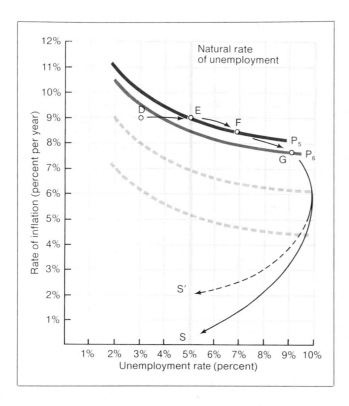

Exhibit 17.5
Continued deceleration toward a soft landing
Continuation of deceleration, beginning from the situation shown in Exhibit 17.4, could eventually bring the economy to a soft landing, with a stabilized rate of inflation and unemployment at the natural rate. The exact path followed by the economy would depend on aggregate demand policies and on how rapidly inflationary expectations declined. Two possibilities are shown here, one ending with a soft landing at zero inflation (Point S), and the other ending at a stable 2 percent rate of inflation (Point S').

occurs while inflationary expectations continue to push up reservation wages will only lengthen the average period of job seeking and raise unemployment still further.

The cost-push theory of inflation thus comes into its own during an inflationary recession. In such a period, demand-pull and cost-push are not conflicting interpretations of the same thing. Instead, the latter occurs as an aftereffect of the former.

Continued Deceleration If the growth rate of nominal output were held to 6 percent for another year, the economy would continue to move down and to the right along Phillips curve P_5 toward Point F. Unemployment would continue to rise, and real output would continue to fall, but now the rate of inflation would begin to fall too. In subsequent years, the Phillips curve would begin to shift downward, as shown in Exhibit 17.5. This process is the mirror image of the continued acceleration shown in Exhibit 17.2.

In principle, through the proper manipulation of aggregate nominal demand, the economy could after a few years be brought to a "soft landing" at some point along the long-run Phillips curve. This could happen at a zero rate of inflation (Point S in Exhibit 17.5) or at some rate of inflation greater than zero (for example, Point S'). With unemployment at its natural rate, maintaining a steady growth of nominal output would result in a steady-state rate of inflation equal to the growth of nominal output minus the growth of potential real output.

The Stop-Go Cycle

In the real world, however, it is difficult to achieve a true soft landing. Just as prolonged acceleration generates political pressure to do something about inflation, so prolonged deceleration brings pressure to do something about unemployment. It is always politically tempting to respond to these pressures by once again accelerating the growth of nominal output.

Reflation The application of expansionary policy after a prolonged period of deceleration is known as **reflation**. In the first stages of a reflation, before inflationary expectations are rekindled, it is possible to get a big drop in unemployment with little penalty in terms of inflation. In fact, if renewed expansion of aggregate demand starts while the Phillips curve is still drifting downward, the unemployment rate may fall to the natural rate while the rate of inflation is still declining. But although reflation temporarily brings the best of all possible economic worlds, unemployment cannot be cut below the natural rate without permitting inflation once again to accelerate. The economy is back to familiar territory, having completed a cycle.

The cycle of acceleration, inflationary recession, deceleration, and reflation is popularly known as **stop-go policy**. Unlike the traditional business cycle, which economists have known about for more than a century, the origins of the stop-go cycle are more political than economic. Perhaps it can even be said that the stop-go cycle is a peculiarity of democratic politics. In an election year, it is particularly difficult to resist the short-run gains of reflation or to take the initial steps to end runaway acceleration.

Reflation An expansion of aggregate demand after a period of high unemployment and decelerating inflation, bringing substantial short-term gains in employment with little or no inflationary penalty.

Stop-go policy A cycle of acceleration, inflationary recession, deceleration, and reflation brought about by alternating political pressures to do something first about inflation and then about unemployment.

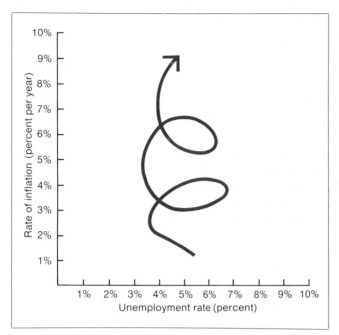

Exhibit 17.6
Stop-go with an inflationary bias
The so-called stop-go cycle means the alternation of acceleration, inflationary recession, deceleration, and reflation, as political pressure builds up first to do something about inflation and then to do something about unemployment. If the pressures to reduce unemployment are, on the average, stronger than the pressures to control inflation, the stop-go cycle may be given an upward bias. Each time around, the cycle spirals higher, as this sketch indicates.

Inflationary Bias

To add the final touch to the discussion of stop-go, a possibility not yet considered must be mentioned. It may be that, on the average, the political system is more sensitive to the political pressures that arise from unemployment than to those arising from inflation. If this is the case, the symmetry of the stop-go pattern is destroyed. The details of what happens when an inflationary bias is added to a policy of stop-go stabilization will

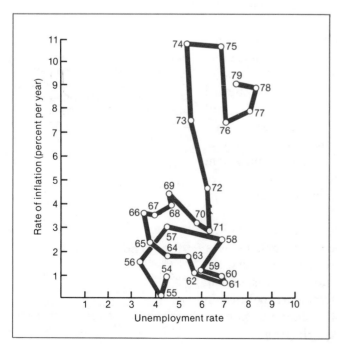

Exhibit 17.7
Recent Canadian experience with inflation and unemployment
Since 1954, inflation and unemployment have spiraled upward in a series of roughly circular loops. One cycle, that following the 1957 recession, was cut off before the previous peak of inflation had been reached. In 1973-75, inflation reached an especially high peak because internationally generated commodity inflation was added to domestic inflationary pressures. Inflation is given as a year-to-year percentage increase in the consumer price index.

Source: Department of Finance, *Economic Review*, April 1980, pp. 202, 216.

not be worked through here, but Exhibit 17.6 gives a sketch of the process. The economy goes into an upward spiral because the upward push that the economy is given during the acceleration phase of the stop-go cycle is longer and more vigorous than the downward push it receives during the recessionary phase.

Turning from the realm of theory to the real world, one can find some striking similarities between the hypothetical stop-go cycle of Exhibit 17.6 and recent experience with inflation and unemployment in Canada. The following case study outlines this experience.

Case 17.2
Recent Canadian Experience with Unemployment and Inflation

Exhibit 17.7 presents actual data on inflation and unemployment in the Canadian economy from 1954 to 1978. One part of this record — the Pearson acceleration — has already been examined. Now some other features will be explored.

The overall impression one gets from the figures for the latter half of the 1950s and for the 1960s is that of roughly circular clockwise loops. Although the lengths and strengths of successive accelerations and decelerations are rather irregular, it does not take much imagination to see an upward spiral of sorts. This figure at least roughly resembles that of Exhibit 17.6.

For the period after 1969, the picture is somewhat different, although the movements are generally in line with the theory presented here. The growing inflation in the latter half of the 1960s brought about a more restrictive monetary policy by 1968. The inflationary process was brought under control, but the result was a sharp increase in the unemployment rate between 1969 and 1971. By 1970, monetary policy was again expansionary and prices began to rise sharply in 1972. Canada then began to go through a period of accelerating inflation, accompanied by only small declines in the unemployment rate, approximating the pattern described in Exhibit 17.2. The inflation was now fed by sharply increased demand from abroad for our agricultural products and other resources, by increased costs for imported foodstuffs, and by the upsurge of oil prices associated with the OPEC oil cartel. (The latter phenomenon is described as "commodity inflation" in Chapter 16.) Rising prices may have been induced by demand forces, but they were soon supported and accentuated by cost-push factors, based on new inflationary expectations. The process began to resemble the inflationary recession described in Exhibit 17.4.

The government stepped in with wage and profit controls in October 1975 and this seemed to dampen inflation in 1976. However, in the years 1977 and 1978 prices again rose sharply, led by increases in food and energy costs. Unemployment remained high, increasing to 8.4 percent in 1978. In view of the increased inflation, one might have expected unemployment to decline. In other words, one would have expected the trend line to move upward to the left after 1976, rather than upward to the right.[2]

---

[2] A recent study by Clarence Barber and John McCallum (see suggestions for further reading) suggests that the unemployment rate would have fallen to 6.9 percent in 1978 if restrictive monetary policy prior to 1977 had not held back our foreign sector by keeping the value of our dollar at an unrealistically high level. By 1979 Canada was benefiting from a depreciated dollar — having overcome the J effect — and the unemployment rate fell to 7.5 percent. Was this the beginning of a new short-run Phillips curve?

Policy Implications This theory of the dynamics of inflation and unemployment contains some important implications for economic policy. It is worth listing three of them here again.

1. Unexpected increases in the rate of inflation pull the rate of unemployment below what it otherwise would be. If policy makers allow inflation to run faster and faster year after year, they can keep unemployment low for quite a while

2. When inflation slows after a long period of acceleration, people end up in the worst of all possible worlds. Inflationary expectations generate cost-push inflation, while the slowdown of demand pushes up unemployment. The worse the inflation, the more distasteful the cure.

3. Recession cures inflation, but only slowly. After the cure is underway and the rate of inflation is falling, a quick step-up of aggregate demand (reflation) temporarily brings the best of both worlds. Until expectations adjust to the reversal of policy, there is falling unemployment without rising inflation.

The theory reviewed here can now be applied to some current policy problems.

FINE TUNING VERSUS POLICY RULES

The primary focus of stabilization policy, as it has developed over the years, has been the management of aggregate nominal demand. Basically, the idea is that if the economy goes into a slump and too many people are out of work, aggregate demand can be boosted with expansionary fiscal or monetary policy, and the economy can be gotten moving again. If a boom gets too hot and prices rise too fast, putting the damper on aggregate demand is supposed to cool things off. The hope is that by judicious use of expansionary and contractionary policy the economy can be fine tuned for prosperity without inflation.

As we have seen, however, things have not worked out particularly well in recent years for the would-be stabilizers, fine tuners, and demand managers. The degree of instability exPerienced in the 1970s, in fact, has seriously called into doubt the adequacy of traditional approaches to stabilization policy. This chapter will now look at the sources of some of those doubts and at some new directions that economic thinking is taking in response to them.

Policies Affecting Aggregate Demand: a Recap

Aggregate demand means the total value of all expenditures by all buyers in the economy. The concept of demand management thus encompasses all policies that affect the consumption plans of households, the investment plans of business firms, the plans of government units regarding the purchase of goods and services, and international trade of goods and services. Demand management policies fall into two groups—fiscal and monetary.

Fiscal policy acts by directly varying the volume of planned expenditures injected into the circular flow through government purchases or withdrawn from the circular flow through taxation. Fiscal policy actions in turn affect private consumption, investment decisions and net exports, and lead to a multiplier effect, which magnifies the impact of changes in taxes and government purchases.

Monetary policy, unlike fiscal policy, does not act by directly injecting new flows of expenditures into the economy. Instead, monetary actions inject new stocks of money into the portfolios of asset holders. The effects of monetary policy actions on aggregate demand are felt indirectly as people readjust their portfolios to accommodate the changed supply of money, thereby affecting the prices of other assets, interest rates, planned investment spending, consumer durables purchases, and so on. Nonetheless, although indirect, the effects of monetary policy are potentially quite powerful.

The Bank of Canada's interest rate policy affects the foreign exchange rate through its impact on capital flows. This type of monetary policy, therefore, influences aggregate demand very profoundly by changing net exports.

Just how powerful monetary policy is relative to fiscal policy is still a matter of some controversy between Keynesian and monetarist economists. Despite differences in emphasis, however, both sides to the debate would agree that fiscal and monetary policy in some appropriate combination can be used to expand or contract aggregate demand, thereby altering the equilibrium level of nominal national income and product.

When economists express a fear that macroeconomic policy has failed, they do not mean that it has failed to have any effect on the economy. Everyone grants that the level of aggregate demand, measured in nominal terms, has a powerful influence on economic life. Disputes about the relative importance of monetary or fiscal tools of demand management should not obscure this agreement. Instead, doubts about demand management are doubts about whether the particular policies that have been pursued have had a stabilizing effect. The fear is that the powerful tools of demand management, if misused, can have results opposite to those intended.

Much of the debate over demand management revolves around two different philosophies of how such policies should be used. Traditionally, Keynesian economists have taken an activist line. They think that the federal government should make frequent and vigorous use of both fiscal and monetary policy tools in order to fine tune the economy. That way, they hope, just the desired mix of high employment, high real growth, and price stability can be achieved. Other economists, including most of those who consider themselves monetarists, argue that attempts to fine tune usually do more harm than good. In their view, the correct policy is instead one of steady-as-you-go, governed by rules that remain unchanged over long periods.

The Case for Fine Tuning

The case for fine tuning is based on three beliefs about the economic and political system of a modern democracy like Canada. The first is the belief that, left to itself, the private economy is unstable. The second is that the tools of demand management work fairly rapidly and predictably. The third is that, with careful scientific argument and patient persuasion, government authorities can be educated to use the tools of demand management in the best long-run interest of the public at large.

The belief that the private economy is unstable has a long history. For nearly two hundred years, there have been alternating periods of boom and depression in market economies. By World War II, a whole branch of economic theory, under the name of business-cycle theory, had grown up to support this view. The Great Depression reinforced the idea of instability in the minds of all those who lived through it.

The idea that fiscal and monetary policies are quick and predictable in their effects on the economy is part and parcel of the Keynesian tradition. It is supported by much of the theory presented in Chapters 8 through 15 of this book.

Then there is the idea that in a democratic nation political power will end up in the hands of politicians who will use the tools of policy wisely. This is an outgrowth of the liberal tradition as it has developed since the 1930s.

Experience with Fine Tuning The fine tuners came into their own in the 1960s. Initially, their policies met with success. The years 1964 to 1969 saw one of the best periods of expansion in the history of Canada. Since that time something has gone wrong. Economic instability has increased. A stop-go policy cycle has pushed the economy into widening swings of unemployment and inflation. It looks, then, as if at least part of the fine tuner's argument must be incorrect. Either the tools of activist monetary and fiscal policy do not work as quickly and predictably as they should, or else the tools have been badly mishandled. What do the opponents of fine tuning have to say?

The Case against Fine Tuning

Opponents of fine tuning challenge every aspect of the case just set forth. They claim that their historical studies show the private economy to be more stable than is often thought. They are skeptical that politicians have the courage to keep long-run economic goals in mind when faced, in the short run, with the need for reelection. But the most telling point in the case against fine tuning is a challenge to the idea that the effects of demand management are either quick or predictable.

Inside lag The delay between the time a policy action is needed and the time it is taken.

Outside lag The delay between the time a policy action is taken and the time its effects on the economy are felt.

Lags In recent years, economists have begun to worry more and more about lags and delays in the operation of fiscal and monetary policy. There are two major kinds of lags. First, there is the so-called **inside lag**—the delay between the time policy action is needed and the time action is taken. Second, there is the **outside lag**—the delay between the time policy action is taken and the time its effects on the economy are felt.

The inside lag has several sources. One is the time it takes to gather accurate economic statistics. A second source of inside lag is the legislative process. This problem is less severe in Canada than in the United States. In our system the executive and legislative branches are not separated, and Parliament can act relatively quickly on cabinet recommendations. However, long lags may still exist between the time a new policy is agreed upon in cabinet and its implementation.

The causes of the outside lag for fiscal and monetary policy are not really very well understood, but it is well established that the lag is a serious one. For monetary policy, it is likely to be at least six months before the first important effects of a policy change are felt and perhaps two years before all the effects have worked through the system. It is sometimes thought that fiscal policy has a shorter outside lag, although just how much shorter is not clear.[3]

Lags and Destabilization Monetarist economists such as Milton Friedman have long argued that the length and variability of policy lags make fine tuning very hard. You can understand this if you have ever stood under a shower when the water temperature changed. First you are scalded. When you try to adjust the taps, you find that there is a lag of a few seconds between the time you turn them and the time the water coming out changes in temperature. You overreact to the scalding and are next frozen. By the time you get the system fine tuned again, the temperature is probably back where it was in the first place. You might just as well have stepped aside and waited.

The point is that when there are lags, policy actions can have a destabilizing rather than a stabilizing effect. A policy that is intended to speed recovery from a recession may take effect only in time to make inflation worse when recovery is already underway. An action intended to cool off a boom may take hold near the bottom of the next recession, when it is least wanted.

Policy Rules as an Alternative to Fine Tuning

What do the opponents of fine tuning offer in its place? Specific suggestions vary. A common theme, though, is that demand management should be made subject to explicit long-term rules rather than being left to the discretion of policy makers.

A Monetary Growth Rule Milton Friedman has for years tried to popularize the idea of a monetary growth rule. He suggests that central banks be required by law to keep money growth to the same steady pace year after year. Friedman thinks the constancy of the pace matters more than the specific rate but suggests that a good target would be equal to the long-run growth of potential real GNP. That would be somewhere in the neighborhood of 4 percent per year at present. In Canada, as we have seen, the Bank of Canada began, in 1975, to follow a less rigid version of Friedman's views. It has tried to keep the growth of the money supply within a range of 8 to 12 percent.

Balanced Budget Rules On the fiscal policy side, a variety of rules that would require the federal government in one way or another to maintain a balanced budget have been proposed. Not all such rules, however, have

---

[3] The Bank of Canada has found that monetary policy makes its greatest impact after sixteen quarters, and fiscal policy after twelve quarters, following the introduction of a new policy. (Bank of Canada, *The Structure of RXD₂, Staff Research Studies No. 7, Ottawa 1971.*)

been put forward for the specific purpose of mproving economic stability. Some are instead aimed primarily at placing a constraint on government spending as a share of national income. Nonetheless, some variants of a balanced budget rule might have stabilizing effects.

Full employment balanced budget rule A rule under which taxes and spending policy would be adjusted so that the federal budget would be in balance if the economy were at full employment.

The leading proposal of this kind is a rule that would require a so-called **full employment balanced budget**. Under such a rule, the federal cabinet would decide the level of government purchases solely on the basis of the actual needs they see for defence, housing, health care, and so on. No attention would be paid at this stage to the macroeconomic effects of these policies. Then, having made the spending decisions, they would adjust taxes so that the budget would be in balance if the economy were at full employment. Because actual net taxes change with the size of nominal income, there would still be actual budget deficits in times of recession and surpluses in times of exceptionally high employment. Fiscal policy of an "automatic" variety would exist. This, it is hoped, would have a stabilizing effect on real output.

In contrast, it is widely feared that any stricter policy rule that required the federal budget to be in balance every year regardless of the state of the economy could have destabilizing effects. During a recession, tax revenues tend to fall and transfer payments to rise. To maintain a year-to-year balanced budget, the government would have to cut purchases as economic activity contracted, thereby further reducing aggregate demand. Such a policy would be pro-cyclical, according to the usual multiplier analysis, and hence destabilizing. (To guard against this problem, some advocates of a strict balanced budget have suggested that in years of high employment, the government could set aside a "reserve fund" for expenditure in time of recession. Such a policy would be tantamount to following a full employment balanced budget rule.)

The Growing Humility of Economic Policy Makers

As of this writing, neither the Bank of Canada nor the fiscal policy makers in the cabinet are inclined to bind themselves to rigid long-term policy rules. Nonetheless, there appears to be a growing realization that the government's ability to steer economic events may be somewhat more limited than it was thought to be in the heady years of the early 1960s.

BEYOND DEMAND MANAGEMENT

It can be seen, then, that although traditional tools of demand management are not likely to be abandoned soon, economists have become pessimistic about the ability of discretionary fiscal and monetary policies alone to return the economy quickly to the desired path of full employment, price stabilityx and balanced economic growth. Not surprisingly, they have cast about for supplementary policy tools. This section will examine one such tool—incomes policies.

Incomes policy A policy that attempts to control wages, salaries, earnings, and prices directly in order to fight inflation.

Incomes Policies

An **incomes policy** is any policy that directly controls wages, salaries, and earnings for the purpose of fighting inflation. Ordinarily, such a policy also includes direct controls on wholesale and retail prices. Canada has experimented with incomes policies, and they have become a permanent feature of economic life in many Western European countries. It will be worthwhile to look at how these policies work and why they are highly controversial.

The Theoretical Case for an Incomes Policy From a theoretical point of view, the case for an incomes policy is strongest when the policy is intended as a temporary measure to fight inflationary recession. This chapter has shown that when policy makers put on the brakes after a long period of accelerating inflation, the economy is thrown for a time into the worst of all possible worlds. Workers and employers base their plans on the expectation of more inflation; yet aggregate demand is actually tailing off. Wages, prices, and unemployment all rise at once—until expectations adjust to reality.

Now enters the timely use of an incomes policy. Suppose that just at the moment the fiscal and monetary brakes are put on, the government announces a program of strict price and wage controls. This is done with great fanfare and a show of grim determination to lick inflation once and for all. What is hoped is that workers and businesspeople will believe that these controls are going to stop inflation. If they do, they will revise their inflationary expectations downward much more rapidly than if they have to wait to learn from experience. This revision of expectations will get rid of the cost-push element of the inflationary recession. Workers will know that they do not have to push for high wages to beat inflation, so they will accept the controls. Firms will know that they will not have to pay higher wages, so they will keep their prices in line and concentrate on increasing their sales. The readjustment to price stability and full employment will be more rapid and less painful than it would be without an incomes policy.

Problems with Controls So much for theory. Granting that wage and price controls are helpful in squeezing the cost-push element out of an inflationary recession, does that mean that they are a cure-all for the country's economic problems? kot really. The problem is that controls can be of help in correcting past mistakes in demand management policy, but they cannot work as a substitute for sound demand management. Unfortunate things can happen if the government tries to use an incomes policy to fight inflation without also slowing the growth of aggregate demand or if it leaves controls in force after a recession is over and a new boom gets underway.

If aggregate demand rises in nominal terms, one of three things must logically happen. First, national product (aggregate supply) may rise in real terms to meet the increased nominal demand without a rise in prices. Second, prices may rise to meet the increase in nominal demand without an increase in output. Finally, neither prices nor output may rise, in which case the aggregate quantity of goods demanded will exceed the aggregate quantity of goods supplied, and there will be an overall shortage of goods. A combination of these three alternatives may sometimes occur, but no fourth alternative is logically possible.

Naturally, the first alternative is the most attractive. It will mean real economic growth without inflation. Real economic growth can come from only two sources, however. One is an increase in potential GNP, which can be hoped for at the rate of about 3 percent per year in the long run. The other is a fall in unemployment. This source of growth is temporary, because unemployment will soon reach a level below which it can fall no further. In the long run, then, real growth without inflation or shortages is possible only if demand management limits the growth of nominal GNP to the potential long-term growth rate of real GNP.

An incomes policy cannot buy real growth without inflation or shortages if that rule of demand management is not followed. All it can do is determine which of the second two alternatives will occur. If aggregate demand is allowed to run away without controls, the result is runaway inflation. If controls are applied and demand still runs away, the result is shortages, rationing, and black markets.

Canadian Experience with Controls

There have been several experiments with wage and price controls in the Canadian economy. One was during World War II. Then, huge wartime government spending made it impractical to control aggregate demand. The effects of controls in those conditions were as predicted. Rationing was introduced, and there were widespread shortages and black markets. All this was tolerated because people felt that rationing was the fairest way to distribute essentials during the emergency. As soon as the war had been won, controls were abandoned with a sigh of relief.

Another experiment, of an entirely voluntary nature, was attempted in the late 1960s when prices started rising after a period of price stability. The government suggested in 1966 that wage increases should not exceed 6 percent annually. However, these guidelines were soon broken by the government itself when it granted a 15 percent increase to members of the Seafarers' Union after a long strike.

In 1969 the government tried to reestablish a voluntary program of restraint by creating a Prices and Incomes Commission. This commission made some thorough studies of the causes of inflation and sought voluntary support for a restraint program, but labor unions, which felt that wages would be more closely monitored than profits, refused to cooperate. These attempts came to an end with the obolition of the commission in 1972.

A third, major experiment with controls was initiated by the Trudeau government in October 1975, after prices in the previous year had risen by more than 10 percent. There is some evidence that inflationary pressures were beginning to ease just at the time the controls were set up. However, an Anti-Inflation Board was established with the mandate, and with considerable powers, to reduce annual price increases to 4 percent by 1978. The price and wage controls applied to about 50 percent of the economic activity of the country. Excluded were the prices of foodstuffs, imports and exports, and the prices of public services. About 2.4 million workers had their wages controlled by the board by late 1976. The board restricted its control to the profits and prices of firms employing more than 500 employees. However, direct price controls were eliminated in June 1976, because of the complex problems that arose in enumerating the huge variety of goods and services. Corporations were still required to justify price increases and large profit margins were seen as evidence of excessive price changes and grounds for ordering price rollbacks.

The Anti-Inflation Board and the control program were discontinued in the Spring of 1978, so the experiment was in effect for about 2 1/2 years. In terms of its major objective, the substantial reduction of annual price increases, the program must be considered a failure. As we saw in Exhibit 17.7, the inflation rate did drop considerably in 1976, to 7.5 percent, but by 1978 the annual rate of increase was up to 9 percent, instead of down to the target of 4 percent.

There are several reasons for this. First, many goods, particularly imports and foodstuffs, were not controlled at all. The Canadian consumer is heavily dependent on both. In late 1976 the problem of import prices was compounded by a serious and prolonged decline in the exchange rate of the Canadian dollar. This helped to boost exports and ease some of the demand pressure on imports, but it also meant a substantial increase in the effective price that Canadians paid for their imports.

The failure of governments to control utility prices also contributed to the maintenance of high inflation. In addition, because many income earners were not monitored at all, or not monitored as closely as those subject to union management negotiations in large corporations, unions understandably did not support the program. Therefore, cost-push factors were not eased nearly as much as had been hoped.

Whether the program helped to diminish inflationary expectations is not clear. Inflation continued to run high in 1979 and profit rates were increasing at much more than 10 percent. It was hoped that workers would settle for wage and salary increases below the level of inflation, but it seems highly unlikely that they will agree to a decrease in their real purchasing power for very long, or at all.

We don't know what inflation would have been like without the program. But the results of this radical incomes experiment in Canada, like similar programs in other countries, have not been very satisfying.

The Future of Controls

Not everyone is willing to give up yet on the idea of controls, though. A very bold British experiment with incomes policy was established in 1976. It had one novel feature. In return for accepting lower wage increases, the government promised to cut taxes for wage earners. The idea was that this would protect workers' real incomes without making labor power so expensive that firms could not afford to hire new workers. In combination, the wage controls and tax incentives were intended to cut both inflation and unemployment at the same time. Incomes policy is likely to be talked about and experimented with as long as inflation remains at its recent unacceptable levels.

CONCLUSIONS

Macroeconomics as it is now known was born in the crisis of the Great Depression. Before that time, the distinction between what is now called macroeconomics and microeconomics was not as sharp as it later became. In particular, part of what made Keynes's ideas catch on was their macro quality. To the followers of Keynes, it seemed that the really important features of national economic life could be captured in a few key relationships between broad aggregate quantities. Macroeconomics meant building with big blocks labeled "consumption," "investment," "aggregate supply," "money," and so on. The demand management policies of the 1960s grew out of this macroeconomic approach.

Today, the distinction between macroeconomics and microeconomics is once more becoming blurred. One thing more than any other unites the critics of the theory and policy of the past — a belief in the great importance of understanding the detailed microstructure of economic life. This is as true of economists who are liberals as of those who are conservatives. It is as true of neo-Keynesians as it is of monetarists. And it is true of those who simply look for the truth with no labels attached.

The exciting topics of macroeconomics today are such micro questions as: How can we understand unemployment in terms of the job search decisions of individual workers? How is cost-push inflation generated in concentrated, as compared with competitive, industries? Which particular sectors of the economy are affected first and which only after a long lag when new money is injected into the economy? How do individual workersx consumers, and businesspeople form their expectations and plans for the future?

We are back, it seems, to the theme with which the book began. Economics is about people. It is not about aggregate demand or expansionary gaps or Phillips curves — except when these things are understood as expressions of the way individual people think and act and plan.

SUMMARY

1. Modern theories of inflation and unemployment place major emphasis on the role of expectations in determining how demand management policies affect the economy. When there are unexpected changes in the rate of inflation, many workers and employers make mistakes and do things they would not otherwise have done. These mistakes show up as changes in the unemployment rate.
2. If the rate of inflation climbs faster and faster each year, unemployment can be kept low for a long period. When the rate slows down, an inflationary recession is likely to result. Recession cures inflation, but only slowly. When aggregate demand first begins to grow again after a recession, unemployment may fall sharply — with little increase in inflation.
3. There are important lags in the use of fiscal and monetary policies. There is an inside lag between the time a policy is needed and the time it is enacted, and there is an outside lag between that time and the time it takes effect. If lags are long enough, attempts to fine tune the economy can have destabilizing rather than stabilizing effects. For this reason,

some economists frown on fine tuning and advocate steady-as-you-go policy rules instead.

4. Incomes policies (wage and price controls) are one kind of stabilization policy that goes beyond demand management. There is good reason to believe that temporary controls may be helpful in easing the effects of inflationary recession. But an incomes policy cannot work as a substitute for good demand management.

DISCUSSION QUESTIONS

1. In what sense does an abnormally high or low rate of unemployment indicate that the market is not performing very well its function of distributing information?
2. What specific reforms in government can you think of that would slow the inside lag of economic policy? The outside lag?
3. Go to the library, and see if you can find the *Annual Review* of the Economic Council of Canada for any of the years since 1963. Do you think those reports generally reflect a confidence in the ability of policy makers to fine tune the economy?

SUGGESTIONS FOR FURTHER READING

Economic Council of Canada. *Sixteenth Annual Review: Two Cheers for the Eighties*. Ottawa: Minister of Supply and Services, 1979.
A general review of economic activity in 1978.

Donner, Arthur W., and Peters, Douglas D. *The Monetarist Counter-Revolution, A Critique of Canadian Monetary Policy, 1975 –1979*. Toronto: James Lorimer, 1979.
A critique of current economic policy —in particular, Bank of Canada policy.

Barber, Clarence L., and McCallum, John C.P. *Unemployment and Inflation, The Canadian Experience*. Ottawa: The Canadian Institute for Economic Policy, 1980.
A critique of recent monetary policy and a defense of traditional Keynesian policies.

THE THEORY OF PRICES AND MARKETS

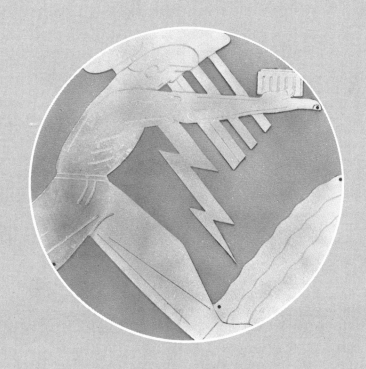

C H A P T E R 18

SUPPLY AND DEMAND: BUILDING ON THE BASICS

WHAT YOU WILL LEARN IN THIS CHAPTER

This chapter begins with a review of the principles of supply and demand, first covered in Chapter 3, for the benefit of those who have just completed the study of macroeconomics. Next it introduces the concept of elasticity as a way of measuring the responsiveness of the quantity of a good supplied or demanded to a change in the price of that good. It then extends the concept of elasticity to apply to changes in variables affecting the demand for a good other than changes in the price of the good itself.

FOR REVIEW

Here are some important terms and concepts that will be put to use in this chapter. If you do not understand them, review them before proceeding.
- *Market equilibrium (Chapter 3)*
- *Shortage and surplus (Chapter 3)*
- *Substitutes and complements (Chapter 3)*
- *Normal and inferior goods (Chapter 3)*

The principles of supply and demand are the most widely applied principles in all of economics. Those readers who have just completed the study of macroeconomics will have seen many applications since the principles were first introduced. In Chapter 4, supply and demand were used as an aid to understanding the incidence of taxation. Chapters 12 and 13 discussed the supply and demand for money. And the principles of supply and demand also underlay the whole discussion of inflation—a process in which the forces of supply and demand, acting in the same direction in many markets at once, produce an increase in the average level of all prices. In Chapter 15, supply and demand analysis was used to explain the short-run determination of exchange rates.

As the text moves from the study of macroeconomics to the study of microeconomics, the principles of supply and demand will become more important than ever. This chapter will set the stage for what is to come by briefly reviewing the principles presented in Chapter 3 and then adding some new details.

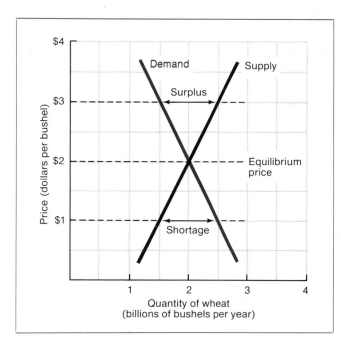

Exhibit 18.1
Equilibrium in the market for wheat
The equilibrium price is found at the point where the downward-sloping demand curve and the upward-sloping supply curve intersect. That is the only price at which there is neither a shortage nor a surplus, so that no person has an incentive to change the price asked or offered.

A REVIEW OF THE BASICS

The Supply and Demand Curves

Exhibit 18.1 uses the market for wheat to set the scene for a review of the basics of supply and demand. The demand curve for wheat is drawn with a negative slope in accordance with the law of demand: as the price of wheat decreases, other things being equal, the quantity demanded increases. The supply curve is drawn with a positive slope, indicating that, other things being equal, farmers are willing to increase the quantity of wheat they will supply if they are offered the incentive of a higher price.

Both the supply and demand curves are drawn on the basis of other things being equal in order to isolate the effects of changes in the price of wheat from the effects of other things that might influence the decisions made by buyers and sellers. To be specific, the demand curve is drawn on the assumption that population, consumer tastes, consumer incomes, the prices of other goods, and consumer expectations about future prices remain unchanged as the price of wheat changes. Similarly, the supply curve for wheat is drawn on the assumption that production technology, the prices of inputs to the production of wheat, and supplier expectations about future prices remain unchanged as the price of wheat changes.

Equilibrium

The price of $2 per bushel, where the supply and demand curves intersect, is shown as the *equilibrium price* in the exhibit. It is the equilibrium price because it is the only price at which no person has an incentive to change the price asked or offered for the product.

Consider, by contrast, any price higher than $2. At a price of, say, $3 the quantity supplied would be 2.5 billion bushels and the quantity demanded only 1.5 billion. There would be a surplus (an excess quantity supplied) of 1 billion bushels per year. Farmers could not sell all they were willing to offer at that price. Those who were unable to find buyers for their crops would then have an incentive to cut the price at which they offered their wheat for sale. As the price fell, the quantity demanded would increase and the quantity supplied would decrease. The surplus would gradually be eliminated, and equilibrium would be restored.

In much the same way, there would be an incentive for price changes if the price of wheat were below $2. As Exhibit 18.1 is drawn, for example, at a price of $1, buyers would want to purchase 2.5 billion bushels of wheat per year, but producers would be willing to supply only 1.5 billion bushels. There would be a shortage (excess quantity demanded) of 1 billion bushels. Not all buyers would be able to get as much wheat as they wanted. Unsatisfied buyers would have an incentive to offer higher prices in order not to be left out altogether. Farmers would willingly accept these offers, and the price would rise toward equilibrium. Eventually the shortage would disappear.

Changes in Equilibrium

As economic conditions change, the equilibrium price and quantity for the market change also. In analyzing changes in equilibrium, it is important to distinguish between shifts in supply or demand curves and movements along those curves.

When a change occurs in the price of a good, other things being equal, the effect is seen in a movement along the demand curve for that good. Economists refer to such a movement as a *change in the quantity demanded*. In contrast, when the behavior of buyers is affected by a change in something other than the price of the good for which the demand curve is drawn, the result is shown as a shift in the entire demand curve. Such a shift is, by convention, referred to as a *change in demand* for the good in question. All the items covered by the other-things-being-equal clause in the law of demand are potential sources of shifts in the demand curve. Changes in the demand for a good can thus occur as the result of changes in population, consumer tastes, consumer incomes, the prices of other goods, or consumer expectations regarding future prices.

The same distinction between movements along a curve and shifts in the curve applies to the supply curve. When a change in the price of the good occurs, other things being equal, the effect is shown as a movement along the supply curve. This is called a *change in the quantity supplied*. A change in one of the things covered by the other-things-being-equal clause — production technology, input prices, or supplier expectations — produces a shift in the supply curve. Such a shift is referred to as a *change in supply*.

The points regarding shifts in curves and movements along curves are illustrated in Exhibit 18.2. In Exhibit 18.2a, an increase in consumer incomes shifts the demand curve for wheat to the right, from the position D_1 to the position D_2. This shift creates a shortage of wheat, which in turn drives up the price. As the price rises, the market moves up along the supply curve, from the original equilibrium position E_1 to equilibrium position E_2. In Exhibit 18.2b, a price rise is touched off by a decrease in supply. An increase in labor costs shifts the supply curve upward, from S_1 to

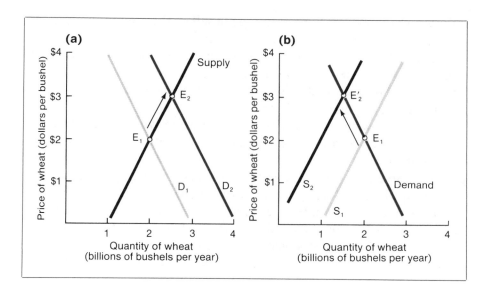

Exhibit 18.2

Changes in price caused by changes in demand and supply

Part a of this exhibit shows the effects of a change in the demand for wheat caused by an increase in consumer incomes. The demand curve shifts to the right, from D_1 to D_2, creating a shortage at the initial price of $2 per bushel. The market moves up along the supply curve, as shown by the arrow, until a new equilibrium is established at E_2, with a price of $3 per bushel. Part b shows the effects of a change in supply caused by an increase in labor costs. The supply curve shifts upward from S_1 to S_2, creating a shortage at the original price. The market moves along the demand curve to the new equilibrium E'_2.

S_2. This creates a shortage of wheat at the initial price, which again pushes the price upward. As the price rises, the market moves along the demand curve from the original equilibrium position E_1 to the new equilibrium position E'_2.

ELASTICITY

Elasticity and Changes in Revenue

The review of supply and demand just presented emphasized the effects of changes in price on the quantity of a good demanded. This section shifts focus somewhat to look at the effects of price changes on the total revenue generated by the sale of a good — total revenue being calculated as the quantity of the good sold multiplied by the price at which it is sold.

As Exhibit 18.3 shows, a change in the price of a good can have one of three effects on total revenue, depending on the shape and position of the demand curve. In the case of good A, a decline in price from $5 per unit to $3 per unit increases the quantity demanded from three units to six units. Total revenue thus increases from $15 to $18 as the price falls. In the case of good B, the same decline in price from $5 to $3 is shown as increasing the quantity demanded by only one unit, from three units to four units. Total revenue thus decreases from $15 to $12. Finally, in the case of good C, a drop in price from $5 to $3 increases the quantity demanded from three units to five units, leaving total revenue unchanged at $15.

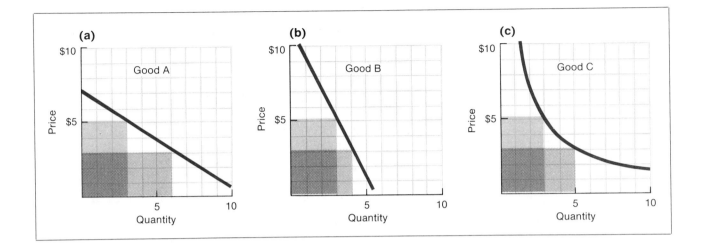

Exhibit 18.3

Elastic, inelastic, and unit elastic demand

This exhibit illustrates the relationship between changes in price and changes in revenue for three different demand curves. As the price of good A decreases from $5 to $3, revenue increases from $15 to $18; the demand for good A is elastic. As the price of good B decreases over the same range, revenue falls from $15 to $12; the demand for good B is inelastic. As the price of good C decreases, revenue remains unchanged; the demand for good C is unit elastic.

The effects of changes in price on total revenue illustrated in Exhibit 18.3 can be expressed in terms of the relationship between the percentage by which the quantity demanded changes and the percentage by which the price changes. The ratio of the percentage change in the quantity demanded of a good to the percentage change in the price of the good is known as the **price elasticity of demand**, or simply the **elasticity of demand**, for that good. If quantity changes by a larger percentage than price, as in Exhibit 18.3a, so that total revenue increases as the price decreases, demand for the good is said to be **elastic**. If quantity changes by a smaller percentage than price, so that total revenue decreases as the price decreases, as in Exhibit 18.3b, demand is said to be **inelastic**. And if price and quantity change by the same percentage, as in Exhibit 18.3c, so that total revenue remains unchanged, demand is said to be **unit elastic**.

In addition to the cases of elastic, inelastic, and unit elastic demand illustrated in Exhibit 18.3, there are two limiting cases illustrated in Exhibit 18.4. Exhibit 18.4a shows a demand curve that is perfectly vertical. No matter what the price, the quantity demanded is a constant five units—no more, no less. Such a demand curve is referred to as **perfectly inelastic**. Exhibit 18.4b shows a demand curve that is perfectly horizontal. Above the price of $5, none of the good can be sold. But as soon as the price drops to $5, producers can sell as much of the good as they care to produce without cutting the price any more. A horizontal demand curve such as this one is described as **perfectly elastic**.

Price elasticity of demand (elasticity of demand) The ratio of the percentage change in the quantity of a good demanded to the percentage change in the price of the good.

Elastic demand The situation in which quantity changes by a larger percentage than price along the demand curve, so that total revenue increases as price decreases.

Inelastic demand The situation in which quantity changes by a smaller percentage than price along the demand curve, so that total revenue decreases as price decreases.

Unit elastic demand The situation in which price and quantity change by the same percentage along the demand curve, so that total revenue remains unchanged as price changes.

Perfectly inelastic demand The situation in which the demand curve is a vertical line.

Perfectly elastic demand The situation in which the demand curve is a horizontal line.

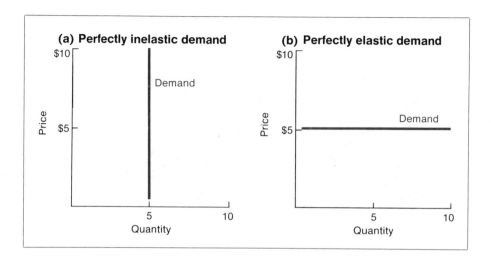

Exhibit 18.4
Perfectly elastic and perfectly inelastic demand.
Part a of this exhibit shows a demand curve that is a vertical line. No matter what the price, the quantity demanded is a constant five units. Such a demand curve is referred to as perfectly inelastic. Part b shows a perfectly elastic demand curve, which is a horizontal line. Above the price of $5, none of the good can be sold. At the price of $5, suppliers can sell as much of the good as they want without further reductions in price.

The Importance of Elasticity

If elasticity were nothing more than another way of describing the shape and position of demand curves, it would not deserve a great deal of attention. But what makes elasticity an important concept is not so much its descriptive usefulness as its analytic usefulness. Decision makers in business and government often would like to know what the elasticity is for particular products. This is illustrated in the following case study.

Case 18.1
Measuring Elasticity of Demand in the Wine Market

The price of beer, liquor, and wine is set by provincial liquor control commissions. In setting prices, the commissions take account of world demand and supply conditions as well as local demand and supply forces. They would like to know something about the elasticity of demand for their various products in order to guess how changes in price will affect the quantity demanded.

The news item below, taken from the *Winnipeg Free Press* of January 19, 1974, illustrates this:

The jump in price of European wines June 1 has shown some pretty predictable results at the local liquor control commission.

(Prices, particularly of French wines, shot up drastically last year as a result of a combination of factors, including increased world demand, increased shipping charges, a few poor vintages and the devaluation of the United States dollar.)

To compensate for the expected decrease in sales of French wines, the Manitoba liquor control commission expanded its range of Italian, German, Spanish, and Portuguese wines last spring.

Statistics made public this week by the commission indicate that, between October 1972, and October 1973, the purchase of French wines had decreased by 13 percent and the sale of Italian wines, by 55 percent. German wines were up 66 percent from October 1972; Spanish and Portuguese wines were up 53 percent.

The statistics on decreased purchases of French wines apply mainly to those which increased drastically in price. For example, until May, Chateauneuf du Pape sold at $3.90 a bottle and, between January and May, the commission sold a total of 5,200 bottles. After June 1, the price of the wine soared to $11.95 and between June and December sales dropped to 400 bottles. It's a wonder even 400 bottles were sold at this terribly inflated price.

The Manitoba liquor control commission was forced to raise the price of French wines because of demand and supply changes noted in the second paragraph of the newspaper article. The commission correctly anticipated that the quantity of French wines demanded by the Manitoba public would decline and that the demand for other wines would increase. However, it could not predict how much the price increase would affect the quantity demanded of French wines. In other words, it couldn't say how elastic or inelastic the demand for a given French wine actually was.

The last paragraph in the news article gives us some useful information about the demand for one particular brand of French wine, Chateauneuf du Pape. In the five-month period before June 1, the value of sales of this wine totaled $20,280 (5,200 × $3.90). In the seven-month period after the June 1 price increase, sales declined to $4,780 (400 × $11.95). Would you say that the demand for this wine is elastic or inelastic? Note that the calculation of elasticity in this example is complicated by the fact that the comparision is drawn out over a full year. Elasticity is meant to measure consumer response to a change in price over such a short period of time that other factors like income and tastes cannot be said to influence consumer behavior. Over a year, of course, such factors do alter, so that it is difficult to say how much of the change in the quantity demanded was caused by the price change.

Measuring Elasticity of Demand

For some purposes, it is useful to put a numerical value on elasticity of demand, rather than simply to classify demand as elastic or inelastic. The basis for such numerical measurements is the definition of the *elasticity of demand* as the ratio of the percentage change in quantity demanded to the percentage change in price.

Percentage Changes In order to apply this definition to the measurement of elasticity, we need to be somewhat more precise than before about how to calculate percentage changes. Suppose, for example, we are dealing with a $.25 increase in the price of strawberries, from $.75 pint to $1 per pint. In everyday usage, we would call this a 33 percent increase in price ($.25/$.75 = 0.33). However, if we observed a $.25 decrease in the price of strawberries, from $1 per pint to $.75, we would call it a 25 percent decrease ($.25/$1 = 0.25).

In measuring elasticity, it would be awkward to have to specify whether we were dealing with a price increase or a price decrease before calculating the percentage change. To get around this difficulty, we will adopt the convention of using the midpoint of the price range as a basis for calculating the percentage. The midpoint in this case is ($.75 + $1)/2 = $.875, so the percentage change, as we define it, becomes $.25/$.875 = 0.285 (approximately). Calculated this way, the percentage is the same for an increase as for a decrease over the specified range of price.

Using P_1 to represent the price before the change and P_2 the price after the change, this convention for calculating the percentage change in price can be written in terms of a general formula as:

$$\text{Percent change in price} = \frac{P_1 - P_2}{(P_1 + P_2)/2}.$$

The same problem arises in defining the percentage change in the quantity demanded that results from a given change in price. Suppose that when the price of strawberries falls from \$1 to \$.75, the quantity demanded increases from 100 pints per day to 150 pints. We can use the average of the higher quantity and the lower quantity to calculate the percentage change in quantity. If Q_1 and Q_2 are the quantities before and after a change in price, the formula for the percentage change can be written as:

$$\text{Percentage change in quantity} = \frac{Q_1 - Q_2}{(Q_1 + Q_2)/2}.$$

Applying this formula to the example just given, we would say that either an increase in quantity from 100 to 150 or a decrease in quantity from 150 to 100 represented a 40 percent change in quantity:

$$\text{Percentage change in quantity} = \frac{150 - 100}{(150 + 100)/2} = 0.40.$$

An Elasticity Formula Defining percentage changes in this way allows us to write a practical formula for calculating elasticities. The formula can be applied to the elasticity of either supply or demand. Using P_1 and Q_1 to represent price and quantity before a change and P_2 and Q_2 to represent price and quantity after the change, the formula is:[1]

$$\begin{array}{c}\text{Price} \\ \text{elasticity} \\ \text{of demand}\end{array} = \frac{(Q_1 - Q_2)/(Q_1 + Q_2)}{(P_1 - P_2)/(P_1 + P_2)} = \frac{\begin{array}{c}\text{Percentage change} \\ \text{in quantity}\end{array}}{\begin{array}{c}\text{Percentage change} \\ \text{in price}\end{array}}$$

The following problem illustrates the use of this formula.

Problem: A change in the price of strawberries from \$1 per pint to \$.75 per pint causes the quantity demanded to increase from 100 pints per day to 150 pints per day. What is the price elasticity of demand for strawberries over the range of price and quantity indicated?

---

[1] Given the definition of percentage changes, we could write the elasticity formula as:

$$\frac{\dfrac{Q_1 - Q_2}{(Q_1 + Q_2)/2}}{\dfrac{P_1 - P_2}{(P_1 + P_2)/2}}$$

This is unnecessarily complicated, however, because the 2s cancel out. The formula given in the text is the simplified equivalent of this one.

Solution:

P_1 = Price before change   = \$1
P_2 = Price after change   = \$.75
Q_1 = Quantity before change = 100
Q_2 = Quantity after change   = 150

$$\text{Elasticity} = \frac{(100 - 150)\,/(100 + 150)}{(\$1.00 - \$.75)\,/(\$1.00 + \$.75)}$$

$$= \frac{-50\,/250}{\$.25/\$1.75}$$

$$= \frac{-0.2}{\$.1428}$$

$$= -1.4.$$

Note that when the formula is applied to a good having a negatively sloped demand curve — as most, if not all, goods do — it yields a negative value for elasticity. The reason is that the quantity changes in the opposite direction to the change in price. It will be the practice in this book to drop the minus sign, however, and to speak of price elasticity of demand as a positive number; that is, the elasticity of demand for a good will be given as 2 or 0.5 or whatever rather than as −2 or −0.5. This convention of dropping the minus sign is widely used in economic writing, although it is not followed universally. If this convention is applied to the preceding problem, the elasticity of demand for strawberries will be said to be 1.4 over the range of price and quantity shown.

Elasticity Values and Changes in Revenue

The chapter earlier introduced the terms *elastic, inelastic, unit elastic, perfectly elastic* and *perfectly inelastic demand*. They were defined in terms of the relationship between change in price and change in total revenue. Each of these elasticity terms corresponds to a certain numerical value or range of numerical values of elasticity as calculated according to the elasticity formula. A perfectly inelastic demand curve has a measured elasticity of 0, because any change in price produces no change in quantity demanded. The term *inelastic* (but not perfectly inelastic) *demand* applies to measured elasticities in the range from 0 up to, but not including, 1. *Unit elasticity*, as the name implies, means a numerical elasticity of exactly 1. *Elastic demand* means any value for elasticity greater than 1. *Perfectly elastic demand*, corresponding to a horizontal supply curve, is not defined numerically; as the demand curve approaches horizontal, the denominator of the elasticity formula approaches 0, so that the measured value of elasticity approaches infinity.

Varying and Constant Elasticity Demand Curves

The formula just given for calculating the elasticity of demand shows the elasticity of demand over a certain range of price and quantity. Measured over some other range of price and quantity, the elasticity of demand for the

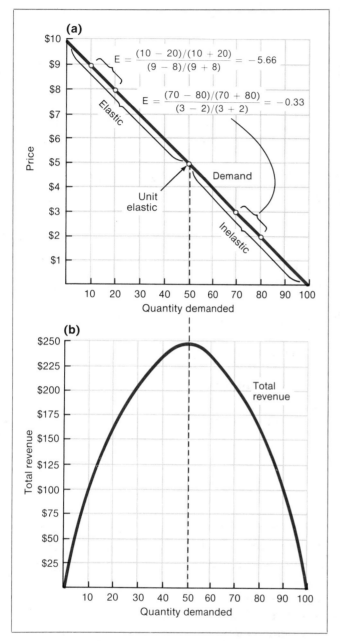

Exhibit 18.5
Variation in elasticity along a straight-line demand curve
This exhibit shows how elasticity varies along a straight-line demand curve. At low quantities, demand is elastic; for example, in the range from ten to twenty units, the elasticity of the demand curve shown in Part a of the exhibit is 5.66. At fifty units of output (halfway down the curve), a point of unit elasticity is reached. From there to a hundred units of output, demand is inelastic; in the range seventy to eighty units, for example, elasticity is 0.33. Part b of the exhibit shows that total revenue increases as quantity increases over the elastic portion of the demand curve and decreases as quantity increases over the inelastic portion. Total revenue reaches a maximum at the point of unit elasticity.

same good may or may not be different. Whether the elasticity of demand for a good changes along the demand curve turns out to depend on the exact shape of the curve. This is illustrated in Exhibits 18.5 and 18.6.

A Linear Demand Curve First consider Exhibit 18.5a, which shows a straight-line demand curve like most of those drawn in this book. The elasticity of demand is not constant for all ranges of price and quantity along this curve. Measured over the price range $8 to $9, for example, the elasticity of demand is 5.66. Measured over the range $2 to $3, it is 0.33. (The full calculations are shown in the exhibit.)

Exhibit 18.6

A demand curve with constant elasticity

It is possible for a demand curve to have constant elasticity throughout its length. The calculations in the exhibit show that this curve has an elasticity of 1.0 wherever it is measured. This particular demand curve is a rectangular hyperbola with the formula P × Q = 100.

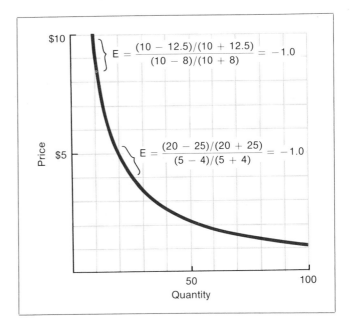

$$E = \frac{(10 - 12.5)/(10 + 12.5)}{(10 - 8)/(10 + 8)} = -1.0$$

$$E = \frac{(20 - 25)/(20 + 25)}{(5 - 4)/(5 + 4)} = -1.0$$

This illustrates the general principle that elasticity declines as one moves down along a straight-line demand curve. It is easy to see why: with a straight-line demand curve, a $1 reduction in price always produces the same absolute increase in quantity demanded. At the upper end of the demand curve, though, a $1 change in price is a small percentage change, while the absolute change in quantity, as a percentage of the small quantity already demanded, is large. At the lower end of the curve, the situation is reversed. A $1 change is now a large percentage of the price, while the constant absolute increase in quantity has now become smaller in percentage terms. Because it is percentages, not absolute amounts, that count in elasticity calculations, the demand curve is less elastic near the bottom than near the top. Because elasticity changes along a straight-line demand curve, it makes sense to apply the formula only to small changes.

Note the relationship between the elasticity of demand and total revenue, as shown by Exhibit 18.5b. In the elastic range of the demand curve, total revenue increases as price decreases. Total revenue reaches a peak at the point of unit elasticity and declines again in the range of inelastic demand.

A Constant Elasticity Demand Curve   If the demand curve is not a straight line, the above results need not always apply. There is an important special case in which the demand curve has just the curvature needed to keep elasticity constant throughout its length. Such a curve is shown in Exhibit 18.6. As the calculations in the exhibit indicate, elasticity is exactly 1.0 everywhere on this curve. It is possible to construct demand curves with constant elasticities of any desired value. Such curves are often used in statistical studies of demand elasticity, as the following case study illustrates.

Case 18.2
Measuring Elasticity of Demand in the Cotton Market

The market for cotton has tended to be relatively unstable in the postwar period. Price changes from one year to the next have been very great. It is thought that one of the reasons for this instability is a very inelastic demand for cotton. With an inelastic demand, the price must fall a long way for producers to dispose of a relatively small surplus, and a considerable rise in price can occur when there is a shortage. Kenneth Lewis, an economist at Boston University, thought it would be useful for those concerned with the cotton market to know just how inelastic demand was.

Lewis began by assembling data on the price of cotton and the quantity of cotton purchased in sixteen industrialized countries during the period 1949 to 1964. To simplify his calculations, he followed a standard econometric practice and assumed that the cotton demand curve would have the shape needed to give constant elasticity throughout the normal range of prices. Next he had to deal with the problem of "other things being equal." A demand curve tells how the demand for cotton responds to the price for cotton when nothing else changes, but in the wide range of countries and years represented in Lewis's data, "other things" could hardly be expected to stand still. To deal with this problem, he used a statistical technique known as multiple regression analysis. This allowed an approximate correction for changes that had occurred over time in population, per capita consumer income, and the prices of other closely related products — particularly wool and synthetic fibers.

Lewis's statistical results confirmed that the demand for cotton was very inelastic — only 0.095, as nearly as he could estimate. This meant that more than a 10 percent change in price from one year to the next would be required to change the quantity demanded by 1 percent. Lewis suggested two reasons for the low elasticity of demand. One was that cotton is a raw material that often accounts for only a small portion of the value of a final product. For example, a 10 percent change in the price of cotton would have far less than a 10 percent effect on the price of a cotton shirt if the cost of manufacturing, labor, transportation, retailing, services, and the like remained unchanged. Second, the products made from cotton were necessities rather than luxuries, for the most part, and hence they too could be expected to have low elasticities of demand.

Source: Based on Kenneth Lewis, "Multi-Market Demand Functions in the Presence of Supply Constraints: International Demand for Cotton and Wool." *Southern Economic Journal* 38 (October 1971), pp. 200-208.

It is important to recognize the limitations of statistical estimates of demand elasticity. To say that the elasticity of demand for cotton is 0.095 is not to measure any inherent quality of the good itself. Neither is the measured elasticity really a constant of consumer behavior. The actual measurement is just a capsulized fragment of economic history. It tells us that at certain times and places in the past, a 1 percent change in price appears to have been associated with approximately a 0.095 percent change in quantity demanded.

Despite their limitations, however, statistical estimates of elasticity can be of considerable practical use. Economic decision makers in business and government must take past experience into account when planning for the future even though they know that market conditions in the future will not be exactly like those in the past.

Determinants of Elasticity of Demand

Why is the price elasticity of demand high for some goods and low for others? One thing helping to determine the elasticity of demand for a good is the availability of substitutes or complements. If a good has close substitutes, demand for that good tends to be elastic, because when its price rises, people can switch to something similar. For example, the demand for olive oil is more elastic than it would be if other salad oils were not available as substitutes. Similarly, the demand for cars is less elastic than it would be if good public transport were available everywhere, because cars and public transportation are reasonably close substitutes for each other. On the other hand, if something is a minor complement to an important good, its demand tends to be inelastic. For example, the demand for motor oil tends to be inelastic, because it is a complement to a more important good — gasoline. The price of gasoline is much more likely to influence the amount of driving a person does than is the price of motor oil.

Elasticity is also influenced by the portion of a person's budget spent on a good. Matches, for example, are no longer really a necessity, and good substitutes exist. Nonetheless, the demand for matches is thought to be very inelastic, just because people spend so little on them that they hardly notice a price change. In contrast, the demand for things like housing and transportation is not perfectly inelastic, even though they are necessities. Since they occupy a large part of people's budgets, changes in prices just cannot be ignored.

Finally, elasticity of demand is influenced by the time perspective being considered. Demand is often less elastic in the short run than in the long run. Consider the demand for home heating fuel, for example. In the short run, people find it hard to cut back the quantity they use when the price goes up. They are accustomed to living at a certain temperature, dressing a certain way, and so on. Given time, though, they may find ways to economize. They can put better insulation in their homes, get in the habit of dressing more warmly, or even move to a warmer climate.

Other Elasticities

The concept of elasticity has, up to this point, been applied only to the price elasticity of demand for a good; but there are many other common applications of the concept. All of them are based on the idea of the ratio of the percentage change in one variable to the percentage change in another. Two of the most commonly used types of elasticity, in addition to the price elasticity of demand, are price elasticity of supply and income elasticity of demand.

Price Elasticity of Supply The definition of the **price elasticity of supply** for a good closely resembles that of the price elasticity of demand: it is the percentage change in the quantity of the good supplied divided by the percentage change in the price of the good. The formula for price elasticity of supply is exactly the same as that for price elasticity of demand. Because price and quantity change in the same direction along a positively sloped supply curve, the formula gives a positive value for the elasticity of supply. Exhibit 18.7 applies the elasticity formula to two supply curves, one having constant elasticity and the other having variable elasticity.

Price elasticity of supply (elasticity of supply) The ratio of the percentage change in the quantity of a good supplied to the percentage change in its price.

Income Elasticity of Demand As shown in Chapter 3 and again earlier in this chapter, changes in consumer income can cause changes in the

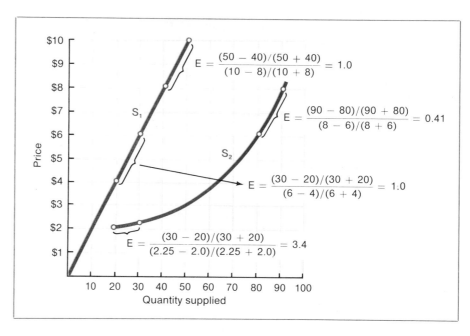

Exhibit 18.7

Calculating price elasticities of supply

This exhibit gives four examples of how supply elasticities are calculated — two for each of the two supply curves shown. The supply curve S_1, which is a straight line passing through the origin, has a constant elasticity of 1.0. The supply curve S_2, which is curved, is elastic for low quantities of output and inelastic for larger quantities. For example, in the range from twenty to thirty units of output, the elasticity of S_2 is 3.4, and in the range from eighty to ninety units of output, the elasticity is 0.41.

Income elasticity of demand The ratio of the percentage change in the demand for a good to the percentage change in the per capita income of buyers.

demand for a good. Such changes are represented by shifts in the demand curve. The concept of elasticity, in the form of the income elasticity of demand, can be applied to measure the size and direction of such changes. The **income elasticity of demand** for a good is defined as the ratio of the percentage change in demand for the good to the percentage change in income. In measuring the income elasticity of demand for a good, the price of the good is assumed not to change. Income is usually measured in per capita terms. Using Q_1 and Q_2 to represent quantities before and after the income change and y_1 and y_2 to represent per capita income before and after the change, the formula for income elasticity of demand can be written as follows:

$$\text{Income elasticity of demand} = \frac{(Q_1 - Q_2)/(Q_1 + Q_2)}{(y_1 - y_2)/(y_1 + y_2)} = \frac{\text{Percentage change in quantity}}{\text{Percentage change in income}}$$

Income elasticity of demand is positive for a normal good and negative for an inferior good. Suppose, for example, that a study of meat buying habits showed that for each 10 percent increase in income, the typical Canadian household tended to consume 12 percent more steak, 5 percent more chicken, and 2 percent less hamburger. One would conclude from these numbers that the income elasticity of demand was 1.2 for steak, 0.5 for chicken, and −0.2 for hamburger. Steak and chicken would thus be classified as normal goods and hamburger as an inferior good.

CONCLUSIONS

This chapter has set the stage for asking a great many questions. First, what really lies behind the supply and demand curves? The text has given general commonsense explanations of why these curves have the shapes they do, but now it must show in more detail how they can be explained in terms of individual people's attempts to deal with the problems of scarcity and choice. This explanation will occupy several chapters.

Next, do the principles of supply and demand apply to all markets or to only certain types of markets? This chapter limited its examples to markets like those for wheat and strawberries, where there are many buyers and sellers and all of them are relatively small. But we need to know also how to apply the principles to markets that may be dominated by only one or a few large sellers.

Finally, how can the principles of supply and demand be applied to help in further understanding the role of government in the economy? In many markets, government regulations have important influences on the prices and quantities of goods that consumers can buy and producers can sell.

In answering all these questions, future chapters will continue to build on the basics reviewed in this chapter.

SUMMARY

1. According to the law of demand, the quantity of a product demanded increases as its price decreases. It is also widely the case that sellers of a good are willing to increase the quantity supplied only if offered the inducement of a higher price. When these conditions hold, there is a market equilibrium price at the intersection of a good's supply and demand curves. That intersection represents the only price at which no one has an incentive to change the price asked or offered.

2. For some goods, a 1 percent change in price produces more than a 1 percent change in quantity demanded, so that revenue increases as price decreases. Such goods are said to have elastic demand. Similarly, goods are said to have an elastic supply if a 1 percent change in price produces more than a 1 percent change in the quantity supplied. At the extreme, where supply or demand curves are horizontal, supply or demand is said to be perfectly elastic. For other goods, a 1 percent change in price will cause less than a 1 percent change in quantity demanded, so that revenue decreases as price decreases. Such goods are said to have inelastic demand. Similarly, goods are said to have an inelastic supply if a 1 percent change in price produces less than a 1 percent change in the quantity supplied. Perfectly inelastic demand or supply means a vertical supply or demand curve.

3. The formula for calculating the elasticity of supply or demand between two points on a supply or demand curve is:

$$\text{Elasticity} = \frac{(Q_1 - Q_2)\,/(Q_1 + Q_2)}{(P_1 - P_2)\,/(P_1 + P_2)}.$$

In applying this formula to demand, it is conventional to drop the minus sign from the result and consider elasticity to be a positive number.

4. Changes in per capita income can cause shifts in demand curves. The

ratio of the percentage change in quantity to the percentage change in per capita income is known as the income elasticity of demand. Income elasticity of demand is positive for a normal good and negative for an inferior good.

DISCUSSION QUESTIONS

1. How much of each of the following goods or services do you buy now in comparison with the quantity you bought a year ago?
   a. Clothing
   b. Movie tickets
   c. Gasoline
   d. Beer
   If the quantity you buy has changed for any of these goods, do you think the change is best described as a movement along your demand curve, a shift in your demand curve, or a combination of the two? Explain.
2. How do firms and consumers recognize market disequilibrium in the real world? What are the specific tangible signs of a surplus or a shortage?
3. If you were the president of a union bargaining for a new contract and asking for higher wages, would you prefer that the demand for your firm's product were relatively elastic or relatively inelastic? Explain.
4. Suppose that Middle Eastern governments cut off imports of petroleum products into Canada and that the Canadian government imposed a price ceiling. Do you think the lines that might form at gas stations would be longer if the demand for gasoline were relatively elastic or if it were relatively inelastic? (You may wish to refer to Exhibit 3.7 on page 52.)
5. Suppose that the supply of tobacco were relatively elastic and the demand relatively inelastic. Under these conditions, who do you think would protest an increase in the cigarette tax more strongly—consumers or producers? What if the elasticities were reversed? (You may wish to refer to Exhibit 4.6 on page 70.)
6. The town manager of River City calls you in as a consultant to explain something puzzling. Last year, the city doubled its fares on its downtown buses. For a few months, the bus line reported a strong increase in revenues, but then the revenues began falling off and ended up lower than they had been to begin with. Does what you have learned about elasticity of demand and the determinants of that demand help you explain what happened?
7. Do you think it makes sense as a general principle to say that the demand for a broadly defined good such as cars, clothing, or meat will be less elastic than the demand for a corresponding narrowly defined good such as Fords, Levis, or pork chops? Explain.
8. Why would the slope of a demand curve not be just as good a measure as elasticity for the responsiveness of demand to price changes? Can you formulate a simple generalization relating the slope of a demand curve to the way in which total revenue changes when price changes?
9. Economists define the *cross elasticity of demand* between good A and good B as the ratio of the percentage change in the quantity of good A to the percentage change in the price of good B. Suppose that the price of olive oil was $5 per quart. Suppose also that a grocer found that customers bought 100 quarts of olive oil a month when the price of safflower oil was $3 per quart and 150 quarts of olive oil per month when the price of safflower oil was $4 per quart. What is the cross elasticity of demand between olive oil and safflower oil? Are the two kinds of salad oil complements or substitutes for each other?

THE LOGIC OF CONSUMER CHOICE

WHAT YOU WILL LEARN IN THIS CHAPTER

According to the law of demand, people tend to buy more of a good when its price goes down. This chapter discusses some of the principles of consumer choice that lie behind the law of demand. It explains how consumers, facing the necessity of choosing among alternatives and having limited budgets, balance the relative satisfactions they get from various goods against the prices they must pay for those goods.

FOR REVIEW

Here are some important terms and concepts that will be put to use in this chapter. If you do not understand them, review them before proceeding.

• *Law of demand (Chapters 3 and 18)*
• *Normal and inferior goods (Chapters 3 and 18)*
• *Substitutes and complements (Chapters 3 and 18)*

People are used to the idea that when the price of a good goes down, the quantity of that good demanded by consumers tends to go up. The law of demand is easy to accept, because common sense and everyday experience show that it is the way things are. Still, knowing that a thing is so does not keep people from asking why it is so. In Newton's day, everyone knew that when apples fell from trees, they fell down and not up; but Newton asked why, and this led him to some valuable new insights about the laws of gravitation. In the same way, economists have often asked why people buy more of a good when its price falls. Trying to answer that question leads to some useful insights.

CONSUMPTION AND UTILITY

The most basic question one can ask about the law of demand is why people demand goods and services at all. The answer seems to be that people want material goods and services because they get pleasure and satisfaction from them. A loaf of bread to eat, a warm bed to sleep in, or a book to read—each serves needs or desires in one way or another. Economists have their own term for this sort of thing. They say that the use or consumption of material goods gives people **utility**.

Utility The economist's term for the pleasure, satisfaction, and need fulfillment that people get from the consumption of material goods and services.

Utility and Psychological Needs

To a psychologist, just saying that people want things because they get utility from them would sound very shallow. Some psychologists, at least, would want to go into detail about the nature and sources of human wants. Followers of Abraham Maslow, for example, find it useful to think in terms of five basic kinds of needs: (1) physiological needs; (2) safety and security needs; (3) affection and belonging needs; (4) the need for self-esteem and the esteem of others; and (5) the need for "self-actualization" or self-fulfillment.[1] For each person, the order of importance of the five needs is different.

This simple list of needs raises some important questions for psychologists. Is there a hierarchy among needs? Why is any given need more important to some people than to others? What factors in people's upbringing affect the needs they seek to satisfy in later life? Questions like these, however, get very little attention from economists. Smith may buy a tennis racket to satisfy a physiological need for exercise. Jones may buy one in order to gratify a need to belong by joining a tennis club. Baker may buy one in order to gain the esteem of others by playing in tournaments. What is true of tennis rackets is true of other goods and services too. People with very different psychological needs all have one thing in common. They get utility of one sort or another from material goods. Most economists feel that they do not really need to know any more psychology than that.

Utility and Demand

Economists may not be interested in the origins of human wants, but they are interested in the intensity of those wants. The reason is that the intensity of people's wants for some goods relative to the intensity of their wants for others determines the quantity of those goods they will demand in the marketplace. Whether a person wants a new car intensely enough to pass up the opportunity to spend the same funds on a three-week Caribbean cruise is clearly an economic as well as a psychological question. It is a question about the demand for automobiles.

Marginal utility The amount of added utility obtained from a one-unit increase in consumption of a good.

Principle of diminishing marginal utility The principle that the greater the rate of consumption of some good, the smaller the increase in utility from a unit increase in the rate of consumption.

Diminishing Marginal Utility Economists made a major step forward in their understanding of the relationship between utility and economic behavior when, in the late nineteenth century, they first clearly formulated the principle of diminishing marginal utility. The **marginal utility** of a good to a consumer means the amount of added utility obtained from the consumption of one additional unit of the good in question. The **principle of diminishing marginal utility** says that the greater the quantity of any good consumed, the less the marginal utility from a unit increase in consumption.

For a simple but vivid example of the principle of diminishing marginal utility in action, imagine yourself in a blackberry patch eating berries by the handful. As you eat more and more berries, you get more and more

---

[1] See Abraham Maslow, *Motivation and Personality*, 2d ed. (New York: Harper & Row, 1970).

satisfaction; but at the same time, the satisfaction from each additional handful diminishes. If you eat enough, you may even get to a point where more berries give you no additional utility at all. Then you stop eating berries, at least until the next day.

Utility, to be sure, is a very subjective concept. No one has yet invented a "utility meter" that can be hooked up to a person's skull to read utility like blood pressure. But suppose, to indulge in a bit of science fiction, that there is such a utility meter. If you allow yourself to be hooked up to the meter during your spree in the blackberry patch, the results can be recorded in numerical or graphical form, as in Exhibit 19.1. The table and the graphs in this exhibit use the "util" as an imaginary unit for measuring utility. Both the table and the graphs show that as the quantity of berries consumed per day increases, total utility increases—but at a decreasing rate. Marginal utility—that is, the added utility obtained from each additional handful of berries—falls as the rate of consumption increases. For example, the third handful of berries increases utility by two units, from 5.5 to 7.5, whereas the fourth handful gives only 1.5 units more.

Exhibit 19.1
Diminishing marginal utility

As the rate at which a person consumes some good increases, the utility derived from one additional unit decreases. The table and figures here show that as the rate of consumption of berries increases, total utility increases—but at a decreasing rate. In Part b, a smooth curve is drawn through the stair-step total utility line, which is based on the table. Part c shows a marginal utility curve. The height of this curve at each point is equal to the slope of the smooth curve in Part b.

(a)

Quantity of Berries (Handfuls per Day)	Total Utility (Utils)		Marginal Utility (Utils per Handful)
1	3.0		2.5
2	5.5		2.0
3	7.5		1.5
4	9.0		1.0
5	10.0		0.5
6	10.5		

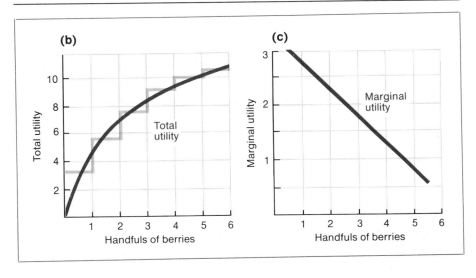

The Consumer as Economizer For better or for worse, the world is not all one big blackberry patch where people can eat as much as they want without making choices. To put the principle of diminishing marginal utility to work in understanding consumer demand, one must look at a world more like the one that really exists. In particular, this is a world in which:

1. There are many different desirable goods.
2. Consumers must pay known prices for the goods they want.
3. Consumers have limited budgets.
4. Consumers try to get the greatest satisfaction they can from their limited budgets.

Pure economizing The aspect of economic decision making that consists of choosing a pattern of activities from among a given set of alternative activities that will best serve a well-defined objective, subject to known constraints.

In such a world, consumers are faced with a classic problem in **pure economizing**: to maximize an objective (their own satisfaction) subject to known constraints (the prices of the goods and their budgets) by choosing among alternative activities (the consumption of various kinds of goods). In such a world, consumers have to make choices, and each choice involves an opportunity cost. If people spend more on one good, they have less to spend on something else. What can be said in a general way about how consumers economize their scarce resources?

Solving the Consumer Problem Begin with the consumer you know best—yourself. Suppose you are deciding how to divide your monthly spending between, say, food and clothing. If you spend an extra dollar a month on food, you get a certain added utility from doing so. At the same time, though, you must bear an opportunity cost equal to the utility you could instead have obtained by spending the dollar on clothing. Whether or not you actually think consciously in such terms, then, your choice will depend on which utility is greater—the extra dollar's worth of food or the extra dollar's worth of clothing.

Which is greater depends in turn on how much of each good you consume. If, relatively speaking, you have a lot of clothing and not much food, the marginal utility of clothing will tend to be low and that of food to be high. By shifting a dollar from clothing to food, you can give up a small utility and gain a large one, which will increase your total utility.

If, instead, you have relatively much food and little clothing, the marginal utilities may be reversed. You will gain a lot of utility from spending an extra dollar on clothing and only a little from spending an extra dollar on food. Again, you can gain in total utility by shifting your pattern of expenditure without spending any more over all.

Consumer Equilibrium It is clear, then, that if the marginal utility of a dollar's worth of clothing is different from that of a dollar's worth of food, you have an incentive to change your pattern of consumption. The only condition in which you will not have an incentive to change your pattern of spending on food and clothing will be if the marginal utility per dollar's worth of the two goods is exactly the same.

Generalizing from this example, it can be said that consumers tend to shift their expenditures from one kind of good to another as long as they can increase their total utilities by doing so. When consumer expenditures are distributed among the various available goods in such a way that, for each consumer, the marginal utility of a dollar's worth of each good consumed is equal to the marginal utility of a dollar's worth of each other good consumed, no further increase in utility is possible within the given budget constraint. A state of **consumer equilibrium** is then said to prevail.

An Alternative Statement There is another, equivalent way to state the conditions for consumer equilibrium. Suppose that a person is consuming just the right quantities of, say, chicken and beef to make the marginal utility of a dollar's worth of chicken equal to the marginal utility of a dollar's worth of beef. It must be true, then, that the marginal utility of a pound of chicken divided by the price of chicken per pound is equal to the marginal utility per pound of beef divided by the price of beef per pound. In equation form, this comes out as:

$$\frac{\text{Marginal utility of chicken per pound}}{\text{Price of chicken per pound}} = \frac{\text{Marginal utility of beef per pound}}{\text{Price of beef per pound}}$$

Suppose, for example, that chicken costs \$1 per pound and beef costs \$3. If the equation just given holds, then an extra pound of beef will give the consumer three times as much utility as an added pound of chicken. This

Consumer equilibrium A state of affairs in which consumers cannot increase the total utility they obtain from a given budget by shifting expenditure from one good to another. (In consumer equilibrium, the marginal utility of a dollar's worth of one good must be equal to the marginal utility of a dollar's worth of any other good.)

The English economist William Stanley Jevons is generally credited with the first systematic exposition of the theory of marginal utility and with its first application to the problem of consumer equilibrium. Jevons was trained in mathematics and chemistry. With this background, it is not surprising that when his interest turned to economics, he would try to strengthen that science by restating its theories in mathematical form. It was the mathematical reworking of economics that led him to the theory of marginal utility.

Although Jevons wrote many books and papers, he is best remembered for his *Theory of Political Economy*, published in 1871. There he set forth the principle of diminishing marginal utility using this illustration:

Let us imagine the whole quantity of food which a person consumes on an average during twenty-four hours to be divided into ten equal parts. If his food be reduced by the last part, he will suffer but little; if a second tenth part be deficient, he will feel the want distinctly; the subtraction of the third part will be decidedly injurious; with every subsequent subtraction of a tenth part his sufferings will be more and more serious until at length he will be upon the verge of starvation. Now, if we call each of the tenth parts *an increment*, the meaning of these facts is, that each increment of food is less necessary, or possesses less utility, than the previous one.

Jevons was the first to put the new theory in print, but he shares credit for the "marginal revolution" in economics with at least three others who were working independently along the same lines at the same time. The Austrian Karl Menger published his version of marginal utility theory in 1871 also. Three years later, the Swiss economist Leon Walras, who did not know of either Jevons's or Menger's work, came out with still another version. Finally, Alfred Marshall worked out the basics of marginal analysis about the same time, although his own major work was not published until 1890.

Jevons had a strong interest in applied economics as well as in pure theory. He wrote on Australian gold mining, on the problem of Great Britain's coal reserves, on monetary questions, and on issues of social reform. As a consultant to the British government, he successfully recommended the abolition of the import duty on corn. In 1880, he resigned his teaching position at the University of London to devote full time to research. Sadly for the science of economics, however, this prolific writer died in a boating accident just two years later, at the age of forty-seven.

William Stanley Jevons (1835-1882)

means, as in the earlier statement of the conditions for consumer equilibrium, that the marginal utility of a dollar's worth (one pound) of chicken is equal to the marginal utility of a dollar's worth (one-third of a pound) of beef.

The equation can be extended to a world with any number of goods and services. MU_A, MU_B, and so on stand for the marginal utilities of goods A, B, and so on. Likewise, P_A, P_B, and so on stand for the prices of the various goods. The general expression for consumer equilibrium then becomes:

$$\frac{MU_A}{P_A} = \frac{MU_B}{P_B} = \frac{MU_C}{P_C} = \frac{MU_D}{P_D} = \ldots$$

From Consumer Equilibrium to the Law of Demand The concepts of consumer equilibrium and diminishing marginal utility can be combined to give an explanation of the law of demand that is intuitively appealing, if not altogether precise. The explanation goes like this: suppose you have adjusted your pattern of consumption until you have reached an equilibrium in which, among other things:

$$\frac{MU \text{ of chicken}}{\$1} = \frac{MU \text{ of beef}}{\$3}$$

As long as this equality holds, it will not be to your benefit to increase your consumption of beef; to do so would, according to the principle of diminishing marginal utility, quickly push down the marginal utility of beef. The marginal utility per dollar's worth of beef would drop below the marginal utility per dollar's worth of chicken, and you would be better off to switch back toward more chicken.

But what if the price of beef were to drop, say to $2.50 per pound, upsetting the equality given above? To make the two ratios equal again, given the new price of beef, either the marginal utility of chicken would have to rise or the marginal utility of beef would have to fall. According to the principle of diminishing marginal utility, one way to get the marginal utility of beef to fall is to consume more beef, and one way to get the marginal utility of chicken to rise is to consume less chicken. Because chicken and beef are substitutes to most people, probably you would do a little of both—that is, cut back a little on chicken and consume a little more beef. In doing so, you would be acting exactly as the law of demand predicts: a fall in the price of beef would have induced you to buy more beef.

SUBSTITUTION AND INCOME EFFECTS AND THE LAW OF DEMAND

The argument just given links the principle of diminishing marginal utility to the law of demand in an intuitively appealing way, but it leaves a few too many loose ends dangling to suit all economists. Is there a way to rationalize the law of demand without relying directly on the slippery, unmeasurable concept of utility? There is. The alternative approach relies on a breakdown of the effects of a change in price into two separate components, known as the substitution and income effect.

The Substitution Effect

Go back in the earlier example to the point where you had adjusted your purchases to an equilibrium, given a price of beef of $3 per pound and a price of chicken of $1 per pound. As before, suppose that the price of beef dropped to $2.50 per pound. With beef relatively cheaper than before, you would tend to substitute beef for chicken in your diet. You might substitute beef for other things too; with the price of a steak dinner cheaper, you might substitute an evening in a restaurant now and then for an evening at the movies. This effect of the change in the price of beef is known as the substitution effect. In general terms, the **substitution effect** of the change in the price of a good is that part of the change in the quantity demanded attributable to the tendency of consumers to substitute relatively cheap goods for relatively expensive ones.

Substitution effect The part of the increase in quantity demanded of a good whose price has fallen that is attributable to the tendency of consumers to substitute relatively cheap goods for relatively expensive ones.

The Income Effect

The substitution effect is not, however, the only reason that a drop in the price of beef would be likely to increase your consumption of beef. Suppose that with the price of beef at $3 per pound, you bought ten pounds per month. The decline in the price to $2.50 per pound would be welcome to you not only because it would allow you to substitute beef for chicken in your diet, but for another reason as well: it would increase the purchasing power of your monthly budget. With beef at $2.50 per pound, you could buy the same quantities of all goods, including beef, and now have $5 left over at the end of the month to spend as you pleased. In short, a fall in the price of any good, other things being equal, produces an increase in real income.[2]

With your increased real income, you would tend to buy more of all normal goods and less of any inferior goods. For most people, beef is a normal good. Some of your new-found $5 in real income, then, would presumably go to the purchase of more beef. This effect of the change in the price of beef on the quantity of beef demanded is known as the income effect. In general terms, the **income effect** of a change in the price of a good is that part of the change in the quantity of the good demanded attributable to the change in real income resulting from the change in price.

Income effect The part of the change in quantity demanded of a good whose price has fallen that is attributable to the change in real income resulting from the price change.

The Law of Demand for Normal and Inferior Goods

The concepts of the substitution and income effects of a price change are very helpful in understanding the law of demand itself and in understanding why the law of demand might, under rare circumstances, permit exceptions. Consider separately the cases of normal and inferior goods.

For a normal good, the law of demand holds absolutely, because the substitution and income effects work together to produce an increase in quantity demanded when the price of a good falls. The example given above

---

[2] Readers who have completed the macroeconomics section of the book will already be familiar with the concept of real income. For the benefit of those who have not read that section, real income means income adjusted for changes in prices to reflect actual purchasing power. The same number of dollars represents more real income when prices fall and less real income when prices rise.

is a case in point. When the price of beef dropped, you bought more beef partly because you substituted beef for chicken and for other goods and services that were now relatively more expensive than before. In addition, you bought more beef still because you spend part of your increased real income on beef—a normal good. Taking the two effects in combination, there is no doubt that a decline in the price of beef would increase the quantity of beef you demanded.

In the case of an inferior good, things are not quite so simple. Suppose that instead of considering a drop in the price of beef in general, you considered the effect of a drop in the price of hamburger only—with the price of all other cuts of beef held constant. Suppose further that you considered hamburger an inferior good—one that you would tend to phase out of your diet as your real income rose. A drop in the price of hamburger, as before, would tend to make you substitute hamburger for other foods that had become relatively more expensive. By itself, this would increase the quantity demanded. However, a drop in the price of hamburger would also produce a slight increase in your real income; and that, considered by itself, would tend to make you buy less hamburger. For an inferior good, then, the substitution and income effects operate in the opposite direction. The law of demand holds for an inferior good only if the size of the substitution effect is larger than that of the income effect.

Are There Really Exceptions to the Law of Demand?

No one has ever come up with a fully convincing real-world case of an exception to the law of demand. It is reasonably certain that there are genuine examples of inferior goods. An earlier chapter cited intercity bus travel and shoe repair services as two likely examples. But as far as anyone knows, in all important cases, the substitution effect outweighs the income effect even for inferior goods, so that demand curves slope downward.

It is possible, however, to construct hypothetical examples of exceptions to the law of demand that, although perhaps farfetched, are logically possible. Chapter 3 suggested the following hypothetical case: a family living in Manitoba spends each January in Florida. One year the price of home heating fuel goes up sharply. The family turns its thermostat down a little; but even so, the heating bills go up so much that it cannot afford to go to Florida that year. Staying home in January means that the house must be kept heated during that month. The extra fuel burned during January is more than what the family has been able to save with a lower thermostat setting in the other months. Thus the total quantity of fuel burned in the season increases as a direct result of the increase in the price of fuel.

This curious case can be analyzed in terms of the income and substitution effects as follows: when the price of fuel goes up, the substitution effect works normally. The family turns its thermostat down, substituting warm clothes for heating fuel as a source of winter comfort. The weekly demand for heating fuel, however, is inelastic; even though the quantity burned per week to heat the house is slightly reduced, total expenditures on it rise, cutting sharply into the real income that the family has to spend on other goods. Now comes the "gimmick" that makes the case work.

Heating fuel may not be an inferior good for most families, but this family is different. For this family, winter vacations spent in Manitoba are an inferior good; the higher the family's income, other things being equal, the less time it spends in Manitoba in the winter. Heating fuel is a complement to winter vacations in Manitoba, and this complementarity makes heating fuel too an inferior good for this particular family. Other things being equal (including the price of heating fuel), the higher the family's real income, the more time it spends in Florida and the less fuel it burns per year.

With heating fuel an inferior good, the slope of the family's demand curve depends on the relative size of the income and substitution effects of the increase in the price of heating fuel. Assume that the substitution effect, although it does act to decrease consumption, is small. Sweaters are something of a substitute for a warm house, but not a particularly good substitute. Assume also that the income effect, which takes the form of spending January, the coldest month of the year, at home, is quite large. More fuel is burned in January than the total of what is saved by wearing sweaters all the rest of the year. The increase in the price of fuel thus increases the consumption of fuel. This is a logically sound, although strictly hypothetical, exception to the law of demand.

CONCLUSIONS

Much of the available evidence concerning the theories of consumer behavior set forth in this chapter is subjective. The principle of diminishing marginal utility, the substitution effect, income effects, and the law of demand are plausible largely because they reflect the way people behave as consumers.

Many economists are content to let the theory of consumer behavior stand on a foundation of subjective evidence. But others are not. Over the years, there have been repeated attempts to expose the theory to various empirical tests. Most of these attempts at testing have used human subjects. Experimenters have set up games or artificial economies in which subjects "buy" goods or services with tokens, or something of the sort. The results of such experiments have been clouded by certain difficulties, though. Human subjects are hard to use. It is impossible to find subjects free of past experience with a market economy. It is also impossible for the subjects not to know that they are only playing a game. It is difficult or very expensive to continue the experiments for long. And it is hard to shut out all outside influences.

A few years ago, in an attempt to surmount these difficulties, a group of experimenters at Texas A & M University and the State University of New York at Stony Brook took a dramatic new approach. Instead of using human subjects to test the theory of human behavior, they used ordinary laboratory rats. Their methods and some of their results are sketched in the following case study.

Case 19.1
Testing Consumer Demand Theory with White Rats

Two male albino rats were placed in standard laboratory cages, with food and water freely available. At one end of each cage were two levers that activated dipper cups.

One dipper cup provided a measured quantity of root beer when its lever was depressed; the other provided a measured quantity of Collins mix. Previous experimentation had shown that rats prefer these beverages to water.

Within this setup, each rat could be given a fixed "income" of so many pushes on the levers per day. The pushes could be distributed in any way between the two levers. Experimenters could also control the "price" of root beer and Collins mix by determining the number of pushes the rat had to "spend" to obtain one milliliter of liquid.

In an initial experimental run lasting two weeks, the rats were given an income of three hundred pushes per day, and both beverages were priced at twenty pushes per milliliter. Under these conditions, Rat 1 settled down to a pattern of drinking about eleven milliliters of root beer per day and about four milliliters of Collins mix. Rat 2 preferred a diet of almost all root beer, averaging less than one milliliter of Collins mix per day.

Next came the crucial test. By manipulating incomes and prices, could the rats be induced to shift their consumption patterns in the way economic theory predicts? To see if they could, the experimenters proceeded as follows. First, the price of root beer was doubled, and the price of Collins mix was cut in half. At the same time, each subject's total income of pushes was adjusted to make it possible for each to afford to continue the previous consumption pattern if it should be chosen. (This adjustment in total income was made in order to eliminate any possible income effect of the price change and to concentrate solely on the substitution effect.) Economic theory predicts that under the new conditions, the rats would choose to consume more Collins mix and less root beer than before, even though they would have the opportunity not to change their behavior.

The rats behavior exactly fitted these predictions. In two weeks of living under the new conditions, Rat 1 settled down to a new consumption pattern of about eight milliliters of root beer amd seventeen milliliters of Collins mix per day. Rat 2, which had chosen root beer almost exclusively before, switched over to about nine milliliters of root beer and twenty-five milliliters of Collins mix.

Source: Adapted by permission from John H. Kagel and Raymond C. Battalio, "Experimental Studies of Consumer Demand Behavior," *Economic Inquiry* 8 (March 1975), pp. 22-38.

This fascinating experiment can hardly be taken as the ultimate proof of the economic theory of consumer choice. Further experiments carried out with the same rats pointed to possible limitations of the theory and suggested important directions for more research. In its way, though, the experiment gave more impressive evidence in favor of the theory than any experiment with human subjects could. The complete control over the subjects' environment permitted the problem of consumer choice to be reduced to its absolute basics. The results of the experiments certainly correspond to our subjective feelings about what *we* would do under similar circumstances.

But even if theories of consumer behavior can be verified empirically, the skeptic might ask what good they are. The answer may be that, in terms of practical applications, they are not very useful. The theories do not describe the way consumers actually think about the choices they make; nor do they permit policy makers to help consumers make the right choices. If they could actually measure utility (perhaps, as suggested earlier, by hooking people up to a utility meter), such practical applications might be possible. Without a utility meter, they are not.

The value of the theories of marginal utility and consumer equilibrium, then, lies elsewhere. Rather than producing practical applications, these theories produce insight and understanding. They help us understand how consumers deal with the universal economic problem of choosing among alternative uses for scarce resources. They give a deeper insight into the logic of the familiar law of demand. These things are important enough to keep the ideas of marginal utility and consumer equilibrium alive as a basic part of modern economics.

SUMMARY

1. People demand goods and services because they get utility from them. Psychologists are able to identify many different reasons that material goods and services give people utility. The same good may fulfill different needs for different people. Economists do not usually find it necessary to distinguish the various possible sources of utility. They are interested primarily in whether people want a good enough to pay for it, not in why they want it.

2. The increase in utility from a one-unit increase in the rate of consumption of some good is called the marginal utility of that good. As the rate of consumption of any good increases, the marginal utility of that good tends to decrease.

3. Consumer equilibrium is a state of affairs in which people cannot increase the utility they get from a given budget by shifting expenditure from one good to another. Consumer equilibrium requires that the marginal utility of a dollar's worth of any good be equal to the marginal utility of a dollar's worth of any other good. Alternatively, the condition for consumer equilibrium can be expressed in the form of the equation:

$$\frac{MU_A}{P_A} = \frac{MU_B}{P_B} = \frac{MU_C}{P_C} = \frac{MU_D}{P_D} = \cdots$$

4. The effect of a change in the price of a good on the quantity of that good demanded can conceptually be broken into a substitution effect and an income effect. For normal goods, the substitution and income effects of a price decrease both act to increase the quantity demanded, guaranteeing that the demand curve for the good will have a negative slope. For inferior goods, the income effect of a price decrease tends to offset the substitution effect. With few, if any, exceptions, however, the substitution effect is stronger, so that demand curves even for inferior goods have negative slopes.

DISCUSSION QUESTIONS

1. Is it true for all goods that more is always better than less, or are there some situations in which marginal utility could become negative? Discuss.

2. Suppose you have a room that will require eight rolls of wallpaper to decorate. If someone gives you seven rolls of wallpaper, you will not get much satisfaction. The eighth roll, however, will be very much appreciated. Do you think this is a valid counterexample to the law of diminishing marginal utility?

3. Who is your favorite classical or popular musician? Do you think a concert by this person that lasted thirty minutes would give you more than ten times as much satisfaction as a concert lasting just three minutes. More than sixty times as much satisfaction as a concert lasting just thirty seconds? Would you bother to go to a concert lasting just thirty seconds even if it were free? What does all this have to do with diminishing marginal utility?

4. Martha Smith consumes two pounds of pork and five pounds of beef per month. She pays $1.50 per pound for the pork and $2 per pound for the beef. What inference can you draw about the ratio:

   Smith's marginal utility per pound of pork
   Smith's marginal utility per pound of beef ?

   Is this ratio equal to 3/4, 4/3, 5/2, 2/5, or none of those alternatives?

5. What would happen to the quantity you demanded of each of the following if its price rose while all other prices remained unchanged:
   a. Your favorite soft drink
   b. All forms of transportation
   c. Greyhound bus tickets
   d. Levis (the genuine brand only)
   In each case, how much of the change in quantity demanded would be attributable to the income effect and how much to the substitution effect?

6. Imagine a very poor country in which people spend most of their income on food. They eat bread when they can afford it, but they cannot afford to eat bread all the time; more than half of their diet is made up of cheaper, but less palatable, oatmeal. One year, the price of oatmeal rises substantially, while the price of bread does not change; despite the price rise, however, oatmeal remains cheaper than bread. Does it seem reasonable to you that the people just described might respond by increasing the quantity of oatmeal they consume? Try to explain how this might happen in terms of the income and substitution effects. If you want to, make up an example with specific prices and quantities.

7. Imagine that you are the director of a slave labor camp and that you are a thick-skinned, antihumanitarian person with absolutely no regard whatsoever for the comfort or welfare of your charges. Do you think you can design an experiment to test the laws of consumer behavior using your prisoners as subjects? What possible pitfalls might you encounter that an experimenter using rats would not encounter? What advantages or disadvantages might you have compared with an experimenter who is restricted to the use of paid human volunteers?

APPENDIX TO CHAPTER 19
AN INTRODUCTION TO INDIFFERENCE CURVES

Chapter 19 gave two versions of the theory of consumer choice underlying the law of demand—one based on marginal utility, the other on income and substitution effects. This appendix gives a third version, using what are known as indifference curves. Indifference curves are not featured in this book, but they are used very frequently in intermediate and advanced level economic writing. Many students and instructors find it worthwhile to cover them at least briefly as part of an introductory course. This appendix will serve the needs of those who are interested.

CONSTRUCTING AN INDIFFERENCE CURVE

Begin by supposing that I am an experimenter and you are my experimental subject. I want to find out how you feel about consuming various quantities of meat and cheese. It would be convenient if I had a utility meter, but I do not. In order to find out your attitudes toward the consumption of meat and cheese, I instead present you with a number of food baskets (two at a time) containing various quantities of the two goods.

As I present each pair of baskets, I ask: would you prefer the one on the left to the one on the right? The one on the right to the one on the left? Or are you indifferent between the two? If you play your role of experimental subject in good faith, I have a reasonable hope of getting a meaningful answer from you. In any event, I certainly have a better chance of getting a meaningful answer than I would have if I asked you how many utils you would get from each basket.

At some point in the experiment, I offer you one basket (A) containing, say, eight pounds of meat and three pounds of cheese and another basket (B) containing, say, six pounds of meat and four pounds of cheese. I ask you the usual questions, and you answer that you are indifferent between the two baskets. The extra pound of cheese in Basket B, you feel, just makes up for the fact that it has two pounds less of meat than does Basket A. This gives me a very useful bit of information: it tells me that, for you, Basket A and Basket B belong to an **indifference set** — a set of consumption alternatives each yielding the same amount of satisfaction, so that no member of the set is preferred to any other. Exploring the matter further, I discover that two other baskets (C and D) also belong to the same indifference set, which now has the following four members:

Indifference set A set of consumption alternatives each of which yields the same utility, so that no member of the set is preferred to any other.

Basket	Meat (pounds)	Cheese (pounds)
A	8	3
B	6	4
C	5	5
D	4	7

With this information in hand, I thank you for participating in my experiment and get out a piece of graph paper. First, I draw a set of coordinate axes, as in Exhibit 20A.1. Pounds of meat are measured on the horizontal axis and pounds of cheese on the vertical. Each basket of goods can be shown as a point on the area between the two axes. The points representing Baskets A through D are shown in their proper spots in the diagram. These points and all the points in between them lying on the smooth curve that has been sketched in joining them are members of the same indifference set. The curve itself is an **indifference curve** — a curve composed entirely of points that are all members of a single indifference set.

Indifference curve A graphical representation of an indifference set.

SOME PROPERTIES OF INDIFFERENCE CURVES

Indifference curves have properties that reflect certain basic regularities in patterns of consumer preferences. Five of these properties are of particular interest.

1. *Indifference curves normally have negative slopes.* For example, the curve sketched in Exhibit 19A.2 is not a possible shape for an indifference curve if both meat and cheese are desirable goods. The consumption basket shown by Point A contains more of both goods than the one shown by Point B. This implies that if greater quantities of meat and cheese give greater satisfaction, A must be *preferred* to B. It cannot then be a member of the same indifference set as B.

2. *The absolute value of the slope of an indifference curve at any point represents the ratio of the marginal utility of the good on the horizontal axis to the marginal utility of the good on the vertical axis.* For an example, refer back to Exhibit 19A.1. Between D and C, the slope of the curve is approximately −2 (or simply 2 when the minus sign is removed to give the absolute value). This shows that the marginal utility of meat is approximately twice the marginal utility of cheese for the consumer — when the quantities consumed are in the area of Baskets C and D. Because the marginal utility of meat is twice that of cheese in this region, the consumer will feel neither gain nor loss in total utility in trading Basket D for Basket C — that is, in giving up two pounds of cheese for one extra pound of meat. Because it shows the rate at which meat can be substituted for cheese without gain

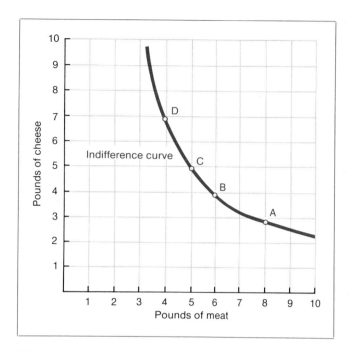

Exhibit 19A.1
An indifference curve
Each point in this diagram stands for a basket of meat and cheese. A, B, C, and D are all baskets among which a certain consumer is indifferent. All give equal utility. Those points and all the others on a smooth curve connecting them constitute an indifference set. An indifference curve, such as the one shown here, is a graphical representation of an indifference set.

Marginal rate of substitution The rate at which one good can be substituted for another without gain or loss in satisfaction (equal to the slope of an indifference curve at any point).

or loss in satisfaction, the slope of the indifference curve is called the **marginal rate of substitution** of meat for cheese.

3. *Indifference curves are convex; that is, their slope decreases as one moves down and to the right along them.* This implies that the ratio of the marginal utility of meat to the marginal utility of cheese (also known as the marginal rate of substitution of meat for cheese) diminishes as one moves down and to the right along the curve. Look once more at Exhibit 19A.1. In the region between D and C, the slope of the curve is approximately −2, indicating that the ratio of the marginal utility of meat to that of cheese is approximately 2:1. By comparison, in the neighborhood between B and A, the slope is only about −1/2. The ratio of the marginal utility of meat to the marginal utility of cheese is now approximately 1:2.

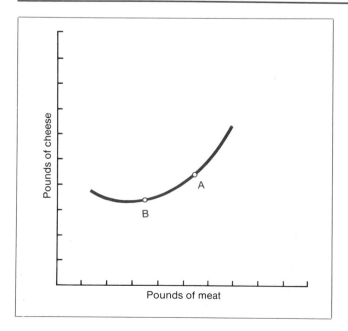

Exhibit 19A.2
Indifference curves normally slope downward
Indifference curves normally have negative slopes. The upward-sloping portion of the indifference curve shown here is impossible if both goods give increased satisfaction with increased quantity. A has more of both goods than B. Point A should thus be preferred to Point B, and therefore it could not lie on the same indifference curve.

Exhibit 19A.3
Multiple indifference curves

An indifference curve can be drawn through any point. Here the indifference curve I_1 represents an indifference set containing points A, B, C, and D, while I_2 represents a set containing Points E, F, and G. All points on I_2 Fare preferred to all points on I_1. A representative selection of indifference curves like the one shown here can be called an indifference map.

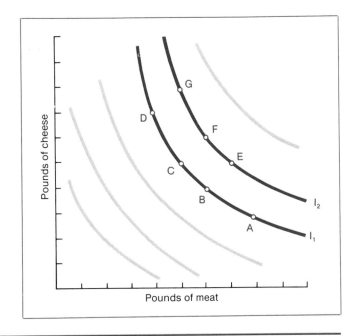

4. *An indifference curve can be drawn through the point that represents any basket of goods whatsoever.* Consider Exhibit 19A.3. Here is the same indifference curve as in Exhibit 19A.1, but labeled I_1. Point E, representing a basket with seven pounds of meat and five pounds of cheese, is not a member of the indifference set represented by this curve. Because it lies above and to the right of Point B and has more of both products than B, it must be preferred to B. There are other points, such as F and G, that have more cheese and less meat than E and, on balance, give the same satisfaction as E. The consumer is indifferent among E, F, G, and all other points on the curve I_2 and prefers all of these points to any of the points on I_1.

Any point taken at random, together with the other points that happen to be equally satisfactory, can form an indifference curve. Several other such curves, unlabeled, are sketched in Exhibit 19A.3. If all possible curves were drawn in, they

Exhibit 19A.4
Crossing indifference curves contradict the assumption of transitive preferences

Because consumer preferences are transitive, indifference curves do not cross. The impossible indifference curves shown here represent contradictory preferences. A and B are both on I_1, so the consumer must be indifferent between them. A and C are both on I_2, so the consumer must be indifferent between them too. Transitivity implies that the consumer is indifferent between B and C, but this is impossible, because C contains more of both goods than does B.

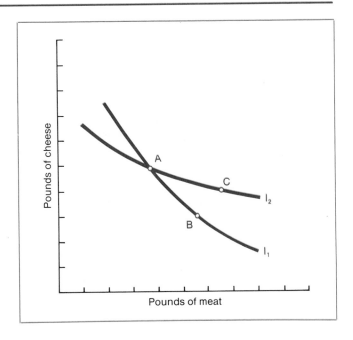

would be so close together that the ink of the lines would run into a solid sheet entirely filling the space between the axes. A representative selection of indifference curves, showing their general pattern but leaving enough space to make the diagram easy to read, is called an **indifference map**.

5. *Indifference curves do not cross, because consumer preferences are* **transitive**— which means that if you prefer A to B and B to C, you will prefer A to C. Looking at Exhibit 19A.4, you can see that crossed indifference curves contradict this assumption of transitivity. Consider Points A, B, and C. A and B both lie on the same indifference curve, I_1; hence the consumer is indifferent between them. A and C both lie on I_2; hence the consumer is indifferent between them also. From the property of transitivity, if B is as good as A and A is as good as C, C is as good as B. But C lies above and to the right of B. It represents a combination of goods with more of both meat and cheese. If more is better, the consumer must prefer C to B. Since crossed indifference curves imply a contradictory set of preferences, the conclusion is that they cannot cross.

Indifference map A representative selection of indifference curves for a single consumer and pair of goods.

Transitivity The situation where if A is preferred to B and B is preferred to C, then A must be preferred to C.

THE BUDGET LINE

The range of consumption opportunities open to a consumer with a given budget and with given prices can be shown on the same kind of graph that has been used for indifference curves. Exhibit 19A.5 shows how this can be done. Suppose that you have a food budget of $10 per week, that the price of meat is $2 per pound, and that the price of cheese is $1 per pound. If you spend all your money on meat, you can have up to five pounds of meat; if you spend all your money on cheese, you can have up to ten pounds of cheese. Combinations such as two pounds of meat and six of cheese or four pounds of meat and two of cheese are also possible. Taking possible purchases of fractional pounds of meat and cheese into account also, these consumption opportunities can be shown on the diagram as a diagonal line running from 10 on the cheese axis to 5 on the meat axis. This diagonal line is called the **budget line** under the assumed conditions.

Using m to stand for meat and c to stand for cheese, the equation for the budget line can be written as $2m + 1c = 10$. This equation simply says that the number of

Budget line A line showing the various combinations of goods that can be purchased at given prices within a given budget.

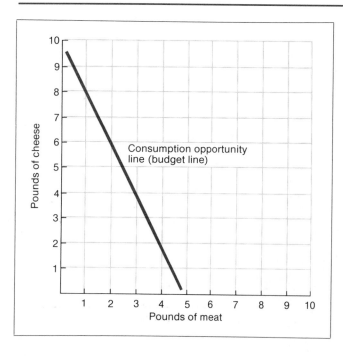

Exhibit 19A.5
The budget line
Suppose you have a budget of $10 per week. You can spend your money on meat at $2 per pound, on cheese at $1 per pound, or on some combination of the two goods. The consumption opportunity line (budget line) shows all the possible combinations available to you, given these prices and your limited budget.

pounds of meat bought times the price of meat plus the number of pounds of cheese bought times the price of cheese must add up to the total budget if no money is left unspent. Expressed in more general terms, the equation for a budget line for goods x and y — with P_x the price of x, P_y the price of y, and B the consumer's total budget — is $P_x x + P_y y = B$. The slope of such a budget line is $-P_x/P_y$. In the case illustrated in Exhibit 19A.5, where the price of meat is $2 per pound and the price of cheese is $1 per pound, the slope of the budget line is -2.

A GRAPHICAL REPRESENTATION OF CONSUMER EQUILIBRIUM

Indifference curves and the budget line can be used to give a graphical representation of consumer equilibrium. Exhibit 19A.6 shows the budget line from Exhibit 19A.5 superimposed on an indifference map similar to that shown earlier in Exhibit 19A.3. Preferences and consumption opportunities can thus be compared easily. For example, Point B is preferred to Point A because it lies on a "higher" indifference curve (one that at some point like C passes above and to the right of A). By similar reasoning, Point D is inferior to Point B. Of all the points on or below the budget line, it is clear that Point E, representing 2.5 pounds of meat and 5 pounds of cheese, is the most preferred, because all the other points on the budget line lie on lower indifference curves. Every point that, like F, is better still lies outside the range of consumption opportunities.

Because E is the point giving the highest possible satisfaction under the conditions set, it is the point of consumer equilibrium. At E, the relevant indifference curve is just tangent to the budget line; this means that the slope of the indifference curve and the budget line are the same at this point. The slope of the indifference curve, as shown earlier, is equal to the ratio of the marginal utility of meat to the marginal utility of cheese. The slope of the budget line is equal to the ratio of the price of meat to the price of cheese. It follows that in consumer equilibrium:

$$\frac{\text{Marginal utility of meat}}{\text{Marginal utility of cheese}} = \frac{\text{Price of meat}}{\text{Price of cheese}}.$$

This is the condition for consumer equilibrium given in Chapter 19.

Exhibit 19A.6

Graphical demonstration of consumer equilibrium
E is the point of consumer equilibrium, given the indifference curves and budget line shown. All points that are better than E (such as F) lie outside the boundary of the budget line. All other points for goods that the consumer can afford to buy (such as A and D) lie on lower indifference curves than E and are thus less preferred.

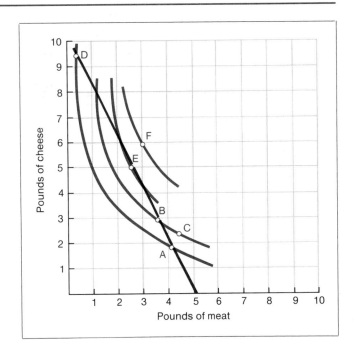

GRAPHICAL DERIVATION OF THE DEMAND CURVE

This appendix concludes with Exhibit 19A.7, which shows how a demand curve for meat can be derived graphically from a set of indifference curves. Together with the indifference curves, Exhibit 19A.7 shows a whole family of budget lines. Each budget line is based on the assumption that the price of cheese is $1 per pound and that the consumer's budget is $10, as before. Now, though, each budget line assumes a different price, P, of meat. The budget line running from 10 on the vertical axis to 2.5 on the horizontal axis assumes P = $4. The budget line running from 10 on the vertical axis to 5 on the horizontal axis assumes P = $2. (This is the same budget line drawn in Exhibits 19A.5 and 19A.6.) The other two budget lines are based on P = $1.50 and P = $1, respectively.

The equilibrium consumption pattern for the consumer will be different for each price of meat, other things being equal. When P = $4, Point A, representing six pounds of cheese and one pound of meat, is the best the consumer can do; when P = $2, Point B is the most preferred point; and so on.

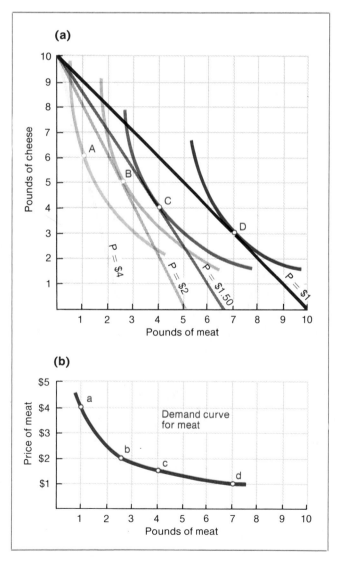

Exhibit 19A.7
Graphical derivation of a demand curve

Part a of this exhibit shows a consumer's indifference map for meat and cheese and a set of budget lines. Each budget line corresponds to a different price, P, of meat, as shown. All four budget lines assume the price of cheese to be $1 and the total budget to be $10. Points A, B, C, and D in Part a show the choices the consumer makes at meat prices of $4, $2, $1.50, and $1, respectively. In Part b of the exhibit, the information on consumption of meat at the various prices is plotted on a new set of axes. The smooth line connecting Points a, b, c, and d is the consumer's demand curve for meat.

Given this information on consumer equilibrium under different price assumptions, it is a simple matter to draw the consumer's demand curve for meat. Exhibit 19A.7b shows a new set of axes, with the quantity of meat on the horizontal axis as before, but with the price of meat now on the vertical axis. From Exhibit 19A.7a, when P = $4, the consumer chooses the consumption combination A, which includes one pound of meat. In Exhibit 19A.7b, Point a is thus marked as the quantity of meat demanded at a price of $4. Then Point b (corresponding to Point B in Part a) is added, and so on. Drawing a smooth line through Points a, b, c, and d in Exhibit 19A.7b thus gives the consumer's demand curve for meat. As expected, it has the downward slope consistent with the law of demand.

SUGGESTIONS FOR FURTHER READING

Blaug, Mark. *Economic Theory in Retrospect.* Rev. ed. Homewood, Ill. Richard D. Irwin, 1968.
Chapter 8 discusses the origins of utility theory and the work of William Stanley Jevons. Chapter 9 discusses Alfred Marshall's refinements of utility theory and the modern restatement in terms of preference and indifference.

Leftwich, Richard H. *The Price System and Resource Allocation.* 7th ed. Hinsdale, Ill.: Dryden Press, 1979.
Chapter 5 provides an intermediate level treatment of the topics covered in this chapter and its appendix.

Nicholson, Walter. *Intermediate Microeconomics and Its Application.* 2d ed. Hinsdale, Ill.: Dryden Press, 1979.
Chapters 3 and 4 treat utility analysis and indifference curves in somewhat more detail than Leftwich does.

C H A P T E R 20
THE NATURE OF THE FIRM

WHAT YOU WILL LEARN IN THIS CHAPTER

The firm is the basic unit of production in the market economy. This chapter explores the nature of the firm and of the economic decision making that takes place within it. Among the issues raised are those of why firms exist at all, how the division of labor is coordinated within and among firms, why firms have differing legal forms of organization, and who really controls large corporations.

FOR REVIEW

Here are some important terms and concepts that will be put to use in this chapter. If you do not understand them, review them before proceeding.
• *Entrepreneurship (Chapter 1)*
• *Pure economizing (Chapter 19)*

Throughout this book, the firm has continually been referred to as the basic unit of business in the market economy; but up to now, little has been said about what a firm really is or how it works. Business firms come in a great variety of sizes and shapes. There are mom-and-pop corner stores, giant automobile and steel corporations, and powerful partnerships of lawyers and stockbrokers. Despite their different purposes and different legal forms of organization, all firms have many things in common. This chapter will explore their common ground, beginning with a look at the most basic task the firm must perform—that of coordinating economic activity.

COORDINATING ECONOMIC ACTIVITY

Market versus Managerial Coordination

Production in any modern economy, as emphasized in Chapters 1 and 2, is based on a vast division of labor. Many people make individual contributions to the whole effort that must somehow be coordinated. It must be determined what goods are to be produced, who is to produce them, and how they are to be produced. There are fundamentally two kinds of coordination for this vast division of labor: market coordination and managerial coordination.

Market coordination
Coordination of economic activity using the price system to transmit information and provide incentives.

Managerial coordination
Coordination of economic activity through directives from managers to subordinates.

Market coordination relies on the price system as a source of incentives and a communications network. As relative prices vary in response to the forces of supply and demand, users are induced to substitute low-priced goods and services for scarcer and more expensive alternatives. At the same time, changing relative prices continually creates new profit opportunities for entrepreneurs who can devise ways of expanding the output of whatever is particularly scarce and thus particularly valuable to users. All of this is accomplished in a decentralized fashion, with no central authority making decisions or issuing demands.

There are substantial areas of economic activity, however, that do not rely directly on market coordination. Consider, for example, the internal organization of work within, say, a furniture factory. Individual employees do not decide each morning, in response to changing relative prices, that they will spend the day making end tables rather than TV cabinets. Instead, they make end tables because that is what their immediate boss tells them to do. This is the realm of **managerial coordination**, which operates on the principle of direct instruction from manager to subordinate. What makes the instruction effective is the fact that subordinates have pledged obedience to the manager (at least within certain agreed limits) as a condition of employment.

Coordination in the Firm

In a famous essay on the nature of the firm, Ronald Coase posed a question about these two ways of coordinating the division of labor: if the market principle works as well as economists say it does, why is the managerial principle ever used at all?[1] Why do the workers in a furniture factory have to be employees taking orders from a boss? If the market principle were applied everywhere, TV cabinets and end tables would all be built by independent artisans. Changes in the relative prices of various items of furniture would keep the right number of workers at each job.

Coase found an answer to his question. He said that the market is not used for every situation where coordination is required because there are transactions costs to using it. There are costs of finding out what prices are. There are also costs of negotiating contracts, writing bills and receipts, and straightening things out when market contracts are not carried through. If, say, a potential car buyer had to negotiate separately with each person who worked on the car, the cost of coordination would make the car too expensive. If the buyer saved negotiating costs by having one or two local mechanics build the car from scratch, the advantages of mass production and the division of labor would be lost, and the vehicle would still cost too much. But when Ford Motor Company acts as an intermediary between the buyer and the workers, thousands of market transactions are eliminated. Cars are sold on the market, but everything in between is coordinated by the managerial principle of simply giving orders and expecting them to be obeyed.

---

[1] Ronald H. Coase, "The Nature of the Firm," *Economica*, new series, 4 (November 1937), pp. 386–405.

Ronald Coase is the intellectual founder of the "new institutional economics." Through his own writings and his editorship of the *Journal of Law and Economics*, Coase has fostered a unification of institutional economics and analytical economics, once separate and even antagonistic branches of the discipline. The method of the new institutional economics is simple and productive of great insights. One selects an economic institution and poses two related questions: what are the effects of this particular institution on the allocation of resources? And how can one account for the evolution and continued existence of the institution *in terms of* an analysis of its effects on resource allocation?

Coase, born and educated in London, began his studies of economic institutions early in his career. In the 1930s he studied the British postal system and the British broadcasting system as well as other public utility industries. The results of these studies were set out in a number of articles and in his book, *British Broadcasting: A Study in Monopoly*, which was published in 1951.

Coase's famous paper on the nature of the firm was published in 1937 and brought him international recognition. He came to the United States in 1951 to teach first at the University of Buffalo, then at the University of Virginia, and finally at the University of Chicago. In 1961, his most famous paper of all, "The Problem of Social Cost," appeared in the *Journal of Law and Economics*. At that time, the journal was new, and the study of law and economics hardly existed as an independent specialty within either profession. Coase's probing analysis of the nature of the law as an economic institution sparked such enormous interest among both economists and lawyers that law and economics soon became one of the most exciting fields of study around. Within little over a decade, all leading law schools had economists on their staffs and were offering courses in the new institutional economics as applied to legal institutions.

One subject on which the new institutional economics has had much to say is government regulation of industry. Coase himself has written extensively on the regulation of broadcasting, and articles on regulation of other industries appear regularly in his journal. Traditionally, the economics of regulation was concerned largely with how regulation ought to be conducted and what beneficial effects would emerge from it under ideal conditions. Coase shifted the focus to an analysis of regulatory institutions as their structure and effects actually exist. The result, on balance, has been highly critical. Coase himself has gone so for as to write, "It is now generally accepted by all students of the subject that most (perhaps almost all) government regulation is anti-competitive and harmful in its effects."

Ronald H. Coase (1910–   )

Coase realized, though, that in answering one question, he had just raised another. If managerial coordination works so well, why use the market at all? Why not run the entire economy as one big firm, with all people as employees and a single, central manager running the whole show? Then it would be a matter of not only giving furniture workers or auto workers orders about what to do that day but also giving high school graduates orders about whether to be auto workers or cabinet makers. Not only would the matter of how many end tables and how many TV cabinets be handled by the managerial principle, but so would matters such as how many firms should be in the industry and where they should be located.

Managerial coordination, however, has transactions costs of its own, as well as savings of transactions costs. Under the managerial system, the person actually doing a job does not need to know all the reasons behind the decision to do it, and that is a saving. Offsetting this is the fact that *managers* have to know a great deal about all the different jobs they coordinate, and that is a cost. Sometimes the costs of supplying information to a manager or other central decision maker are greater than the costs of supplying information to people close to the job. When this is the case, managerial coordination loses its advantage over market coordination.

The Limits of the Firm

Coase saw that the two coordination principles give the key to understanding the nature of the firm and its role in the economy. A firm, he said, is an organization that uses the managerial principle of coordination internally and uses the market to coordinate its activities with those of other firms and individuals. Each firm tends to grow until the transactions cost of organizing one extra task within the firm becomes equal to the cost of organizing the same task outside the firm through the market. In some industries (as will be shown shortly), this rule dictates that firms grow to enormous size. In others, the limit to the growth of the firm occurs at a very small size. By allowing each firm to grow to its optimal size and by leaving coordination among firms to the market, the total costs of organizing economic activity can, in principle, be minimized.

Coase's insights into the nature of the firm have survived the test of time well. They should be kept in mind as the chapter turns from abstract principles to some of the practical details of the organization of business firms.

ALTERNATIVE FORMS OF BUSINESS ORGANIZATION

Textbook discussions of economic theory inevitably tend to portray business firms as well-defined, homogeneous units of analysis. In the real world, however, they take on a very wide variety of forms. Some firms are tiny, consisting of a single individual doing all production and managerial jobs. At the other extreme are corporate giants like General Motors or ITT. These firms employ more people and dispose of more assets than the governments of all but the world's largest countries. Firms differ not only in size but in their legal form of organization as well. The following three sections will discuss the advantages of the three main types of firms — sole proprietorships, partnerships, and corporations.[2]

Sole Proprietorships

Sole proprietorship A firm owned and usually managed by a single person, who receives all profits of the firm and who personally bears all of the firm's liabilities.

A **sole proprietorship** is a firm that is owned and usually managed by one person. In most cases this person is also an operative employee. Responsibility for the success or failure of the firm rests solely on the proprietor's shoulders. From a legal point of view, he or she owns all the assets and owes all the debts of the organization.

A good way to get a perspective on the organization of a sole proprietorship is to look at such a firm's balance sheet. The balance sheet shown in Exhibit 20.1 is that of Van Appleman's grocery store. All the property Appleman owns for use in his business is listed on the left-hand side of the

---

[2] Much of the material in this section is adapted from Robert D. Hay, *Introduction to Business* (New York: Holt, Rinehart and Winston, 1968), pp. 140-148. Reprinted by permission of the author.

Exhibit 20.1

Balance sheet of Van Appleman's sole proprietorship

In a sole proprietorship, all assets are owned by one person, and that person is solely liable for all debts. The difference between the firm's assets and its liabilities is the proprietor's equity — that is, the proprietor's own stake in the business.

Assets		Liabilities and Equity	
Cash	$ 2,000	Accounts payable	$ 500
Inventory on the shelves	10,000	Mortgage payable	5,000
Equipment	2,000	Total debts	$ 5,500
Land and buildings	20,000	Appleman's equity	28,500
Total assets	$34,000	Total liabilities plus equity	$34,000

balance sheet under the heading "assets." All the debts he owes in connection with his business are listed on the right-hand side of the balance sheet under the heading "liabilities and equity." The difference between the firm's assets and liabilities is its net worth, which represents Appleman's equity in the business. It is, in principle, the sum he would have left over if he sold all the firm's assets at the values listed and paid all the listed debts. In this case, Appleman has business assets of $34,000 and debts of $5,500; his equity in the firm is thus $28,500.

Advantages One of the most important advantages for the owner of a sole proprietorship is the complete ownership of all the assets and the right to all the profits of the business. The sole proprietor is legally entitled to 100 percent of any rewards. This right to all the profits is a powerful incentive to the owner to invest money and to work hard to get the revenue from customers from whom profits are derived.

Another of the reasons the sole proprietorship is so widely used is because it is relatively easy to organize. There are very few legal requirements to meet. Consequently, little or no costs of organization are involved. Practically anyone can develop an idea into a sole proprietorship form of organization. (Of course, the firm may not succeed, but at least it can be formed with little effort.) To an owner of private property wishing to manage a business, the advantage of ease of organization may be a factor in choosing this form of legal organization.

Still another factor in choosing the sole proprietorship may be the advantage of receiving a high degree of personal satisfaction from the management of the firm. People who like to have the freedom to exercise their personal judgment in management decisions and who want to be able to make decisions promptly without the consultation or approval of other owners or managers derive great personal satisfaction from the sole proprietorship of a firm. So do people who do not work well with other managers or under supervision.

Finally, ease of dissolution may be an important advantage of the sole proprietorship. Just as there are few legal complications about going into business, there are very few in going out of business. Dissolution may simply mean selling the inventory, paying the debts, and locking the door. Ease of dissolution allows the owner to retire or enter another type of business quickly and easily.

Disadvantages   The sole proprietorship form of organization also has some disadvantages, however. First and foremost among them is unlimited financial liability. This means that in the event of bankruptcy, the sole proprietor's personal property may have to be sold to pay business debts.

Also, because the expansion of a sole proprietorship is limited by what the owner can contribute or borrow, he or she may find it difficult to expand. This difficulty is magnified by the sole proprietor's inability to get into other lines of business because of a lack of capital or of managerial ability. Expansion often increases financial risks, and the owner's refusal or inability to bear these risks may make expansion impossible. If the minimum amount of capital required is more than one person can safely provide, the sole proprietorship will not work.

Finally, the death, injury, imprisonment, or bankruptcy of the owner may terminate the legal life of the firm. This lack of continuity stems from the legal fact that the individual and the business are one and the same in a sole proprietorship.

Partnerships

Partnership A firm formed by two or more persons to carry on a business as co-owners. Each partner bears full legal liability for the debts of the firm.

A **partnership** is an association of two or more persons who will carry on a business as co-owners by voluntary legal agreement. Instead of one person being the owner, there are at least two who own all the assets, owe all the liabilities, and have an equity in the business. For example, imagine that Janet Kerwich and Alice Appleman decide to go into business together. If Kerwich and Appleman each put $28,500 cash into the business, the balance sheet might look like the one in Exhibit 20.2. Note that Appleman and Kerwich together own $62,500 worth of assets and owe $5,500; and each has an equity of $28,500, for a total equity of $57,000.

Advantages   Like the sole proprietorship, the partnership as a form of legal organization enjoys simplicity and ease in getting started and, in some cases, savings in income taxes. The partnership is able to obtain more equity capital than the sole proprietorship, because the amount available is determined by the personal fortunes of the partners. Many sole proprietorships evolve into partnerships in order to raise more equity capital. For example, a person with a new idea may find another person who is willing

---

Exhibit 20.2
Balance sheet of the Kerwich and Appleman partnership
In a partnership, all assets are owned jointly by the partners. Each partner is individually liable for all the firm's debts. The difference between the firm's assets and its liabilities is the owners' equity, shared among the partners.

Assets		Liabilities and Equity	
Cash	$30,500	Accounts payable	$ 500
Inventory	10,000	Mortgage payable	5,000
Equipment	2,000	Total debts	$ 5,500
Land and building	20,000	Alice Appleman's equity	28,500
		Janet Kerwich's equity	28,500
Total assets	$62,500	Total liabilities plus equity	$62,500

to contribute a major share of the needed capital to turn the idea into a profitable business operation for both of them. Thus the necessary amount of capital is acquired through the formation of a partnership.

An advantage closely related to raising equity capital is the enlarged credit standing, or ability to borrow capital, of the partnership. Because the personal wealth of all the partners is available to pay debts of the business organization, a partnership may enjoy a higher credit rating than a sole proprietorship.

Many partnerships are formed to take advantage of greater managerial ability. Because numerous functions are involved in the operation of a business, partners proficient in different functions may complement each other. This combined effort leads to the greater managerial ability.

Disadvantages A partnership form of organization does not offer all the answers because it too has certain disadvantages. As in the sole proprietorship, the chief disadvantage is the unlimited financial liability. In the case of a partnership, the responsibility for the debts of the business is shared individually as well as jointly. Consequently, the unlimited financial liability could result in one partner being forced to pay not only his or her own share but all the debts of the firm.

Suppose, for example, that the Kerwich and Appleman partnership finds itself unable to operate at a profit and must go out of business in order to avoid further losses. At the time of liquidation, suppose that the firm still has $62,500 in assets, as shown in Exhibit 20.2, but has in the meantime incurred total debts of $100,000. This leaves the partners with a negative equity of $37,500 — the amount by which liabilities exceed assets. Suppose further that Appleman has no significant personal assets but that Kerwich does. In the process of liquidating the firm, Kerwich could be forced to sell $37,500 of her personal assets to cover debts of the partnership in addition to losing her original $28,500 investment in the firm. Her partner would lose only the original investment.

One further disadvantage of a partnership is that one partner cannot easily withdraw without the cooperation of the others. The partner who wants to withdraw must either find a new partner willing to buy his or her share in the partnership or get the other partners to agree to buy the share. Meanwhile, although the partner wishing to withdraw continues to own a share of the partnership's equity, that equity is "frozen"—it cannot be turned into cash or invested in another undertaking.

In forming a partnership, each partner must accept the others for better or for worse. Although better decisions usually result from the combined judgments of the partners, the division of decision making can cause personal difficulties. More partnerships have been dissolved because of such difficulties than for any other reason.

Any change in the combination of partners automatically causes a dissolution of the firm; thus the partnership has limited life. Like the sole proprietorship, the death, incapacity, or withdrawal of any of the partners terminates the original partnership agreement. The admission of a new partner or the sale of a partner's interest also ends the old partnership. Simply because there are more people involved, the limited life poses a larger problem in the partnership than in the sole proprietorship.

Corporations

Corporation A firm in which the ownership is divided into equal parts called shares, with each shareholder's liability limited to the amount of his or her investment in the firm.

Unlike a sole proprietorship or partnership, a **corporation** is a legal entity separate and apart from its owners. The ownership of a corporation is divided into equal parts called shares of stock. Persons who own the shares are called shareholders or stockholders. They elect officers to manage the business. Of course, if they own the majority of voting stock, they can, and often do, elect themselves as managers.

A major legal feature of the corporation is that it can be dealt with separately just like an individual. This means that the corporation serves as a buffer between the firm's owners and their customers, employees, suppliers, and creditors, as well as between the owners and the government and community. The corporation can hold, buy, sell, and exchange property in its own name. In a sole proprietorship or partnership, property must be held in the name of the individual owners.

Suppose that the partnership of Kerwich and Appleman decides to incorporate. It can transfer its owners' equity from a partnership interest to a stockholder interest. The balance sheet will appear as in Exhibit 20.3.

Notice that the $57,000 of owner's equity (in a sole proprietorship and partnership) is now called capital stock. The ownership remains essentially the same but is called something else. Why would an owner prefer a corporation as the legal form of organization?

Advantages The main advantage of having the firm as a separate entity is that the owners carry only limited financial liability. This means that creditors can look only to the assets of the corporation for settlement of their claims. They cannot hold the owners liable for the debts of the corporation. If the corporation fails, the shareholders lose only the amount of their investment; their personal assets cannot be attached to pay the corporate debts.

This is not the case for a sole proprietorship or a partnership, where the owners are held liable for all the debts and are forced, when necessary, to pay them out of their personal assets. In a corporation, the owners' liability is limited only to their investment.

A corporation can grow to a larger size than a sole proprietorship or partnership because it can attract capital from thousands of individuals. It can expand or increase its size because the advantage of limited financial

Exhibit 20.3
Balance sheet of a corporation
A corporation owns all its assets in the name of the firm. Ownership of the firm's capital stock is the equity. Shareholders are liable for the firm's debts only to the extent that they have invested money in the firm.

Assets		Liabilities and Equity	
Cash	$30,500	Accounts payable	$ 500
Inventory	10,000	Mortgage payable	5,000
Equipment	2,000	Total debts	$ 5,500
Land and buildings	20,000	Capital stock (equity)	57,000
Total assets	$62,500	Total liabilities plus equity	$62,500

liability makes investors more willing to purchase additional shares of stock. It is easier for a corporation to raise $1 million by having a thousand people invest $1,000 each than it is for a sole proprietorship to have one person invest $1 million.

The transfer of ownership in a corporation is easily accomplished, especially for those corporations whose capital stock is listed and traded on the major stock exchanges and in the over-the-counter market. Thousands of shares of capital stock change hands daily. As a general rule, corporations allow shareholders to transfer their ownership to anyone at any time (assuming that the price is agreeable to both buyer and seller) without the approval of the other shareholders.

The transferability of ownership of a corporation contributes to the continuity of the firm. Shareholders may withdraw by selling their shares or may die, leaving their shares to their heirs without disturbing the legal existence of the corporation.

A further advantage may be the lower income tax paid by a corporation. Canadian-controlled private business corporations pay only about 25 percent tax on the first $150,000 of income, while an individual earning that much could be paying twice as much.

Disadvantages The first disadvantage of the corporate form of business organization is the cost of chartering a corporation. The chartering can be done on either the provincial or the federal level and can cost from about five hundred dollars to several thousand dollars in legal fees.

A corporation is subject to special government regulations, and therefore is involved in more red tape and less privacy than other business firms. For example, little is known about the sales and profits of Eaton's in Canada because it is a private company. Corporations, on the other hand, must report such information to their shareholders.

A further disadvantage is the "double taxation" of corporate income. Corporate profits are taxed first before they are paid out as dividends, and dividend income is subsequently taxed when it reaches the shareholders. However, dividend income is subject to "dividend tax credits" that reduce the effective tax rate considerably.

The Co-operative

The co-operative form of organization is quite important in the Canadian economy, much more so than in the United States. A co-operative is an organization that pools the resources of its members, just as a corporation does, but grants only one vote to each member regardless of the member's investment. Further, earnings not retained are paid out according to the amount of business conducted by the member. Co-operatives may incorporate in order to obtain the benefits of limited liability and continuous existence. Co-operatives are of several types: consumer co-operatives, which engage in retail trade; marketing co-operatives, which sell members' agricultural products; financial co-operatives (for example, credit unions—and in French Canada—*caisses populaires*); insurance co-operatives and service co-operatives (for example, funeral co-operatives).

The chief advantages of the co-operative are the one-member, one-vote form of democracy, the possibility of buying goods and services more cheaply, and the special tax privileges enjoyed under Canadian law. Patronage dividends are not taxable because they are considered to be either volume rebates for goods purchased by members or additional payments for members' goods received by the co-operative.

The chief disadvantages of the co-operative are the difficulty it may have in raising funds, because increased investment by members does not lead to increased control, and the possibility that radical democratic control may lead to inefficient management.

Government Enterprises

As noted in Chapter 4, governments play an active role in the Canadian economy, and numerous government enterprises have been created to carry out this role. Provincially owned utilities such as Quebec and Ontario Hydro are huge industrial complexes, ranking first and second in assets, respectively, among all industrial corporations in Canada.[3]

Federally controlled businesses operate in various forms. The Post Office, for example, is run as a regular government department, although a plan is underway to change it into a Crown corporation. Crown corporations are uniquely Canadian government businesses. They have the legal status of independent entities, but have all or most of their assets owned by the government and are ultimately accountable to Parliament through a minister.

Some Crown corporations, like the Canadian National Railways and Air Canada (which ranked seventh and thirty-seventh in assets, respectively, among all industrial corporations in 1979), have special provisions that allow them to finance their operations independently of the government. Others, like Atomic Energy of Canada Limited, are tied more closely to government and are called *agency* Crown corporations.

Some Data on Business Organizations

According to Coase's theory, described earlier in this chapter, a firm exists because some business tasks are more easily coordinated by managerial directive than by prices and markets. The theory predicts that each firm will grow until the cost of coordinating one more task within the firm exceeds the cost of coordinating one more task via the market. This limit to growth occurs at vastly different stages of development for different firms.

In 1976 there were approximately 1 million firms in Canada, with total sales of $103.8 billion. About three-fourths of the total number of firms were single proprietorships or partnerships. There were about 2,500 co-operatives in Canada and between forty and fifty business-type crown corporations.

In a recent survey of most industries, not including finance, 237,464 corporations were recorded. Exhibit 20.4 divides these corporations into eight major groupings.

---

[3] *The Financial Post 500: The 1980 Ranking of Canada's 500 Largest Companies* (June 14, 1980), p.66.

Exhibit 20.4
Number of corporations in major industry grouping, 1976

Industry	No. of Corporations
Agriculture, forestry and fishing	12,003
Mining	3,994
Manufacturing	29,233
Construction	37,061
Utilities	13,673
Wholesale Trade	34,189
Retail Trade	52,055
Services	55,256
Total	237,464

Source: Statistics Canada, *Annual Report of the Minister of Industry, Trade and Commerce under the Corporations and Labour Unions Returns Act* (Part I: *Corporations*), 1976, p. 161.

Only about 10 percent of the more than 300,000 farm holdings in Canada are organized in a corporate form. In manufacturing, the picture is quite different, and it has changed considerably over the years, as illustrated in Exhibit 20.5.

As the manufacturing industry has grown in the post-World War II period, more and more firms have found it advantageous to adopt the corporate form of business organization. In 1947, only 34.3 percent of manufacturing firms were incorporated; by 1974 this had increased to 74.4 percent.

The association of size with type of organization can be observed in the manufacturing industry by examining the relationship of the type of organization to the number of employees and value added, as shown in Exhibit 20.6.

The evidence indicates that individual ownership offers some advantages to small firms, but the corporate form offers clear advantages to larger firms.

OWNERSHIP AND CONTROL OF CORPORATIONS

Sole proprietorships are owned and controlled by their proprietors and partnerships by their partners. Corporations are legally owned by their shareholders, but the matter of control is much less clear-cut than for other types of firms. Because corporations account for such a large part of Canadian business, no discussion of the nature of the firm would be complete without some mention of the controversy over control of the corporation.

Exhibit 20.5
Percentage distribution of establishments in manufacturing
by type of organization

Year	Individual Ownership	Partnership	Incorporated Companies	Co-operatives	Total
1947	46.3	16.1	34.3	3.2	100.0
1974	19.2	5.2	74.4	1.2	100.0

Source: Statistics Canada, *Manufacturing Industries of Canada, Type of Organization and Size of Establishment*, 1974, p. 3.

Exhibit 20.6

Type of organization in manufacturing, 1974, and average size of establishment

Type of Organization	Number of Establishments	Average Number of Employees per Establishment	Average Value of Value Added per Establishment
Individual ownerships	6,039	2.7	$ 36,195
Partnerships	1,593	5.7	87,078
Corporations	23,536	74.2	1,572,000
Co-operatives	367	39.7	757,324

Source: Statistics Canada, *Annual Report of the Minister of Industry, Trade and Commerce under the Corporations and Labour Unions Returns Act* (Part I: *Corporations*), 1976, pp. 4–5.

Shareholder Rights

One of the advantages of the corporate form of business organization is that capital can be raised from many thousands of separate individuals, who need not invest a large share of their own portfolios in any one firm. Legally, those shareholders have the power to control the corporation. The principal channel for control is the shareholders' power to elect the corporations's board of directors, who decide company policy.

However, most shareholders do not actively exercise their ownership rights. Small shareholders are not really in a position to know what goes on inside their corporation and why decisions are made as they are. They tend to accept the policies set by managers as being for the best. If they disapprove of management policies, it is easier for them to sell their stock and buy shares in a better managed company than to try to throw their weight around at annual shareholder meetings. The result is a degree of separation of ownership from control unknown in sole proprietorships and partnerships.

Shareholders versus Managers

Why is the separation of ownership and control an important issue? The answer given by many economists is that the interests of shareholders and managers may differ. Most shareholders have only one interest in the corporation whose stock they own — that the corporation earn a maximum profit for them. Managers do not always think of their relationship to the corporation in such simple terms.

For one thing, managers are naturally concerned about the security of their own jobs. They know that they must earn at least a respectable minimum of profits or the shareholders may rebel and throw them out. But when it comes to delicate decisions involving marginal trade-offs between risk and profitability, their interests and those of the shareholders may diverge. Shareholders do not normally put all their eggs in one basket. They hold diversified portfolios. If by taking prudent risks they can earn higher average returns, an occasional failure is no disaster. Because a manager's career is more closely tied up with the fate of a single corporation, or even a single project of a corporation, managers may tend to be excessively cautious from the shareholders' point of view.

Corporate growth is another possible area of conflict of interest. Shareholders are interested in growth to the extent that growth means more profit per share, but managers may sometimes favor growth purely for its own sake. The power and prestige of managers, the number of employees they have working under them, and even their salaries are enhanced by growth, regardless of whether that growth increases profit per share.

Finally, it is claimed that managers who identify personally with their firms may be more willing than shareholders to spend money to improve their corporations's image. Lavish headquarters, charitable contributions, community relations projects, and the like may in some cases attract customers and swell profits; but because they also swell managerial pride, there can be a temptation to carry such expenditures too far.

In short, the picture offered by some observers of the corporate scene is one of contrast between the traditional firm singlemindedly pursuing the goal of profit maximization and the modern management controlled corporation for which profits are only one goal among many — and not always the highest ranking one.

Constraints on Managers

How much truth is there in this picture? The picture offered so far cannot be regarded as complete. There are strong reasons to believe that managers cannot really act as independently of the profit maximizing interests of owners as the preceding arguments might suggest.

For one thing, many corporations have plans that permit management to share directly in company profits. One of the most important types of profit sharing plans is the stock option. Stock options give managers the right to buy a certain number of shares of stock in the corporation at a guaranteed price at some time in the future. For example, say that in July 1980, a manager is given the option to buy a thousand shares of the company's stock in July 1981 at the 1980 price of, say, $25. If the manager, together with other managers, does a good job running the firm in the meantime, the price of the stock stands a good chance of rising. If the market price rises to $35 by July 1981, the option to buy a thousand shares at $25 will be worth $10,000, and the manager will reap a rich reward. But if the company is poorly managed and the share price falls, the option is worthless.

A second important constraint on the power of managers to slacken their pursuit of profits is the threat of a takeover. It is true that when ordinary shareholders do not like a corporation's policy, they may simply sell out and buy other stocks rather than attempt to exercise their influence directly. But what if a great many shareholders sell out? If they do, the price of the stock falls below the value it would have if the corporation were managed by profit maximizers. When this happens, an alert stock market entrepreneur can engineer a takeover bid. The takeover may be made by an individual, a group, or, often, another corporation. The idea is to buy a controlling percentage of the corporation's shares and use the power thus gained to replace current managers with more profit-minded ones. If the gambit succeeds, the listed value of the stock's price will rise as the new management policies attract other buyers. Then the original takeover group will reap very handsome gains.

In periods when stock prices are low by historical standards (for example, during the late 1970s), corporate takeovers become common. Large conglomerate firms that make a specialty of them go on the prowl, and weakly managed companies whose stock is selling at prices not reflecting their long-run profit potential are particularly likely to be bought up. Often, the managers of companies threatened with unfriendly takeovers cast around for a "white knight"—an alternative buyer who will take over the company and let the managers keep their jobs, provided they can convince the white knight of their competence.

The effectiveness of the corporate takeover as a device for keeping management on the profit maximizing track should not be measured solely in terms of the number of takeovers that actually occur. The threat of takeover is a powerful disciplinary device that can work without being used every day.

CONCLUSIONS

This chapter has offered just a glimpse of some of the complexities lying behind the simple concept of the firm. In many branches of economic theory, firms are treated as simple, homogeneous building blocks. In reality, they are neither simple nor homogeneous. Except for the smallest one-person operations, each firm is an organization of separate individuals united for a common purpose—the purpose of carrying out the division of labor effectively. Depending on circumstances, this purpose may best be served by the legal form of a sole proprietorship, a partnership, or a corporation. The next few chapters will set aside most of these details and complexities and will treat firms as simple units devoted to the maximization of profits. This simplifying assumption may not be altogether appropriate in each individual case, however. The information given in this chapter will be of help in keeping the firm in perspective and in avoiding acceptance of the simplifications of theory as the whole picture.

SUMMARY

1. There are two major forms of coordination for the division of labor—market coordination and managerial coordination. Market coordination uses the price system for communication and the profit motive as a source of incentives. Managerial coordination proceeds through directives from superiors to subordinates. It organizes the division of labor within a firm, while market coordination organizes the division of labor among firms. Firms tend to grow until the cost of organizing one more task by managerial means exceeds the costs of organizing that task through the market.

2. Firms may be organized as sole proprietorships, partnerships, corporations or co-operatives. Proprietorships are very common among small firms. They are easy to set up and have the advantage of giving the proprietor rights to all of the firm's profits. They have the disadvantage of unlimited liability. Partnerships also suffer from unlimited liability, but they can allow a firm to grow by bringing in new partners with new skills and new capital. Corporations protect their shareholders with limited

liability and permit huge sums of capital to be raised. They suffer the disadvantages of higher taxes and closer regulations than other kinds of businesses, however. Co-operatives have one-member, one-vote democracy, are able to buy goods and services more cheaply than individuals can, and enjoy tax privileges. However, they may have difficulty in raising funds, and their democratic management may be inefficient.

3. It is sometimes argued that managers, rather than shareholders, exercise effective control over corporations. This is an important issue, because the interests of managers and shareholders sometimes conflict. Managers may be less willing than owners to take risks and may sometimes pursue growth at the expense of profits. There are limits to the ability of managers to pursue policies opposed to shareholder interests, though. The most important single constraint is the threat of takeover if profits are too much neglected.

DISCUSSION QUESTIONS

1. Your college or university uses a type of managerial coordination to determine which courses should be offered and which professors should teach them. In principle, market coordination could be used instead. The college or university could limit itself to providing classrooms, dormitories, library facilities, and so on. Professors would then be independent businesspeople, advertising certain courses for so much per credit hour and collecting fees directly from the students. Compare the advantages and disadvantages of each system. Why do you think the managerial system predominates? As far as you know, is the market system ever used in education? Explain.

2. Holt, Rinehart and Winston of Canada, the publisher of this book, does not perform "in house" all the operations necessary to bring out the book. Instead, many particular jobs, such as copy editing, drawing the artwork, composition, and printing are done on a subcontract basis by independent firms. How does Coase's theory of the firm help you understand why Holt, Rinehart and Winston does not maintain on its own payroll all the necessary artists, compositors, printers, and so on?

3. On graduation, a classmate whom you barely know suggests that you go into business together selling sports equipment to the students in your university town. He wants to make the business a partnership. "You supply the brains; I'll put up the money," he says. Do you think you might be better off if he set the business up as a sole proprietorship, with you as his employee? As a corporation, with the two of you holding some of the stock? What would be the advantages and disadvantages to you of each alternative?

4. Why are corporations dominant in some lines of business and not in others? As the economy becomes more service oriented, do you think the importance of the corporation will decline? Explain.

SUGGESTIONS FOR FURTHER READING

Coase, Ronald H. "The Nature of the Firm," *Economica*, new series, 4 (November 1937), pp. 386–405.
The seminal article on the nature of the firm, it explains why there are such things as firms at all.

Galbraith, John Kenneth. *The New Industrial State.* Boston: Houghton Mifflin, 1967.
In this provocative and decidedly unorthodox book, Galbraith develops the thesis that the market plays little or no role in coordinating economic activity in the U.S.

economy and that the corporation is run not by its stockholders but by something called the technostructure.

Gordon Scott. "The Close of the Galbraithian System." *Journal of Political Economy* 76 (July-August 1968), pp. 635 –644.

A short but trenchant critique of Galbraith's view of the economic system and the corporation.

C H A P T E R 21

FOREIGN OWNERSHIP AND CONTROL OF CANADIAN BUSINESS

WHAT YOU WILL LEARN IN THIS CHAPTER

When considering the ways in which Canadian businesses are owned and operated, it is important to distinguish not only among sole proprietorships, partnerships, corporations, and co-operatives and between private and government ownership (as was done in the previous chapter), but also between Canadian and foreign ownership. The effect of foreign ownership on the nature of the Canadian firm is examined in this chapter. The issue of foreign control of Canadian business is part of a larger issue involving Canada's heavy dependence on other economies. The latter topic will be discussed briefly, but the main purpose of this chapter is to examine the extent to which Canadian firms are owned and controlled by foreigners, the effect this may have on those firms, the possible costs and benefits to Canadians, and the policies that are being used — or might be used — to reduce foreign ownership.

FOR REVIEW

Here are some important terms and concepts that will be put to use in this chapter. If you do not understand them, review them before proceeding.

- *Staple production and foreign dependence (Chapter 1)*
- *The National Policy (Chapter 4)*
- *Balance of international payments (Chapter 6)*
- *The foreign sector and the multiplier (Chapter 15)*
- *The corporation (Chapter 20)*

One of the most hotly debated topics in Canada today is the dependence of the Canadian economy on that of other countries, particularly that of the United States. Canada is dependent on other economies in many different ways and has been throughout its history. First, Canada depends on foreign demand for about one-quarter of its total output. This pattern began, as we saw in Chapter 1, with the early stress on staple or primary production for export markets. As late as 1960, over 90 percent of Canadian exports consisted of natural resources in crude or processed form. In the 1960s, finished products as a proportion of total exports increased from 8 percent to 38 percent, but in the 1970s the composition of exports showed no further significant change. The Canadian economy, then, continues to rely heavily on the export of primary products to other countries.

Second, Canada depends to a considerable extent on the importation of consumer durables and capital machinery. Its trade balance on end products was generally in deficit during the 1970s, and it reached a record deficit of $17 billion in 1979.

Third, Canada depends on foreign funds to finance the expansion of its output. This too has a long history. In the last half of the nineteenth century, foreigners provided much of the funding for the building of roads, canals, and railways, and for the development of mining and manufacturing. Most of this capital came from Great Britain. After World War I, the United States began to invest heavily in Canada. This investment often resulted in the establishment of new firms or the purchase of existing firms by "parent" companies in the United States. It is this development of numerous "subsidiary" firms in Canada (subsidiary to foreign parents) that has come to typify the way Canada is in general subservient to foreign interests.

THE EXTENT OF FOREIGN INVESTMENT IN CANADIAN BUSINESS

Canada has actively encouraged foreign investment by erecting tariff barriers to trade, which have discouraged foreign firms from selling goods to Canada and encouraged them instead to establish subsidiaries in this country, and by selling bonds and shares abroad to finance large public and private undertakings. There seems to have been a pervasive feeling through much of our history that Canadian development desperately required the infusion of foreign funds. In the 1960s, when the United States tried to discourage its citizens from investing in other countries, Canada frantically — and successfully, as it turned out — sought exemption from such restrictions. Part of the concern was that inflows of foreign capital were necessary to finance the perennial current account deficit (as discussed in Chapters 6 and 15), but part was also the result of the long-standing conviction that Canada continually needs new infusions of foreign capital for the expansion of its industry.

One result of such favorable attitudes to foreign investment is that Canada has become, next to the United States (which has large short-term claims against it because its currency is virtually the world's currency), the world's largest net international debtor. The official value of our indebtedness is now over $55 billion, or about $2,400 for every person in the nation.[1] This net indebtedness is increasing at about $4 to $5 billion annually, and it costs about $6 billion annually just to service the debt, through interest and dividend payments and retained earnings. About 75 percent of total foreign assets are owned by Americans.

Portfolio Investment and Direct Investment

Not all foreign financing guarantees control of Canadian industry by foreigners. An important distinction must be made between portfolio investment and direct investment.

---

[1] Bruce W. Wilkinson, "Long-Term Capital Inflows and Balance of Payments Policy," *The Walter L. Gordon Lecture Series, 1978–79*, Vol. 3, p. 30.

Portfolio investment includes minority holdings of corporate shares, which may or may not have voting power, and bond holdings, which do not carry voting rights. Most British investment in the pre-World War I period was of this kind, with Canadian bonds being sold in the London bond market. Such investment is more in the nature of a loan. For example, Canadian utilities like Quebec and Ontario Hydro do much of their current financing by selling bonds in the New York market. Such sales do not give Americans any control over those utilities because the bonds carry no voting rights.

Portfolio investment
Purchase of securities that involves no control of the company selling the securities.

Direct investment refers to holdings of securities with voting rights that are substantial enough to give the holder of those shares control over the business. It includes the establishment of subsidiaries by foreign companies that are financed through the earnings of the home company. Control is assumed when the investors own 50 percent or more of the securities or assets with voting rights. In contrast to Great Britain, American investors chose to put a large part of their financing into direct investments. Between 1945 and 1967, long-term investment by the United States in Canada increased from $5 billion to $28 billion, with direct investment rising from $2 billion to $17 billion. About half of the increase in direct investment was used to give Americans control of Canadian natural resources.

Direct investment Purchase of securities with voting rights substantial enough to give the investors control of the company invested in.

Direct investment by foreigners in Canada is generally carried out by corporations that have come to be called **multinationals**. These are companies that carry on business on a world-wide scale, and organize their world operations from a central headquarters. There are many foreign multinational firms operating in Canada, including such giants as General Motors, the Ford Motor Company, and Exxon Corporation. Canada also has its own multinational firms, such as Canadian Pacific Enterprises and Seagrams, which have large operations in other countries.

Multinationals Corporations that have enterprises in a number of countries.

Exhibit 21.1
Percentage of assets in Canadian corporations that are foreign-controlled (excluding finance), 1976

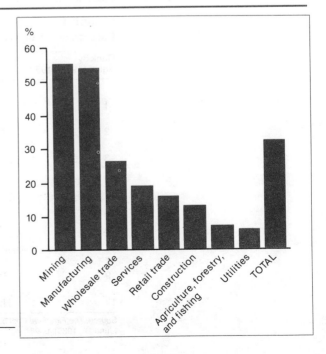

Source: *The Financial Post*, May 12, 1979, p. 8.

Foreign Ownership of Canadian Industry

Our main concern here is with direct foreign investment in Canada. A greater proportion of Canada's industry is foreign owned than that of any other industrialized country. As Exhibit 21.1 shows, between 50 and 60 percent of all assets in Canadian mining and manufacturing in 1976 were held by corporations in which foreigners had a controlling interest (that is, foreigners held more than 50 percent of the voting shares), and the proportion for all industry was 31 percent. Foreign-controlled companies accounted for 46 percent of all industry profits.

Utilities have only about 4 percent foreign ownership, because most are owned by provincial governments. Financial businesses, including banks, also have a low ratio of foreign ownership (about 10 percent) because of special legislation prohibiting substantial foreign investment. Current revisions to the Bank Act will open the door to more foreign banks, however, in order to increase competition in that field.

Some important subsectors of Canadian industry are almost completely owned by foreigners. For example, the proportion of foreign-owned assets is about 99 percent in petroleum and coal products and about 80 percent in transport equipment (including automobiles).

More detail on individual firms in Canada is given in a recent survey of Canada's largest industrial companies. Exhibit 21.2 indicates that five of the ten largest Canadian industrial companies are owned by nonresidents. Only three have foreign ownership of less than 30 percent.

Of the 400 largest "Canadian" companies surveyed in that same report, 193 are owned 50 percent or more by nonresidents, and 128 companies are owned 100 percent by foreigners. Companies that are completely foreign owned include Chrysler, Canada Safeway, F.W. Woolworth, International Harvester, and IBM Canada, all among the fifty largest companies in Canada.

Exhibit 21.2

Foreign ownership in Canada's ten largest industrial corporations

Rank by Sales (1979–1980)	Company	Major Shareholders	Foreign Ownership
			(Percentage)
1	General Motors of Canada Ltd.	General Motors Corp. Detroit	100
2	Canadian Pacific Ltd.	Wide distribution U.S. 22%, Britain 6%	35
3	Ford Motor Co. of Canada	Ford Motor Co. Dearborn, Mich.	89
4	Imperial Oil Ltd.	Exxon Corp. N.Y.	71
5	George Weston Ltd.	Weston family	
6	Bell Canada	Wide distribution	4
7	Alcan Aluminum Ltd.	U.S. 53%, other 8%	61
8	Massey Ferguson Ltd.	Wide distribution Hollinger Argus Ltd.	37
9	Shell Canada Ltd.	Royal Dutch/Shell Group	71
10	Hudson's Bay Co.	Thomson family 75%	

Source: *The Financial Post 500: The 1980 Ranking of Canada's 500 Largest Companies*, (June 14, 1980), p. 96.

In addition to ownership, economists are interested in the actual control of Canadian companies by nonresidents. Ownership may not always be a good indicator of control. Some subsidiaries wholly owned by foreigners will be much less tightly controlled than others by the parent company, while many companies in Canada that are technically owned by Canadians are influenced substantially by foreign interests. For instance, movie houses in Canada owned by Canadians show movies in accordance with agreements made with foreign movie producers. Fast-food businesses in Canada are, in many cases, franchised from U.S. companies, and the nature of the product and service are determined almost entirely by the American firms.[2]

There is no doubt, however, that foreign ownership of Canadian firms will affect the behavior of those firms. Why else would foreign firms want to own and control Canadian resources? Some academic economists have disputed this, but as others have pointed out, "The argument that foreign ownership does not matter is clearly false. If certain Canadian resources are worth more to a foreign firm than they are to a Canadian firm [which must be the reason why a foreign firm rather than a Canadian firm has come to own them], some change in the allocation of the Canadian resources must take place if they are under the control of an international firm. If the acquisition of Canadian resources by a foreign firm had no effect at all on the employment of those resources, their value to the foreign firm and a Canadian firm would have to be equal. The reason the foreign firm succeeds in bidding Canadian resources away from Canadian firms is that it expects to be able to make changes in the allocation of those resources that will be to its advantage."[3]

Whether the changes made to the Canadian economy by foreign ownership of its resources are good or bad for that economy is another and much more difficult question. It is necessary, therefore, to examine the possible costs and benefits, to Canadians, of the extensive foreign investment in this country.

THE BENEFITS AND COSTS OF FOREIGN OWNERSHIP OF CANADIAN BUSINESS

Economists have tried in various ways to determine the benefits that Canadians derive from the foreign ownership of Canadian business, and to compare such benefits with the apparent costs.

Before examining some of the approaches used to measure these things and the results obtained, it is important to note one point that is beyond dispute and that is central to the whole debate. Regardless of what foreign control may or may not do to Canadians, it clearly compromises their sovereignty. Sovereignty has been defined as "the capacity to develop and exercise choice."[4] One leading Canadian economist has posed this issue in

---

[2] This point is made by Jack Carr, Frank Mathewson, and John C. McManus in *Cents and Nonsense: The Economics of Canadian Policy Issues* (Toronto: Holt, Rinehart and Winston, 1972), p. 90.

[3] Carr, Mathewson, and McManus, *Cents and Nonsense*, p. 92.

[4] John J. Shepherd, "An Economic Strategy for Canada: Our Political Economy Regained," *The Walter L. Gordon Lecture Series, 1978–79*, Vol. 3, p. 10.

the following way: "To those who want to be shown how the political interests of domestic and foreign controlled firms differ, I would say: 'Suppose the right to vote in Canadian elections were confined to the inhabitants of, let us say, Cleveland, Ohio. Would that be all right? Would that not be an infringement of Canadian independence in and of itself? Would it be necessary to show that the resulting Canadian government was worse than one elected by residents of Canada?'"[5]

To use an even more prosaic analogy, it may not be too facetious to suggest that Canada is in many ways like a young couple who prize their high standard of living and their apparent ability to stand on their own feet, but have in fact achieved at least some of their success through borrowings from their parents. Could they have done as well on their own? It is difficult, if not impossible, to tell. Will the parents interfere? They will not necessarily interfere overtly, or very often, but it would certainly be an illusion for the young couple to think that they are truly independent or, when it comes to a difference of opinion as to how they should spend their money, that pressure will not be brought to bear on their decision. In addition, their dependence on "outside" financing may create a spirit of caution and dependence that will retard their future financial development.

Empirical studies of the Canadian economy have anticipated these possibilities and others. On the positive side, a number of economists have drawn attention to the superior technology and management skills that foreign capital often brings with it. It is argued that if investment were restricted to the portfolio type, foreign firms would not be as likely to risk the application of some of their best techniques in other countries. Harry G. Johnson (introduced in Chapter 14) in particular has argued that American-owned corporations have made possible the low-cost diffusion of technology and ideas in Canada, and have undoubtedly contributed to the growth of the Canadian economy.[6] One study reported that in the years 1950–1956 net foreign investment (both portfolio and direct) contributed from 8 to 20 percent of the growth in per capita real income in Canada.[7] Another study indicated that if only Canadian capital had been used, the gross domestic product in Canada would be 16.5 percent lower.[8]

Studies of this kind are based on assumptions that are themselves very difficult to verify, but they represent a serious effort to measure the possible benefits derived from foreign investment and ownership.

On the negative side, economists and other social scientists have stressed, in addition to the general loss of sovereignty already noted, the

[5] Gideon Rosenbluth, "Canadian Policy on Foreign Ownership and Control of Business," in *The Canadian Economy: Problems and Policies*, ed. G.C. Ruggeri (Toronto: Gage, 1977), p. 346.

[6] H.G. Johnson, "Economic Benefits," in *Nationalism and the Multinational Enterprise*, ed. H.R. Hahlo, Graham Smith, and Richard W. Wright (Leiden, The Netherlands: Sijthoff, 1973).

[7] Rudolph G. Penner, "The Benefits of Foreign Investment in Canada, 1950–1956," *Canadian Journal of Economics and Political Science*, May 1966, pp. 172–83. Cited by A.E. Safarian, "Issues Raised by Foreign Direct Investment in Canada," in *Issues in Canadian Economics*, ed. L.H. Officer and L.B. Smith (Toronto: McGraw-Hill Ryerson, 1974), p. 82. The estimate deducts Canadian investment abroad; the contribution of gross inflows alone would be greater.

[8] Philip A. Neher, "Capital Movement, Foreign Ownership and Dependence on Foreign Investment in Canada and British Columbia," and John Helliwell and Jillian Broadbent, "How Much Does Foreign Capital Matter?" both in *B.C. Studies*, Department of Economics, University of British Columbia, Spring 1972, 13, pp. 31–42. Cited by Safarian, "Issues," p. 82.

possibility that Canadian subsidiaries of foreign multinationals may be induced to do things that are in the interest of the parent company rather than in the interest of the subsidiary or the Canadian economy.

First, the influx of managerial talent that often accompanies a foreign takeover and may contribute to increased efficiency in the firm that has been taken over, may simultaneously cause a long-run dependence on expertise and services lodged in the parent company. This represents a loss of business to Canadian firms that might otherwise supply such a company with architectural, legal, and advertising services. The tendency to limit the development of services and skills in the foreign-owned subsidiary, because they are concentrated in the parent company, is known as **trunca-tion**. It has been estimated that the migration of services to the United States will result in a projected $1.5 billion dollar deficit in our balance of payments by 1985.[9]

Truncation Limits placed on the development of skills and services in and by a Canadian subsidiary because they are concentrated in the parent company.

Related to this is the concentration of research and development (R & D) activities in the parent company, at the possible expense of such activities being undertaken in the Canadian subsidiary. Early studies of this subject indicated that foreign-owned firms were as committed to research and development as Canadian-owned firms, but recently developed data show that, in several sectors of the economy, Canadian-owned companies per-form more R & D per dollar of sales than do foreign-owned companies.[10]

The impact of foreign ownership on exports and imports has also been examined. It has been conjectured that subsidiaries of foreign companies would be constrained from exporting, because their exports might compete with exports of the same commodity produced by the parent company, while at the same time they would import more than similar domestically owned companies because of their reliance on services and capital equip-ment from the parent company. (Though in the absence of the foreign subsidiary, Canadian imports of goods produced by that subsidiary might increase.) In view of Canada's chronic deficit on current account, this possibility has been viewed with great concern. The detailed studies of A.E. Safarian, a Toronto economist, indicate that foreign-owned firms seem to export as freely as their Canadian-owned counterparts. At the same time they also import more.[11] The net impact on the balance of payments of the export and import behavior of foreign-owned firms does not appear to be as serious as some have thought. At the same time, it should not be forgotten that the capital flows that are part and parcel of foreign investment have a profound impact on the balance of payments. Insofar as they represent the creation of new foreign debt for Canada, which must be paid back in the form of interest and dividends, they increase the already serious deficit in Canada's current account—a deficit that we have traditionally tried to cover by even larger inflows of capital and larger current account deficits. Simultaneously, the inflow of capital, under a system of flexible exchange rates, increases the value of the Canadian dollar and reduces the cost of imports. However, this beneficial result must be balanced against the fact that our exports are simultaneously made more expensive.

---

[9] John J. Shepherd, "An Economic Strategy for Canada: Our Political Economy Regained," *The Walter L. Gordon Lecture Series, 1978–79*, Vol. 3, p. 17.

[10] John J. Shepherd, "Economic Strategy," p. 23.

[11] A.E. Safarian, *Foreign Ownership of Canadian Industry* (Toronto: McGraw-Hill, 1966).

The net effect of such capital flows in this respect is hard to gauge.

General, tentative conclusions of this kind should not obscure the fact that, in many individual cases, Canadians have come to feel that they have good reason to want more control of their economy.

In 1971, Robert L. Perry, a reporter for *The Financial Post*, made a detailed examination of the foreign control of Canadian industry in Galt, Ontario. His award-winning study was called *Galt, U.S.A.* He discovered that many American-owned firms in Galt were tightly controlled by their American headquarters and were making decisions that, in the opinion of Canadian personnel of these firms, were not in the best interests of Canada. As one of the Canadian managers of a subsidiary noted, "I was being manipulated and controlled by Americans — by people outside the day-to-day work environment." This manager thought it was in the interest of the company to purchase a steel mill owned by Bethlehem Steel just across the border from Ontario, but the American parent firm vetoed the idea because "the American market belonged to the parent."[12]

Eight years later, in 1979, Perry returned to that same community to bring his research up to date. He found now that many American firms were selling their branch plants because they had discovered what their Canadian-based managers had been trying to tell them: that many of the subsidiaries had been performing badly under absentee ownership and control. It is too early to tell whether the movement of some American firms out of the Galt area (since renamed Cambridge) represents a nationwide trend that will reduce the American presence in Canadian industry.

Another experience linked to foreign ownership is described in Case 21.1 American firms like Westinghouse may decide at any time that it would pay them to consolidate their multinational operations at the expense of individual plants somewhere in their operation.

Case 21.1
Who Decides for Westinghouse Canada Ltd.?

Early in 1979, Westinghouse of Canada Ltd., with headquarters in Hamilton, Ontario, announced plans to "decentralize" its Hamilton operations. The 700 workers in the Hamilton plant were naturally concerned. What did "decentralization" mean? Would they lose their jobs? Would they be dispersed to other parts of Canada? Would the operation be moved to the United States, where the parent company seemed to make the decisions? The Ontario government and the labor unions demanded clarification. As the following news item indicates, it was Westinghouse of Canada's dependence on its U.S. parent that created much of the concern, illustrating a problem created for the Canadian economy by foreign ownership. As *The Financial Post* reported:

The gut issue in the controversy swirling about the possible decentralization of Westinghouse Canada Ltd.'s switchgear and control division is who exactly is calling the shots? Executives in Hamilton, Ont., or chiefs back in Pittsburgh, Pa., home-base of Westinghouse Electric Corp.?

The other key question is why is the move necessary when even company officials admit the division, which produces devices to distribute and measure electrical power, is the second most profitable at Westinghouse?

Leaders of the United Electrical Radio & Machine Workers Union of America say Pittsburgh has snapped its fingers.

---

[12] Robert L. Perry, *Galt, U.S.A.*, rev. ed. (Toronto: The Financial Post, 1979). Excerpt reprinted in *The Financial Post*, Sept. 1, 1979, p. 15.

"They just want to get the heck out of Canada, and away from the union," says John Ball of Local 504.

The union claims the switchgear plant is viable for future growth and that the division will become a "warehousing and service operation" if decentralized.

With the support of provincial opposition parties and Hamilton city council, the union is pressing the Ontario government to introduce legislation that would guarantee the jobs of 700 Hamilton workers and force Westinghouse to accept its "social responsibility" to the community.

Late last week, Westinghouse management finally issued a point-by-point reply to the charges.

C. F. MacNeil, vice-president, told *The Post* the decision to move to a multi-location operation "with internal strategies to match" will be Canadian. "There is a 1% chance the division will leave Canada, but that is not part of our study," he says.

Source: *The Financial Post*, March 31, 1979, p. 5.

Another major problem associated with foreign-owned firms is **extraterritoriality**: the intrusion of foreign law and policy into Canada. The United States, in particular, has always insisted that subsidiaries of American corporations operating in Canada are subject to American laws. This has had a number of important, and highly publicized, repercussions for Canadian subsidiaries of American firms. For example, under the U.S. Trading with the Enemy Act, trade by American-owned corporations with countries like Cuba, China, Vietnam, and North Korea has at times been expressly prohibited. Several sales of goods to Cuba by Canadian subsidiaries were stopped by the U.S. government in the 1970s, though after a vigorous appeal by the Canadian government one of them eventually went through. The U.S. government has also extended its antitrust laws into Canada, and on several occasions has warned Canadian subsidiaries to bring their behavior into line with American law. Such actions may actually benefit Canadians, but it is not surprising that they are also resented as unwarranted interference from outside the country.

Extraterritoriality The application of foreign laws to Canadian companies.

The problems just cited do not amount to indisputable evidence that foreign-owned corporations have done serious and irreparable damage to the Canadian economy. In fact, on balance it would be extremely difficult to prove whether or not the costs have outweighed the benefits. However, as was observed at the beginning of this section, there is no question that the extensive foreign ownership of Canadian firms represents a substantial diminution of Canadian sovereignty.

POLICIES TO CURB THE FOREIGN OWNERSHIP OF CANADIAN BUSINESS

Though Canada has generally welcomed the inflow of foreign capital to support the development of its industry, in the last decade or so a large number of Canadians, including governments at both the provincial and federal levels, have become concerned about the extent of foreign ownership. A number of policies have been undertaken by governments to reduce the size of new capital inflows and to repatriate some of the assets already owned by nonresidents. A federal government study in 1972 described three types of policies that have emerged.[13]

[13] *Foreign Direct Investment in Canada*, a report prepared under the direction of the Hon. Herb Gray (Ottawa: Information Canada, 1972).

First, legislation has been passed limiting direct foreign investment in sectors of the economy deemed crucial to Canada's cultural and financial development. In the field of broadcasting, no broadcasting system in Canada is permitted to have more than 20 percent nonresident participation. In the field of publishing, attempts have been made, through tax laws and government subsidies, to discourage Canadian advertising in foreign magazines and to establish Canadian publishing houses in a field largely dominated by American companies. In banking, the Bank Act revision of 1967 limits to 25 percent the proportion of shares that can be transferred to nonresidents. The actual participation of foreigners in this important field is considerably smaller than that. Similar legislation applies to insurance companies.

A second strategy has been to provide guidelines for the behavior of American (and other foreign) firms in Canada. In 1975, the federal minister of Industry, Trade and Commerce issued a document entitled *The New Principles of International Business Conduct*, advising foreign corporations on matters such as interference in the operation of Canadian subsidiaries and the need for more research and technological development in Canada. It is doubtful, however, that such public relations efforts have had much impact on the performance of foreign-owned corporations.

An important exception to this may be the Foreign Investment Review Agency (FIRA), which was established in 1973 by the federal Parliament to monitor prospective foreign takeovers, and to encourage more Canadian participation at the management level and more use of Canadian resources and skills by foreign corporations permitted to enter the Canadian market. The review agency has denied few applications and is generally felt to have exercised little real control over the entry of new foreign firms, but in 1980 the federal government issued a statement that appeared to renew its commitment to its general purpose.

A third type of policy consists of encouraging increased Canadian ownership of business firms. Many measures have been adopted to accomplish this. For example, corporations that are partly Canadian owned pay lower dividend taxes than those that are wholly foreign owned; pension funds, which are an extremely important source of capital funding, are required to pay a special tax if they do not keep at least 90 percent of their assets in Canada.

In 1971, the federal government established the Canada Development Corporation (CDC) as an independent company, to channel Canadian funds into the purchase of companies currently controlled by foreigners or operating in sectors largely controlled by foreigners. In fact, its first major purchase was of a successful Canadian Crown corporation, Polymer, and for this it was severely criticized. It has since made substantial investments in the oil and pharmaceutical fields, which are heavily dominated by foreign firms. In 1979 it was listed, in terms of sales, as the twenty-eighth largest nonfinancial corporation in Canada, with assets of $2.8 billion.[14]

Despite all of these efforts, Canada remains an economy peculiarly dependent on other economies, particularly that of the United States. It is

---

[14] *The Financial Post 500: The 1980 Ranking of Canada's 500 Largest Companies* (June 14, 1980).

clear that Canadian business firms are profoundly affected by foreign ownership, though the actual costs and benefits of such ownership are extremely difficult to assess.

SUMMARY

1. Canada's economy has, throughout its history, been dependent on the economies of other countries. Canada depends heavily on its exports of primary goods and on its imports of finished products. Further, Canada has always encouraged foreign investment for industrial expansion. This has led to the development of numerous "subsidiary" firms, operating in Canada but responsible to parent companies in other countries.

2. Even without much documented evidence that foreign multinational firms interfere frequently in decisions made by their Canadian subsidiaries, the very fact that such Canadian enterprises have been purchased by foreigners is reason enough to believe that their performance is different from the way it would have been under Canadian control.

3. Whether the difference mentioned works for or against Canada is a matter for legitimate dispute. Recent evidence seems to indicate that, in terms of its balance of payments position, research and development, and in the development of highly skilled Canadian managers, the costs may exceed the benefits.

4. A number of approaches have been developed by governments to restrain foreign investment, to make foreign investors conform to Canadian needs and practices, and to encourage a partial repatriation of foreign-owned assets by Canadians.

DISCUSSION QUESTIONS

1. Does it appear to you, from what has been said in this chapter and on the basis of your previous reading, that the problem of Canada's dependence on other countries is primarily a political, social, or economic one? Explain.

2. Why do you think multinational corporations want to own the firms in which they invest? Why don't they just use contractual agreements, franchises, etc., to purchase the resources that they want from Canada?

3. Suggest ways, other than those being followed today, by which Canada might "buy back" the companies now owned by foreigners. Try to obtain data from the sources listed in this chapter on how expensive this might be. Do you think Canadians are willing to pay a considerable price for an increase in their economic autonomy?

THE THEORY OF COST

WHAT YOU WILL LEARN IN THIS CHAPTER

Further exploration of microeconomic theory requires a better under-standing of what lies behind the supply curve, which in turn requires a theory of cost. This chapter explains exactly what economists mean by cost. Then it discusses the relationship between costs and the quantity of output produced by a firm and shows why this relationship depends on (among other things) the time horizon under consideration.

FOR REVIEW

Here is an important term that will be put to use in this chapter. If you do not understand it, review it before proceeding

• *Opportunity cost (Chapter 1)*

Many upward-sloping supply curves have been presented in earlier chapters. These curves have indicated that suppliers are willing to offer more of their product for sale when prices are high than when they are low. In a general way, it has been suggested that the positive slope of supply curves has something to do with costs; now it is time to take up that suggestion in more detail. The theory of cost developed in this chapter will be used as a basis for the construction of supply curves in Chapter 23 and for the analysis of many kinds of business decisions in later chapters.

THE NATURE OF COSTS

One of the most basic principles of economics is that all costs arise from the necessity of choosing among alternative uses of scarce resources. All costs of producing goods or services are opportunity costs; the true measure of the cost of doing something is always the value of the best alternative use of the same resources.

Implicit and Explicit Costs

In practical terms, the opportunity costs that a firm incurs in the course of business consist of the payments the firm must make to suppliers and the incomes it must provide to resource owners in order to attract labor, capital, and natural resources away from their alternative uses. These costs, in turn, fall into two categories—explicit costs and implicit costs.

Explicit costs Costs taking the form of explicit payments to nonowners of a firm.

Explicit costs are costs that take the form of payments to nonowners of the firm. They include payments made for the labor and raw materials used in actual production operations, the services of hired managers and salespeople, insurance, legal advice, transportation, and a great many other things.

Implicit costs The opportunity costs to a firm of using resources owned by the firm itself or contributed by owners of the firm.

Implicit costs are the opportunity costs to the firm of using resources owned by the firm itself or contributed by owners of the firm. Like explicit costs, they represent real sacrifices to the firm; but unlike explicit costs, they do not take the form of explicit payments to outsiders. For example, when a firm occupies a building or uses machinery that it owns, it forgoes the opportunity to use that building or machinery in some other way. For another example, the proprietor of a small firm who works alongside the firm's hired employees forgoes the opportunity to work elsewhere. Firms do not normally record costs of this sort in their accounts because no explicit payments are made to outsiders, but that does not make the costs any less real. Implicit costs represent the sacrifice of income that could have been earned by selling or hiring out the firm's resources to others.

Costs and Profits

Pure economic profit The sum remaining after both explicit and implicit costs are subtracted from total revenue.

The proper distinction between explicit and implicit costs is very important for understanding the concept of *profit* as it is used in economics. **Pure economic profit** means the difference between a firm's total revenues and total costs, including both explicit and implicit costs; the term *profit* as used in this book always means pure economic profit.

Much to the confusion of generations of economics students, the everyday language of business and accounting uses the term *profit* in another, quite different, sense—namely, to mean the sum remaining after only explicit costs are subtracted from total revenue. This kind of profit will be referred to as **accounting profit** to distinguish it from the pure economic profit defined above. Putting the two definitions together produces the relationship:

Accounting profit Total revenue minus explicit costs.

Pure economic profit = Accounting profit − Implicit costs.

A Numerical Example The numerical example given in Exhibit 22.1 further illustrates the difference between pure economic profit and accounting profit for a firm called the Smith Tool Company. The firm was formed

Total revenue	$500,000
Less explicit costs:	
Wages	200,000
Salaries	100,000
Materials and other	50,000
Equals accounting profit	$150,000
Less implicit costs:	
Forgone salary, Andrea Smith	40,000
Forgone salary, Ralph Smith	40,000
Interest forgone on invested savings	20,000
Equals pure economic profit	$ 50,000

Exhibit 22.1

Accounts of Smith Tool Company, 1980

Accounting profit is a firm's total revenue less its explicit costs. The accounting profit of Smith Tool Company for 1980 is thus $150,000. To arrive at pure economic profit, implicit costs must also be subtracted from revenue. In this case, the implicit costs consist of income forgone by Andrea and Ralph Smith, owners of the company— including $80,000 in forgone salaries and $20,000 in forgone interest on their invested savings. After these items are deducted, it can be seen that pure economic profit for the firm in 1980 is just $50,000.

when Andrea and Ralph Smith left their jobs at a large corporation (where he had worked as a manager and she as an engineer) to set up a small firm of their own. Initial capital for the new firm was provided by $200,000 in personal savings that the Smiths had accumulated while working for their corporate employer.

During its first year, 1980, Smith Tool Company earned total revenues of $500,000. Total explicit costs, consisting of purchased materials and wages and salaries paid to persons other than the owners, came to $350,000, which left an accounting profit of $150,000.

The explicit costs of the new firm, however, did not represent all of the opportunity costs incurred by the firm during its first year of operation. Both Andrea and Ralph Smith gave up high-paying jobs to start the firm. Their combined former salary of $80,000 is listed in Exhibit 22.1 as an implicit cost of production because it represents the income they had to expect to derive from the firm in order to be attracted away from their former jobs.[1] Also listed as an implicit cost in Exhibit 22.1 is $20,000 of forgone interest income. This item is discussed in the next section.

After both implicit and explicit costs are subtracted from the firm's income, the firm is left with a pure economic profit of $50,000. This sum is profit, not cost, because it represents what the Smiths earned from their new company over and above the $100,000 assumed to be necessary to attract their labor and capital away from the best alternative use. It is their reward for acting as entrepreneurs — that is, for recognizing and entering a potentially profitable niche in the machine tool market that no other entrepreneur had yet exploited.

Profit and Return to Capital

For some purposes, it is useful to calculate a firm's earnings in relation to the capital invested in the firm. In order to attract funds for investment, a firm must be able to provide prospective investors with the expectation of earning at least as much income as they would expect to earn from the best alternative use of their funds. Stated in terms of percent per year, this amount can be called the **normal rate of return to captial**. The normal rate of return represents the opportunity cost of capital to the firm. In the case of the Smith Tool Company, the normal rate of return to capital was assumed to be 10 percent per year. The Smiths could thus have earned $20,000 per year by putting their $200,000 of savings at the disposal of other firms in which they did not participate in an entrepreneurial capacity — for example, by using their savings to buy stocks and bonds of other companies.

As things worked out, the success of the Smith Tool Company permitted Andrea and Ralph Smith to earn much more than they would have if they had put their savings at the disposal of other firms. To be precise, they earned not only the $20,000 listed in Exhibit 22.1 as the opportunity cost of capital but also $50,000 in pure economic profit. The opportunity cost of

Normal rate of return to capital The opportunity cost of capital to a firm — that is, the rate of return necessary to attract funds for investment from their best alternative uses.

---

[1] The $80,000 combined former salary is really only an approximation of what would have been required to attract the Smiths away from their former jobs. Perhaps, because starting a new firm is a risky venture, the true opportunity cost — including lost peace of mind — would be more. Or perhaps, because the Smiths place some value on being their own boss, the true opportunity cost would be less.

Total rate of return to capital The opportunity cost of capital plus pure economic profit, expressed as a percentage of the capital invested in a firm.

capital plus pure economic profit, expressed as a percentage of capital invested in the firm, can be called the **total rate of return to capital** for the firm. In the case of the Smith Tool Company, the total rate of return to capital for 1980 was 35 percent:

$$\frac{\$20,000 + \$50,000}{\$200,000} = 0.35.$$

From these definitions, it follows that a firm earning a total rate of return to capital greater than the normal rate of return is earning a positive pure economic profit; a firm earning a total rate of return less than the normal rate of return is earning a negative pure economic profit (that is, a pure economic loss); and a firm earning a total rate of return just equal to the normal rate of return is earning zero pure economic profit.

PRODUCTION AND COSTS IN THE SHORT RUN

Now that the economic meaning of cost is clear, the next step is to build a theory of cost. The main purpose of such a theory is to explain how costs vary as the quantity of output produced by a firm varies. The exposition of the theory of cost will be divided into two parts corresponding to two time perspectives—the short run and the long run. The distinction between these two perspectives requires just a bit more preliminary explanation before the theory of cost itself is presented.

The Long Run and the Short Run

A firm uses many kinds of inputs to produce its output. By varying the quantities of inputs it uses, the firm can vary the quantity of output produced. The quantities of some things a firm uses can often be adjusted very quickly, whereas others are not so easy to adjust. The inputs that cannot easily be varied as the level of output changes define the size of plant the firm must work with. The physical size of structures, the production capacity of major items of machinery, and specialized or not easily replaceable employees are among the inputs determining the size of a firm's plant. These inputs are known as **fixed inputs**. They can be distinguished from **variable inputs** — inputs that can be varied quickly and easily to adjust the quantity of output produced within a plant of a given size. Raw materials, energy, and hourly labor are among the major variable inputs for most firms.

Fixed inputs Inputs to the production process that cannot easily be increased or decreased in a short period of time (the quantity of fixed inputs employed by a firm defines the size of the firm's plant).

Variable inputs Inputs to the production process that can quickly and easily be varied to increase or decrease output within a plant of a given size.

The distinction between fixed and variable inputs in turn forms the basis for the distinction between the short run and the long run in cost theory. The **short run** is a time perspective too short to change the size of a firm's plant, so that variations in output can come only from changes in the quantities of variable inputs used. The **long run**, in contrast, is a time horizon long enough to permit changes in the quantities of fixed inputs and the size of the firm's plant.

Short run A time perspective within which output can be adjusted only by changing the quantities of variable inputs within a plant of fixed size.

Long run A time perspective long enough to permit changes in the quantities of all inputs, both fixed and variable.

Production in the Short Run and Diminishing Returns

Production with One Variable Input With these preliminaries out of the way, the discussion of short-run cost theory can begin with a simple story about the relationship between inputs and outputs in the short run for the Smith Tool Company. Imagine, for the sake of discussion, that the company has only one input that is variable in the short run—namely, labor—and that it produces only one product—say, a small, portable drill press. Beginning from a zero level of output, imagine that the rate of production of this tool is to be gradually increased, varying the quantity of labor while keeping the size of the plant fixed.

Initially, the firm might hire just one worker. This worker would have to walk from machine to machine, doing every step in the production process alone. The worker would lose time moving from machine to machine and would not become skilled at any particular task. This would not be very efficient, so costs would be relatively high in relation to output.

As more workers were taken on, output would increase rapidly. In fact, because workers could become more productive by specializing in particular tasks, it is very likely that the quantity of output produced per added unit of variable input would increase initially.

However, the rate of output per added unit of variable input could not continue to rise indefinitely. Eventually, a point would be reached beyond which the useful possibilities for specialization and division of labor within the plant would be exhausted. More workers might still increase output, of course. Each worker standing at a machine could be given a helper to pass along materials and carry away finished parts. Still more helpers could be added to pick up metal shavings for recycling or wave fans to keep the machine operators more comfortable and productive. Musicians could be hired to play string quartets to keep up morale in the stockroom. But obviously, long before that point was reached, each additional unit of variable input would be adding less and less to output. The fixed quantity of inputs other than labor would become increasingly inadequate to support the growing labor force. Eventually, additional workers would contribute nothing at all.

A Numerical Example The preceding story, although somewhat fanciful, is put more precisely in the numerical example of Exhibit 22.2. This exhibit, like the story on which it is based, assumes that labor is the firm's only variable input. Columns 1 and 2 show the quantity of output, measured in units (drill presses) per day, and the quantity of the variable input, measured in labor hours per day. Output reaches one unit per day only after labor input reaches 38 hours per day. Seventy-two labor hours per day suffice to raise output to two units per day; 102 labor hours are enough to produce three units per day, and so on. By the time labor input rises to 880 hours per day, output has risen to twenty-four units per day.

Columns 3 and 4 of Exhibit 22.2 illustrate the relationship between inputs and outputs in marginal terms. Column 3 shows the number of added labor hours required to produce each added unit of output. Column 4 shows the number of units of output added by each added unit of labor. The entry in Column 4 is thus the reciprocal of the entry in Column 3. For example, to increase output from four units to five units requires that labor input be increased from 130 hours per day to 155 hours per day, an increase of 25 labor hours. In the range between four and five units of output, then, each added labor hour contributes 1/25th of a unit (0.04 units) of output.

Quantity of Output (units per day) (1)	Quantity of Labor (labor hours per day) (2)	Added Labor Hours per Added Unit of Output (3)	Added Units of Output per Added Labor Hour (marginal physical product of labor) (4)
1	38.0		
2	72.0	34.0	0.029
3	102.5	30.5	0.032
4	130.0	27.5	0.036
5	155.0	25.0	0.040
6	178.0	23.0	0.043
7	199.5	21.5	0.047
8	220.0	20.5	0.049
9	240.0	20.0	0.050
10	260.5	20.5	0.049
11	282.0	21.5	0.047
12	305.0	23.0	0.043
13	330.0	25.0	0.040
14	357.5	27.5	0.036
15	388.0	30.5	0.032
16	422.0	34.0	0.029
17	460.0	38.0	0.026
18	502.5	42.5	0.024
19	550.0	47.5	0.021
20	603.0	53.0	0.019
21	662.0	59.0	0.017
22	727.5	65.5	0.015
23	800.0	72.5	0.014
24	880.0	80.0	0.013

Exhibit 22.2

Short-run inputs and outputs for the Smith Tool Company

This exhibit shows hypothetical input and output data for the Smith Tool Company. One variable input (labor) and one output (drill presses) are assumed. As the quantity of the variable input is increased—the quantities of fixed inputs remaining constant—output increases. Column 4 shows the additional output produced by each added labor hour for each one-unit range of output up to twenty-four units; this is called the marginal physical product of labor. Note that the marginal physical product of labor first rises but after nine units of output begins to fall again.

Marginal physical product (of an input) The quantity of output, expressed in physical units, produced by each added unit of the input.

For present purposes, the entries in Column 4 are of particular interest. The quantity of output added per unit of added labor is called the **marginal physical product of labor**. Exhibit 22.3a, based on Columns 1 and 2 of Exhibit 22.2, shows how the total physical product of labor (that is, the total quantity of output) varies as the total quantity of labor varies. Exhibit 22.3b, based on Columns 2 and 4 of Exhibit 22.2, shows how the marginal physical product of labor varies as the quantity of labor used varies. Both graphs are based on the same assumption as the table in Exhibit 22.2—namely, that labor is the only variable input; the size of the plant and the quantities of all other inputs are assumed to remain fixed.

The Law of Diminishing Returns Notice that in Exhibit 22.3b, as the quantity of labor input varies, the marginal physical product of labor at first rises but then falls. This increase and then decrease in marginal product gives the total physical product curve its characteristic S-shape. The curves shown in Exhibit 22.3 illustrate a principle known as the **law of diminishing returns**, which says that as the quantity of one variable input used in a production process is increased, with the quantities of all other inputs remaining fixed, a point will eventually be reached beyond which the quantity of output added per unit of added variable input (that is, the marginal physical product of the variable input) will begin to decrease.

Law of diminishing returns The law stating that as the quantity of one variable input used in a production process is increased (with the quantities of all other inputs remaining fixed), a point will eventually be reached beyond which the quantity of output added per unit of added variable input (that is, the marginal physical product of the variable input) begins to decrease.

The law of diminishing returns is quite general. It applies to all known production processes and to all variable inputs. In the example above, the

Exhibit 22.3
Total and marginal physical product curves for Smith Tool Company

The curves in this exhibit are drawn from the data given in Exhibit 22.2. Part a shows the total quantity of output produced by various quantities of the variable input labor, given the size of the firm's plant as defined by the quantities of fixed inputs. It is labeled the total physical product curve. Part b shows how much extra output is produced by each additional unit of labor. It is labeled the marginal physical product curve. Note that after labor input reaches approximately 230 hours per day, the marginal physical product of labor begins to decline. The downward-sloping section of the marginal physical product curve illustrates the law of diminishing returns.

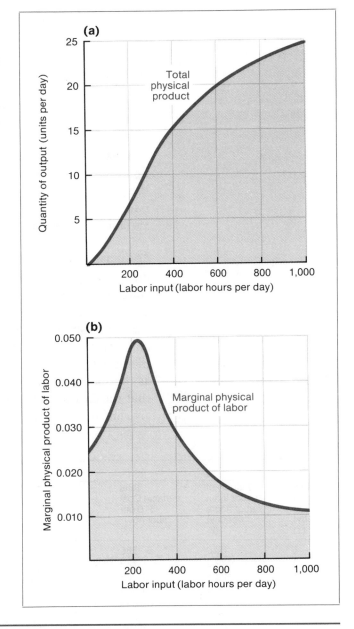

law was illustrated by the case of a manufacturing firm, with labor as the variable input. It could have been illustrated equally well by an example from farming, with, say, fertilizer as the variable input: as the quantity of fertilizer used per acre of land increases, all other inputs remaining fixed, the number of bushels of output per acre increases; but beyond some point, the quantity of output added per added unit of fertilizer begins to decrease. Or an example from the energy industry could have been used: as the number of tons of coal burned per week in a power plant of a given size increases, the output of electricity increases; but beyond some point, the capacity of the plant is approached, and the added output of electricity per added ton of coal per week decreases. In every case, the limited quantity of fixed input is unable, after a certain point, to adapt to increasing quantities of the variable input without a decline in marginal physical product of the variable input.

Diminishing Returns and Short-Run Costs

It is a short step from the law of diminishing returns to an analysis of the short-run relationship between output and costs. To explore this relationship, return to the example of the Smith Tool Company. Assume that the company is able to hire production workers at a constant wage of $10 per hour. If, beyond a point, each added hour of labor adds less to output than the previous one, and each added labor hour costs the same as the previous one, it follows that beyond the point where diminishing returns begin, variable costs per unit of output must rise.

Marginal Costs and Total Costs The relationship between the law of diminishing returns and the behavior of short-run variable costs is illustrated numerically in Exhibit 22.4 and graphically in Exhibit 22.5. Exhibit 22.4 is based directly on Exhibit 22.2, assuming a labor cost of $10 per hour. Column 3 shows the total variable cost, at $10 per labor hour, of producing any given level of output. Column 4 shows the amount of added cost incurred to produce each added unit of output. This cost increase is known as the short-run **marginal cost** of production at that level of output. Note that the entries in Column 4 are equal to the differences between successive entries in Column 3.

Marginal cost The increase in cost required to increase output of some good or service by one unit.

Quantity of Output (units per day) (1)	Quantity of Labor Input (labor hours per day) (2)	Total Variable Cost ($10 per labor hour) (3)	Marginal Cost (4)
1	38.0	$ 380	
2	72.0	720	$340
3	102.5	1,025	305
4	130.0	1,300	275
5	155.0	1,550	250
6	178.0	1,780	230
7	199.5	1,995	215
8	220.0	2,200	205
9	240.0	2,400	200
10	260.5	2,605	205
11	282.0	2,820	215
12	305.0	3,050	230
13	330.0	3,300	250
14	357.5	3,575	275
15	388.0	3,880	305
16	422.0	4,220	340
17	460.0	4,600	380
18	502.5	5,025	425
19	550.0	5,500	475
20	603.0	6,030	530
21	662.0	6,620	590
22	727.5	7,275	655
23	800.0	8,000	725
24	880.0	8,800	800

Exhibit 22.4

Total variable cost and marginal cost for the Smith Tool Company

The data given in this exhibit are based on those given in Exhibit 22.2; they assume a labor cost of $10 per hour. Column 3 gives the total variable cost (assuming labor to be the only variable input) of producing a given quantity of output per day. Column 4 shows the marginal cost at each level of output — that is, the added cost of increasing the level of output by one unit.

Exhibit 22.5 is derived directly from the numbers given in Exhibit 22.4. A comparison of Exhibits 22.3 and 22.5 shows that the marginal cost and total cost curves are, roughly, the mirror images of the marginal product and total product curves. In particular, over the range of diminishing returns, marginal product falls and marginal cost rises. Correspondingly, the slope of the total product curve becomes flatter as one moves to the right in the range of diminishing returns, while the slope of the total cost curve becomes steeper.

A Family of Short-Run Cost Curves

The marginal cost and total variable cost curves shown in Exhibit 22.5 are only two of a whole family of short-run cost curves that can be constructed for the Smith Tool Company. The complete family is shown in numerical form in Exhibit 22.6c and graphically in Exhibits 22.6a and 22.6b.

Total variable cost, from Exhibit 22.4, appears in Column 2 of Exhibit 22.6c. Not all costs are variable in the short run. Fixed cost, which repre-

Exhibit 22.5

Total variable and marginal cost curves for Smith Tool Company

The total variable and marginal cost curves shown in this exhibit are plotted from data given in Exhibit 22.4. Because marginal cost measures the amount by which total cost increases each time output is increased by one unit, the height of the marginal cost curve at each quantity of output is equal to the slope of the total variable cost curve at that output. Notice in particular that just at the point of minimal marginal cost, the total variable cost curve stops getting flatter and begins to get steeper.

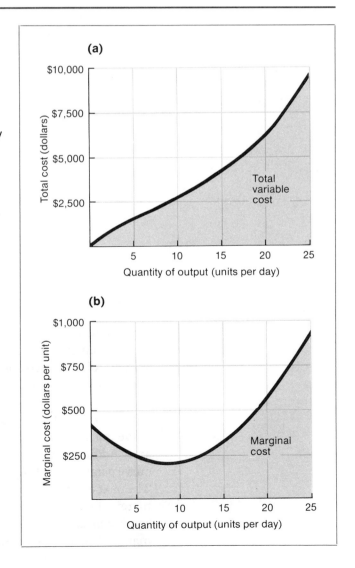

Exhibit 22.6

A family of short-run cost curves

A whole family of short-run cost curves can be derived from the cost data shown in Part c of this exhibit. Three kinds of total cost curves are shown in Part a, while average and marginal cost curves are shown in Part b. Note that the marginal cost curve intersects the average total cost and average variable cost curves at their lowest points.

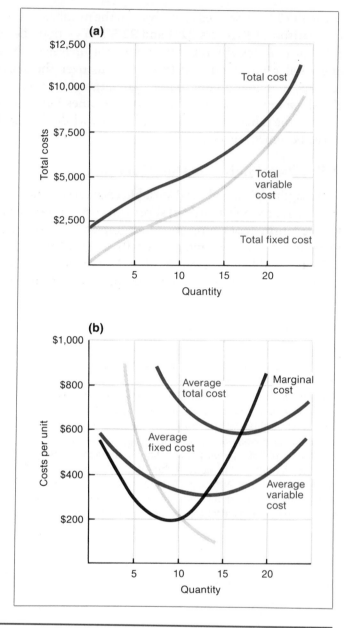

sents the costs of maintaining the plant within which the variable input labor is put to work, is assumed to amount to $2,000 per day in the case shown. Adding fixed cost (Column 3) to variable cost gives short-run total cost, shown in Column 4. The three total cost curves — total variable, total fixed, and total cost — are shown graphically in Exhibit 22.6a. Because fixed cost by definition does not vary as output varies, the total fixed cost curve is a horizontal line at a distance equal to $2,000 above the horizontal axis. Adding fixed cost to variable cost gives total cost, so the total cost curve parallels the total variable cost curve at a level exactly $2,000 higher. The next entry in Exhibit 22.6c is again a familiar one — marginal cost. The marginal cost data given here are the same as those in Exhibit 22.4. They again appear on lines between the total cost entries to emphasize that marginal cost shows how total cost changes as the level of output changes.

(c)

Quantity of Output (units) (1)	Total Variable Cost (2)	Total Fixed Cost (3)	Total Cost (4)	Marginal Cost (dollars per unit) (5)	Average Variable Cost (dollars per unit) (6)	Average Fixed Cost (dollars per unit) (7)	Average Total Cost (dollars per unit) (8)
0	$ 0	$2,000	$ 2,000				
1	380	2,000	2,380	$380	$380	$2,000	$2,380
2	720	2,000	2,720	340	360	1,000	1,360
3	1,025	2,000	3,025	305	342	667	1,009
4	1,300	2,000	3,300	275	325	500	825
5	1,550	2,000	3,550	250	310	400	710
6	1,780	2,000	3,780	230	296	333	629
7	1,995	2,000	3,995	215	285	286	571
8	2,200	2,000	4,200	205	275	250	525
9	2,400	2,000	4,400	200	266	222	488
10	2,605	2,000	4,605	205	260	200	460
11	2,820	2,000	4,820	215	256	181	437
12	3,050	2,000	5,050	230	254	169	421
13	3,300	2,000	5,300	250	254	154	408
14	3,575	2,000	5,575	275	255	143	398
15	3,880	2,000	5,880	305	259	133	392
16	4,220	2,000	6,220	340	264	125	389
17	4,600	2,000	6,600	380	271	118	389
18	5,025	2,000	7,025	425	279	111	390
19	5,500	2,000	7,500	475	289	105	394
20	6,030	2,000	8,030	530	302	100	402
21	6,620	2,000	8,620	590	315	95	410
22	7,275	2,000	9,275	655	331	91	422
23	8,000	2,000	10,000	725	348	87	435
24	8,800	2,000	10,800	800	367	80	450

The marginal cost curve drawn in Exhibit 22.6b is the same as the one appearing in Exhibit 22.5.

The last three columns in Exhibit 22.6c are all average cost concepts: average variable cost, average fixed cost, and average total cost. Average variable cost is equal to total variable cost divided by the quantity of output; average fixed cost is equal to total fixed cost divided by output; and average total cost is equal to total cost divided by output. The three average cost curves are also drawn in Exhibit 22.6b.

Some Geometric Relationships

A careful examination of Exhibits 22.6a and 22.6b reveals some important geometric relationships among the various average, marginal, and total cost curves represented there. First compare the marginal cost curve with the total variable cost curve drawn directly above it. The bottom of the U-shaped marginal cost curve occurs at exactly the same level of output where the slope of the reverse S-shaped total variable cost curve stops getting flatter and starts getting steeper. This occurs because the slope of the total variable cost curve is the *rate* at which the total variable cost curve is rising, just as marginal cost measures the *rate* at which total variable cost is rising. In graphical terms, then, the *height* of the marginal cost curve is always equal to the *slope* of the total cost curve.

A second feature of the cost curves drawn in Exhibit 22.6 deserves special comment. The marginal cost curve intersects both the average variable cost and average total cost curves exactly at their lowest points. This is not just coincidence. It is a consequence of a relationship that can be called the **marginal average rule**. This rule can be explained as follows: beginning at any given point, ask what will be the cost of producing one more unit. The answer is given by marginal cost. Then ask whether this cost is more or less than the average cost of all units produced up to that point. If the added cost of the next unit produced is less than the average cost of previous units, then producing it will have the effect of pulling down the average. If the next unit costs more, its production will pull up the average. It follows that whenever marginal cost is below average variable cost, the average variable cost curve must be falling (that is, negatively sloped); and whenever marginal cost is above average variable cost, the average variable cost curve must be rising (that is, positively sloped). This in turn implies that the marginal cost curve cuts the average variable cost curve at its lowest point. All this is equally true of the relationship between marginal cost and average total cost.

Marginal average rule The rule that marginal cost must be equal to average cost when average cost is at its minimum.

LONG-RUN COSTS AND ECONOMIES OF SCALE

Short-Run and Long-Run Average Costs

Shifting perspective from the short run to the long run now, take another look at the costs of production for the Smith Tool Company. Remember the crucial distinction between the long run and the short run: in the long run, there are no fixed inputs. Not only can quantities of labor, raw materials, energy, and the like be varied, but, given time, the size of the firm's plant can be changed by building new structures, buying new capital equipment, and adding other fixed inputs as necessary.

It is sometimes said that firms operate in the short run and plan in the long run. This slogan reflects economists' distinction between variable and fixed costs: in the short run, one varies output within a plant of fixed size; and in the long run, one plans (and executes) expansions or contractions of the plant itself. Thinking of the long run as the firm's planning perspective and the short run as the firm's operating perspective makes it easier to understand the relationship between short-run and long-run average costs.

Planning for Expansion Put yourself in the position of an entrepreneur just setting out to establish a small firm such as the Smith Tool Company. You think it will be wise to start with just a small plant, but you want to do some long-range planning too. After consulting with production engineers and

Exhibit 22.7
Alternative short-run average total cost curves
The position of the short-run average total cost curve for a firm depends on the size of the plant it constructs. In the long run, the firm has a choice of operating with any size plant it chooses. Each plant size can be represented by a different U-shaped short-run average total cost curve. Five such curves are shown in this exhibit. A new firm might begin with a plant corresponding to a curve such as the first one shown here. Then, as demand for its product expanded, it might move to those farther to the right.

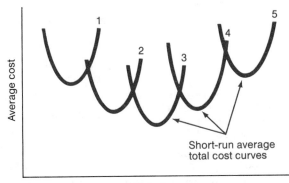

other specialists, you sketch some average cost curves for various possible sizes of plant. Five such curves are drawn in Exhibit 22.7. The first one shows short-run average costs for the range of output that is feasible with a very small plant, the second one corresponds to a slightly larger plant, and so on. As you build up the market for your product, you hope to be able to expand your plant and move from one of these curves to the next.

Of course, the five short-run cost curves in the exhibit represent only a sample of plant sizes. Intermediate positions are also possible. The size of plant you actually choose to build will depend, in the long run, on the quantity of output you expect to produce. For any given level of output, you will choose the size of plant that will permit that output to be produced at the lowest possible average total cost.

The Long-Run Average Cost Curve As your firm gradually expands, then, you can envision moving along a *long-run average cost curve* of the kind shown in Exhibit 22.8. This curve is the "envelope" of all possible short-run average cost curves. The size of plant chosen in the long run for each output will be the one that produces a short-run average total cost curve just tangent to the long-run average total cost curve at that point.

Exhibit 22.8
Derivation of a long-run average cost curve
A firm can build a plant of any size, and each possible plant size implies a different short-run total cost curve. Here are drawn a large number of possible short-run total cost curves, but even these curves are only a sample of all possible curves. As the firm expands, in the long run, it moves from one curve to another, always choosing the size of plant that minimizes the average total cost for the output the firm plans to produce at any particular time. The path along which a firm will expand — the firm's long-run average cost curve — is thus the "envelope" of all the possible short-run average total cost curves.

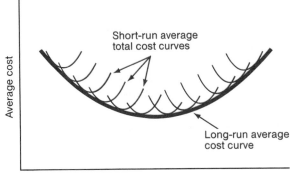

Economies of Scale

Economists have developed some special terminology to describe what happens to long-run average costs as output increases. In any range of output where long-run average cost *decreases* as output increases, the firm for which the cost curves are drawn is said to experience **economies of scale**. In any range of output where long-run average cost *increases*, the firm is said to experience **diseconomies of scale**. Finally, if there is any range of output for which long-run average cost does not change as output changes, the firm is said to experience **constant returns to scale** in that range.

The long-run average cost curve in Exhibit 22.8 is smoothly U-shaped, but that is not the only possible shape for such a curve. In fact, statistical studies suggest that L-shaped long-run average cost curves are the rule, at least in many manufacturing industries. Such a curve appears in Exhibit 22.9, which shows an initial range of economies of scale followed by a range of approximately constant returns to scale. The curve could turn out to be a flat-bottomed U if it were followed out far enough (as the broken extension of the curve in Exhibit 22.7 indicates). In any single industry, however, there may be no firms large enough to show diseconomies of scale. If there are none, that range of the curve remains invisible to statistical observation.

Statistical studies of long-run average cost often concentrate on measuring the level of output where economies of scale are exhausted and constant returns to scale begin. This level is called the **minimum efficient scale** for the firm. As shown in Exhibit 22.9, it corresponds to the point where the L-shaped long-run average cost curve stops falling and begins to level out. If the cost curve does not have a sharp kink at this point — and there is no reason to think it must have — the minimum efficient scale can be identified only approximately. This is not a major problem, however, since statistical studies of cost must deal in approximations in any event.

Where do economies of scale come from? Why is it ever true that a large firm can produce at a lower unit cost than a smaller firm? Economists who have investigated these questions have found that there is no single source of economies of scale for all industries. Rather, there are a number of different sources, some of which are important in certain industries and others in other industries.

Economies of scale
A phenomenon said to occur whenever long-run average cost decreases as output increases.

Diseconomies of scale
A phenomenon said to occur whenever long-run average cost increases as output increases.

Constant returns to scale
A phenomenon said to occur when there are neither economies nor diseconomies of scale.

Minimum efficient scale
The level of output at which economies of scale are exhausted.

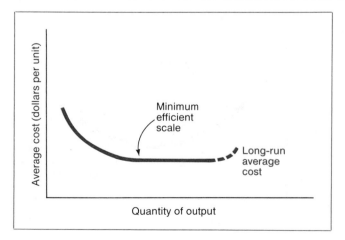

Exhibit 22.9

An L-shaped average cost curve showing minimum efficient scale

Statistical studies of long-run average cost suggest that long-run average cost curves are often L-shaped, as shown here. The point at which economies of scale are exhausted and the curve begins to flatten out is called the minimum efficient scale for the firm. Probably, if a firm continued to expand without limit, long-run average costs would eventually begin to rise. However, in many industries, there are no firms operating at a large enough scale to make the range of decreasing returns to scale visible to statistical observation. The upward-sloping portion of the curve is thus shown here as a broken line.

Economies of Scale at the Plant Level When most people think of econ-omies of scale, what probably comes to mind first is an automobile assem-bly plant or a large steel mill. Costs per unit tend to decrease with the rate of output per plant per day in such industries as automobiles and steel for a number of reasons. One is that a metal-forming machine or steel furnace capable of producing twice as much as another usually costs less than twice as much to build. Another is that larger plants can take advantage of more specialized division of labor. The automobile assembly line, on which each worker performs a single operation on each car as it moves by, is the classical example of this effect. Economies of scale associated with the rate of output per plant per day can be referred to as *plant-level* economies of scale. The following case study describes one attempt to measure plant-level economies of scale for a sample of sixteen industries.

Case 22.1
Measuring Plant-Level Economies of Scale

In 1967, two University of Toronto economists, H.C. Eastman and S. Stykolt, published the results of an ambitious study of economies of scale in sixteen major Canadian industries. These industries accounted for about 22 percent of value added by manufacturing industries in Canada. The study was based on a series of interviews with engineers and industrialists carried out in the years 1955 to 1960. The respondents were asked questions relating to the level of technology in the industry at that time. Information was obtained on the smallest size of a new plant at which costs of production were minimized (that is, the point at which the L-shaped long-run average cost curve for a typical plant in each industry stopped falling and began to level out).

Exhibit 22.10 gives some of the major findings of this study. The first column of the table shows the study's estimates of how many plants each industry would contain if each plant were the minimum efficient size. The second column shows how many plants actually existed in the industries in the years indicated. In twelve of the sixteen industries, the actual number of plants exceeded the number that the market would contain if each plant were the minimum efficient size. In other words, in most industries plant size was smaller than the minimum size required by efficiency. The implication of this for the efficiency of Canadian industry is revealed in Column 3. In eight of the sixteen industries, half of the output or less was produced by plants operating at efficient size.

It appears from this study that a large number of plants in Canada are of sub-optimal size. This contrasts with similar studies in the United States, in which most plants appear to be near or slightly larger than optimal size. The result is that, in Canada, costs of production in manufacturing usually exceed the lowest level technically achievable. The authors of the study conjecture that the relatively small market in Canada makes firms reluctant to enlarge capacity because increased output would tend to depress prices. Limiting output enables Canadian firms to keep their prices high. These high prices can be maintained in the marketplace because the prices of competing goods from foreign countries are made artificially high by tariffs. Indeed, the study revealed that Canadian firms took the price of foreign goods entering the Canadian market as the level to which they could raise their own.

Other Sources of Economies of Scale Not all economies of scale are associ-ated with increases in the rate of output of a single plant. Sometimes, for example, they have their origin in the total quantity of a product or model produced rather than in the rate at which it is produced. With a long production run, costs associated with product design, equipment set-up,

Exhibit 22.10

Minimum efficient scale for sixteen industries

This table presents the results of the study described in Case 22.1 The first column shows the number of plants that the existing Canadian market could contain if each plant were the smallest efficient size (that is assuming that each plant was operating at the point where the average cost curve stops falling and begins to level out). The second column shows the actual number of plants in each industry. The third column shows the percent of industry output produced by plants actually operating at the most efficient level.

Industry	Year of Study	Number of Plants of Smallest Efficient Size the Existing Canadian Market Could Contain	Actual Number of Plants	Percent of Output Produced by Plants at Most Efficient Size
Fruit canning	(1958)	4	13	0
Vegetable canning	(1958)	24	43	50
Cement	(1957)	17.8	18	80
Containerboard	(1960)	4.7	10	57
Shipping containers	(1958)	28	37	72
Synthetic solid detergents	(1959)	7	3	100
Synthetic liquid detergents	(1959)	49	?	75
Refrigerators	(1960)	0.6	10	0
Electric ranges	(1960)	0.9	23	0
Wringer washing machines	(1960)	8	14	58
Newsprint	(1958)	36	39	80
Beef packing	(1959)	42	47	68
Pork Packing	(1959)	16	45	9
Petroleum refining	(1956)	7	40	0
Primary steel	(1955)	4	4	0
Rubber tire	(1959)	7	9	20

Source: H.C. Eastman and S. Stykolt, *The Tariff and Competition in Canada* (Toronto: Macmillan 1967).

and specialized training can be spread over a large number of units. A comparison of General Motors with Volkswagen can serve to illustrate the difference between economies of scale associated with the rate of production and those associated with the volume of production. General Motors achieves important economies of scale through a high rate of production but changes models frequently. Volkswagen, by comparison, produces fewer cars per year but keeps each model in production longer. Its famous Beetle, for example, was produced with minor variations for more than four decades.

In addition to the rate and volume of production at a single plant, attention must be given to economies of multi-plant operation. The McDonald's hamburger chain provides a good example. The minimum efficient scale for a single plant (a single restaurant) is obviously very small in the fast-food industry. Nonetheless, McDonald's apparently realizes important economies by operating many restaurants as an integrated system. Some of the economies are production economies: individual food items and ingredients can be produced in efficient centralized kitchens, personnel can be trained at the famous "Hamburger University," and so on. A multi-plant firm such as McDonald's also realizes significant economies of scale with such functions as finance, advertising, and marketing.

CONCLUSIONS

This chapter has only scratched the surface of the theory of cost. Advanced books on the subject go into a wealth of extensions, additional details, mathematical formulations, and special cases. Nonetheless, the limited treatment given here will serve quite well as a basis for the analysis of individual firms and industries in the following chapters.

Chapter 23 will show how short-run and long-run cost curves can be used to derive supply curves for an industry in which there are a large number of competing firms. Chapter 24 will then use cost curves to analyze business behavior in markets where a single firm has a monopoly. Chapter 25 will examine agricultural markets. Then, Chapter 26 will turn to the case of markets dominated not by a single firm but by a relatively small number of firms. At that point, the discussion will return to the theme of economies of scale, which are an important factor in determining the number of firms that exist in the market for a given product. Chapters 27 and 28 will develop a variety of applications of cost theory to important questions of public policy.

SUMMARY

1. A firm's costs of production include all the sacrifices it must make in order to carry on production. Some of these sacrifices take the form of explicit payments to outsiders and are called explicit costs. Others are opportunity costs of using resources owned by the firm itself and are called implicit costs.

2. Economists use the term *profit* in a special sense: *pure economic profit* means the difference between a firm's revenues and its total costs, including both implicit and explicit costs. In everyday language, the term *profit* is instead often used to mean the difference between total revenue and explicit costs; economists refer to this difference as *accounting profit*.

3. The short run is a time period so short that not all of a firm's inputs can be varied in response to changes in output. According to the law of diminishing returns, in the short run, there must be some point beyond which the marginal physical product of a variable input diminishes. Short-run average and marginal cost curves for the typical firm are U-shaped. The marginal cost curve cuts the average variable cost and average total cost curves at their lowest points.

4. In the long run, a firm can adjust the quantities of all inputs in response to changes in output. A firm will choose the size of plant that will allow the expected long-run output to be produced at the minimum possible average cost. A long-run average cost curve can be constructed as the envelope of a set of short-run average total cost curves, one for each possible size of plant.

5. A firm is said to experience economies of scale over any range of output where its long-run average cost curve slopes downward. Over any range of output where the long-run average cost curve slopes upward, the firm experiences diseconomies of scale. If there are flat spots on the long-run average cost curve, the firm is said to experience constant returns to scale there.

DISCUSSION QUESTIONS

1. Consider the costs of owning and operating an automobile. Which of the costs are implicit, and which are explicit? Are there any economy-wide opportunity costs of operating an automobile that do not show up at all in your tally of private costs?

2. Now divide the costs of owning and operating an automobile into fixed costs and variable costs. Suppose you were deciding whether to drive to a neighboring college to a football game or to take the bus instead. Would you take both fixed and variable costs into account? Suppose you were deciding whether to buy a house in a neighborhood where you could walk to work or a house located where you would have to buy a second car to drive to work every day. Would you then take both fixed and variable costs of the car into account?

3. What are the economies of scale and diseconomies of scale involved in running a university? Give specific examples.

4. Do you see any parallel between the law of diminishing returns and the principle of diminishing marginal utility? Do you think that both could be lumped together in a "law of diminishing marginal everything"? Try stating such a general law.

5. Take a piece of graph paper and draw, freehand, a typical reverse S short-run total cost curve. Then, as accurately as you can, construct the corresponding average total cost, average variable cost, average fixed cost, and marginal cost curves. When you have mastered these curves, try something harder. Draw some non-typical short-run total cost curves—curves with, say, funny kinks or bends or perhaps bumps like those on a roller coaster. They will not make much economic sense, but trying to draw the average and marginal cost curves for them will be an excellent test of whether you can really understand a graph like the one in Exhibit 22.6. If you cannot do this exercise successfully, you may need to review the Appendix to Chapter 1.

6. Turn to Exhibit 22.8. Copy this diagram onto a sheet of graph paper, drawing the long-run average cost curve and just one of the short-run average total cost curves. Use the curves you have drawn to construct the corresponding long-run and short-run cost curves. The total cost curves you get should both be reverse S-shaped and should be tangent to one another at the same level of output at which the average cost curves are tangent.

7. Suppose you had investigated the relationship between quantities of coal burned per week in a power plant of a given size and the output of electricity per week at that plant and had found the following: for tiny quantities of coal, not enough even to heat up the boiler, no electricity could be produced. After a critical minimum of coal was burned, the added electricity per added ton of coal burned was constant over a considerable range. Then, abruptly, a capacity limit was reached beyond which putting more coal in would produce no added electricity at all. Sketch the marginal and total physical product of coal curves for the plant. Do they conform to the law of diminishing returns?

8. It has been said that if it were not for the law of diminishing returns, all the food that the world needs could be grown in a flowerpot. Discuss. (Hint: think of land as the only fixed factor and fertilizer as the only variable factor. How much food could be grown in the flowerpot if the marginal physical product of fertilizer were constant regardless of the quantity of fertilizer applied per unit of land?)

C H A P T E R 23
SUPPLY UNDER PERFECT COMPETITION

WHAT YOU WILL LEARN IN THIS CHAPTER

The theory of cost developed in Chapter 22 provides a foundation for a theory of the supply curve. That theory will be developed in this chapter, using the concept of a perfectly competitive market. The chapter will first explain how a typical firm adjusts its quantity supplied to short-run changes in market prices. Next, it will show how a short-run supply curve for the market as a whole can be built up from the supply curves of separate firms. Then it will develop the relationship between short-run and long-run adjustments for both the firm and the market. Finally, it will briefly discuss what is perfect about perfect competition.

FOR REVIEW

Here are some important terms and concepts that will be put to use in this chapter. If you do not understand them, review them before proceeding.
- *Supply and demand (Chapters 3 and 18)*
- *Elasticity of supply (Chapter 18)*
- *Pure economizing (Chapter 19)*
- *Theory of cost (Chapter 22)*

The last two chapters have examined the nature of the firm and the cost structure of a typical firm. The discussion has supplied the background needed to develop a theory of what lies behind the supply curves so frequently drawn in earlier chapters. This chapter will begin with the simplest case — one in which the firm's supply decision is limited solely to determining how much to produce. Chapter 24 will extend the analysis to markets in which firms must also decide what price to put on their products as well as how much to produce.

THE STRUCTURE OF PERFECT COMPETITION

The nature of the decisions a firm must make depends in large part on the structure of the market in which it operates. **Market structure** in this sense means such characteristics as the number of firms that operate in each industry, the extent to which the products of different firms are varied, and the ease or difficulty firms have in getting into and out of the market.

There are many possible market structures. This chapter will be occu-

Market structure Important characteristics of a market, including the number of firms that operate in it, the extent to which the products of different firms are diverse or homogeneous, and the ease of entry into and exit from the market.

Perfect competition A market structure characterized by a large number of relatively small firms, a homogeneous product, good distribution of information among all market participants, and freedom of entry and exit.

pied with one known as perfect competition. As a market structure, **perfect competition** has four defining characteristics:

1. There are many sellers and buyers, each of which sells or buys only a small fraction of all that is bought and sold in the market.
2. The product traded in the market is entirely homogeneous; that is, the product sold by one firm is just like that sold by any other.
3. All participants in the market, buyers and sellers alike, are well-informed about prices, sources of supply, and so on.
4. Entry into and exit from the market are very easy.

The Perfectly Competitive Firm as Price Taker

Price taker A firm that sells its outputs at fixed prices that are determined entirely by forces outside its own control.

These four characteristics of perfect competition, taken together, ensure that all firms in the market will be **price takers**—firms that sell their outputs at fixed prices determined entirely by forces outside their own control. If a firm makes, say, steel nails, and steel nails sell for $1.50 a pound, that is that. The firm makes all its decisions and all its plans as if nothing it can do will change the $1.50 price tag.

It is easy to understand why firms operating in a perfectly competitive market are price takers. Because each producer contributes only a small fraction of the total output, its individual supply decisions will have no significant effect on the total quantity supplied in the market—and thus no significant effect on the market price as determined by supply and demand. Because the product is homogeneous, buyers are just as happy to buy from one firm as another. Thus a firm that raised its price even a fraction above what its competitors were charging would quickly lose all its customers. And because all buyers and sellers are well-informed, no one would, out of ignorance, be willing to pay or be able to get a price higher than the prevailing one.[1]

Under perfect competition, then, the decisions facing individual firms are very simple. The firm does not have to decide at what price to sell because price is completely beyond its control. It does not have to worry about product design or marketing decisions because, by definition, the product is the same for all firms and never changes. The only decision the firm needs to make is about quantity—how much to produce.

Perfect Competition: The Ideal and the Reality

Perfect competition, as defined here, is an abstraction or ideal. Economists study it because it is a theoretically interesting benchmark, useful in judging the performance of real-world industries. No industry exactly fits all the conditions of perfect competition. Agriculture is often considered to be a very competitive industry, because there are thousands of independent producers of very standardized products. However, as Chapter 25 will show, farmers have reduced the competitive element through the creation of marketing boards. Before going on, it is important to take note of a

---

[1] The fourth feature of perfect competition—easy entry and exit—is not strictly necessary, in the short run, to make firms price takers. But, as will be explained later in the chapter, it has considerable importance for how competitive markets work in the long run.

paradox associated with perfect competition. The paradox is that perfect competition, as defined, is in many respects the exact opposite of competition as many people think of it in everyday business life.

When we think of business competition, we ordinarily think of rivalry and struggle. We think of Ford and General Motors battling for shares of the market. We think of advertising people talking up one product and putting down another. We think of Kodak working in secrecy to build an instant camera as good as Polaroid's.

Perfect competition, though, is none of these things. In a perfectly competitive market, there is no reason to battle for market shares because there is plenty of room for each small firm to sell as much as it wants at the going price. There is no advertising in such a market, because buyers are already well-informed, and goods are perfectly homogeneous — not only in fact but in the eyes of their consumers as well. There is no need for secrecy about techniques or innovations, because all technological knowledge is widespread and there are no innovations. The market environment is still competitive in the sense that any firms that fail to make their cost and supply decisions as accurately as their rivals may be forced out of the market. Firms are not sheltered from that kind of competition by any special privileges. Nonetheless, many more colorful or personalized aspects of competition are absent. Much more will be said about the relationship of "perfect" competition to real-world competition in the next few chapters.

SHORT-RUN SUPPLY UNDER PERFECT COMPETITION

Short-Run Profit Maximization for a Typical Firm

Now that the concept of perfect competition has been introduced, it is time to turn to the main subject of the chapter — what lies behind the supply curve in a perfectly competitive market. The investigation will begin at the level of the individual firm, using the Smith Tool Company as a typical example. The discussion will assume throughout that this firm and all others in the market make their production decisions with the object of earning maximum economic profits for the firms' owners, given prevailing prices of inputs and outputs and the production technology available. If prevailing market conditions make it impossible to earn positive economic profits, the firms will try to minimize losses.

A simple numerical example will show how a perfectly competitive firm adjusts the quantity of output it supplies to maximize profits. Exhibit 23.1a shows short-run cost data for Smith Tool Company (as first given in Chapter 22). It also shows the revenue earned by Smith Tool from the sale of each quantity of output, assuming a constant price of $500 per unit. The price per unit does not vary as output per day varies because it is assumed, for the sake of discussion, that the drill press produced by Smith Tool is essentially the same as that produced by a large number of other companies in this perfectly competitive market. The company is thus a price taker.

Subtracting total cost in Column 3 from total revenue in Column 2 gives the total profit the firm earns at each level of output. The maximum is reached at nineteen units per day, where a profit of $2,000 per day is earned.

Nineteen units per day is thus the quantity the firm will choose to supply at the price of $500 per unit, assuming that it wants to earn the maximum profit.

This profit maximizing quantity of output is also identified graphically in Exhibit 23.1b. In that diagram, the firm's total profit is indicated by the vertical distance between the total revenue and total cost curves. As shown, that distance is greatest at nineteen units of output.

A Marginal Approach As an alternative to comparing total cost and total revenue, a marginal approach can be used to determine the profit maximiz-

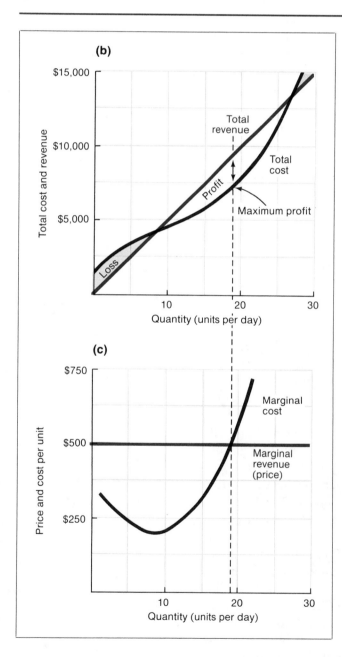

Exhibit 23.1
Short-run profit maximization under perfect competition — Smith Tool Company

This exhibit shows the profit maximizing quantity of output chosen by a perfectly competitive firm — Smith Tool Company. The output can be found by comparing total cost and total revenue in Columns 2 and 3 of Part a. This approach is shown graphically in Part b, where total profit appears as the gap between the total revenue and total cost curves. Alternatively, the profit maximizing output can be found by comparing marginal cost and marginal revenue in Columns 5 and 6 of Part a. Profit increases up to the point where marginal cost begins to exceed marginal revenue and declines thereafter. Part c of the exhibit gives a graphical representation of the marginal approach. Whatever approach is used, the profit maximizing output is seen to be nineteen units per day, and the maximum profit per day is seen to be $2,000.

(a)

Quantity of Output (1)	Total Revenue (2)	Total Cost (3)	Total Profit (2)–(3) (4)	Marginal Cost (5)	Marginal Revenue (6)
1	$ 500	$ 2,380	$ –$1,880		
2	1,000	2,720	–1,720	340	500
3	1,500	3,025	–1,525	305	500
4	2,000	3,300	–1,300	275	500
5	2,500	3,550	–1,000	250	500
6	3,000	3,780	–780	230	500
7	3,500	3,995	–495	215	500
8	4,000	4,200	–200	205	500
9	4,500	4,400	100	200	500
10	5,000	4,605	395	205	500
11	5,500	4,820	680	215	500
12	6,000	5,050	950	230	500
13	6,500	5,300	1,200	250	500
14	7,000	5,575	1,425	275	500
15	7,500	5,880	1,620	305	500
16	8,000	6,220	1,780	340	500
17	8,500	6,600	1,900	380	500
18	9,000	7,025	1,975	425	500
19	9,500	7,500	2,000	475	500
20	10,000	8,030	1,970	530	500
21	10,500	8,620	1,880	590	500
22	11,000	9,275	1,725	655	500
23	11,500	10,000	1,500	725	500
24	12,000	10,800	1,200	800	500

ing level of output for the competitive firm. Turn first to Columns 5 and 6 of Exhibit 23.1a. Column 5 gives data on marginal cost. As in Chapter 22, these data are printed on lines between the entries in the first four columns to indicate that marginal cost is the change in cost as output moves from one level to another. Column 6 presents a new concept—marginal revenue. **Marginal revenue** is the amount by which total revenue increases when output increases one unit. For a firm that is a price taker, as this one is, marginal revenue is equal to the price of the product. Each extra unit of output sold by the Smith Tool Company thus adds $500 to total revenue.

As Exhibit 23.1 is constructed, every unit increase in output adds to both total cost and total revenue. If the increase in revenue exceeds the increase in cost (that is, if marginal revenue is greater than marginal cost), increasing output by one unit increases total profit. If the increase in cost exceeds the increase in revenue (that is, if marginal cost is greater than marginal revenue), increasing output by one unit reduces profit. It follows that in order to maximize profit, a competitive firm should expand output so long as marginal revenue exceeds marginal cost. It should stop as soon as marginal cost begins to exceed marginal revenue. A comparison of Columns 5 and 6 of Exhibit 23.1 shows that for Smith Tool Company, this means producing nineteen units of output per day—the same number arrived at through a comparison of total cost and total revenue.

The marginal approach to short-run profit maximization is represented graphically in Exhibit 23.1c. Up to nineteen units of output, the marginal cost curve lies below the marginal revenue curve, so that each added unit of output increases profit. Beyond nineteen units, the marginal cost curve is above the marginal revenue curve, so that each added unit of output reduces profit. Note that the point of profit maximization, where the marginal cost and marginal revenue curves intersect, corresponds exactly to the point in Part b where the spread between total revenue and total cost is greatest.

Minimizing Short-Run Losses In the example just given, Smith Tool Company was able to make a comfortable profit at the prevailing market price of $500 per unit. But market conditions need not always be so favorable. Suppose, for example, the market price were to drop to $300. The firm, being a price taker, could do nothing about the price and would simply have to adjust its quantity of output as best it could to meet the new situation. The necessary adjustments can be determined from the table and diagrams of Exhibit 23.2. The table shows that there is no level of output at which the firm can earn a profit. *Unable to earn a profit, the firm must turn its attention to minimizing losses.* With a price of $300 per unit, the minimum loss occurs at fourteen units of output. As in the previous case, this is the level of output beyond which marginal cost begins to exceed the price of the product.

The two diagrams in Exhibit 23.2 give additional insight into the loss minimizing supply decision under the given market conditions. Exhibit 23.2b shows clearly why the firm cannot earn a profit: the total cost curve is everywhere higher than the total revenue curve. Nonetheless, total revenues come closest to meeting total costs at fourteen units of output.

Exhibit 23.2c is perhaps the most helpful of all for understanding why it

Marginal revenue The amount by which total revenue increases as the result of a one-unit increase in quantity.

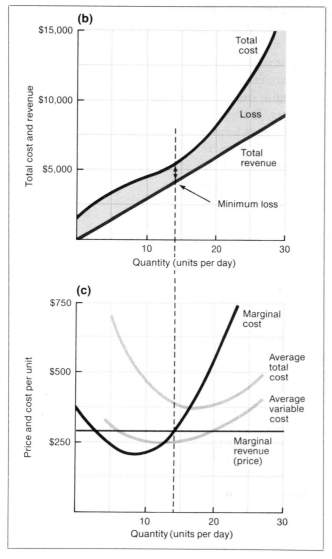

Exhibit 23.2
Short-run loss minimization under perfect competition — Smith Tool Company

If the product price is too low for the firm to earn a profit, the firm must turn its attention to minimizing losses. The same techniques illustrated in Exhibit 23.1 can be used to find the loss minimizing level of output, which is fourteen units of output for a price of $300 per unit, as shown here. Part c of this exhibit shows that the marginal revenue curve intersects the marginal cost curve at a point higher than average variable cost but lower than the average total cost. Each unit of output sold earns more than its share of average variable cost but not enough to pay its share of average total cost (including its share of average fixed cost).

(a)

Quantity of Output (1)	Total Revenue (2)	Total Cost (3)	Total Profit or Loss (4)	Average Total Cost (5)	Average Variable Cost (6)	Marginal Cost (7)	Marginal Revenue (8)
0	$ 0	$2,000	−$2,000	—	—	$380	$300
1	300	2,380	−2,080	$2,380	$380	340	300
2	600	2,720	−2,120	1,360	360	305	300
3	900	3,025	−2,125	1,009	342	275	300
4	1,200	3,300	−2,100	825	325	250	300
5	1,500	3,550	−2,050	710	310	230	300
6	1,800	3,780	−1,980	629	296	215	300
7	2,100	3,995	−1,895	571	285	205	300
8	2,400	4,200	−1,800	525	275	200	300
9	2,700	4,400	−1,700	488	266	205	300
10	3,000	4,605	−1,605	460	260	215	300
11	3,300	4,820	−1,520	437	256	230	300
12	3,600	5,050	−1,450	421	254	250	300
13	3,900	5,300	−1,400	408	254	275	300
14	4,200	5,575	−1,375	398	255	305	300
15	4,500	5,880	−1,380	392	259	340	300
16	4,800	6,220	−1,420	389	264	380	300
17	5,100	6,600	−1,500	389	271		300

is worthwhile for the firm to produce fourteen units of output even though it loses money by doing so. In addition to the marginal cost and marginal revenue curves, it shows average variable cost and average total cost curves. Notice that the point where marginal cost is equal to price lies between the two average cost curves. The vertical distance between the average variable cost and average total cost curves is equal to average fixed costs. Thus, at fourteen units of output, the price of $300 is more than enough to cover each unit's share of variable costs but not quite enough to cover each unit's share of fixed costs.

Without referring to technical terminology, it is easy to see that the firm's loss minimizing decision corresponds to simple common sense. Assume that the only variable input for Smith Tool Company is labor, and substitute the term *payroll* for the term *variable cost*. Similarly, assume that the firm's only fixed input is its factory building, and substitute *mortgage payment* for *fixed cost*. Clearly, with a price of $300, the firm is better off producing fourteen units of output than no units of output, because each unit more than pays for its share of the payroll and makes at least some contribution toward paying the mortgage.

Shutting Down to Minimize Short-Run Losses What would happen if the price dropped even lower? Would it always be worthwhile for the firm to keep grinding out drill presses even though it was losing money? The answer, as shown in Exhibit 23.3, is no.

Exhibit 23.3 is based on an assumed price of $225 per unit. The table in Part a shows that there is no way for the firm to make a profit with the price so low. Any supply decision will produce a loss. But this time, the loss can be minimized at a zero level of output. The best thing for the firm to do in the short run is to shut down. If things get better and the price rises again, the firm can restart production. If things never do get better, then, in the long run, the firm will have to wind up its affairs and go out of business altogether.

Notice that in this case it can be misleading to look only at the marginal revenue and marginal cost columns of the table. After seven units of output, marginal cost drops below the price of $225 and stays below until an output of eleven units is reached. *If* the firm were to stay in production, eleven units of output would give it a lower loss than any slightly greater or smaller level of output. But in this case the firm takes a still smaller loss by not producing at all.

As in the previous examples, the graphs tell the same story as the table. Exhibit 23.3b shows once again that the total revenue curve never reaches the total cost curve. It comes fairly close at eleven units of output but not as close as it comes at zero output.

Exhibit 23.3c shows that marginal cost and price are equal at eleven units of output. However, even at eleven units, the price does not cover average variable cost. Losses are minimized by shutting down. Once again, it may help to put the problem in payroll and mortgage terms. If the firm produced eleven drill presses per day and could sell them for only $225 apiece, it would not earn enough even to meet its payroll. Better to send the workers home, suffer a loss equal to the mortgage payment, and hope for things to get better.

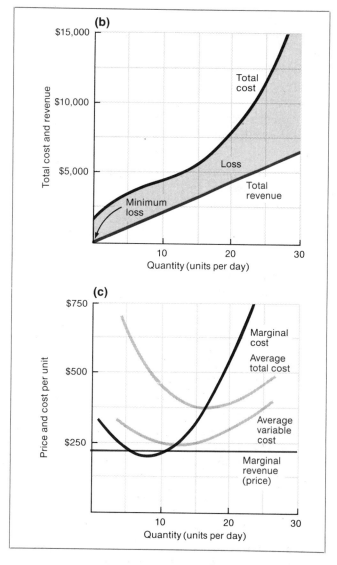

Exhibit 23.3

Shutting down Smith Tool Company to minimize short-run losses

Sometimes the price of a firm's output may drop so low that the firm must shut down altogether to minimize short-run losses. That possibility is illustrated here at the price of $225 per unit. Notice that eleven units of output yield a smaller loss ($2,345 per day) than any slightly greater or smaller output. However, the loss can be reduced to just $2,000 per day if the firm shuts down. Notice also that in Part c of the exhibit, the marginal cost curve intersects the marginal revenue curve at a point below minimum average variable cost. That is the signal to shut down.

(a)

Quantity of Output (1)	Total Revenue (2)	Total Cost (3)	Total Profit or Loss (4)	Average Total Cost (5)	Average Variable Cost (6)	Marginal Cost (7)	Marginal Revenue (8)
0	$ 0	$2,000	−$2,000	—	—		
1	225	2,380	−2,155	$2,380	$380	$380	$225
2	450	2,720	−2,270	1,360	360	340	225
3	675	3,025	−2,350	1,009	342	305	225
4	900	3,300	−2,400	825	325	275	225
5	1,125	3,550	−2,425	710	310	250	225
6	1,350	3,780	−2,430	629	296	230	225
7	1,575	3,995	−2,420	571	285	215	225
8	1,800	4,200	−2,400	525	275	205	225
9	2,025	4,400	−2,375	488	266	200	225
10	2,250	4,605	−2,355	460	260	205	225
11	2,475	4,820	−2,345	437	256	215	225
12	2,700	5,050	−2,350	421	254	230	225
13	2,925	5,300	−2,375	408	254	250	225
14	3,150	5,575	−2,425	398	255	275	225
15	3,375	5,880	−2,505	392	259	305	225
16	3,600	6,220	−2,620	389	264	340	225
17	3,825	6,600	−2,775	389	271	380	225

Exhibit 23.4
Derivation of the short-run supply curve for Smith Tool Company
This diagram traces Smith Tool Company's short-run supply curve. When the price is $500, the firm will produce at Point E_1. As the price falls, the firm moves down along its short-run marginal cost curve, as shown by Points E_2 and E_3. The firm will continue to produce where price equals marginal cost, until marginal cost falls below average variable cost. At that price, the firm will do just as well to shut down — that is, to produce at Point E_4.

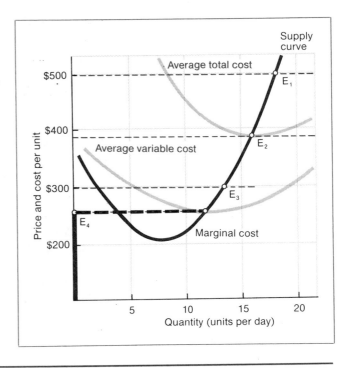

The Firm's Short-Run Supply Curve

The preceding examples supply everything needed to construct a short-run supply curve for the profit maximizing firm in a perfectly competitive market. Exhibit 23.4 shows how this curve is constructed.

Work through this exhibit beginning with a price of $500. As before, Smith Tool Company would choose to produce nineteen units of output at this price. Point E_1 of the firm's short-run marginal cost curve must therefore be a point on the firm's supply curve.

Suppose now that the market price of the firm's product begins to fall as a result of forces beyond its control. As it does, the point where price equals marginal cost moves down along the firm's marginal cost curve. Soon Point E_2 is reached — the point where marginal cost and average total cost are equal. This occurs at an output of approximately seventeen units and a price of approximately $385. At this price, the best the firm can do is break even. Either a greater or a smaller output would result in a loss.

If the price falls still lower, the firm's problem becomes one of minimizing loss rather than maximizing profit. At a price of $300, for example, the firm minimizes losses by producing fourteen units, at Point E_3. In the range of prices lying between minimum average total cost and minimum average variable cost, the supply curve continues to follow the marginal cost curve.

Below a price of about $254, a change occurs. As before, when price is lower than the lowest point on the average variable cost curve, the firm minimizes losses by shutting down, rather than continuing to produce up to the point where marginal cost begins to exceed price. For a price of $254, then, Point E_4 on the vertical axis is the preferred point of operation. This point must then be a point on the firm's short-run supply curve. As the diagram shows, for this and all lower prices, the supply curve coincides with the vertical axis.

All that has been learned so far about the firm's short-run supply decision can now be stated in the form of an important generalization: *the short-run supply curve for a profit maximizing firm operating in a perfectly competitive market coincides with the upward-sloping part of the marginal cost curve lying above its intersection with the average variable cost curve.*

The Short-Run Industry Supply Curve

The supply curve for a whole industry can now be constructed on the basis of the supply curves of the individual firms. As a first approximation, an industry supply curve can be obtained by the horizontal addition of individual firms' supply curves, as shown in Exhibit 23.5. It is necessary to make one qualification, though. The assumption has been that any individual firm can expand output without any change in input prices; but if all firms in an industry expand simultaneously, input prices will rise unless the supply curve of the input is perfectly elastic. If input prices rise as industry output expands, the short-run industry supply curve will be somewhat steeper than the sum of the individual supply curves.

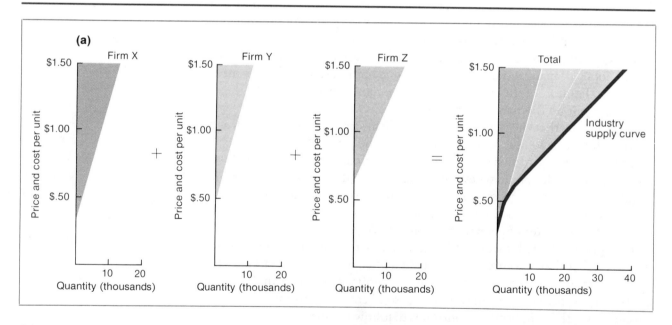

(b)

Price	Quantity Supplied			
	Firm X	Firm Y	Firm Z	Total
$ .40	1,500			1,500
$ .80	5,500	3,000	3,333	11,833
$1.20	9,500	7,000	10,000	26,500
$1.50	12,500	10,000	15,000	37,500

Exhibit 23.5

Approximate derivation of short-run industry supply curve

An approximation to the short-run industry supply curve can be obtained by horizontal summation of individual firms' supply curves. Here the method of summation is shown for an industry with just three firms. If the prices of inputs vary as industry output varies, it will be necessary to make an adjustment in the industry supply curve.

LONG-RUN EQUILIBRIUM UNDER PERFECT COMPETITION

Entry and Exit

For the individual firm, the long run is distinguished from the short run by the fact that all, not just some, inputs can be varied. In the long run, firms can go out of business entirely. (Sometimes firms go peaceably, with the owners selling off the assets and banking what is left. Other times they go with a crash, leaving their creditors to collect perhaps only pennies on the dollar for the mortgages, bonds, and other debts they hold.) Also in the long run, new firms can come into a market, building new plants and buying new equipment, which then become their short-run fixed inputs. As firms enter and exit, whole industries expand and contract.

One of the defining characteristics of perfect competition is that there must be no barriers to this free flow of firms into and out of the industry. This characteristic played no direct role in the discussion of a firm's short-run supply decision, but free entry and exit are crucial to explaining how a competitive market works in the long run.

Equilibrium

Equilibrium, as explained here in many different contexts, is a state of affairs in which economic decision makers have no incentive to change their current patterns of behavior. In a perfectly competitive industry, short-run equilibrium means that each firm must have no incentive either to increase or to decrease its quantity of output. That requires the firm to adjust its output to the point where marginal cost is equal to the price of the product. (Keep in mind that a perfectly competitive firm is a price taker, so price and marginal revenue are always equal.) In the long run, equilibrium in a perfectly competitive industry requires two other things as well. One is that each firm have no incentive to change the size of plant it uses to produce its current output, and the other is that firms have no incentive either to enter or to leave the industry.

Exhibit 23.6 shows graphically how all these requirements are satisfied simultaneously in long-run equilibrium for a perfectly competitive firm. First, marginal cost is equal to price at the equilibrium quantity of output. This equality ensures that there is no incentive in the short run either to increase or to decrease output.

Second, the firm is operating with a plant of just the size necessary to make short-run average total cost equal to the minimum possible long-run average cost at the equilibrium quantity of output. No change in the quantity of fixed inputs employed can reduce average cost, so the firm has no long-run incentive to change its plant size.[2]

Third, average total cost (both long-run and short-run) is equal to price at the equilibrium quantity of output. As always, average total cost includes an allowance for a normal rate of return on capital—no more, no less. Thus, when average total cost is equal to price, there is no incentive for

---

[2] The reader may wish to review Exhibits 22.7 and 22.8, which show the relationship between short-run and long-run average cost curves for various plant sizes.

firms either to enter the industry (to seek pure economic profit in excess of the normal rate of return on capital) or to leave the industry (in order to avoid pure economic loss — that is, a rate of return on capital less than the normal rate).

The long-run equilibrium conditions shown graphically in Exhibit 23.6 can also be expressed in the form of the following equation:

$$\text{Price} = \frac{\text{Marginal}}{\text{cost}} = \begin{array}{c}\text{Short-run}\\ \text{average}\\ \text{total cost}\end{array} = \begin{array}{c}\text{Long-run}\\ \text{average}\\ \text{cost.}\end{array}$$

If any part of this equation does not hold, there will be an incentive for firms to change the quantity of output they are producing within their current plants, to change the size of the plants they are using to produce their current output, or to enter or leave the industry. That is, unless all parts of the equation hold, the market cannot be in long-run equilibrium.

Industry Adjustment to Falling Demand

A particular position of long-run equilibrium, such as the one shown in Exhibit 23.6, can continue undisturbed only so long as outside conditions remain unchanged. Exhibit 23.7, for example, shows how a perfectly competitive industry reacts to a long-run decrease in the demand for its product.

The exhibit consists of two parts. Part a shows a set of cost curves, much like those shown in Exhibit 23.6, for a typical individual firm in the industry. Part b is a simple supply and demand diagram representing the market in which the typical firm sells its output. The curves drawn there are short-run industry supply curves built up from the short-run supply curves of all the individual firms in the market (see Exhibit 23.5). The

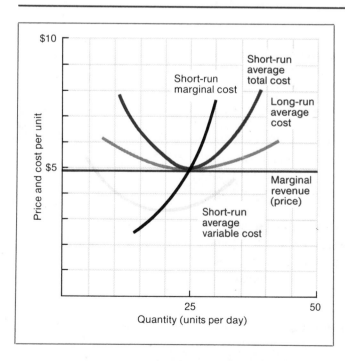

Exhibit 23.6
The typical perfectly competitive firm in long-run equilibrium
Long-run equilibrium in a perfectly competitive industry requires that the typical firm (1) have no short-run incentive to change the quantity of output currently produced, (2) have no long-run incentive to change the size of plant used to produce its current output, and (3) have no long-run incentive to enter or leave the industry. This requires that price, short-run marginal cost, short-run average total cost, and long-run average cost all have the same value in equilibrium, as shown.

demand curves are short-run market demand curves of the usual kind.

Suppose that, initially, short-run supply curve S_1 and short-run demand curve D_1 applied. That would produce a market equilibrium price of $5. The individual firm would take this price as given and adjust its output accordingly, producing twenty-five units of output, as shown. At this price and output, it would be just breaking even. Remember, though, that breaking even in the economic sense means earning enough to cover all costs including the implicit cost of a normal rate of return on the owner's invested capital.

Suppose now that something happens — say, a change in consumer tastes or incomes — that shifts the demand curve to the new position, D_2. The short-run result of this demand shift will be a drop in the market price to $4 per unit. The individual firm, being a price taker, will consider this decline in price as something beyond its control and will adjust to it as best it can. As shown in Part a of the exhibit, this means cutting back output a little to minimize loss but not shutting down completely. The movement of each individual firm back down along its marginal cost curve is what produces the movement of the market as a whole down and to the left along short-run supply curve S_1.

But the situation that the market is now in cannot prevail in the long run. The reason is that the typical firm and its fellows are operating at a loss. They are not giving their owners the normal rate of return they need to make an investment in this industry worthwhile. If the demand curve does not show any hope of shifting back to the right, some owners will become

---

Exhibit 23.7

Long-run adjustment to a decline in demand

In this exhibit, Part a represents a single typical firm and Part b the entire industry. Initially, both the firm and the industry are in long-run equilibrium at a price of $5. Then something happens to shift the demand curve leftward from D_1 to D_2. In the short run, the price falls to $4, at the intersection of D_2 and S_1. The firm's short-run reaction is to retreat down along its marginal cost curve. Eventually, some firms (not the one shown) get tired of taking losses and exit from the industry. Their exit causes the supply curve to shift toward S_2 and the market price to recover. The typical firm returns to breakeven operation. The market has traced out part of its long-run supply curve, as shown by the large arrow.

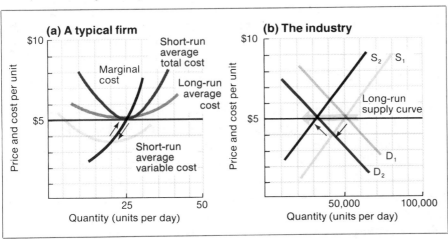

discouraged and will pull their capital out of the industry. Perhaps their firms will actually go bankrupt, or perhaps they will sell off their plant and equipment and get out while the going is good. Perhaps they will keep their firms intact but set to work to produce other goods for other, more profitable, markets. The particular form of exit does not much matter.

There is no real way to tell which firms will be the first to go; but for convenience, assume that the typical firm shown in the exhibit is not one of the first. Look what happens to it now as some of the others leave. As some firms withdraw, the market loses their contribution to the total supply. The market supply curve, now added together from fewer individual supply curves, shifts to the left toward S_2. As it does so, the market price begins to rise up along demand curve D_2. When the price gets all the way back up to $5, the firms still left in the industry will no longer be losing money. The exodus from the industry will stop, and the market will have reached a new long-run equilibrium. In the new equilibrium, price, marginal cost, short-run average total cost, and long-run average cost will once again be equal.

The entire sequence of events has traced out a portion of this industry's *long-run* supply curve, as shown by the arrow. A long-run supply curve for an industry shows the path along which equilibrium price and quantity move in response to persistent changes in demand, given time for individual firms to adjust the sizes of their plants, if necessary, and given time for entry and exit to occur. The long-run supply curve shown in Exhibit 23.7 is perfectly elastic, at least in the region shown. In the long run, the leftward shift of the demand curve causes no change in price, only a decrease in the quantity supplied.

Industry Adjustment to Rising Demand

Freedom of entry plays the same role in the long-run adjustment of a perfectly competitive market to rising demand as freedom of exit plays in the adjustment to falling demand. This is illustrated in Exhibit 23.8.

The starting position in this exhibit is exactly the same as in Exhibit 23.7. Short-run supply curve S_1 and demand curve D_1 give an equilibrium price of $5. The individual firm just breaks even producing twenty-five units of output at this price. Now follow what happens as the demand curve shifts, this time to position D_2, to the right of D_1.

The short-run result of the shift in the demand curve is an increase in the market price to $6. The typical firm adjusts to this new price by moving up along its marginal cost curve to a somewhat higher level of output. As all firms do this, the market moves up and to the right along short-run supply curve S_1.

But again, this short-run adjustment does not result in a state of affairs that can last in the long run. For now, all the firms are making profits in excess of the minimum needed to attract capital to the industry. Entrepreneurs elsewhere in the economy will soon spot this healthy, expanding market as a prime investment opportunity. Some of them may start brand new firms to produce for this market. Others may shift plants and equipment previously used to produce something else to making goods for this industry. It does not matter whether the entry is by brand new firms or by

Exhibit 23.8
Long-run adjustment to an increase in demand

In this exhibit, both the firm and the industry are again initially in equilibrium at a price of $5. Then something happens to shift the demand curve rightward to D₂. In the short run, the price rises to $6, at the intersection of D₂ and S₁. The firm's short-run reaction is to move up along its marginal cost curve, earning better than normal profits. These high profits eventually attract new firms into the industry. As new firms enter, the supply curve shifts toward S₂. Profits for the typical firm return to normal, and entry activity ceases. Again, the market has traced out part of its long-run supply curve, as shown by the large arrow.

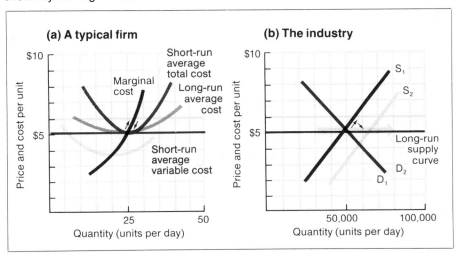

firms already existing in other industries that devote part of their capital to this particular market for the first time. In either case, new entry will cause the supply curve to shift to the right, toward S_2.

As the supply curve shifts, the price falls. It does not fall far enough to drive the new entrants back out again, but it does fall enough to drive everyone's profits back to the normal level. Entry will stop, and the market will be in a new long-run equilibrium at the intersection of S_2 and D_2.

Once again, a portion of the long-run supply curve for the industry has been traced out, as shown by the large arrow. And once again, this long-run supply curve is horizontal in the region investigated. A rightward shift in the demand curve has, in the long run, produced an increase in quantity supplied but no increase in price.

Other Long-Run Supply Curves

In the examples just given, the industry long-run supply curve was a horizontal straight line, at least in the region examined. That is not the only possible shape such a supply curve can take, however. Exhibit 23.9 shows some other possibilities — upward-sloping, downward-sloping, and U-shaped.

Which shape the long-run industry supply curve takes depends primarily on what happens to the industry's input prices in the long run as output expands. If the long-run supply curve for all inputs is perfectly elastic, the price of those inputs will not change as the quantity of them demanded by the industry increases. Or perhaps the industry will use such a small part of the total supply of each unspecialized input that whatever change in input price does occur will be negligibly small. Industry output can thus expand without affecting the underlying costs of the individual firms. Thus the long-run supply curve of the industry using the outputs will be perfectly horizontal (that is, perfectly elastic) too. This is the case in Exhibits 23.7 and 23.8. Exhibit 23.9a shows a succession of short-run supply and demand curves lying along such a horizontal long-run supply curve. Each pair of short-run curves represents one stage in the industry's long-run expansion.

Suppose, though, that the industry uses some specialized input, the supply of which cannot easily be increased. Perhaps some special skilled labor is needed, and more workers can be induced to acquire the skill only by bidding up the wage rate. The rising price of this important input will cause an upward shift in the cost curves of all the firms in the industry as new firms enter the industry and output expands. In this case, the industry long-run supply curve will slope upward, as in Exhibit 23.9b.

It is also possible that the price of some important input can decrease as output of the industry expands. For example, as sales of electronic equipment expand, the firms making the components that go into that equipment may be able to adopt cheaper methods of production. If this occurs, the cost curves for all firms will drift downward as new firms enter the

Exhibit 23.9

Possible long-run supply curves for a competitive industry

The shape of an industry's long-run supply curve depends largely on what happens to the prices of the industry's inputs as demand and output expand in the long run. If input prices do not change significantly, the long-run supply curve willl be horizontal, as in Part a of this exhibit. If input prices rise, the long-run supply curve will slope upward, as in Part b. Falling input prices will produce a downward sloping long-run industry supply curve, as in Part c. Finally, mixed cases, where the long-run supply curve first falls and then rises are possible, as in Part d.

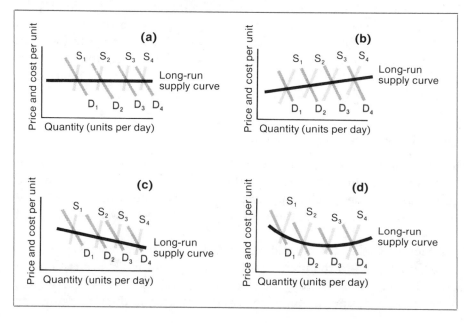

industry. The long-run supply curve will then be downward-sloping, as in Exhibit 23.9c.

Finally, it is possible that a combination of forces can be at work. In the industry shown in Exhibit 23.9d, long-run supply is at first influenced by the falling price of one specialized input; but beyond a point, some other specialized input becomes a bottleneck that causes the long-run supply curve to bend upward. Many variants are possible. Only actual observation of particular industries can determine which possibility applies.

WHAT IS PERFECT ABOUT PERFECT COMPETITION?

The discussion of perfect competition is now very nearly complete. We have a fairly good picture of how perfectly competitive markets work. But there is one remaining question that deserves more attention than it has yet been given: what is so perfect about perfect competition?

As suggested early in the chapter, the answer is not that such a market is the perfect place to observe all forms of business rivalry. Far from it. Many familiar forms of rivalry are completely absent from perfectly competitive markets. Under perfect competition, business managers go blandly about their pure economizing without caring a whit what any particular other firm in the industry does. After all, those other firms cannot, by definition, be big enough to have any individual impact on market prices. They cannot, by definition, be getting ready to introduce a new, distinctive version of the industry's product. And they cannot, by definition, have any secrets. So it is not in any of these senses that perfectly competitive markets are perfect.

They are instead perfect in another sense. Think, for a moment, about just what a market really is. Very simply, it is a mechanism for getting buyers and sellers together to carry out mutually beneficial transactions. It would seem to make sense, then, to say that *a perfect market is one in which all potential mutually beneficial transactions are in fact carried out—a market in which none is missed*. That is exactly the sense in which perfectly competitive markets are perfect.

To see why, look at Exhibit 23.10. This is a quite ordinary supply and demand diagram (long-run variety) just like many shown before. But now look at it in a slightly different way.

Start with the demand curve. Usually, one thinks of a demand curve as showing the quantity that consumers are willing and able to buy at any given market price. But the demand curve can also be thought of as showing the maximum amount consumers are willing to pay for a marginal unit of the good, given the quantity already available. This particular demand curve, for example, has a height of $12 at 100 units of output. That means someone is willing to pay barely $12 for the marginal 100th unit and someone is willing to pay almost, but not quite, that much for the 101st.

The supply curve can be interpreted in much the same way. Usually, one thinks of it as showing how much producers are willing to supply at a given price. But it also shows the minimum amount necessary to induce producers to supply the marginal unit. The supply curve in this exhibit, for example, has a height of $6 at an output of 100 units. That means someone is barely willing to supply the 100th unit for $6 and that no one will supply a 101st unit unless offered just a little bit more.

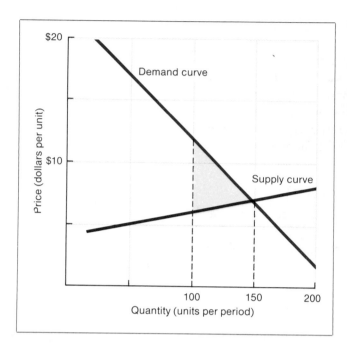

Exhibit 23.10
Why perfectly competitive markets are perfect
Think of the demand curve in this diagram as showing how much consumers would be willing to pay for additional units of output and the supply curve as showing how much producers would have to be offered to supply them. If production were limited to a rate of 100 units per period, mutually beneficial opportunities for exchange would be passed up. Consumers would be willing to pay nearly $12 for the 101st unit, while producers would have to be given barely more than $6 to produce it. Not all such worthwhile trades would take place until output were raised to 150 units. The shaded area provides a rough measure of the opportunities for mutual benefit that would be wasted if production were limited to 100 units. But a competitive market would carry output all the way to 150 units.

Now, suppose that for some reason, producers in fact are supplying goods to this market at a rate of only 100 units per period. At that level of output, the demand curve is above the supply curve. Some consumer out there is willing to pay nearly $12 for the 101st unit. And some producer is willing to supply it for anything just over $6. If production stops at 100 units, then, buyers and sellers will be passing up an opportunity for a mutually beneficial transaction. The market will not be perfect.

The same will be true, to a slightly lesser degree, if output stops at 101, 110, or 149 units. Even the production and sale of the 150th unit represents a mutually beneficial exchange, although only barely so. It can be said, then, that the whole shaded area in the diagram gives a measure of the accumulated potential for mutual benefit that will be wasted if production stops short at 100 units.

Now we can see the sense in which perfectly competitive markets, when they are in equilibrium, are perfect. In such markets, production is carried out up to, but not beyond, the point where the long-run supply and demand curves intersect. All possible mutually beneficial transactions between consumers and producers are thus carried out. And, as shown in the previous section, each firm in long-run perfectly competitive equilibrium produces at the minimum possible average total cost. That means no further gains are possible on the production side, at least within the limits of current technology. With no improvements possible through changes in either the quantity of output traded or the way that output is produced, the market does as well as it can in satisfying the needs of consumers. In that sense, it is a perfect market.

CONCLUSIONS

It would be tempting to draw broad generalizations from the preceding section. Would not an economy in which all markets displayed all the structural characteristics of perfect competition be a perfect one in every economic respect? There is a sense in which this proposition is true, but its truth is hedged with a number of qualifications.

One very important qualification is that technology does not cooperate. Economies of scale make it altogether impractical in many industries to scatter production among a large number of very small firms.

A second qualification is the refusal of consumers to be indifferent between the products of different firms. Consumers demand variety, not homogeneity, from the firms they patronize. To enforce homogeneity in the name of perfect competition would be to pass up many mutually beneficial opportunities for firms to cater to the differing individual tastes of consumers.

A third qualification is inherent in the whole concept of perfect competition. General propositions about the efficiency of perfect competition place little weight on the entrepreneurial element in business life. The theories set forth in this chapter say little about how efficiently resources are allocated in a world where change occurs, where knowledge is not perfectly distributed, and where markets are not always in equilibrium. Do markets with large numbers of small firms guarantee efficient entrepreneurial decision making in a world of change and uncertainty? Are such markets most productive of new and better ways to satisfy human wants? The theory of perfect competition says nothing one way or the other in answer to these questions. Later chapters will return to them.

When all is said and done, perfect competition is one of the great abstractions of economics. As such, it produces many valuable insights. It makes it possible to think more clearly about what lies behind the law of supply and demand. It makes it easier to understand the element of pure economizing in business decision making—an important part of the real world of business but not all of it. It provides some insights into economic efficiency that, if not overgeneralized, can be of real use in comparing alternative economic policies. And, finally, for some kinds of markets, it is not so very far from the mark in a descriptive sense.

SUMMARY

1. A firm is a price taker if it can do nothing to affect the prices of the outputs it sells. The characteristics of perfect competition are sufficient to make firms behave as price takers. Firms are too small to influence output prices by varying their own quantities supplied. The fact that consumers are indifferent between the products of different individual firms makes it impossible for those firms to raise their prices above the prevailing level without losing all their customers. The "other things being equal" assumption applies in a particularly strong way to the price taking, perfectly competitive firm, which makes all its managerial calculations as if whatever it did would not affect in any way what others did.

2. Perfect competition, as the technical name of a particular market structure, must be carefully distinguished from real-world business competition. Many common types of business rivalry among entrepreneurs are absent in perfect competition.

3. For the typical firm with U-shaped short-run cost curves, the short-run supply curve is that upward-sloping portion of the short-run marginal cost curve that lies above the average variable cost curve. If price falls below average variable cost in the short run, the firm minimizes its losses by temporarily shutting down. The short-run industry supply curve is approximated by the summation of the supply curves of individual firms. An adjustment must be made, though, for any change in input prices that may occur when all firms in the industry expand or contract simultaneously.

4. In long-run equilibrium, product price, short-run marginal cost, long-run average cost, and short-run average total cost must all be equal for the competitive firm. If price rises above long-run average cost, new firms will be attracted to the industry, driving the price back down. If price is below long-run average cost, some firms will leave the industry, allowing the price to rise again. In the long run, variations in industry output take place primarily through the entry or exit of firms rather than through changes in the quantity produced by each individual firm.

5. Competitive markets are perfect in the sense that when they are in equilibrium, they leave no unrealized opportunities for mutually beneficial transactions between producers and consumers. One must, however, be cautious about generalizing from the perfection of particular markets, in this sense, to broad propositions about the economy as a whole.

DISCUSSION QUESTIONS

1. Instead of saying that a perfectly competitive firm is a price taker, it is sometimes said that such a firm faces a perfectly elastic demand curve. Why are these two ways of putting the matter equivalent?
2. The concept of being a price taker can apply to consumers as well as producers. A price taking consumer is one who cannot influence the price paid for a product by changing the quantity purchased. For which of the goods and services that you buy are you a price taker? Are there any goods or services you buy for which you are not a price taker?
3. If the government imposes a price ceiling on some product, does that make the firms that sell the product price takers, regardless of whether their industry fits the market structure of perfect competition? Explain.
4. Make a list of half a dozen products that you purchase frequently. Do you buy any of these things from firms that are perfect competitors? If the firms you buy from are not perfect competitors, do they compete, in some other sense, with rivals for your business?
5. Explain the role that the free entry and exit assumption plays in determining the nature of long-run equilibrium in a competitive industry.
6. Here is a definition of efficiency that economists often use: an economy is said to be operating efficiently if and only if there is no possible change that will make at least one person better off and no person worse off. Can you show that perfectly competitive markets are efficient in this sense?

THE THEORY OF MONOPOLY

WHAT YOU WILL LEARN IN THIS CHAPTER

This chapter is devoted to the analysis of pure monopoly, a market structure in which the entire quantity sold is supplied by a single firm. It will show that under pure monopoly a firm can potentially earn pure economic profits, even in long-run equilibrium. At the same time, it will show that pure monopoly is a less efficient market structure than perfect competition. In addition to the theory of pure monopoly, the chapter will discuss the closely related problems of price discrimination and cartels.

FOR REVIEW

Here are some important terms and concepts that will be put to use in this chapter. If you do not understand them, review them before proceeding.

- *Price elasticity of demand (Chapter 18)*
- *Pure economizing (Chapter 19)*
- *Pure economic profit (Chapter 22)*
- *Normal rate of return on capital (Chapter 22)*
- *Perfect competition (Chapter 23)*
- *Marginal revenue (Chapter 23)*

Perfect competition, with its very large number of very small firms, is one polar extreme of market structure. The other extreme is **pure monopoly**—the name given to a market structure in which one firm supplies 100 percent of industry sales.

As the sole supplier to its market, the pure monopolist is assumed not only to have no current competitors but also to be protected against the potential competition of new entrants into the market. Various kinds of barriers to entry can protect a pure monopolist from potential competition. In some cases, the barriers are technological, as when the nature of the product makes it inefficient for more than one firm to serve a market. Local utilities—such as the electric power, gas, water, and telephone companies—are the classic examples, in that it is likely to be wasteful for competing firms to provide duplicate lines or mains to any one neighborhood. Monopolies protected by technological barriers to entry are called **natural monopolies**. Monopolies based on the ownership of a unique natural resource can also be considered natural monopolies.

Pure monopoly A market structure in which one firm accounts for 100 percent of industry sales.

Natural monopoly A monopoly protected from competition by technological barriers to entry or by ownership of unique natural resources.

Franchised monopoly A monopoly protected from competition by a government grant of monopoly privilege, such as an exclusive license, permit, or patent.

Other monopolies are created or perpetuated by government grants of monopoly privilege that make it illegal for new firms to enter even when it is technologically feasible for them to do so. Monopolies protected by law against the entry of new competitors are called **franchised monopolies**. The Canadian Post Office is the classic example of a franchised monopoly. The law permits private carriers to compete with the Post Office in the transportation of parcels, but competition in first class mail has been prohibited. Monopolies based on patented inventions or processes can also be considered franchised monopolies.

The barriers to entry protecting natural and franchised monopolies from competition have their origin in technological or legal factors not directly created by the monopolistic firm itself. In addition, it may sometimes be possible for a firm or a group of firms acting in concert to erect other, artificial barriers to the entry of new competitors. This possibility will be discussed in Chapter 26, which examines certain market structures that are intermediate between perfect competition and pure monopoly.

Having defined pure monopoly, the chapter will turn now to an analysis of how a pure monopolist decides what quantity to supply to the market it dominates. As in the case of perfect competition, it will look first at the short run and then at the long run.

PROFIT MAXIMIZATION FOR THE PURE MONOPOLIST

The Monopolist Is Not a Price Taker

The short-run profit maximization decision for a pure monopolist, like that for a perfectly competitive firm, is a problem in pure economizing. With market demand conditions, the technology of the production process, and the prices of inputs given, the problem is to determine the quantity of output to supply in order to earn the maximum profit or minimum loss.

The supply decision for the pure monopolist, however, does differ from that of the perfectly competitive firm in one major respect: the pure monopolist is not a price taker. The perfectly competitive firm is assumed to be so small in relationship to its market that its individual supply decision has no noticeable impact on the market price. Not so for a monopolist. The pure monopolist, as the sole supplier to the market, must take into account the fact that the market demand curve has a negative slope. As the monopolist increases output, it must reduce the price at which it offers its product for sale in keeping with the law of demand.

Output and Revenue Consider Exhibit 24.1a, for example. Columns 1 and 2 give market demand for a typical pure monopolist. Exhibit 24.1b presents the same demand graphically. This demand curve provides the relationship between the quantity of output that the monopolist chooses to supply and the price at which that quantity can be sold. The greater the output, the lower the maximum price the monopolist can charge without leaving an excess supply unclaimed by any buyer.

The information contained in the demand curve can be used to determine what happens to the firm's revenue as its output changes. For any output, total revenue is equal to price times quantity. Column 3 of Part a

Exhibit 24.1
Demand, total revenue, and marginal revenue for a pure monopolist

This exhibit shows the relationships among demand, total revenue, and marginal revenue for a typical monopolist. Total revenue is found by multiplying price times quantity at each point on the demand curve. Marginal revenue is the increase in total revenue resulting from a one-unit increase in output. Part b of this exhibit shows the demand curve and marginal revenue curve in graphical form. Note that for a straight-line demand curve, the marginal revenue curve lies halfway between the demand curve and the vertical axis and that it cuts the horizontal axis at the point where price elasticity of demand is equal to zero. This point corresponds to the point of maximum total revenue, as shown in Part c.

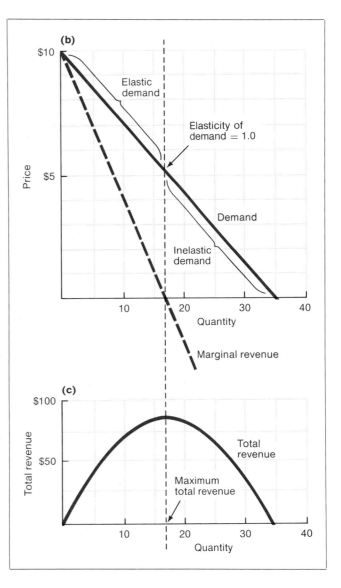

(a)

Quantity (1)	Price (2)	Total Revenue (3)	Marginal Revenue (4)
1	$10.00	$10.00	$9.40
2	9.70	19.40	8.80
3	9.40	28.20	8.20
4	9.10	36.40	7.60
5	8.80	44.00	7.00
6	8.50	51.00	6.40
7	8.20	57.40	5.80
8	7.90	63.20	5.20
9	7.60	68.40	4.60
10	7.30	73.00	4.00
11	7.00	77.00	3.40
12	6.70	80.40	2.80
13	6.40	83.20	2.20
14	6.10	85.40	1.60
15	5.80	87.00	1.00
16	5.50	88.00	.40
17	5.20	88.40	−.20
18	4.90	88.20	−.80
19	4.60	87.40	−1.40
20	4.30	86.00	−2.00
21	4.00	84.00	−2.60
22	3.70	81.40	−3.20
23	3.40	78.20	−3.80
24	3.10	74.40	−4.40
25	2.80	70.00	−5.00
26	2.50	65.00	−5.60
27	2.20	59.40	−6.20
28	1.90	53.20	−6.80
29	1.60	46.40	−7.40
30	1.30	39.00	−8.00
31	1.00	31.00	−8.60
32	.70	22.40	−9.20
33	.40	13.20	−9.80
34	.10	3.40	−3.40
35	.00	.00	

and the graph in Part c of the exhibit show that as output increases, total revenue first rises, then reaches a maximum at about seventeen units of output, and then falls. Notice the similarity between this exhibit, and

Exhibit 18.6, which appeared as part of the discussion of price elasticity of demand. There it was demonstrated that when demand is *elastic*, a decrease in price causes total revenue to increase. (The reason is that in percentage terms, the quantity sold increases by more than the price decreases, so the product of the two increases.) In contrast, when demand is *inelastic*, revenue falls when the price goes down. (That is because, with inelastic demand, the percentage increase in quantity is less than the percentage decrease in price.) With a straight-line demand curve like that of Exhibit 24.1b, the upper half is elastic and the lower half inelastic. That accounts for the shape of the "revenue hill" in Part c of this exhibit.

Marginal Revenue The relationship between output and revenue for the pure monopolist can also be viewed in marginal terms. Chapter 23 defined *marginal revenue* as the change in total revenue resulting from a one-unit increase in a firm's output. Column 4 of Exhibit 24.1a gives data on marginal revenue for the firm in this example. Notice that the figures in this column are simply the differences between successive entries in Column 3. Part b of the exhibit shows a graph of marginal revenue. Notice that the marginal revenue curve is above the horizontal axis when total revenue is increasing (elastic demand) and below the axis when total revenue is decreasing (inelastic demand). It intersects the horizontal axis just at the point of maximum total revenue.[1]

Profit Maximization

The relationship between output and revenue for the pure monopolist forms the basis for an analysis of short-run profit maximization. Profit maximization for a pure monopolist can be demonstrated by means of a numerical example similar to that used for the case of perfect competition.

Exhibit 24.2 incorporates the demand and revenue data for a typical pure monopolist from Exhibit 24.1 and gives total and marginal cost data for the same firm. One way to determine the profit maximizing quantity of output for the firm is to compare total cost and total revenue, as given in Part a of the exhibit. Subtracting total cost in Column 6 from total revenue in Column 2 gives total profit in Column 7. A glance down Column 7 shows the profit maximizing level of output to be thirteen units. The total-revenue, total-cost approach to profit maximization is shown graphically in Exhibit 24.2b. Total profit appears in that exhibit as the vertical gap between the total cost and total revenue curves; it reaches a maximum at thirteen units of output, where the two curves are the maximum distance apart.

Note that maximizing profit is not the same thing as maximizing revenue. Between thirteen and seventeen units of output, total revenue continues to rise; but total cost rises even faster, so profit declines.

---

[1] Here is an easy rule that will help in sketching the marginal revenue curve corresponding to any straight-line demand curve: *the marginal revenue curve for a straight-line demand curve always cuts the horizontal distance from the demand curve to the vertical axis exactly in half*. This rule does not work for curved demand curves, but the examples in this book will be kept simple.

Exhibit 24.2
Profit maximization for a pure monopolist

This exhibit demonstrates that a pure monopolist maximizes profits by producing that quantity of output for which marginal cost is equal to marginal revenue. Notice that maximizing profit is not the same as maximizing revenue. As this example is constructed, the profit maximizing output is thirteen units. In the range from thirteen to seventeen units of output, total revenue continues to increase. But because total cost increases even faster in this range, profits decline. Notice also that the profit maximizing price for the monopolist is determined by the height of the demand curve (not the marginal cost or marginal revenue curve) at the profit maximizing quantity of output.

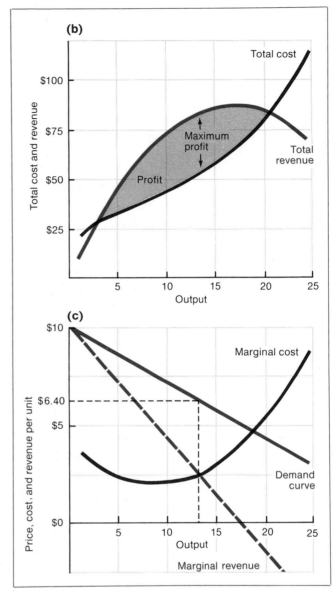

(a)

Output (1)	Price (2)	Total Revenue (3)	Marginal Revenue (4)	Marginal Cost (5)	Total Cost (6)	Total Profit (7)
1	$10.00	$10.00			$23.80	−$13.80
			$9.40	$3.40		
2	9.70	19.40			27.20	−7.80
			8.80	3.05		
3	9.40	28.20			30.25	−2.05
			8.20	2.75		
4	9.10	36.40			33.00	3.40
			7.60	2.50		
5	8.80	44.00			35.50	8.50
			7.00	2.30		
6	8.50	51.00			37.80	13.20
			6.40	2.15		
7	8.20	57.40			39.95	17.45
			5.80	2.05		
8	7.90	63.20			42.00	21.20
			5.20	2.00		
9	7.60	68.40			44.00	24.40
			4.60	2.05		
10	7.30	73.00			46.05	26.95
			4.00	2.15		
11	7.00	77.00			48.20	28.80
			3.40	2.30		
12	6.70	80.40			50.50	29.90
			2.80	2.50		
13	6.40	83.20			53.00	30.20
			2.20	2.75		
14	6.10	85.40			55.75	29.65
			1.60	3.05		
15	5.80	87.00			58.80	28.20
			1.00	3.40		
16	5.50	88.00			62.20	25.80
			.40	3.80		
17	5.20	88.40			66.00	22.40

The Marginal Approach Alternatively, the profit maximizing level of output for the pure monopolist can be found by comparing marginal cost and marginal revenue, as shown in Columns 4 and 5 of Exhibit 24.2a. Marginal revenue is the amount by which total revenue increases as the result of a one-unit increase in output, and marginal cost is the amount by which total cost increases. It follows that so long as marginal revenue exceeds marginal cost, adding one more unit of output will add more to total revenue than to total cost and will hence add to total profit. Beyond thirteen units cf output, marginal revenue falls below marginal cost, so further expansion of output reduces total profit.

Exhibit 24.2c makes the comparision between marginal revenue and marginal cost graphically. The profit maximizing quantity is found where the marginal cost and marginal revenue curves intersect. It corresponds to the point of maximum profit, shown in Exhibit 24.2b as the point where the gap between the total revenue and total cost curves is greatest.

The intersection of the marginal cost and marginal revenue curves in Exhibit 24.2c gives the profit maximizing quantity of output for the pure monopolist; the corresponding profit maximizing price is given by the height of the demand curve for this quantity. For the pure monopolist, this price is always above marginal cost. Marginal cost at thirteen units of output for the firm in the example is $2.50 per unit, but according to the demand curve, consumers would be willing to buy thirteen units of output for as much as $6.40. The price of $6.40 is thus what the monopolist will charge for the thirteen units of output in order to earn the maximum profit.

Profit Maximization or Loss Minimization?

Just as for a perfectly competitive firm, profit maximization for a monopolist can sometimes mean loss minimization, at least in the short run. Whether there are actual profits to be made or only losses to be minimized depends on the position of the demand curve relative to the monopolist's average cost curves.

One possibility is illustrated in Exhibit 24.3. Here, demand is high enough relative to average cost for the monopolist to make a pure economic profit, above and beyond the normal rate of return on capital that is built into the definition of average total cost. As in Exhibit 24.2, the profit maximizing quantity, at the intersection of the marginal cost and marginal revenue curves, is roughly thirteen units of output. The demand curve indicates that the profit maximizing price for that quantity of output is approximately $6.40 per unit.

At thirteen units of output, average total cost is only $4 per unit. That means the monopolist earns a pure economic profit of $2.40 per unit above and beyond all costs, including the implicit cost of a normal rate of return on invested capital. At thirteen units of output, total profit is $31.20. This is shown graphically in Exhibit 24.3 as the shaded rectangle. The base of the rectangle is equal to the quantity of output (thirteen units). Its height is equal to the difference between the price of $6.40 per unit and the average total cost of $4 per unit — that is, to the $2.40 average profit the firm earns.

Under less favorable demand conditions, however, the same firm may be able to do no better than to minimize losses. This possibility is illustrated

Exhibit 24.3

A pure monopolist earning positive profits

The profit actually earned by a pure monopolist depends on the relationship of price to average total cost. In this example, the monopolist's demand curve is high enough to enable a pure economic profit to be earned. Total profit is shown in the diagram as the shaded rectangle with a height equal to the difference between price and average total cost and a width equal to the profit maximizing quantity of output.

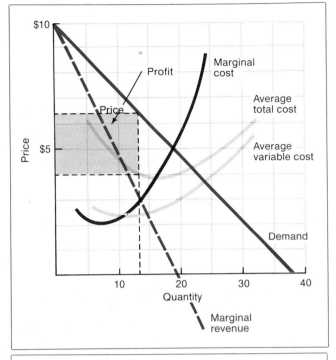

Exhibit 24.4

Short-run loss minimization for a pure monopolist

Sometimes demand may not be sufficient to permit a pure monopolist to earn a pure economic profit. As this exhibit is drawn, for example, the demand curve lies below the average total cost curve at all points. The best the monopolist can do, in the short run, is to minimize losses by producing at the point where marginal cost equals marginal revenue. If the demand curve were to shift downward even farther, so that the firm could not obtain a price covering average variable cost, the short-run loss minimizing strategy would be to shut down.

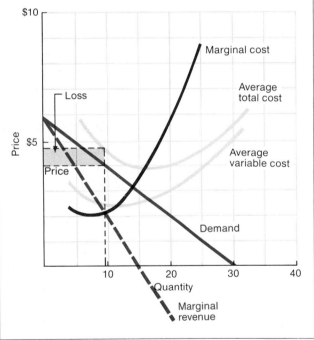

in Exhibit 24.4. The demand curve in the diagram lies below the average cost curve at all points. This can happen, for example, during a severe recession, when consumer incomes are abnormally low. Following the usual rule, the profit maximizing quantity of output is found to be about ten units, as Exhibit 24.4 is drawn. According to the demand curve, that much output can be sold for $4 per unit, but average total cost at ten units of output is $4.75. At a price of $4 per unit, the monopolist will lose $.75 on each unit sold. This total loss is shown in the exhibit by the shaded rectangle.

Although the monopolist suffers a loss at ten units of output, no other choice of output will yield a smaller loss. As Exhibit 24.4 is drawn, $4 per unit is more than enough to cover average variable costs. The monopolist, like the perfectly competitive firm, is better off staying in production in the short run, even at a loss, so long as the price at which the output can be sold is greater than the average variable cost. If the demand curve shifts so far to the left that it falls below the average variable cost curve at all points, the pure monopolist, like the perfectly competive firm, will minimize short-run losses by shutting down. In the long run, if demand conditions do not improve, the firm will go out of business.

Long-Run Profit Maximization under Pure Monopoly

One of the most important conclusions reached in Chapter 23 was that, in the long run, pure economic profits are impossible under perfect competition. The reason is that if an increase in demand for the product raises the market price above average total cost, new firms will be attracted into the industry. As the new firms enter, the total quantity supplied to the market increases, driving the market price back to the level of average total cost.

Under pure monopoly, in contrast, pure economic profits can continue indefinitely if demand conditions are favorable. The reason is that a monopolist is assumed to be protected against competition by barriers to entry. Even if short-run demand conditions permit a higher than normal rate of return on capital, as in Exhibit 24.3, no other firm can enter the market. If nothing happens to disturb the favorable position of its cost and demand curves, a pure monopolist can earn pure economic profits above and beyond the normal rate of return even in the long run.

Indirect Competition and Long-Run Profits

Although protection from direct competition makes it possible in some cases for pure monopolists to earn pure economic profits in the long run, there are other cases in which long-run profits are eroded by indirect competition. In one limiting case, a monopolist faced with indirect competition might find itself in the position pictured in Exhibit 24.5. In that exhibit, the demand curve just touched the average total cost curve at the quantity of output for which marginal revenue equals marginal cost, so that the best the firm can do is break even. It earns sufficient revenue to cover all its costs, including a normal rate of return on capital, but nothing more.

Two kinds of indirect competition in particular might push a monopolist toward this long-run breakeven position. One is competition in the process of establishing a monopoly in the first place. A firm may have to bid competitively for a key patent or for access to key natural resources in order to establish its monopoly. Perhaps it will have to hire expensive lawyers and consultants to convince a government agency that it, and not some other firm, should get a key license or permit. If entrepreneurs compete vigorously to establish a monopoly, it may very well turn out that the winner never does better than break even. Its initial efforts, although successful, may cost so much that it ends up in the position shown in Exhibit 24.5.

Exhibit 24.5
The breakeven position for a pure monopolist
Being a pure monopolist in a market may make it possible to earn a pure economic profit in the long run, but it does not guarantee that positive profits will be earned. This exhibit shows a monopoly that is only breaking even (that is, earning only a normal rate of return on invested capital). Among other possibilities, this could be the result of high costs of obtaining or defending the firm's monopoly position or of erosion of demand through indirect competition from substitute products.

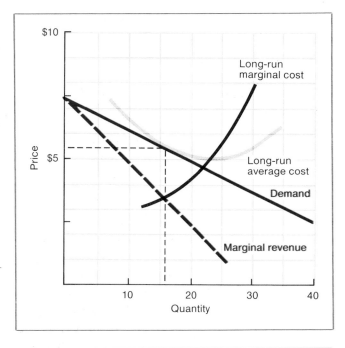

Competition from substitute products can also force a monopolist to the breakeven position. A firm with a monopoly of steel production, for example, may find that, over time, clever entrepreneurs in the aluminum or plastics industries are stealing away more and more of its customers. The competition of substitutes may gradually erode demand for the monopolist's own product until, in the limiting case, the demand curve falls all the way to tangency with the average cost curve.

The likelihood of actually reaching the limiting position of zero profits depends on the closeness of the substitutes offered by the other firms. For example, a firm whose monopoly consists in owning the only Italian restaurant in town will clearly feel more competitive pressure than will a firm owning the only restaurant of any kind. In fact, when a firm's "monopoly" is so narrowly based that many competing firms offer products that are very close substitutes, economists no longer classify the firm as a pure monopolist. Instead, they call a market structure in which a large number of firms offer products that are relatively close substitutes for one another **monopolistic competition**. Chapters 26 and 27 will have more to say about monopolistic competition and about other forms of competition lying between pure monopoly and perfect competition.

Monopolistic competition
A market structure in which a large number of firms offer products that are relatively close substitutes for one another.

MONOPOLY, CONSUMER WELFARE, AND PRICE DISCRIMINATION

Pure Monopoly as an Imperfect Market Structure

Chapter 23 showed that production is carried out in a perfectly competitive market up to the point where price is equal to marginal cost. This, it was argued, makes perfect competition a "perfect" market form in the sense that all potential mutually beneficial transactions are carried out. Beyond the point of competitive equilibrium, consumer welfare cannot be further improved without imposing an actual loss on producers.

Under pure monopoly, in contrast, production stops short of the quantity necessary to bring market price down to the level of marginal cost. Consider Exhibit 24.6, for example. There, the monopolist maximizes profit by producing 2,000 units of output per month and selling each unit for $3. At a rate of output of 2,000 units per month, marginal cost is only $1 per unit. There is a $2 gap between marginal cost and the market price. This gap represents a market imperfection; it indicates that some potential mutually beneficial transactions are not being carried out.

One way to understand the nature of this market imperfection is to think of the monopolist as a middleman standing between the consumer and resource owners. The height of the demand curve at 2,000 units of output in Exhibit 24.6 represents what consumers are willing to pay for the 2,000th unit of output. The height of the marginal cost curve at this point represents what the firm has to pay resource owners for the various inputs necessary to produce the 2,000th unit. Clearly, production of the 2,000th unit is worthwhile; consumers value it at $3, and resource owners value the resources used up in producing it at only $1.

Reasoning in the same way, it would also be worthwhile to produce a 2,001st unit of output. Consumers would value the 2,001st unit at only slightly less than $3, and resource owners would be willing to release the necessary inputs for only a little more than $1. If it were feasible for consumers to negotiate directly with resource owners for production of the 2,001st unit, it would presumably be produced at a mutually agreeable price, such as $2. In this case, however, consumers do not deal with resource owners directly. They deal instead through the monopolist as an intermediary, and it is not worthwhile for the monopolist to produce a 2,001st unit of output. Even though the 2,001st unit could be sold at a price higher than its marginal cost, the marginal revenue earned by the monopolist from the transaction would be less than marginal cost. And it is not profitable for the monopolist to increase output beyond the point where marginal revenue falls below marginal cost.

What is true of the 2,001st unit is also true of the 2,002nd, the 2,003rd, and all units up to and including the 3,000th. Each of these units could be produced and sold at a price higher than marginal cost — that is, at a price high enough to fully compensate resource owners and low enough to still be agreeable to consumers. But so long as consumers deal with resource owners only at arm's length, through the agency of the monopolist, this potential mutual benefit, represented in Exhibit 24.6 by the shaded triangle, will not be realized. It is in this sense that pure monopoly is an imperfect market structure.

Price Discrimination

This is a good place to emphasize an assumption that has been only implicit in the discussion to this point — the assumption that the pure monopolist sells all units of output at a uniform price. Such a pricing policy is forced on the monopolist whenever the nature of the product makes resale among buyers possible. For example, it is highly unlikely that your campus bookstore (a monopoly on many campuses) could get away with selling economics texts at list price to third year students and at a 25 percent discount to everyone else. If it tried to do so, it would not be long before some enterprising first year student went into buying books for resale to seniors at some split-the-difference price. The bookstore's list-price sales would soon fall to zero.

Some firms, however, do not sell their product to all customers at the same price. Such sellers are said to practice **price discrimination**. Two things are required if price discrimination is to be possible. First, resale of the product among consumers must be impossible, or at least inconvenient. And second, the seller must be able to classify potential customers into groups with highly inelastic demand, who can be charged high prices, and groups with more elastic demand, who will be driven away unless offered low prices. The following case study illustrates price discrimination in action.

Price discrimination The practice of charging more than one price for different units of a single product, when the price differences are not justified by differences in the cost of serving different customers.

Case 24.1
Price Discrimination in Private Schools

Private schools in Canada very commonly practice price discrimination in selling their main product — education. Usually, it works this way. First, the business office sets tuition at some ambitiously high level. Then, the admissions office gives its stamp of approval to a certain number of qualified applicants. After this is done, the financial aid office gets busy working out a price discrimination strategy. The strategy consists of offering selective price rebates, called scholarships, to those students who it thinks will not be willing or able to attend if charged full tuition.

A private school is in an ideal position to practice price discrimination. For one thing, the product is completely nontransferable. If you get admitted to both Upper Canada College in Toronto and Lower Canada College in Montreal, you can't sell your Upper Canada College admission to someone who didn't get into either place! Furthermore, the school collects a great deal of information that allows it to classify students according to willingness and ability to pay.

If the price discrimination strategy is successful, everyone involved may benefit. Students who would not have been able to attend a private school at all without financial aid probably benefit most. Students who pay full tuition find their school experience enriched by the diversity of a student population with a wider variety of backgrounds and abilities than could have been attracted without a scholarship program. Meanwhile, the school itself benefits by keeping its classrooms full with the help of scholarship students and its budget balanced with tuition and fees collected from those without scholarships.

Pros and Cons of Price Discrimination

Price discrimination is widely perceived as unfair, especially by those who pay a high price while others pay less. Attempts have been made to outlaw price discrimination in some markets. However, as the preceding case study suggests, price discrimination should not be condemned without considering the alternatives.

The key question to ask in evaluating any price discrimination scheme is whether it moves the market closer to or farther from the ideal state in which all potential mutually beneficial trades are carried out. When price discrimination allows buying by those who are willing to pay a price at least equal to marginal cost but not as high as what a nondiscriminatory monopolist would charge, it may very well be beneficial. For example, price discrimination makes it possible for some students to attend schools they otherwise could not afford. It allows parents to take their young children to

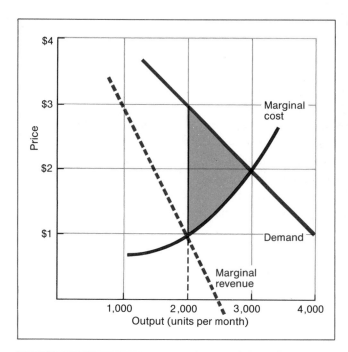

Exhibit 24.6
Why monopoly markets are imperfect
A perfect market is one in which all potential mutually beneficial exchanges are carried out and none is missed. Monopoly markets are not perfect in this sense. In the case illustrated here, a pure monopolist will maximize profits at a quantity of 2,000 units per month and a price of $3 per unit. But at that price and quantity, there is a gap between the demand curve and the marginal cost curve, which indicates that, in principle, further production can be carried out to the mutual benefit of consumers and resource owners. The shaded triangular area indicates the value of potential benefits forgone.

the movies. And it makes it possible for standby passengers, who could not afford the full fares business travelers pay, to fill airplane seats that would otherwise go empty. These forms of price discrimination almost certainly represent improvements in market performance compared with what would realistically be possible under uniform pricing.

On the other hand, price discrimination can sometimes be carried too far. In particular, it is important that the lowest price charged not fall below marginal cost. If that were to happen, another kind of market imperfection would be introduced: output would be too large, rather than too small, in comparison with a perfectly competitive market. Too many, rather than too few, resources would be attracted to the industry in question. For example, public utility commissions in some areas encourage electric utilities to discriminate against industrial users and in favor of residential users even to the point that some power for residential use is sold below long-run marginal cost. Many economists believe that this has encouraged wasteful use of electricity by homeowners and has thus made it necessary for utilities to overexpand their generating capacity.

Later chapters will discuss a number of additional examples of price discrimination. Case by case evaluations will show that some are good and others bad.

CARTELS

Pure Monopolies and Cartels

To the extent that it is motivated by profit maximization, every firm would like to be a monopolist. But most firms have no realistic chance of becoming pure monopolists. In most markets, firms face competitors that are far too numerous and far too vigorous ever to be bought up or driven away. Furthermore, in most markets, decreasing returns to scale would make it highly inefficient to concentrate all production in a single firm.

For would-be monopolists in such markets, there is a tempting alternative to the pure, single-firm monopoly. That alternative is a **cartel**—an agreement among a number of independent firms to stop competing and, instead, to coordinate their supply decisions so all of them will earn a monopoly profit.

Cartel An agreement among a number of independent suppliers of a product to coordinate their supply decisions so all of them will earn monopoly profits.

How Cartels Work

A simple example will show just how cartels work. Imagine an industry composed of one hundred identical small firms. For simplicity, assume that the marginal cost of production for all firms in the industry is a constant $1 per unit, regardless of the quantity produced. Because marginal cost is the same for all units of output, the marginal cost curve also serves as the long-run average cost curve and the long-run supply curve for the industry. This perfectly elastic long-run supply curve is shown, together with a hypothetical demand curve for the industry, in Exhibit 24.7.

The equilibrium price and quantity of output of the industry depend on how the market is organized. Suppose initially that all firms behave as perfect competitors. Under the theory set forth in Chapter 23, this situation will result in an equilibrium in which the market price is $1 per unit (equal to long-run average cost and long-run marginal cost) and in which 400,000 units of output are produced each month. In this equilibrium, each firm earns a normal rate of return on its capital and earns no pure economic profit.

Suppose now that one day the heads of the hundred firms get together to form a cartel. It is their hope that by replacing competition with cooperation, they can advance their mutual interests. They elect one of their number as cartel manager. The manager is instructed to work out a production and marketing plan that will maximize total profits for the industry and to share these profits fairly among the members.

The profit maximizing problem faced by the cartel manager is exactly the same as that faced by a pure monopolist. Industry profits are maximized at the output where marginal revenue for the industry equals marginal cost. That output is 200,000 units per month for this example. By restricting output to that quantity, the price can be raised to $2 per unit, and $200,000 per month of pure economic profit will be generated. To share this profit among all cartel members, each firm will be given an output quota of 2,000 units a month, half as much as it had been producing as a competitor. By this arrangement, the member firms will reap the benefits of pure monopoly despite their small size and large numbers.

The Stability Problem for Cartels

For its members, a successful cartel is a wonderful thing. Each firm is able to share in the profits of a monopoly while maintaining its organizational independence. But for buyers of the product, a cartel is clearly no blessing. In this example, buyers end up spending the same amount of money on the product as under competition but getting only half the quantity.

Fortunately for consumers, relatively few markets are organized as cartels. Partly, this is because most cartels are illegal under Canadian law. (More on this subject in Chapter 28.) Even more importantly, though,

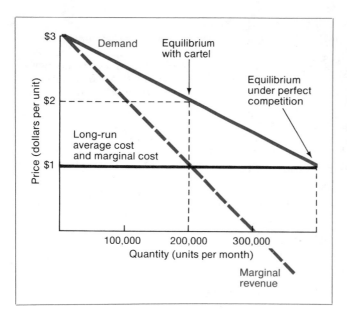

Exhibit 24.7
The effects of a cartel
This exhibit represents an industry composed of one hundred identical firms, each producing at constant long-run average and marginal cost. If the firms behave as perfect competitors, the industry will be in equilibrium where the demand curve and marginal cost curve intersect. If the firms form a cartel, however, they can jointly earn profits by restricting output to the point where marginal cost is equal to marginal revenue and by raising the product price from $1 to $2.

cartels suffer from two big built-in problems that prevent most potential cartels from being formed at all and keep others from surviving for long if they are formed.

Control over Entry The first problem that cartels suffer from is control over entry. As long as competition in an industry keeps price down to the level of long-run average cost, membership in the industry tends to be stable. As soon as a cartel raises price above this level, however, the industry becomes a magnet for new entrants. The entry of new firms does not increase the total quantity that the cartel can sell at the profit maximizing price. It increases only the number of members among which profits have to be shared. Unless there is a way for a cartel to control entry into its market, it cannot effectively serve the interests of its members.

Enforcement of Output Quotas The second, even more serious, built-in problem of cartels is the enforcement of output quotas. In every cartel, each individual member always has an incentive to cheat on its quota by producing extra, unauthorized output. Take the cartel in Exhibit 24.7. The quota for each of the one hundred members is 2,000 units per month, just half of what each firm would produce under competitive conditions. What would happen if any single firm cheated on its quota by stepping up output to the precartel level while the others continued to play by the rules?

The answer is simple. An extra 2,000 units per month by one firm would have a negligible effect on the market price, because it would represent only a 1 percent increase in industry output. By producing 4,000 units a month, the cheater would double its monthly profit—as long as others did not cheat too.

What if the others did cheat? What if all the other ninety-nine firms stepped up output to 4,000 units while only one firm stuck to its quota? With industry output at 398,000 units, the price would be forced down virtually all the way to the competitive level of $1. The firm that played fair would gain nothing for its honesty.

Because cartels are potentially so profitable, cartel organizers sometimes undertake elaborate measures to suppress cheating and enhance stability. In the case of illegal cartels, these efforts go on behind locked doors, and outside observers rarely have a chance to learn the details. The following case study shows that such cartels suffer chronically from the stability problems identified here.

Case 24.2
Instability in an Actual Cartel

Mining is by no means a risk-free business. A single mine can cost hundreds of millions to develop, and interest on that money alone may mean high fixed payments for five or ten years. In the meantime, strikes, government intervention, and price fluctuations can chop out large chunks of revenue.

So mining companies seek out any way they can to reduce uncertainty. Their most common tactic is to form producers' cartels to prop up prices and regulate production. Recently, though, the cartel solution hasn't been working.

Cartels were originally organized by the great international mining finance houses such as Rio Tinto-Zinc, Le Nickel, Anglo American Corporation, and Charter Consolidated. Acting more as banks than operating companies, these firms would take participation in one another's projects, organize transportation and marketing, work out deals with governments, and set production and price levels.

As one mining finance man says, "The old cartels worked because the guys on top were willing to cut production ruthlessly when the market turned down. If a mining company attempted to produce more than its quota, it could find itself in trouble with its bankers and customers." All this was possible because governments didn't have the leverage to force companies to keep up payrolls and exports at unprofitable price levels.

The system also tended to work to the disadvantage of the new, small producer. As the head of the British copper cartel once said, "A high copper price is the cheapest form of exploration." Boom periods would suck in new, risk-taking prospectors and developers. The new guys would build new properties, and then find themselves overextended when the price dropped. Then the mining finance houses would come in and pick up the pieces. Their close ties to the banks made it possible for them to find the cash even as the doors were being closed on the entrepreneurs.

That system hasn't been working for a while. The mining finance houses are still around, to be sure. In Canada, for example, Britain's Rio Tinto-Zinc controls Rio Algom, the country's biggest uranium producer, and South Africa's Anglo American controls Hudson Bay Mining and Smelting Company. Increasingly, though, governments, rather than companies, are setting production and price policy, and they're not doing an especially good job.

In copper, for example, the old producers' cartel has been replaced by an organization called CIPEC, a sort of copper exporters' version of OPEC. Its members are Third World countries like Zaire, Zambia, Peru, and Chile. They have enormous burdens of debt, and they'll ship out copper at almost any price to meet the interest payments. This means that, unlike the old private cartel, they've been unable to cut production and prop up the price.

The breakdown of the international system has had serious effects on Canadian copper producers. They had their own cozy arrangement, the "North American Producer Price," which smoothed out fluctuations in the copper market. Now, in the face of attacks from the U.S. Justice Department and their industrial customers, most of the copper companies are being forced to go to something approaching a free market system. There are more competitive price cuts and fewer "orderly marketing arrangements" — the old euphemism for market-rigging deals.

Source: *Saturday Night*, Oct. 1978, pp. 80–81.

The Exception: OPEC

Despite the very serious problems that cartels encounter, there are a few known exceptions to the rule that cartels are unstable and short-lived. In modern times, by far the most conspicuously successful cartel has been the Organization of Petroleum Exporting Countries, commonly known as OPEC. When OPEC quadrupled the price of oil in 1974, many prominent economists believed that it had overreached itself and would soon collapse. Instead, it remained strong and at this writing appears to be in no immediate danger of falling apart.

Why has OPEC been able to succeed as a cartel when many other cartels have failed? All observers agree that its success has been aided, more than anything, by the enormous time and expense required to develop alternative sources of supply. True, non-OPEC supplies, such as Alaskan and North Sea oil, did appear in response to the escalation of world prices; but at least through the 1970s, these new supplies were barely enough to offset a part of the increase in world oil demand and did not cut seriously into OPEC revenues. Development of such enormous potential non-OPEC reserves as those of Mexico and China appears to be many years in the future.

Beyond this primary advantage of very high barriers to entry, certain other factors have enhanced OPEC's stability. One of these is that a single producer, Saudi Arabia, is so large that it is able to make production cutbacks single-handedly when other members are tempted to supply more than they ought to. Another advantage is the unity of political purpose of the Arab members of OPEC, which dominate the cartel. Still another advantage is a very inelastic demand for the cartel's output. Finally, OPEC has sometimes been rescued by sheer good luck. In the winter of 1978–79, for example; just as OPEC seemed to be threatened by a temporary world oil glut, the revolution in Iran took the cartel's second largest producer temporarily out of action and led to renewed upward movement of world prices.

In short, although OPEC is to some degree subject to the same problems as other cartels; it is better equipped than most to cope with those problems. Someday, no doubt, it will go the way of most of its fellow cartels throughout history, but economists have grown cautious about predicting the day and the hour.

CONCLUSIONS

It would be tempting to conclude this chapter with some sweeping comparisons of monopoly and competition. Competition is perfect; monopoly is flawed. So three cheers for competition, and down with monopoly! But not so fast. The implications that can legitimately be drawn from a comparison of the two market structures are more limited than they initially appear. And a lot more groundwork must be laid before even those limited conclusions can be drawn.

For one thing, remember that all of the analysis of perfect competition and pure monopoly has taken place on the level of pure economizing. We should be reluctant to draw any conclusions about the relative merits of alternative market structures until we know something about how they affect entrepreneurial decision making as well. That is a topic to be taken up in Chapters 26 and 27.

Second, even within the realm of pure economizing, we have seen only how to compare two *different* markets—one competitive and the other monopolistic. That is not at all the same thing as making an evaluation of how a single market would perform under two alternative forms of organization. In practice, it is rarely, if ever, possible to change the structure of a market without making other changes in it as well. In particular, any change in market structure that involves increasing or decreasing the number of firms among which production is divided is very likely to affect costs and product characteristics as well. If competition reduces costs and improves product characteristics, its degree of superiority over monopoly may be very much greater than the little triangle in Exhibit 24.6 indicates. On the other hand, if excessive fragmentation of production has adverse effects on cost or product quality, those effects may more than outweigh competitive benefits of the type looked at so far.

Finally, it would simply be premature to make any comparisons between perfect competition and pure monopoly until we have examined many other market structures that are neither one nor the other. That job will occupy most of the next five chapters.

SUMMARY

1. Pure monopoly is a market structure in which one firm accounts for 100 percent of market supply. A firm operating as a pure monopolist is potentially much more profitable than one operating as a perfect competitor. Any short-run profits earned by a competitive firm will soon be eaten away by new entrants. But under pure monopoly, a price high enough to allow short-run profits need not immediately be driven down by competitors because, by definition, there are no competitors in that particular market.

2. The monopolist is not a price taker. Because the firm can expand sales only by lowering the price at which the product is sold, marginal revenue is always less than price. With a straight-line demand curve, the marginal revenue curve always lies exactly halfway between the demand curve and the vertical axis.

3. Once the demand curve, marginal revenue curve, and cost curves are given, profit maximization for the monopolist can be treated as a problem in pure economizing. To find the profit maximizing quantity, locate the point where marginal cost and marginal revenue curves intersect. Then, to find the profit maximizing price, go vertically up from that point to the demand curve.

4. Whether the profit maximizing supply decision actually yields a profit over and above the normal rate of return on invested capital or merely minimizes losses depends on the location of the demand curve relative to the average cost curves. If the demand curve is above the average total cost curve at the point where marginal cost and marginal revenue are equal, the firm will earn a positive profit. If the demand and average total cost curves are tangent at that point, the firm will break even. If the

demand curve passes below the average total cost curve but above the average variable cost curve, the firm will minimize losses in the short run by producing where marginal cost equals marginal revenue. If the demand curve is everywhere below average variable cost, the firm will minimize losses by shutting down.

5. A perfect market is one in which all potential mutually beneficial transactions are carried out. Pure monopoly is not perfect in this sense. At the profit maximizing quantity of output, there is a gap between the demand curve and the marginal cost curve; this indicates that further production will be beneficial to both consumers and resource owners. Sometimes these additional gains from trade, wasted under pure monopoly, can be realized if the monopolist engages in price discrimination. Price discrimination may result in some buyers paying even higher prices than under pure monopoly, but it also may permit buying by some who would be shut out of the market altogether under nondiscriminating monopoly.

6. A cartel is an agreement among a number of independent suppliers in a market to stop competing and, instead, to coordinate their activities in order to earn a monopoly profit. The profit maximizing rule for a cartel is the same as that for a pure monopolist: produce where industry marginal cost equals industry marginal revenue. Cartels are less common than they might otherwise be partly because they are often illegal and partly because they are often unstable. They are unstable because each firm has an incentive to cheat on the cartel's price and output decisions in order to earn more than its agreed-upon share of the cartel's total profits.

DISCUSSION QUESTIONS

1. One sometimes hears it said that a firm with a monopoly in its particular market will charge "the highest price it can get" for its product. What is the fallacy in this statement?

2. The common form of price discrimination involves charging different prices to different customers when the price difference is not justified by differences in the cost of serving those customers. Can you think of any examples where the different prices a firm changes *are* justified by differences in the cost of service? Alternatively, can you think of any instances in which a firm charges the same price for all units it sells, even though the cost of serving various customers is not the same? Should this too be considered price discrimination? Explain.

3. Some postal services have traditionally maintained a special low rate for shipments of books. Can you think of any likely economic reasons for this particular instance of price discrimination? Do you think the policy is a desirable one? Explain.

4. In what respect do you think labor unions resemble cartels? In what respects do they differ from cartels? Do you think labor unions ever suffer from the instability problems that plague product market cartels?

5. What is the best example you know of a pure monopoly? What protects this monopoly from the entry of direct competitors? How significant is the indirect competition by substitute products that this monopoly faces?

C H A P T E R 25

COMPETITION AND PUBLIC POLICY IN AGRICULTURE

WHAT YOU WILL LEARN IN THIS CHAPTER
This chapter discusses Canadian agriculture and agricultural policy. First, it explains why farmers regard the almost perfectly competitive structure of agricultural markets as a mixed blessing. Next it analyzes selected farm policies, applying the theories of competition and monopoly described in previous chapters.

FOR REVIEW
Here are some important terms and concepts that will be put to use in this chapter. If you do not understand them, review them before proceeding.
- *Price and income elasticity of demand (Chapter 18)*
- *Perfect competition (Chapter 23)*
- *Pure monopoly (Chapter 24)*
- *Cartels (Chapter 24)*
- *Price discrimination (Chatper 24)*

The theories of perfect competition and pure monopoly are two of the most important items in the economist's tool kit. They provide patterns for thinking about the complex and varied market structures of which the Canadian economy is composed.

This chapter applies the theories to agricultural markets. Agriculture is a sufficiently important sector of the Canadian economy to be worth studying for its own sake. Consumers in Canada devote nearly a quarter of their consumption expenditure to farm products, despite the fact that only about 6 percent of the population actually lives on farms. But the chapter is not just descriptive. It has a theme as well as a subject. This theme is the tension between the inherently competive structure of agricultural markets and the departures from perfect competition introduced by government agricultural policy.

THE STRUCTURAL ORIGINS OF THE FARM PROBLEM

The Mixed Blessings of Perfect Competition

Many agricultural markets come very close to fitting the four structural requirements of perfect competition: large numbers of small firms, homogeneous products, good information flows, and easy entry and exit. In Canada, there are some 300,000 farms altogether, about 90 percent of which are sole proprietorships — traditional family farms. Large corporate farms are gradually becoming more common, but more than half of all farm operators in 1971 had sales of less than $10,000. Most agricultural markets are characterized by a high degree of product homogeneity. Only rarely do consumers know or care about which particular farm produced the products they buy. The flow of information in agricultural markets is accomplished through highly organized commodity exchanges for major crops. The last structural requirement for perfect competition, easy entry and exit, is also well satisfied in agriculture.

As explained in Chapter 23, perfectly competitive markets have some important virtues. Whenever consumers are willing to pay more for a good than its marginal cost, a competitive market will bring forth the additional supply. If existing firms cannot handle the demand, new firms will enter. Similarly, if consumers are unwilling to buy all that is produced at a price at least equal to marginal cost, competition will accomplish the required reduction in supply. If a long-run reduction in supply is needed, some firms will withdraw from the market. In every case, the necessary adjustments occur in response to changes in the market price of the good, as determined by supply and demand. No central planner is needed to give orders; Adam Smith's "invisible hand" is at work.

Left alone, agricultural markets really do work in something quite close to this ideal fashion. But for farmers the ideal is a mixed blessing. In the short run, competition means unpredictable prices and unstable incomes as supply and demand curves shift with the weather and with patterns of world trade. In the long run, competition has driven more and more farmers from the land as new technology has increased crop yields per worker. So not despite but because of the perfectly competitive structure of agricultural markets, there is a farm problem.

The farm problem, it must be added, is a problem for *farmers*. From the consumer's point of view, and even more so from the detached point of view of the economist, fluctuating prices and declining farm population may not be problems at all; they may be merely the healthy functioning of competitive markets. Nonetheless, the farmer's point of view has traditionally dominated the Canadian government's farm policy. That being the case, it is worth examining more closely the cause of the problem, in order to evaluate the policies designed to cure it.

Instability and Price Inelastic Demand

In a competitive market, the response of price and revenue to changes in the quantity supplied depends on the price elasticity of demand. This response is illustrated by Exhibit 25.1. Market A in the exhibit is characterized by relatively low price elasticity of demand and Market B by relatively high elasticity.

In both markets, the time horizon is the **very short run** — a time so short that producers cannot make any adjustments in inputs or outputs in response to a change in price. This is the case in the market for a perishable agricultural good after the crop has been harvested and before the farmers have a chance to respond to prices by adjusting their supply decision for the next year.

Suppose now that in the first year, 100,000 units of each crop are harvested. When the quantity of output is brought to market, an equilibrium price of $2 is established for both goods. The next year, because of improved weather, increased planting, or some other reason, output in both markets increases to 125,000 units. This is represented in the exhibit by a shift in the short-run supply curve from S_1 to S_2. What happens to price and revenue?

Very short run A time horizon so short that producers are unable to make any changes in input or output quantities in response to changing prices.

Exhibit 25.1
Demand elasticity and price instability

The stability of prices and revenues in the face of changing supply conditions depends on the price elasticity of demand for the product. In Market A, where demand is relatively inelastic, an increase in supply from 100,000 units to 125,000 units brings the price down from $2 to $1 and revenue down from $200,000 to $125,000. In Market B, where demand is relatively elastic, the same increase in supply causes the price to drop to $1.80 and revenue to increase from $200,000 to $225,000.

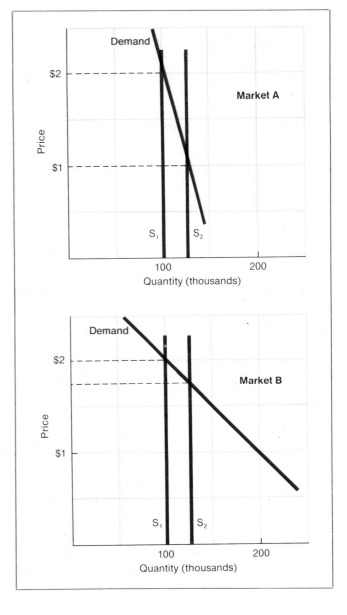

Farm Product	Demand Elasticity
Cattle	0.68
Calves	1.08
Hogs	0.46
Sheep and lambs	1.78
Chickens	0.74
Turkeys	0.92
Eggs	0.23
Milk used for:	
Fluid milk and cream	0.14
Evaporated and condensed	0.26
Cheese	0.54
Ice cream	0.11
Butter	0.66
Other use	0.36
Soybean	0.61
Cottonseed	1.03
Potatoes, sweet potatoes	0.11
Dry beans, peas, peanuts	0.23
Wheat	0.80
Corn	0.50
Oats	2.00

Source: G. E. Brandow, "Interrelations among Demands for Farm Products and Implications for Control of Market Supply," *Bulletin 680* (University Park, Pa.: Pennsylvania State University Agricultural Experiment Station, 1961), pp. 59, 64, 80, 81, and 96. Reprinted by permission.

Exhibit 25.2
Price elasticity of demand for selected farm products
This table shows estimated price elasticities of demand for selected farm products. The low demand elasticities for many major products are a factor contributing to chronic price instability.

In Market A, where demand is inelastic, a large decrease in price is necessary to bring about the required increase in quantity demanded. As the price falls from $2 to $1, total revenue earned from the sale of the crop declines from $200,000 to $125,000. In Market B, however, a relatively small decline in price, from $2 to $1.80, is sufficient to increase the quantity demanded to 125,000 units. Because the price declines by a smaller percentage than the quantity of output increases in this market, revenue rises from $200,000 to $225,000.

Studies of actual agricultural markets indicate that they are more like Market A than Market B. Exhibit 25.2 presents some statistical estimates of demand elasticity for farm products. The striking thing about this table is how low most of the elasticities are. With the exceptions of sheep, calves, cottonseed, and oats, all the elasticities listed are less than 1.

The Historical Instability of Prices

Because demand for farm products is price inelastic, changing supply and demand conditions result in disproportionately large year-to-year price changes. The instability of agricultural prices is evident from Exhibit 25.3, which shows fluctuations in farm prices of Canadian agricultural products from 1961 to 1978. During that eighteen-year period, there were eight years in which agricultural prices actually declined. On the other hand, in 1973, when there appeared to be a worldwide shortage of agricultural commodities, accentuated by crop failures in the Soviet Union, the price of agricultural products in Canada rose by 49.3 percent. This was followed by

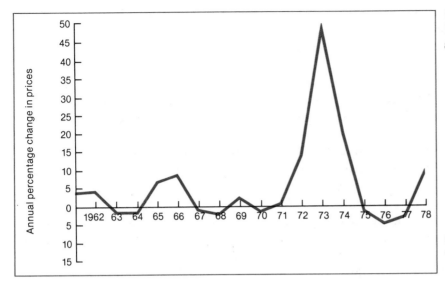

Source: Department of Finance, *Economic Review*, April 1979, p. 181.

Exhibit 25.3
Fluctuations in farm prices of agricultural products, 1961–1978

a further 20.6 percent increase in 1974. This trend was abruptly reversed in 1975, when agricultural prices fell by 1.0 percent.

This price record tells the story of one aspect of the farm problem: short-term instability. There is a second aspect of the farm problem as well: long-term adjustment to rising productivity and slowly growing demand.

Canadian farmers, like farmers in most western countries, have increased output at an extraordinary rate. In 1946, one farm worker in Canada produced enough agricultural output for the consumption of fifteen people. By the 1970s, the worker produced enough for the consumption of fifty people. However, this increase in productivity has not been matched by increased demand. The demand for farm products is not only price inelastic, but *income* inelastic as well. As per capita income grows, the quantity of agricultural output demanded increases, but less than in proportion to the increase in income.

The result of slowly growing demand and rapidly growing farm productivity has been a steady decline in the farm population and a relatively poor income record for farmers. We noted that currently about 6 percent of our population lives on farms. In 1929, one-third of the population lived on farms. In the fifty-year period to 1979, the farm population shrank by about 2 million people.

The competitive market knows just one way to bring about the exit of resources from an industry in which they are no longer needed: reduce the amount those resources are paid. Not surprisingly, then, per capita farm income has fared more poorly than the income of many other groups in our society.

For most postwar years per capita farm income has been considerably below that of the population as a whole.[1] In the 1970s, the sharp increase in agricultural prices of 1973 and 1974 raised per capita agricultural incomes

---

[1] See O.J. Firestone, *Canada's Economic Development 1867–1953* (London: Bowes & Bowes, 1958), Table 70, p. 193; and Agriculture Canada, *Selected Agricultural Statistics for Canada*, annual.

above the national average, but those years have been exceptions to the general rule.

Because of declining agricultural population and slowly growing income, the farm income share of net national income has declined from about 4 percent in 1962 to just over 2 percent in 1978. This is illustrated in Exhibit 25.4. The heavy line indicates how the share has fluctuated, demonstrating the instability of farm income, while the fine straight line indicates the long-run trend.

However, it would be quite misleading to assume, because only about 6 percent of Canada's population lives on farms and farm income is only about 2 percent of net national income, that the farm sector is of little importance to the Canadian economy. We depend on the agricultural sector for many of the most important products that we consume. In addition, a large segment of our nation's industry is in the **agribusiness** sector of the economy. This includes those industries that produce goods and services for farmers and those that process farm materials, such as manufacturers of farm machinery, meat packers, dairies, and flour mills. It was estimated by the Agricultural Economics Research Council of Canada that the agribusiness sector, including the farm sector itself, constituted 42 percent of Canada's gross national product.[2]

Agribusiness All those business firms that are linked directly to agricultural producing, including food processing firms and agricultural implement manufacturers and dealers.

[2] N. J. Beaton, "Economic Problems and Policies in Canadian Agriculture," in *The Canadian Economy: Problems and Policies*, ed. G. C. Ruggeri (Toronto: Gage, 1977), pp. 259–260.

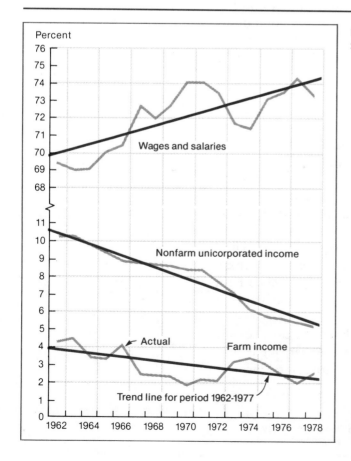

Exhibit 25.4
Shares of net national income at factor cost

Source: Statistics Canada, *National Income and Expenditure Accounts Quarterly*, Cat. 13-001; and Department of Finance, *Economic Review*, April 1979.

Because of the continuing importance of the farm sector, and its unique demand and supply conditions, farmers have been able to make successful appeals to government for various types of assistance. Farm markets are by nature competitive. The farmers' very sensible response has been to wish: *if only they were not so competitive.*

These wishes have not gone unheeded. Helpful policy makers in Ottawa and in the provincial capitals have heard the farmers' complaints and agreed that something should be done. Piece by piece, over the past half-century, a farm policy has been assembled that places a number of ingenious restrictions on competition. As a result, Canadian agriculture not only supplies textbook writers with some good illustrations of perfect competition in action, but also gives them a chance to develop applications of the theory of monopoly.

FARM POLICY

Competition versus Coordination

Farmers could solve many of their own problems if only they could coordinate their activities instead of competing with each other. The theory developed in Chapter 24 suggests that one way to do this would be to form a comprehensive system of agricultural cartels. The cartel for each crop could limit the quantity supplied to the market and hold prices up. It could also carry one year's surplus over for sale at a higher price in a year when the crop was not so abundant. If there were more farmers than required to produce the profit maximizing output, the cartel could assign each member a fair share of the limited production while planning orderly withdrawal of unneeded resources.

But organizing such a system of agricultural cartels on a private, voluntary basis would be a completely hopeless undertaking. As Chapter 24 showed, cartels have built-in stability problems of their own. To be successful, a cartel must be able to restrict the entry of nonmembers into the industry, and it must be able to enforce its rules among its own members. Because the number of farms is so large and the barriers to entry are so low, these problems would quickly prove fatal for any privately organized agricultural cartel.

Unable to overcome their problems through voluntary coordination, then, it is not surprising that farmers have turned to the government for help.

The federal and provincial governments in Canada have helped to coordinate and support the activities of farmers in many different ways. Some assistance policies go back a long way, like the granting of agricultural land to new settlers in the late nineteenth century, and the use of subsidized railway rates — known as the Crow's Nest Pass Agreement — to encourage the export of grain and flour. However, with the creation of the Canadian Wheat Board in 1935, and the passing of the Agricultural Prices Support Act in 1944, Canadian governments began to develop institutions and procedures to support farm prices and incomes in the direct manner characteristic of cartels.

Farm Policy: Price Supports, Acreage Controls, and Subsidy Prices

There are, essentially, three ways that government supported agencies can help farmers to control prices:

1. They can establish a minimum price and agree to buy all or a certain amount of the output at that price.
2. They can restrict output and guarantee a price for that output.
3. They can subsidize the price paid by the consumer.

Price Supports

Price support A program under which the government guarantees a certain minimum price to farmers by undertaking to buy any surplus that cannot be sold to private buyers at the support price.

Price supports are the most venerable of all instruments of farm policy. Exhibit 25.5 shows how they work, taking the market for wheat as an example. As the figure is drawn, the competitive equilibrium price is $2 per bushel, and the equilibrium quantity of output is 2 billion bushels per year. The supply curve is not completely inelastic because a longer period of time extending into another growing season is contemplated.

Suppose now that in order to raise farm incomes, the government declares a support price of $3 per bushel. At this price, farmers will produce 2.5 billion bushels of wheat, but consumers will buy only 1.5 billion. The government will maintain the price at the support level by buying the 1 billion bushels of surplus wheat at the support price and putting it in storage.[3]

But what is to be done with the surplus wheat? During the 1960s, the quantities of wheat stored by the government became a national problem.

---

[3] Through the Canadian Wheat Board the government allocates a wheat delivery quota to each farmer, and the wheat is sold by the board either at home or abroad. The farmer is paid an initial price (for example, $3 per bushel), which is in effect the support price. If demand on the world market enables the price to rise higher than $3, farmers receive additional payments.

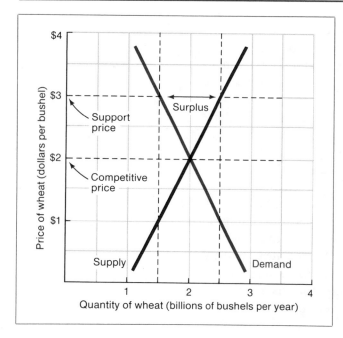

Exhibit 25.5
The effects of direct price supports
To carry out its price support policy, the government agrees to pay $3 per bushel for all wheat that cannot be sold at that price in the open market. Because the support price is above the equilibrium price for a competitive market, this policy will reduce the quantity of wheat demanded and increase the quantity of wheat supplied. The resulting surplus will be purchased by the government and put into storage[3] or otherwise disposed of.

Luckily, most of the vast accumulation (or at least the part of it that had not spoiled) was cleared out during the 1973 world food crisis. Because of the surplus problem, the government has experimented with two other instruments of farm policy that potentially avoid the problem.

Acreage Controls

Acreage controls are one of the instruments intended to avoid the problem of surpluses. Exhibit 25.6 shows how they work. The demand curve, D, and supply curve S_1 in this exhibit are the same as in Exhibit 25.5. The objective of government policy is also the same: raise the price of wheat from its equilibrium level of $2 per bushel to the desired level of $3 per bushel.

The method of pushing the price up is different this time, however. Instead of offering to buy any wheat that goes unsold at the price of $3 per bushel, the government attempts to restrict the quantity of wheat produced in order to drive the price up to the desired level. It does this by requiring each farmer to take some land out of wheat production.

The effect of the artificial restriction of acreage is to raise the marginal cost of producing wheat. Ordinarily, farmers who want to grow more wheat will minimize their cost of production by adding a little more land, a little more labor, and a little more capital (machinery and fertilizer) in certain cost minimizing proportions. Now those same farmers face a new constraint: they can use more labor and capital but not more land. It is still possible to grow more wheat if the price is high enough to justify the added cost, so the new supply curve, S_2, still has an upward slope. But the increased marginal cost resulting from the constraint on farming practices pushes the supply curve to a higher level. If acreage is restricted by just the right amount, as it is in Exhibit 25.6, the same price ($3 per bushel) will be reached as was reached through direct price supports in the previous example.

Acreage controls Policies designed to raise agricultural prices by limiting the acreage on which certain crops can be grown.

Exhibit 25.6

The effects of acreage controls

This exhibit shows how the government can raise the price of wheat to the desired level of $3 per bushel through the use of acreage controls. Acreage controls raise the cost of producing wheat, shifting the supply curve from S_1 to S_2. The effect is to push up the price of wheat without creating a surplus. However, more resources must be used to produce each bushel of wheat than would have been the case without acreage controls.

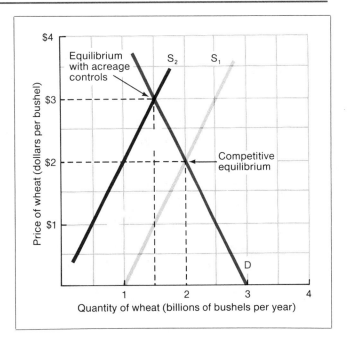

Subsidy Prices

Subsidy price A price guaranteed to farmers by the government; if the market price falls below the subsidy price, the government pays the farmers the difference.

Neither price supports nor acreage controls offer much to consumers but the prospect of spending more and getting less. With policy makers becoming more sensitive to consumer complaints, a third instrument of farm policy, **subsidy prices**, has received increased attention.

Exhibit 25.7 shows how such prices work. It begins with the same supply and demand curves as before and the same goal of getting the revenue received by farmers up to $3 per bushel. Now, however, the government does not try to control either the quantity of wheat produced or the actual market price. Instead, it sets a target price of $3 per bushel and promises farmers a " deficiency payment" equal to the difference between the target price and the market price for each bushel produced. Knowing they will receive $3 per bushel regardless of how low the market price falls, farmers follow their supply curve up to an output of 2.5 billion bushels. When this quantity of wheat is thrown on the market, the price falls to $1 a bushel. Consumers get lots of cheap wheat, and the government pays most of the bill.

Alternative Policies Compared

Which of these three policy instruments — price supports, acreage controls, or subsidy prices — is the best? The answer turns out to depend on whose viewpoint is taken — the farmer's, the consumer's, the taxpayer's, the economist's, or the government policy maker's.

From the farmer's point of view, direct price supports and subsidy prices tie for best, and acreage controls are clearly inferior. As the examples here have been constructed, both price supports and subsidy prices raise total farm revenues from $4 billion to $7.5 billion, without any adverse impact on productivity. Acreage controls, in contrast, raise revenues to only $4.5

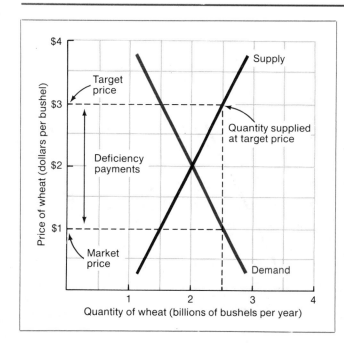

Exhibit 25.7
The effects of subsidy prices

Subsidy prices are a third way of raising the price of wheat to the desired level of $3 per bushel. The government announces a subsidy price of $3 per bushel but does not actually offer to buy any wheat at this price. Farmers responding to the subsidy price increase the quantity they supply from 2 to 2.5 billion bushels. The increased quantity drives the market price down to $1 per bushel. The government then makes a "deficiency payment" to farmers equal to the difference between the market price and the subsidy price.

billion and simultaneously raise costs per unit. Valuable labor and capital was wasted cultivating some land too intensively, while other land lies altogether idle.

From the consumer's point of view, subsidy prices are by far the best, with price supports and acreage controls equally bad. Subsidy prices give consumers more wheat at a lower price per unit, while the other two instruments give them less wheat at greater cost.

From the taxpayer's point of view, acreage controls are the cheapest, involving only administrative costs. Both price supports and subsidy prices involve large payments directly to farmers. Which of the two is more expensive for taxpayers depends on the exact shape and position of the supply and demand curves.

It is not quite so easy to say which of the three policies looks best from the economist's point of view. The answer may again depend on the exact shape and position of the supply and demand curves. However, most economists would agree that, other things being equal, the cost required to secure a benefit of a given size should be minimized, regardless of who gets the benefit.

All three of the policy instruments discussed in this chapter involve some administrative costs. All three also distort resource allocation in that they result in the wrong amount of wheat being produced. Under subsidy prices and price support, too much wheat is grown; and under acreage controls, too little is grown. Nonetheless, price supports and acreage controls involve certain additional costs that subsidy prices do not have. In the case of price supports, the cost is that of keeping wheat in storage to shore up the market price, instead of letting people eat it. In the case of acreage controls, the cost is the extra labor and capital required to grow each bushel of wheat when the use of land is artificially restricted. Without the alternative of a freely competitive market in wheat, many economists would therefore choose subsidy prices as the best of the three alternatives.

Some Current Farm Policies

Now comes the question of which policy instrument looks best from the point of view of government policy makers. Clearly, the answer depends on which interest groups they want to please. Because politicians normally want to please everyone at once, it is not surprising that actual farm policy employs a mixture of all three major instruments.

Under the Agricultural Prices Support Act of 1944, the federal government received the power to establish a price support policy for any agricultural product. It proceeded to support a wide range of products, most notably eggs and butter. By 1958, the cost of supporting surplus commodities had reached about $100 million. This, however, did not discourage the government. In 1958 it enlarged the support program through the Agricultural Stabilization Act. Under this new Act, it agreed to support the prices of nine major commodities, including cattle, hogs, butter, and eggs, at 80 percent of the previous ten-year average price.

Because of large surpluses of hogs and eggs, the government modified the support program by changing to a subsidy price policy. It encouraged farmers to sell surpluses in the consumer market at "market clearing" prices, and it then paid farmers the difference between this price and the base target price.

In most cases, farmers were also given quotas under these support programs, which are similar to acreage restrictions. Such restrictions have also been imposed for a number of other products. Until 1970, wheat farmers had no acreage restrictions placed on their output, though they had quota restrictions. By that year, such a large surplus of wheat had developed that acreage restrictions were imposed. As noted previously, the problem was finally relieved by the sharp increase in world demand in 1973.

Through the Agricultural Stabilization Act and the Canadian Wheat Board Act, the federal government has created government agencies that support prices in the ways just described. In addition, both the federal and provincial governments have helped farmers to form their own price support agencies, known as *marketing boards*

There are now more than 120 such marketing boards in Canada, controlling more than one-quarter of total agricultural output. Governments support these boards by making it compulsory for all producers of a given commodity to adhere to the regulations of their marketing board. The most powerful boards are the fluid milk boards or commissions, which directly fix prices and establish marketing quotas for dairy farmers.[4] Poultry product marketing boards set marketing quotas and minimum sales prices.

These boards have helped to ensure for all farmers the same basic price for their product, as well as uniform and fair quality standards. They are all, however, "monopoly" adaptations to what would otherwise be an extremely competitive industry.

This completes the discussion of specific agricultural problems and policies. A great many details have been left out, of course, because of space limitations and because the details of policy change almost every year.

CONCLUSIONS

Throughout this chapter, the theme has been the tension between the inherently competitive structure of Canadian agriculture and the desire of farmers to shield themselves from what they perceive to be the mixed blessing of competition. The intent is not to condemn farmers for wanting protection. They owe no moral allegiance to the economist's abstract theory of perfect competition. But not all criticisms of farm policy by nonfarmers come down to a simple tug-of-war between contending interest groups, each wanting more for itself and less for others.

First, the critics find that current farm policies are very expensive for consumers. Furthermore, as a means for transferring income from consumers to farmers, they are a very leaky bucket. Administrative costs and misallocation of resources mean that for each dollar in cost to consumers, farmers gain only pennies in real net profits.

Second, critics claim that farm policies have lost sight of their own goal of short-term stabilization. All farm policies involve built-in trade-offs

---

[4] This information is based on G. A. Hiscocks and T. A. Bennett, "Marketing Boards and Pricing in Canada," in *The Canadian Economy*, ed. Ruggeri, pp. 265–272.

between the goal of stabilization and the goal of enhancing farm incomes. A pure stabilization policy would operate to raise prices in some years and depress them in other years, so the average price would be close to that of a competitive equilibrium. In practice, many farm policies are designed to take advantage of each year's changing supply and demand conditions to raise farm prices as high as possible in that year. That is a major reason why, despite fifty years of activist farm policies, price stability has not in fact been achieved.

Third, farm policies are criticized for giving little attention to the goals of long-term adjustment and elimination of rural poverty. The most prosperous farmers get the lion's share of all subsidies, while poor farmers get little or none. How else could it be in a system where subsidies are paid out in proportion to acres planted or bushels harvested?

All in all, then, Canadian farm policy is not a very inspiring picture. But at least it supplies economists with plenty of opportunities to put the tools of their trade to use.

SUMMARY

1. Many agricultural markets fit the structural requirements of perfect competition very closely. They have large numbers of small firms, homogeneous products, good information systems, and free entry and exit. Farmers, however, regard perfect competition as a mixed blessing. The demand for most farm products is price inelastic; as a result, prices fluctuate sharply as the size of the crop varies from year to year. Demand is also income inelastic, with the result that the growth of demand for farm goods has not kept pace with the growth of farm productivity. This has led to depressed farm incomes.

2. One way for farmers to enhance their incomes and stabilize prices would be to form cartels. However, it would be very difficult to form purely voluntary cartels in agriculture because of the large number of producers and the ease of entry. In some cases, government policy makes it possible for farmers to engage in cartel-like practices.

3. Price supports are an instrument of farm policy that can be used to stabilize prices and enhance farm incomes. The government announces a support price higher than the competitive equilibrium price. That induces farmers to move up along their supply curve, increasing total quantity supplied. To maintain the support price, the government must purchase the excess quantity supplied and keep it off the market. Price supports result in high prices to consumers and substantial storage costs for taxpayers.

4. Acreage controls are a policy sometimes used to raise farm prices without encouraging surplus production. They shift the supply curve upward, which means a higher equilibrium price and a lower equilibrium quantity than without controls. However, farmers respond to these controls by applying increased labor and capital to each acre of land, thereby raising the cost of production. These increased production costs offset the advantage that farmers get from the high prices.

5. Subsidy prices are a method of raising farm incomes without raising consumer prices. Under this policy, the government announces a sub-

sidy price above the competitive equilibrium price but does not agree to buy surplus output. Farmers increase output, thereby driving down the market price. The government makes up the difference between the market price and the subsidy price with deficiency payments to farmers.

6. Canadian farm policies are subject to many criticisms. One objection is that the policies are very expensive for consumers. Another is that they pay too little attention to the goal of short-run stabilization and place too much emphasis on raising farm incomes. Still another is that they are ineffective in dealing with the problem of rural poverty, because most subsidies go to relatively prosperous farmers.

DISCUSSION QUESTIONS

1. What aspects of the farm problem are problems from the farmer's point of view only, and what aspects are problems from the consumer's point of view as well? Is a low average level of farm prices a problem for consumers? For a given average level of farm prices, are unstable prices a problem for consumers? Explain.

2. Turn to the table of demand elasticities for farm products that is presented in Exhibit 25.2. Can you find any examples there that seem to illustrate the rule that elasticity will be greater for products with close substitutes than for those without close substitutes? The rule that the greater the proportion of the consumer's budget spent on the good, the greater the elasticity? What other explanations of differences in the elasticities shown can you think of?

3. Other things being equal, we would expect that a policy of acreage quotas but no output quotas would cause an increase in output per acre. (Explain why.) Would this policy also be expected to cause an increase in output per worker hour? Why or why not? If not, how could you explain the sharp rise in productivity per worker hour in agriculture that took place during the 1950s?

C H A P T E R 26

OLIGOPOLY: COMPETITION AMONG THE FEW

WHAT YOU WILL LEARN IN THIS CHAPTER

Most markets have neither a single firm, as required for pure monopoly, nor the many firms required for perfect competition. Markets in which there are only a few firms, at least some of which have a large share of industry sales, are called oligopolies. This chapter will explain how to measure the degree of concentration in an oligopolistic industry and what determines the degree of concentration. It will examine several attempts to construct formal theories of oligopoly and explain why none of these attempts has been entirely successful. It will also examine evidence regarding the relationship between profits and market concentration. Throughout the chapter, a major question will be how well oligopolistic markets perform.

FOR REVIEW

Here are some important terms and concepts that will be put to use in this chapter. If you do not understand them, review them before proceeding.
- *Economies of scale (Chapter 22)*
- *Minimum efficient scale (Chapter 22)*
- *Perfect competition (Chapter 23)*
- *Pure monopoly and cartels (Chapter 24)*

As pointed out before, the term *competition* has two distinct meanings in economics. Used in "perfect competition," it refers to market structure. A market is said to be perfectly competitive if it has large numbers of small firms, a homogeneous product, well-informed buyers and sellers, and easy entry and exit. In contrast, when used as the verb "to compete," competition refers to business rivalry. In this sense, it is a matter of conduct rather than market structure. Two firms are said to compete if they treat each other as rivals in their independent efforts to do the best they can in the marketplace.

Up to this point, the emphasis has been almost entirely on the structural side of things. Rivalry has played little role in the theories that have been introduced. There is no rivalry in perfectly competitive markets because each firm sees each other firm as too small to have much influence on market conditions. Rivalry is absent from pure monopoly because there is only one firm in the market. And, in a cartel, rivalry disappears as the result of an explicit decision to replace competition with coordination.

In the vast majority of markets, however, rivalry plays too big a role to be pushed into the background. Most markets have more than a single firm but fewer than the large number required for perfect competition. Most such markets also lack explicit agreements among competing firms to refrain from business rivalry. Such markets are known as **oligopolies**.

Oligopoly A market structure in which there are two or more firms, at least one of which has a large share of total sales.

Under oligopoly, it matters very much to each firm what its rivals do. This is true even for the simplest kind of oligopoly, in which all firms produce a homogeneous product, because each firm is so large that a change in the quantity it supplies can significantly affect the market price. It is even more true in more complex forms of oligopoly, where the products of rival firms are not exactly alike. There, each firm must be prepared to react to moves that its rivals make in terms of style changes, product innovations, and promotional techniques as well as to changes in price and quantity of output and in many other areas.

The need to focus on the interaction of many firms rather than on the behavior of each firm in isolation makes it difficult to formulate a completely satisfactory theory of oligopoly. Rather than presenting a single, unified theory, then, this chapter will look at a number of fragmentary theories all tied together by one central question: *is perfect competition necessary for satisfactory market performance, or is competition among a few large rival firms good enough?* Some economists have argued that even without explicitly agreeing to do so, oligopolists can coordinate their actions to restrict output and raise prices almost as effectively as do members of formal cartels. Others reject this idea and argue instead that competition among the few works very efficiently to serve consumer needs. Still others hedge their bets by saying that some oligopolies seem to perform better than others for reasons that are not completely understood. Although the controversy cannot be settled here, at least a map of the territory can be provided.

MARKET CONCENTRATION AND ITS DETERMINANTS

The main purpose of this chapter is to develop some insight into the performance of oligopolistic markets, but two preliminary questions need to be asked. First, how many markets are really dominated by just a few firms (and how many is "a few")? And second, what determines the number of firms in a market and the size of their market shares? Knowing the answers to these questions will make it easier to understand both how markets work and what government policy is toward monopoly and oligopoly.

Measuring Market Concentration

Concentration ratio The percentage of all sales contributed by the four or eight largest firms in a market.

Concentration ratios provide a rough-and-ready measure of the extent to which markets are dominated by a few firms. The most common of these ratios are the four-firm concentration ratio (which measures the percentage of sales attributed to the top four firms in a given market) and the eight-firm concentration ratio (which measures the share of the top eight firms).

Exhibit 26.1 gives concentration ratios for a representative selection of manufacturing industries. At the top of the figure are industries that are classic oligopolies; they consist of a handful of firms that control virtually the entire market. For other industries, shown in the middle of the chart, the top four firms account for less than half of industry sales, although these firms are clearly large enough not to fit the strict requirements of perfect competition. Only in the case of services, such as hairdressing salons and shoe repair shops, does it appear safe to say that there are "many" firms, each one of which is "small" relative to the size of the market. All in all, close to one-half of Canadian manufacturing output comes from markets in which the top four firms control half the markets or more. Canadian industry is considerably more concentrated than American industry.[1]

---

[1] A Canadian study showed that, in Canada, industries in which four or fewer firms produced 50 percent or more of total output accounted for 45 percent of all industries; in the United States such highly concentrated industries account for about 28 percent of industries. See B. Bock, "Is Concentration Rising" *The Conference Board Record*, Vol. 13, No. 9, 1976, pp. 46 –50.

Exhibit 26.1

Four-firm and eight-firm concentration for selected industries, 1976

Concentration ratios measure the percentage of industry output contributed by the largest firms. This representative selection of thirty-three Canadian industries shows a wide range of concentration ratios. The figures given here do not take into account foreign competition or the fact that some industries produce mainly for local markets.

Source: Statistics Canada, *Annual Report of the Minister of Industry, Trade and Commerce under the Corporations and Labour Unions Returns Act* (Part I: *Corporations*), 1976, p. 36.

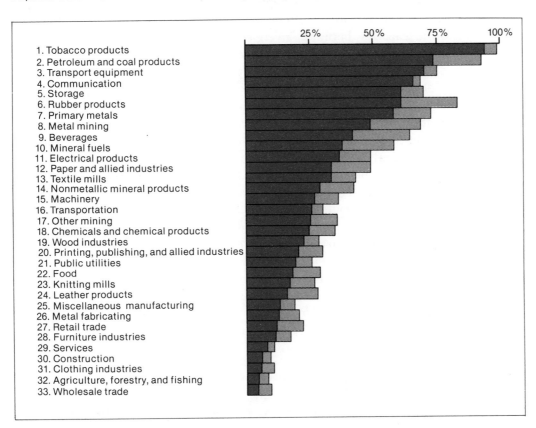

1. Tobacco products
2. Petroleum and coal products
3. Transport equipment
4. Communication
5. Storage
6. Rubber products
7. Primary metals
8. Metal mining
9. Beverages
10. Mineral fuels
11. Electrical products
12. Paper and allied industries
13. Textile mills
14. Nonmetallic mineral products
15. Machinery
16. Transportation
17. Other mining
18. Chemicals and chemical products
19. Wood industries
20. Printing, publishing, and allied industries
21. Public utilities
22. Food
23. Knitting mills
24. Leather products
25. Miscellaneous manufacturing
26. Metal fabricating
27. Retail trade
28. Furniture industries
29. Services
30. Construction
31. Clothing industries
32. Agriculture, forestry, and fishing
33. Wholesale trade

Exhibit 26.1 gives a rough indication of the extent of industrial concentration. The next important question is: why are some industries more concentrated than others? The phenomenon of economies of scale provides a logical place to start answering this question.

Economies of Scale

Chapter 22 introduced the concept of economies of scale. A firm is said to experience economies of scale if its long-run average costs decline as its scale of output increases. Shapes of long-run average cost curves vary from one industry to another, but statistical studies have indicated that many industries fit the pattern of an L-shaped long-run average cost curve. Such a cost curve shows economies of scale initially, followed by a range of constant returns to scale.

The point at which the average total cost curve stops falling and begins to flatten out is known as the minimum efficient scale for the firm — an important determinant of market concentration. The study of economies of scale by Eastman and Stykolt, discussed in Chapter 22, indicated that many industries in Canada appear to have *too many* plants. In contrast to American firms, which often build plants that appear to be larger than required by economies of scale, Canadian firms often build plants that are smaller than would be necessary to realize efficiencies of scale. Where this is the case, the concentration ratio might be said to be too low rather than too high. In view of the relatively small Canadian market and the existence of economies of scale, much of Canadian industry may be unavoidably oligopolistic in structure.

As was conjectured in Chapter 22, the reason Canadian firms build plants too small for economies of scale may be that they are reluctant to expand capacity because, given a relatively small market, substantial increases in capacity might require considerable reductions in price. Price reductions would threaten the profit margins of the firms in the industry.

It should also be noted that production costs of individual plants are not the only criteria used by firms in deciding the most efficient scale of operation. A recent study on the Canadian food processing industry observes that "plants which are too small to minimize production costs are often optimal in the sense of minimizing overall costs of production, assembly, and distribution."[2] Small tomato-canning plants in Ontario, for instance, can survive because they can locate close to raw materials and can specialize. These factors lead the multi-plant firms that we have in the meat packing, fish processing, and dairy processing industries to assume the higher production costs associated with small operations while retaining the advantages of size in bargaining, raising capital, advertising, and spreading overhead. Given such multi-plant economies, more industries may be operating at or close to their minimum efficient scale than otherwise appears to be the case.

Despite this, it is unlikely that economies of scale entirely determine the

---

[2] John Morris, "The Competitive Characteristics of the Canadian Food Processing Industry," in *Competition and Public Policy on Competition in the Canadian Food Industry, Proceedings of Agricultural and Food Marketing Forum*, ed. R. M. A. Loyns and R. L. Louks, Department of Agricultural Economics and Farm Management, University of Manitoba, Occasional Series No. 7, May 1977.

market concentration ratios presented in Exhibit 26.1. Many Canadian economists are convinced that, in a large number of industries, there are more plants now in operation than are warranted by considerations of efficiency, while simultaneously there are fewer firms than desirable. In other words, a relatively small number of firms — often operating numerous production or distribution units of less-than-efficient size — have come to dominate many industries.[3] Determinants other than efficiency must account for the maintenance of such market structures and for the absence of new rivals challenging existing firms. It is thus worth considering other possible determinants.

Barriers to Entry Not Related to Economies of Scale

One reason why an industry may be more or less concentrated than economies of scale alone would indicate is that there may be barriers to entry of new firms. Even if profits in the industry are unusually high, prospective entrepreneurs may for some reason be unable to duplicate the performance of existing firms. As demand for the product expands, then, growth can come only through the expansion of existing firms, even after all economies of scale have been exhausted, or even if existing firms merely duplicate undersized production units.

Legal Barriers As in the case of pure monopoly, barriers to entry into oligopolistic industries are sometimes created on purpose by federal, provincial, or municipal government policy. In such industries, policy stops short of creating a pure franchised monopoly but still limits the number of competitors to fewer than would exist under free entry. For example, entry into many segments of the broadcasting industry was for years tightly controlled by the Canadian Radio-Television Commission (CRTC). Despite some recent reforms, these legal barriers to entry have still not been entirely dismantled. At the provincial level, entry into many professions — law, medicine, plumbing, hairdressing, and dozens of others — is limited by licensing boards. Entry into rental housing or retailing in many communities is limited by local zoning regulations. The list of such legal barriers to entry goes on and on.

Ownership of Resources A second kind of barrier to entry is ownership of some nonreproducible resource. For example, entry into the ski resort industry is limited by the availability of suitable mountains. Entry into extractive industries is, in at least some cases, limited by ownership of the best available natural resources by existing firms. In other markets, the nonreproducible resources in question are human. Entry into the movie industry might be difficult, for example, if the top-quality stars were all under contract to existing firms. Whatever the reason, ownership of a nonreproducible resource gives existing firms an advantage over new entrants and thus constitutes a barrier to entry.

---

[3] A recent study of the Canadian food retailing industry concludes that consumers are probably being harmed by the dominance of only four corporate chains in that industry (Dominion, Steinberg's, Canada Safeway, and Weston-Loblaw), which have simultaneously created overcapacity in the industry. (See Bruce Mallen, "Competition in Canadian Food Retailing," in *Competition and Public Policy on Competition in the Canadian Food Industry*.)

Market performance The ability of a firm to realize economies of scale through efficiency of operation.

Market Power We have seen that there may be barriers to entry in a given industry that are related to market performance. By **market performance** we mean the ability of a firm to realize economies of scale through very efficient operation. Where large size is the result of genuine economies of scale, no economist objects to the existence of large firms, and economists have little sympathy for a smaller firm struggling to remain in existence when it is not large enough to be as efficient as its competitors.

However, the strength of some large firms, and their ability to beat down the opposition of smaller firms, may be due to market power. Market power is not the same thing as market performance, though in cases where economies of scale exist, it may depend at least partly on efficient performance. By **market power**, economists mean the strength that a firm may possess for a whole host of reasons—exclusive control of resources, prior build-up of profits, or networks of influence and command—strength that gives it advantages over potential rivals.

Market power The strength that a firm possesses—because of exclusive control of resources, prior build-up of profits, or networks of influence and command—that gives it an advantage over its rivals.

The following hypothetical example illustrates one aspect of market power. A young engineer in Montreal develops a new method of manufacturing cement that, he claims, can reduce the cost of producing a certain type of cement by one-third. He arranges the financing, builds the plant, installs his new machines, and hires the necessary employees. Assume that his calculations are correct. On the day he opens his plant he announces a price for his cement that is one-third lower than the price charged by the large, single, long-established cement firm in the area. This larger firm cannot produce cement at that price, but, relying on its accumulation of past profits and its network of cement plants across the country, it cuts its price in the Montreal area by one-half. The new firm will now be driven out of business, not because it is unable to achieve efficient operation—it is *more* efficient than its rival—but because it doesn't have the market power of its older rival. The established firm does not have to lose much money, because it can retain higher prices in its other markets, nor does it have to lose money for long, because it can raise the price again as soon as the challenger declares bankruptcy. Incidentally, the practice of the hypothetical established firm in this case would be a violation of Canadian law. It is an example of "predatory pricing," meaning the temporary, localized use of below-cost prices to drive a rival out of business. However, such practices are difficult to prosecute, and the fines levied may be a small price to pay for the elimination of a competitor.

Firms may increase their market power by appointing bank presidents or other persons with specialized knowledge and influence to their boards of directors. Such appointments may give them advantages when it comes to examining new markets or arranging their financing. Several Canadian sociologists have documented the existence of a "corporate elite" in Canada: a social and economic network of about 1,000 business leaders who occupy most of the important directorships in the country.[4] One doesn't have to suffer from paranoia to assume that the social and economic

---

[4]The classic study of this phenomenon remains John Porter, *The Vertical Mosaic* (Toronto: University of Toronto Press, 1965). See also Wallace Clement, *The Canadian Corporate Elite, An Analysis of Economic Power* (Toronto: McClelland and Stewart, 1975), and Peter Newman, *The Canadian Establishment* (Toronto: McClelland and Stewart, 1977), Vol. I.

connections thus established may provide benefits to the participants that place them at an economic advantage over those who operate outside the network.

Firms may also attempt to expand their power and control through formal mergers. Mergers can take many forms. A firm can merge *vertically* with a supplier or purchaser of its products, or *horizontally* with a competitor. It can engage in a *conglomerate* merger with firms producing completely different types of product and services. Horizontal mergers may result in economies of scale, and conglomerate mergers may give the firms more stability by reducing the danger of having all eggs in one basket. Almost always, however, one objective is increased market power, and, from the point of view of potential competitors, the result may be increased barriers to entry. The largest conglomerate in Canada in 1978 was Canadian Pacific Investment, which employed 107,000 people directly or through its many subsidiaries.

Some businesspeople are able to "pyramid" their investments from one company to another, in order to establish effective control over a huge industrial empire without formal mergers. This is illustrated in Exhibit 26.2 which shows how Conrad and Montegu Black in 1978–79 wrested control of the $200 million assets of Argus Corporation and, through that

Exhibit 26.2
The kingdom of Conrad and Montegu Black

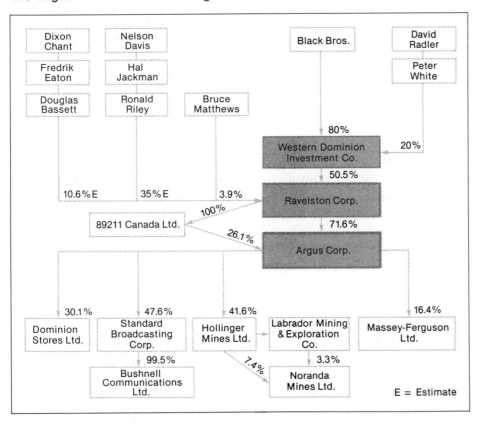

Source: *The Financial Post*, March 3, 1979.

holding corporation, gained substantial control of firms with about $4 billion in assets.

The Black brothers, together with David Radler and Peter White, owned Western Dominion Investment Co. They used this company to obtain 50.5 percent of the voting shares of Ravelston Corporation. In turn they used this corporation to purchase 71.6 percent of Argus Corporation (another 26.1 percent of which they obtained through 89211 Canada Ltd.). Through the assets of Argus they were able to gain large enough interests in such companies as Dominion Stores Ltd. and Massey-Ferguson to assume major control of them.

Patents and Copyrights   Patents and copyrights, another important class of barriers to entry, operate under oligopoly as well as under pure monopoly. A patent or copyright can be treated as a restrictive government regulation. Alternatively, ownership of a patent or copyright can be treated just like ownership of any other nonreproducible resource. Whichever point of view is adopted, patents and copyrights clearly can make entry difficult and thus can contribute to market concentration.

As the term is used here, a *barrier to entry* is something that prevents new entrants from duplicating the performance of existing firms in terms of cost or quality of product. It does not mean that every effort or expense that a firm must undertake to enter a market should be considered such a barrier. To start a new firm, a prospective entrepreneur must be willing to bear risks, must find investors to put up capital, must recruit a labor force, must attract customers, and so on. All these things are hard work—often hard enough to discourage less enterprising individuals from making the effort. Nonetheless, the need for hard work is not itself a barrier to entry in the economic sense. It is when entrepreneurs are not freely able to go out and buy the various building blocks of their new firms in the same market where existing firms buy their inputs, that barriers to entry become a determinant of market structure.

Random Influences

Suppose there is a market with no economies of scale and no barriers to entry. Will such a market necessarily be inhabited by a large number of firms, all of roughly equal size? Not necessarily, it seems. Even after all other factors have been allowed for, pure chance appears to play a very significant role in determining market concentration. Just how significant is suggested by the following case study.

Case 26.1
Chance as a Determinant of Economic Concentration

How much market concentration can be expected in a world from which economies of scale, mergers, government policies, and all other identifiable determinants of concentration are absent? Northwestern University professor F. M. Scherer once performed a computer simulation experiment to try to find out. The answer, he discovered, is that even in such a world, a high degree of market concentration appears not only possible but likely.

Scherer began by constructing an imaginary industry composed of fifty identical firms, each with a 2 percent share of the market. He assumed zero economies of scale. Each year the industry as a whole would grow by 6 percent, but each individual firm in the industry would have a certain random probability of growing a little faster or a little slower than the average. The average rate of growth and the variability of individual firm growth around this average were set equal to the actual rates observed for *Fortune*'s list of the five hundred top industrial corporations. Having gotten all firms off to a fair start, Scherer programmed his computer to follow the industry through 140 years of simulated history. His results for sixteen repetitions of the experiment are shown in Exhibit 26.3.

Exhibit 26.3
Concentration in a simulated market

This exhibit shows the results of a computer simulation experiment on market concentration conducted by F. M. Scherer. Scherer began by assuming a hypothetical industry of fifty firms, all identical and all experiencing no economies of scale. He assumed that the industry would grow at a rate of 6 percent per year but that, by luck, various individual firms would grow faster or slower. In sixteen repetitions of the experiment, shown here, chance alone soon resulted in a moderate to substantial degree of concentration, even when other sources of concentration, such as economies of scale and barriers to entry, were entirely absent.

Four-Firm Concentration Ratios Resulting from Sixteen Simulation Runs of a Stochastic Growth Process Model, with Mean Growth of 6 Percent per Annum and a Standard Deviation of 16 Percent

	Four-Firm Concentration Ratio at Year:							
	1	20	40	60	80	100	120	140
Run 1	8.0	19.5	29.3	36.3	40.7	44.9	38.8	41.3
Run 2	8.0	20.3	21.4	26.1	37.5	41.6	50.8	55.6
Run 3	8.0	18.8	28.9	44.6	43.1	47.1	56.5	45.0
Run 4	8.0	20.9	26.7	31.8	41.9	41.0	64.5	59.8
Run 5	8.0	23.5	33.2	43.8	60.5	60.5	71.9	63.6
Run 6	8.0	21.3	26.6	29.7	35.8	51.2	59.1	72.9
Run 7	8.0	21.1	31.4	29.0	42.8	52.8	50.3	53.1
Run 8	8.0	21.6	23.5	42.2	47.3	64.4	73.1	76.6
Run 9	8.0	18.4	29.3	38.0	45.3	42.5	43.9	52.4
Run 10	8.0	20.0	29.7	43.7	40.1	43.1	42.9	42.9
Run 11	8.0	23.9	29.1	29.5	43.2	50.1	57.1	71.7
Run 12	8.0	15.7	23.3	24.1	34.5	41.1	42.9	53.1
Run 13	8.0	23.8	31.3	44.8	43.5	42.8	57.3	65.2
Run 14	8.0	17.8	23.3	29.3	54.2	51.4	56.0	64.7
Run 15	8.0	21.8	18.3	23.9	31.9	33.5	43.9	65.7
Run 16	8.0	17.5	27.1	28.3	30.7	29.9	37.7	35.3
Average	8.0	20.4	27.0	33.8	42.1	46.7	52.9	57.4

Source: F. M. Scherer, *Industrial Market Structure and Economic Performance* (Chicago, Rand-McNally, 1970), Table 4.4, p. 126. Copyright © 1970 by Rand McNally College Publishing Company. Reprinted by permission.

Why do industries become so highly concentrated when everyone has a fair start and when there are no economies of scale? The answer, according to Scherer, is pure luck. By chance, some firms get an early run of luck and grow faster than the average several years in a row. Once they lead the pack, it is hard for the followers to catch up, since, by definition, each firm has an equal chance to grow by a given *percentage* amount each year. The result is that the imaginary industries end up with just about the same degree of market concentration observed in the real world.

Source: The experiment is described in F. M. Scherer, *Industrial Market Structure and Economic Performance* (Chicago: Rand McNally, 1970), pp. 125–130.

**Joan V. Robinson
(1903–)**

Joan Robinson is best known as a pioneer in the study of the behavior of firms in less than perfectly competitive markets. When she was a young assistant lecturer at Cambridge University, she decided to stand the accepted procedures of economics on their head. "It is customary," she wrote, "in setting out the principles of economic theory, to open with the analysis of a perfectly competitive world, and to treat monopoly as a special case.... This process can with advantage be reversed.... It is more proper to set out the analysis of monopoly, treating perfect competition as a special case." These words and the analysis to support them appeared in her *Economics of Imperfect Competition* in 1933. The book established her reputation immediately and remains one of the basic pioneering contributions to this branch of economics. (As often happens in economics, a similar theory was developed independently and published in the same year — by E. H. Chamberlin.)

Microeconomics was not Robinson's only interest, however. She was a pioneer of macroeconomic thinking. Even as her work on imperfect competition came out, she was involved in the debate that preceded the publication of Keynes's *General Theory*. In fact, in much of her later macro work, she is critical of the very kind of "partial" analysis on which her theory of imperfect competition rests.

Robinson has always been intensely interested in policy questions. In all her policy writings, she is a vehement critic of the market. In 1945, she wrote in *Private Enterprise and Public Control*:

The system of private property in its modern developments leads to great evils. Its inequality is not only an outrage on social justice, but also on common sense. It leads to large scale waste through unemployment, while the development of monopoly creates artificial scarcities and the dominance of the interests of property over the interests of human beings twists the whole system into a form for which it is impossible to find any reasonable justification.

Her opposition to the market and her interest in broad normative questions also led her to write *An Essay on Marxian Economics* (1956), *Economic Philosophy* (1962), and *Freedom and Necessity* (1970). Now long past retirement age, Robinson continues an active life as debater, social critic, and economic heretic.

COORDINATION AND INTERDEPENDENCE UNDER OLIGOPOLY

After this explanation of why some industries are more concentrated than others, the chapter can turn to the behavior of firms in concentrated markets. In particular, it will examine the interdependence of firms in an oligopolistic market and the conditions under which the firms may be able to coordinate their price and output decisions to their mutual advantage.

Oligopolistic Interdependence

Oligopolistic interdependence The necessity, in an oligopolistic market, for each firm to pay close attention to the behavior and likely reactions of its rivals when planning its own market strategy.

When there are only a few firms in a market, it matters very much to each firm what its rivals do. Economists call the situation **oligopolistic interdependence**. This interdependence makes it very difficult to develop a theory of pure economizing in highly concentrated markets. A simple example will explain the problem.

Imagine a market in which there are only two firms — Alpha Company and Zed Enterprises. Their product costs $1 per unit to make. If both firms set their price at $5 per unit, each will sell 100 units per month at a profit of $4 per unit, for a total monthly profit of $400. If both firms set their price at $4 per unit, each will sell 120 units at a profit of $3 per unit for a total profit of $360. Which price will the firms actually set? Clearly, $5 is the price that will maximize their joint profits; but under oligopoly, this price may not represent a stable equilibrium.

Exhibit 26.4 shows why. It presents the alternative pricing strategies available *as they appear to Alpha Company*. In addition to the two possibilities already mentioned, Alpha must consider two more. One new possibility is to cut its price to $4 while Zed holds at $5. That will allow Alpha to steal away a lot of Zed's customers and to sell 150 units, for a profit of $450. The other new possibility is for Alpha to hold its price at $5 while Zed cuts to $4. Then Zed will steal a lot of Alpha's customers and leave Alpha selling only 60 units, for a total profit of $240.

So what will happen? We just don't know! The theories that have helped explain many other market structures do not work for this simple oligopoly problem. We know how the firms can maximize joint profits if they coordinate their efforts. We know how to maximize Alpha's profits if we know what Zed is going to do. We know how to maximize Zed's profits if we know what Alpha is going to do. But none of that is enough. Something is still missing. The missing link needed to solve the problem of oligopolistic interdependence is some assumption about *how Alpha thinks Zed will react* to each possible move that Alpha might make.

Types of Oligopolistic Interdependence All formal theories of oligopoly include some assumption about oligopolistic interdependence—about how each firm will react to its rival's market behavior. Although none of these can be upheld as the single correct theory, several are interesting enough to be worth describing briefly.

One very important possibility is that the rival firms in an oligopolistic market will recognize that they are all in the same boat and will tacitly coordinate their activities. Do unto others as you would have them do unto you will be the golden rule in such a market. Each firm will choose the price

Exhibit 26.4

Profits for Alpha Company under different pricing strategies

This exhibit shows the profits that Alpha Company would earn under different pricing strategies for Alpha and its rival, Zed Enterprises. If both firms price at $5, each earns $400. If both cut their price to $4, they continue to split the market; and each earns $360. If Alpha cuts its price while Zed does not, Alpha steals many of Zed's customers and earns $450. If Zed cuts its price while Alpha's remains at $5, Zed steals many of Alpha's customers, leaving Alpha with only $240 in profit.

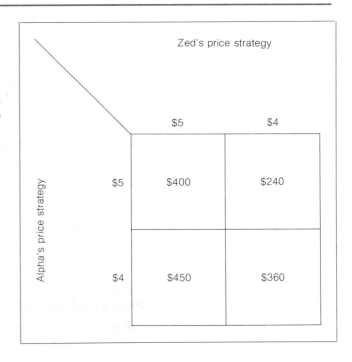

and output strategy that, if chosen by all the others, will maximize joint profits. In terms of the example in Exhibit 26.4, each firm will choose a price of $5. In the more general case, the golden rule will lead to a market equilibrium under oligopoly that will be the same as for a pure monopoly or a perfect cartel.

At the opposite extreme from the assumption of tacit coordination is the assumption that each firm will expect its rivals to do the worst thing possible. In the example, Alpha's managers will ask themselves what is the best they can do if Zed does the worst — that is, cuts its price. The answer is that Alpha must cut its price too. If Zed follows the same reasoning, both firms will end up charging $4.

A more general variation of this theory is based on the assumption that each firm will expect its rivals to match its price decreases but not its increases. Under this assumption, a firm will be reluctant to lower its price because it knows that will only touch off a mutually destructive price war. At the same time, the firm will be reluctant to raise its price because its rivals will keep their prices down and steal customers. This theory has the curious property of saying that, under oligopoly, prices are not likely to change — without saying why prices are at one particular level rather than another in the first place. Nonetheless, it is claimed that some oligopolists actually do have exactly these expectations about their rivals' pricing strategies.

Objection to Formal Theories

Unfortunately, all the assumptions about oligopolistic interdependence just described suffer from a common failing: they make business managers sound terribly naive.

Consider first the assumption of tacit coordination. The best evidence available is that rival firms are not likely to be able to achieve true joint profit maximization through tacit coordination alone. Cartels are explicit agreements among rivals to coordinate price and output strategies. Often cartel agreements are written up in a great detail, with elaborate enforcement and penalty clauses. Yet cartels are notoriously unstable. For each one that works, many fall apart before they get off the ground. And if explicit coordination is so difficult to achieve, how can tacit cooperation have any hope of working very well for very long?

On the other hand, it has been argued that it is just as naive for business-people always to assume that their rivals will do the very worst, when such behavior can clearly be mutually harmful. People have devised ingenious games in which, under controlled conditions, with carefully measured rewards and penalties, experimental subjects play the roles of rival managers. The results of some of these games have shown that after an initial period of all-out competition, opponents gradually learn to play cooperatively, even if they never meet or communicate directly.

Case 26.2
Oligopoly Pricing: Meters and Automobiles

The following news items illustrate how closely oligopoly firms attempt to work with others in setting prices. In Winnipeg two producers of hydro house meters, Westinghouse and Sangamo, submitted the same price on the meters when responding to a tender from Winnipeg Hydro. A representative of Sangamo Co. Ltd. admitted openly that "all firms in the industry attempt to match prices," and Hydro's chief engineer observed that tenders in the last three years had resulted in identical price bids. One of the spokesmen for Westinghouse makes an interesting complaint about what would happen if the firms behaved as if they were independent of each other: "You would see prices juggling all over the place if one company's prices went up and another didn't." There was no price choice, so the city finally chose Westinghouse because it was situated in the city and paid taxes.

Winnipeg's works and operations committee had some difficulty finding an advantage in either of two identical bids submitted by two different firms on a Winnipeg Hydro tender for house meters.

After an hour-long debate, the committee awarded its $246,855 contract for kilowatt-hour meters and base adapters to Westinghouse Canada Ltd., on the grounds that the firm paid property taxes while its competitor did not.

Ted Glass of Westinghouse told committee members the industry has seen the pricing practice for 20 years.

"We are not about to change it," said Glass when asked if the firm would give the city a cost reduction.

"You would see prices juggling all over the place if one company's prices went up and another didn't," said the company representative.

The meters manufactured and distributed by both Canadian companies are almost identical in quality and performance, admitted Glass.

Glass appealed to the committee to accept his firm's bid to help it recover from a four-month strike by United Electrical Workers at its Hamilton plant this year.

Delivery of the meters will be delayed until four weeks after receipt of the order because of stock shortages, said Glass.

R. J. Brown of Sangamo Co. Ltd., which also submitted an identical price of $31.30 a meter, said all firms in the industry attempt to match prices.

Chief engineer, K. H. Hallson, said the city had received identical bids during all of the last three years and had awarded its annual contract to a different firm each time.[5]

The pricing of automobiles in Canada is quite similar. As the second news article indicates, General Motors, which is not only the biggest automobile company but also the biggest company (in sales) overall in Canada, acts as a price leader for the other automobile companies. This creates at least a semblance of price competition. Each fall General Motors announces its price increases on new models. The other automobile manufacturers then follow suit, perhaps over a period of a few weeks. Their increases may not be exactly the same as General Motors', but after a few adjustments back and forth the companies adopt virtually the same increases.

Despite a slight downturn on the sales charts, the Big Four auto makers in Canada will increase prices later this month, The Post has learned.

Paced by an average increase of 5.5 percent by General Motors of Canada Ltd., the North American makers should have new prices on their product lines by February 1.

The GM increase, which averages $255 per car, went into effect this week, but it will take at least a week before the other manufacturers can restructure their prices in line with GM, the traditional price leader. The auto firms always wait for the company's final lists before publishing their own price changes.[6]

[5] "Identical Bid Wins City Contract," *Winnipeg Free Press*, November 15, 1978, p. 10.
[6] Douglas Mepham, "Auto Makers to Follow GM Price Rise," *The Financial Post*, January 15, 1977, p. 1.

Informal Theories of Oligopoly

Many economists have simply given up the hope of developing a workable formal theory of oligopoly. Instead, they have resorted to various informal theories and rules of thumb that may be of some use in judging the performance of oligopolistic markets. These theories can be presented simply as a list of circumstances under which tacit coordination among oligopolists is likely to be more or less successful.

Number and Size of Firms There is little doubt that the number and size of firms in a market make a lot of difference. Tacit coordination in a market with only two or three big firms of roughly equal size is surely more plausible than, say, coordination in a market with an eight-firm concentration ratio of 40 percent. A major reason is that the larger the number of firms, the more likely it is that any one firm can cut prices under the table without its rivals' knowledge.

Price leadership A situation in an oligopolistic market where increases or decreases in price by one dominant firm, known as the price leader, are matched by all or most other firms in the market.

The relative size of the various firms in the market is probably also important. Many observers have suggested that tacit coordination of prices is easier in an industry where there is one clearly dominant firm. That firm may then be able to act as a price leader. Under the strongest form of **price leadership**, firms are no longer uncertain about how their rivals will react to price changes. The leader can be confident that the others will follow it both up and down. The others can be certain that if they follow the leader, others will too; but if they initiate price increases (or decreases) of their own, others will not follow. Ideally, this arrangement can lead to joint monopoly profits for the industry.

However, tacit coordination cannot always be inferred solely from the timing of price changes. In any industry, someone has to be the first to change prices if underlying market conditions change. Even if one particular firm is usually the first to make a move, its role may be no more than that of a barometer telling others that the pressure of demand or cost has made a change necessary.

Nature of the Product The nature of the product is also believed to affect the ease or difficulty of achieving tacit coordination. A homogeneous product with a smooth flow of orders tends to make coordination easier. A variable product with lumpy or irregular orders tends to make it more difficult. With a nonhomogeneous product, there are simply too many things to coordinate. It is not enough that all firms tacitly agree to sell at the same price. They also have to agree on a schedule of allowances above and below the basic price for changes in quality, accelerated or delayed delivery, size of the customer's order, and so on. Under these conditions, an agreement to raise the price above the competitive level, even if it can be sustained, will probably not lead to higher profits. It will more likely lead instead to an outbreak of competition in terms of quality, scheduling, volume discounts, and so on. These things will add to the cost of doing business until excess profits disappear. The next two chapters will return to this theme of nonprice competition several times.

Information Tacit coordination under oligopoly, if possible at all, is probable only in a market where firms have fairly good information about what their rivals are doing. Clearly, there can be no tacit understanding that all firms will charge the same price or follow a price leader if prices are kept secret. So there is little doubt that secrecy is an enemy of coordination under oligopoly.

There is a subtle danger in trying to reverse this formula, however. If secrecy is the enemy of coordination, does that make secrecy the friend of competition? From there it is only a short step to the proposition that bad information is the friend of good market performance. But this last statement is clearly nonsense. The primary function of the market system, after all, is to facilitate the flow of information among potential buyers and sellers. Perfect markets require perfect information, not perfect secrecy.

Growth and Innovation The rates of growth and innovation in a market are a final factor likely to affect the ease or difficulty of tacit coordination among rival oligopolists. In a market where product characteristics, production technologies, and the personalities of individual buyers and sellers do not change from year to year, an agreement among firms, whether tacit or explicit, need never be reworked once it is established. In a market where things change rapidly, any agreement that is reached will soon be rendered obsolete by changing circumstances or disrupted when newly entering buyers or sellers have to be accommodated. Given the uncertainties of establishing tacit agreements and the illegality of establishing explicit agreements, one would expect rival firms to be able to coordinate their activities less successfully the more rapid the pace of growth and change.

MEASURING MARKET PERFORMANCE UNDER OLIGOPOLY

Neither the formal nor the informal theories of oligopoly just discussed give conclusive answers to the question asked at the outset of this chapter—namely, whether rivalry among a few firms in a concentrated market is sufficient to secure good market performance. Good market performance, in this context, means performance resembling that of a perfectly competitive market, with prices equal or close to marginal cost and all major opportunities for mutually competitive transactions among consumers, firms, and resource owners carried out. Poor performance means performance resembling that of a monopoly or cartel, in which efforts of firms to secure higher profits result in equilibrium prices higher than marginal cost and unrealized opportunities for potentially mutually beneficial trades between consumers and resource owners.

With pure theory unable to answer questions about market performance, it is natural for economists to try to answer the questions by the statistical examination of empirical data. Because it is usually difficult to measure directly whether a gap exists between a firm's output prices and its marginal costs, the most common approach taken is an indirect one. If firms in concentrated industries can be shown, on the average, to earn higher than normal rates of return on capital, it is reasoned, the inference that they are behaving more like monopolists than like perfect competitors can be drawn. If, on the other hand, firms in concentrated industries appear to earn rates of return no higher, on the average, than firms in relatively unconcentrated industries, it can be inferred that oligopolies perform about as well as more competitively structured industries.

Early Empirical Studies

The first person to try this approach in a systematic way was University of California professor Joe Bain. In 1951, he published the results of a study of forty-two selected industries for the years 1936–1940. These results are shown in Exhibit 26.5. According to Bain's interpretation of the data, industries with concentration ratios over 70 earned higher profits than less concentrated industries. The relationship between profits and concentration was not perfect and not overwhelmingly strong, but it did exist.

During the 1950s and 1960s, many of Bain's students and followers repeated his studies for other industries and other years. Most of them got the same results—a weak but persistent relationship between profits and concentration. It became part of the conventional wisdom of economics that the more highly concentrated an industry, the more likely its performance would resemble that of a cartel or monopoly. This would be true even if there were no conspiracy among rivals to raise prices and divide markets.

More Recent Results

As faith in this proposition grew, economists tried harder and harder to verify it, using the more powerful statistical techniques and better data that became available year by year. Curiously, the harder they tried, the more elusive the relationship became. Some studies showed that if adjustments were made for the absolute size of firms in different markets, the relationship between concentration and profits tended to disappear. Other studies showed that if adjustments were made for differences in advertising expenditures, the relationship would disappear. Still other studies seemed to show that results like Bain's held only in years of depression and recession and disappeared with prosperity.

Average of Industry Average Profit Rates, by Concentration Groups, Forty-two Selected Industries, 1936–1940

Eight-Firm Concentration Ratio	Average Profit Rate	Number of Industries
90–100	12.7	8
80–89	9.8	11
70–79	16.3	3
60–69	5.8	5
50–59	5.8	4
40–49	8.6	2
30–39	6.3	5
20–29	10.4	2
10–19	17.0	1
0–9	9.1	1

Source: Joe S. Bain, "Relation of Profit-Rate to Industry Concentration," *Quarterly Journal of Economics* 65 (August 1951), p. 293. Copyright © 1951 by the President and Fellows of Harvard College; all rights reserved. Reprinted by permission.

Exhibit 26.5

The relationship of market concentration to profits

This table shows the relationship between market concentration and profits, according to a pioneering study published in 1951. The table appears to indicate that firms in industries with concentration ratios over 70 earn higher profits, on the average, than firms in less concentrated industries. The validity of the relationship shown by the figures has been the subject of lively debate ever since.

What is more, even as the relationship between concentration and profits was becoming less certain, economists were also becoming less certain about how such a relationship should be interpreted even if it were confirmed. New reasons were discovered why firms in more concentrated industries might appear to earn higher profits than firms in less concentrated industries. These reasons had nothing to do with monopoly pricing or tacit collusion. For example, a concentrated industry that was growing rapidly might need to earn high profits to attract the new capital it needed. Or the high profits of the largest firms in each concentrated industry might simply reflect the firms' superior efficiency relative to smaller firms in the same industry. Finally, the higher profits that some concentrated industries appeared to earn might not be profits at all in the economic sense. They might reflect only the fact that the categories used by accountants to classify business transactions are different from those used by economic theorists.

It is still too early to tell which team of econometricians will have the last word in the debate over concentration and profits or which team of theorists will have the last word on what the relationship means, if there really is one. For the moment, however, it appears that the empirical approach is not much more successful than the theoretical approach in solving the riddle of oligopoly behavior.

CONCLUSIONS

This chapter began with the question of whether rivalry among the few is enough to guarantee satisfactory market performance. After reviewing the apparent determinants of market concentration, the informal theories of oligopoly behavior, and the empirical evidence on the relationship between concentration and profits, the answer is maybe yes, maybe no—it all depends.

Perhaps, though, economists are looking in the wrong place for an answer. The search for a theory of oligopoly is a search for a theory that is analogous to the theories of perfect competition and monopoly but lying somewhere in between. The theories of monopoly and competition, however, are theories of pure economizing. They deal with only a part of business reality—the search for maximum profits under *given* conditions of demand, technology, and resource availability. Perhaps economists would do better in their efforts to understand competition among the few if they broadened their focus to take into account more of the entrepreneurial elements in business decision making.

There have already been some hints that this is where they should look. The subjects of advertising competition and nonprice competition have come up more than once. These forms of competition involve entrepreneurial decision making. The question of barriers to entry has been raised. Entry of a new firm into an industry is an entrepreneurial decision. And such entrepreneurial variables as product homogeneity, growth, and innovation play major roles in determining how firms behave in concentrated markets. Without further delay, then, a new chapter will look into some of these things.

SUMMARY

1. Markets that have more than one firm but fewer than many firms are called *oligopolies*. Any study of oligopoly must pay close attention to the phenomenon of business rivalry. The conduct of oligopolistic firms is very much influenced by what each firm expects its rivals to do in the competitive struggle for sales and profits.

2. The four-firm (or eight-firm) concentration ratio for a market is the percentage of industry output contributed by the top four (or eight) firms in the market. Close to one-half of all manufacturing output in Canada comes from markets with a four-firm concentration ratio of 50 or more.

3. Economies of scale are one major determinant of market concentration. Plant level economies alone, however, are not enough to explain observed concentration ratios. Economies of multi-plant operation must also be taken into account. Even when multi-plant scale economies are accounted for, some market concentration remains to be explained by barriers to entry and random influences.

4. Many attempts have been made to construct a formal theory of oligopoly. Such a theory would resemble the theories of perfect competition and pure monopoly but would lie somewhere between the two. However, the formal theory of oligopoly to date has not been conspicuously successful. The reason is that it is very difficult to know how firms will react to the price and output decisions of their rivals. No simple assumption works for all cases.

5. Even in the absence of a formal theory of oligopoly, an attempt can be made to list factors that are likely to facilitate or hamper tacit coordination among rival firms. Among the most important factors are the number and size of firms in the market, the nature of the product, the availability of information about rival firms, and the rates of growth and innovation in the market.

6. Partly because oligopoly theory does not give clear answers about market performance in concentrated industries, economists have made many efforts to see whether firms in such industries are more profitable than those in less concentrated industries. If they were, that might indicate that oligopolists were able to achieve tacit coordination of their price and output decisions. Initial results reported during the 1950s appeared to indicate that concentrated industries were more profitable. More recent studies, however, have called these early results into question.

DISCUSSION QUESTIONS

1. What is the difference between rivalry and competition? What does it mean to say that rivalry is a matter of conduct, while competition is a matter of structure?

2. The data on market concentration in Exhibit 26.1 relate only to manufacturing, the sector of the economy that has been studied most closely in this respect. How highly concentrated do you think the following sectors of the economy are: Agriculture? Transportation? Services? Retail trade? Communications? What factors do you think probably account for concentration or lack of concentration in each of these sectors?

3. Evaluate the following statement: barriers to entry are lower in the restaurant industry than in the airline industry, because a restaurant requires only a few workers and a few thousand dollars in capital, while even a small airline requires hundreds of workers and millions of dollars in capital.

4. Would you consider the market for university education to be an oligopoly? What factors do you think determine the structure of the university "industry"? How important are economies of scale? Barriers to entry? Chance factors?

5. Oligopoly has sometimes been called a game, because each player's behavior depends on thinking ahead to outguess the strategies and reactions of rivals. How does oligopoly resemble such games as chess? Bridge? Tennis? War? Would it surprise you to learn that the formal theory of games is not much more practical help in understanding actual games than formal theories of oligopoly are in understanding actual oligopoly behavior? Explain.

C H A P T E R 27

ADVERTISING AND MONOPOLISTIC COMPETITION

WHAT YOU WILL LEARN IN THIS CHAPTER

This chapter introduces a number of topics in competition and market performance. First, it reviews an ongoing controversy concerning the conditions under which advertising can act as a barrier to entry into a market or industry. In connection with the discussion of advertising and nonprice competition, it introduces a formal theory of monopolistic competition. Finally, it distinguishes between static and dynamic efficiency and explains why both kinds of efficiency must be considered when evaluating the effects of market structure on market performance.

FOR REVIEW

Here are some important terms and concepts that will be put to use in this chapter. If you do not understand them, review them before proceeding.
- *Positive and normative economics (Chapter 1)*
- *Pure economizing (Chapter 19)*
- *Theory of consumer choice (Chapter 19)*
- *Pure monopoly and monopolistic competition (Chapter 24)*

There are still large pieces missing from the picture of competition assembled in the last four chapters. For one thing, up to this point the emphasis has been mainly on price and output decisions. Advertising, product innovation, and other forms of nonprice competition have remained in the background. In addition, the focus has been more on pure economizing than on entrepreneurial aspects of business conduct. This chapter will try to fill in some of the gaps and broaden the understanding of the process of competition.

It will begin with a discussion of advertising—first its effects on consumers and then its possible role as a barrier to entry into markets or industries. From there, it will move to a discussion of monopolistic competition—the market structure under which there are numerous firms and no barriers to entry but under which nonprice competition is very important. Finally, it will discuss the relationships among market structure, innovation, and competition for entrepreneurs.

ADVERTISING AND THE CONSUMER

The Consumer as Economizer and Entrepreneur

Chapter 19 presented the outlines of a long established economic theory of consumer choice. This theory sees consumer choice as a classic problem in pure economizing. Consumers are presented with certain givens — namely, their tastes, the size of their budgets, the characteristics of available goods, and the prices of those goods. Using these givens, consumers must calculate the mix of purchases that will give them the greatest satisfaction. They do this by equalizing the marginal utility per dollar's worth of goods for all goods.

In certain important respects, this theory of consumer choice resembles the theories of perfect competition and monopoly developed in Chapters 23 and 24. All are theories of pure economizing, which is to say that all are concerned with situations in which the decision maker confronts objectives, alternative activities, and constraints as givens — clearly known and not subject to manipulation. In addition, all these theories are concerned with decision-making situations in which price and quantity are the primary variables.

In reality, though, consumer choice is a matter of more than just pure economizing. Consumers are not fully aware of prices and product characteristics. They are not givens; they are constantly changing. Consumer decision making is not costless or instantaneous. Instead, it requires significant time and effort. The practical consequence is that consumers, just as much as business managers, must constantly be making entrepreneurial decisions. They have to be alert to new information, and they have to be willing to explore innovative ways of satisfying their wants.

Recognizing the entrepreneurial element in consumer decision making is the key to understanding how advertising works. It is not possible to understand why businesses spend money on advertising until it is understood why advertising affects the way consumers spend their money.

Overcoming Consumer Ignorance

Any explanation of how advertising works must begin with the simple fact that because information is costly to acquire, consumers are always ignorant to some degree. They may have some idea how much eggs cost, but they do not automatically know whether this week eggs are cheaper at Dominion or at Loblaws. They know beds are bought in furniture stores, but they are not able to reel off a list of all the furniture stores in town — at least not if the town is very big. They know what a car is, but they do not always know which ones have front-wheel drive or which have side-window defrosters. Every firm can feel certain that there are consumers who would buy its product if they knew about it. By telling consumers of the price and characteristics of products and the places where they can be bought, advertisements attract enough customers to pay for the resources spent to produce the ads.

Inducing Changes in Demand

Other kinds of advertising are aimed not at informing consumers about prices and products but at changing their tastes. If consumer tastes are changeable, firms can make profits by changing them. Making consumers like a firm's product more can increase the demand for the product and in some cases can make the demand more inelastic. Sales or prices or both can then be increased, which will raise profits. To understand advertising, then, it is useful to know something about the mechanisms by which consumer tastes are produced and modified.

Changing Tastes For one thing, people's tastes and preferences do not originate spontaneously. Instead, they are strongly influenced by the tastes and preferences of others. Some people are innovators and take up new styles or products of their own accord, but more people are imitators and change their buying patterns only after they see others change. The interaction of innovators and imitators in the consumer community keeps tastes and styles in flux. Through advertising, firms can hope to control the direction and pace of change. Controlled and predictable change is more profitable and less risky than random change. It can be worth the advertising resources invested to produce it.

Changing Perceptions Changing tastes is not the whole story, though. Market researchers have found that advertising changes not only tastes but also perceptions. It can influence not only which product people will like but how well they will like a given, unchanged product. The following case study provides an interesting illustration.

Case 27.1
Advertising and the Perceived Taste of Turkey Meat

In 1965, James C. Makens of Michigan Technological University conducted an experiment to determine the effect of a well-known brand name on consumers' preferences for turkey meat. In Part 1 of the experiment, 150 subjects from Detroit were presented with two plates, each containing a slice of turkey meat. Although the two slices were actually from the same turkey, they were labeled differently. One bore a brand name heavily advertised and well known in Detroit, and the other bore an unfamiliar brand name. Of the 150 subjects, only 10 percent indicated that they thought the two samples tasted alike; 56 percent expressed a definite preference for the known brand, and 34 percent preferred the unknown brand. Makens concluded that in the presence of brand name clues, the subjects tended to perceive identical portions of turkey as being different, and they tended to prefer the more familiar name.

In Part 2 of the experiment, sixty-one consumers were presented with two plates. One plate contained a slice of tender turkey meat and the other a slice of tough turkey meat. This time, no brand names were used. The tender sample was marked with one symbol and the tough sample with another. Forty-nine subjects said they preferred the tender meat, four said they preferred the tough meat, and eight said they could not tell the difference. The conclusion was that, in the absence of brand name clues, consumers generally can perceive an actual difference in quality.

In the final part of the experiment, the sixty-one subjects who had tasted the samples marked with symbols were asked to indicate which brand they thought each sample belonged to — after they had said which they preferred. Thirty-four subjects said that the turkey they preferred must have been the known brand; eighteen identified the preferred turkey as probably the unknown brand; and one did not express an opinion. The conclusion was that consumers tended to think it likely that the high quality product was the one with which they were familiar.

Makens summarized his results in these terms: "Brand preference for one well-known turkey brand was strong enough to influence the perceived taste for turkey meat among the subjects....[Also] the consumers expect a well-known brand to be of superior quality to an unknown brand" (p. 263).

Similar results have been reported elsewhere. These experiments leave us a long way from the idea that taste and preferences are a given of the consumer choice process.

Source Based on James C. Makens, "Effect of Brand Preferences upon Consumers' Perceived Taste of Turkey Meat," *Journal of Applied Psychology* 49 (November 4, 1965), p. 261-263. Used by permission.

Brand Loyalty In the idealized world of economic theory, the decisions consumers make are neither costly nor time-consuming. In the real world, this is not so. The shortcuts consumers take to simplify the decisions they have to make sometimes create openings for advertisers. An example is the phenomenon of brand loyalty.

A brand loyal consumer keeps decision costs down by choosing the same brand again and again. Where does brand loyalty come from? It can perhaps be explained to some degree on the basis of innate differences in tastes among consumers. (Some people may just be born with a liking for Molson Golden and others with a liking for Labatt 50.) The following case study, though, shows that there is more to brand loyalty.

Case 27.2
An Experimental Study of Brand Loyalty

In 1968, J. Douglass McConnell of the Stanford Research Institute reported the results of an experimental study of brand loyalty. The product chosen for the experiment was beer. It was chosen because people buy beer frequently and because McConnell judged that the nature of the product would help motivate subjects to stay with the experiment over the two-month period required. A random sample of sixty beer drinkers was drawn from Stanford University students living in married student housing. The subjects were told that the experiment was part of a marketing test of three types of beer produced by a local brewer.

Once a week, the subjects were presented, in their homes, with an opportunity to choose one bottle from among three bottles labeled "M," "L," and "P." They were told that Brand M was a high-priced beer, Brand L a medium-priced beer, and Brand P a bargain-priced beer. The subjects did not actually have to pay for their beer; but to make the price difference seem realistic, the medium-priced beer, had a $.02 "refund" taped to the bottle, and the low-priced beer had a $.05 "refund." The subjects could keep the refunds.

In point of fact, the three brands of beer were identical. They were all drawn from the same production run at the brewery, and they differed only in terms of the labels added by the experimenter. This, however, did not prevent the development of fierce brand loyalties by many of the subjects. One measure of brand loyalty that McConnell used was the occurrence of four consecutive choices of the same label. Although at first the subjects experimented with different brands, by the end of twenty-four trials, fifty-seven of the sixty had developed brand loyalty, as measured by the four-choice criterion. Of these fifty-seven, twenty-six chose Brand M, twelve Brand L, and nineteen Brand P.

Another measure of brand loyalty is the probability of making a switch in brands from one trial to the next. The lower the probability of switching, the more loyal. Exhibit 27.1 shows how the probability of switching decreased rapidly over the first twelve trials of the experiment.

Because the beer was actually all the same, these results could not be explained by any "given" differences in tastes. The results instead suggest that, by convincing themselves that one brand was better than another, the subjects avoided the painful task of having to make up their minds from scratch at each trial.

Exhibit 27.1

Effects of repeated tasting on brand loyalty

In the experiment, subjects were given a choice of three bottles of beer on each trial. The bottles had different labels, but their contents were the same. At first, consumers experimented, switching from brand to brand to find one they liked. Soon, though, the frequency of switching fell to a low level as brand loyalty developed.

Source J. Douglass McConnell, "The Development of Brand Loyalty: An Experimental Study." *Journal of Marketing Research 5* (February 1968), Table 3. Reprinted from *Journal of Marketing Research* published by the American Marketing Association.

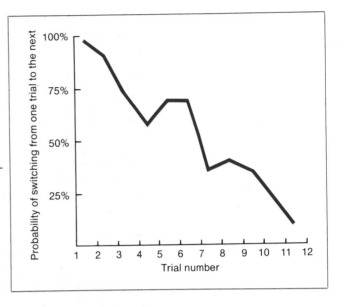

Given the nature of the choice the subjects were offered, it is remarkable how firmly set in their opinions some of them became. One woman reported, "M is a good strong malty beer, but I like L because it is lighter. Mmm!!! P would poison me — make me ill." A man who developed an enthusiasm for P once deviated to experiment with a bottle of M and reported, "Worst I've ever had; you couldn't give it away."

Source: Based on J. Douglass McConnell, "The Development of Brand Loyalty: An Experimental Study," *Journal of Marketing Research* 5 (February 1968), pp. 13-19. Used by permission.

Normative Implications

So far, the chapter has discussed advertising and the consumer purely from the point of view of positive economics. It can, for example, be experimentally verified that external clues, such as exposure to advertising or differences in price, change consumer perceptions of unchanged products. This kind of positive analysis of the effects of advertising is all that is really needed in order to understand the role of advertising in the competitive process. In practice, though, advertising is an emotionally charged subject that invites normative as well as positive analysis. Before moving on to a discussion of advertising and market structure, then, the chapter will look at some of the normative issues that advertising raises.

The Case against Advertising   It is not hard for opponents of advertising to get an audience. Anyone who has ever been interrupted in the middle of a favorite Bogart film on late-night television is an automatic convert. But the case against advertising rests on much more than just the complaint that it is intrusive, annoying, ugly, and distracting. Following are some of the most common normative objections to advertising that economists make.

Heading the list of arguments against advertising is the complaint that it violates consumer sovereignty. Producers, it is said, do not adjust their output to consumer preferences. Instead, they use advertising to force consumers to buy whatever it is that they feel like producing. Harvard professor John Kenneth Galbraith has been one of the most vocal proponents of this view. In his book, *The Affluent Society*, he put the matter this way:

Were it so that a man arising each morning was assailed by demons which instilled in him a passion sometimes for silk shirts, sometimes for kitchen ware, sometimes for chamber pots, and sometimes for orange squash, there would be every reason to applaud the effort to find the goods, however odd, that quenched this flame....

Consumer wants can have bizarre, frivolous, or even immoral origins, and an admirable case can still be made for a society which seeks to satisfy them. But the case cannot stand if it is the process of satisfying wants that creates the wants. For then the individual who urges the importance of production to satisfy those wants is precisely in the position of the onlooker who applauds the efforts of the squirrel to keep abreast of the wheel that is propelled by his own effort.[1]

Advertising is identified as the chief method by which the people who satisfy the wants (that is, the economy's business firms) also create those wants. According to Galbraith, a distinction must be made between wants that are innate within the consumer and those that producers create through advertising. Consumer sovereignty means guiding production purely in accordance with innate wants. Advertising and all other means of want creation are a violation of that sovereignty.

Twenty years after the appearance of Galbraith's book, the ideas he expressed remain popular. Now they often take the form of the doctrine of consumer alienation, to use a term favored by Marxist-oriented economists. The doctrine is based on the idea that people have two sets of preferences. One set reflects their "true" wants and needs; the other reflects the "false" wants and needs created by advertising and other evils of modern capitalism. In this view, consumer sovereignty is a mockery unless preceded by consumer liberation from false needs and desires.

---

[1] John Kenneth Galbraith, *The Affluent Society* (Boston: Houghton Mifflin, 1958), pp. 153-154.

**John Kenneth Galbraith
(1908–   )**

John Kenneth Galbraith, a native Canadian who has been teaching economics at Harvard University in Boston for many years, enjoys a unique distinction among economists today: his books regularly hit the best-seller list and stay there for long periods. Galbraith represents the opposite extreme from economists who, like Paul Samuelson, write primarily to gain the applause of other economists. On the contrary, his major books — *The Affluent Society* (1958) and *The New Industrial State* (1967) — are all-out attacks on conventional economics, written to be read by the widest possible nonprofessional audience.

Galbraith lumps everything he dislikes about modern economics under the heading of "the conventional wisdom." By this phrase, he means all the ideas that he claims are widely believed not because they are true but simply because they are often repeated. He saves his sharpest barbs for two particular elements of the conventional wisdom: consumer sovereignty and the law of supply and demand.

Consumers are not sovereign, Galbraith says, because their tastes and preferences are heavily manipulated by advertising. The ability of business to manipulate consumers knocks the "demand" leg out from under supply and demand theory. The "supply" leg is then knocked out with a second deftly aimed kick. The supply curve is valid only in an economy where firms aim to maximize profits. In the U.S. economy, says Galbraith, firms do not do this. How, then, can supply and demand determine price? The kinds of goods that consumers are persuaded to buy and the prices at which these goods are sold are determined by the whims of the "technostructure," Galbraith's name for the managerial-professional-academic elite who run the country.

Galbraith is many things other than an economist. He is a political activist, always promoting liberal and ultraliberal causes. He served as chairman of the Americans for Democratic Action, and he played a key role in securing the Democratic presidential nomination for George McGovern. He is also a diplomat and served as John Kennedy's ambassador to India. (At six feet eight inches, he towered almost comically over his local diplomatic counterparts there.) He once even turned his hand to writing a novel, *The Triumph*.

Few economists take the complete Galbraithian system seriously, but many admit that he is a useful critic. Economics, like other social science disciplines, is in fact always in danger of becoming excessively abstract and formalistic. Economists who talk only to other economists, and then only in mathematical language, do indeed often end up saying things that are just plain silly. Galbraith is determined that they not get away with it.

Another Point of View But by no means do all economists accept the view that advertising is a violation of consumer sovereignty or an attempt to exploit some shameful, perverse side of human nature. Those who adopt a less hostile attitude toward advertising usually begin by making the point that there are no such things as natural, given, or innate consumer preferences, at least not if one means by this preferences for specific kinds of goods and services. People may well be born with basic needs for food, security, affection, self-esteem, and the rest; but there is an infinite variety of particular goods that can satisfy these needs. If the advertisers of one generation persuade people that their need to keep their feet dry is best satisfied with pointy-toed boots and those of the next that square-toed boots do the job better, so what? One should not be silly enough to think that, left to their own devices, people's "true" tastes in boot-toes would magically emerge, making everyone better off.

Perhaps, some go so far as to say, the idea of true and false preferences itself poses a potential threat to consumer sovereignty. Perhaps the so-called true preferences are just the preferences of a cultural elite who do not like the lowbrow life-styles of their neighbors. Because the members of this elite prefer Beaujolais to Baby Duck, or "tastefully" styled European cars to "tasteless" North American cars, they think that everyone else ought to share their preferences. It is a short step from a policy of forbidding the advertising of Baby Duck and Buicks to a policy of forbidding their production in the name of giving the people what they really want. And then what becomes of consumer sovereignty?

The economists's case against advertising, however, does not consist entirely in the claim that it violates consumer sovereignty. There is also a group of issues concerning the effect of advertising on market performance under oligopoly and monopolistic competition. These issues too, as will be shown, are highly controversial.

Is Advertising a Barrier to Entry?

Perhaps the most controversial issue of all is that of advertising as a barrier to entry. If advertising does represent a barrier to entry, then it may contribute to high levels of market concentration. And as shown in the last chapter, market concentration in turn may lead to poor market performance.

Advertising as a Barrier The mechanism by which advertising acts as a barrier to entry is said to be the creation of brand loyalties. Consumers who might otherwise treat all cola drinks as very close substitutes are divided into opposing camps, some fiercely loyal to Pepsi, others to Coca-Cola. Each firm can then raise its price with little fear that doing so will cause its customers to go elsewhere. And each firm will have to worry less that the resulting high profits will attract new entrants, because the new firms will not only have to spend money to build plants and hire workers but will also have to mount fabulously expensive advertising campaigns.

In 1967, this view of the effects of advertising received a substantial boost from W. S. Comanor and T. A. Wilson, who looked at the statistical relationship between advertising expenditures and profits in forty-one industries and reached the following conclusion:

It is evident that . . . advertising is a highly profitable activity. Industries with high advertising outlays earn, on the average, at a profit rate which exceeds that of other industries by nearly four percentage points. This differential represents a 50 percent increase in profit rates. It is likely, moreover, that much of this profit rate differential is accounted for by the entry barriers created by advertising expenditures and by the resulting achievement of market power.[2]

An Alternative View of Advertising and Entry Neither the theory of advertising as a barrier to entry nor the result of the Comanor and Wilson study have been accepted by everyone, however. Other economists, notably Yale Brozen of the University of Chicago business school, see the relationship between advertising and competition in a rather different light.[3]

According to Brozen, the theory that advertising is a barrier to entry stands reality on its head: advertising is not an impediment to competition; it is a means of competition. Existing firms have no advantage over new firms in buying advertising; ad agencies stand ready to sell their services to anyone willing to pay the proper fee. In fact, advertising is even more important for new firms than for existing firms. In Brozen's view, firms aim their advertising not so much at building loyalty in their own customers as at getting their rivals' customers to try something different. The real way to create a barrier to entry and protect established oligopolies, he says, would be to outlaw advertisng. Then it would be far harder for a new firm to break into a market.

What about the Comanor and Wilson study, though? Brozen treats the apparent relationship between profits and advertising as an example of the fallacy of confusing accounting categories with the categories of economic theory. Encouraged by certain features of the tax laws, accountants treat advertising as a current expense, like wages or purchases of materials. In fact, Brozen contends, advertising is an investment having long-term

---

[2] W. S. Comanor and T. A. Wilson, "Advertising, Market Structure, and Performance," *Review of Economics and Statistics* 49 (November 1967), p. 437.

[3] For a representative exposition of Brozen's views, see Yale Brozen, "Entry Barriers: Advertising and Product Differentiation," in *Industrial Concentration: The New Learning*, ed. Harvey J. Goldschmid, H. Michael Mann, and J. Fred Weston (Boston: Little, Brown, 1974), pp. 115-137. For a Canadian defense of advertising in somewhat similar terms see O. J. Firestone, *The Economic Implications of Advertising* (Toronto: Methuen, 1967).

effects. A brand image takes years to develop; and once developed, it is a valuable, long-lasting asset for the company that created it. If an adjustment is made to treat advertising as an investment, companies that advertise intensively no longer appear to be more profitable than the average.

Advertising and Monopolistic Competition

Up to this point, the discussion of advertising and market performance has centered on markets that are oligopolistic in structure. Critics of advertising have charged that in such markets, advertising acts as a barrier to entry, that it contributes to market concentration, and that it is associated with excessively high rates of profit. Now attention will be given to the claim that even in markets where none of these things is true, advertising may have adverse effects on market performance. This effort will require a closer look at a type of market structure that has been mentioned before only in passing: monopolistic competition.

According to the definition given in Chapter 24, a monopolistically competitive market is one in which there are a large number of small firms, a differentiated product, and no significant barriers to entry. Examples can be found in such industries as restaurants, gasoline retailing, and personal services.

Equilibrium for the Firm under Monopolistic Competition The theory of monopolistic competition, like its definition, is a blend of monopolistic and competitive elements. The theory can be understood with the help of Exhibit 27.2, which shows short-run and long-run equilibrium positions for a typical firm under monopolistic competition.

Exhibit 27.2
Short-run and long-run equilibrium under monopolistic competition
Under monopolistic competition, each firm has a downward-sloping demand curve, but there are no barriers to entry. In the short run, a firm producing at the point where marginal cost is equal to marginal revenue can earn profits in excess of the normal rate of return, as shown in Part a of the diagram. In the long run, however, new competitors are attracted. This diverts part of the demand from firms originally in the market, and the original firms may fight to retain their market shares, using promotional techniques that add to total costs. Entry will continue until a long-run equilibrium in which profits are eliminated is reached, as shown in Part b.

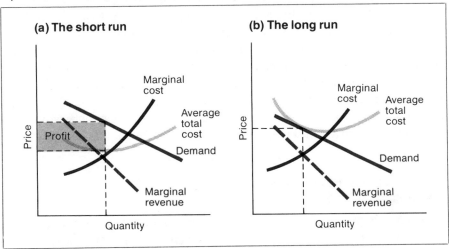

The demand curve for a monopolistically competitive firm, like that for a pure monopolist, slopes downward, although it is likely to be more elastic than that of a monopolist. Each firm's product is a little different from the products of its competitors. Each firm can therefore raise its price at least a little without losing all its customers, because some customers attach more importance than others to the special style or location or whatever that the firm offers. Given this downward-sloping demand curve, the short-run profit maximizing position shown is analytically the same as that for a pure monopolist. The quantity of output is determined by the intersection of the marginal cost and marginal revenue curves, and the price charged is determined by the height of the demand curve at that point.

But this short-run equilibrium cannot also be a long-run equilibrium under monopolistic competition. The reason is freedom of entry. In the short-run position shown in Exhibit 27.2a, the firm is earning profits in excess of the normal rate of return on investment. (This is shown by the fact that price exceeds average total cost.) High profits attract new competitors. As new competitors come in, the demand curves of firms that are already there will shift downward, because the new entrants will sell products that are reasonably good substitutes for those of the original firms. If the original firms try to resist the shift in demand by improving their products or marketing them more aggressively, those efforts will raise their average total costs. The downward shift in the demand curve of the original firms and/or the upward shift in their cost curves will continue until there are no more profits to attract new entrants. The result is the long-run equilibrium position shown in Exhibit 27.2b.

Market Performance In this long-run equilibrium position, it is claimed, markets perform poorly. For one thing, as under pure monopoly, each firm produces too little of its product. The gap between price and marginal cost indicates an unrealized potential for further mutually beneficial transactions. In addition, the monopolistically competitive firms do not operate at the minimum points on their long-run average cost curves. If there were fewer firms, each producing a greater quantity of output, the same quantity of products could be provided to consumers at a lower total cost. The hallmarks of monopolistic competition, then, are said to be too many gas stations, supermarkets, and restaurants, each operating at only a fraction of capacity and each charging inefficiently high prices, yet each earning no more than the minimum return needed to stay in business.

And what does advertising have to do with all this? Advertising is said to make the effects of monopolistic competition worse than they otherwise would be. The reason is that advertising exaggerates the differences among the products of various firms and thus makes each firm's demand curve less elastic than it would otherwise be. The performance gap between monopolistic competition and perfect competition is thus made even wider.

Are Perfect Competition and Monopolistic Competition Different?

The analysis of market performance under monopolistic competition just given has not been accepted by all economists. Many scholarly articles have been written on the subject, and many elaborate mathematical variations on the theory have been suggested. Setting aside differences in detail, most of the attempts to defend monopolistic competition come down to the simple idea that monopolistic competition and perfect competition are not really significantly different.

One argument is that the illusion of a difference comes from a mistaken idea about the nature of the product being sold. Take restaurants, for example. The restaurants in any town sell meals that are highly differentiated according to location, national cuisine, atmosphere, service, and many other characteristics. But perhaps meals are not really the relevant product. Instead, think of all restaurants as selling a homogeneous good called dining pleasure. The differences among restaurants should be thought of not as differences in product but rather as differences in the technology used to produce dining pleasure and differences in the size of the package of dining pleasure being sold. By analogy, different farmers grow potatoes in assorted sizes and use a variety of farming methods, but the potato market is still considered to be close to perfectly competitive. The dining pleasure market, according to this line of reasoning, is no different from the potato market.

A variation of this defense of monopolistic competition acknowledges differences among products but points out that product diversity is valuable in and of itself. Suppose it were true, as the theory of monopolistic competition suggests, that prices would be a little lower if there were fewer barbershops, each not quite so conveniently located, or fewer supermarkets, each a little more crowded, or fewer flavors of ice cream. Would a move in that direction benefit consumers? Not necessarily, if consumers are willing to pay something for variety. Imagine that there were some way to split the market for, say, ice cream into two markets—one for the good called ice cream and the other for the good called variety. If that were possible, then each good could have its own separate price, and each market could be perfectly competitive. But such a split is simply impossible. In the real world, a single market for both goods, having the structure described as monopolistic competition, is as close as one can come to the ideal.

Evidence on Advertising and Market Performance

As in so many cases where economic theorists disagree, attempts have been made to use empirical methods to settle the controversy about advertising and market performance under monopolistic competition. The studies on advertising and profits are not really relevant here, because firms would not be expected to earn profits under either perfect or monopolistic competition. Instead, evidence bearing more directly on the effect of advertising on market structure is needed. Is the natural state of the world one in which consumers tend to view all sources of supply as just alike and to move freely among them in response to small changes in price? Or is the natural state one in which inertia and ignorance on the part of consumers cause them to cling to familiar sources of supply, giving each firm a local monopoly vis-à-vis its own customers? And advertising—does it set up unnatural barriers between firms, thereby adding to their monopoly power, or does it break down natural barriers, thereby destroying monopoly power? A number of kinds of evidence might help answer these questions.

One kind of evidence comes from studies of consumer behavior, such as the two case studies earlier in this chapter. But these studies by themselves do not entirely settle the issue. Case 27.1, for example, showed that advertising affected the perceived taste of turkey meat that was actually all from the same turkey. This indicates that advertising can increase brand loyalty. On the other hand, Case 27.2 showed that in the case of beer, people not subjected to advertising also perceived great differences among actually identical goods and were very reluctant to switch from one "brand" to another. This indicates that brand loyalty can arise even in the absence of advertising.

Another kind of evidence comes from studies of how advertising is actually used by firms. For example, it has been shown that new products are advertised more intensively than old products. This may indicate that makers of old products tend to depend on consumer inertia and that advertising is a way of breaking down that inertia. It has also been shown that consumers in markets where advertising is heavy are less loyal to one brand than are consumers in markets where advertising is light. This too might indicate that advertising helps overcome consumer reluctance to try substitute products.[4]

MARKET DYNAMICS AND COMPETITION AMONG ENTREPRENEURS

Static Efficiency versus Dynamic Efficiency

Static efficiency The ability of an economy to get the greatest consumer satisfaction from given resources and technology.

Dynamic efficiency The ability of an economy to increase consumer satisfaction through growth and innovation.

Up to this point, the discussion of market structure and economic performance has focused almost entirely on the problem of **static efficiency** — the ability of an economy to get the greatest output of consumer satisfaction from given resources and technology. Static efficiency is a measure of how close an economy operates to its production possibility frontier. But market structure may also have an important impact on the economy's **dynamic efficiency** — its success in achieving growth in the rate of output per unit of resources. Dynamic efficiency is thus a measure of the rate at which the production possibility frontier of an economy shifts outward over time.

Of the two kinds of efficiency, dynamic efficiency is by far the most important in the long run. During the 1960s, Canada's real gross national product grew at an average rate of about 3.7 percent per year. One of the most important factors contributing to this growth was the improvement of knowledge — that is, innovation and technological change. Improvement in knowledge accounted for about a third of all economic growth, or 1.2 percent per year. The remaining economic growth is attributable to capital accumulation, population growth, increased education, and other factors. The contribution of innovation and technological change is very large compared to the estimate of the loss in static efficiency caused by

---

[4] The article by Brozen, cited in footnote 3, contains references to and discussions of these and several similar studies.

monopolistic and oligopolistic market imperfections. The largest estimate of the static efficiency loss ever seriously put forward is about 2.5 percent of gross national product. Innovation and technological change add more than that to GNP each two years.

The Schumpeter Hypothesis

If every policy promoting static efficiency also contributed to dynamic efficiency, the distinction between the two would not be important in a chapter dealing with market structure and economic performance. Unfortunately, however, it is not certain that things work out that way. In fact, there is a widely shared hypothesis according to which some sources of dynamic efficiency are to be found in just those concentrated markets that are suspected to be sources of static inefficiency. This will be referred to as the Schumpeter hypothesis, after economist Joseph Schumpeter, who first brought it to widespread attention.

According to Schumpeter, the source of innovation and growth is competition—but not the kind of competition found in those markets classified as perfectly competitive. Instead, he wrote:

Joseph Alois Schumpeter (1883–1950)

Joseph Schumpeter was born in Trietsch, Moravia, then a part of Austria. He studied law at the University of Vienna, also attending the seminars of the leading economists of the Austrian school of the day. In 1906, he received a doctor of laws degree and briefly practiced law before turning to teaching as a career. He taught at several European universities, taking time out in 1919-1920 to serve as the Austrian minister of finance. In 1932, he emigrated to the United States. There, he accepted a post at Harvard University, which he held until his death in 1950. In 1948, he was honored with the presidency of the American Economic Association.

Schumpeter's writings are characterized by a broad scope rare in twentieth century economics. In his writings on economic development, business cycles, the history of economics, and economic systems, he attempted to portray the whole of the economic process. He had little use for the kind of economics that reduces everything to problems of managerial calculations and then reduces those problems to an arid set of mathematical equations. To him, the crucial figure in economic life was the entrepreneur, not the clerk or manager. What is more, he saw the entrepreneur as operating in an environment shaped as much by history, politics, and religion as by simple forces of supply and demand.

Although his *History of Economic Analysis* is probably Schumpeter's greatest scholarly achievement, it is *Capitalism, Socialism, and Democracy* that holds the most interest for the greneral student of economics. The book is, among other things, Schumpeter's reply to Karl Marx. The opening chapters of the book contain one of the most lucid and perceptive analyses of Marx's system ever written. Schumpeter went on to explain why he believed that capitalism would inevitably come to an end and be replaced by socialism. Unlike Marx, however, Schumpeter believed that capitalism would be killed not by its failures but by its successes. In the process of explaining this paradoxical proposition, he offered an analysis of the role of the entrepreneur in the market economy and explained why, in the twentieth century, the entrepreneur has come to face an increasingly hostile intellectual environment. A minor but significant role in the downfall of capitalism, Schumpeter believed, would be played by the economic profession's myopic focus on the fairyland of perfect competition and its blindness to the nature and importance of entrepreneurship.

The competition that counts is the competition from the new commodity, the new technology, the new source of supply, the new type of organization (the largest scale unit of control, for instance)—competition which commands a decisive cost or quality advantage and which strikes not at the margins of the profits and the outputs of the existing firms, but at their foundations and their very lives. This kind of competition is as much more effective than the other as a bombardment is in comparison with forcing a door, and so much more important that it becomes a matter of comparative indifference whether competition in the ordinary sense functions more or less promptly; the powerful lever that in the long run expands output and brings down prices is in any case made of other stuff.[5]

"In this respect," he added in another place, "perfect competition is not only impossible but inferior, and has no title to being set up as a model of ideal efficiency."[6]

Just how is it that market concentration can actually promote, rather than retard, the kind of competition on which dynamic efficiency depends? There appear to be two mechanisms at work.

First, monopoly power is often the goal of competition among entrepreneurs and the chief incentive to engage in such competition. The first firm to seize on new knowledge and put it to use is able to make profits in excess of the normal rate of return precisely because its new discovery establishes a temporary monopoly that it can exploit until its competitors successfully imitate or outflank it. If each new product had to be introduced at a price that just covered costs, or if each cost-reducing innovation had to be followed immediately by a matching reduction in price, there would be little reason to introduce such innovations at all. If the first firm to adjust to changing circumstances were not able to increase the gap between its costs and its revenues by doing so, there would be no incentive to be first. Competition among entrepreneurs is competition for monopoly power of at least a temporary kind. In this sense, monopoly is not the opposite of competition but a normal result of it.

Second, monopoly power, once achieved, acts as a spur to competition. This is not only true in the now familiar sense that an industry where monopoly profits are being made tends to attract new entrants. It also applies to competition among different industries and product groups for the consumer's dollar. The OPEC countries' exploitation of their oil monopoly has subjected oil to greatly intensified competition from other sources of energy. The rate of innovation in methods of energy production and the rate of introduction of known energy-conserving technology have been greatly speeded up. Even if the oil cartel were now to be broken up, world energy markets would not return to their former equilibrium pattern. In this sense, monopoly is not the opposite of competition but a spur to it.

Can the Schumpeter Hypothesis Be Tested?

The Schumpeter hypothesis poses a sweeping challenge to economic theory and policy. Not surprisingly, many attempts have been made to verify or refute it by examining the available data on economic growth,

---

[5] Joseph Schumpeter, *Capitalism, Socialism, and Democracy* (New York: Harper & Bros, 1942), pp. 84-85.
[6] Ibid, p. 106.

market concentration, and innovative activity. The results to date, however, are somewhat inconclusive.[7]

The major difficulty with testing the Schumpeter hypothesis lies in measuring innovative activity. Schumpeter had a fairly broad concept of innovation in mind. Inventing new products or processes, developing practical applications of new inventions, working out new forms of business organization, discovering new ways of financing investment, and creating new methods of marketing and distribution were, to Schumpeter, all equally important sources of dynamic efficiency. But clearly, most of these sources can be measured only indirectly, and some not at all. As a result, attempts to test the Schumpeter hypothesis have had to make do with rather crude approximations to the central concepts involved.

Looking at all the studies in perspective, it appears that firms of all sizes in markets of all levels of concentration are, under favorable circumstances, able to contribute positively to the dynamic efficiency of the economy. This implies that neither a policy of indiscriminately breaking up large firms into smaller ones nor a policy of indiscriminately welding small firms into larger ones can be counted on to speed the pace of innovation. The ability of the largest corporations to mass huge research and development teams on a difficult technical problem is important, but so is the flash of insight that may come to a lone inventor. In short, for all we know, the present mix of large and small firms may be just about right from the point of view of dynamic efficiency.

CONCLUSIONS

Much of this chapter and the preceding one have been devoted to describing unresolved issues of market structure and performance, but they have been unable to offer firm conclusions. In preparation for the next chapter, which discusses public policy toward competition and market structure, it will be useful to summarize what has been covered up to this point in terms of two major areas of controversy.

The first area concerns the extent to which perfect competition, or something reasonably close to it, can be regarded as the natural state of the economy. If a substantial degree of concentration is necessary in most markets in order to take advantage of economies of scale, perfect competition appears to be an exceptional market structure, unattainable in most cases. On the other hand, if most market concentration can be explained on the basis of artificial barriers to entry, such as government franchises or the advertising and marketing strategies of firms dominating the market, public policies aimed at reducing such barriers may realistically be expected to be effective. Somewhat similarly, in the case of unconcentrated but monopolistically competitive industries, one can ask whether the existing degree of product differentiation is natural or contrived.

The second area of controversy concerns the question of whether perfect competition, or something closely approximating it, is a necessary or even a sufficient condition for good market performance. If, in concentrated

---

[7] For a survey of the most important efforts, see Jesse W. Markham, "Concentration, Stimulus or Retardant to Innovation," in *Industrial Concentration*, ed. Goldschmid, Mann, and Weston, pp. 247-272.

markets, tacit or explicit cooperation among firms is the exception and vigorous rivalry is the rule, perfect competition may not be necessary. And if, at least in some markets, economic concentration and large-scale operations are necessary to ensure dynamic efficiency, perfect competition may not be even a sufficient condition for good market performance.

Disagreements over these analytical issues, as will be shown in the next chapter, underlie many of today's public policy debates.

SUMMARY

1. Some economists think that advertising may act as a barrier to new competition in concentrated industries. Their argument is twofold: (1) that advertising creates strong brand loyalties, thereby making the demand for each firm's product less elastic; and (2) that the necessity of mounting an advertising campaign adds to the start-up costs of a new firm. Other economists disagree; they see advertising as a means of competing rather than a barrier to competition. They argue that advertising is a way of attacking established brand loyalties and facilitating the entry of new firms.

2. A monopolistically competitive market is one in which there are large numbers of small firms, no significant barriers to entry, and a strongly differentiated product. Each firm in such a market faces a downward-sloping demand curve and maximizes profits at the point where marginal cost and marginal revenue are equal. If firms earn profits in the short run, then new firms will enter the market until those profits are eliminated. In long-run equilibrium under monopolistic competition, price must be equal to average total cost.

3. Economists disagree about market performance under monopolistic competition. Some argue that, in equilibrium, there will be too many firms in the market, each producing too little output. Others think that there is really little or no difference between monopolistic competition and perfect competition.

4. An economy's static efficiency is its ability to get the most out of given resources and technology; its dynamic efficiency is its ability to grow through innovation and technical change. According to the Schumpeter hypothesis, large firms in concentrated industries are the economy's major source of dynamic efficiency.

DISCUSSION QUESTIONS

1. Discuss the controversy over advertising as a barrier to entry in terms of the following statement: a barrier to entry is something that prevents new entrants from duplicating the performance of existing firms in terms of cost or quality. Nonetheless, the need for hard work is not in itself a barrier to entry in the economic sense. When entrepreneurs are freely able to go out and buy the various building blocks of their new firms in the same markets where existing firms buy their inputs, barriers to entry are not a determinant of market structure.

   Do you think it is important that the market for advertising services is itself highly competitive?

2. In downtown Moscow, there are far fewer restaurants than in comparable Canadian cities. These restaurants are, on the average, much larger and much more crowded than their Canadian counterparts. The quality of food served is high, although service leaves something to be desired by Canadian standards. Do

these facts suggest to you that the central planners who control Moscow's restaurants have designed their system to perform better than the restaurant market in most Canadian cities? Using what you have learned about monopolistic competition, make a serious attempt to argue both sides of this question.

3. A landmark American study found that eyeglasses were cheaper in states where advertising was freely permitted than in states where it was restricted. Where advertising was completely banned, glasses cost an average of $37.48 per pair; where there were no restrictions, the average was $17.98.[8] Explain these results in terms of what you have learned in this chapter.

4. Evaluate the following argument in terms of what you have learned in this chapter: the apparent association between dynamic innovation and large firm size is an artificial result of the patent system, which allows firms to grow fat on the monopoly profits of their inventions. Without patents, new inventions could be equally shared among a large number of small firms, and there would be just as much dynamic efficiency without the need to suffer the present degree of market concentration.

SUGGESTIONS FOR FURTHER READING

Department of Consumer and Corporate Affairs. *A Study on Consumer-Misleading and Unfair Trade Practices*. Ottawa: Information Canada, 1976.
A critical examination of problems in Canada created by questionable forms of advertising.

Firestone, O.J. *The Economic Implications of Advertising*. Toronto: Methuen, 1967.
A quite deliberate but well-reasoned Canadian defense of advertising.

Galbraith, John Kenneth. *The Affluent Society*. Boston: Houghton Mifflin, 1958.
Contains Galbraith's well-known attack on advertising as a violation of consumer sovereignty.

Goldschmid, Harvey J.; Mann, H. Michael; and Weston, J. Fred. *Industrial Concentration: The New Learning*. Boston: Little, Brown, 1974.
Chapter 3 is a debate between Yale Brozen and H. Michael Mann on the topic of advertising as an impediment to competition. In Chapter 5, Jesse W. Markham discusses market concentration and innovation, citing several attempts to bring empirical evidence to bear on the Schumpeter hypothesis.

Hayek, Friedrich A. von. "The Non Sequitur of the Dependence Effect." *Southern Economic Journal* 27 (April 1961).
A reply to Galbraith's views on advertising and consumer sovereignty.

Schumpeter, Joseph. *Capitalism, Socialism, and Democracy*. New York: Harper & Bros., 1942.
Part 2 of this book contains Schumpeter's famous discussion of the relationship between market concentration and dynamic efficiency.

---

[8] Lee Benham, "The Effect of Advertising on the Price of Eyeglasses," *Journal of Law and Economics* 15 (October 1972), pp. 337-352.

C H A P T E R **28**

GOVERNMENT AS REGULATOR AND PRODUCER

WHAT YOU WILL LEARN IN THIS CHAPTER

There has been a long-standing concern in Canada about the growth of big business and the use of business practices that threaten competition. In 1889, Canada passed its first anticombines legislation. Through anticombines policy the federal government has tried to check anticompetitive business practices like price fixing, but it has not engaged in the vigorous "trust-busting" that has occasionally been carried out in the United States. Anticombines policy is not the only way in which government intervenes in the market economy. Sometimes a private monopoly or oligopoly is subjected to other forms of regulation. Further, as an alternative to regulating a private producer, government can itself become a producer of goods and services, as was noted in Chapters 4 and 21.

Do our current anticombines laws do the right job and do it well? Do regulatory agencies simply guard the status quo? Do government corporations really help to keep the private sector "on its toes"? These and other questions are part of the continuing controversy over public policy toward monopoly.

FOR REVIEW

Here are some terms and concepts that will be put to use in this chapter. If you do not understand them, review them before proceeding.

- *Positive and normative economics (Chapter 1)*
- *Public goods (Chapter 4)*
- *Government corporations in Canada (Chapter 21)*
- *Price discrimination (Chapter 24)*
- *Oligopoly and barriers to entry (Chapter 26)*
- *Market power and mergers (Chapter 26)*

THE CASE AGAINST BIG BUSINESS, AND ANTICOMBINES LAWS

Bigness in business, as George Stigler wrote some twenty-five years ago,[1] can have one of two meanings. It can mean that a firm is large relative to the market it serves, or large in absolute size. Some firms are big in one way, but

---

[1] George J. Stigler, "The Case against Big Business," first published in *Fortune*, May 1952, and widely reprinted since.

not the other. Eaton's department store is large in absolute size, but still accounts for only a fraction of all retail sales in Toronto. The Red River Brick and Tile Co. of Winnipeg has a huge share of the local brick market, but is a pigmy on a nationwide scale. The serious problems of government policy toward big business do not arise for businesses like these. The case against big business is a case against those relatively few firms — General Motors, Canadian Pacific, Imperial Oil, Alcan Aluminum, and a short list of other famous names — that are *both* big relative to their market *and* big in absolute size.

The case against big business rests on two kinds of charges. First, the charge is made that big business is inefficient. This contention largely rests on the theory set forth in Chapter 24. Monopolies — and, to some extent, oligopolies and monopolistic competitors too — are able to restrict output and raise prices above marginal costs. Critics of monopoly charge that this results in inefficient resource allocation. They argue that monopolistic industries would use more resources to produce more goods and services if they were competitively organized.

The second part of the case against big business rests on the fear that bigness confers the power to break the rules of the free market economy. These rules call for open access to all markets, and the elimination of force and coercion from economic life. Sometimes big business breaks these rules through directly illegal acts. In the nineteenth century, for example, some businesses hired private armies to settle labor disputes. In our own time, many giant firms have been caught paying huge bribes or making illegal campaign contributions. But breaking the rules of the free market does not always mean stepping outside the law. Firms often operate within the political system to write new rules restricting competition and establishing further monopoly privileges for themselves. These actions of big business encourage countervailing political power plays by labor and the general public. The result, it is often feared, is a drift toward a society of big business, big government, and big labor, in which the individual counts for little, and large collective bodies count for everything.

The Anticombines Laws

Anticombines laws A set of laws, including the acts of 1889 and 1923 and subsequent amendments, that seek to control market structure and the competitive behavior of firms.

Legislative attempts to curb monopoly in Canada — **anticombines laws** — go back to the Anticombines Act of 1889, which made it a misdemeaner "to conspire, combine, agree or arrange unlawfully, to unduly limit the transportation, production, or storage facilities for any trade commodity, to restrain the trade of such a commodity, or to unduly prevent or lessen competition in the production, sale, or price of any commodity."

In 1892 this act became a part of the Criminal Code, and an offense under the act became indictable. Subsequently, in 1910 and 1923, 1951 and 1960, further Combines Acts were enacted and revised, providing investigative and administrative support for prosecutions carried out under the Criminal Code.

When one compares these anticombines acts of Canada with the Sherman Antitrust Act, and other antitrust laws in the United States, it becomes clear that the Canadian approach to monopoly is much less aggressive than the American.

A Canadian expert on anticombines legislation has noted: "Perhaps the most striking aspect of the history of the legislation dealing with restraints on competition in Canada is the mixed character of the economic beliefs and policies it discloses. For example, the early debates in the House of Commons on the Combines Investigation Act—and the more recent debates for that matter—display no broad support for a general policy of competition."[2]

Canadian economic development, as we noted in Chapter 4, was promoted by the creation of virtual monopolies, such as the Hudson Bay Company and the Canadian Pacific Railway. There was considerable resentment toward abusive practices of these corporations, but there was simultaneously a widespread belief that large companies were necessary to develop the chief resources of the country. There was, therefore, no strong commitment to what Skeoch calls "a general rule of competition."

This helps to explain several important features of our anticombines policy. First, no attempt has been made to break up monopolies, as was done with Standard Oil of New Jersey in the United States in 1911. In Canada, the law has been primarily concerned with the prevention of such individual abuses as price fixing and price discrimination. Second, large sectors of the economy—banking and real estate, for instance—have until recently been exempt from prosecution. Third, the limited financial resources allotted by the government to anticombines investigation have never permitted more than a token approach to the problem.

Until 1967, anticombines investigation and prosecutions were carried out through a special branch of the Department of Justice. Since 1967, the Department of Consumer and Corporate Affairs has assumed responsibility for combines, mergers, monopolies, and other forms of restraint of trade. A new Competition Bill, before Parliament since 1977, would place strict limits on mergers and monopolies and would allow for their adjudication and even dissolution by a special civil tribunal. Strong lobbying by business groups has delayed the passage of this bill.

Over the years, the federal government has used its anticombines legislation to deal with two types of offenses: those that were considered to be illegal *per se*, and those that could be declared illegal only if it was shown that they had been detrimental to the public.

The pursuit of *per se* offenses has led to numerous successful prosecutions. Such offenses include *price fixing* (where firms agree to sell their similar products at a set price), *price discrimination* (charging different customers different prices for no justifiable economic reason), and *exclusive dealing and tied selling* (product supplied on condition that the purchaser buy other products as well). Interestingly, *resale price maintenance*, wherein manufacturers or wholesalers try to force a certain price on the retailer, is illegal in Canada (there can be only a "suggested price"), while in many American states it is protected by law. Canadian law seems to favor the consumer, while the United States is more concerned about protecting small businesses.

---

[2] L.A. Skeoch, *Restrictive Trade Practices in Canada* (Toronto: McClelland and Stewart, 1966), p. 3. Much of this section is based on this book.

The prosecution of offenses involving mergers and monopolies has been uncommon. Before World War II, there was only one prosecution for a merger offense, the Western Fruits and Vegetables case, and it resulted in an acquittal. In 1959, charges were brought against Canadian Breweries and the Western Sugar Company, but both of these cases ended in acquittal. The Electric Reduction Company of Canada Limited pleaded guilty to a merger charge in 1970. K.C. Irving Limited, a Maritimes conglomerate, was convicted of merger charges in 1974, but the decision was reversed by the Supreme Court of Canada on grounds that detriment had not been proven. In Canada, therefore, there has never been a conviction after a full trial that was not reversed on appeal. As we have noted, new and tougher legislation has been stymied by strong business groups, calling into question the ability of a modern, industrial democracy to curb the power of important economic interests.

In addition to the protests of those who might be adversely affected by a more vigorous anticombines policy, there are arguments advanced by others against a basic change in policy.

Almost all economists would agree that, under given conditions of cost, competitive markets perform more efficiently than markets in which competition is restricted. But a major problem with anticombines policy, according to many critics, is that the law fails to recognize that cost conditions are not always given. Mergers, for example, may result in economies of scale. In condemning such mergers, the courts may prevent business from cutting costs, and the consumer may end up paying higher, rather than lower, prices as a result of anticombines or antitrust enforcement.

The Royal Commission on Corporate Concentration

The idea that mergers may benefit consumers has been articulated by the Royal Commission on Corporate Concentration, which was established by Parliament in 1975. In its 1978 report, the Commission argued that the anticombines laws did not need any basic strengthening, because concentration had not been increasing in the past decade or more and there is nothing wrong with concentration in itself. Indeed, the report maintained that many industries would fare better in the international market if firms were able to become larger and utilize economies of scale. This, the report argued, should be allowed to happen "through internal growth and through mergers and acquisitions, even if this expansion resulted in higher concentration levels."[3]

In its recommendations, the Royal Commission advocated a form of *workable competition*, rather than the perfect competition idealized by economists, as a suitable model for the Canadian economy. It noted several important conditions for such workable competition.[4]

First, small and medium-sized firms must not be unfairly prevented from operating and expanding and must not face artificial barriers to entering new industries.

---

[3] *Report of the Royal Commission on Corporate Concentration*, 1978, p. 214.
[4] Royal Commission Report, pp. 215 ff.

Second, there should be selective reductions in the tariff and nontariff barriers that protect most Canadian manufacturing industries. Such reductions, which would put more pressure on firms to achieve international standards of efficiency, should be accompanied by government sanction of specialization agreements under which competitors in a market would be allowed to allocate production among themselves to achieve longer production runs and greater economies.

Third, there must be disclosure of accounting and profit information so that conglomerate firms are unable to hide areas of high profitability behind a protective shield of consolidated reporting.

Fourth, competition policy must be strong and vigorously enforced, particularly in the areas of restrictive trade practices and attempts to build or maintain barriers to entry.

Finally, another possible condition necessary for workable competition is that the proportion of the Canadian economy constrained by government regulation or ownership should be reviewed and possibly reduced.

While economists are aware of the difference between their model of perfect competition and the real world of imperfect competition, and while most are probably in favor of recognizing and protecting some form of workable competition, there is wide disagreement over the methods that should be pursued in achieving even this limited goal. The Royal Commission report has been severely criticized for downplaying the dangers of increased concentration and for not supporting more wholeheartedly the attempts made by the federal government in the 1970s to strengthen anticombines legislation. It is clear that government policy has been quite ineffective in lowering barriers to entry and in preventing mergers and other forms of business concentration.

OTHER FORMS OF GOVERNMENT REGULATION AND INTERVENTION

Up to now we have discussed one important kind of government intervention in the market economy, anticombines policy. Now we turn to two others. If government is not willing to accept the outcome that the operation of the market produces in some industry, it does not need to limit itself to changing the market structure of that industry. One alternative is to leave the structure of the market untouched, but to subject producers to direct regulation. Another is for government itself to enter the market as a producer, either supplementing or supplanting the private firms operating there. Both of these alternatives are widely employed in the Canadian economy. No discussion of *what, how, who,* and *for whom* would be complete if it did not consider such strategies at least briefly. The discussion of regulation can begin with a fairly simple case, that of utility regulation. Here, regulation presents itself as a direct alternative to anticombines policy. For various technical reasons, public utilities tend to be **natural monopolies**. A natural monopoly is an industry in which total costs are minimized by having just one producer serve the entire market. Consider electricity, telephone service, water, or gas, to take the most common examples. It is easy for one utility to hook up extra customers in a neighborhood once it has run its basic lines, but wastefully expensive for

Natural monopoly An industry in which total costs are minimized by having just one producer serve the entire market.

separate companies to run duplicate sets of lines down each street. The problem is how to keep that one firm from restricting output and raising its price as a profit-maximizing pure monopolist would do.

A graphical example will help make the problem clear. Consider Exhibit 28.1. The firm represented there has roughly constant marginal costs and an L-shaped long-run average cost curve. The demand curve intersects the long-run average cost curve at a quantity Q_1, not far above the minimum economic scale of production. If this output were divided between even as many as two firms, each producing half the quantity Q_1, cost per unit would be substantially higher.

If a single firm operates in the market, it will tend to behave as a pure monopolist. Instead of producing Q_1, it will produce Q_2, which corresponds to the intersection between the firm's marginal revenue and marginal cost curves. The price corresponding to this output is P_2, far in excess of marginal cost. This would be a smaller output and higher price than efficient resource allocation requires.

Rate Regulation

In this analysis, then, competition by two or more firms is wasteful, and monopoly pricing by a single firm is wasteful too. The standard solution in the U.S. is to allow just one firm to operate, but to impose rate regulation on it. Instead of permitting the firm to charge the price P_2, the regulatory commission limits the price to no more than P_1, the price where the demand curve intersects the long-run average cost curve. The firm is forced to be a price taker, in effect, and chooses the quantity Q_1. Actually, maximum efficiency would require a price equal to *marginal* cost, and an output a little greater than Q_1. The problem is that the firm would then suffer a loss and eventually go bankrupt unless it were paid a subsidy. Most economists would agree that the price P_1, which avoids the necessity of paying a subsidy, is close enough to the ideal for practical policy purposes.

Practical Problems

The argument for rate regulation of public utilities is based on the theories presented in Chapters 24 and 26. It is worth recalling the assumption on which those theories were based. For one thing, the theories assume that all participants in the market (including the regulators) possess accurate knowledge of cost and demand conditions. Second, they assume that when rate regulation is imposed on the monopoly, it will treat the rates as determined by forces beyond its own control, and will consequently behave as a price taker. Finally, they assume that underlying cost and demand conditions are stable and not subject to change.

In the real world, none of these conditions is wholly fulfilled. As a result, it is not quite so easy to make rate regulation work as Exhibit 28.1 suggests.

A major problem is that the regulators do not really know the shapes and positions of the firm's demand and cost curves. Not knowing these, they cannot directly identify the price and quantity where the demand and average cost curves intersect. They must use an indirect approach to finding the correct price instead, reasoning as follows: with the cost and demand curves shown in Exhibit 28.1, if the price were set above average cost, the firm would earn a higher rate of return than the average for other firms in the economy. If the price were set too low, the firm would earn a lower than average return. Therefore, if a price can be found that will allow the firm to earn just an average rate of return, that will be the price to charge.

Armed with this reasoning, the rate-setting process proceeds in five steps. First, the regulators measure the value of the firm's capital, which for our hypothetical firm is, say, $1,200,000. This is called the firm's *rate base*. Second, they measure the average rate of return for the economy, which, let us say, turns out to be 10 percent per year. (In practice, neither of these first two steps is quite as easy as it sounds, but we can afford to give the regulators the benefit of the doubt.) Third, they multiply the rate base by the permitted rate of return to figure out a total profit target for the firm. Step 4 is to ask the firm to propose a price or schedule of prices that it thinks will allow it to earn the target profit. Finally, as time goes by, the regulators monitor the firm's profits, cutting the price if profits rise too high and allowing the price to rise if profits fall below the target.

In an unchanging world where business decision makers behaved as price-taking managerial calculators, this approach might work fairly well. In a changing world, where business decision makers are entrepreneurs as well as calculators, rate regulation is less successful.

Cost Control

For one thing, the procedures of rate regulation tend to weaken the firm's incentive for cost reduction. The regulated firm is not really a price taker. Its managers know that if they let costs rise, they will be able to complain

---

Exhibit 28.1

Cost and revenue curves for a natural monopoly

Because of the L-shaped average cost curve, one firm could supply the market with the quantity Q_1 more cheaply than could two firms, each producing half that much. A single unregulated firm, however, would behave as a monopolist, producing only Q_2 and selling at the price P_2. By imposing the price ceiling P_1, the firm is forced to act as a price taker and produces the desired quantity Q_1.

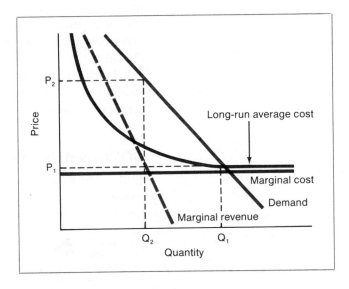

about low profits to the regulatory commission, which will be bound to grant a rate increase big enough to restore the target rate of return. Cost minimization, after all, is hard work for managers. Why not relax and take things easy? Why not take Wednesday mornings off for golf? Why not install new carpets on the boardroom floor, give a job to the president's incompetent nephew, and generally make life more pleasant at the expense of operating efficiency?

In addition to just slacking, a regulated firm is often tempted to over-expand its rate base. An unregulated firm will invest in additional capital only if the value of the extra output is sufficient to cover the cost of the investment. For a regulated firm, investment can be profitable whether it is productive or not. As an extreme case, imagine a regulated utility that spends $1 million on an investment project that adds absolutely nothing at all to output. The next time it goes before the regulatory commission, it can point to a million-dollar increase in its rate base, and legitimately ask for a corresponding increase in the profits it will be permitted to earn. Of course, because the new investment does not produce any new output, the only place the added profit can come from is a price rise. Not good for efficiency, but from the firm's point of view, profits from rate-base expansion are just as good as any other kind of profits.

Canadian governments regulate many industries in the manner described in Exhibit 28.1. Railways, electricity, gas, and telephone utilities (both private and government-owned), banks, pipelines, trucking companies, airlines, taxicabs, broadcasting companies, securities and insurance firms, as well as numerous agricultural products mentioned in Chapter 25, are all subject to regulatory boards that concern themselves with their operation.[5] In some cases, for example railways and telephone companies, there is close scrutiny of prices, profits, and levels of service. In others, like insurance, banking, and securities, the regulatory authorities are interested mainly in financial integrity and do not control prices and profits. In broadcasting, the chief concern seems to be with service. In the transportation industry the government has allowed more self-regulation by the Canadian Transport Commission, but recently it has tried to increase direct government control because it has felt that the public interest has not been well served by such policies as railway relocation. At the same time, de-regulation is occurring in the airline industry, where private airlines have not been permitted to compete on even terms with Air Canada.

It is estimated that about 29 percent of Canada's total gross domestic product (which includes government activities) is subject to some form of direct regulation.[6]

GOVERNMENT AS PRODUCER

If the government does not like the way resources are allocated or the way income is distributed by free markets, it can, as we have seen, regulate

---

[5] For a good brief discussion, on which this part of the chapter is based, see the *Report of the Royal Commission on Corporate Concentration*, Chapter 17.

[6] *Responsible Regulation: An Interim Report by the Economic Council of Canada*, November 1979.

those markets. There is another alternative as well. Rather than leave production to private firms, regulated or unregulated, the government can itself become a producer.

What Kinds of Goods?

There is really no restriction on the kind of goods or services that government can supply. In communist countries, virtually all firms are government owned and all goods and services government supplied. In many Western European countries, the leading firms in such industries as steel, automobiles, shipbuilding, and aircraft are "nationalized," that is, owned and run by the government. Also in Western Europe, government ownership is widely used instead of regulation to accomplish political control of transportation, communications, and utilities.

In the United States, the role of government as a producer is somewhat more limited. Few goods or services are produced for direct sale to users. Instead, most government-produced goods and services are supplied to the public free of charge. These fall into two categories. First, the government supplies a certain number of public goods, national defense being perhaps the best example. As we saw in Chapter 4, the special properties of public goods make it difficult for private firms to produce and sell them at a profit. If they are provided to one citizen, their benefits are shared by all, so the problem arises of how to get would-be "free riders" to pay their share of costs. The government solves this free-rider problem by employing its power to tax.

In addition to public goods, the government also supplies a number of so-called **merit goods**. These include such things as education, police protection, and some kinds of medical services that are distributed free of charge on the ground that each citizen as a matter of human right merits his or her fair share.

Merit goods Goods that are produced by government and supplied free of charge on the grounds that each citizen merits his or her fair share.

Canada has generally tended to follow the Western European example rather than the American in its approach to government ownership of business. For purposes of development and regulation, governments in Canada have become owners of virtually all major utilities and have established giant government enterprises in broadcasting, in air and railway transportation, and in such resources as chemicals (Polysar), petroleum (Petrocan), forest products (Churchill Forest Products), and potash (Saskatchewan government).

A good example of how governments are using their own corporations to give them more control over the operation of an industry is provided by the federal government's controversial purchase of Petrocan. Petrocan began operations on January 1, 1976, as an attempt by the federal government to get a foothold in Canada's important oil industry, much of which, as we saw in Chapter 21, is controlled by foreign companies. Petrocan has since become the largest Canadian-owned oil company, through purchases of such American-controlled companies as Atlantic-Richfield and Pacific Petroleums Limited. By mid-1979 it had assets of around $2.5 billion and 2,000 employees. It is still considerably smaller than the half dozen Canadian subsidiaries of multinational corporations in the oil industry, but it has become significant enough to become the object of criticism and political controversy. Private critics have argued that because of its close ties to government it has been able to arrange financing (backed by government guarantees) at terms not available to the private sector. Others have simply maintained that it has no place in a private sector economy.

The new Conservative government in 1979 announced that it would sell Petrocan to private interests, but shortly after its election, during energy talks in Japan in which national control over energy supplies was discussed, the new government announced that "privatization" of Petrocan would be delayed indefinitely. Once again, the Canadian public, through the government it elected, indicated that in Canada there is no doctrinaire opposition to government ownership of industry in itself. If there appear to be developmental or regulatory arguments in favor of it, it becomes a legitimate form of government activity.

SUMMARY

1. Anticombines policy is that area of public policy designed to control market structure and the competitive behavior of firms.
2. The foundations of anticombines policy in Canada go back to the first Anticombines Act of 1889, which preceded the Sherman Antitrust Act in the United States by one year. This act, together with amendments and subsequent court interpretations, places constraints on business behavior. The prohibition of price fixing has been the most important constraint on what firms can do. In addition, laws prohibiting certain kinds of *vertical restraints* — such as tied-sale contracts and resale price maintenance — and many forms of price discrimination have also been enforced with some success. However, attempts to limit the growth of companies through merger have largely failed.
3. Economists are far from united on what course anticombines policy should take in the future. Attempts by the federal government to establish a civil tribunal to adjudicate mergers and other forms of enterprise coordination have been stymied by strong opposition from the business community.
4. A natural monopoly is an industry in which total costs are minimized by having just one producer serve the entire market. The policy problem raised by natural monopoly is how to keep the single producer from exploiting its monopoly power to raise prices and restrict output. The traditional solution is to impose maximum price regulation in order to limit the firm's rate of return to a normal level. In practice, however, the effectiveness of such regulation may be rather limited.
5. Regulation, at least as currently practiced, is not highly regarded by most economists today. The economic case against regulation can be expressed in terms of two fundamental propositions. First, regulatory agencies and proceedings become dominated by efforts to redistribute income and wealth among participants in regulated markets, and this inevitably has a negative impact on economic efficiency. Second, even when regulators conscientiously try to make markets work more efficiently, they more often than not fail because regulation is not as effective as the market for making economic decisions and utilizing economic information.

6. In Canada, as in many Western European countries, government ownership of utilities and transportation, communication, and resource companies is a technique frequently used to regulate industry. Proponents of government ownership would say that it fosters public control over basic resources, encourages development of facilities that private enterprise might not otherwise undertake, and checks the monopolistic behavior of other giant firms in the industry. Canadians do not appear to be ideologically committed to government ownership as such, but neither are they committed to "the rule of competition" or to uncontrolled free competition.

DISCUSSION QUESTIONS

1. A young economist working for the Combines Branch in Ottawa was assigned to an investigation of a firm in Toronto accused of price fixing. When the young investigator confronted the president of the firm and informed him that he would need to look at all of the firm's files, the president retorted: "The trouble with this country is government bureaucrats like you interfering in the operation of a free market economy. Why don't you leave us alone? Haven't you ever heard of Adam Smith?" How would you have responded to these remarks?
2. Compare and contrast anticombines laws and regulation as alternative policies toward monopoly. Why is sometimes one and sometimes another used?
3. In the case of a true natural monopoly, do you think it would be best to have regulated private monopoly, public ownership of the monopoly, or an unregulated private monopoly? How do considerations of efficiency enter into your choice? Considerations of equity?

Factor Markets and Income Distribution

FACTOR MARKETS AND MARGINAL PRODUCTIVITY THEORY

WHAT YOU WILL LEARN IN THIS CHAPTER

This chapter is the first of three that discuss the operation of factor markets — the markets in which labor, capital, and natural resources are bought and sold. These markets are much like the product markets studied earlier, with one major exception: in factor markets, households are the sellers and firms the buyers. Accordingly, a theory of factor supply can be developed as an outgrowth of the theory of consumer choice, and a theory of factor demand can be developed as an outgrowth of the theory of the firm. The factor market theory discussed in this chapter covers both perfectly competitive and less than perfectly competitive cases.

FOR REVIEW

Here are some important terms and concepts that will be put to use in this chapter. If you do not understand them, review them before proceeding.

- *Factors of production (Chapter 1)*
- *Determination of saving and investment (Chapter 8)*
- *Marginal utility and consumer equilibrium (Chapter 19)*
- *Income and substitution effect (Chapter 19)*
- *Marginal physical product (Chapter 22)*
- *Pure economic profit (Chapter 22)*
- *Law of diminishing returns (Chapter 22)*
- *Normal rate of return (Chapter 22)*

One very important set of markets in the economy has been referred to so far only indirectly: **factor markets** — the markets in which labor, capital, and natural resources are bought and sold. (In Chapter 1 entrepreneurship — the innovative, risk-taking function — was identified as a possible fourth factor of production. It is discussed later in this chapter in relation to profit income.) Factor markets perform two major functions in a market economy. They help determine how goods and services are produced and for whom they are produced. This chapter and the next three chapters will look at both functions.

Factor markets are important in determining how goods and services are produced because most goods and services can be produced in more than

Factor markets The markets in which the factors of production — labor, natural resources, and capital — are bought and sold.

one way. Wheat, for example, can be grown by extensive cultivation of large areas of land with a lot of machinery and little labor or by intensive cultivation of small areas with little machinery and much labor. The choice of production methods depends on the relative prices of the various factors. As those prices change, production methods can change too. Factors that are relatively cheap are used intensively, while those that are relatively expensive are used sparingly.

At the same time, factor markets help determine for whom output is produced, because most people earn their incomes by selling whatever factors of production they own. The greatest number sell their labor services. Many also sell or rent land or capital that they own. Because markets determine factor prices, they also determine how much of the total product will go to the owners of labor services, capital, and natural resources.

Functional distribution of income The distribution of income according to factor ownership — that is, the distribution among workers, natural resource owners, and owners of capital.

Personal distribution of income The distribution of income among individuals, taking into account both the functional distribution of income and the distribution of factor ownership among persons.

The distribution of income among factor owners is called the **functional distribution of income**. Functional distribution partly explains for whom output is produced, but it is not the whole story. The **personal distribution of income** — which specific people receive the income — depends both on the functional distribution of income and on the way ownership of factors is distributed among people. This chapter and the next will be largely concerned with the functional distribution of income. First, the outlines of marginal productivity theory will be presented and applied to the factor markets for natural resources and capital. Chapter 30 will apply this theory to labor markets and use it to help explain the nature and functions of labor unions.

Finally, Chapter 31 will take up the subject of the personal distribution of income and, in particular, the problem of poverty. It will show how the operation of factor markets helps determine the incidence of poverty and will discuss various government policies aimed at reducing or eliminating poverty.

THE DEMAND FOR FACTORS OF PRODUCTION

The Firm in Factor Markets

In many ways, factor markets are much like the product markets already studied. The theories of supply and demand and the tools of marginal analysis apply to factor markets just as to product markets. But factor markets do differ from product markets in one major respect. In factor markets, it is firms that are the buyers and households that are the sellers, rather than the other way around. A theory of the demand for factors of production must be based on the same considerations of price, revenue, and profit that determine the supply of products. A theory of factor supply must be an extension of the theory of consumer choice.

In taking the first steps toward a theory of factor demand the assumption, as earlier, will be that firms aim to maximize profits. Each profit maximizing firm must take three things into account when it makes its hiring decisions. The first is the quantity of output produced by a unit of the factor in question, the second is the revenue derived from the sale of the output that will be produced, and the third is the cost of obtaining the factor.

Marginal Physical Product

Chapter 22 defined the *marginal physical product* of a factor as the increase in output resulting from a one unit increase in the input of that factor when the quantity of all other factors used remains unchanged. For example, if employing one additional worker hour of labor in a light bulb factory yields an added output of five light bulbs, when no other inputs to the production process are increased, the marginal physical productivity of labor in that factory is five bulbs per hour. To take another example, if giving a farmer one more acre of land makes it possible for the farmer to produce twenty more bushels of wheat per year—without any increase in the amount of work performed, the amount of machinery used, or anything else—the marginal physical product of land on that farm is twenty bushels per acre. Finally, if having one extra dollar of capital allows a taxi company to carry one extra passenger one extra mile each year, that puts the marginal physical product of capital for the company at one passenger mile per dollar's worth of capital.

Exhibit 29.1

Total and marginal physical product of a factor of production

As the quantity of one factor increases with the quantity of other factors remaining unchanged, total physical product increases, but at a decreasing rate. Marginal physical product, as Part c of this exhibit and Column 3 of the table in Part a show, decreases as the quantity of the factor employed increases. This decrease in marginal physical product is a direct consequence of the law of diminishing returns.

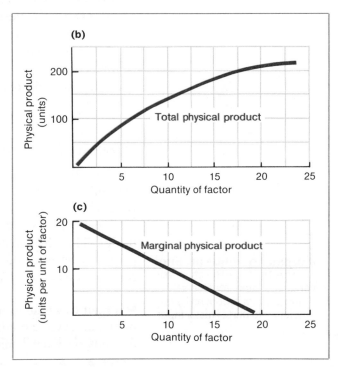

(a)

Quantity of Factor (1)	Total Physical Product (2)	Marginal Physical Product (3)
0	0	
		20
1	20	
		19
2	39	
		18
3	57	
		17
4	74	
		16
5	90	
		15
6	105	
		14
7	119	
		13
8	132	
		12
9	144	
		11
10	155	
		10
11	165	
		9
12	174	
		8
13	182	
		7
14	189	
		6
15	195	
		5
16	200	
		4
17	204	
		3
18	207	
		2
19	209	
		1
20	210	

Law of Diminishing Returns   As Chapter 22 showed, the marginal physical product of a factor varies as the quantity of the factor used varies, other things being equal. In particular, as the quantity of a single variable factor increases, with the quantities of all other factor inputs remaining fixed, a point will be reached beyond which the marginal physical product of the variable factor will decline. This principle is known as the *law of diminishing returns*.

Exhibit 29.1 shows total and marginal physical product curves for a firm subject to the law of diminishing returns throughout the range of zero to twenty units of factor input. (At this point, it does not matter whether the factor in question is labor, capital, or natural resources; the principle is the same for all.) As the quantity of this one factor is increased, with the quantities of all other factors used held constant, output increases — but at a diminishing rate. The first unit of the factor yields a marginal physical product of twenty units of output, the second a marginal physical product of nineteen units of output, and so on. After the twentieth unit of output, as the example is constructed, marginal physical product drops to zero. This implies that some absolute capacity ceiling has been reached, so that adding more of the variable factor cannot produce more output unless the quantities of some of the fixed factors are also increased. For example, if the variable factor in question is labor, it may be that adding more than twenty workers will do nothing to increase output unless, say, the quantity of machinery available for use by the workers is also increased. Note that beyond twenty units of output, where the marginal physical product of the variable factor drops to zero, the total physical product curve becomes horizontal.

Marginal Revenue Product

To determine what quantity of each factor of production it should hire to maximize profit, a firm must take into account the revenue that will be earned from the sale of the product of an added unit of factor input as well as the size of the marginal physical product. Here, a new term will be useful. The change in revenue resulting from the sale of the product produced by one additional unit of factor input is called the **marginal revenue product** of that factor.

Marginal revenue product (of a factor) The change in revenue resulting from the sale of the product produced by one additional unit of factor input.

Marginal Revenue Product for a Competitive Firm   What happens to the marginal revenue product of a factor as the quantity of that factor is varied depends on what happens to both the marginal physical product of the factor and the marginal revenue earned by selling the product. The simplest case to consider is that of a perfectly competitive firm. Because such a firm is a price taker, as shown in Chapter 23, the quantity of output it produces has no effect on the price at which its output is sold. Marginal revenue for the competitive firm is thus equal to the price of the firm's output, which is constant for all quantities of output. To calculate marginal revenue product of a factor for such a firm, then, the marginal physical product of the factor is multiplied by the price of the output.

Exhibit 29.2 gives an example of how marginal revenue product is calculated for a perfectly competitive firm. The marginal physical product

Exhibit 29.2

Marginal revenue product for a typical price taking firm

For a price taking firm, the marginal revenue product of a factor is equal to the factor's marginal physical product times the price of the product. This table is constructed on the assumption that the product price is $1 per unit and that marginal physical product is the same as in Exhibit 29.1.

Quantity of Factor (1)	Total Physical Product (2)	Marginal Physical Product (3)	Revenue per Unit (Price) (4)	Marginal Revenue Product (5)
0	0			
		20	$1	$20
1	20			
		19	1	19
2	39			
		18	1	18
3	57			
		17	1	17
4	74			
		16	1	16
5	90			
		15	1	15
6	105			
		14	1	14
7	119			
		13	1	13
8	132			
		12	1	12
9	144			
		11	1	11
10	155			
		10	1	10
11	165			
		9	1	9
12	174			
		8	1	8
13	182			
		7	1	7
14	189			
		6	1	6
15	198			
		5	1	5
16	200			
		4	1	4
17	204			
		3	1	3
18	207			
		2	1	2
19	209			
		1	1	1
20	210			

schedule is the same as that given in Exhibit 29.1, and a constant price of $1 per unit of output is assumed.

Marginal Revenue Product for a Monopolist If the firm in question is not perfectly competitive, the price at which it sells its output will tend to vary as the quantity of output varies. Suppose, for example, that the firm is a pure monopolist. As Chapter 24 demonstrated, a pure monopolist must decrease the price at which its product is sold each time it wants to increase the quantity sold, in accordance with the downward-sloping demand curve for its product. Because the price per unit decreases as output increases, marginal revenue per unit of output is always less than price per unit for a monopolist.

To calculate the increase in revenue resulting from a one unit increase in factor input for a monopolist, then, requires taking changes in both marginal physical product and marginal revenue into account. Exhibit 29.3 illustrates how this is done. The exhibit is constructed using the same total physical product schedule as Exhibits 29.1 and 29.2; but this time, the firm is assumed to be a monopolist. Column 3 gives the firm's demand curve, showing that the price at which output can be sold drops from $1.40 per unit at 20 units of output to $.45 at 210 units of output. Multiplying price times total physical product gives the total revenue corresponding to each quantity of factor input, shown in Column 4.

The differences between successive entries in the total revenue column give the marginal revenue product data, shown in Column 5. For example, as the quantity of factor input increases from 4 units to 5 units, the total output increases from 74 units to 90 units, while the price falls from $1.13 per unit to $1.05. As Column 4 shows, total revenue increases from $83.62

when 4 units of factor input are used to $94.50 when 5 units of factor input are used. This gives a marginal revenue product of $10.88 in the range from 4 to 5 units of factor input.

As the price continues to fall, marginal revenue eventually becomes negative. Beyond that point, additional units of factor input, even though they increase total physical product, reduce total revenue. The turning point comes at 10 units of factor input, as Exhibit 29.3 is constructed. Beyond that point, marginal revenue product is negative, even though marginal physical product remains positive.

At every level of factor input, the marginal revenue product of the factor is equal to the marginal physical product times the marginal revenue per unit of output. This relationship is shown in Columns 5 through 7 of Exhibit 29.3. Note that the marginal revenue figures in Column 7 are expressed in terms of dollars per unit of output, whereas the marginal revenue product figures in Column 5 are expressed in terms of dollars per unit of factor input.

Exhibit 29.3
Marginal revenue product for a monopolistic firm

This exhibit shows how marginal revenue product varies as the quantity of factor input varies for a firm that is a pure monopolist. As Column 3 shows, price falls as outputs increase, in accordance with the demand for the firm's product. Total revenue begins to decline after ten units of output, as marginal revenue per unit of output becomes negative, even though marginal physical product remains positive. Marginal revenue product can be calculated either as the difference between successive entries in the total revenue column or as the product of marginal physical product and marginal revenue per unit of output.

Quantity of Factor (1)	Total Physical Product (2)	Price of Output (3)	Total Revenue (4)	Marginal Revenue Product (5)	Marginal Physical Product (6)	Marginal Revenue per Unit of Output (7)
0	0	—	0			
1	20	$1.40	$28.00	$28.00	20	$1.40
2	39	1.31	50.90	22.90	19	1.21
3	57	1.22	69.26	18.36	18	1.02
4	74	1.13	83.62	14.36	17	.84
5	90	1.05	94.50	10.88	16	.68
6	105	.98	102.38	7.88	15	.52
7	119	.91	107.70	5.32	14	.38
8	132	.84	110.88	3.18	13	.24
9	144	.78	112.32	1.44	12	.12
10	155	.73	112.38	.06	11	.01
11	165	.68	111.38	−1.00	10	−.10
12	174	.63	109.62	−1.76	9	−.20
13	182	.59	107.38	−2.24	8	−.28
14	189	.56	104.90	−2.48	7	−.35
15	195	.53	102.38	−2.52	6	−.42
16	200	.50	100.00	−2.38	5	−.47
17	204	.48	97.92	−2.08	4	−.52
18	207	.47	96.26	−1.66	3	−.55
19	209	.46	95.10	−1.16	2	−.58
20	210	.45	94.50	−.60	1	−.60

Figures in Columns 3, 4, 5, and 7 are rounded to the nearest cent.

Marginal Factor Cost

The third consideration a firm must take into account to determine the profit maximizing quantity of a factor is the cost of obtaining each additional unit of that factor—the factor's **marginal factor cost**.

To keep things simple for the moment, consider only the case where a firm is a price taker in the market where it buys its factors of production. This will happen if the firm is only one among a large number of firms competing to hire that particular factor and if the quantity of the factor it uses is only a small fraction of the total used by all firms. For a firm that buys as a price taker, marginal factor cost is simply equal to the market price of the factor. If, for example, the market wage rate for typists is $7 per hour, then the marginal factor cost for this particular type of labor is $7 per hour for any firm that is a price taker in the market for typists.

Marginal factor cost The amount by which a firm's total factor cost must increase in order for it to obtain an additional unit of that factor.

Profit Maximization

Profit maximization requires that a firm hire just enough of each factor of production to equalize marginal revenue product and marginal factor cost. If marginal revenue product exceeds marginal factor cost, hiring one more unit of the factor will add more to the revenue than to the cost and hence will increase profit. If marginal factor cost exceeds marginal revenue product, reducing input of the factor by one unit will reduce cost by more than revenue and hence will also increase profit. Only when marginal revenue product and marginal factor cost are equal will it be impossible for any change in factor input to raise profit. This rule applies both to a firm that is a perfect competitor in its output market and to a monopolist.

Exhibit 29.4 illustrates this profit maximization rule. The exhibit, which contains both a table and a corresponding diagram, is constructed on the assumption that the firm is a perfect competitor in the output market and that it sells its product at $1 per unit, as in Exhibit 29.2. The firm is also assumed to be a price taker in the factor market, buying inputs of the factor at $5 per unit. Notice that profit rises as more of the factor is hired—up to the fifteenth unit of input. The firm just breaks even on the hiring of the sixteenth unit of input, and profit declines thereafter. It is between the fifteenth and sixteenth units of factor input that marginal revenue product becomes exactly equal to marginal factor cost.

Factor Demand Curves

It follows from this analysis of profit maximization that a firm's marginal revenue product curve for a factor is also the firm's demand curve for that factor. A demand curve must indicate the quantity demanded at each price, and it has just been shown that the quantity of the factor demanded will be whatever quantity makes the factor's price (more precisely, its marginal factor cost) equal to marginal revenue product.

Individual firm demand curves for a factor of production can be added together to get a market demand curve for that factor. Such a market demand is said to be a *derived* demand curve, because the demand for a factor of production does not arise from the usefulness of the factor services themselves. Instead it is derived indirectly from the usefulness of the products the factor can produce. The market demand for farmland is derived from the market demand for food, the market demand for printers from the market demand for books, and so on.

Changes in Factor Demand

The demand for factors, like the demand for products, changes in response to changes in economic conditions. Consider Exhibit 29.5. Suppose that the demand curve D_0 is the market demand curve for some factor of production. A change in the market price of that factor will cause the quantity of the factor demanded to change. This is represented by a movement along the demand curve. (See the arrow drawn parallel to D_0.) Changes in economic conditions other than a change in the factor's price

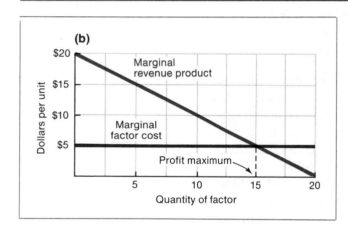

Exhibit 29.4
Profit maximization for a price taking firm

Profit maximization requires that a firm hire just enough of each factor of production to equalize marginal revenue product and marginal factor cost. Here it is assumed that the firm is a price taker, as in Exhibit 29.2. The point of profit maximization falls between fifteen and sixteen units of the factor.

(a)

Quantity of Factor (1)	Marginal Revenue Product (2)	Marginal Factor Cost (3)	Total Factor Cost (4)	Fixed Costs (5)	Total Revenue (6)	Total Profit (7)
1			$5	$100	$ 20	−$85
2	$19	$5	10	100	39	−71
3	18	5	15	100	57	−58
4	17	5	20	100	74	−46
5	16	5	25	100	90	−35
6	15	5	30	100	105	−25
7	14	5	35	100	119	−16
8	13	5	40	100	132	−8
9	12	5	45	100	144	−1
10	11	5	50	100	155	5
11	10	5	55	100	165	10
12	9	5	60	100	174	14
13	8	5	65	100	182	17
14	7	5	70	100	189	19
15	6	5	75	100	195	20
16	5	5	80	100	200	20
17	4	5	85	100	204	19
18	3	5	90	100	207	17
19	2	5	95	100	209	14
20	1	5	100	100	210	10

can cause a change in demand for a factor—for example, a shift in the demand curve from D_0 to D_1 or D_2.

Three kinds of changes in particular are capable of causing shifts in the demand curve for a factor of production. First, an increase in demand for the product that the factor produces will shift the factor demand curve to the right. Similarly, a decrease in demand for the product will cause the factor demand curve to shift to the left. Second, a change in the price of another factor of production used in combination with the given factor can also cause the demand for the given factor to shift. An increase in the price of a factor that is a substitute for the given factor will cause the demand curve for the given factor to shift to the right, while an increase in the price of a factor that is a complement to the given factor will cause the demand curve of that factor to shift to the left. Third, any change in technology that increases the marginal physical productivity of a factor will cause its demand curve to shift to the right, other things being equal, while a decrease in the marginal physical product of the factor will shift the curve to the left.

SUPPLY AND DEMAND IN THE LABOR MARKET

Up to this point, marginal productivity and factor demand have been discussed in general terms. It is time now to turn to the specifics of markets for particular factors. This section begins the analysis of such markets by looking at the supply and demand for labor, land, and capital. It concludes with a discussion of a unique and controversial form of income called profit. The discussion on labor will be limited at first to the case where individual workers compete with one another for jobs. The next chapter will take up the case of organized labor markets, where workers join together into unions to bargain with employers rather than competing with one another for jobs on an individual basis.

Exhibit 29.5
Movements along a factor demand curve and shifts in the curve
Changes in the price of a factor, other things being equal, will produce movements along a given factor demand curve, as shown by the arrow. Other kinds of changes can shift the factor demand curve. An increase in demand for the product produced by the factor might shift the curve from D_0 to D_1. An increase in the price of another factor that is a complement to the given factor might shift the curve from D_0 to D_2.

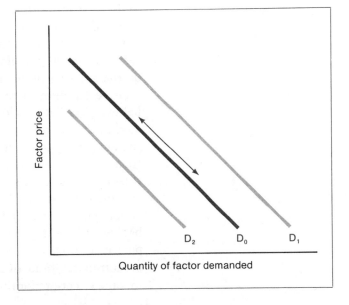

The Labor Supply Curve

The general analysis of a factor demand given in the previous section can be applied to the labor market without special modification. A labor supply curve is now needed to go with the labor demand curve. A look at the labor supply decision for an individual worker will begin the analysis.

Labor Supply for the Individual As individuals, people's decisions regarding how much labor to supply to the market are part of the general problem of consumer choice and can be analyzed in terms of the theory developed in Chapter 19. The best way to approach the problem is to think in terms of a trade-off between two alternative sources of utility—leisure and the consumption of purchased goods and services. Leisure is valued for relaxation, recreation, and the accomplishment of assorted household tasks. Time spent at leisure is time taken away from work, however, and thus is time taken away from earning income that can be used to buy goods and services. Within the limits of a twenty-four-hour day, people balance the relative advantages of work and leisure to achieve a consumer equilibrium in which, ideally, the marginal utility per hour of leisure exactly equals the marginal utility of the goods that can be bought with an hour's earnings.

The hourly wage rate can be thought of as the price—or, more precisely, as the opportunity cost—of leisure to the worker, in that it represents the dollar equivalent of the goods and services that must be sacrificed in order to enjoy an added hour of leisure. As the wage rate increases, it affects work versus leisure decisions in two ways. First, there is a substitution effect; the increased wage rate provides an incentive to work more, because each hour of work now produces more income to be spent on goods and services. In effect, purchased goods and services are substituted for leisure. Second, however, the increase in the wage rate has an income effect that tends to reduce hours worked. The higher wage rate, assuming that the prices of goods and services in general remain unchanged, increases workers' real incomes. With higher real incomes, they tend to consume more of all goods that are normal goods and less of those that are inferior goods. Leisure is a normal good. Other things being equal, people generally seek more leisure, in the form of shorter working hours and longer vacations, as their incomes rise. Taken by itself, then, the income effect of a wage increase is the reduction of the quantity of labor supplied by workers.

It can be seen, therefore, that the net effect of an increase in the wage rate on the quantity of labor supplied by an individual worker depends on the relative strength of the substitution and income effects. It is generally believed that for very low wage rates, the substitution effect predominates, so that the quantity of labor supplied increases as the wage increases. As the wage rises, however, the income effect becomes stronger. People tend to treat leisure as a luxury good; after they have assured themselves of a reasonable material standard of living, they begin to consider "spending" any further wage increases on increased time off from work. The labor supply curve for an individual to whom this generalization applies has a backward-bending shape, like the one shown in Exhibit 29.6. Over the positively sloped low wage section, the substitution effect of wage changes predominates, and over the negatively sloped high wage section, the income effect predominates.

Market Labor Supply Curves Even though the labor supply curves for all individual workers may bend backwards, at least over some range of wages, the supply curve for any particular type of labor as a whole is likely to be positively sloped throughout. Consider, for example, the supply of electrical engineers, the supply of typists in Montreal, or the supply of farm laborers in Saskatchewan. Each individual engineer or typist or laborer might, beyond some point, respond to an increased wage by cutting back on hours worked; but for the market as a whole, this tendency would be more than offset by new workers drawn into that particular labor market from other occupations or areas. Thus, other things being equal, if the wage rate for electrical engineers rose, more engineering students would take up that specialty; if the wage rate for typists in Montreal rose, more people would become typists than, say, filing clerks; and if the wage for farm laborers in Saskatchewan rose, workers would be drawn in from Alberta, Manitoba, and Ontario. As a result, for any discussion of the market for a particular category of labor at a particular time and place, it is reasonable to draw the labor supply curve with the usual positive slope, as in Exhibit 29.7, regardless of the shape of the individual labor supply curves underlying it.

Competitive Equilibrium

Determining the wage rate in a labor market that is fully competitive on both sides is a straightforward exercise in supply and demand analysis. Exhibit 29.8, for example, shows a supply and demand curve representing the labor market for typists in Montreal. It assumes that a large number of typists compete with one another for jobs and that a large number of employers compete with one another for typists, so that both are price takers. The demand curve for typists is the employers' combined marginal revenue curve. The supply curve is the same as that in Exhibit 29.7.

Equilibrium in this market requires a wage rate of $7 per hour, with 200,000 typists employed. If the wage rate were lower, there would be a

---

Exhibit 29.6

An individual's labor supply curve

On the one hand, a higher wage tends to increase the amount of work an individual is willing to do, because the extra money compensates for time taken away from leisure activities. On the other hand, a higher wage allows a person to take more time off work and still enjoy a high standard of living. Taken together, the two effects tend to give the individual labor supply curve the backward-bending shape shown here.

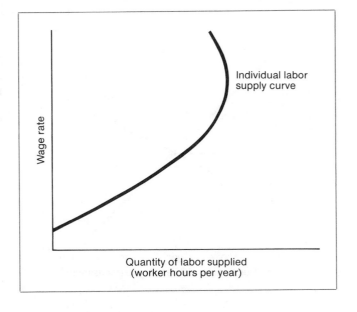

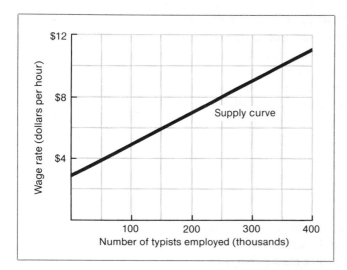

Exhibit 29.7

Hypothetical supply curve for typists

Although each individual typist may have a backward-bending supply curve, the supply curve for typists in any particular local market will have the usual upward-sloping shape. As the wage rises, people will be drawn into this occupation from other kinds of work or other localities.

shortage of typists. Some firms, unable to fill all their job openings, would offer premium wages to workers from other jobs or other regions. The wage rate would be driven up to the equilibrium level. If, on the other hand, the wage rate were above $7 per hour, there would be a surplus of typists. Many people would be looking for typing jobs and not finding them. After sufficient fruitless search, some would become willing to accept work at lower than expected wages, thus pushing the wage rate down toward equilibrium. Others would drift into other occupations or regions.

In a labor market such as this one, where both employers and employees are price takers, the equilibrium wage rate is equal to the marginal revenue product of labor. In the special case where all employers are price takers (perfect competitors) in the market where they sell their output as well as in the market where they purchase inputs, the equilibrium wage rate is equal to the marginal physical product of labor times the price per unit of output.

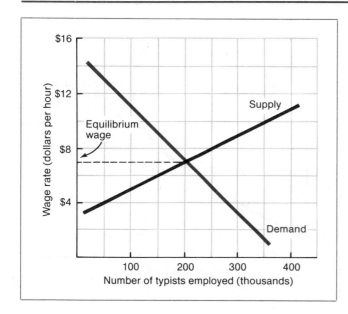

Exhibit 29.8

Determination of the equilibrium wage in a competitive labor market

When both employers and workers are price takers in the labor market, the point of equilibrium is found where the supply and demand curves intersect. Here the equilibrium wage rate is $7 per hour, and the equilibrium quantity of labor is 200,000 typists employed.

Monopsony

Not every factor market has a large number of buyers competing with one another. The extreme situation where there is only one buyer in a market is called **monopsony**.

There is an important difference between the case of competition and the case of monopsony. For a monopsonist, marginal factor cost is not equal to the price of the factor. Exhibit 29.9 shows why. The table and graph in this exhibit represent the supply side of the market for typists in a small town where there is just one big employer—an insurance company—which employs all or almost all the town's typists.

The supply schedule of typists shows that no one will work as a typist if the wage rate is $3 per hour or less. Above that wage, each extra two cents per hour will attract one more worker. Suppose that the monopsonistic employer has hired 150 typists, paying them $6 per hour. The total labor cost for a labor force of this size is $900 per hour. What will happen to the firm's total labor cost if it expands its labor force by one additional worker?

According to the supply curve, to hire 151 typists requires a wage of $6.02 per hour. That wage must be paid not just to the 151st worker but to all workers. The total cost of a labor force of 151 typists, then, is $6.02 times 151, or $909.02. The addition of one more worker has raised the total labor cost from $900 to $909.02, a marginal factor cost of $9.02. Similar results can be obtained by choosing other starting points from the table. In every case, the marginal factor cost for the monopsonist is greater than the factor price (the wage rate).

Exhibit 29.9b shows a marginal factor cost curve based on the marginal factor cost column of the table in Part a. This curve lies above the supply curve at every point. The relationship between the supply curve and the marginal cost curve for a monopsonist, as shown in this figure, is analogous

Monopsony A market in which there is only one buyer; from the Greek words *mono* ("single") and *opsonia* ("buying ").

Exhibit 29.9
Marginal factor cost under monopsony
Under monopsony, marginal factor cost exceeds factor price. Consider an increase in quantity from 150 to 151 units of labor in this exhibit. The wage rate must be raised from $6 to $6.02 not just for the 151st employee but for all the previous 150 as well. Marginal labor cost in this range is thus $9.02 per hour, not $6.02 per hour.

(a)

Quantity of Labor Supplied (1)	Wage Rate (2)	Total Factor Cost (3)	Marginal Factor Cost (4)
1	$3.02	$ 3.02	$ 3.06
2	3.04	6.08	3.10
3	3.06	9.18	
150	6.00	900.00	9.02
151	6.02	909.02	9.06
152	6.04	918.08	
200	7.00	1,400.00	11.02
201	7.02	1,411.02	11.06
202	7.04	1,422.08	

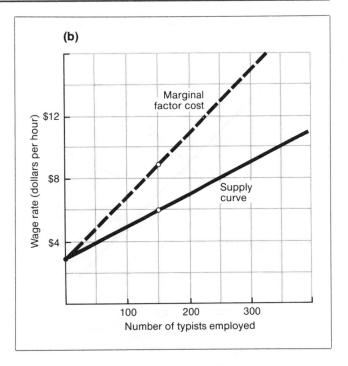

to the relationship between the demand and marginal revenue curves for a monopolist.

Monopsony Equilibrium

Given the monopsonist's marginal factor cost curve—derived from the factor's market supply curve—determining the equilibrium level of employment for the firm is a matter of routine. Exhibit 29.10 shows the monopsonistic employer's marginal revenue product curve along with the labor supply and marginal factor cost curves from Exhibit 29.9. Following the general rule that profit is maximized where marginal factor cost is equal to marginal revenue product, it can be seen that the monopsonist will hire 150 typists at a wage rate of $6 per hour.

Note that when a labor market is in monopsony equilibrium, the wage rate is lower than the marginal revenue product of labor. In the example shown, the equilibrium wage rate is $6 per hour, although the marginal revenue product is $9 per hour. Despite the gap between the wage rate and the marginal revenue product, this increase in the quantity of labor hired will not increase revenue by enough to offset higher labor costs. The reason is that the cost of hiring another worker is not just the $6.02 per hour that must be paid to the 151st worker but that sum plus the extra two cents per hour by which the wages of all 150 previously hired workers must be raised. The complete marginal factor cost for the 151st worker is thus $6.02 + $3.00, or $9.02 per hour.

RENT, INTEREST, AND PROFITS

Wages and salaries are a big part of the income distribution picture in the Canadian economy. In 1980, they accounted for some three-quarters of all net national income. They are not the whole picture, however.

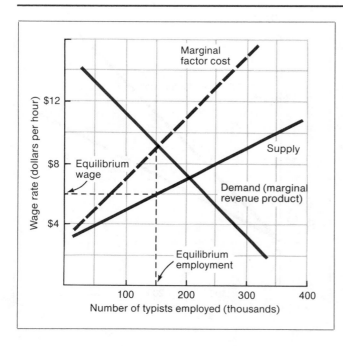

Exhibit 29.10
Wage determination under monopsony

Here are a monopsonist's marginal revenue product of labor curve, labor supply curve, and marginal factor cost curve. The quantity of labor required to maximize profits is found where the marginal revenue product curve and the marginal factor cost curves intersect. Note that the equilibrium wage rate is *not* shown by the intersection of the marginal factor cost and marginal revenue product curves. Instead, the rate is equal to the height of the supply curve directly below that intersection.

The remaining quarter of personal income (excluding transfer payments) is composed of rent, interest, and profits. These sources of income, although relatively small, deserve the same careful analysis given to wages and salaries. Rent, interest, and profits play a key role in the resource allocation process. They also play an important role in determining the overall personal distribution of income, since they are distributed somewhat less equally than labor income.

Rent

Economic Rent   **Pure economic rent** is the income earned by a factor of production that is in completely inelastic supply. The classic example of such a factor is land, which in this context means the natural productive powers of the earth and the locational advantages of particular sites. It does not include artificial improvements; nor does it include such matters as destruction of the soil through erosion or creation of new land through reclamation.

Exhibit 29.11 shows how rent is determined by supply and demand in a competitive market. It considers a particular category of land — Saskatchewan wheatland. The supply curve for Saskatchewan wheatland is a vertical line, because the quantity of land supplied does not vary as the rent that it earns varies. The demand curve is the marginal revenue product curve for that land as seen by Saskatchewan wheat farmers. The marginal product of land falls as more land is used in combination with fixed quantities of labor and capital because of diminishing returns. The demand curve thus slopes downward to the right.

The rent the land earns is determined by the intersection of the supply curve, representing the scarcity of land, and the demand curve, representing its productivity. If the rent is higher than the equilibrium shown, not all land will be put to use. The rent will then fall as landowners compete with

Pure economic rent The income earned by any factor of production that is in perfectly inelastic supply.

Exhibit 29.11
Determination of rent by supply and demand
Pure economic rent is earned only by a factor that has a perfectly inelastic supply curve. This figure shows hypothetical supply and demand curves for Saskatchewan wheatland. No account is taken of any possibilities for creating or destroying such land, so the supply curve is vertical. The demand curve, as for other factors, is based on the land's marginal revenue product.

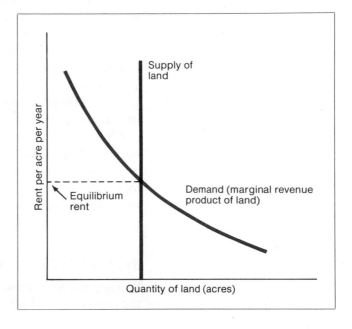

one another to find tenants. If the rent is lower than the equilibrium rate, farmers will be unable to find all the land they want. They will bid against one another for the limited available supply and drive rents up.

Capitalization of Rents The price of land is called rent; but much land, of course, is used by the person who owns it and is therefore not rented by a tenant from a landlord. That use does not change the way supply and demand determine the value of land. It does mean, though, that it is sometimes useful to speak of the price of land in terms of a lump-sum sales price rather than as a rent per month or year.

There is a simple relationship between the value of a piece of land expressed as a rent and the price at which that piece can be sold in the market. The market price of a piece of land is said to be the **capitalized value of its rent**—that is, the sum that would earn an annual return equal to the annual rent if it were invested at the market rate of interest.

Consider, for example, a piece of land with an expected real rental value of $1,000 per year in perpetuity. If the expected real rate of interest were 5 percent per year, a buyer would be willing to pay $20,000 for title to the land. If the expected real rate of interest were 2 percent per year, the price of the land would rise to $50,000, and so on. In general, the price of a parcel of land having a perpetual expected real annual rental value of R dollars per year, capitalized at the real rate of interest r is given by the formula R/r.

Capitalized value of a rent
The amount equal to the value of the sum of money that would earn a periodic interest return equal to the rent if invested at the current market rate of interest.

Other Rents The term *rent* can refer to the market return earned by any factor of production that is unique or that is in perfectly inelastic supply. Consider the very high incomes of people with unique talents, such as singers, actors, and some executives. These incomes are more plausibly thought of as rents earned on talents rather than as wages earned for work done. Artificially created legal privileges can be said to earn rents, too. For instance, part of the earnings of a Winnipeg taxicab can be counted as rent earned from the license that gives it the legal privilege to operate, so long as the supply of licenses is strictly limited by city authorities.

The hallmark of pure economic rent is inelasticity of supply. Pure economic rent should not be confused with what is loosely called the rental income earned by manufactured assets that are not in perfectly inelastic supply. Consider rental income of an apartment house owner, for example. It may in part be pure economic rent earned by some uniquely convenient site on which the building is located. In addition, though, the owner's income includes implicit wages for any custodial work done in the building, implicit interest on the money invested to build it, and so on.

What is pure economic rent and what is not depends in part on the time framework within which the income is considered. In the short-run—say a period too short for new buildings to be constructed—a case could be made for considering the income earned from buildings as a pure economic rent. In the long run, however, when additional buildings can be supplied at a price, such rental income is clearly not a pure economic rent.

INTEREST AND CAPITAL

Two Aspects of Interest The theory of capital and interest is in many ways the most complicated part of factor market theory, and care must be taken to understand the relationship between two different aspects of interest. The term *interest* is used to express both the price paid by borrowers to lenders for the use of loanable funds and the market return earned by capital as a factor of production. A person who loans $1,000 to another in return for a payment of $100 per year (plus eventual repayment of the principal) is said to earn 10 percent interest per year on the money. At the same time, a person who buys a machine for $1,000 and earns $100 a year by employing the productive services of that machine is said to earn 10 percent interest on capital.

Consumption Loans The discussion of interest and capital will begin by looking at how credit markets work in a simplified economy where households are the only suppliers of credit — that is, of loanable funds. Savers are households that earn incomes now but consume less than they earn in order to put something aside for expected future needs. Not all households in the economy are savers, however; some want to consume more than their current incomes permit. The latter may be households that want to tide themselves over a temporary decrease in income, or they may be households with steady incomes that just do not want to wait to buy a car or take a vacation. These and other households that borrow for any number of reasons are one source of demand for loanable funds. The loans they take out are called consumption loans.

The Productivity of Capital Nothing has yet been said about production or capital. Opportunities to use capital as a factor of production are a second source of demand for loanable funds, in addition to the demand for pure consumption loans. To understand the demand for loans of this kind, it is necessary to understand why capital is productive.

Using capital means using a roundabout method of production rather than a direct method. Consider, as an example, a person whose business is making bricks. There are two ways to make bricks. The direct way is to form them by hand out of raw clay scooped up from the ground and to bake them over an open fire. Suppose that by using this method, a worker can make 100 bricks per month. The alternative way of making bricks is a roundabout one. The brickmaker first spends a month forming bricks by hand and putting them together to make a kiln. When the kiln is completed, its hotter fire and lower fuel consumption make it possible to produce 110 bricks per month from then on. The roundabout method using capital (the kiln) lengthens the period between the time work starts and the time finished bricks begin to appear. In return, it increases the eventual rate of output. That is the sense in which capital is productive.

The brickmaker's experience is repeated in a more elaborate way whenever a firm makes a capital investment. Producing automobiles on an assembly line is a roundabout method of production compared to producing them one by one with hand tools. Constructing a building in which to hold economics classes is a roundabout method of education compared with holding classes in the woods under a tree. In every case, time is taken to construct aids to production in order to produce more effectively later on.

Investment Loans The brickmaker in the example invested directly by actually building the needed capital equipment. In a market economy, firms need not build their own capital equipment. Anyone who sees an opportunity for increasing output by using a more capital intensive (that is, a more roundabout) production process can borrow money and buy capital. The productivity of capital thus creates a source of demand for loanable funds in addition to the demand for consumption loans. Loans for increasing productivity can be called investment loans.

Exhibit 29.12 shows how the rate of interest is determined when the demand for investment loans is added to the demand for consumption loans. The demand curve for loans is downward sloping because consumers experience diminishing satisfaction from extra consumption and will borrow more, in order to finance increased consumption, only if they can do so at lower rates of interest. Because of the diminishing marginal productivity of capital (see Chapter 8), business'es will be inclined to borrow more money for building more capital equipment only if they can do so at lower interest rates. The supply of loanable funds slopes upward to the right because those who provide the funds sacrifice current consumption. The more they sacrifice, the more painful it becomes, the greater will be the interest they demand in compensation. The equilibrium interest rate is simply the price that those who supply the funds exact for their sacrifice, and a reflection of the increased benefits anticipated by those who borrow the funds. In other words, at the equilibrium interest rate, S = D.

PROFIT AND ENTREPRENEURSHIP

The term *pure economic profit* was introduced in Chapter 22 to refer to the income, if any, remaining to owners of a firm after they deduct all implicit and explicit costs of production. Explicit costs include factor payments to

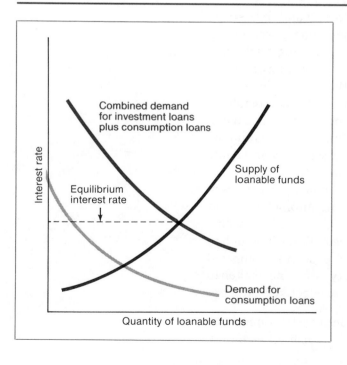

Exhibit 29.12
Determination of the interest rate with both consumption and investment loans
The demand for investment loans must be added to the demand for consumption loans to get the combined demand curve for loanable funds.

workers, resource owners, and suppliers of capital, together with the cost of semifinished inputs, if any, purchased from other firms. Implicit costs include a normal rate of return on capital supplied by owners of the firm plus the opportunity costs of using natural resources or labor supplied by owners of the firm or owned by the firm itself. What is left over is pure economic profit.

This definition of profit leaves unanswered two very important questions that have not yet been raised explicitly. Why does a firm ever earn any pure economic profit at all? Why is the entire value of the product of all firms not divided up among the owners of the labor, natural resources, and capital used in the production process? These are subtle questions that have occupied the minds of many great economists, who have not yet come up with answers that everyone agrees with. Still, it will be worthwhile to look at some of the kinds of answers that have been suggested.

Theories of Profit

Risk and Profit According to one theory, profits are a reward that the owners of business receive for bearing risk. Every business venture is subject to the risk of failure. That is the nature of economic life in a world where the future is not known with certainty. People who merely hire out their factor services largely escape risk. A new business is usually expected to offer workers contractual guarantees that the payroll will be met even if the firm loses money. It is also expected to offer security against default to banks or bondholders who provide capital. The owner or owners of the firm (stockholders if the firm is organized in the corporate form) bear most of the risk of loss if the firm fails. In return, they get the privilege of keeping the profits if revenues turn out to be more than enough to pay off the obligations to hired factors. Why is it, though, that the profits earned by successful risk takers are not exactly offset by the losses of the unsuccessful? The answer has to do with people's attitudes toward risk.

It is possible that some people are indifferent to risk. A person who is indifferent to risk will be indifferent between the opportunity to earn $10,000 a year with absolute certainty and the opportunity to try for $20,000, subject to a fifty-fifty chance of failing and earning nothing. People who are indifferent to risk may launch new businesses even when the expected profit if the business succeeds is exactly offset by the expected loss if the business fails.

In practice, though, most people dislike risk. If they know they can earn a secure $10,000 a year, they will not launch a business with a fifty-fifty chance of failure unless that business, if successful, will pay more than $20,000. Because most people dislike risk, somewhat fewer business ventures are launched than would be otherwise. That makes opportunities a little more favorable, on the average, for those who are willing to bear some risk. When successes and failures are averaged out over the whole economy, profits more than offset losses. The excess of profits over losses is the reward earned by the people who bear business risks. Factor owners are willing to accept less than the whole value of the product of the firm to the extent that they are shielded from these risks.

Arbitrage The activity of earning a profit by buying a good for a low price in one market and reselling it for a higher price in another market.

Profits as Arbitrage A second theory equates profits with the return to the activity of **arbitrage**—buying a good at a low price in one market and selling it at a higher price in another. Examples of pure arbitrage can be found in markets for agricultural commodities, precious metals, foreign currencies, and other markets where completely standardized goods are traded at different points in the world. Consider, for example, the gold markets in London and Hong Kong. Economic policies, daily news developments, and other events may initially affect supply and demand in these two gold markets differently.

A political crisis in the British government, for example, might prompt an increase in demand in the London market, sending the price of gold there up relative to the price in Hong Kong. Before the prices got far apart, however, alert arbitrageurs in Hong Kong would start buying gold at the low Hong Kong price for resale at the higher London price. This activity would raise demand in Hong Kong and increase supply in London until the price in the two markets was equalized. (In practice, because of various transactions costs, the prices would be only approximately equalized on any given day.) In the process of acting as a crucial link in the international transmission of information through the price system, the arbitrageurs would turn a handy profit.

Arbitrage cannot always be seen in a form so pure as the international gold market. However, New York University economist Israel Kirzner has pointed out in an influential book that there is an element of arbitrage in every profit-making transaction.[1] Consider the entrepreneur-owner-manager of, say, a small shoe factory. This person buys inputs in one set of markets at the lowest prices possible and, after combining the inputs to form finished shoes, sells the product in other markets at the highest prices possible. In a hypothetical world where all markets were in perfectly competitive long-run equilibrium, it would no more be possible to make a profit by buying labor and leather and selling shoes than it would be by buying gold in Hong Kong and selling it in London. In such a world, the price of the leather and labor would be bid up to just equal the price of the finished shoes. In the real world, though, the alert entrepreneur can find arbitrage opportunities in a great variety of markets and can earn profits accordingly.

Profits and Innovation A third theory associates the profit and the activity of innovation. This theory has achieved considerable popularity through the writings of Joseph Schumpeter.[2] In subtle contrast to the entrepreneur as arbitrageur, taking advantage of spontaneously occurring opportunities to buy low and sell high, the entrepreneur as innovator creates new profit opportunities by devising a new product, a new production process, or a new marketing strategy. If successful, the entrepreneur achieves a position of temporary monopoly that permits pure economic profits to be earned until rival firms catch on or leap ahead with innovations of their own.

---

[1]Israel Kirzner, *Competition and Entrepreneurship* (Chicago: University of Chicago Press, 1974).
[2]See, for example, Joseph Schumpeter, *Capitalism, Socialism, and Democracy* (New York: Harper & Bros., 1942). Schumpeter's theories are also discussed in Chapter 27 of this text.

Further Comments on the Nature of Profit

Entrepreneurship as a Factor of Production It is probably pointless to argue which of the three theories of profit just discussed is the correct one. The economic activity that, since Chapter 1, has been called entrepreneurship is best thought of as an inseparable blend of risk taking, alertness to opportunities for arbitrage, and innovation.

Because entrepreneurs, like workers, resource owners, and suppliers of capital, earn a reward for their contribution to production, entrepreneurship is sometimes spoken of as a fourth factor of production. In some ways, it is indeed a little like the three factors of production—labor, natural resources, and capital. First, entrepreneurship, like the others, is scarce. Not everyone possesses the ability to organize business undertakings and recognize new economic opportunities. Second, entrepreneurs do earn an income in the form of the profit that remains after all the costs of their firms have been covered. Third, as is true for labor, natural resources, and capital, production cannot take place without entrepreneurship.

There is a limit, however, to how far the parallel between entrepreneurship and other factors can be pushed. The chief problem is that entrepreneurship is an intangible, not subject to measurement. There is no quantitative unit of entrepreneurship and hence no way to determine a price per unit. Applying supply and demand analysis to this fourth factor of production just does not work.

Monopoly Profits Up to this point, no distinction has been made between the profits earned in the short run by a competitive firm (before those profits are eroded by the competition of new entrants) and the profits earned by a monopolist (which under proper conditions of demand can persist indefinitely). Some writers have suggested that monopoly profits are a separate category of income that cannot be explained either as a reward to labor, capital, or natural resources or in terms of the entrepreneurial activities of risk bearing, arbitrage, and innovation. On close inspection, however, it turns out that most, if not all, of monopoly profit can be explained without introducing a special new category of income.

Consider, for example, the case of a monopoly based on a patented invention. When explicit costs are subtracted from revenue for such a firm, more than enough will be left over to provide a normal rate of return on capital. The firm might be said to earn a pure economic profit, but it would more accurately be said to earn an implicit rent as owner of the patent. It could, after all, sell or lease the patent rights to some other firm, in which case the patent owner would earn an explicit rent and the firm using the patent would earn only a normal return on capital after paying to acquire the patent. The opportunity cost to a monopolist of not renting the patent to another firm should thus be counted as an implicit cost, not as part of pure economic profit. The same applies to firms having a monopoly based on any other unique advantage that is in perfectly inelastic supply, such as a government franchise, a uniquely suitable location, or a unique natural resource.

If a monopolistic firm does not possess any unique advantage, its monopoly cannot be more than temporary. Sooner or later, other entrepreneurs will enter into competition with the firm and begin the process of reducing its pure economic profits to zero. Temporary monopoly profits of this type are not a separate category of income; they are simply the return earned by the monopolistic entrepreneur who was alert enough to get into the market before any competitors did so.

In Exhibit 29.13 are listed the sales, assets, earnings, and rates of return on capital investment for a select number of large and well-known corporations in Canada in 1978. These data help us to see how profit rates are calculated and how they vary from one corporation to another.

Column 2 shows the value of sales, and Column 3 lists the estimated value of all assets owned by each company. Column 4 indicates the net income earned by each corporation. Net income is close to the business-person's definition of profit. It is the value of sales recorded in Column 2, *minus* operating expenditures (but not minus extraordinary expenditures).

To determine the profit *rate*, we should calculate net income as a percent-age of the funds or assets that investors have committed to a particular corporation. But how does one determine the amount committed? Column 3 provides one such measurement—the estimated market value of the company's assets. This value will usually be considerably higher than the amount actually invested in the company by shareholders. Many assets will have been purchased over the years out of the company's retained earnings. However, if Column 3 accurately measures the current value of the company's assets, and if these assets could be pulled out of the company at any time by the shareholders and sold for that value, then Column 3 represents the amount that shareholders actually have tied up in the corporation. Under such circumstances, shareholders should compare profit calculated as a percent of asset value with the best alternative return they might enjoy if they sold their assets and invested them elsewhere. For example, Column 5 tells us that, for the Bell Telephone Company, net income was only 4 percent of asset value in 1978. If Bell Telephone could actually sell its assets for $9.2 billion, it should clearly do so. It could direct the $9.2 billion that it received from the sale of its assets into bonds earning about 10 percent, which would give it net earnings of about $920 million instead of only $370.6 million.

However, it is extremely unlikely that the sales value of the assets would be anywhere near $9.2 billion. Used equipment will seldom bring to its

Exhibit 29.13
Sales, assets, earnings, and rates of return for selected Canadian corporations, 1978

Company (1)	Sales or Operating Revenue $000's (2)	Assets $000's (3)	Net Income $000's (4)	Net Income as Percent of Assets (5)	Net Income as Percent of Shareholders' Equity[a] (6)	Net Income as Percent of Sales (7)
General Motors	7,721,138	1,624,529	202,990	12.4	28.8	2.6
Ford Motor Co.	6,868,100	2,055,900	35,900	1.7	4.2	0.5
Bell Canada	4,374,355	9,205,283	370,562	4.0	12.1	8.5
Dominion Stores	2,405,385	392,087	24,077	6.1	15.8	1.0
Canada Safeway	1,985,126	500,744	46,276	9.2	13.6	2.3
McDonald's Restaurants	365,000	162,121	10,096	6.2	27.5	2.8

[a]After taxes.

Source: *The Financial Post 500: The 1979 Ranking of Canada's 500 Largest Companies* (June 16, 1979).

owners the value that accountants attribute to it, even though the value of such assets is depreciated. Still, the ratio of net earnings to assets does give the owners (shareholders) of a corporation some idea of how well the company is using its resources.

Another more common way of measuring the profit rate is to calculate net income as a percentage of the amount that shareholders have actually invested in the company (shareholder's equity). We don't have these figures, but *The Financial Post* used them to calculate such a profit rate in Column 6. That column informs us that all of the corporations listed, except the Ford Motor Company, earned a higher rate of profit on investment in 1978 than the going interest rate of about 10 percent. Ford shareholders in that year earned considerably less on their actual investment than they could have earned in many alternate forms of investment.

Sometimes corporations will calculate their profit as a percentage of sales. Supermarkets often do this because, in their case, sales are unusually large in relation to their investment, so that the profit/sales ratio will be much lower than the profit/investment ratio. By focusing on sales, supermarkets can try to counteract consumer criticism that they are earning high profits. They may also have good internal reasons for keeping track of profits in relation to sales, but for purposes of comparing their profit rates with other corporations, the profit/investment ratio is much more meaningful.

Profits and Loot One final kind of financial gain that is sometimes confused with profit is the acquisition of wealth not through production and voluntary exchange, as in the case of profit and factor incomes, but coercively, through the expropriation of other people's property. Suppose, for example, that a service station owner, instead of paying a mechanic the market wage of $10,000 per year, hires a gang of thugs to threaten to burn the worker's house and molest the worker's children unless he agrees to work for $6,000. The station's accounting profit will then appear to be $4,000 greater than otherwise. The extra $4,000 is not really pure economic profit, however, but something else. The vocabulary of economics lacks an accepted general term for the proceeds of coercive activity, but perhaps the word *loot* can serve as well as any. Looting need not be as crude as in the example just given. If a firm earns money by misrepresenting its product and defrauding consumers, that money is loot, not profit. If it gets rid of industrial wastes by dumping them on unwilling bystanders, then part of the firm's apparent profit is really loot. Loot is not only not profit; properly speaking, it is not a form of income because it is not a payment for newly produced goods or for services currently rendered.

CONCLUSIONS

The introduction to this chapter mentioned that factor markets determine not only how productive inputs are allocated among competing uses but also how total output is divided among individual factor owners. Consider the case in which several factors of production are used by a firm and factor markets are competitive. Profit maximization then requires that each factor be used up to the point where its marginal revenue product is equal to its price.

This suggests that each unit of each factor receives a reward that is equal to the contribution it makes to the firm's revenue. The idea that factors are rewarded according to their marginal productivity is know as the **marginal productivity theory of distribution**. The theory applies only to cases in which all factors are purchased in competitive input markets.

In an economy where all markets are perfectly competitive—not only input markets but output markets as well—the marginal productivity theory applies in an even stronger form. It has been shown that when output markets as well as factor markets are competitive, marginal revenue product is equal to output price times marginal physical product. In such an economy, the reward that each unit of each factor receives is exactly equal to the value of its marginal physical product. If an extra hour's labor in a T-shirt factory produces two extra T-shirts, and each T-shirt sells for $5, the wage rate must be $10 per hour—no more, no less.

This principle of distribution, in which every factor receives a reward equal to the value of its marginal product, appeals to many people as the most just one possible. The reward of every worker is exactly equal to the contribution of that worker to the productive process. If a worker or factor owner were to decide to withhold a unit of productive services from the market, that person would suffer a loss of earnings exactly equal to the value of production that would be lost to the economy as a whole.

Not everyone favors distribution according to marginal productivity, however. Some people do not believe it leads to the best personal distribution of income. There are two main lines of criticism. Some critics argue that it is fine for factors to earn their marginal products but that a just personal distribution of income also requires that the ownership of factors be justly distributed among people. Others argue that productivity is completely irrelevant as a basis for distribution. Instead, distribution should be carried out on the principle of "to each according to needs." These issues lie somewhat beyond the scope of this chapter, but the chapters on poverty and on capitalism versus socialism will return to them.

Marginal productivity theory of distribution A theory of the functional distribution of income according to which each factor receives a payment equal to its marginal revenue product.

SUMMARY

1. In factor markets, firms are the buyers, and households are the sellers. The theory of demand for a factor of production is thus an extension of the theory of the firm. A profit maximizing firm must take three things into account when it makes a hiring decision for any factor: (a) the quantity of output produced by a unit of the factor in question (marginal physical product), (b) the revenue derived from the sale of the output that will be produced by the extra unit of the factor (marginal revenue product), and (c) the cost of obtaining an extra unit of the factor (marginal factor cost).

2. A profit maximizing firm will hire just enough of each factor of production to equalize marginal revenue product and marginal factor cost. In the special case where a firm is a price taker both in the market where it buys its inputs and in the market where it sells its outputs, profit

maximization requires that each factor's price be equal to its marginal physical product times the product price. So long as the firm is a price taker in the factor market, its demand for a factor of production is that factor's marginal revenue product curve.

3. The theory of labor supply for an individual household is an extension of the theory of consumer choice. Given the alternatives of work and leisure, each consumer works just enough that the marginal utility per hour of leisure exactly equals the marginal utility of the goods that can be bought with an hour's wage. The labor supply curve for a single individual tends to have a backward-bending shape. The market labor supply curve for a particular occupation or locality, however, ordinarily has the conventional upward-sloping shape.

4. In a market where both workers and employers are price takers, the equilibrium wage rate and equilibrium quantity of labor are found at the intersection of the labor supply and labor demand curves. If the workers are price takers but their employer is a monopsonist, the equilibrium quantity of labor is found at the intersection of the marginal revenue product curve and the marginal factor cost curve, and the equilibrium wage rate is determined by the height of the supply curve directly below this intersection.

5. In a competitive market where there are several factors of production, profit maximization requires that each factor be used up to the point where its marginal product is equal to its price. Each factor thus receives a reward equal to its marginal revenue product. This distribution is thought by some to be the most just distribution of income possible.

6. Pure economic rent is the income earned by any factor of production that is in completely inelastic supply. Land is the classic example of a factor that earns a pure economic rent. Rent can be expressed in terms of either a periodic payment or a lump-sum price paid when a piece of land is transferred from one owner to another. The market price of a piece of land is the capitalized value of the rent it can earn. Rent can also be said to be earned by other factors that are in perfectly inelastic supply. The special talents of uniquely gifted persons earn rents, as do artificially created legal privileges.

7. The term *interest* expresses both the price paid by borrowers to lenders in credit markets and the income earned by capital as a factor of production. The interest rate is determined in credit markets. The supply of credit depends on the willingness of savers to lend. The demand for credit is composed of the demand for consumption loans plus the demand for investment loans. There is a demand for investment loans because capital using, roundabout methods of production are more productive than direct methods.

8. There are several theories about the true nature of profits. One theory holds that profit is the reward that entrepreneurs earn for performing the function of bearing risks. Another sees profits as earned primarily through arbitrage. Still another emphasizes innovation. In practical terms, profit usually appears to arise from a mixture of these three sources.

DISCUSSION QUESTIONS

1. What is meant by the statement that factor markets help determine for whom things are produced? Is it that workers consume exactly the things they produce? Do they ever do this? When they do not, what other markets also help determine for whom things are produced?

2. The text examined only factor markets in which the buyers are firms. Are households ever the buyers of factors of production? Are you the direct purchaser of a factor of production when you hire someone to type a term paper for you? When you get your hair cut? When you buy or rent a plot of land for a vegetable garden? What changes would have to be made in the theory of factor markets to take into account the case where both buyers and sellers are households?

3. Is a monopsonist necessarily a monopolist, and vice versa? Try to imagine a firm that is a monopolist in its product market but not a monopsonist in its factor markets. Then try to imagine a firm that is a monopsonist but not a monopolist.

4. Do you think there is any close connection between the value of what somebody produces and the amount that person earns? Consider these specific examples: an auto worker; a real estate salesperson; a rock star; your economics professor. Why does the connection between earnings and product seem closer in some cases than in others?

5. Suppose a friend said to you that it was just fine to let factor markets determine how things were produced, but the matter of for whom ought to be handled according to the principle of "to each according to need." Sketch a reply to this remark that begins: "But that won't work. If you don't let markets determine for whom, they won't be able to determine the how...."

6. In 1978, Canadian farmers had cash receipts of $11.9 billion. Part of this income went to cover explicit private costs of about $7.4 billion, leaving farmers with $4.5 billion of net income. Is that net income best thought of as wages, rent, interest, or profit? How can one go about making a rough breakdown of net farm income into these categories? Do you think that any farm income ought to be considered loot?

7. The chapter has suggested that part of the income of persons with exceptional talents might best be considered pure economic rent earned on those talents. Suppose a certain opera singer makes $100,000 per year. How could you tell what part of that income is wages and what part is rent? Here are three possible tests for finding what part is rent: (a) ask how big a pay cut the singer would take before switching to a job where singing talent would be of no use; (b) measure the difference between this singer's income and the income of a singer with the same training but only average natural talent; (c) measure the difference between the singer's income in opera and the income he or she could earn in the next-best nonsinging job available. Which test is best? Do they all give about the same answer? Explain.

8. Turn back to Chapter 4 and Exhibit 4.7, and refresh your memory about the theory of tax incidence. How would the burden of a tax on pure economic rent be divided between resource owners and consumers? What about a tax on the "rental" income of apartment house owners?

9. Suppose you decide to start a Christmas tree farm. You already own a suitable piece of land. You get seeds from pine cones picked in the woods. You plant the seeds with your bare hands, using no tools or equipment of any kind. Five years later, you harvest the trees, breaking them off with your hands rather than using any tools whatsoever. You sell the trees and earn a handsome income. How should that revenue be divided into wages, rent, interest, and profit? Did you use any capital? If so, what form did it take? (Hint: did you use a roundabout method of production?)

10. Suppose a contractor places an ad for laborers in the newspaper, offering to pay them $1 per cubic yard for removing rocks and dirt from a cellar hole. Four workers show up and start the job. Alice is a person of average build. She uses a

simple shovel and bucket for the job and manages to earn $2 a day. Baker, a giant of a man, also uses a shovel and bucket but earns $5 a day. Charles brings a wheelbarrow with him and earns $6 a day even though he is no stronger than Alice. Donna uses a bucket and shovel and, like Alice, earns only $2 a day at first. Not satisfied with this, she takes a month off to go through an intensive course of physical conditioning. When she comes back, she can earn $5 a day. How should the income of each worker be categorized in terms of wages, rent, income, and profits?

C H A P T E R 30

LABOR UNIONS AND COLLECTIVE BARGAINING

This chapter completes the discussion of labor markets begun in the previous chapter. It explains how labor markets operate when workers organize into unions and bargain collectively with their employers. It begins with a brief history of the union movement in Canada. Next, it shows how to interpret the effects of unionization in terms of supply and demand curves. Finally, it reviews the history of public policy toward labor unions and discusses some contemporary issues in labor union economics.

FOR REVIEW
Here are some important terms and concepts that will be put to use in this chapter. If you do not understand them, review them before proceeding.
- *Cost-push inflation (Chapter 15)*
- *Incomes policy (Chapter 18)*
- *Anticombines Act (Chapter 28)*
- *Monopsony (Chapter 29)*

WHAT YOU WILL LEARN IN THIS CHAPTER
In 1978, 3,277,968 Canadian workers belonged to labor unions—approximately 39 percent of all nonagricultural employees and 31.3 percent of the total labor force. About 66 percent of the union members were in unions affiliated with or directly chartered by the Canadian Labour Congress (CLC), over 20 percent were in unaffiliated national unions, and 5.4 percent were affiliated with the Confederation of National Trade Unions (CNTU), the Quebec-based federation. Unions with headquarters in the United States accounted for 47.4 percent of total Canadian membership.

Canadian union membership, although substantial, is not large by European standards. In Austria and Sweden, more than two-thirds of all workers belong to unions. In England, Germany, and the Netherlands, more than one-third are members. Only France, among the major European countries, has a comparably low level of unionization, with just 29 percent of the labor force unionized.

In the United States the largest unions are virtually all "blue collar" unions, representing manufacturing and transportation workers. In Canada the practice is quite different. The single largest union is the Canadian

Exhibit 30.1

**Membership of the twelve largest
Canadian unions, 1978**

About 41 percent of all union members belong to these
twelve largest unions. Of the twelve, only the International
Brotherhood of Teamsters, the Ontario Public Service
Employees, and the Quebec Teaching Congress are
independent.

Name of Union	1978 Membership
1. Canadian Union of Public Employees (CLC)	231,000
2. United Steelworkers of America (AFL-CIO/CLC)	199,000
3. Public Service Alliance of Canada (CLC)	154,432
4. International Union, United Automobile, Aerospace and Agricultural Implement Workers of America (CLC)	130,000
5. National Union of Provincial Government Employees (CLC)	128,061
6. United Brotherhood of Carpenters and Joiners of America (AFL-CIO/CLC)	89,010
7. International Brotherhood of Teamsters, Chauffeurs, Warehousemen and Helpers of America (Ind)	86,603
8. Quebec Teaching Congress (Ind)	85,000
9. Social Affairs Federation (CNTU)	70,000
10. International Brotherhood of Electrical Workers (AFL-CIO/CLC)	63,914
11. Ontario Public Service Employees (Ind)	61,049
12. Labourers International Union of North America (AFL-CIO/CLC)	61,029

Source: Labour Canada, *Labour Organizations in Canada*, 1978, pp. 8–9.

Union of Public Employees (CUPE), representing mostly "white collar"
government employees. The unions ranked third, fifth, eighth, ninth, and
eleventh represent similar types of workers. Exhibit 30.2 illustrates the
strength of the union movement in public administration.

Apart from the much smaller fishing and trapping sector, the public
sector is the most highly unionized industry in Canada. It is also significant that virtually all of the public administration workers belong to
national unions. International unionism is strongest in such private industrial sectors as construction, mines and oil wells, and manufacturing.

In Europe, union membership is associated with political support for
socialist political parties. In the United States, the popular image of union-
ists is somewhat the reverse. Union workers are often represented as being

Exhibit 30.2

**Percent of workers unionized, by industry and by international and national
unions, 1976**

Industry Group	Percent of Workers Unionized	Percent in International Unions	Percent in National Unions
Public administration	67.4	3.2	64.2
Construction	52.1	48.9	3.2
Transportation and utilities	50.0	25.2	24.8
Forestry	42.0	32.5	9.5
Mines and oil wells	39.7	33.4	6.3
Manufacturing	43.5	34.5	9.0
Fishing and trapping	73.5	16.8	56.7
Service industries	22.6	6.2	16.4
Trade	8.5	6.8	1.7
Finance	2.7	1.2	1.5

Source: *Statistics Canada, Annual Report of the Minister of Industry, Trade and Commerce under the
Corporations and Labour Unions Returns Act* (Part II: *Labour Unions*), 1976, pp. 74, 77.

more conservative on political and social questions than the nonunion public. In fact, on a broad range of issues, including social programs, national defense, and foreign affairs, surveys in the United States have shown that the opinions of union members differ very little from the opinions of the rest of the public.

In Canada, the leadership of the Canadian Labour Congress and of some of the major unions is openly committed to the New Democratic Party, but rank-and-file union members have voting preferences similar to those of the rest of the public. A concerted effort by union leaders to rally their workers behind the NDP in the 1979 federal election had little success.

So much for generalities. These statistics and observations are enough to show that Canadian unions, although not as strong as in some other countries, are large enough to play quite a significant role in the economy. Let us now turn to a more detailed look at their origins and functions.

THE HISTORY OF CANADIAN UNIONISM

The history, structure, and philosophy of Canadian unions have been shaped by the various forces that we have discussed earlier in this book: the extreme regional disparities of the country, the large-scale development of resources requiring considerable capital investment and resulting in concentration levels higher than those in the U.S., the extreme seasonal and cyclical fluctuations, and the close economic dependence on the United States. These factors have, in the words of one scholar, "all worked to produce a Canadian labor movement that could be described as decentralized, fragmented, relatively weak, and strongly influenced by American international unions."[1]

The development of local unions in Great Britain and the United States at the beginning of the nineteenth century found an echo in scattered industrial centres in Canada by the 1820s and 1830s. Small **craft unions**, which were unions of skilled workers all practicing the same craft were formed in the shops of tailors, printers and foundry operators in several places in Quebec, the Maritimes, and Ontario. These early attempts at unionization usually failed, because of sharp opposition from owners, generally hostile courts, and poor organization. In 1873, in Toronto, the first attempt was made to form a coordinating body, the Canadian Labour Union. It lasted only until 1877. A somewhat more successful effort was made by an American union, the Knights of Labor, which began to organize Canadian unions shortly after Confederation. It was founded as a secret society (the Noble Order of the Knights of Labor), but its growth began only after it abandoned secrecy in 1878. It reached a peak membership of about 12,000 in Canada in 1887.

Many local unions of skilled craftsmen were affiliated with the Knights of Labor, but the Knights' principles went far beyond the narrow bounds of craft unionism. They welcomed anyone who worked for a living, including farmers and unskilled laborers. In this they resembled an **industrial union**,

Craft unions Unions of skilled workers practicing a single craft.

Industrial unions A union representing all workers in an enterprise, regardless of trade.

[1]M. Saunderson, "Labour Relations in Canada," in *The Canadian Economy: Problems and Policies*, ed. G.C. Ruggeri (Toronto: Gage, 1977), pp. 274–275.

which is a union of all workers in an industry, including both skilled and unskilled workers and workers practicing various trades. Only such "undesirables" as bankers, liquor dealers, Pinkerton detectives, and lawyers were excluded by the Knights. Their program was not limited to narrow economic concerns. It stressed workers' education and producer co-operatives that would help counteract the "evil of wealth."

The Knights ran into conflict with other craft unions and declined rapidly after they were associated (without proof) with the killing of a policeman during Chicago's Haymarket Riot of 1886.

Despite the ultimate failure of the American-based Knights of Labor, many Canadian workers found it advantageous to turn to American unions for financial and organizational support in establishing unions in their craft. Naturally, most of these unions became affiliates of the American unions.

The United Brotherhood of Carpenters and Joiners in the United States had dozens of affiliates in Canada, from Nova Scotia to British Columbia, by 1890.

One of the first successful confederations of labor in Canada, the Trades and Labour Council of Canada (TLC) was founded in 1886, and affiliated itself with the rapidly growing American Federation of Labor (AFL). Thereafter, the philosophy of the AFL, as expressed by its founder Samuel Gompers, came to dominate much of the Canadian labor scene. No Canadian labor leader has so influenced the philosophy of unionism in Canada as this powerful American unionist. Gompers sought to avoid the mistakes that had led to the downfall of the Knights of Labor. The AFL owes its success largely to three features of its organization and philosophy that were prominent from its earliest years:

1. The AFL was based solidly on the principle of craft unionism. Its leaders thought that the dangers of economic depressions and employer opposition could be overcome only by relying on skilled workers who could not easily be replaced during strikes. The AFL itself was, in effect, an umbrella organization of national craft unions.

2. The AFL emphasized business unionism; that is, it devoted most of its energies to bread-and-butter issues of pay and working conditions. Unlike many European labor unions, it was content to work within the capitalist system. It did not seek the overthrow of private property or the establishment of socialism.

3. The AFL limited its political role to that of a lobbyist on labor's behalf. Again in contrast to European labor movements, it did not found a labor party. Gompers thought that excessive political involvement would lead to internal conflict within the labor movement and would weaken its ability to achieve concrete economic objectives.

The TLC, through its affiliation with the businesslike and highly successful AFL, was the guiding force for unionism in Canada for half a century after its founding.

Partly because of the strength of the international unions affiliated with the TLC and the AFL, several rival, autonomous confederations were established on a provincial basis, notably the B.C. Federation of Labour in 1911 and the Federation of Catholic Workers of Canada (Quebec) in 1921. Until the rise of strong, independent public workers' unions after World

Samuel Gompers was born in a London tenement, the son of a skilled cigar maker. When he was thirteen, his family moved to the United States and settled on the East Side of New York. Gompers followed his father into the cigar trade.

Although his formal education ended at the age of ten, Gompers was very active in the workers' self-education movement of the time. In the cigar-making shops, jobs were organized on a piecework basis. Groups of workers would have one of their members read to them while they worked, "paying" the reader by making his cigars for him. Gompers became acquainted with the works of Marx, Engels, and other European socialists in this way. Often he was chosen as the reader.

The cigar makers' union to which Gompers belonged fell apart during the depression of 1873. Gompers rebuilt it as a model of the craft unions he was later to unite under the American Federation of Labor. Key features of this union were high membership dues, central control of funds, national officers with control over local unions, and union-organized accident and unemployment benefits for members.

Gompers became disillusioned with radical socialism. The main role of unions, in his view, was to watch after the economic interests of their members. He wrote:

Unions, pure and simple, are the natural organization of wage workers to secure their present material and practical improvement and to achieve their final emancipation.... The working people are in too great need of immediate improvements in their condition to allow them to forgo them in the endeavor to devote their entire energies to an end however beautiful to contemplate.... The way out of the wage system is through higher wages.

Samuel Gompers (1850–1924)

During the 1890s, a socialist faction emerged within the AFL. It adopted a program calling for the collective ownership of all means of production and other radical measures. Gompers opposed the group, and in the 1895 election for the AFL presidency, he was defeated. He fought back, however, and succeeded in regaining the presidency the next year. He remained president until his death in 1924.

Gompers was an ardent patriot throughout his career. During World War I, he opposed pacifism and supported the war effort. In 1918, he said: "America is a symbol; it is an ideal; the hopes of the world can be expressed in the ideal — America."

War II, these provincial federations formed the main bulwark against the complete dominance of the TLC.

The period 1914 to 1919 saw the development of a more radical form of unionism. Union membership increased sharply in this period, partly as a result of the increased union activity permitted by the federal government in all industries devoted to the war effort. The war itself brought Canadian union members in touch with more militant forms of industrial conflict in Europe, particularly the aims and methods of the 1917 Bolshevik Revolution. There is also evidence that rising prices immediately after the war, and a poor job market, led to a decline in real wages for many workers. The result of such new opportunities, ideas, and economic pressures was growing political action by labor in British Columbia, the formation of the One Big Union (OBU) by western radicals in 1918, and the most dramatic event in Canadian labor history, the Winnipeg General Strike of 1919. The police put down the strikers in Winnipeg, and several, including J.S. Woodsworth, later the founder of the CCF (the precursor of the NDP party), were put in jail. In 1920, however, eleven labor members were elected to the Manitoba Legislature, and J.S. Woodsworth became a member of Parliament for Central Winnipeg.

However, despite (and because of) the new radicalism and the political successes, the union movement showed few new advances in the interwar period. There were approximately 400,000 union members in Canada in 1920, and about the same number in 1940. As we shall see, social, legal, and legislative changes were required to give the union movement new momentum.

New union structures were also needed. The TLC and the AFL had turned their backs on the type of industrial unionization favored by the Knights of Labor. In the 1920s and 1930s, several unions in Canada and the United States promoted industrial unionism and laid the foundation for a major change in union strategy. In the United States, the fight was carried on by the Congress of Industrial Organizations (CIO) led by the Mineworkers leader, John L. Lewis. In Canada the Canadian Brotherhood of Railway Employees (CBRE) led the way, creating first the All-Canadian Congress of Labour (ACCL) and assisting, in 1940, in the formation of the Canadian Congress of Labour (CCL). The CCL, in turn, affiliated with the CIO but never came under the latter's dominance (unlike the TLC, which was clearly subservient to the AFL).

After World War II, the AFL in the United States modified its stand on craft unionism and began to espouse industrial unionism. This helped to lead to a merger of the AFL and the CIO in 1955. A similar merger occurred in Canada in 1956, when most of the members of the TLC and the CCL created one confederation of labor, the Canadian Labour Congress (CLC). Most unions outside of Quebec are now affiliated with the CLC. In Quebec, the CNTU continues to represent most of the provincial trade unions.

Since the beginning of World War II, union membership has grown rapidly. Between 1955 and 1978, membership increased by more than 250 percent, from 1,268,000 to 3,278,000. However, the labor force has also grown rapidly, and union members as a percentage of non-agricultural paid workers only went up from 33.7 percent in 1955 to 39.0 percent in 1978. Major efforts now underway to organize professionals (for example, university professors) and such previously impervious sectors as banking and finance, though they have met with some success, have not yet provided a major new breakthrough for the union movement in Canada.

COLLECTIVE BARGAINING AND WAGE RATES

Union Goals

Labor unions have done many things for their members and pursued many goals. They have bargained for shorter working hours and better health and safety conditions. They have founded pension funds for their members, promoted worker education, and engaged in party politics. For Canadian unions, however, the number one goal has long been to achieve higher wages for their members. This section will look at the means unions have to achieve higher wages. Later sections will examine how successful they have been.

The Union in a Competitive Market

The discussion will begin with the case of a union that is formed in a previously competitive market and now seeks higher wages through the threat of a strike. Consider Exhibit 30.3. This figure shows a labor market in which the competitive equilibrium wage rate is $8 per hour and the equilibrium level of employment is 300,000 worker hours per year. (See Point E_1 in the exhibit.)

Exhibit 30.3

Effect of unionization in a competitive labor market
A union formed in a previously competitive labor market can use a strike threat to bargain for higher wages. Here, the union threatens to strike unless the wage is raised from its competitive level of $8 per hour ($E_1$) to $10 per hour. With the strike threat in force, the supply curve of labor to employers becomes horizontal at $10 per hour up to 400,000 labor hours per year, as shown. A new equilibrium is reached at E_2, where the new supply curve intersects the demand curve. The wage is higher than initially, but the quantity of labor employed is smaller.

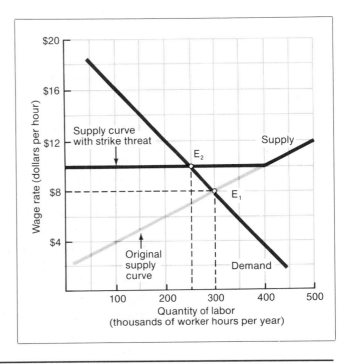

Suppose that the newly organized workers in this industry tell employers that they want $10 per hour, or else they will go on strike. The strike threat is shown in the diagram by a change in the shape of the supply curve. Originally, the supply curve had the usual upward-sloping shape. After the strike threat, employers face a supply curve with a kink in it. The horizontal left-hand branch of the new kinked supply curve indicates that if the employer does not pay at least $10 per hour, no workers at all will be available. Up to 400,000 worker hours will be supplied at $10 per hour. To hire more labor than that, the wage will have to be raised higher than the union is demanding.

Suppose that the employers decide they have no choice but to accept the union demand. They will react by shifting to a new equilibrium at Point E_2 in Exhibit 30.3, where the demand curve and the horizontal part of the new supply curve intersect. There they will hire 250,000 worker hours per year at $10 per hour. The union will have succeeded in raising the wage of its members, although only at the expense of reducing the amount of work available from 300,000 worker hours per year to 250,000 worker hours per year.

The trade-off in this example between increased wages and reduced employment is a rather general one when workers bargain collectively with competitive employers. Given the inevitable trade-off, just how far back along the employers' demand curve for labor should the union try to push?

There is no easy answer—no easy way to calculate an optimal wage demand. If the union wants to keep as many of its workers employed as possible, it may simply accept the competitive wage and confine its bargaining to nonwage issues. Perhaps, though, the union wants to raise the total income of its members. If the demand curve is inelastic in the region of the competitive wage, this can be done by pushing the wage up a bit. Although employment will fall, total labor income will increase.

In Exhibit 30.4, the labor demand curve is inelastic up to a wage of $10 per hour, unit elastic at that point, and elastic beyond. The $10 wage thus gives the largest possible total labor income—$2.5 million per year. Unfortunately, keeping the wage at this level creates a surplus of labor. Workers will be willing to supply 400,000 hours per year, but only 250,000 will be demanded. The union can simply allow workers to compete for jobs on a first-come, first-serve basis and not worry about those who cannot get a job. Alternatively, it can try to parcel out the available work among all who want a job in the industry. Each worker will then be limited in the number of hours that can be put in. Whichever route is taken, a union that keeps the wage above the equilibrium level must be well enough organized to prevent nonunion workers from undercutting it.

Sometimes a strong union will ask for a wage even higher than the one that gives the maximum labor income. Suppose, for example, that the union takes an elitist attitude, restricting membership to certain racial or ethnic groups or to friends and relatives of current members. Look at Exhibit 30.4 again. An elite group of workers may push the wage up to, say, $16 per hour, if 100,000 hours per year is all the work members of the group want. To hold a card in such a union, needless to say, will be a jealously guarded privilege.

Featherbedding

Featherbedding The practice of negotiating purposefully inefficient work rules so that more workers will be needed to do a job.

Sometimes powerful unions try to get around the trade-off between wages and jobs through the practice of **featherbedding**—insisting on purposefully inefficient work rules so that more workers will be needed to do a job. There have been some notorious examples of featherbedding in Canadian industry. Railroad unions, for example, have required fire fighters on diesel locomotives.

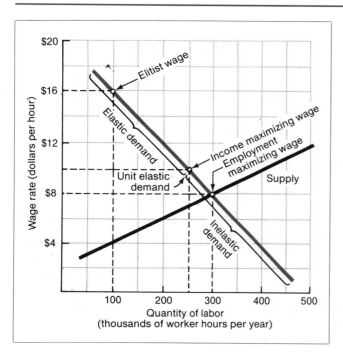

Exhibit 30.4

The wage-job trade-off

Unions facing employers who are price takers may choose various ways of dealing with the wage-job trade-off. If the union's objective is to maximize employment, it will not bargain for a wage higher than the competitive equilibrium. If the labor demand curve is inelastic at the competitive equilibrium point, total income of union members can be increased by raising the wage to the point where the demand curve becomes unit elastic. If the union restricts membership to a limited elite group, it may push wages even higher.

If featherbedding simply meant that some workers stood idly by while others worked normally, it would just be another form of work sharing. To the extent that it involves technical restrictions that lower productivity, though, it creates problems that simple work sharing does not. Lowering productivity means shifting the labor demand curve to the left. In the end, total earnings for a group of featherbedding workers must be lower than earnings for an equal number of workers who practice a form of work sharing that does not restrict productivity.

Union versus Monopsonist

There is one exception to the trade-off between jobs and wages — the case where a union faces a monopsonistic employer. Consider Exhibit 30.5. This figure shows a labor market in which a monopsonistic employer faces a group of workers who are initially unorganized. The wage rate in equilibrium is $6.50 per hour, and only 220,000 hours of labor per year are hired. This point is labeled E_1.

Now consider what happens if a union confronts the monopsonist with a demand for a wage of $10 per hour and backs the demand with a strike threat. As in Exhibit 30.3, this demand puts a kink in the labor supply curve. What is more important, along the horizontal part of the new labor supply curve, the monopsonist's marginal labor cost is equal to the wage rate. The union says, in effect, that the firm can hire as many workers as it wishes at no more and no less than $10 per hour — which means that changes in the quantity of labor hired no longer require changes in the wage rate. One more worker hour raises total labor costs by no more and no less than $10.

Suppose that the union is strong enough to make the monopsonist accept its wage demand on a take-it-or-leave-it basis. The new equilibrium will

Exhibit 30.5
The effects of unionization in a monopsony labor market

When a union faces a monopsonistic employer, it can sometimes raise both wages and employment. Here, the original monopsony equilibrium wage is $6.50 per hour with 220,000 worker hours per year (E_1). A strike threat puts a kink in the monopsonist's marginal labor cost curve, because the union's take-it-or-leave-it $10 per hour bargaining position makes the employer a price taker in the labor market at that wage rate. The new marginal labor cost curve intersects the demand curve at 240,000 worker hours per year, which becomes the new equilibrium point, E_2. Both the wage rate and the quantity of labor employed are higher than at E_1.

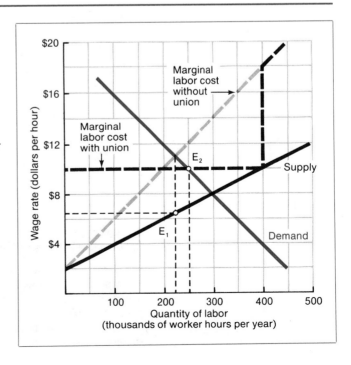

then be found where the new marginal labor cost curve intersects the demand curve, at Point E₂. The wage rate there is $10 per hour, and 240,000 worker hours per year are employed. Both the wage rate and employment are higher than in the previous monopsonistic equilibrium.

Notice, however, that there is a limit on the power of a union facing a monopsonist to raise wages without losing jobs. This limit is set by the extent to which the original monopsony wage fell short of the competitive wage. Once the wage rate begins to exceed the level where the supply and demand curves intersect, further raises reduce employment. In fact, as Exhibit 30.5 is drawn, the wage of $10 per hour is already in the trade-off region. Maximum employment is achieved with a wage rate of $8 per hour, equal to the competitive wage.

Bilateral Monopoly

Bilateral monopoly A market in which both buyer and seller exercise monopoly power and neither passively accepts the demands of the other.

The example just given assumes that the monopsonistic employer will accept the union demand on a take-it-or-leave-it basis. Not all employers react this way. A strong employer may counter the union demand with the threat of a lockout or of some take-it-or-leave-it offer of its own. The kind of bargaining situation that develops when neither party to the labor contract acts competitively and neither passively accepts the demands of the other is called **bilateral monopoly**. The outcome of bargaining under bilateral monopoly is impossible to predict with the type of analysis used here. Economic theory can only specify a range of outcomes within which a settlement can take place. The actual outcome depends simply on the relative bargaining strength and skill of the two sides. The headline-making disputes in which "big labor" clashes with "big business" often fall into the category of bilateral monopoly.

Relative Wages

How successful unions are in raising the relative wages of their members depends primarily on three things: (1) whether the unions are strong enough to make a creditable strike threat; (2) how willing they are to sacrifice jobs in order to gain higher wages; and (3) what the demand conditions are in their sector of the labor market. No purely theoretical analysis can tell which unions will be able to win higher relative wages and which will not. This is an empirical question that has drawn the attention of many economists. The following case reviews some of the results they have reached.

Case 30.1
Labor Unions and Relative Wages

In 1963, H.G. Lewis of the University of Chicago published a study of the effects of unionism on relative wages. As part of his work, he made an exhaustive survey of previous studies of individual industries. The main results of the earlier studies, as presented by Lewis, are shown in Exhibit 30.6.

This table suggests that unions do have some measurable power over their members' relative wages. Often, however, this power is not great. Cases in which

Exhibit 30.6

Effects of unionization on relative wages in selected American industries

Unions vary in their ability to win higher relative wages for their members. Cases where union wages are at least 25 percent higher than nonunion wages appear to be rare. Many unions gain only a very slight relative wage advantage for their members.

Author of Study	Industry	Years Covered	Effect of Unionization on Relative Wages
Rees	Steel	1945–1948	Zero or negative
Scherer	Hotels	1939–1948	Negligible, 6–10%
Sobel	Tires	1936–1938	10–18%
		1945–1948	5–9%
Sobotka	Construction (skilled)	1939	25%
	Construction (unskilled)	1939	5%
Greenslade	Coal	1909–1957	Variable; 0–82%
Maher	Seven manufacturing industries	1950	0–7%
Craycroft	Barbers	1948	2%
		1954	19%
Rayaek	Men's clothing	1919	20%
		1926	12%
Sobotka	Airline pilots	1956	24–30%
Laurie	Local transit	1920s	15–20%
		1948	10%
Rapping	Seamen	1939–1957	6–35%

Source: Data from H.G. Lewis, *Unionism and Relative Wages in the U.S.* (Chicago: University of Chicago Press, 1963), pp. 184–186. © 1963 The University of Chicago. Reprinted by permission.

unions were found to raise relative wages more than 25 percent above the nonunion level are rare. Lower figures are common, and in more than one instance the relative wage power of unions declined over time. Their greatest impact was in the first years of organization.

Source: Based on H.G. Lewis, *Unionism and Relative Wages in the U.S.* (Chicago: University of Chicago Press, 1963), pp. 184–186.

Unions and Absolute Wages

It seems well established, then, that unions can affect relative wages. Are they also able to raise the average wages of all workers, as measured by the share of wages in national income? That is a quite separate question. This time, there is little theoretical basis for believing they can. Except in cases of true monopsony, which are likely to be temporary and purely localized, unions win their higher wages at the expense of fewer jobs. As the wage in unionized industries rises, the supply of labor to nonunionized sectors increases, keeping nonunion wages down.

National income statistics show labor's share of national income to be remarkably stable over time. Unadjusted figures show the proportion of wages in national income rising from about 60 percent in the 1920s to around 75 percent today, but this change reflects factors other than unionization. It is largely explained by the relative growth of sectors of the economy that employ much labor (especially government and services) and the decline of sectors using less labor in proportion to other inputs. When an adjustment is made for this, labor's share of national income appears to have increased by only about 2 percent over the past half-century. Since this period coincides with the period of fastest union growth, the impression left is that the impact of unionization on average wages has been minimal.

PUBLIC POLICY TOWARD UNIONS

What should be the government's policy toward unions? This question has been a topic of impassioned political debate ever since unions began. Some have argued that all unions should be suppressed as illegal restraints on trade. Others have advocated government support for unions to promote industrial stability and high living standards for all. Still others have favored a laissez-faire policy, letting workers and management bargain without government interference. The debate has been clouded by disagreements about the true effect of unions on relative and absolute wages and on industrial efficiency. Without taking a position, the next section will survey the changing course of government policy over time, showing how first one and then another opinion has become dominant.

Unions had trouble with the courts from their earliest days. Under precedents from English common law, they were often treated as illegal conspiracies in restraint of trade. Businesses were able to get the support of the courts in most cases to have the unions declared illegal. Often they didn't bother resorting to courts. Workers who were caught participating in the formation of a union, or just listening sympathetically to a union organizer, were summarily fired. Such workers were often blacklisted, so that they had trouble getting a job anywhere else. Confrontations were often violent, both in Canada and the United States. Some employers used "yellow-dog" contracts, whereby workers signed an agreement not to engage in union activity. This then became a condition of employment.

In the United States, the Sherman Antitrust Act was used vigorously against unions as a form of restraint of trade, but in Canada the anticombines legislation was not used in a similar fashion. Canadian governments, both provincial and federal, created few laws either for or against unions, so that unions had neither the disadvantages of the Sherman Act nor the advantages of pro-union laws passed in the U.S. in the 1930s. The first supportive act was passed by Parliament in 1900. This set out a framework of conciliation to handle disputes between labor and management. This was followed by the Industrial Dispute Act of 1907, which included the acceptance of the right of workers to organize and bargain collectively, but did not require management to recognize a union.

It was only in 1939 that changes in the Criminal Code made it an offence for an employer to harass employees who were unionizing with threats of dismissal. During World War II, a special Order-in-Council laid the basic foundation for collective bargaining, by forcing management to bargain with an elected union "in good faith."

A unique Canadian decision in 1946, by Mr. Justice Ivan Rand of the Supreme Court of Canada, who had been appointed to arbitrate and settle a bitter strike at the Ford Motor Company, gave unions a new type of power and security. His ruling which has come to be known as the *Rand Formula*, required both union and nonunion members at Ford to pay union dues. This has given strong support to the practice of compulsory union dues.

Exhibit 30.7
Person-Days Lost from Industrial Disputes

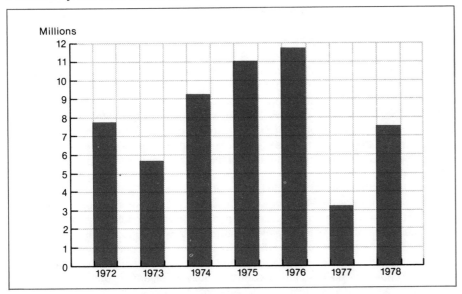

Since World War II, unions have enjoyed the right to organize, to bargain collectively with the employer, and to strike if a settlement cannot be reached. Despite such obvious power, the Canadian experience in management-labor relations is one of the most disappointing among western industrialized nations.

Union leaders in Canada generally frown on the cozy relationship that some American union leaders seem to have with their employers, which may have made the American unions less militant and which has also led to many glaring abuses of power and finances by American union leaders. At the same time, both union and management are skeptical of experiments in "industrial democracy" in such countries as Sweden and West Germany, where a greater spirit of cooperation has been developed between employers and employees by granting workers considerable rights in the management of companies.

Canadian labor and management seem to prefer the adversary system of bargaining, based on the assumption of class conflict. The result is continued industrial strife, millions of hours of work lost through strikes and lockouts, and the use of tactics that sometimes seem to fall just short of war. In 1976, almost 11 million person-days were lost through industrial disputes, or about 1,200 days per 1,000 workers. This compares with 20 lost days per 1,000 workers in West Germany and 6 lost days per thousand workers in Sweden. The U.S. had 392 lost working days per 1,000 workers.[2] Exhibit 30.7 shows that the number of person-days lost was less in 1977 and 1978 than in the strike-plagued years from 1974 to 1976, but Canada still has one of the worst records in the west.

---

[2]International Labour Office, *1977 Year Book of Labour Statistics*, Geneva, 1978.

Case 30.2
Continuing Conflict between Labor and Management

The news article reproduced here from *The Financial Post* shows that Canada's deeply rooted management-labor conflicts are far from resolved. Perhaps no area of our economy is more in need of innovation and change.

Following hard on the heels of a remarkable growth membership, union organization drives show signs of degenerating into brutal trench warfare with managements that shudder at the thought of union shops.

It's been that way for some time in Quebec, where celebrated battles such as that between the Canadian Tire outlet in Sherbrooke and the Retail Clerks International Union stayed on the boil for months in and out of court. And there've been some tough battles in British Columbia. But the fighting seems now to have spread to Ontario with a vengeance.

In two rulings this year, the Ontario Labor Relations Board (OLRB) — more noted for its restraint than anger — has come down hard on management. In one ruling, it said Toronto-based Norseman Plastics Ltd. conducted what "could only be described as a concerted campaign of terror aimed at employees who supported the union."

Then late last month, Dylex Ltd. was charged with criminal conspiracy to commit unfair labor practices. Dylex manufactures and distributes clothing through such well-known chains as Tip Top, Harry Rosen and Suzy Shier, among others.

The charges related to an unsuccessful attempt to organize the 175 employees in Dylex's central distribution centre in Toronto $2\frac{1}{2}$ years ago. Included in the indictments were two Dylex executives — marketing director, Lewis Pearsall and manager Gunter Leverenz — and private detective firm Centurion Investigation Ltd. (which has since had its license suspended) and its president, Daniel McGarry. The charges include the claim that Dylex hired two Centurion employees to pick a fight with the two leading union organizers on Dylex's payroll, giving the company reason to fire all four of them.

Dylex officials declined to comment when contacted by The Post.

Sam Fox, Canadian director of the Amalgamated Clothing & Textile Workers' Union (which was conducting the organizing campaign), claims there is a "whole new breed of labor experts advising management how to beat or break a union drive."

Fox says Dylex is just one of a series of companies that have started to dig in against the unions. S. S. Kresge Co. and Radio Shack, Barrie, are examples. But labor leaders say most are within the "ghetto industries" — small companies of less than 50 employees, labor intensive, such as metal fabrication or clothing, and employing immigrants. Generally they are less sophisticated in labor relations and belong to industries without a tradition of trade union organization.

Source: Peter Silverman, "Unions Facing Tough Battles in Ontario as Managements 'Dig In,'" *The Financial Post*, May 12, 1979, p. 36.

SUMMARY

1. The first local craft unions in Canada were established in the early decades of the nineteenth century. In the 1870s and 1880s a confederation of labor was attempted by the U.S.-based Knights of Labor. The Knights were soon succeeded by the Trades and Labour Council of Canada (TLC), in affiliation with the AFL in the United States. The philosophy and practice of the latter was shaped by the strong leader Samuel Gompers. The TLC emphasized craft unionism and concentrated on the bread-and-butter issue of higher wages. There were some early successes in industrial unionism in some provinces and in some independent unions, but it became widespread only with the formation of the Canadian Congress of Labour (CCL) in 1940, in affiliation with the CIO in the U.S. At first the TLC and CCL feuded bitterly, but in 1956,

following the merger of the AFL and the CIO, the two organizations united and formed the Canadian Labour Congress (CLC). Today about two-thirds of all union members in Canada are in unions affiliated with the CLC.

2. The strike threat is a union's ultimate weapon in bargaining with employers for higher wages. A union wage demand backed up by a strike threat has the effect of bending the labor supply curve so that it becomes horizontal at the level of the wage demand. In a market where employers are price takers, a higher wage can usually be won only at the expense of jobs lost. Sometimes, featherbedding or other kinds of work sharing are used to spread available work among all union members. Within certain limits, a union can win higher wages from a monopsonistic employer and gain higher employment at the same time.

3. Empirical studies show that many unions actually do succeed in raising the relative wages of their members. Often, though, the relative wage advantage of union members is only a few percent. It is doubtful that unions have a significant effect on the average wages of all workers, as measured in terms of the share of wages in national income.

4. Public policy toward unions has gone through several phases. Until the 1930s courts were generally hostile toward unions. Beginning in 1900, but accelerating in the late 1930s and during World War II, legislation was passed giving unions the rights they now enjoy. The Rand Formula of 1946 has provided the foundation for compulsory payment of union dues, a source of new security for unions. Despite legislative progress, labor and management operate in a sometimes fierce adversary system, resulting in a comparatively high rate of days lost through industrial disputes.

DISCUSSION QUESTIONS

1. Why do you think that unions are stronger in the public service and, for example, in manufacturing, than in service industries and in such sectors as banking and agriculture?
2. Why has socialism never been a strong political force in Canadian unionism, even though the labor movements of almost every other country are strongly socialist or communist?
3. Is the nonteaching staff of your college or university unionized? If so, what union or unions represent them? Is the teaching faculty unionized? If not, are there any active attempts underway to unionize the faculty? Describe.
4. Why do some unions encourage wasteful featherbedding rather than simple work sharing in the form of, say, shorter hours or longer vacations?
5. In what ways do labor unions resemble cartels? Do you think labor unions deserve more public policy support than cartels of producers? Explain.
6. Do you think public employees should be allowed to form unions? Should they have the right to strike? What changes need to be made in the analysis of unions and labor markets in order for it to apply to unions of public employees? (Hint: what determines the labor demand curve of a unit of government?)

SUGGESTIONS FOR FURTHER READING

Crispo, John. *The Canadian Industrial Relations System*. Toronto: McGraw-Hill Ryerson, 1978.
Ostry, Sylvia. *Labour Economics in Canada*. Toronto: Macmillan, 1974.

Williams, Jack. *The Story of Unions in Canada*. Toronto: J.M. Dent, 1975.

Woods, H.D. *Labour Policy in Canada*. Toronto: Macmillan, 1974.

The book by Williams provides an excellent history of the Canadian labor movement. The others are more analytical and emphasize current policies concerning labor.

CHAPTER 31

THE PROBLEM
OF POVERTY

WHAT YOU WILL LEARN IN THIS CHAPTER

Factor markets do not distribute income equally among Canadian families. Even in an economy that supplies households with a median income of almost $15,000 (in 1977), some three to four million Canadians are officially classified as poor. Federal, provincial, and local governments have many ambitious antipoverty programs. These have somewhat reduced the inequality of income distribution over recent decades, but they have not eliminated the problem. Current programs are so expensive that there has been much discussion of streamlined transfer schemes such as the negative income tax. Not all economists think that transfers are the best answer to the poverty problem. Policies that aim to improve poor workers' chances in the job market also generate much current interest.

FOR REVIEW

Here are some important terms and concepts that will be put to use in this chapter. If you do not understand them, review them before proceeding.
- *Tax incidence (Chapter 4)*
- *Economic functions of government (Chapters 4 and 28)*
- *Functional distribution of income (Chapters 29 and 30)*

A PROFILE OF POVERTY IN CANADA

The Personal Distribution of Income

The factor markets that we have been studying distribute income very unequally among Canadian families. Exhibit 32.1 gives an idea of who received how much in 1977. The table shows a median household income in 1977 of $14,962. A household is a family or a single individual living alone. Although this median was sufficient to provide a comfortable standard of living, it is worth noting that about a quarter of all families received less than half of that. It is the lower end of the income distribution profile that will particularly concern us in this chapter.

Exhibit 31.1

Personal distribution of income in Canada, 1977

Income is not distributed equally among households in Canada. About a quarter of all households receive less than half the median income.

Income Bracket (by Households)	Percent of Households in Each Bracket	Percent of Households in Each Bracket and Below
Under $3,000	7.7	7.7
$3,000–$4,999	8.5	16.2
5,000– 6,999	7.2	23.4
7,000– 8,999	7.0	30.4
9,000–10,999	6.4	36.8
11,000–12,999	6.6	43.4
13,000–14,999	6.8	50.2
15,000–16,999	6.8	57.0
17,000–19,999	9.5	66.5
20,000–24,999	12.8	79.3
25,000–34,999	14.3	93.6
35,000 and over	6.5	100.0

Average Income $16,602
Median Income $14,962

Figures do not add up to exactly 100, because of rounding.
Source: Statistics Canada, *Income Distributions by Size in Canada*, 1977, Preliminary Estimates, p. 12.

Effects of Government Spending on Income Distribution

Exhibit 31.1, we should note, records only the distribution of before-tax money income, including government transfer payments. To get a more accurate picture of the relative welfare of upper and lower-income households, and of changes in the distribution of income over time, we must make certain adjustments. First, we have to correct for the different impact of taxes on households at different levels of income. Second, we should adjust for differences in the average size of household. Unfortunately this is not done by Statistics Canada.

Exhibit 31.2 shows that when some of these adjustments are made, the income distribution in Canada has become somewhat more equal over time.

Exhibit 31.2

Effects of government taxes and expenditures on income distribution in Canada, 1961–1969

Income Group (1)	Percent of Households in Group (2)	Percent of Broad Income by Group 1961 (3)	Percent of Adjusted Broad Income, 1961 (4)	Percent of Broad Income by Group, 1969 (5)	Percent of Adjusted Broad Income, 1969 (6)
1. Poorest	21.7	3.1	5.8	3.3	6.9
2. Lower-middle	25.5	15.7	18.2	14.9	17.9
3. Middle	25.5	27.5	27.6	25.8	25.7
4. Upper-middle	22.2	33.6	31.6	35.7	32.0
5. Richest	5.0	20.1	16.8	20.3	17.6
Total	100.0	100.0	100.0	100.0	100.0

Source: W. Irwin Gillespie, "On the Redistribution of Income in Canada," *Canadian Tax Journal*, No. 24, 1976, p. 432, 450.

The data in Exhibit 31.2 are based on a study in which income groups were selected, not on the basis of a constant level of income, but on the basis of constant percentages of households in each group. Thus, in both 1961 and 1969, the two years chosen for comparison, the poorest group consisted of the bottom 21.7 percent of all households; the next group consisted of the next 25.5 percent of households, and so on. Column 3 indicates the percent of income that would have been received by each group in 1961 if governments at all levels had not intervened with both taxes and transfer payments (and with expenditures on such items as hospitals and schools, whose benefits for each group are also calculated). Column 4 illustrates the difference in these percentages after income has been adjusted by taking account of such government activity.

Comparing Columns 3 and 4, we see that in 1961 the three lowest income groups had income redistributed in their favor by government taxation and expenditure programs. In general this occurs not because of the tax system — which tends on the whole to be only slightly progressive — but because of government expenditures that favor lower-income groups. In 1969, only the two lowest income groups had income redistributed in their favor by the combination of government taxes and expenditures. Based on the experience of those two years, it can be said that government activities redistribute income from higher to lower-income classes.

Income Distribution over Time

What happens to income distribution over time? Comparing Columns 3 and 5 we see that the picture is extremely ambiguous. Without the presence of government, the percentage of income going to the poorest group would have increased slightly, from 3.1 to 3.3 percent. In fact, an even greater shift occurred for this group, because of government activity. The adjusted broad income share (columns 4 and 6) increased from 5.8 percent to 6.9 percent. However, the lower-middle class fared quite differently. Both when government activity is considered, and when it is not, the share of this group declined between 1961 and 1969. The same holds true for the middle class. On the other hand, both the upper-middle and the richest classes enjoyed a greater share of income, adjusted and unadjusted, in 1969 than in 1961. It seems that the poorest and the richest classes benefitted in the interval at the expense of the middle-income groups. One can hardly say, therefore, that income was clearly distributed in favor of lower-income people in the decade of the 1960s. It appears that government programs do not bring about much change in income shares.

This rather dismal conclusion was challenged in 1979, however, by Professor Clarence Barber of the University of Manitoba. "A more careful look suggests that Gillespie's conclusion, widely shared among economists, has a major pitfall. The studies assume that the structure of households today is roughly the same as 20–25 years ago. In fact, there have been quite major changes. And when allowance has been made for these, it is no longer clear just what changes have occurred in our income distribution."[1]

---

[1] Clarence Barber, *The Financial Post*, July 14, 1979, p. 8.

As we noted previously, a household may be a family or a single person living alone. Barber notes that in recent years many young people who previously would have been at home contributing to family income have established separate households. Since many of these young people are just starting out, their incomes will be relatively low. This will increase the number of low-income households in the data, but we would not be justified in saying that these young people are worse off than their counterparts a generation earlier. He notes other changes in family living that would have a similar effect. He concludes, therefore, that "the contention that the growth in government welfare spending...has had little effect on income distribution is a contention no one is justified in making."[2]

POVERTY AND INCOME DISTRIBUTION

If we are to discuss poverty as a policy problem, we must know how income distribution and poverty are related. We might say, in a sense, that income distribution is a matter of numbers, while poverty is a matter of people and values. Measuring income distribution is just a routine task of positive economics. Measuring poverty, however, requires a normative judgment. It requires us to say how far down the income scale a family can fall before they do not have enough or have less than they ought to have.

Definitions of Poverty

There is no single definition of poverty that everyone accepts. Some want an absolute income figure, indicating the minimum income that a household would need to satisfy its basic wants. Others see poverty in relative terms. When income in general is rising the income of the poor may also rise, but if their relative position is unchanged their sense of being poor will remain. By a definition of this kind it is possible to have "poor" in Canada who are better off than the "rich" in some other countries, but they are poor in relation to the rest of society, with which they will inevitably compare their situation.

Statistics Canada and the Economic Council of Canada have tried to establish absolute poverty lines for different-sized families in different locations. These lines were originally calculated on the basis of studies in the 1960s that indicated Canadian families spent, on average, about half of their income on the basic essentials of food, clothing, and shelter. It was arbitrarily decided that a family which spent a considerably greater proportion of its income on such essentials — say 70 percent — could be considered poor. The "poverty line" was drawn at that point, any household spending 70 percent or more on essentials was considered to be below it. Since then, with rising real incomes, the line has been lowered to those income levels that require the expenditure of 62 percent or more of income on food, shelter, and clothing.

Exhibit 31.2 indicates how much income different-sized households, in rural and urban areas, would require in 1977 to be able to spend no more than 62% percent of their income on essentials (or to be able to devote 38 percent of their income to non-essentials).

---

[2] Ibid.

Exhibit 31.3

Poverty lines by household size and location, 1977

Persons Per Household	Poverty Line for Large Cities (500,000 plus)	Poverty Line for Rural Areas
1	$ 4,446	$ 3,231
2	6,443	4,688
3	8,221	5,980
4	9,778	7,110
5	10,930	7,951
6	11,999	8,726
7 or more	13,158	9,567

Source: Statistics Canada, *Income Distribution by Size in Canada, 1977*, Preliminary Estimates, p. 7.

There is, of course, much room for debate about the validity of these figures. Some critics contend that the figures are too high because, for example, some households below the poverty line are seemingly able to afford cars and television sets. Others argue that the figures are too low, because people do not live "by bread alone" and many families close to the poverty line are unable to share in the cultural and social amenities which their society offers. The debate will never be settled, but the figures at least give social planners something definite to work with. We shall use them in other parts of this chapter.

Who Are the Poor?

As of 1977, more than three million Canadians, or about 15 percent of the population, were living below the official poverty line. The poor were not distributed evenly across the population, either demographically or geographically. A majority of poor people (52.6 percent) lived in cities with populations of 100,000 or more. However, a higher proportion of families in rural areas (13.2 percent) were poor than were families in cities (for example, 10.2 percent of families in cities with populations from 100,000 to 500,000). This was true despite the fact that for a family of two persons, for example, the poverty line in rural areas was only $4,688 while in cities from 100,000 to 500,000 population the line was drawn at $6,034.

Exhibit 31.4

The geographical distribution of poverty in Canada, 1977

The data presented in this table show the percentage of families in each province who fell below the poverty line in 1977.

Province	Percentage of Families below Poverty Line
Newfoundland	16.6
Prince Edward Island	12.7
Nova Scotia	12.6
New Brunswick	15.1
Quebec	13.6
Ontario	10.5
Manitoba	13.2
Saskatchewan	14.4
Alberta	10.6
British Columbia	9.6

Source: Statistics Canada, *Income Distributions by Size in Canada, 1977*, Preliminary Estimates, p. 19.

Poverty is also unevenly distributed across the country. Exhibit 31.4 shows the percentage of families below the poverty line by province in 1977. British Columbia had the lowest proportion of families below the line (9.6 percent) and Newfoundland had the highest (16.6 percent).

Still other data can shed light on why some persons or families fall below the poverty line. Exhibit 31.5 shows that 44 percent of households headed by a woman, usually widowed or divorced, live in poverty, as compared to only 8.5 percent of households in which the head is a male.

Age is also important, as Exhibit 31.5 indicates. Both very young (age of family head below 25) and old families (age of family head 65 and over) have a very high poverty rate.

Not surprisingly, employment is also very important. Only 5.7 percent of families in which the head is an employee live in poverty, compared to 16.3 percent of the self-employed and 32.2 percent of families in which the head is not in the labor force.

About ten years ago the Special Senate Committee on Poverty determined in the course of extensive hearings that the poor can be classified in three general categories:

1. About one-quarter of the poor are unable to work because of severe disability.
2. About one-half of the poor are working, but are not able to earn an adequate income.
3. The remaining quarter of the poor are seemingly able to work but can't or won't find employment.[3]

---

[3] Special Senate Committee on Poverty, *Poverty in Canada*, 1971. See also T. Courchene, "Some Reflections on the Senate Hearings on Poverty," in *Economic Canada: Selected Readings*, eds. B.S. Keirstead, J.F. Earl, et al. (Toronto: Macmillian of Canada, 1974), pp. 205–206.

Exhibit 31.5
Incidence of Poverty by Selected Characteristics 1977

Characteristics	Incidence of Poverty (Percentage of families below poverty line)
Sex of family head	
Male	8.5
Female	44.1
Age of Family Head	
24 and under	17.1
25–34	11.4
35–44	10.1
45–54	9.1
55–64	10.2
65–69	16.3
70 and over	22.3
Labor status of head	
Employee	5.7
Self-Employed	16.3
Not in Labor Force	32.2

Source: Statistics Canada, *Income Distribution by Size in Canada, 1977*, Preliminary Estimates, p. 19.

The first group can be helped through special assistance programs and personal charity. The second group, the working poor, poses many special problems. Its members are the victims of erratic employment patterns related to swings in the business cycle; low-productivity jobs and low pay, often associated with low levels of education; and low mobility. Some members of this group may also be the victims of discrimination.

The third group, made up of those who are not working but are potentially able to work, also poses acute problems. To what extent are they simply not motivated to work, either because of generous social assistance programs that reduce the penalty for not working, or because of the absence of inner drive and a sense of responsibility? To what extent are they unable to match their limited skills with the prevailing job market? We simply don't have many reliable answers to these questions. We noted in a previous chapter that unemployment insurance provisions have undoubtedly contributed to some of the unemployment in the country. Some feel that generous welfare programs do the same. However, a recent study of welfare in Manitoba observed: "Contrary to a popular view, the typical individual on welfare is not an able-bodied person with a large family who prefers living in idleness drawing his welfare cheque to taking a job and supporting himself. Indeed, insofar as the provincial welfare rolls are concerned, the employable category makes up only a small proportion of the total, usually five percent or less."[4]

WHAT IS TO BE DONE ABOUT POVERTY?

This profile of poverty in Canada gives us an idea of the dimensions and diversity of the problem. Next we shall look at what is being done to alleviate poverty, and what else might be done but is not.

We have divided the poor into three main categories, and this suggests that three different types of approaches may be necessary to alleviate poverty in Canada.

For those who are clearly disabled or unable to participate in the work force because of age, a program of social assistance, involving transfer payments, is required. We noted in Chapter 4 that all three levels of government in Canada have instituted programs of this type. At least a dozen transfer programs are now in existence, coordinated through the Canada Assistance Plan (1966). Programs include the Old Age Security Pension, Blind Persons' Assistance, Veterans' Benefits, Family Allowances, and Workmen's Compensation. In addition there are social insurance schemes, in which the amount paid out is related to premiums paid by the recipient. These include the Canada (and Quebec) Pension plans and unemployment insurance.

Such assistance programs are generous enough to prevent extreme hardship among most of the unemployed poor in the country, but it could be argued that, in a wealthy nation like Canada, assistance to the disabled and the aged could and should be sufficient to lift them above the poverty line entirely.

---

[4]Clarence L. Barber, *Welfare Policy in Manitoba*, A Report to the Planning and Priorities of Cabinet Secretariat, Province of Manitoba, December, 1972, p. 8.

For the employable poor, other types of programs are required. In Chapters 4 and 17, we mentioned various types of manpower training programs and fiscal and monetary measures that governments currently utilize to create more and better jobs. These need to be supplemented by other measures. It would appear, for example, that more vigorous efforts are necessary to moderate excessive wage and income differentials by curbing the monopolistic power of large corporations, professional groups, and labor unions.

A comprehensive approach to poverty through changes to the income tax act, which would use "negative taxes" to provide assistance without discouraging work incentives, has also been advocated in Canada. This is related to what is known as a Guaranteed Annual Income policy (GAI) for Canada. In November 1970 the federal government published a White Paper, "Income Security for Canadians," calling for study of "an overall guaranteed income program for the whole population." The government agreed to cooperate with provincial governments in researching the feasability of such a program. The only provincial government to take up the offer was Manitoba, which launched a three-year research project in 1975 (see Case 31.1). In 1973 the federal government issued a "Working Paper on Social Security in Canada," which gave broad support to new initiatives in the area of social security including a negative income tax approach.

The Negative Income Tax

Economists concerned about the disincentive effects of the present welter of poorly coordinated transfer programs have long advocated "cashing out" all in-kind transfers and rolling all transfer programs into a single negative income tax program. The basic idea behind a negative income tax is very simple. Under a positive income tax — the kind currently used — individuals pay the government an amount that varies according to how much they earn. A **negative income tax** puts the same principle to work in reverse. It makes the government pay individuals an amount that varies in proportion to their earnings.

Negative income tax A general name for transfer systems that emphasize cash benefits, beginning with a basic benefit available to households with zero earned income that is then subject to a benefit reduction rate of substantially less than 100 percent.

Exhibit 31.6 shows how a negative income tax could be set up. The horizontal axis of the figure measures the income a household earns. The vertical axis measures what it actually receives after payments from or to the government. The 45 degree line represents the amount of disposable income households would have if there were no tax of any kind. The negative and positive income tax schedules show the disposable income of families with the negative income tax program in force.

As the exhibit is drawn, the benefit received by a family with no income at all is just equal to the average low income level, assumed to be $6,000. That is necessary if the scheme is to eliminate officially measured poverty entirely. Starting from zero earnings, benefits are reduced by $.50 for each $1 earned. When earned incomes reach a level equal to twice the low income level, a breakeven point where no taxes are paid and no benefits received is reached. Beyond that point, a positive income tax schedule of the familiar kind takes over.

The negative income tax has the great advantage of maintaining work incentives for all beneficiaries. The marginal tax rate for poor families is

Exhibit 31.6

Possible schedules for a negative income tax

A negative income tax redistributes income without imposing extremely high marginal tax rates on either taxpayers
or beneficiaries. In order to maintain low marginal tax
rates, some benefits are given to nonpoor families, and
some poor families are given more than they need to
reach the low income level. The cost of a negative income
tax scheme must therefore always be greater than the
aggregate income deficit.

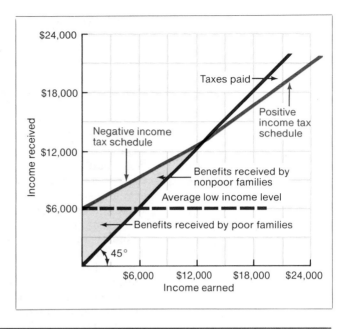

only 50 percent as the exhibit is drawn. This rate is presumably low enough
to prevent widespread withdrawal of effort. Note, however, that the cost of
the program is still much greater than the initial size of the aggregate
income deficit. All but the very poorest families receive more than the
minimum they need to reach the low income cutoff. What is more, many
nonpoor families—those with earned incomes in the $6,000 to $12,000
range—also receive benefits.

Many practical questions about the cost and workability of a negative
income tax cannot be answered by armchair economics. They can be
answered only on the basis of actual experience with running such a
program. Some significant experiments have now been carried out; one of
them is described in the following case study.

Case 31.1
The New Jersey Graduated Work Incentive Experiment and the Basic Annual Income Experiment in Manitoba

From 1968 to 1972, a negative income tax experiment involving 1,300 low-income
families was carried out in four eastern cities. The program was called the New Jersey
Graduated Work Incentive Experiment. A variety of different benefit schedules were
used with different groups of subjects. The level of guaranteed minimum income
ranged from 50 to 100 percent of the poverty-level income, and the marginal tax rate
for the beneficiaries varied from 30 to 70 percent. Only households headed by a male
were included in the experimental group.

The central objective of the experiment was to investigate the effect of the negative
income tax on work incentives and labor supply. Results of the experiment indicated
strongly that the labor supply effects of such a program are small. Over all, it
appeared that there might be a 5 to 10 percent reduction in the amount of work done
by participants in the program. Somewhat surprisingly, no statistically measurable
differences in labor supply response were observed within the range of 30 to 70
percent marginal tax rates. Some experimenters tentatively took this to indicate that
marginal tax rates of at least 50 percent could be used without seriously eroding work
incentives.

A detailed study of the labor supply response of beneficiaries revealed some further items of interest. In particular, it appeared that the 5–10 percent overall reduction in hours worked did not take the form of total withdrawal from the labor force of any significant number of workers. Rather, reductions came from fewer hours worked, fewer dual jobs and, in some cases, longer periods of job search between jobs. Reductions in labor supply appeared to be more pronounced for secondary than for primary workers. They were also more pronounced for whites that for blacks or Spanish-speaking workers.

A secondary purpose of the experiment was to test the administrative feasibility of a negative income tax. Results were encouraging in this respect also. Despite problems of interpreting some of the data, and lack of clearcut statistical results in some areas, it was felt that, as an experiment in experimentation, the New Jersey program had been a success. It has encouraged further investigation of the negative income tax as a practical policy alternative.

Manitoba decided to initiate further experimentation in 1975, under a three-year program called Mincome Manitoba, costing over $17 million. This was financed jointly by the federal government (75 percent) and the Manitoba government (25 percent).

Several areas in Manitoba were selected for the experiment, and participants were chosen on a random basis. In addition, the community of Dauphin was chosen for saturation experimentation. In total over a thousand families were involved. Participants were guaranteed a minimum level of income, to be paid in full if they had no other form of income. For each dollar of income earned through employment the assistance was reduced by 50 percent (up to a limit of $7,600 for a family of four, with the guaranteed income level set at $3,800). Unfortunately, when the experiment was concluded in 1978 further funding became uncertain. Without more funding the basic results of the experiment may never be determined.

Source: Joseph A. Pechman and Michael Timpane (eds.), *Work Incentives and Income Guarantees. The New Jersey Negative Income Tax Experiment*, (Washington, D.C.: Brookings Institution, 1975).

Political Problems

In addition to problems posed by the need for more practical information on cost and effects, the negative income tax scheme faces a number of political problems. One such problem is posed by the diversity of living standards in different parts of the country. The business of setting benefits would be greatly complicated by the need to reconcile regional interests. A further problem is how the negative income tax should relate to other programs. Many economists believe that it would make great sense to use a comprehensive negative income tax to replace all existing social insurance and public charity programs. Existing programs are not easy to eliminate, however. Each has its own army of lobbyists among beneficiaries, politicians, and public officials. Yet simply to tack a negative income tax onto the existing welter of programs would increase rather than diminish the total cost of all transfer programs. It would increase rather than diminish the complexity, overlaps, and conflicting incentives that characterize the current system. For the moment, it appears that political realities will keep the negative income tax in the textbooks, but interest in the scheme has become so widespread that it may not stay there forever.

HELPING THE POOR: JOB MARKET STRATEGIES

Transfer strategies for helping the poor are based on the diagnosis that people are poor because they do not have enough money. The implied cure is to give them additional resources in cash or in kind. A different approach to the problem of poverty is based on the diagnosis that poverty results from a failure of factor markets to allocate human resources properly. By implication, putting wasted labor to work would make many poor households self-supporting.

The diagnosis that poverty is a matter of factor market failure must be broadly interpreted if it is to have any credibility at all. The data in Exhibit 31.5 suggest that very few of the poor are adults in households headed by unemployed, able-bodied males aged eighteen to sixty-five. A narrowly conceived jobs-for-the-poor approach that focused just on this group would not make much of a dent on the overall poverty picture. In a broader sense, though, much more poverty is attributable to job related sources. The number of elderly poor and working poor would be reduced if the market provided higher paying jobs. The number of families headed by women, where the highest proportion of poor children are concentrated, would be less if it were not for the destructive effect on family life of men's inability to get good jobs. In the long run, job market strategies for alleviating poverty could benefit all the poor.

The Dual Labor Market Theory

Job market failure as a source of poverty is not just a matter of unemployment. According to one theory, the problem lies in the existence of a dual labor market. One sector of the labor market contains high wage jobs with profitable firms. These jobs not only pay more but are more likely to be unionized, to offer opportunities for advancement, and to be less affected by macroeconomic fluctuations. The secondary job market, in contrast, contains low paying jobs with marginal firms. These jobs are held by unorganized workers with unstable work patterns. They are largely dead-end jobs with few opportunities for advancement, and they are heavily hit by cyclical swings in unemployment.

According to proponents of the dual labor market theory, the two parts of the job market are kept separate by a complex of interacting factors. Discrimination, attitudes, motivation, and work habits determine which sector a worker is in. Once in the secondary sector, a worker develops attitudes and work habits that make discrimination more likely. The dual labor market theory has clear implications for antipoverty policy—namely, that such a policy must aim at breaking down the barriers between the two market sectors. The following section looks at some possible means of doing this.

Education Economists like to view education as an investment. By spending money and taking time away from current employment, people can improve their skills and productivity. Later, they can sell their services at higher wages in the labor market. One antipoverty strategy, then, is to make good quality education available to the poor and to the children of the poor, in the hope that this education will make them self-supporting.

There are actually two different ways in which education can have an impact on the problem of poverty. On the one hand, education benefits the particular individuals who are educated, thus taking people one by one out of poverty. On the other hand, improved education has a general impact on the equality of income distribution; by increasing the supply of highly educated workers, it lowers their relative wages. Both effects are slow, however, and far from foolproof.

Looking first at elementary education, one encounters the problem of an uncertain relationship between the quantity of educational inputs and the quality of educational outputs. Despite numerous studies, it is by no means clear that spending more on schools improves the performance of the pupils who go to them. To a considerable extent, the home and community environment may be more powerful than formal education in transmitting the crucial attitudes, motivations, and work habits that decide which sector of the labor market a person will end up in.

Increased spending on higher education appears to be an even less certain method for combating poverty. It is true that a college education gives upward mobility for many individuals from impoverished backgrounds. Those who succeed in college, however, are likely to be those with the attitudes and abilities that would bring them success in any event, even if they never had the chance to go to college. There is some evidence that in the early 1970s, salaries for college trained workers began to fall in response to an increased supply of college graduates. This may be having some effect on the inequality of income distribution. There are probably other, better ways to achieve the same effect, though. It would seem better to bring up the income of the poor rather than to push down the income of college graduates by encouraging their oversupply.

One thing remains to be said in favor of education as an antipoverty measure. Although the economic effects of subsidizing education may be difficult to measure, a good education is something that most disadvantaged parents want for their children. Improvements in education thus fill a perceived need. This may be important in itself.

CONCLUSIONS

The economics of poverty is, in many ways, the most discouraging branch of economics to study. Economists, of course, have plenty of simple and elegant solutions. If we really want to eliminate poverty, what we need to do is abolish all existing programs and replace them with a single, stream-lined negative income tax, or something like it. But our political system is not built to pursue a goal such as eliminating poverty in a straightforward, single-minded way. It is a system of give and take that responds to many opposing interests, and the current array of poverty programs is the natural outcome.

SUMMARY

1. In 1977, some three to four million Canadians were officially classified as poor, according to poverty lines established by Statistics Canada. These lines are based on the amount of income required by different-sized families in different locations of the country to enable them to spend no more than 62 percent of their income on basic necessities. In classifying families as poor or nonpoor, only before-tax money incomes are taken into account. This practice leads to an overstatement of the

difference between the two groups. If the effects of taxes and all benefits are taken into account, the distribution of income in Canada appears to have become somewhat more equal in recent decades.

2. The Canada Assistance Plan of 1976 is the heart of government transfer efforts. Many benefits are paid to families on the basis of need. Social insurance benefits are paid with some relationship to premiums that have been contributed.

3. The negative income tax is a simplified transfer scheme often suggested as an alternative to current antipoverty efforts. A key feature of the negative income tax is a relatively low marginal tax rate for families at all income levels. Limited local experiments tentatively confirm the practicality of the negative income tax. The idea is not yet as popular in governments, however, as it is among economists.

4. Job market strategies for aiding the poor approach poverty as a problem of factor market failure. More is involved than just unemployment. One theory states that antipoverty efforts must aim at breaking down a dual labor market. Some think that the government should approach the problem from the supply side with education and job training programs. Others emphasize demand-side programs including antidiscrimination measures and public employment.

DISCUSSION QUESTIONS

1. It is sometimes said that poverty is not the fault of individuals, but the fault of society. Do you agree? What do you think the statement means? Because "society" is itself composed of individuals, does it mean that certain nonpoor individuals are responsible for the poverty of poor individuals? If so, which individuals are responsible? Do you think that any of your own actions may be at fault in causing someone else to be poor?

2. According to the logic of the federal government's low-income standard, an officially poor family is likely not to be able to afford an adequate diet. Do you think it odd that so many poverty-level families, who cannot afford adequate nutrition, do seem able to afford cars, television sets, clothes dryers, and air conditioners? Is it natural and reasonable that a poor family should own such things? Would you favor legislation that attempted to force poor families to spend more on food and less on seemingly unnecessary appliances? Could the data on appliances indicate a defect in the official method of measuring poverty?

3. What are the relative merits of cash versus in-kind transfers? Review Chapter 19, paying particular attention to the concepts of marginal utility and consumer equilibrium. Suppose that program A gives a family a $1,000 cash benefit, and program B gives the family $1,000 worth of goods in kind, in proportions not selected by the family itself. Which program do you think would be likely to give the family greater utility? To make the question easier to answer, assume a simplified economy where there are only two goods, food and clothing. What if the two goods were food and whiskey?

4. Suppose that there were a universally effective negative income tax in force, so that measured poverty was entirely eliminated. Would you then be willing to see other social insurance programs, including social security (retirement), unemployment insurance, and medicare abolished? Why or why not?

5. What are the relative merits of job market versus transfer strategies for combatting poverty? Do you think either one could ever entirely replace the other? Why or why not?

THE WORLD ECONOMY

C H A P T E R 32

THE ECONOMICS OF POPULATION AND DEVELOPMENT

WHAT YOU WILL LEARN IN THIS CHAPTER

Most of the inhabitants of the planet earth are very poor, and the numbers of the poor are increasing more rapidly than those of the more well-to-do. This chapter discusses some of the economic problems faced by the inhabitants of the less developed countries. It begins with a lesson in basic population arithmetic. Then it compares population growth trends over time in the developed and less developed countries and shows why the population problem of the less developed world is in many respects more serious than that faced in earlier times by the now developed countries. Finally, the chapter turns from the population problem itself to the problem of producing sufficient food to feed the ever-growing third world population.

FOR REVIEW

Here is an important concept that will be put to use in this chapter. If you do not understand it, review it before proceeding.
• Sources of economic growth (Chapter 7)

How will the ever-increasing numbers of people in the world find room to live? How are they going to be fed? These are among the most pressing worldwide problems to be faced in the closing years of the twentieth century.

The problems of food and population have largely been solved in the world's industrialized market economies. For that reason, this chapter will focus on the less developed countries, where two-thirds of the world's people already live. It begins with a brief discussion of the nature of the economic development process itself. Next, it turns to the topic of population. Finally, it reviews the status of world food production, on which the solution of the problems of development and population so heavily depend.

THREE FACES OF ECONOMIC GROWTH

Economic Development as Growth

The less developed countries that make up what is called the "third world" differ from one another and from the developed countries in many ways, but

$3,001 to more than $7,000

Australia	Gabon	Norway
Austria	Greenland	Oman
Bahamas Islands	Iceland	Qatar
Bahrain	Israel	San Marino
Belgium	Italy	Saudi Arabia
Bermuda	Japan	Spain
Brunei	Kuwait	Sweden
Canada	Libya	Switzerland
Czechoslovakia	Liechtenstein	United Arab Emirates
Denmark	Luxembourg	United Kingdom
East Germany	Monaco	United States
Faroe Islands	Nauru	USSR
Finland	Netherlands	West Germany
France	New Zealand	

$201 to $1,000

Albania	Dominica
Algeria	Dominican
Angola	Republic
Antigua	Djibouti
Belize	Ecuador
Benin	Egypt
Bolivia	El Salvador
Botswanna	French Guiana
Cameroon	Gambia
Chili	Ghana
Colombia	Gibraltar
Congo	Gilbert Islands
Cook Islands	Grenada
Cuba	Guadeloupe

$1,001 to $3,000

Andorra	
Argentina	
Barbados	
Brazil	
Bulgaria	
Costa Rica	
Cyprus	
Falkland Islands	
Fiji	
French Polynesia	
Greece	
Hong Kong	
Hungary	Portugal
Iran	Puerto Rico
Iraq	Romania
Ireland	Singapore
Jamaica	South Africa
Malta	Surinam
Martinique	Taiwan
Mexico	Trinidad and
Netherlands Antilles	Tobago
New Caledonia	Turkey
Panama	Uruguay
Poland	Venezuela
	Yugoslavia

Exhibit 32.1
Gross national product per capita, 1977 (in 1977 U.S. dollars)
The countries of the world exhibit an enormous range in per capita incomes. There is no sharp dividing line between the developed and less developed countries. Here, four groups are distinguished. The most poverty stricken countries are those with incomes of less than $201 GNP per capita. Those with per capita incomes of less than $1,001 are also very poor, but many are experiencing promising self-sufficient

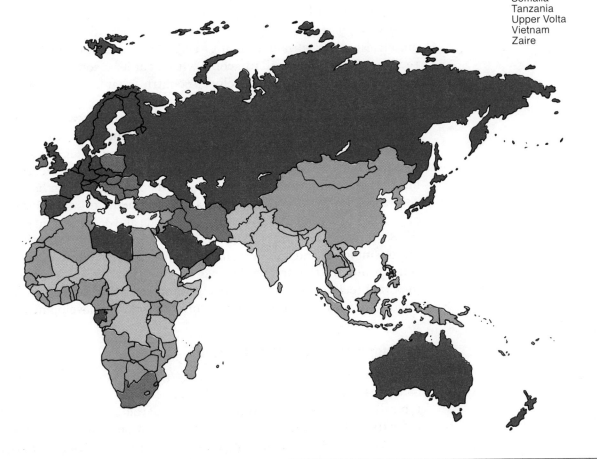

Guatemala	Malaysia	Peoples Republic of China	South Yemen	**Less than $201**
Guyana	Mauritania	Peru	Sri Lanka	Afghanistan
Haiti	Mauritius	Phillippines	Sudan	Bangladesh
Honduras	Mongolia	Rhodesia	Swaziland	Bhutan
Indonesia	Morocco	St. Christopher-	Syria	Burma
Ivory Coast	Mozambique	Nevis-Anguilla	Thailand	Burundi
Jordan	Namibia	St. Lucia	Togo	Cambodia
Kenya	Nicaragua	St. Vincent	Tonga	Cape Verde Islands
Lebanon	Nigeria	Sao Tome/Principe	Tunisia	Central African Empire
Lesotho	North Korea	Senegal	Uganda	Chad
Liberia	North Yemen	Seychelles	Western Sahara	Equatorial Guinea
Macao	Papua-New	Sierra Leone	Western Samoa	Ethiopia
Madagascar Republic	Guinea	South Korea	Zambia	Guinea-Bissau
	Paraguay			India

Guatemala
Guyana
Haiti
Honduras
Indonesia
Ivory Coast
Jordan
Kenya
Lebanon
Lesotho
Liberia
Macao
Madagascar
  Republic

Malaysia
Mauritania
Mauritius
Mongolia
Morocco
Mozambique
Namibia
Nicaragua
Nigeria
North Korea
North Yemen
Papua-New
  Guinea
Paraguay

Peoples Republic
  of China
Peru
Phillippines
Rhodesia
St. Christopher-
  Nevis-Anguilla
St. Lucia
St. Vincent
Sao Tome/Principe
Senegal
Seychelles
Sierra Leone
South Korea

South Yemen
Sri Lanka
Sudan
Swaziland
Syria
Thailand
Togo
Tonga
Tunisia
Uganda
Western Sahara
Western Samoa
Zambia

Less than $201

Afghanistan
Bangladesh
Bhutan
Burma
Burundi
Cambodia
Cape Verde Islands
Central African
  Empire
Chad
Equatorial Guinea
Ethiopia
Guinea-Bissau
India
Laos
Malawi
Mali
Nepal
Niger
Pakistan
Rwanda
Somalia
Tanzania
Upper Volta
Vietnam
Zaire

economic growth. Countries in the $1,001 to $3,000 range belong in the less developed category in some respects; but in other ways, they more closely resemble the countries with more than $3,000 per capita GNP. This last group includes the oil-rich countries of the Middle East as well as the industrialized countries of Europe and North America.

Source: Adapted from U.S. Central Intelligence Agency, National Foreign Assessment Center, *Handbook of Economic Statistics* (Washington, D.C., 1978), Figure 1, p. 1.

they have one conspicuous thing in common — low per capita income. No magic number divides the rich countries from the poor; there is a continuous range of degrees of poverty, as shown in the map in Exhibit 32.1. At the very bottom of the range are the poorest of poor countries — those with per capita GNP of less than $200 per year. These countries are found in southern Asia, from Afghanistan to Vietnam, and in a band through central Africa reaching from Guinea on the west coast to Tanzania on the east. The map also distinguishes countries with per capita GNP in the range of $201 to $1,000, clearly in the less developed group but somewhat better off. A third group, in the $1,001 to $3,000 range — including much of Latin America as well as such countries as Portugal, Yugoslavia, and Taiwan — straddles the ill-defined border between developed and less developed status. Countries with still higher levels of per capita GNP include the truly developed countries as well as the somewhat anomalous oil-rich countries of the Middle East.

To draw these distinctions in terms of per capita incomes implies that economic development equals economic growth. That is the traditional view of the matter, and it is a view that still has much truth to it. Economic growth can occur without bringing a better life to everyone, but it is hard to see how a better life for all can come without at least some growth. This is especially true for the least developed countries that have less than $200 of GNP per capita.

Much of development economics, then, focuses on ways to enable a country to grow. Growth oriented development studies usually emphasize capital accumulation as the great key. Capital accumulation has accounted for only about 20 percent of economic growth in Canada in recent years, but it is more important for less developed countries, which have a great shortage of capital. Typically, saving and investment are only 5 to 7 percent of GNP, compared to over 15 percent in Canada and 35 percent in Japan and the Soviet-type economies. Without capital accumulation, it is difficult to put unemployed and underemployed people to work. Without capital it is equally difficult to improve the level of education or to take advantage of imported technology. Yet, although capital accumulation and growth are important, they are not the whole story of economic development.

Development as Industrialization

The developed countries are not only richer than the less developed countries; they are also more highly industrialized. Developed countries typically have between a fifth and a quarter of their populations engaged in industry. In the less developed countries, the proportion is likely to be 10 percent or less. A second interpretation of economic development, then, is that it means industrializing, just as the advanced countries have done in the past.

The view that development means industrialization, like the view that development means economic growth, has much truth to it. The less developed countries have large and growing urban populations. Only industrialization offers them much hope of employment. As incomes rise in a developing country, the demand for manufactured goods increases rapidly. It makes sense to meet many of these needs with domestic sources of supply. Many less developed countries have valuable raw materials that they now export for processing; these materials could be processed domestically instead. Still, despite all this, the importance of industrialization to development should not be exaggerated.

For one thing, an overemphasis on industrialization may cause resources to be wasted on ill-conceived showcase projects. Not every less developed country needs a steel mill and an automobile plant. Even small-scale industrial projects may be inappropriate if they mean building an exact replica of some plant originally designed for Manchester or Milwaukee, where relative factor scarcities and other market conditions are completely different.

What is more, an overemphasis on industrialization can lead to the neglect of other development objectives. The third face of economic development shows why.

Development as Depauperization

It is a widely shared opinion that a major goal of economic development should be a better life for the poorest of the poor — the people at the low end of the income distribution in the poorest countries. They are the true paupers — lacking adequate food, often lacking all access to medical care, and not infrequently lacking even the most primitive shelter.

Development economists once were confident that the benefits of growth and industrialization would automatically trickle down to the poorest of the poor. Unfortunately, this optimism may not be justified, as the research of Irma Adelman and C.T. Morris has shown.[1] Their work focuses on the range of development from sub-Saharan Africa to the poorest countries of South America — that is, from about $100 to $500 per capita income. In these countries, development tends to bring both relative and absolute impoverishment to the poorest 60 percent of the population. At very low levels of development, there appears to be no trickling down at all. The poor begin to benefit only after an intermediate level of development has been reached.

Adelman and Morris have concluded that the policies needed to benefit the poor are different from those needed to maximize growth rates. The ideas of development as growth or industrialization, they say, should be replaced with the idea of **depauperization** — the provision not only of the necessary material basis for life but also of access to education, security, self-expression, status, and power. Depauperization stresses the removal of social, political, and spiritual deprivation as much as physical deprivation. It has as much to do with equity as with growth.

Depauperization Economic development of a kind that benefits the poorest of the poor, providing them not only with the material necessities of life but also with access to education, status, security, self-expression, and power.

Two Strategies

The choice of development goals strongly influences the strategy that can best promote the development process. The Soviet Union represents one extreme. For early Soviet planners, development meant industrialization

[1]Irma Adelman and C.T. Morris, *Society, Politics, and Economic Development* (Baltimore: Johns Hopkins University Press, 1967).

above all else. Through high rates of saving, they sacrificed consumption to achieve rapid growth. Through collectivization, they sacrificed the growth of agriculture to achieve the growth of industry. Eventually, the benefits of successful industrialization began to trickle down to the population at large. Initially, though, living standards declined, and the overall distribution of income shifted in favor of industrial workers and against peasants.

Even where industrialization as an end in itself is not made a higher priority than overall growth, the benefits of development may be spread unevenly. Many less developed countries suffer from what is called a **dual economy**. In such an economy, a modern, Westernized industrial sector provides high wages for better educated workers and a tax base to pay a middle class of civil servants. Meanwhile, a secondary, traditional sector remains largely untouched. Sometimes, the overall growth rate of GNP can be maximized by concentrating available development resources on the modern sector, at least in the short run. Often also foreign aid and the investments of multinational corporations are concentrated on the modern sector of dual economies.

There is a second kind of development strategy that contrasts with the industry-first approach. It emphasizes redistribution and mass education first and growth later. Redistribution in the context of less developed countries means, most importantly, the redistribution of land ownership. Education means mass education in literacy and general knowledge, rather than just specialized training for participation in the modern sector. If this strategy works, redistribution can provide the basis for rural development and education the basis for the growth of broadly based, labor-intensive industry. Adelman and Morris cite Israel, Japan, South Korea, Singapore, and Taiwan as countries that have successfully followed this strategy. China should probably be added to the list. In the last century, U.S. economic development followed this strategy much more than did economic development in Europe.

Dual economy An economy that is sharply divided into a modern, westernized industrial sector capable of rapid growth and a traditional rural sector that remains stagnant.

POPULATION AND DEVELOPMENT

Whatever development strategy they choose, all less developed countries face certain common problems that they must somehow solve. None is more serious than the problem of population growth. As background for a discussion of population problems in the less developed countries, here is a review of some basic population arithmetic.

Population Arithmetic

For a population to increase, it is obvious that more people must be born than die each year. (In this section and in what follows, immigration and emigration are ignored.) The number of people born into a population per thousand per year is the **crude birthrate** for that population. The number who die per thousand per year is the **crude death rate**. The difference between the two is the **rate of natural increase**.

Exhibit 32.2 shows crude birthrates, crude death rates, and rates of natural increase for a selection of countries, according to the latest available data. In interpreting data such as these, it sometimes helps to translate

Crude birthrate The number of people born into a population per thousand per year.

Crude death rate The number of people in a population who die per thousand per year.

Rate of natural increase The current growth rate of a population calculated as the crude birthrate minus the crude death rate.

Exhibit 32.2
Birthrates, death rates, and natural increase of
population for selected countries
The current rate of population growth for a country can be found by subtracting the crude death rate from the crude birthrate. The faster the rate of population growth, the shorter the time period required for the population to double.

Country	Year	Crude Birth-Rate	Crude Death Rate	Rate of Natural Increase	Approximate No. of Years for Population to Double
Ecuador	1970–75	41.8	9.5	32.3	21
Mexico	1970–75	42.0	8.6	33.4	21
Algeria	1970–75	48.7	15.4	33.3	21
Kenya	1970–75	48.7	16.0	32.7	21
Zambia	1970–75	51.5	20.3	31.2	22
India	1974	34.5	14.4	20.1	35
Argentina	1970	22.9	9.4	13.5	52
Japan	1976	16.4	6.3	10.1	69
Australia	1976	16.7	8.3	8.4	83
U.S.S.R.	1976	18.5	9.5	9.0	78
United States	1976	14.7	8.9	5.8	121
France	1976	13.6	10.5	3.1	229
U.K.	1976	12.1	12.2	−0.1	Never
Canada	1976	15.8	7.2	8.6	81

Source: United Nations, *UN Statistical Yearbook*, 1977.

Exhibit 32.3
Typical S-shaped curve of population growth
A living population cannot grow indefinitely in a finite environment. Under laboratory conditions, populations of bacteria or fruit flies or other organisms tend to follow S-shaped growth curves such as the one shown here. In the long run, it seems inevitable that the growth curve of human population will also begin to decrease.

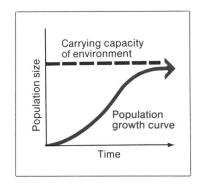

rates of natural increase into population doubling times. This is done in the last column of the table. The faster the rate of natural increase, the shorter the period of time required for the population to double in size.

Growth Curves A population that grew indefinitely at a constant rate of natural increase would double each time a fixed number of years elapsed. It would reach 2, 4, 8, 16, 32, 64 (and so on) times its original size, following the same sort of growth path as that followed by the value of a sum of money invested at compound interest.

Normally, however, living populations are not able to grow exponentially without limit. Suppose that bacteria are allowed to multiply in a glass jar of nutrient, or a population of fruit flies is allowed to grow in a glass cage or room of fixed size, or a breeding pair of dogs is introduced on an island previously inhabited only by rabbits. Under such conditions, the growth of the population of bacteria, fruit flies, or dogs typically follows the kind of S-shaped growth curve shown in Exhibit 32.3. At first, the population will expand at the exponential rate. The biological characteristics of the species in question determine the population doubling time under optimal conditions. Sooner or later, though, the population will begin to fill up its jar or cage or island or whatever. Then, under more crowded conditions, the time needed to double the population will increase. Eventually, overcrowding will bring population growth to a halt.

Must the growth of human population also be subject to this S-curve pattern? In the long run, it surely must. Estimates of the maximum human population of earth vary widely, but no one doubts that there is some finite ceiling. (One admittedly fanciful estimate places the limit as high as 20 million times the present world population. This would require people to live 120 to the square meter in a two-thousand-story building covering the entire earth. Even that limit would take only 890 years to reach at the present growth rate of world population!)

In the short run, though, the growth of human population has not followed the simple S-curve pattern. In fact, over as long a period as any kind of population estimates can be made, the world rate of natural increase has been accelerating, not slowing down. World population has doubled in about the last forty-five years and would double again in the next thirty-five if the current growth rate were to continue. The last preceding doubling of population took about eighty years, from 1850 to 1930. The doubling before that took some two hundred years. It is hard to imagine that this trend will continue. There are now indications that the world is reaching the bend in the population growth curve and that world population growth, for the first time, is beginning to slow.[2]

Population Equilibrium

There can be no doubt that in the long run the level of human population is headed for an equilibrium state in which births will just balance deaths. The really interesting question is: what will that equilibrium look like? Let's explore some possibilities.

First, imagine a market economy in which people earn money to buy the necessities of life only by selling factor services. The population begins to approach some fixed limit to population growth defined, for example, by the food supply. Income is distributed unequally in this society. As population nears the ceiling, the price of food rises relative to the wage rate. The lowest income groups find their standard of living reduced, and this eventually affects their birth and death rates. At some point, an excess of deaths over births will occur among the poorest classes. This will be accompanied by a balance between births and deaths for those living just at the margin of subsistence. An excess of births will be possible only among the well-to-do. When enough people have finally been pushed down to or below the margin of subsistence, population growth as a whole will cease. The result can be called a marginal subsistence equilibrium for population.

---

[2]For example, Donald J. Bogue and Amy Ong Tsui, in "Zero World Population Growth," *Public Interest*, no. 55 (Spring 1979), pp. 99–113, go so far as to declare the once-feared population bomb a dud. Between 1968 and 1975, they report, fertility declined in 103 countries having a total population of 3.2 billion and increased or was unchanged in only 45 countries with a total population of 749 million.

This equilibrium assumes great inequality. It implies affluence for a few against the backdrop of destitute masses whose members are continuously replenished by the excess children of the rich driven down into poverty. If the assumption of inequality is removed, the result is a second type of population equilibrium, which can be called the absolute subsistence equilibrium. Under this solution, as crowding begins to lower the living standards of a population, taxes and transfers are used to divide the burden equally among all. This equality permits population growth to go on longer; no one is starved or crowded to the point of being unable to reproduce until everyone reaches that point. The total number of people living in poverty in the absolute subsistence equilibrium is greater than in the marginal subsistence equilibrium.

Population projections like these were what once caused economics to be called the "dismal science." As long ago as 1798, Thomas Malthus forecast a marginal subsistence population equilibrium for humanity that would come about through the operation of the law of diminishing returns, as a growing population caught up with a fixed supply of agricultural land. According to Malthus's theory, only the landlords, who owned the means of producing precious food, would escape eventual poverty. Even the capitalists would eventually be ground down and their profits reduced to zero.

Malthus's prophecy has not come true for Great Britain, the United States, or other advanced industrial countries. These countries have instead achieved, or nearly achieved, a nonsubsistence population equilibrium with low birthrates, low death rates, and high living standards. The process by which this equilibrium has been achieved is a good illustration of how economic and demographic processes interact.

Thomas Robert Malthus was born in England in 1766 and received what was, for his time, a radical upbringing. His father was an admirer of Rousseau and Condorcet, and one of his tutors was imprisoned for expressing the wish that the French revolutionaries would invade and liberate England. Malthus studied at Cambridge, took holy orders, and became a curate.

In 1793, a book appeared that had a great impact on the circles in which young Malthus moved. The book was *Enquiry Concerning Political Justice and Its Influence on Morals and Happiness* by the anarchist and socialist, William Godwin. As a result of many lively debates over this book and subsequent essays by Godwin, Malthus decided to write down his own view that population growth constituted an insurmountable barrier to a society of absolute equality and abundance. This writing appeared as *An Essay on the Principle of Population* in 1798.

The heart of Malthus's argument was the doctrine that population tended to grow in geometric progression (2, 4, 8, 16, and so on) while the means of subsistence grew only in arithmetic progression (2, 4, 6, 8, and so on). As population increased, increasingly less fertile land would have to be brought into cultivation. Population would outstrip food production, and wages would be driven down to the subsistence level.

Famine, vice, misery, and war could be avoided only if people engaged in "moral restraint" — later marriages with fewer children per family. Schemes such as the Poor Laws or subsidized housing for the poor were worse than useless, according to Malthus. They simply encouraged population growth and led to an actual deterioration of conditions.

Thomas Robert Malthus (1766–1834)

Malthus's views influenced Darwin in developing his survival of the fittest doctrine in the nineteenth century. More than anyone else, it was Malthus who was responsible for earning political economy the name of the "dismal science." Not everyone has interpreted the man in such a negative light, however. John Maynard Keynes placed Malthus firmly in "the English tradition of humane science...a tradition marked by a love of truth and a most noble lucidity,...and by an immense disinterestedness and public spirit."

The Demographic Transition

In a preindustrial society, birthrates and death rates are both very high, and the rate of natural increase of population is low. With industrialization and economic development, per capita incomes begin to rise. The first demographic effect of rising income is a reduction in the death rate brought about by better nutrition, better hygiene, and better medical care. With the birthrate remaining high, the drop in the death rate increases the rate of natural increase. Population enters a phase of very rapid growth.

If there are sufficient natural resources and enough investment in new capital, economic growth can outstrip population growth. Per capita income then rises. This has happened in all the major industrialized countries of the world. In these countries, rising per capita incomes have eventually caused the birthrate to fall. Population growth has then slowed, and population equilibrium has been approached.

Demographic transition A population cycle that accompanies economic development, beginning with a fall in the death rate, continuing with a phase of rapid population growth, and concluding with a decline in the birthrate.

The whole cycle, from falling death rates to rapid population growth to falling birthrates and equilibrium is called the **demographic transition**. Exhibit 32.4 provides a graphical view of the demographic transition. Part a represents the course of the crude birthrate and death rate over time. Part b shows what happens to the rate of natural increase as it first rises and then falls. Part c shows the familiar S-curve pattern of population growth that results from the demographic transition. The human population growth curve shown in Part c differs in an important respect from that of flies in a jar or dogs on an island; it levels off at an equilibrium population below the biologically maximum level set by subsistence requirements.

Exhibit 32.4

The demographic transition

In a preindustrial society, both birthrates and death rates are high, so that population growth is slow. The first effect of economic development is a drop in the death rate. This brings on a period of rapid population growth. As economic development continues, the birthrate begins to fall. Population growth decelerates and eventually may fall to zero.

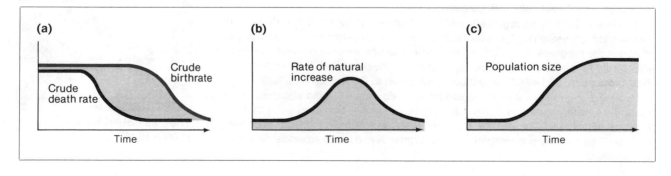

The crucial part of the demographic transition is the fall in birthrates produced by rapid economic development. Demographers do not completely understand the mechanisms that bring about this decline. In large part, it is probably caused by increasing urbanization. Traditionally, a large number of children is an economic asset to a farm family, because children can contribute to production from an early age. In the city, children tend to be an economic burden. There is no guarantee of remunerative jobs for them, and their food, clothing, and housing cannot be produced at home. More subtle changes in life-styles and attitudes toward family life, which occur as income rises, also seem to be involved in the demographic transition.

Net Reproduction

To complete the demographic transition and approach an equilibrium population takes many decades. To understand why the transition takes so long, one needs to know more about population growth than crude birthrates and crude death rates alone can offer.

Crude birthrates and death rates can be misleading because they depend on both the underlying reproductive behavior of a population and its age structure. A more direct measure of reproductive behavior is the **net reproduction rate** for a population—the average number of daughters born to each female child in the population over her lifetime. If the net reproduction rate is equal to 1, then the population is, in the long run, just replacing itself. If it is greater than 1, then the population has a long-run tendency to grow. If it is less than 1, it has a long-run tendency to shrink.

Net reproduction rate The inherent long-term growth rate of a population, measured as the average number of daughters born to each female child over her lifetime.

In the short run, the rate of natural increase in a population may be positive even when the net reproduction rate is 1 or less. In particular, this will happen when population growth has been slowing in the recent past. The present situation in Canada provides a case in point. The Canadian net reproduction rate is now less than 1, but it has fallen to that level only recently. The elderly people now in high mortality brackets are members of the relatively small generation born around the turn of the century. People in the high fertility range are members of the much larger generation who were born immediately after World War II. The disproportion in the size of the generations causes the crude death rate to be lower—and the crude birthrate to be higher—than will be the case in the long-run equilibrium. If there is no further change in reproductive behavior, and if the net reproduction rate remains slightly less than 1, it will take some forty to sixty years for the rate of natural increase to fall to 0. Only at that point will the demographic transition in this country be complete.

Turn back for a moment to Exhibit 32.2, which gives population growth data for a selected group of developed and less developed countries. The countries are grouped by rates of population growth. Near the middle of the table we find Zambia, which, with both the highest crude birthrate and crude death rate, most closely fits the traditional pattern. Even there, though, modern medicine has had an effect on the death rate. The rate of increase is very substantial, at 31.2 per 1,000 per year. Near the bottom of the table are the United Kingdom and France, where birth rates and death rates are very nearly in equilibrium. The U.K.'s slight negative growth may

Exhibit 32.5
The demographic transition and the economic growth
Here, the effects of the demographic transition are shown in terms of economic growth and population growth. It is assumed that death rates begin to fall once per capita income reaches Level A, and that birthrates begin to fall once per capita income reaches Level B. During the transition, population growth speeds up and per capita income growth slows. Economic growth always stays above population growth, however.

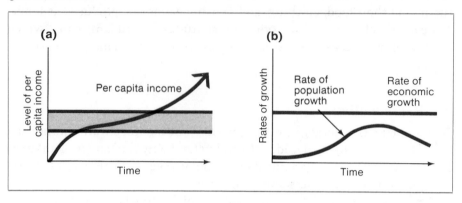

be the pattern for other developed countries in the future. At the top are Ecuador and Mexico—by no means the poorest of less developed countries—where death rates are as low as those in the United States or the U.S.S.R., but birthrates are nearly as high as in the poorest parts of Africa. These are the countries where, to use the popular phrase, the "population bomb" is ticking away.

The Population Trap

Birthrates, death rates, economic growth, and income levels are in very delicate balance during economic development. Countries that develop successfully undergo a process called the demographic transition. During that process, rising income levels first depress death rates, causing population growth rates to accelerate, and then depress birthrates, causing population growth to slow.

Exhibit 32.6
The population trap
If at some point during the demographic transition the rate of population growth exceeds the rate of economic growth, a country may be caught in a population trap. As this exhibit is drawn, the country enters the trap at Time T. At that point, per capita income begins to fall and the demographic transition is aborted.

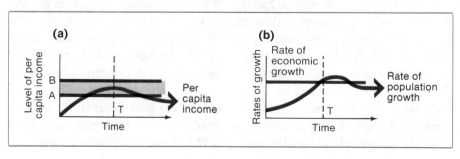

Exhibit 32.5 shows what happens to per capita income and population growth, assuming steady economic growth, during the demographic transition. In Part a, the vertical axis measures the level of per capita income. When income is below Level B, people are so poor that death rates are high, and when it is above A, people are prosperous enough that birthrates are low. (Of course, things are really more complicated than this. There are not really any sharp cutoff levels of income, but this simple assumption makes the point.) In Part b, the vertical axis measures growth rates of total GNP and population. Note that population growth never exceeds the growth of GNP. The curve of per capita income in Part a always moves upward, although it rises less rapidly in the zone between A and B while the demographic transition is under way.

Can today's less developed countries complete this process as the developed countries have done? It is to be hoped that they can, but it is by no means certain. There is a real danger that they will get caught in a **population trap**, which will abort their attempt to make it through the demographic transition.

Exhibit 32.6 shows schematically how a country can fall foul of the population trap. Suppose that such a country begins development normally, as did the country represented in Exhibit 36.5. This time, though, either population growth is more rapid or economic growth is slower. At Time T, population growth begins to exceed the growth of income, and per capita income starts to fall. Instead of completing the demographic transition, the country falls back into a subsistence equilibrium with birth and death rates both high and per capita income stagnant.

Population trap A situation in which the rate of population growth rises above the rate of economic growth, halting the growth of per capita income and aborting the demographic transition.

Escaping the Population Trap In the nineteenth century, when Western Europe and North America were industrializing, death rates fell only slowly—and only after living standards had already begun to improve. Population growth rates did not rise above 1 percent per year in most cases. Today, modern death control techniques have reached almost every corner of the globe, no matter how poor. That makes it more difficult for today's less developed countries to escape the population trap. During the nineteenth century, the Canadian economy experienced growth rates of GNP in the range of 3.5 to 4.5 percent per year. Growth rates in that range are no longer good enough for less developed countries, where population itself can grow as fast as 3.5 percent per year. Any growth rate for GNP slower than 6 to 7 percent per year gives little hope for escaping the population trap just by outrunning it. Countries like South Korea or Taiwan may make it, but those like Haiti, Chad, or Dahomey, where per capita incomes are already falling, will not.

The only other way to escape the population trap is to bring down the birthrate while per capita incomes are still low. Although headway has been made in some countries, serious problems remain elsewhere, as the examples in the following three-part case study show.

Case 32.1
Three Experiments in Population Control

Saying that less developed countries need to bring population growth under control is one thing; accomplishing the feat is another. Here is a report on population programs in three of the largest countries of the third world. Each has made major efforts, but the results are not uniformly encouraging.

Pakistan. Few countries have a more serious population problem than Pakistan. Development planners were thus delighted when, in 1973, Pakistan was chosen as the laboratory for a massive experiment in the "inundation" approach to family planning. Using $58 million in U.S. aid as well as local resources, the plan was literally to flood the countryside with condoms and birth control pills at a price so low — 2.5 cents for a month's supply — that even the poorest people could afford them. The flood of birth control devices was to be followed by teams of "continuous motivators," who were to visit each household three or four times a year to give encouragement and instruction.

Today, the program appears to be a total failure. The birthrate has gone up, not down. Only 9 percent of fertile couples in the country have ever tried birth control, and only 6 percent practice it regularly. Why the failure? Poor administration is part of the reason, but the real flaw in the program was its assumption that families *wanted* to have fewer children. In rural Pakistan, each child, male and female, begins to contribute positively to the support of the family as early as the age of four by tending goats or chickens, running errands, or driving a bullock cart. And in this conservative Moslem society, children are a source of social prestige. The condoms were turned into children's playthings or melted down by contractors to make caulking material.

India. India, a neighbor of Pakistan, faces a population problem of much the same magnitude. Under the leadership of Prime Minister Indira Gandhi and her controversial son, Sanjay, however, India adopted a very different approach to birth control. To make certain that families stayed on the birth control track once they got on it, the government emphasized sterilization and insertion of IUDs as the main birth control techniques. An elaborate program of incentives and disincentives included transistor radios; the disincentives included disqualification for government housing for men not willing to accept sterilization after two children. When even this program proved unequal to the task of getting the birthrate down to a level of 25 per 1,000, the government turned to outright coercion. At a rate of a million a month, men were herded into sterilization clinics.

It soon became apparent, though, that the Gandhi policy had gone too far. After a period of nationwide political disruption, Gandhi was swept out of office by India's voters, who feared and detested the birth control program. Under the new government, birth control efforts collapsed, and the birthrate began to creep up again. It has already risen to 35 per 1,000 from its low of 33 in 1977 and is likely to reach 40 soon unless the government takes strong action — something that is now almost impossible politically.

Indonesia. Meanwhile, on the Indonesian island of Bali, a population program is achieving heartening success. In the tiny village of Banjar Kangin, for example, 218 of the village's 243 fertile couples are practicing some form of birth control. At monthly town meetings, each man is asked what he has done about birth control that month — and then the next month's supply of condoms and pills is handed out.

Why the contrast? Several things appear to contribute to it. For one thing, the Hindus of Banjar Kangin have much more open and permissive attitudes toward sex than do the Moslem Pakistanis. (But even Moslem areas of Indonesia do better than Pakistan.) For another, the administrative structure of the village is much stronger. But perhaps most important of all is that the village economic structure is such that children are perceived as liabilities, not assets. Even with these successes, though, Indonesia's population is expected to soar from 132 million in 1978 to 215 million in 2000.

Source: The descriptions of the programs in Pakistan and Indonesia are based on Bill Peterson, "Battling the Birth Boom — Small Wins, Big Failures," *Washington Post*, May 19, 1978, p. A-1. India's story is based in part on Barry Kramer. "The Politics of Birth Control," *Wall Street Journal*, May 8, 1978, and in part on William Borders, "Birth Control Slows in India," *New York Times*, February 6, 1978, p. A-2.

FOOD AND DEVELOPMENT[3]

Hunger

The aspect of economic development that causes the greatest concern of all is the problem of hunger. Hunger comes in varying degrees. People are said to be undernourished if they suffer from a quantitative lack of calories. They are said to suffer from malnutrition if the food they do get contains insufficient protein and other nutrients, even if energy requirements are met. Undernourishment leads to actual starvation. In recent years it has been a major problem in the countries just south of the Sahara in Africa; in India, Bangladesh, and Sri Lanka in Asia; and in Bolivia, Haiti, and El Salvador in the Americas, to list only a few. Malnutrition is much more widespread and has long-run effects that are hardly less devastating. A protein insufficiency in the diets of young children and breast-feeding women is especially dangerous, because it retards brain development. People who survive a malnourished childhood are likely to suffer from lethargy and lack of productive ability in later life. These are hardly the traits required for the labor forces of poor countries struggling to achieve development.

Accurate statistics on world hunger are hard to come by. Definitions vary, and the governments of some of the worst-hit countries are reluctant to supply information. Some who have studied the problem believe that as many as two-thirds of the world's population may suffer from undernourishment or malnutrition in some form. The data in Exhibit 32.7 are based on much more conservative methods of estimation, but they still show an appallingly serious problem.

---

[3]This section draws on many points in the useful survey *World of Hunger*, by Jonathan Power and Anne-Marie Holenstein (London: Temple Smith, 1976). Used by permission.

Exhibit 32.7

Estimated numbers of people with insufficient protein/energy supply, by regions, 1970

According to the relatively conservative estimates reported in this table, some 388 million people had less than minimum standards of nutrition in 1970. Some observers think that nearly two-thirds of the world's population may suffer from malnutrition to some extent.

Region	Population (billions)	Percentage below Lower Limit	Number below Lower Limit (millions)
Developed regions	1.07	3	28
Developing regions (excluding Asian centrally planned economies)	1.75	20	360
Latin America	0.28	13	37
Far East	1.02	22	221
Near East	0.17	20	34
Africa	0.28	25	68
World (excluding Asian centrally planned economies)	2.83	14	388

Source: Jonathan Power and Anne-Marie Holenstein, *World of Hunger* (London: Temple Smith, 1976). Reprinted by permission.

Hunger and Population

The relationship between hunger and population is complex. It is natural to think of overpopulation causing hunger, with a Malthusian growth of numbers of people outstripping food production. Hunger can be a spur to population growth, too, however. Malnutrition leads to high infant mortality. High infant mortality in turn leads to the desire to have a large family, so that at least some children will survive. Perhaps the relationship between malnutrition and desired family size is part of the reason why birthrates have fallen earliest in those countries that have distributed the benefits of development widely among their populations.

When the world food problem is presented as a race between production and growth of demand, the results are sobering. Information presented at the World Food Conference in 1974 placed seventy-one less developed countries in three groups according to food and population trends during the period 1953–1971. In twenty-four of these countries, the rate of increase in food production fell short of population growth. In an additional seventeen, the rate of increase of food production exceeded the rate of population growth but fell short of the growth rate of domestic demand. Because rising incomes permitted people to eat more, these countries had to increase food imports (or decrease food exports), thereby making things harder yet for the countries in the first group. In the thirty remaining countries, the growth rate of food output exceeded the growth rate of demand, but even some of these countries experienced regional problems because of maldistribution within their borders.[4]

What can be done about the world food problem? The remainder of this section will examine some possible approaches.

Food Aid

Canada, the United States, and many other Western countries are giving direct aid, including food, medical supplies, and other necessary products and services, to the less developed countries. Food surpluses created by government support programs described in Chapter 25 have been used on occasion as part of the aid program. Canada gives its aid through the Canadian International Development Agency (CIDA). Such aid has recently averaged about $1 billion a year, or about 0.5 percent of Canada's GNP. This is far less than the 1 percent or more of GNP that Prime Minister Pearson set as a goal for Canada in the 1960s, but it is considerably higher, on a per capita basis, than some other countries, including the United States, are giving. Canada has concentrated much of its aid in the form of special development programs, assisted by more than 1,500 Canadians serving abroad. The United States has tended to focus much of its attention on food distribution. During the 1960s, the United States gave up to 84 percent of all world food aid. The less developed countries were able to rely on food aid for 30 to 45 percent of their food imports.

But food aid, as given under the American program, has several important disadvantages, as American economists have noted.

---

[4]Preliminary Assessment of the World Food Situation, World Food Conference, 1974, UNIE/Conf. 65/ Prep./6. Data also presented as Table 7 in Power and Holenstein, *World of Hunger*, pp. 41–43.

First of all, American food aid is a somewhat uncomfortable mixture of charity and self-interest. As such, it is liable to disruption from the self-interest side. In periods when American farmers produce large grain surpluses, voters and consumers are happy to see the surpluses given away. In the early 1970s, however, a combination of circumstances caused American food surpluses suddenly to disappear. This put upward pressure on domestic food prices, and exports began to meet opposition from consumer groups. By 1974, the amount of food delivered under aid programs fell to a third of its 1972 level.

There is a second serious problem in the tendency of some receiver governments to rely on food aid as a substitute for domestic agricultural development. In some cases, the motivation has been political. Necessary agricultural reforms would have threatened the privileges of entrenched ruling classes, so American aid seemed like an easy way out. In other cases, food aid has disrupted domestic markets. It has, for example, kept prices low in the less developed countries; this is fine for the landless poor, but it greatly reduces incentives to farmers. Sometimes, the effect of food aid on relative prices has made the growth of nonfood cash crops more attractive than food crops.

Finally, some critics of food aid are unhappy about the standards by which recipients have been selected. Food aid recipients have often been chosen more with political than with nutritional considerations in mind. As a result, say the critics, too small a portion of total food aid has gone to the countries where hunger and malnutrition are the most serious.

Need for Rural Development

Throughout the world, less developed countries are urbanizing rapidly — far more rapidly than today's developed countries did at comparable stages of their own growth. The reasons for this urbanization are complex. Partly the modernity and the promise of a better life in the city attract people. Partly the problem is education systems that do not emphasize agricultural topics. Whatever the causes, cities are not able to meet the aspirations of all those who arrive in them. Urban unemployment rates are very high. Many people who are employed work in tertiary services — from shining shoes to hustling — that contribute little to economic development or to the development of the individuals. Huge shantytowns surrounding third world cities are the rule rather than the exception.

Current rates of urbanization far exceed the potential for industrial development in most poor countries. One study calculated that, just to keep urban unemployment from rising in a typical less developed country, industrial output would have to grow at 18 percent per year.[5] Even in Brazil, which has had outstanding success with industrialization and urban development, industrial growth has run at only 15 percent per year. To get rid of the 20 to 25 percent unemployment common in cities of less developed countries, industry would have to grow at something like 30 to 35 percent per year for a decade.

[5]David Turnham, *The Employment Problem in Less Developed Countries* (Paris: Organization for Economic Cooperation and Development, 1971), as cited by Power and Holenstein, *World of Hunger*, pp. 74–75.

When urban unemployment and the food problem are considered together, it is not surprising that many development economists believe that the real hope for the less developed countries lies in the countryside. The hope is to hold people on the land and to make them productive there within a meaningful community structure. If the third world nations can do that, they may be able to feed themselves, distribute what little they have more equitably, meet the nonmaterial aspirations of their populations, and retain their independence. That, at least, is what the advocates of rural development say. They all recognize that there are problems, though.

Technological Problems Rural development does not mean just the introduction of new agricultural methods. It also means the growth of small-scale industry in villages and towns, which is necessary to meet local needs and provide employment for those whom even the most ambitious land reform program would leave landless. Is the technological basis for such development available?

In some respects, technological progress has been remarkable. The most talked-about development is the appearance of new, high-yield varieties of wheat and rice. Under laboratory conditions, these new varieties can triple food output per acre. They provide the best hope for less developed countries to escape from the sheer shortage of land.

Unfortunately, high-yield wheat, rice, and other grains cannot just be stuck in the ground and expected to do their magic. The secret of their success lies in their ability to absorb huge quantities of fertilizer. If ordinary varieties of grain are overfertilized, they produce only luxuriant growth of stems and leaves or seedheads so heavy that they break the stalk of the plant. With high-yield varieties, extra fertilization produces growth where it is needed. Without such fertilization, the new varieties actually produce less than traditional crops. (In many cases, heavy use of pesticides and irrigation is needed as well.)

As the use of high-yield varieties has spread, less developed countries have become more dependent on imported fertilizers. They now produce barely half their own fertilizer needs. What is worse, fertilizer production depends critically on oil. This is particularly true of nitrogen fertilizers, which make up half the total used. These are made almost entirely from natural gas and petroleum products. The "green revolution" has been extremely hard hit by high oil prices, because outside the Middle East, few less developed countries have their own oil supplies.

Rural industrial development faces technological problems that are, if anything, greater than those faced by agricultural development. Western industrial research has developed technology designed to use cheap capital and save expensive labor. The opposite conditions prevail in rural areas of the third world. Too little research has gone into the development of simple but sophisticated labor-intensive ways of doing things.

Institutional Problems A number of institutional problems also threaten rural development. Chief among them are the problem of land reform and the problem of supplying credit to rural areas.

Advocates of rural development support land reform, which involves buying (or sometimes confiscating) the large holdings of absentee landlords

In October 1979, the Royal Swedish Academy awarded the Nobel Memorial Prize in Economic Science jointly to two men noted for their work in the economics of development. The two — Sir William Arthur Lewis, professor of economics at Princeton University, and Theodore Schultz, professor of economics at the University of Chicago — had never worked together directly. Their writings, however, shared a common theme: the importance of the agricultural sector in the development process, and the hazards of a development strategy overemphasizing industrialization.

Lewis was born on the island of St. Lucia in the British West Indies. He was educated in London and lectured at the University of London from 1938 to 1948. Before coming to Princeton in 1963, he served for several years as vice-chancellor of the University of the West Indies and was knighted by Queen Elizabeth for this work. The author of a number of books on development and development planning, he is best known for *The Theory of Economic Growth*, published in 1955. Lewis has served as an adviser to the governments of many developing nations, to the British government, and to the United Nations. It was this practical experience in particular that led him to recognize the central importance of agriculture in the economies of the less developed countries.

Theordore Schultz grew up on a farm in South Dakota in a community of German settlers. In 1930, he received a Ph.D. from the University of Wisconsin; in that same year, he joined the faculty at Iowa State College. During the 1930s and 1940s, Schultz worked to make agricultural economics a branch of general economics that would benefit from advances in other parts of the discipline. The numerous New Deal farm programs of the period provided many opportunities for research, and he published a series of books on U.S. agricultural policy. At the same time, he developed an interest in the process of economic growth — in particular, the contribution of investment in human capital to growth and development. This line of research led eventually to the publication, in 1964, of his book *Transforming Traditional Agriculture*. In this book, he argued that traditional farmers were efficient in the use of whatever resources they had available and would quickly adopt new methods of production when given the chance to do so. The popularity among third-world farmers of the new, high-yield crop varieties stands as a case in point.

Both men continue to be active scholars and advocates of their common point of view. The Nobel award will no doubt act as a further spur to their work in the economics of agricultural development.

**William Arthur Lewis
(1915–   )**

**Theodore W. Schultz
(1902–   )**

and distributing the land in the smallest feasible parcels among those who actually till the soil. The effects of land reform, if it works, are threefold. First, a small landowner has a greater incentive than a tenant farmer to improve the land and introduce better production techniques. Second, wide distribution of ownership means wide distribution of the product, with all the benefits this is believed to bring. Third, land reform can lead to more stable rural community structures, which help stop the rush to the city. They also help provide the dignity and sense of personal worth that are part of the process of depauperization.

Many countries have carried out thorough land reforms, but many others have not. Two problems hold back further land reform. One major problem is political. The land-owning classes often dominate the political structures of less developed countries and are reluctant to relinquish their hold. The second problem is economic. Under some circumstances, technological considerations may make it more productive to consolidate land holdings into bigger farms to realize economies of scale. To some extent, land reform can involve a trade-off between growth and depauperization.

The other major institutional weakness that holds back small-scale rural development is a weakness of credit markets. In many less developed countries, small farmers have no access to banks and other modern credit facilities. They must rely on local money lenders or merchants, who charge extremely high interest rates.

High-yield crops have made the credit problem more serious than ever. The green revolution can actually work against the small farmer. Higher yields drive land rents up and put downward pressure on output prices. The new varieties cannot be used without expensive fertilizers and pesticides, but buying these goods puts the small farmer more at the mercy of the money lender. Thus, if land reform is carried out without credit reform, it can in fact retard the introduction of new techniques.

CONCLUSIONS

The tone of much of this chapter has been pessimistic. There is no doubt that the problems of the less developed countries will be very difficult to surmount and that some countries will fail. There is every doubt of the ability and the will of the industrialized countries to carry the burden of development. Nonetheless, there are places where things are going right rather than wrong. It is fitting to end this chapter with one of these success stories.

Case 32.2
Daniel Benor's Agricultural Revolution

In India, Turkey, Thailand, Nepal, Sri Lanka, and Indonesia, Daniel Benor, a slender, balding Israeli, is producing a remarkable agricultural revolution. His revolution, sponsored by the World Bank, is quite different from the highly technological green revolution that has been so widely publicized. And it works. Small farmers are doubling and tripling their crop yields wherever the system is tried.

Benor's program is deceptively simple. It is based on what he calls the "T&V" (training and visitation) system of passing information from top experts to farmers in the field. The key link in the system consists of a network of village level extension workers whose responsibility it is to pass carefully limited and digestible doses of information along to a limited group of farmers. The extension worker visits each assigned village on a regular schedule, each week to two weeks. The emphasis is on such labor-intensive basics as proper spacing, weeding, and the use of the most promising seeds.

Even more importantly, in some cases, the program guards against misuse of the green revolution technologies. Take insecticides, for example. In the Gujarat area of India, cotton is the principal crop. The hybrid variety most widely grown responds well to good fertilization and care, but it is vulnerable to insect pests. The farmers' instinctive reaction was to spray heavily with insecticides. They sprayed so heavily, in fact, that they not only increased costs but upset the entire regional ecology. The pest problem actually got worse, not better.

Benor's solution to this problem was to put his T&V system to work teaching farmers when *not* to spray. He trained special "scouts," armed with magnifying glasses, to count the number of pests per plant. The fields would be sprayed only when a threshold — say twenty pests per plant — was reached. As soon as the number started to decline, spraying stopped. Using this simple approach, one agricultural cooperative of two hundred members increased its profits by a third in a single year. Elsewhere, the same principle is applied to prevent overfertilization.

Benor has become a hero to Asian farmers. Traditional development specialists were skeptical of his method at first, but it has now been so widely validated that they too are convinced of its effectiveness. World Bank President Robert S. McNamara, once a skeptic, is now one of Benor's biggest boosters. Countries all over the world are now eager to try the T&V system in the hope that as agricultural yields rise, the race between population and food may one day be won by food.

Source: Based on Hobart Rowen, "Poorest of Poor's Crop Yield Soars," *Washington Post,* November 12, 1978, p. K–1. © 1978 The Washington Post. Used by permission.

SUMMARY

1. Economic development is a complex phenomenon, a major part of which is sheer economic growth—increasing the size of GNP as a whole. Development also means industrialization. In countries that have already developed, industry has grown more rapidly than agriculture. In extreme cases, such as that of the Soviet Union, the agricultural sector has actually been stripped of resources to aid the more rapid growth of industry. A third aspect of economic development is depauperization—not only growing but distributing the benefits of growth to the poorest classes. An industry-first growth strategy may hamper depauperization.

2. A population grows whenever its crude birthrate exceeds its crude death rate. In a finite environment, living populations cannot grow indefinitely. If the birthrate does not fall to the death rate, overcrowding will force the death rate up to the birthrate. Population growth in developed countries has undergone a process known as the demographic transition. In preindustrial society, both birth and death rates were high. As industrialization began, death rates fell and a period of rapid population growth began. Economic growth was even more rapid than population growth, however, so per capita incomes rose. This brought birthrates down and reduced the rate of population growth.

3. Virtually all less developed countries face serious population pressures. Modern death control techniques have been introduced to all corners of the globe, no matter how poor. Where birthrates are still high, population growth rates are more rapid than they ever were during the demographic transition in developed countries. If the growth rate of GNP does not keep up with the growth of population, a country may be caught in a population trap. In order to complete the demographic transition successfully, many countries will have to find a way of lowering birthrates while per capita incomes are still at a very low level.

4. Some observers believe that as many as two-thirds of the world's people suffer from undernourishment or malnutrition in some form. In many developing countries population growth is outstripping food production, thereby making the problem worse. In the past, food aid has been an important stopgap measure, but food aid alone is not the long-run solution. Rural development is needed if less developed countries are to be able to feed themselves. Technological advances, including high-yield grains, provide a potential basis for rural development. Economic and institutional problems remain, however. Some way must be found to provide the fertilizers, pesticides, and capital needed to make the best use of high-yield grains. Land reform and credit reform are also necessary parts of successful rural development.

DISCUSSION QUESTIONS

1. In what ways are the problems faced by the less developed countries similar to the problems faced by Canada one hundred years ago? In what ways are they different? Will today's less developed countries follow a similar path to economic development, or is a different route more promising? Explain.

2. In early phases of industrialization, urbanization seems to be a major factor in bringing birthrates down. Today, birthrates are still falling in Canada, even though the degree of urbanization is no longer changing rapidly. What other factors do you think are at work causing the continued decline in birthrates?

3. Less developed countries are short on capital. Foreign firms are often willing to invest in such countries. Is foreign investment a good way for the countries to solve their capital shortage? What are the advantages and disadvantages to the countries of such foreign investment?

4. Less developed countries tend to have less equally distributed incomes than do developed countries. Why do you think this is so? Why does development sometimes increase inequality rather than reduce it?

5. Do you see any similarity between the dual economy of some less developed countries and the dual labor market that some economists believe exists in Canada?

6. People in Canada eat huge quantities of meat. Each pound of meat requires up to ten pounds of grain to produce. It is sometimes said that the world food problem could be solved in part simply by people eating less meat. Suppose that this advice were taken to heart, and meat consumption in Canada were cut in half, with more bread eaten instead. Would the grain thus saved ever actually reach the hungry poor in the developing countries? If so, explain how shifts in market prices and changes in supply and demand conditions would operate to get it there. If not, explain why the market would fail to move the grain in the desired direction.

7. It is sometimes said that it is pointless to give money to developing countries to buy food, because this money will just end up lining the pockets of Saskatchewan farmers without doing the less developed countries themselves any good. Is this concern wholly justified, partly justified, or wholly unjustified? Why?

SUGGESTIONS FOR FURTHER READING

Bogue, Donald J., and Ong Tsui, Amy. "Zero World Population Growth." *Public Interest*, no. 55 (Spring 1979), pp. 99–113.
A report on recent declines in fertility in many countries that are disproving some of the more pessimistic population forecasts made only a few years ago. The authors suggest that the "population bomb" may turn out to be a dud.

Ehrlich, Paul, and Ehrlich, Ann. *Population, Resources, and Environment*. 2d ed. San Francisco: W. H. Freeman, 1972.
A good introduction to population arithmetic, the debate over optimal population size, and population control techniques.

Johnson, D. Gale. *World Food Problems and Prospects*. Washington, D.C.: American Enterprise Institute, 1975.
A survey of the world food outlook from the perspective of 1975.

Meier, Gerald M., ed. *Leading Issues in Economic Development*. 3rd ed. New York: Oxford University Press, 1976.
A good introduction to the field of development economics.

C H A P T E R 33

CAPITALISM VERSUS SOCIALISM

WHAT YOU WILL LEARN IN THIS CHAPTER

Beyond all the particular issues of economic policies lies the wider issue of capitalism versus socialism. This chapter begins by defining the two terms and distinguishing several particular varieties of each type of economic system. Next, it surveys major elements of the long-standing debate over the relative merits of capitalism and socialism, first from the point of view of efficiency and then from the point of view of equity.

FOR REVIEW

Here are some important terms and concepts that will be put to use in this chapter. If you do not understand them, review them before proceeding.
- *Market justice and distributive justice (Chapter 1)*
- *Managerial and market coordination (Chapter 20)*
- *Efficiency and perfect competition (Chapter 24)*
- *Functional distribution of income (Chapter 29)*

The term *economic system* refers to the whole pattern of economic institutions that determine the way resources are allocated in a society. In most branches of economics, systems and institutions are among the givens. For example, macroeconomics develops theories about how an increase in the money supply will affect prices and interest rates, assuming a given institutional structure of the banking system and credit markets. Sometimes it examines the effects of the change in one particular institution while assuming that others do not change. An example is the study of the effects of fixed versus flexible exchange rates on world trade. In the branch of economics called comparative economic systems, though, the scope of analysis is much broader. Institutions and whole systems of institutions become the variables rather than the givens of analysis.

Economic systems can be grouped into broad categories on the basis of certain common traits. One way to classify them is on the basis of property rights. Property can be owned privately, owned cooperatively by voluntary associations of individuals, or owned by the government. In practice, examples of each kind of ownership can be found in almost every economic system, but often one form or another predominates. In economies called capitalist, for example, there is widespread private ownership of nonlabor factors of production. In socialist economies, cooperative or government ownership prevails.

Economic systems can also be classified in terms of their organizational structure. Chapter 22 introduced two general principles by which the division of labor in an economy can be coordinated. One is the managerial principle, which depends on centralized decision making; coordination is accomplished by means of orders passed from superiors to subordinates within a hierarchical organization. The other is the market principle, which depends on decentralized decision making and the use of the price system as a means of coordination. In capitalist economies, there is a tendency for managerial coordination to be confined to the internal business of individual firms. Relationships among firms are coordinated on a market basis. In socialist economies, there is usually an attempt to introduce managerial coordination on a larger scale, in the form of national economic planning.

This chapter will show how the two bases of classification can be used in various combinations to identify a variety of different subtypes of capitalist and socialist economies. It will also enter briefly into the general debate on the relative merits of the various systems. Chapter 34 will take a more detailed look at one of the largest socialist economies — that of the Soviet Union.

CAPITALISM

Capitalism Any economic system based on private ownership of all factors of production in which owners of capital act as entrepreneurs and coordinate their activity through use of the market.

The discussion of capitalism begins with a formal definition. **Capitalism** is any economic system based on private ownership of all factors of production in which owners of capital act as entrepreneurs and coordinate their activity through use of the market. Under capitalism, the principle of managerial coordination is limited to the internal workings of firms. Capitalism is sometimes also referred to as a *free enterprise system* because production and consumption activities are carried out on the basis of free contracts and voluntary exchange. The rules of the game under which capitalism operates formally prohibit the use of force, violence, threats, and fraud in market transactions.

The term *capitalism* has been applied to so many economic systems that it is necessary to distinguish several different varieties. The following sections will discuss three kinds of capitalism that differ from one another in terms of the economic role played by government. This role can range from nothing at all to very substantial.

Classical Liberal Capitalism

Classical liberal capitalism A capitalist economic system in which government performs only the limited role of protecting property rights and settling private disputes.

Under the tenets of **classical liberal capitalism**, the government plays an important, but strictly limited, role in the economy. In the classical liberal conception, government is a referee that enforces the rules of the game. It has just two functions: (1) to maintain a police force, a system of courts, and, if necessary, a military establishment to protect property rights against criminal activity and foreign aggression; and (2) to provide a court system for the peaceable settlement of disputes that arise over the terms of private contracts. Marxist opponents of capitalism say that this means that the government simply acts as the "executive committee" of the capitalist class and settles all disputes in favor of the owners of capital. Classical liberals deny the executive committee doctrine. Their ideal is a government that is impartial—one that is as vigilant in protecting the personal and property rights of consumers and workers as in protecting those of capitalists.

Under classical liberal capitalism, the government has a monopoly on the legitimate use of force, but it used its coercive powers only against those who violate the personal and property rights of others. The sole exception is that the government can force private citizens to pay whatever minimal taxes are needed to finance its defense and law enforcement agencies.

Anarcho-capitalism

Some supporters of capitalism are even more strongly opposed to the use of force in economic affairs and even more strongly in favor of the free market than are the classical liberals. They believe that even the limited government of classical liberalism is too much. If it is right to protect private property, then the government need have no monopoly in this field. Furthermore, if it is wrong to use force in economic life, then the use of force by the government to collect taxes is also wrong. Following this reasoning, society should dispense with the institution of government altogether. This combination of a radical attack on government (anarchism) with a defense of private property (capitalism) is called **anarcho-capitalism**, or, alternatively, **radical libertarianism**.

Radical libertarians believe that in an anarcho-capitalist society, profit-seeking private firms would take over all the legitimate functions now performed by government. Like classical liberals, they believe that private firms could deliver the mail, dispose of garbage, and collect tolls from motorists to pay for the construction and repair of highways. Unlike classical liberals, they believe that private arbitration firms could settle disputes between parties to business contracts, that private insurance companies could provide protection against criminal activity, and that the criminals themselves could be tracked down by private detectives (hired by the insurance companies) and locked up in privately run jails. A few hours spent with a radical libertarian tract such as Murray Rothbard's *For a New Liberty* have convinced many a skeptic that the principles of private enterprise are much more widely applicable than they ever imagined.[1]

Anarcho-capitalism (radical libertarianism) A capitalist system under which no state exists and all goods and services—including defense, police, and court services—are supplied by private firms.

State Capitalism

At the opposite end of the capitalist spectrum from radical libertarianism are systems that are basically capitalist but in which government plays a much larger role than just enforcing the rules of the game. The term **state capitalism** serves to describe these systems.

Under state capitalism, government provides an alternative to the market as a means by which individuals and firms can win control over resources. If a firm wishes to increase its profits, it can cut costs and

State capitalism A capitalist system under which government intervenes widely in the market and provides an alternative to the market as a means by which individuals and firms can win control over resources.

---

[1]Murray N. Rothbard, *For a New Liberty* (New York: Macmillan, 1972).

improve its product. Alternatively, it can lobby the government for regulations that will drive its competitors out of business and permit it to charge monopoly prices. If homeowners want to improve the value of their houses, they can buy larger lots to build on. Alternatively, they can persuade local zoning officials to force their neighbors to buy larger lots for their houses. If people want to live comfortably in retirement, they can save from their own wages during their working lifetimes. Alternatively, they can arrange that other people's wages be taxed to pay them social security.

In effect, in every sphere of economic life under state capitalism, the government and the market provide parallel structures for resource allocation. To the extent that most factors of production continue to be privately owned, such a system can still legitimately be called capitalist. Clearly, though, it is a rather different form of capitalism than that envisioned by classical liberals.

SOCIALISM

The doctrines and systems that have been called socialist are so diverse that any short definition is bound to offend at least some people who call themselves socialists. If these cautionary words are kept in mind, however, there is no reason not to at least try a definition. As the term is used here, **socialism** means any of a number of doctrines that include two tenets: (1) that some major share of nonlabor factors of production ought to be owned in common or by the state; and (2) that justice requires incomes to be distributed at least somewhat more equally than under classical liberal capitalism. No more will be said here about socialism in general; instead, the chapter will turn to a number of particular types of socialism.

Socialism Any of a number of doctrines that include the following tenets: (1) that some major share of nonlabor factors of production ought to be owned in common or by the state, and (2) that justice requires incomes to be distributed at least somewhat more equally than under classical liberal capitalism.

Centralized Socialism

Perhaps the most widely discussed variety of socialism — and, to many, the only "pure" variety — is **centralized socialism**. In such a system, all capital and natural resources are government owned. The government sets up some kind of central planning board that coordinates all production according to managerial principles. The board issues plans that have binding force on all individual units where production is actually carried out. In a literal sense, the entire economy is one big firm.

Centralized socialism A socialist system under which all capital and natural resources are owned by the government, which plans all production as if the economy were one big firm.

In the most commonly described form of centralized socialism, planning is carried out in physical terms. The plans drawn up by the central planning board specify the number of tons of steel or number of yards of cloth or whatever to be made in each factory. The plans also specify the number of tons of coal or pounds of yarn or whatever to be used up in producing the output. Labor is the only factor of production not directly owned by the state. Workers are free to choose their own jobs within the framework of the plans. (Forms of centralized socialism in which workers are assigned to specific jobs are by no means unknown, however.) Governments that have espoused centralized socialism have generally tried to bring agriculture as well as industry under the sway of central planning.

Socialism as an economic system is inseparably associated with the name of Karl Marx. Although Marx was notoriously reluctant to draw up blueprints for the socialist future he foresaw, a careful study of his writings suggests that he thought of the socialist economy in centralized terms. As will be shown in the next chapter, that has certainly been the interpretation placed on Marxism by ideological authorities in the Soviet Union. Today, however, one often encounters people who think of themselves as Marxian socialists without being strict centralists on economic matters. Many Eastern European reformers and Western Marxist radicals are non-centralists.

Lange's Market Socialism

From the early days of this century, one aspect of centralized socialism has been consistently criticized by economists: the principle of planning in physical terms. Opponents of socialism have argued that it is beyond the capacity of central planners to specify the physical quantities of the millions of inputs required for thousands of firms. Even if workable sets of plans could be drawn up, planners could not guarantee that they had found the most efficient combination of inputs for production of the given outputs and the most efficient pattern of outputs to satisfy consumer demands.

During the 1930s, economist Oskar Lange issued a justly famous reply to these critics. In a series of articles entitled "On the Economic Theory of Socialism," Lange claimed that central planning in physical terms was neither the only nor the best way of running a socialist economy. Instead, he proposed a system — **market socialism** — in which the socialist managers of individual firms would mimic the behaviour of managers under perfectly competitive capitalism. A central planning board would exist, but its major function would no longer be to issue commands; instead, it would set prices for goods and factors of production. Managers would take these prices into account and would conduct the actual operation of their firms according to two rules:

Market socialism A socialist system in which details of resource allocation are made through market mechanisms rather than through central planning.

1. The quantity of output produced by each firm would be the quantity that would make the marginal cost of production equal to the assigned price of the product.
2. A combination of factor inputs would be chosen to produce each product; this would make the marginal physical product per dollar's worth of each factor equal to the marginal physical product per dollar's worth of any other factor.

Managers would requisition whatever quantities of factors of production they needed to produce according to these rules. They would produce whatever quantities of outputs the rules required. In any particular period, the uncoordinated actions of individual firms might result in a surplus or shortage of some goods or factors. If this were to occur, the central planning board would correct any imbalances. It would raise the prices of any factors or goods of which there was a shortage, thereby discouraging their use. Similarly, it would lower the prices of any goods or factors of which there was a surplus, thereby encouraging greater use. In this way, production and use would be brought into equilibrium and the plans of individual firms coordinated.

Lange's system, of which this is only the barest sketch, immediately

Karl Marx (1818–1883)

Karl Marx—German philosopher, international revolutionary, and patron saint of Soviet communism—was also a prominent member of the British classical school of economics. His study of economics began in earnest when he moved to London in 1849 at the age of thirty-one. As it was for his contemporary, John Stuart Mill, the study of economics for Marx was first and foremost the study of the works of David Ricardo. But whereas other economists of the classical school were for the most part sympathetic to the capitalist system, Marx took the tools of Ricardian economic analysis and turned them against the social system that had spawned them.

The keystone of classical economics was the labor theory of value—the doctrine that the values and relative prices of various goods are determined primarily by the number of labor hours that go into their production. For Ricardo, the labor theory had been just a description of how the economy worked; but Marx went on to argue that if labor is the source of all value, workers ought to receive the whole product of their labor. Instead, under capitalism, a large part of that product was siphoned off into the pockets of capitalists in the form of profits or "surplus value."

Marx did not limit himself to exposing the inner workings of the capitalist system and condemning it as unjust. In addition, he attempted in his massive work, *Capital*, to prove that capitalism was headed for an inevitable breakdown, to be followed by a socialist revolution. Marx worked all his life with international revolutionary groups to prepare the way for this coming revolution.

Despite his faith in the inevitability of the socialist revolution, Marx had practically nothing to say about the operation of a socialist economy. The few remarks he did make suggest, however, that the socialism he envisioned would be of a centralized variety in which the "planning principle" would replace the "anarchy of the market." The rest he left to be worked out by future socialists in the course of their practical experience.

---

caught the imagination of his readers. It appeared to offer two major advantages over centralized socialism with physical planning. First, the burden of work on central planners would be lessened because they would be responsible only for prices. Individual managers would do their own planning of physical input and output requirements. Second, Lange's rules for managers closely resembled the rules of managerial calculation under perfect competition. That resemblance made it seem likely that inputs and outputs would be chosen more efficiently than under a regime of physical planning. (These points will be discussed in more detail later in the chapter.)

Participatory Socialism

Participatory socialism A socialist system under which the means of production are owned collectively by the workers of individual firms, who participate democratically in the process of management and share the profits of their firms.

Under **participatory socialism**, the third socialist system to be looked at, the means of production belong neither to the state nor to private capitalists. Instead, they are owned in common by the workers who actually operate them. The workers of each firm participate democratically in management; hence the name. Relationships among firms and between firms and consumers are coordinated by markets, as in a capitalist economy. The role of the government need not be greater than under state capitalism.

Under participatory socialism, workers, not capital owners, are the entrepreneurs. If successful, they share in the profits. The functional distribution of income is determined by marginal productivity principles, much as under capitalism; but the principles that govern the personal distribu-

In his sixty-one years, Oskar Lange achieved not one but two distinguished careers as an economist. Born in Tomaszow, Poland, he came to the United States to study at the University of California and Stanford University. He remained in the United States to teach at the University of Michigan, Stanford University, and the University of Chicago. His famous article, "On the Economic Theory of Socialism," appeared in the *Review of Economic Studies* in 1937 and gave him an international reputation.

Lange's interests as an economist went beyond the question of the economics of socialism. He was a pioneer in econometrics and did important early work in macroeconomics as well. In 1944, he wrote *Price Flexibility and Full Employment*, in which he attempted to establish Keynes's employment theory as a special case within a general equilibrium theory.

By this time, Lange had acquired U.S. citizenship. In 1945, however, he renounced it to become the Polish ambassador to the United States. After serving as ambassador, he became Poland's delegate to the United Nations. Finally, in 1947, he returned to Poland to begin the second phase of his career as an economist. He held various positions in the Communist Party and government and in 1957 became the chairman of the Polish Economic Council.

As a leading economist in communist Poland, Lange turned to electronic computers and cybernetics to reconcile his earlier views on market socialism with Soviet-type central planning. He described the market as a cumbersome and slow-working servomechanism—the best available in the days before computers, but now obsolete. Without repudiating his earlier work, he characterized its proposed trial-and-error system as quaintly out of date. He continued to write on econometrics and economic cybernetics until his death in 1965.

Oskar Lange (1904–1965)

tion of income are quite different. The ownership of nonlabor factors of production is not highly concentrated, as it is under capitalism; instead, it is widely shared by all workers. As a result, workers receive in addition to their wages a bonus or "social dividend" that represents their share of the profits and of the product of resources owned in common. To the extent necessary, of course, this principle of distribution can be supplemented by social insurance to meet the needs of the elderly, the disabled, and the nonworkers.

Participatory Socialism in Yugoslavia Participatory socialism is not just a creature of abstract theory. An entire national economy, that of Yugoslavia, has operated under a system of worker management since the early 1950s. In the Yugoslav economy, a new firm can be created by central or local government, by an existing firm, or by a group of individuals. Once it comes into being, it takes on an independent life of its own, entering into market relationships with its customers and suppliers. The basic governing unit of a Yugoslav firm is the workers' council, in which all workers participate. The council directly reviews and approves basic long-run policy decisions, including the important decision regarding distribution of the firm's income. The council also elects a smaller executive council and a director to handle the day-to-day business of the firm. Although Yugoslavia's communist government claims to find authority in Marx's writings for this brand of socialism, the system could hardly be in greater contrast to the centralized blueprint of official Soviet doctrine.

In many respects, participatory socialism has worked well in Yugoslavia. Although the country was very nearly the poorest one in Europe at the end of World War II, over the next two decades it enjoyed one of the fastest economic growth rates in Europe. Furthermore, Yugoslavs have enjoyed a far greater degree of political and personal freedom than their comrades in other Eastern European countries. This fact is by no means unrelated to the difference in economic systems. Yugoslavia has its share of economic problems, ranging from high inflation and regional disparities in income to complaints that workers spend too much time at factory meetings and not enough on the production line. Nonetheless, it is a system from which there is much to be learned in both the East and the West.

European Social Democracy

The fourth kind of socialism to be looked at is European social democracy. Social democratic parties have either held power or been a strong opposition party in most countries of Western Europe and Scandinavia since World War II. Although there are important differences among the parties of various countries, the main principles of social democracy can be illustrated with the example of the British Labour Party. The defining characteristics of British social democracy are an overriding concern for the poor and a belief in equality. By equality, in the words of a leading member of the Labour Party, "we mean more than a simple redistribution of income. We want a wider social equality embracing the distribution of property, the educational system, social class relationships, power and privilege in industry—indeed, all that is enshrined in the age-old socialist dream of classless society."[2] In pursuit of this goal of equality, the Labour Party, like its counterparts on the continent of Europe, instituted wide-ranging "welfare state" policies. These policies were supposed to guarantee to every citizen, as a matter of political right, minimum standards of health care, education, food, and housing. At the other end of the scale, confiscatory rates of taxation were imposed on people with inherited wealth (or even simply high earned incomes). Great Britain's Labour governments also made strong efforts to reduce selectivity in education in an attempt to eliminate an important source of class distinction.

On the matter of ownership of the means of production, the more moderate Labour Party leaders are not dogmatists. The same person just quoted writes that a "mixed economy is essential to social democracy. For while a substantial public sector is clearly needed to give us the necessary control over the economy, complete state collectivism is without question incompatible with liberty and democracy."[3] Great Britain's public sector is indeed substantial by Canadian standards. In its various periods in power, Labour governments extensively nationalized steel, coal, railroads, shipbuilding, aircraft, automobiles, and several other important industries, although still leaving a large part of the private sector. British nationalized industries are supposed to be run on competitive business principles and are supposed to turn a profit to help finance the government's welfare state policies. In practice, though, the managers of nationalized industry have complained of capricious political interference in their affairs. Many of the

---

[2]Anthony Crosland, *Social Democracy in Europe*, Fabian Tract 438 (London: Fabian Society, 1975), p. 1.
[3]Ibid.

largest nationalized industries have operated at a loss and have required heavy subsidies from the taxpayers. The new Conservative government elected in 1979 pledged to return some nationalized industry to private hands and to improve management of the rest.

As economic systems, social democracy and state capitalism are not far apart. Although they lie to the "left" of the two major Canadian political groupings, the European social democrats represent the "right" within the broad spectrum of possible socialisms.

SOCIALISM: PRO AND CON

Having made this catalog of capitalist and socialist economic systems, the chapter turns now to a brief survey of the ongoing debate over the relative merits of various systems. Socialist slogans have long proclaimed the superiority of socialism over capitalism. Socialism, it has been said, replaces the "anarchy of the market" with the "planning principle." It also replaces "production for profit" with "production for use" and replaces capitalist exploitation of the working classes with a system in which the whole product goes to the real producers. Such slogans are impressive to hear but difficult to evaluate. What exactly is the planning principle? What is the difference between production for profit and production for use? And what is meant by "exploitation"? Can a discussion in terms of mundane economic standards shed some light on the merits of socialism?

Static Efficiency

The first standard that can be used for comparing economic systems is static efficiency. In comparative economics, static efficiency is the efficiency of resource allocation under hypothetical conditions of universal equilibrium. In this system, resources, production technologies, and consumer tastes are known to everyone and are forever unchanging.

Lange's Claims for the Static Efficiency of Socialism Under perfect competition, a capitalist economy can, in principle, operate with complete static efficiency. If claims are to be made for socialism on grounds of static efficiency, then, it must be shown that it can do at least as well as capitalism under the same ideal conditions. That is what Oskar Lange set out to prove. He accepted the idea that any kind of socialism relying on central planning in physical terms would score poorly in terms of static efficiency. In his own system, however, efficiency would be guaranteed. Managers would be instructed to make the proper adjustments in marginal costs and marginal products, while central planners would be instructed to adjust prices to market-clearing, equilibrium levels.

That was only a starting point. It was not enough for Lange to show that under ideal circumstances, his socialist system could function at least as efficiently as capitalism. He went on to argue that under the circumstances that actually prevailed in the real world, his system would do better. First, he claimed that his system solved the problem of monopoly. Under capitalism, in an industry with only one or a few firms, managers tend to equate marginal cost with marginal revenue rather than with price. That tendency violates static efficiency conditions. In Lange's system, in contrast, managers would be instructed to follow the same rule—marginal cost equals price—no matter how few firms there were in a market.

Furthermore, Lange pointed out that even competitive markets would not operate efficiently when pollution or other distorting factors caused private costs to deviate from opportunity costs. Under his system, central planners could automatically correct for such things. They would simply build the appropriate incentives or penalties into the prices they set.

Counterclaims Lange's claims for the superior static efficiency of his system have brought forth three kinds of counterclaims. First, some critics have attacked the system directly in Lange's own terms. They have suggested, for example, that the trial-and-error pricing system that Lange's central planners were to use would be too time-consuming and might even be unstable. Also, they have pointed out that it is not clear how the trial-and-error method for finding market-clearing prices could be applied to goods that were custom-made, as much important industrial equipment is. Finally, they have argued that Lange's system would do poorly where considerations of time and risk played an important role in the pricing process.

A second, rather different, kind of criticism comes from advocates of state capitalism and moderate social democrats. They argue that a full transition to socialism is not necessary to achieve the desired gains in static efficiency. Instead, it would make more sense to keep a market economy and to introduce ad hoc corrections to deal with problems such as monopoly and pollution where necessary.

Finally, the most important of all the criticisms of Lange's system is a simple rejection of static efficiency as a standard of evaluation. Any gains in static efficiency from Lange's system, according to the critics, would be offset by disadvantages. This rejection raises the issues of dynamic efficiency and economic growth, to which the chapter now turns.

Dynamic Efficiency and Economic Growth

Dynamic efficiency and economic growth are standards for evaluating economic systems that accept the world as it is, with changing technologies, resource availabilities, and consumer preferences. The two standards are closely related. Economic growth measures the overall rate of expansion of output of goods and services. Part of any increase in economic growth that occurs may be attributable to increased supplies of factors of production. More capital is accumulated through saving, more labor through population growth or more hours of work per capita, and more natural resources through mineral discoveries or territorial expansion. Dynamic efficiency refers to the growth rate that can be sustained with a given rate of expansion of factor supplies. High dynamic efficiency depends partly on the ability of a system to generate scientific and technical advances. It depends even more on the ability of its entrepreneurs to take advantage of opportunities as they emerge, quickly and effectively.

Claims for the Dynamic Efficiency of Socialism Some claims have been made for socialism on the ground of dynamic efficiency. One such claim is that the absence of private patent rights under socialism speeds the spread of innovations. Another is that monopolistic firms under capitalism consciously obstruct technological progress because they have vested interests in traditional products and methods of production. More commonly, though, the emphasis of socialist writers has been on the ability of their systems to raise the rate of economic growth through better mobilization of the factors of production.

One way socialist planners can increase the rate of economic growth is by diverting a larger share of national product into saving and investment than would be forthcoming under a free market system. It was once popular to claim that individual consumers had a "faulty telescopic facility." Thus people underrated the value of increased future incomes that could be earned by saving more now and overrated the value of present consumption. Socialist planners could feel justified in cutting present consumption to increase investment, because whether consumers realized it or not, such policies would make them better off in the long run.

Socialist planners have pursued other policies as well to increase factor supplies. These policies have included encouragement of long work hours, increased labor force participation by women, mobilization of surplus rural labor for work in industry, and intensified exploitation of new agricultural land and mineral resources. Socialists of almost every variety have advocated some policies to accelerate economic growth. Lange thought that his socialists should opt for more investment. The Yugoslav government has taken a variety of steps to ensure that the country's labor managed enterprises do not distribute too large a share of their revenues among workers for current consumption. As will be shown in the next chapter, though, it is the advocates of centralized socialism who have placed the greatest emphasis on growth. In fact, the ability of centralized socialism to mobilize massive factor supplies is sometimes said to more than outweigh the inferior static and dynamic efficiency of that system. Factor mobilization is alleged to give centralized socialism an edge over all alternatives in terms of economic growth.

Counterclaims Critics have long claimed that dynamic efficiency is the area of socialism's greatest economic weakness. This was brought out very early in the protracted "socialist controversy," to which Lange's famous papers were a contribution. The beginning of the controversy is usually given as 1922, the year the Austrian economist, Ludwig von Mises, published a paper in German, entitled "Economic Calculation in the Socialist Commonwealth."[4] In this paper, Mises attacked socialism for what he saw as its inability, in the absence of markets and a price system, to put collectively owned means of production to efficient use in pursuing the socialist planners' chosen ends. Lange began his own defense of socialism by acknowledging that Mises had identified an important weakness in the writings of socialists of his day. He went so far as to suggest that in the future socialist commonwealth, a statue should be erected in Mises's

---

[4]Translated in Friedrich A. von Hayek, ed., *Collectivist Economic Planning*, 6th ed. (London: Routledge & Kegan Paul, 1963).

honor, so no one would forget that prices and markets would be essential under socialism too. Lange then set forth his own proposals, as described earlier.

Mises and his Austrian colleague, Friedrich von Hayek, were by no means satisfied with Lange's solution to the problem of resource allocation under socialism. What Lange had done, they said, was only to solve the problem of managerial calculation under socialism. But Lange completely neglected to deal with the even more important problem of entrepreneurship. As Mises put it:

> The cardinal fallacy implied in this and all kindred proposals is that they look at the economic problem from the perspective of the subaltern clerk whose intellectual horizon does not extend beyond subordinate tasks. They consider the structure of industrial production and the allocation of capital to the various branches and production aggregates as rigid, and do not take into account the necessity of altering this structure in order to adjust it to changes in conditions. What they have in mind is a world in which no further changes occur and economic history has reached its final stage.[5]

Hayek added to the force of Mises's criticism with his insights into the role of the market as a mechanism for using knowledge. Effective entrepreneurship requires making use of particular knowledge of time and place as well as general knowledge of the opportunity cost of widely marketed goods. The existence of a price system makes the general information on opportunity costs available to people on the spot. Perhaps Lange's artificial price system would also be able to serve this purpose. To make use of the equally important particular knowledge of time and place, though, the people on the spot need independence of action and adequate incentives.

Under capitalism, the necessary independence is provided by private ownership of the means of production. The necessary incentives are provided by the opportunity to earn profits when decisions are taken correctly and the responsibility for bearing losses when things go wrong. Under socialism, the person on the spot is inevitably an economic civil servant whose independence in the economic hierarchy is limited. Furthermore, the civil servant's incentives operate in the direction of playing it safe and not rocking the boat.

The critics do not deny, for the most part, that a socialist economy can achieve a high rate of economic growth despite low dynamic efficiency by means of forced savings and, in some cases, forced labor mobilization. Such growth, however, may be growth at too high a price. This point is underlined by the fact that high saving and growth rates can, if desired, be achieved under state capitalism (as in Japan) and without any substantial sacrifice of dynamic efficiency.

CONCLUSIONS

It would be very misleading to think that socialism owes its widespread support solely to its purportedly superior economic performance. There are many socialists for whom the problems of production are secondary to the

---

[5]Ludwig von Mises, *Human Action* (New Haven: Yale University Press, 1949), p. 703.

Ludwig von Mises was born when the "marginal revolution" that established modern economics was just getting under way, and he lived to celebrate the centenery of that revolution. In the meantime, he became one ot the foremost economists of the twentieth century.

Mises was born in Lemberg, Austria, and was educated at the University of Vienna. He taught at the University of Vienna until the Nazis arrived and then moved to Switzerland. In 1940, he came to the United States, and in 1946, he became a U.S. citizen. In I'945, he joined the faculty of New York University, where he remained until his retirement in 1969, at the age of eighty-eight.

Mises's most original theoretical work is his *Theory of Money and Credit*, published in German in 1912. In that work, he became the first to apply the general principle of consumer choice to explain the demand for cash balances. He went on to use the principles as an explanation of expansions and contractions in economic activity. This pioneering insight, that macroeconomic fluctuations have their roots in microeconomic behavior, was lost sight of by mainstream economists during the Keynesian era. Today, however, the importance of the phenomena about which Mises wrote is widely recognized.

In 1922, Mises set forth his famous critique of socialism, "Economic Calculation in the Socialist Commonwealth." This work had a major influence on socialist writers of the day. Oskar Lange in the United States and Abba Lerner in England took Mises's criticism very seriously, and they set out to create a new market socialism that would solve the allocation problem as elegantly and accurately as any capitalist market. Mises, however, was unimpressed. To him, it was impossible to separate the market as an allocation mechanism from the real-world striving of owners after rents and entrepreneurs after profits. He dismissed Lange's and Lerner's work as that of "men playing at markets as boys play at trains."

In 1949, Mises published his monumental *Human Action*. This work is a treatise on all of economics, a grand work on the scale of Adam Smith's *Wealth of Nations* and John Stuart Mill's *Principles*. In *Human Action*, Mises elaborated on all his views on theory, methodology, and policy at great length. Throughout the book, and indeed throughout his whole career, he championed the libertarian doctrine that all government intervention in the economy is to be regarded with intense suspicion. Mises was a great teacher, and his influence lives on through the many students he taught over the years.

Ludwig von Mises (1881–1973)

---

problems of economic justice. Economic justice, of course, means different things to different people, but here are at least some of the things it means to socialists.

First, socialists conceive of economic justice as equality. In their time-honored phrase, it means "from each according to ability, to each according to need." Some socialists are willing to accept the degree of inequality of labor income that would result from wage payments proportional to marginal productivity. Even these people, however, advocate supplementing wages with interest, rent, and profits earned by collectively owned nonlabor factors.

Second, socialist economic justice is supposed to mean an end to exploitation. In this view, the profits, rents, and interest earned by nonworkers under capitalism do not reflect any real productive contribution of inanimate factors of production. They are instead unfairly deducted from the just earnings of labor. Socialists thus often oppose the nonwage earnings even of small-scale shopkeepers, land owners, and moneylenders, despite the fact that these earnings may not raise their recipients very high up the ladder of income distribution.

Finally, many socialists hold that economic justice requires not only that workers get a fair share of the product but also that they have some voice in the actual management of business affairs. Some socialists pay only lip service to this principle. They promote systems in which workers end up as remote from the functions of the central planning bureaucracies as they are from boardroom management under capitalism. Others—the participatory socialists—make this the first and foremost element of economic justice.

Whatever the specific content given to the concept of economic justice, any argument that a socialist economy is inefficient can, in the last resort, be met by the reply that one can afford to tolerate inefficiency in the name of equity.

Two kinds of counterclaims are advanced against the contention that socialism is necessary to achieve economic justice. One comes from left-wing state capitalists. These people are basically in sympathy with the egalitarian aims of socialism. They simply argue that the government of a capitalist country can, if it has the will to do so, use tax and transfer policies to distribute income however desired. As mentioned earlier, this variety of opinion merges imperceptibly at some point with the position taken by moderate European social democrats.

The less moderate view on capitalism, socialism, and economic justice is heard from classical liberals and radical libertarians. These people conceive of economic justice primarily in terms of what has been called market justice. What economic justice requires, they say, is a system in which all people are able to devote their own energies and abilities exclusively to the pursuit of their own chosen objectives, without coercive intervention by anyone. In this view, the first requirement is a free market in which workers, consumers, and resource owners can participate on a purely voluntary basis. In such a system, no person has a right to demand that another turn over property or produce without offering a fair exchange. Nationalization of the means of production and redistributive taxation are thus unjust per se; equality has nothing to do with the matter.

SUMMARY

1. Any market economy in which all factors of production are privately owned and in which the owners of capital for the most part play the role of entrepreneurs can be called a capitalist economy. In both theory and practice, there is a broad range of kinds of capitalism. The Canadian economy is a form of state capitalism in which government intervenes widely in the affairs of the market. Classical liberals advocate limiting the role of government to the provision of police, defense, and court services. Anarcho-capitalists favor reducing the role of government all the way to zero; with even the minimal functions of the classical liberal state being performed by private firms.

2. Any system can be called socialist if at least substantial parts of nonlabor factors of production are collectively owned and if an attempt is made to distribute incomes more equally than under classical liberal capitalism. Socialist systems differ widely from one another in the role they assign to the market. Centralized socialism envisions an economy run as one big firm in which the market plays no role at all. Lange's socialist

economy, participatory socialism, and European-style social democracy all depend heavily on the market as a mechanism of resource allocation but use redistribution policies to modify the personal distribution of income.

3. The static efficiency of an economy is its theoretical efficiency under idealized conditions in which resources, production technologies, and consumer tastes are completely known and unchanging. A capitalist economy could achieve complete static efficiency under perfect competition. Centralized socialism is widely thought to score poorly in terms of static efficiency. Lange built the case for his own brand of socialism largely on consideration of static efficiency. He argued that under ideal conditions his system would operate as well as a capitalist market economy and that under real-world conditions it could achieve higher static efficiency.

4. Dynamic efficiency and economic growth are additional standards by which to judge the performance of an economic system. Centralized socialism claims a superior growth potential because of its ability to mobilize resources of capital and labor and focus them on the task of economic expansion. Questionable dynamic efficiency is seen as a major weakness of Lange's system.

5. Socialists claim that their systems provide greater economic justice than does capitalism. By economic justice, they mean distributive justice. Some state capitalists claim that the welfare state can achieve distributive justice without socialism. Other critics of socialism emphasize the standard of market justice and see capitalism as superior to socialism according to that standard.

DISCUSSION QUESTIONS

1. Why is it that owners of capital so often perform the entrepreneurial function in an economy where factors of production are privately owned? Why should land owners not play this role? Why not workers? Why not people who own no resources at all but who hire everything they need on a contract basis? Can you think of exceptions to the rule that entrepreneurs are also owners of capital? Explain.

2. What position do you think an advocate of classical liberal capitalism would take on each of the following issues that were discussed in earlier chapters: Antitrust policy? Regulation? Poverty? Pollution? Protectionism? How would the classical liberal position on these issues differ from the anarcho-capitalist position—if at all?

3. Of all the kinds of economic systems discussed in this chapter, which kind would you expect Canadian "big businesses" to favor? Why? On what evidence do you base your answer?

4. Explain just what it means to say that under centralized socialism the whole economy is run as one big firm. In an anarcho-capitalist economy, which would entirely lack any government antitrust policy, do you think private businesses would grow and merge with one another to the point that the whole economy would become one big private firm? Explain.

5. There are no serious legal barriers to the emergence of participatory socialist firms in the Canadian economy. If the workers in a private firm pooled all their resources (perhaps making temporary sacrifices to increase their rate of saving), they could buy up the firm's stock share by share until they owned a controlling interest. They would then be in more or less the same position as the worker-owners of a Yugoslav firm. Why do workers so rarely do this in the Canadian

economy? Do you know of any example of worker-owned and operated firms in the Canadian economy? Explain.

SUGGESTIONS FOR FURTHER READING

Crosland, Anthony. *Social Democracy in Europe*, Fabian Tract 438. London: Fabian Society, 1975.
An articulate defense of European social democracy by a leading British Labour Party spokesman.

Friedman, Milton. *Capitalism and Freedom*. Chicago: University of Chicago Press, 1972.
A classic defense of classical liberal capitalism.

Lange, Oskar, and Taylor, Fred M. *On the Economic Theory of Socialism*. New York: McGraw-Hill, 1964.
This volume conveniently reprints Lange's classical articles of the 1930s together with a closely related essay by Taylor.

Rothbard, Murray N. *For a New Liberty*. New York: Macmillan, 1973.
An exposition of the theory of anarcho-capitalism by the leading proponent of that economic system.

Vanek, Jaroslav. *The Participatory Economy*. Ithaca, N.Y.: Cornell University Press, 1971.
A discussion of participatory socialism, both as a general concept and as practiced in Yugoslavia.

C H A P T E R 34

THE SOVIET ECONOMY

WHAT YOU WILL LEARN IN THIS CHAPTER

This chapter surveys the economic problems and achievements of the Soviet economy, the largest experiment ever in centrally planned socialism. The chapter begins with a discussion of the ideological origins and early history of the Soviet economy. It then surveys the formal structure of the Soviet planning system and points out that the informal structure of the system also plays an important role in how it works. Next, it reviews the Soviet growth record and discusses the Soviet Union's prospects for the future. The chapter concludes with some comments on economic reform in the Soviet system.

FOR REVIEW

Here are some important terms and concepts that will be put to use in this chapter. If you do not understand them, review them before proceeding.
- *Price indexes (Chapter 6)*
- *Centralized socialism (Chapter 33)*

The last chapter discussed many different kinds of economic systems, including several varieties of socialism. This chapter turns from theoretical comparisons to an extended case study of one kind of socialism—the centralized socialism of the Soviet Union. The very size of the Soviet Union as an industrial, political, and military power makes it worth taking a close look at the Soviet economic system. Another reason for studying it is to learn more about the general problem of resource allocation and what must be done to solve it successfully. Following is a survey of the origins, structure, and performance of the Soviet economy.

ORIGINS

Marxism-Leninism

The discussion of the Soviet economy begins with an explanation of its ideological origins as a system founded on the principles of Marxism-Leninism. The voluminous writings of Karl Marx are devoted largely to the evolution and structure of capitalism. Marx wanted to pave the way for revolution by demonstrating that capitalism was headed for a breakdown, but he did not attempt to draw a detailed blueprint for the coming socialist economy. There is little doubt, though, that he envisioned the socialist economy in highly centralized terms. Private ownership of nonlabor factors of production would be abolished, and planning would replace the market as the primary means of resource allocation.

V. I. Lenin, the leader of the Russian Revolution, was, if anything, more of a centralist than Marx himself. The secret of Lenin's political success in Russia was the highly centralized, disciplined structure of the Bolshevik Communist Party he led. It was natural for him to apply the same methods of administration to the economy. In a book written just before he came to power, Lenin likened the task of running the economy to that of running the post office or any other bureaucratic administrative agency. The important thing would be a strong party leadership to define economic goals clearly and to provide the discipline and the will necessary to carry them out.

War Communism

Within months of the revolution of October 1917, the Bolsheviks were engaged in a civil war with their White Russian opponents. From the beginning of the civil war, the market economy was abandoned. Trade between the city and countryside was replaced with forced requisitioning of agricultural products. Virtually all industry was nationalized, including many small-scale businesses. Retail trade was also nationalized, although a substantial black market soon emerged. Industrial labor was put under semimilitary discipline, with workers sent to jobs wherever the need was most pressing. As a final blow to the market, a massive outpouring of paper currency from the new government sent inflation spiraling so high that money became useless. Workers in essential positions were paid in food or other goods. Party ideologists proudly proclaimed that socialism had come to the Russian economy.

Either the civil war or the government's radical policies taken one at a time would have produced economic chaos. In combination, they were a disaster. Militarily, the Bolsheviks scraped through against the odd assortment of White Russians and Western armies of intervention who opposed them. By 1921, however, with the war over, the economy was in sad shape. Agricultural production was down by one-third, and industrial workers had fled to the countryside in search of food. It was time for a change of direction.

The NEP

With the threat of war removed, Lenin launched his New Economic Policy, known as the NEP. It was a step backward, taken, as he put it, in order to prepare for two steps forward. Lenin had endorsed the centralist and antimarket policies of war communism, which fitted closely the views he had expressed before the revolution.[1] Now he set those policies aside in

---

[1] On Lenin's attitude toward war communism, see Paul Craig Roberts, *Alienation and the Soviet Economy* (Albuquerque, N.M.: University of New Mexico Press, 1971), chap. 2.

order to get production back on its feet. Trade and small industry went back to private hands. Buying replaced forced requisitioning in agriculture. The peasants once again found it worth their while to sow the fields they had let go fallow. Currency reform put the brake on inflation, and the money economy reappeared. The "commanding heights"—heavy industry, transportation, banking, and foreign trade—remained in government hands, while the rest of the economy followed its own course. Planning was reduced to the issuance of "control figures," which were not directives but merely forecasts intended to help guide investment decisions.

As an instrument for economic recovery, the NEP was a great success. By 1928, prewar production levels had been surpassed in both industry and agriculture. Lenin died in 1924, and Stalin was busy consolidating his power in the party. It was time to take the two steps forward that Lenin had promised.

Collectivization and the Five-Year Plan

The two steps forward taken in 1928 were the Five-Year Plan for industry and the policy of collectivization in agriculture. These steps were designed to overcome two features of the NEP that Stalin saw as serious defects. First, as long as the NEP was in force, central authorities were altogether unable to control the direction of the market economy. Events went their own way while the nominal planners sat on the side and collected statistics after the fact. Second, the NEP provided no mechanism for transferring resources from agriculture to industry. The party needed such a transfer in order to pursue its industry first development strategy. Higher taxes, lower agricultural prices, or forced requisitioning of grain would result only in a withdrawal of effort by the peasants, as during the civil war.

In industry, the Five-Year Plan was, for the first time, supposed to set the course of development in advance. Annual operational plans were to be drawn up in accordance with it. These plans were to include assignments of the necessary raw materials to producers on a nonmarket basis. Above all, the Five-Year Plan envisioned a massive program of capital investment.

Industrial growth was to be financed by obtaining more agricultural produce. Collectivization was the technique used to make sure that the needed grain moved from the country to the city. Between 1928 and 1932, some 15 million peasant households—about two-thirds of the rural population—were formed into 211,000 collective farms. On the collectives, land and livestock were owned in common, while agricultural machinery was supplied by independent machine-tractor stations. Land was worked in common too, and a complex system of payment to collective farmers was introduced. Party control over the peasantry was immeasurably strengthened. Party policy could be imposed on the collectives in a way that had never been possible while agriculture was in private hands.

Collectivization was at least a qualified success. The policy wreaked havoc with agricultural production. The number of livestock fell nearly by half as peasants slaughtered them rather than turn them over to the collectives. Grain output also fell sharply, both because of the general chaos accompanying collectivization and because the incentive structure of the collectives themselves discouraged effort. Despite the disruption of production, though, the flow of goods from the countryside to the city increased; and that, after all, had been a major objective of the policy.

The increased flow to the cities occurred partly because collectivization put the grain where party authorities could get their hands on the first share, before the remainder was distributed to the peasants, and partly because there were fewer livestock left to eat it in the countryside. There were fewer people in the countryside too. Several millions died in the initial turmoil of collectivization and the subsequent famine of 1932-1934.

Emerging Outlines

Out of the disorder of the early 1930s emerged an economic system that displayed most of the major features of the Soviet economy today. Industry, trade, banking, transportation, and foreign commerce were all completely nationalized—with only the most trivial exceptions. Agriculture was almost entirely collectivized. At the top of the system sat Gosplan, the state planning agency. This agency and the ruling party guided the economy with a development strategy emphasizing centralization and planning in physical terms.

The next section of this chapter will look at some details of the structure and functioning of this system. Then, the final section will evaluate its performance.

STRUCTURE

Central Hierarchy

According to the official party handbook, *Fundamentals of Marxism-Leninism*, the Soviet economy functions as a single enterprise, directed by a single will. At the top of the economic hierarchy are the highest political organs of the Soviet government—the Supreme Soviet and its Council of Ministers. Under the Council of Ministers come a number of specialized agencies, including Gosplan, the Central Statistical Administration, and the State Bank. Also under the Council of Ministers are a long list of ministries with specific industrial responsibilities, such as coal, railroads, and ferrous metallurgy. Subordinate to these ministries are numerous regional agencies that act as intermediaries between the central government and the individual firms that stand at the bottom of the hierarchy.

Parallel to the government administrative structure is a Communist Party hierarchy, which also has important economic responsibilities. One of them is to observe, check, and report to the party leadership what is going on in firms and administrative agencies throughout the economy. A second responsibility is to control appointments to administrative and managerial posts at all levels. A third is to mobilize and exhort the labor force to greater efforts in service of the plan. In addition to these specific responsibilities, local party officials consult and participate in many kinds of managerial decision making at the enterprise level.

Enterprise Status

Operation of the individual Soviet enterprise is governed by a so-called technical-industrial-financial plan. This plan, issued annually, is broken down into quarterly and monthly segments. Its most important part is the production plan, which specifies how much output is to be produced, what assortment of products is to be included in total output, and when output is to be delivered. Other parts of the plan specify the quantities of labor and material inputs allotted to individual firms. A financial section gives targets for costs, wage bills, profits, use of short-term credit, and so on. In all, the plan may contain two dozen or more specific physical and financial targets that a particular firm is to meet.

The plan has the binding force of law on enterprise management. In principle, criminal penalties can be imposed for failure to fulfill the plan, although administrative penalties such as demotion or transfer to less desirable jobs are more commonly used. Positive incentives are also provided. Very substantial bonuses are given to managers who successfully fulfill or overfulfill the various parts of their plans.

Planning Procedures

The heart of the planning process is a set of material balances — summaries of the sources and uses of two hundred or three hundred of the most important industrial commodities — drawn up by Gosplan. The purpose of each balance is to ensure that the sources (supply) and uses (demands) for each good are equal and that there will be no shortages or surpluses.

In a simplified form, the process by which material balances are drawn up works something like this. As soon as Gosplan receives directives from the political authorities indicating the general rate of projected development and the most important priorities, work begins on a preliminary set of balances called control figures. These figures show roughly how much of each good must be produced and how much must be used in each sector of the economy if the overall goals are to be met. The next step is to pass the control figures down through the planning hierarchy, where the main balances are broken down into requirements for each region of the country and finally for each enterprise.

When enterprise managers receive these preliminary control figures, they are supposed to suggest ways they can increase outputs or reduce inputs to achieve more ambitious targets. They also have an opportunity to complain if they think the plans exceed their capacity for output or do not provide sufficient inputs. Enterprise responses to the control figures are then sent back up through the hierarchy to Gosplan at the center.

When the original control figures are corrected in the light of information collected from below, it is likely that the sources and uses of materials will no longer balance. People actually responsible for carrying out the plans will often have tried to make their jobs easier by asking for reduced output targets or increased supplies of inputs. What follows is a complex procedure of adjustment and bargaining in which Gosplan tries to eliminate threatened material shortages without sacrificing overall targets. In some cases, shortages may be covered by imports or by drawing down reserve inventories. More commonly, Gosplan responds by tightening the plan — putting pressure on producers to accomplish more with less. If the tightening process goes too far, the result will be a balance on paper only.

The plan will contain concealed shortages that will emerge during its execution.

The final balances are then broken down again. In addition to the crucial two hundred or three hundred materials subject to central balancing, individual ministries or regional authorities will in the meanwhile have prepared balances on thousands of other goods that are not of economy-wide significance. These material balances together eventually become the technical-industrial-financial plans for all firms through the economy. This is a very time-consuming process. Often the final plans are not completed until the planned year is several weeks or even months underway.

Labor Planning

The planning process for one important resource needs special treatment. Allocating labor is partly a matter of how goods are to be produced and partly a matter of who is to do any particular job. Indirectly, the decisions made on the hows and whos also affect income distribution.

Roughly speaking, the how is decided by central planners. Gosplan draws up labor balances for various kinds of work in much the same way that material balances are drawn up. Basic policy on how much labor each enterprise is to use to accomplish the tasks is specified in the technical-industrial-financial plan.

The who of labor allocation, in contrast, is handled largely by markets. For the most part, individual workers are free to choose their occupation and place of work. Two methods are used by the central authorities to ensure that the right number of workers is available in each sector of the economy. One method is to offer substantial wage differentials, paying premiums for skilled work or for work that is unattractive. The other is to manipulate the labor supply through education and training programs.

Individual enterprises are able to exercise some degree of control over the wages they pay. They do this both by adding bonus payments to standard wages and by deciding the skill bracket to which any particular worker is assigned. The overall result is a system where variations in wages are used to ensure a balance between the supply and demand for labor. This is the most important instance of the use of the market for resource allocation in the Soviet economy.

The Informal Structure

The formal administrative structure of the Soviet economy exactly fits the model of centralized socialism. Communications follow vertical paths up and down the planning hierarchy. The messages passed to enterprise management have the binding force of law. Managers are rewarded or reprimanded in accordance with their degree of obedience to the plan. Only the method of assigning particular workers to particular jobs provides a major exception.

A close study of the informal structure of the Soviet economy, however, shows that central control is not absolute. A good deal of informal "horizontal" communication and exchange occurs among firms. Plans are not always treated as binding; sometimes they are treated as only one among a number of factors influencing management behavior. And the attainment of a comfortable and prosperous life for a Soviet manager is not always just a matter of obeying commands to the letter.

The Safety Factor Soviet managers do not passively wait for plans to arrive from above and then do the best they can to fulfill them. Instead, they direct considerable efforts to making sure that they have a safety factor that will cushion them against the danger of being assigned impossible tasks and then being punished for failing to achieve them.

Safety factors often take the form of large inventories of inputs or semi-finished products. Inventories have always been a problem in the Soviet Union. Sometimes, when there are shortages, inventories get squeezed so low that any break in deliveries disrupts production. At other times, when an enterprise manages to get its hands on more than it needs of some essential material, it hoards the scarce material as a safety factor against future shortages.

A rather different safety factor takes the form of deliberately concealed productive capacity. By hiding its true capacity, an enterprise hopes to get an easy plan. Suppose that when provisional control figures come down to some textile mill, they call for an output of, say, 100,000 yards of fabric in the next year. The manager knows that this is just about all the enterprise can squeeze out, given the inputs the control figures say will be available. It does not pay to let Gosplan know that, however. Instead, the manager complains that it will not be possible to produce more than 90,000 yards unless the labor force is substantially increased and the enterprise is given a bigger allotment of synthetic yarn. The easy 90,000-yard plan provides the needed safety factor. The target will be met even if something goes wrong during the year.

Of course, the people in Gosplan know that managers always try to develop a safety factor of some kind. They act on that knowledge when they are juggling their material balances to make them come out even. They do not hesitate to tighten up the plan even when told from below that it cannot be done. The whole thing develops into a sort of game, which greatly increases the degree of uncertainty involved in the planning process.

Procurement According to the formal structure of the Soviet economic system, individual enterprise managers are not responsible for procuring their own raw materials, energy supplies, equipment, or other inputs. As part of the plan, each user of, say, copper tubing is given a schedule of expected deliveries. At the same time, some supplier is given a corresponding schedule of deliveries to make. The user and supplier do not even need to communicate directly with one another. The necessary plans are all supposed to be set up on the basis of information passed vertically to higher authorities.

In practice, however, managers who passively wait for carloads of copper tubing to roll up to their factory gate are likely to be in trouble. Instead, they must be concerned that either their assigned supplies may be behind schedule on their production plan or that the suppliers may be trying to tuck away a hoard of tubing as a safety factor against future demand.

Managers of the user enterprises take appropriate measures to deal with this problem. For one thing, they keep on their payrolls people colorfully known as "pushers." The pushers' job is to go around wining and dining and wheedling suppliers, much as the salespeople of a capitalist firm go after potential buyers. Of course, technical industrial-financial plans do not allow for funds to hire pushers. They have to be worked in under the title of consulting engineer or something of the sort.

Sometimes all pushers have to do to get supplies moving on time is to twist a few arms. Other times they may have to pay outright bribes. On still other occasions they may have to work out a black market barter deal under which one firm will come up with a hoarded carload of copper tubing in exchange for a desperately needed crate of ball bearings. All in all, the telephone lines are always busy, despite the fact that such things are theoretically unneccessary in a centrally planned economy.

Selective Fulfillment   The plan specifies not one but many targets for each enterprise. There are targets for total production, for assortment of production, for cost reduction, for technological improvements, and for numerous other things. Sometimes the end result of issuing so many different targets is to give managers more, rather than less, freedom to maneuver. This happens when it becomes impossible to fulfill all targets at once, so managers must decide which part of the plan will be most impressive to fulfill. The following much-repeated anecdote illustrates the nature of the problem.

Case 34.1
Fulfilling the Plan in a Soviet Nail Factory

There was once a factory whose business it was to manufacture nails for use in the construction trade. In a certain year, the plant was assigned the task of producing x tons of nails, which were to be distributed among a variety of sizes according to the needs of Soviet carpenters. Before the planned year was far underway, the unfortunate manager of the enterprise realized that he could not achieve his target for total output if he kept to the planned assortment. His past experience had taught him that the authorities were much more interested in the total output than in the assortment plan, so he decided on an ingenious strategy. He gave up making little nails, which were a bother to produce and weighed hardly anything, and concentrated on enormous spikes. In that year, he turned out far more than x tons of output. He was gloriously rewarded for overfulfilling the plan.

Naturally, the long-suffering Soviet carpenters complained. They had no way of fastening together anything smaller than two railroad ties! An ingenious Gosplan official hit on a solution. The next year, when the plan was issued, the total output target for the enterprise was stated not in tons but in number of nails, by count. The reader can guess how the enterprise manager responded. He gave up entirely on huge spikes, which took altogether too much hard-to-produce steel. Instead, he concentrated on producing the tiniest pins and brads, which used hardly any metal and counted millions to the ton.

Naturally, the long-suffering Soviet carpenters complained.

Perhaps this anecdote has become exaggerated with the telling, but not by much. In real-life Soviet stores, one finds the assortment of shoe sizes out of step with the assortment of feet, because big sizes take too much leather and bonuses are based on the number of pairs produced. One finds paint mixed so thinly that two coats are needed instead of one, because bonuses are paid on the basis of number of gallons. One finds new models and styles very rarely, because the innovation plan is less important than the output plan. All in all, the very multiplicity of plan targets reduces the real degree of control the planners achieve over what is actually produced.

Planners' Reactions

Naturally, the central authorities are not unaware of the games managers play. They know that the letter of the law is sometimes broken, that reserves are hidden, and that some parts of the plan are less important than others. They could crack down severely on managerial independence, but they do not. They know that the economy could not function if they did. Planners know that the best plans they can make are full of inconsistencies and contradictions. They have to rely on local initiative and ingenuity to overcome these defects, even if the local initiative involves breaking the law. As a result, the authorities take a pragmatic attitude of selective toleration toward the independent behavior of enterprise managers. If a manager acting on local initiative manages to fulfill the plan, nothing is said. Bonuses are paid, and all is well. Only if illegal methods are used and the plan still is not fulfilled is the manager liable to be called on the carpet. In short, it is recognized that the pushers, the bribes, and the safety factors are the grease that keep an imperfectly fashioned machine running.

Exhibit 34.1

Growth rates of GNP: The Soviet Union and the United States

The Soviet Union has a very impressive record of economic growth. Western and Soviet estimates of this growth use different methods and arrive at different numbers; but even by Western measures, growth has consistently been more rapid in the Soviet Union than in the United States until quite recently.

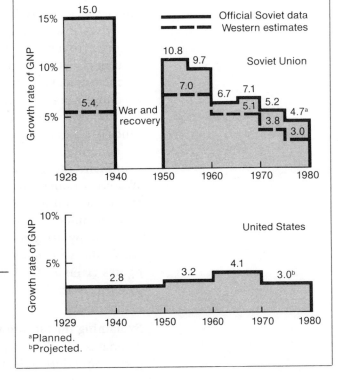

Sources: From Paul R. Gregory and Robert C. Stuart, *Soviet Economic Structure and Performance* (New York: Harper & Row, 1974), p. 378. (Soviet data recomputed from Abram Bergson). Also from "Breznhev's Russia," *Economist*, February 14, 1976, p. 63. All Soviet official data from published sources. Early Western estimates from Abram Bergson, *Real National Income of Soviet Russia since 1928* (Cambridge, Mass.: Harvard University Press, 1961), pp. 180, 210, 261. Most recent estimates from U.S. Joint Economic Committee, *Western Perceptions of Soviet Economic Trends* (Washington D.C.: Government Printing Office, 1978), pp. 3-4.

PERFORMANCE

Growth Record

Soviet leaders, and indeed ordinary Soviet citizens, are extremely proud of one aspect of their economy's performance: its growth record. Within the lifetimes of millions, Russia has been transformed from an economic backwater into one of the world's leading industrial powers. In 1917, Russia had achieved only something like the level of economic development of today's Brazil. It had only a small industrial sector set against a backdrop of vast rural poverty. Today, Soviet living standards are comparable to those of, say, Italy. Soviet industrial capacity exceeds that of West Germany; and in certain particular fields, such as steel output and military technology, it equals or surpasses that of the United States.

Exhibit 34.1 presents the Soviet growth record and compares it to growth in the United States. In the upper figure, representing economic growth in the Soviet Union, two sets of data are presented. The official Soviet statistics show an enormous surge of growth during the 1930s, interrupted by the devastation of World War II and continuing at very high, but gradually declining, rates thereafter. On the same chart, a Western estimate of Soviet growth also shows very respectable growth rates in the earlier periods, but by no means so spectacular a growth as the official Soviet figures show. In the 1970s, both Soviet and Western estimates indicate a slowdown.

Explaining Differing Estimates Why do Western and official Soviet estimates of early Soviet growth differ so much? The answer is largely a matter of the accounting conventions used. Real GNP statistics are always derived by using some index of prices to adjust nominal GNP data in a way that will make it possible to compare data for different years. It turns out to make a great deal of difference which base year is chosen for the index. Choice of an early base year gives rise to numbers that exaggerate the growth rate, especially for an economy that is undergoing rapid structural changes. Soviet statisticians like to use the earliest possible year. The 15 percent growth rates of the 1930s reflect the use of 1928 prices as a basis for calculations. Western practice makes use of a later base year. Soviet accounting practices differ from Western ones in other ways as well, including the way output of services is measured, the way introduction of new kinds of products is taken into account, and the way agricultural harvests are computed.

In many cases, it is not a matter of Soviet statistics being wrong and Western calculations of Soviet performance being right; it is merely a matter of arbitrary choices of accounting convention. What is important for comparative purposes is to express the growth performance of different countries by using conventions that are as nearly the same as possible. It is the Western estimates of Soviet growth that ought to be compared with the figures given for the United States in the lower part of Exhibit 34.1. Compare this with Canadian growth figures given in Chapter 7.

Explaining the Slowdown Soviet economic growth, according to Western estimates, slowed markedly during the 1970s and is unlikely to recover to earlier rates during the 1980s. Over the next decade, Soviet growth is judged unlikely to exceed 3.5 percent, with 2.5 percent a realistic possibility. Various explanations are offered for the slowdown. For one thing, the growth rate of the Soviet labor force is slowing, and population growth in the relatively little-industrialized Central Asian republics is exceeding that in the industrialized areas. The Soviet energy outlook also is not bright. The U.S. Central Intelligence Agency projects a decline in Soviet oil and natural gas production in the 1980s; the Soviet Union may be forced to stop oil exports to Eastern Europe and in the worst case may even become a net oil importer. This would drain scarce reserves of Western currency away from much-needed industrial imports. Finally, weather conditions for Soviet agriculture are not likely to be as favorable on the average during the 1980s as during the 1970s. Comparing these projections of Soviet economic growth with the estimated 3 percent growth rate of potential real GNP in the United States, one can see that the historic gap between Soviet and U.S. growth rates may be drawing to an end.

Sources of Soviet Economic Growth

In the past, the major source of rapid economic growth in the Soviet Union was the ability of the centrally planned economy to mobilize vast new supplies of factor inputs. In the decades immediately before and after World War II, the number of labor hours employed in the Soviet economy increased at a rate of 2.2 percent per year, while they were increasing at only 0.5 percent per year in the United States. Even more impressive, the Soviet capital stock grew at a rate of 7.4 percent per year, compared with just 1 percent per year in the U.S. economy. These very rapid growth rates of factor supplies more than compensated for the inferior dynamic efficiency of centralized socialism. The type of growth experienced by the Soviet Union, based primarily on expansion of inputs, is often called **extensive growth**; the type of growth experienced in the United States, based on better utilization of inputs, is called **intensive growth**.

Extensive growth Growth based predominantly on the mobilization of increasing quantities of factor inputs.

Intensive growth Growth based predominantly on improvements in the quality of factor inputs and in the efficiency with which they are utilized.

Extensive growth is just as effective as intensive growth in adding to the economic power and prestige of a nation as a political unit, but it has certain disadvantages for individual citizens. Most important, a much larger share of GNP has been diverted from consumption into investment in the Soviet Union than in the United States. The figures for 1964 were 35 percent versus 17 percent. As a result, Soviet consumption per capita is only about a third that of the United States, even though GNP per capita is nearly half. It is also worth noting that Japan, the only noncommunist industrial nation to invest as high a fraction of GNP as the Soviet Union, has grown twice as fast in recent years. The Japanese experience shows what can be accomplished when rapid growth of inputs is combined with high dynamic efficiency rather than employed as a substitute for it.

Pricing and Efficiency

As nearly as it can be measured (which is, in fact, only very roughly), the Soviet economy is inefficient in static terms as well as in dynamic terms. Western estimates indicate that it gets only about half as much output per unit of input as does the U.S. economy. There are a number of reasons for this. It may have to do with the structure of managerial incentives, and it may have to do with the motivation and work attitudes of Soviet workers in industry and agriculture. But it is likely that the major source of the Soviet economy's poor static efficiency is the lack of a price system capable of communicating information on opportunity cost to the economy's decision makers.

Consider two functions performed by the price system in a capitalist economy. The first is an accounting function. Prices make it possible to add apples and oranges and come up with a total expressed in dollars' worth of fruit. The second is an allocative function. The prices of inputs measure the opportunity cost of doing a thing or doing it in a certain way, and the prices of outputs measure the value of doing it.

In the Soviet economy, the price system performs the first of these functions but not the second. Industrial goods and consumer goods are all given prices so that industrial accountants can turn in reports on the number of rubles' worth of output produced. The prices, however, are based on custom and arbitrary accounting conventions that have little relationship to opportunity costs. Without knowledge of opportunity costs as reflected in a price system, Soviet planners often have difficulty deciding what to produce and how to produce it. Exact economic calculations are, in fact, impossible. In their place, Soviet planners can use one of three methods of deciding the what and how of resource allocation. First, they can give up calculations in terms of prices altogether and employ rough rules-of-thumb based strictly on engineering considerations. Second, they can do profit-and-loss calculations in terms of their own imperfect prices, even though the answers will at best be only approximately right. Third, they can imitate Western practice. As the following case study shows, though, none of these methods is foolproof.

Case 34.2
The Great Dieselization Blunder

During the 1950s, Soviet planners were faced with a classic problem in resource allocation. The problem was to decide what proportion of truck and tractor engines should be diesel-powered and what proportion gasoline-powered. The decision taken was in favor of massive dieselization. It is revealing to look at the considerations that influenced this important decision.

First, from a strictly engineering point of view, diesels seemed quite attractive. They offer substantially higher mechanical efficiency and are in many ways more elegant and technically sophisticated devices than gasoline engines. Second, the price of diesel fuel in the Soviet economy was low relative to gasoline — about 30 rubles a ton for diesel compared with 60 to 100 rubles for gasoline in the late 1950s. Finally, an examination of Western experience showed extensive dieselization of transportation equipment and heavy tractors.

Far from being a wise piece of economic calculation, though, the dieselization program turned out to be a great blunder. For one thing, diesels require greater initial costs. In part, then, the diesel versus gasoline decision is a matter of proper capital budgeting, in which higher initial costs must be balanced against discounted future gains. One defect in the Soviet price system is that the discount rate used by planners in such decisions is too low. Because the discount rate is, in effect, the "price" of future gains in terms of present costs, there is a bias in favor of techniques involving efficiently large initial costs. This no doubt played a part in the dieselization blunder.

What is more, available evidence indicates that the official Soviet price for diesel oil was too low in comparison to gasoline in the 1950s. Thus the price far underestimated the relative opportunity cost of the heavier fuel. In the United States, the refinery price of diesel is very little less than that of gasoline.

Finally, imitation of Western experience failed to take into account the special circumstances of the Soviet economy. The kinds of crude oil available in the Soviet Union are less suitable than those available in the United States for making diesel fuel. In order to provide fuel for all the new diesel engines, refineries were given plans that they could fulfill only by letting the quality of diesel fuel decline. The oil they used to make diesel should have been made into kerosene or furnace oil. Even worse, they allowed the sulfur content of diesel fuel to rise substantially. Cylinders and pistons wore out quickly when fed a diet of inferior fuel. Under these circumstances, the operating cost of diesel engines turned out to be higher than that of gasoline engines, not lower.

In the 1960s, planners realized their mistake and reversed their earlier decision. A program of de-dieselization began, and perhaps the right ratio of the two kinds of engines has now been reached. If so, the discovery was made not as a result of rational economic calculation but as a result of an enormously expensive process of trial and error.

Source: Based on Robert W. Campbell, *The Economics of Soviet Oil and Gas*, Resources for the Future Series (Baltimore: Johns Hopkins University Press, 1968), pp. 164-167.

Soviet Agriculture

If rapid industrial growth is the Soviet Union's proudest accomplishment, agriculture is its most distressing failure. While Soviet industry grew at a rate of 6.5 percent per year in the first half of the 1970s, agriculture crept ahead at only 2 percent (both official figures). In 1961, then-Premier Nikita Khrushchev set a target of 302 million tons of grain for 1980. In 1975, with three-quarters of Khrushchev's allotted time span elapsed, output was a mere 140 million tons. That was an exceptionally bad year, to be sure, but even the official 1980 target has been scaled down to 218 million tons.

The roots of Soviet agricultural problems date from the earliest days of collectivization. In the Stalin era, agriculture was a cow to be milked for the benefit of industrial development. Now that it has become a serious constraint on industrial development, it is proving difficult to reverse the effects of decades of neglect.

The heart of the Soviet agricultural system is the collective farm, or **kolkhoz**. On paper a kolkhoz is a cooperative, not very different from such participatory social institutions as the Yugoslav worker-managed firm or the Israeli kibbutz. In practice, the collective farm is a far cry from the ideal. Three institutions exercise close control over it from outside. First, the Communist Party controls the selection of collective farm management and directs internal decision making. Second, the kolkolz, like the industrial enterprise, is subject to a plan specifying inputs, outputs, production methods, capital investment projects, and dozens of other details. Third, until 1958 collective farms did not own their agricultural machinery but instead depended on rural "machine-tractor stations." These stations were able to use their monopoly on equipment to control the collective's affairs even further.

In the 1930s, the whole structure of agricultural administration was aimed at one purpose only: moving the indispensable minimum of grain from farm to city. To that end, delivery targets for the kolkhoz were set not

Kolkhoz A Soviet collective farm.

at a percentage of output but at a fixed rate per acre sown. If bad weather brought yields down, the collective farmers bore the entire burden of the shortfall. The state and industry were guaranteed their share. Although it would seem that this would create a strong incentive for the collective to work hard to avoid shortfalls, the effect was blunted by a complex and inefficient system of distributing collective income among kolkhoz members. The system left individuals with few incentives to contribute to the common effort.

Khrushchev must be credited with recognizing that the agricultural problem needed a solution. He abolished the hated machine-tractor stations and made important changes in internal work organizations and management systems. Unfortunately, he diverted much energy and resources into ill-conceived crusades that soaked up resources and offered few long-term results. One cursade was the famous "virgin lands" campaign that put millions of acres of semidesert to the plow for the first time ever. Another was the attempt to introduce the growing of corn, which followed his trip to the United States in 1955. Even more than dieselization (which was also touted as a boon to agriculture), the corn campaign was a naive imitation of foreign practice with little attention paid to radical differences in local conditions.

Agricultural policy in the last decade, like so much else under the Brezhnev leadership, has been characterized by caution mixed with sober determination. Agricultural investment rose from 14 percent of all investment in 1960 to 31 percent in 1976. In the next five years, the farms were to be flooded with some 2 million new tractors and a half million harvesters. Unfortunately, this investment has not been accompanied by the further radical institutional reforms that seem necessary to raise the appallingly low level of agricultural productivity. Nearly a quarter of the entire Soviet labor force still works in agriculture. Productivity per worker is only about a fifth of the Canadian level.

CONCLUSIONS

What sort of future does the Soviet economy face? Since the early 1960s, there has been a great amount of talk, both in the Soviet Union and in the West, about economic reform. To many, the declining Soviet growth rate indicates a necessity to switch from an extensive to an intensive growth strategy, and that cannot be done within current economic institutions. These institutions were designed to mobilize resources and to implement vast structural changes, not to use scarce resources as efficiently as possible.

Reform proposals have centered on three areas. First, there is a need to reform managerial incentives so that, in the Soviet phrase, the interests of management will coincide with the interests of the national economy. The most important part of reforming incentives must be to make profit replace the dozens of indicators of output, assortment, cost, and productivity. Second, there must be a radical price reform. Profit cannot be used as an indicator of economic performance unless industrial prices reflect opportunity costs. Third, there is a need for decentralizing some decision making and establishing direct links among firms, bypassing the cumbersome planning bureaucracy.

The Soviet government has responded to these reform proposals by encouraging discussion, but it has done little else. Compared to the radical changes envisioned by some reformers, what has actually been accomplished is very little. Two official sets of reforms have been attempted. In 1965, Premier Aleksei Kosygin announced one set of reforms: to reduce the number of plan targets for each enterprise from two dozen or more to about eight and to place profit high among the eight as a source of managerial bonuses. In a related group of reforms, there was an attempt to restructure industrial prices during the years 1966 and 1967.

These reforms have eliminated some of the worst previous abuses. The old practice under which plants were rewarded for their achievements in gross output regardless of whether the output could be sold has been replaced by an emphasis on realized output, or actual sales. This practice helps reduce such problems as the production of shoes all of one size that rot in a warehouse for lack of users. Price reform did make some progress in bringing prices in line with average production costs. This eliminated the need to pay enormous subsidies to some firms whose output had always been undervalued. For the most part, though, the reforms have been very limited. A system with eight separate and often conflicting plan targets is a long way from introduction of profits as a single indicator. (Furthermore, since 1971, the direction of change has shifted, with the number of plan indicators increasing again.) By the same token, making prices equal to average cost is by no means the same as making them equal to opportunity cost on the marginal unit.

Explanations for the slow pace of reform vary. Some blame the political conservatism of the Brezhnev regime and the opposition of vested interests within the economic bureaucracy. Others say there is a fear that if economic reforms are introduced, political reforms will have to follow. Still others point out that reform is just not easy. You cannot reform incentives until you have reformed prices, you cannot reform prices until you have greater managerial independence, and you cannot give managers greater independence until you have rationalized their incentives. But, then, you cannot do everything at once either, so you end up doing nothing and hoping for the best!

What the future will bring is a matter of speculation. The most hopeful sign is the great amount of reform and experimentation being carried out in Eastern Europe. Every country in Eastern Europe except Albania has introduced reforms that go far beyond anything tried in the Soviet Union. Each set of reforms is different from the others. Perhaps when a new, more daring leadership comes on the scene in the Soviet Union, it will find in one or another of these experiments a path worth following.

SUMMARY

1. The origins of the Soviet economic system are found first in the Marxist-Leninist ideology and second in the practical experience of the first years of Soviet rule. After the 1917 revolution, an overambitious attempt to abolish the market economy all at once (war communism) was followed by a temporary restoration of the market (the new economic policy). The main features of what is now known as the Soviet-type economy—central planning in physical terms plus collectiviza-

tion of agriculture—were established around 1928. They were designed to serve the government's objectives of complete political control of the economy and extensive, industry-first economic growth. The combination of planning plus collectivization was effective in achieving those objectives.

2. In its formal structure, the Soviet economy is a fully centralized hierarchy. Individual firms receive plans that specify inputs and outputs in physical terms, along with many other targets. These plans are legally binding on firms. In practice, managers of Soviet firms have considerable room to maneuver in fulfilling their plans. They bargain for safety factors, exercise initiative in procuring scarce inputs, and fulfill plans selectively. Central authorities tend to tolerate a certain degree of managerial independence as long as independent action results in fulfillment of the most important plan objectives.

3. The outstanding feature of Soviet economic performance has been rapid economic growth. The rate of growth, has, however, slowed in recent years. The need to switch from a strategy of extensive growth to one of intensive growth has focused attention on the inefficiency of the Soviet system. Soviet economic efficiency is hampered by inadequate managerial incentives and a price system that does not reflect opportunity costs. Many proposals have been put forward for reforming the system, but there has been little practical progress with reform in the Soviet Union. In the Soviet-type economies of Eastern Europe, however, a number of interesting and far-reaching reform experiments have been carried out.

DISCUSSION QUESTIONS

1. During the early war communism period of the Soviet Union, many leading economists seriously proposed the complete abolition of money as part of the transition to a centralized socialist system. Money was restored during the NEP, however, and no further attempt was made to abolish it after central planning began in earnest in the 1930s. Why does even a centrally planned socialist economy find it difficult to get along without money?

2. Any economist who has studied the Soviet economy closely can supply dozens of horror stories like that of the nail factory (Case 34.1). What kind of horror stories involving flagrant misallocation of resources do you know for the Canadian economy? Would you look for such stories in independent private enterprise? In regulated industries? In government itself? Explain.

3. How can you be certain that the right proportion of gasoline and diesel engines is used in the Canadian economy? Or can you? Explain.

4. In the Soviet Union, market mechanisms are used to match workers to jobs, and wage differentials between jobs and regions are largely determined by supply and demand considerations. Do you think this means that labor resources are likely to be more efficiently allocated than other factors of production in the Soviet Union? Explain. In answering this question, you may wish to compare the determinants of labor demand curves in the Canadian and Soviet economies.

5. In reforming a Soviet-type economy, why is it difficult to introduce profit as the major success indicator for management before there has been a thoroughgoing price reform? Why is it difficult to reform prices before managerial incentives have been reformed?

6. In what ways do you think a centralized socialist economy of the Soviet type might be better equipped than a capitalist economy to deal with problems of population, resources, and pollution? In what ways is it less well equipped?

SUGGESTIONS FOR FURTHER READING

Gregory, Paul R., and Stuart, Robert C. *Soviet Economic Structure and Performance*. New York: Harper & Row, 1974.
A short textbook on the Soviet economy, covering all major aspects of history, structure, and performance.

U.S. Congress, Joint Economic Committee.
The Joint Economic Committee publishes numerous reports annually on the economies of the Soviet Union, China, and other Communist countries.

GLOSSARY

Absolute advantage In trade theory, the ability of a region or country to produce a good at absolutely lower cost, measured in terms of factor inputs, than its trading partners.

Accommodating monetary policy A policy under which the Bank of Canada expands the money supply in an attempt to keep interest rates from rising when the government sells bonds to cover a budget deficit.

Accounting profit Total revenue minus explicit costs.

Acreage controls Policies designed to raise agricultural prices by limiting the acreage on which certain crops can be grown.

Adaptive expectations Expectations about the rate of inflation or other future economic events formed primarily on the basis of experience in the recent past.

Aggregate A term used in economics to describe any quantity that is a grand total for the whole economy.

Aggregate demand Total planned expenditure for an economy, consisting of consumption, planned investment, government purchases, and net exports.

Aggregate nominal demand schedule A graph showing the relationship between aggregate nominal demand (the nominal value of total planned expenditure) and nominal national income.

Aggregate nominal supply schedule A graph showing the relationship between aggregate nominal supply (nominal national product) and nominal national income. The schedule has the form of a 45 degree line passing through the origin.

Aggregate supply The total value of all goods and services supplied in the economy; identical to national product.

Agribusiness All those business firms that are linked directly to agricultural producing, including food processing firms and agricultural implement manufacturers and dealers.

Allocation of resources Determination of what will be produced, how it will be produced, who will produce it, and for whom it will be produced.

Anarcho-capitalism (radical libertarianism) A capitalist system under which no state exists and all goods and services — including defense, police, and court services — are supplied by private firms.

Anticombines laws A set of laws, including the acts of 1889 and 1923 and subsequent amendments, that seek to control market structure and the competitive behavior of firms.

Arbitrage The activity of earning a profit by buying a good for a low price in one market and reselling it for a higher price in another market.

Automatic stabilizers Changes in taxes, transfers, and government purchases that occur automatically as nominal GNP rises or falls.

Autonomous consumption The level of consumption shown by a consumption schedule for a zero disposable income level.

Balance of payments A record of all economic transactions between Canada and other countries in a given year. The balance is in surplus when receipts in the current and capital account exceed total payments to foreigners. It is in deficit when such receipts are less than total payments.

Balance of payments equilibrium A situation in which transactions in the capital account exactly match transactions in the current account, so that there is no loss or build-up of foreign currency reserves.

Bank rate The interest rate paid by chartered banks to borrow reserve funds from the Bank of Canada. Acts as a signal as to desired changes in interest rates charged by chartered banks.

Bilateral monopoly A market in which both buyer and seller exercise monopoly power and neither passively accepts the demands of the other.

Budget line A line showing the various combinations of goods that can be purchased at given prices within a given budget.

Capital As a factor of production, all manufactured productive resources such as tools, industrial equipment, structures, and artificial improvements to land.

Capital consumption allowance The amount by which a nation's capital goods, including buildings and equipment, are estimated to wear down (depreciate) in a given year.

Capitalism Any economic system based on private ownership of all factors of production in which owners of capital act as entrepreneurs and coordinate their activity through use of the market.

Capitalized value of a rent The amount equal to the value of the sum of money that would earn a periodic interest return equal to the rent if invested at the current market rate of interest.

Cartel An agreement among a number of independent suppliers of a product to coordinate their supply decisions so all of them will earn monopoly profits.

Centralized socialism A socialist system under which all capital and natural resources are owned by the government, which plans all production as if the economy were one big firm.

Circular flow of income and product The flow of goods from firms to households and factor services from households to firms, counterbalanced by the flow of expenditures from households to firms and factor payments from firms to households.

Classical liberal capitalism A capitalist economic system in which government performs only the limited role of protecting property rights and settling private disputes.

Commodity inflation A variety of cost-push inflation in which a spontaneous increase in commodity prices is the initial source of general price increases.

Comparative advantage In trade theory, the ability of a region or country to produce a good at lower opportunity cost, measured in terms of other foregone goods, than its trading partners.

Complements A pair of goods for which an increase in the price of one causes a decrease in the demand for the other, other things being equal.

Concentration ratio The percentage of all sales contributed by the four or eight largest firms in a market.

Constant returns to scale A phenomenon said to occur when there are neither economies nor diseconomies of scale.

Consumer equilibrium A state of affairs in which consumers cannot increase the total ultility they obtain from a given budget by shifting expenditure from one good to another. (In consumer equilibrium, the marginal utility of a dollar's worth of one good must be equal to the marginal utility of a dollar's worth of any other good.)

Consumer price index (CPI) A price index based on a "representative market basket" of almost 400 goods and services purchased by urban wage earners and clerical workers. This index is calculated using base year quantities.

Consumption schedule A graphical or numerical representation of how nominal consumption expenditure varies as nominal income varies, other things being equal.

Contractionary gap The difference between planned expenditures and national product at the target level of national income when aggregate supply exceeds aggregate demand at that level.

Contractual savings institutions Financial intermediaries such as insurance companies and pension funds, to which individuals and groups commit savings on a long-term contractual basis.

Corporation A firm in which the ownership is divided into equal parts called shares, with each shareholder's liability limited to the amount of his or her investment in the firm.

Cost-push illusion The phenomenon that demand-pull inflation often looks like cost-push inflation to those caught up in it, because inventories cushion the immediate impact of demand on prices at each link in the chain of distribution from producers to retailers.

Cost-push inflation Inflation that is initially touched off by a spontaneous rise in wages, profit margins, commodity prices, or other elements of cost during a period of slack aggregate demand.

Craft unions Unions of skilled workers practicing a single craft.

Crowding out effect The tendency of expansionary fiscal policy to cause a drop in private planned investment expenditure as a result of a rise in the interest rate.

Crude birthrate The number of people born into a population per thousand per year.

Crude death rate The number of people in a population who die per thousand per year.

Currency Coins and paper money.

Deficit In referring to government budgets, an excess of government purchases over net taxes.

Demand curve A graphical representation of the relationship between the price of a good and the quantity of it demanded.

Demand deposits Deposits at chartered banks that permit the depositor to make payments to others by writing a cheque against the deposit. Demand deposits are what we commonly call chequing accounts.

Demand schedule A table showing the quantity of a good demanded at various prices.

Demand-pull inflation Inflation that is initially touched off by an increase in aggregate demand.

Demographic transition A population cycle that accompanies economic development, beginning with a fall in the death rate, continuing with a phase of rapid population growth, and concluding with a decline in the birthrate.

Depauperization Economic development of a kind that benefits the poorest of the poor, providing them not only with the material necessities of life but also with access to education, status, security, self-expression, and power.

Depreciation and appreciation of the exchange rate The Canadian dollar is said to depreciate when its price falls in terms of foreign currency, and to appreciate when its price rises in terms of foreign currency.

Direct investment Purchase of securities with voting rights substantial enough to give the investors control of the company invested in.

Discretionary fiscal policy Changes in the levels of taxes, transfers, or government purchases made for the specific purpose of economic stabilization.

Diseconomies of scale A phenomenon said to occur whenever long-run average cost increases as output increases.

Dissaving Negative saving — the difference between disposable income and consumption expenditure when consumption exceeds disposable income.

Distributive justice The principle of distribution according to innate merit. Roughly, the principle of "from each according to abilities, to each according to needs."

Division of labor The division of the production process for a commodity into numerous specialized functions.

Draw downs and redeposits Transfer of government deposits between the Bank of Canada and the chartered banks.

Dual economy An economy that is sharply divided into a modern westernized industrial sector capable of rapid growth and a traditional rural sector that remains stagnant.

Dynamic efficiency The ability of an economy to increase consumer satisfaction through growth and innovation.

Econometrician A specialist in the statistical analysis of economic data.

Economic ideology A set of judgements and beliefs concerning efficiency, market justice, and distributive justice as goals of economic policy, together with a set of prejudices or beliefs concerning matters of positive economics.

Economies of scale A phenomenon said to occur whenever long-run average cost decreases as output increases.

Effective demand The quantity of a good that purchasers are willing and able to buy at a particular price.

Efficiency The property of producing or acting with a minimum of expense, waste, and effort.

Elastic demand The situation in which quantity changes by a larger percentage than price along the demand curve, so that total revenue increases as price decreases.

Empirical A term referring to data or methods based on observation of actual past experience or on controlled experiments.

Entrepreneurship A unique form of business activity that consists in inventing new ways of doing things, being alert to new opportunities, taking risks, overcoming constraints, and developing new products and organizations.

Excess quantity demanded The amount by which the quantity of a good demanded exceeds the quantity supplied when the price of the good is below the equilibrium level.

Excess quantity supplied The amount by which the quantity of a good supplied exceeds the quantity demanded when the price of the good is above the equilibrium level.

Excess reserves Reserves held by chartered banks in excess of required reserves.

Expansionary gap The difference between planned expenditures and national product at the target level of national income when aggregate demand exceeds aggregate supply at that level.

Expected rate of interest The nominal rate of interest minus the expected rate of inflation.

Expected real rate of return The annual real net improvement in a firm's cost or revenue that it expects to obtain by making an investment; it is expressed as a percentage of the sum invested.

Explicit costs Costs taking the form of explicit payments to nonowners of a firm.

Extensive growth Growth based predominantly on the mobilization of increasing quantities of factor inputs.

Extraterritoriality The application of foreign laws to Canadian companies.

Factor markets The markets in which the factors of production — labor, natural resources, and capital — are bought and sold.

Factor payments The payments with which firms purchase factors of production (natural resources, labor, and capital).

Factors of production The basic elements of natural resources, labor, and capital used in the production of all goods.

Featherbedding The practice of negotiating purposefully inefficient work rules so that more workers will be needed to do a job.

Final goods and services Goods and services sold directly for household consumption, business investment, or government purchase. Excludes intermediate goods sold for use as inputs in the production of other goods.

Financial intermediary Any financial institution that performs the function of channeling funds from savers to investors.

Fiscal policy The collective term for the policies that determine the levels of government purchases and meet taxes.

Fixed inputs Inputs to the production process that cannot easily be increased or decreased in a short period of time (the quantity of fixed inputs employed by a firm defines the size of the firm's plant).

Fixed investment Purchases by firms of newly produced capital goods, such as production machinery, newly built structures, and office equipment.

Flows Processes occurring continuously through time, measured in units per time period.

Foreign exchange market The complex of institutions through which the currency of one country may be exchanged for that of another.

Franchised monopoly A monopoly protected from competition by a government grant of monopoly privilege, such as an exclusive license, permit, or patent.

Fraser Institute An independent economic and social research organization with headquarters in Vancouver. It is firmly committed to the study and preservation of a competitive market system.

Full employment The greatest possible utilization of the labor force consistent with price stability and allowing for unavoidable unemployment of workers between jobs.

Full employment balanced budget rule A rule under which taxes and spending policy would be adjusted so that the federal budget would be in balance if the economy were at full employment.

Functional distribution of income The distribution of income according to factor ownership — that is, the distribution among workers, natural resource owners, and owners of capital.

General equilibrium analysis An approach to the study of markets along the lines of: if Event X occurs, the effect on Market Y will be Z, provided that other markets also adjust fully to the event in question.

GNE implicit price deflator (GNE deflator) A measure of the price level equal to the ratio of current nominal GNP to current real GNP times 100.

Government purchases of goods and services (government purchases) Expenditure made by federal, provincial, and municipal governments to purchase goods from private firms and to hire the services of government employees.

Gross national expenditure A measurement of aggregate economic activity arrived at by adding together the nominal expenditure of all economic units on newly produced final goods and services.

Gross national product (GNP) The dollar value of current market prices of all final goods and services produced annually by the nation's economy.

Homogeneous Having the property that every unit is just like every other unit.

Hyperinflation Very rapid and sustained inflation.

Implicit costs The opportunity costs to a firm of using resources owned by the firm itself or contributed by owners of the firm.

Income approach A method of estimating aggregate economic activity by adding together the incomes earned by all households.

Income effect The part of the change in quantity demanded of a good whose price has fallen that is attributable to the change in real income resulting from the price change.

Income elasticity of demand The ratio of the percentage change in the demand for a good to the percentage change in the per capita income of buyers.

Income velocity of money (velocity) The ratio of nominal income to the quantity of money.

Incomes policy A policy that attempts to control wages, salaries, earnings, and prices directly in order to fight inflation.

Indexing The practice of automatically adjusting wages, salaries, or other payments to compensate for changes in the price level.

Indifference curve A graphical representation of an indifference set.

Indifference map A representative selection of indifference curves for a single consumer and pair of goods.

Indifference set A set of consumption alternatives each of which yields the same utility, so that no member of the set is preferred to any other.

Industrial unions A union representing all workers in an enterprise, regardless of trade.

Inelastic demand The situation in which quantity changes by a smaller percentage than price along the demand curve, so that total revenue decreases as price decreases.

Inferior good A good for which an increase in the income of buyers causes a leftward shift in the demand curve.

Inflationary recession A period of rising unemployment during which the rate of inflation remains high or even continues to rise.

Injections The part of total expenditures that does not originate from domestic households — that is, investment, government purchases, and exports.

Inside lag The delay between the time a policy action is needed and the time it is taken.

Intensive growth Growth based predominantly on improvements in the quality of factor inputs and in the efficiency with which they are utilized.

Inventory investment Changes in the stocks of finished products and raw materials that firms keep on hand. If stocks are increasing, inventory investment is positive; if they are decreasing, it is negative.

Investment The sum of fixed investment and inventory investment.

J-curve effect The tendency for the depreciation of a country's currency to worsen its current account deficit in the short run and to improve it only after a lag.

Keynesian cross A figure formed by the intersection of the aggregate nominal demand and aggregate nominal supply schedules.

Kolkhoz A Soviet collective farm.

Labor As a factor of production, the contributions to production made by people working with their minds and their muscles.

Labor force All members of the noninstitutionalized civilian population over the age of 15 who are either officially employed or looking for employment.

Law of demand The law that the quantity of a good demanded by buyers tends to increase as the price of the good decreases and tends to decrease as the price increases, other things being equal.

Law of diminishing returns The law stating that as the quantity of one variable input used in a production process is increased (with the quantities of all other inputs remaining fixed), a point will eventually be reached beyond which the quantity of output added per unit of added variable input (that is, the marginal physical product of the variable input) begins to decrease.

Law of increasing costs As resources are shifted from one use to another, an additional unit of output of one good requires an increasing rate of sacrifice of other goods as greater and greater shifts occur.

Leakages The part of national income not devoted to consumption (saving plus net taxes) plus domestic expenditures on foreign-made goods (imports).

Liquid Description of an asset that can be used as a means of payment without risk of gain or loss in nominal value.

Long run A time perspective long enough to permit changes in the quantities of all inputs, both fixed and variable.

Lump sum taxes Taxes that do not vary as income varies.

M_1 The money supply defined as currency plus demand deposits in chartered banks.

M_2 The money supply defined as M_1 plus notice (savings and term) deposits at chartered banks.

Macroeconomics The branch of economics devoted to the study of unemployment, inflation, economic growth, and stabilization policy.

Managerial coordination Coordination of economic activity through directives from managers to subordinates.

Marginal average rule The rule that marginal cost must be equal to average cost when average cost is at its minimum.

Marginal cost The increase in cost required to increase output of some good or service by one unit.

Marginal factor cost The amount by which a firm's total factor cost must increase in order for it to obtain an additional unit of that factor.

Marginal physical product (of an input) The quantity of output, expressed in physical units, produced by each added unit of the input.

Marginal productivity theory of distribution A theory of the functional distribution of income according to which each factor receives a payment equal to its marginal revenue product.

Marginal propensity to consume The fraction of each added dollar of disposable income that goes to added consumption. Algebraically it can be written: $MPC = \dfrac{\Delta C}{\Delta D1}$, where MPC is the marginal propensity to consume, C is consumption, and D1 is personal disposable income.

Marginal propensity to import The fraction of each added dollar of disposable income (D1) that goes to added imports.
$$MPM = \dfrac{\Delta M}{\Delta D1}$$
In our model of the economy, where the only difference between disposable income and national income is a lump-sum tax, the marginal propensity to import out of disposable income will be the same as the marginal propensity to import out of national income. For purposes of analysis we will often express MPM in terms of national income, i.e.
$$MPM = \dfrac{\Delta M}{\Delta Y}, \text{ where}$$
Y = national income.

Marginal propensity to save. The fraction of each added dollar of disposable income that is not consumed. Algebraically, it can be written:
$$MPS = \dfrac{\Delta S}{\Delta D1},$$
where MPS is the marginal propensity to save, S is saving, and D1 is personal disposable income.

Marginal rate of substitution The rate at which one good can be substituted for another without gain or loss in satisfaction (equal to the slope of an indifference curve at any point).

Marginal revenue The amount by which total revenue increases as the result of a one-unit increase in quantity.

Marginal revenue product (of a factor) The change in revenue resulting from the sale of the product produced by one additional unit of factor input.

Marginal utility The amount of added utility obtained from a one-unit increase in consumption of a good.

Market coordination Coordination of economic activity using the price system to transmit information and provide incentives.

Market equilibrium A condition in which the separately formulated plans of buyers and sellers of some good exactly mesh when tested in the marketplace, so that the quantity supplied is exactly equal to the quantity demanded at the prevailing price.

Market justice The principle of distribution according to acquired merit. The observance of property rights and the honoring of contracts. Roughly, the principle of "value for value."

Market performance The ability of a firm to realize economies of scale through efficiency of operation.

Market power The strength that a firm possesses — because of exclusive control of resources, prior build-up of profits, or networks of influence and command — that gives it an advantage over its rivals.

Market structure Important characteristics of a market, including the number of firms that operate in it, the extent to which the products of different firms are diverse or homogeneous, and the ease of entry into and exit from the market.

Markets All the various arrangements people have for trading with one another.

Merit goods Goods that are produced by government and supplied free of charge on the grounds that each citizen merits his or her fair share.

Microeconomics The branch of economics devoted to the study of the behavior of individual households and firms and to the determination of the relative prices of individual goods and services.

Minimum efficient scale The level of output at which economies of scale are exhausted.

Monetarists Economists who believe that movements in the money supply are the primary causes of ups and downs in business activity.

Money Anything that serves as a unit of account, a medium of exchange, and a store of purchasing power.

Money demand schedule A schedule showing the quantity of money that people desire to hold in their portfolios given various values for the nominal interest rate and the level of nominal income.

Money multiplier The ratio of the quantity of money to the total reserves in a banking system. Various money multipliers can be defined, depending on the definition of money used. In the simplified banking system, the formula for the money multiplier is:

$$\text{Money multiplier} = \frac{1}{\text{Required reserve ratio}}$$

Monopolistic competition A market structure in which a large number of firms offer products that are relatively close substitutes for one another.

Monopoly power A seller's power to raise the price of a product without losing all, or nearly all, customers.

Monopsony A market in which there is only one buyer; from the Greek words *mono* ("single") and *opsonia* ('buying").

Moral suasion Direct attempts by the Bank of Canada to influence the practices of the chartered banks.

Multinationals Corporations that have enterprises in a number of countries.

Multiplier The ratio of an induced change in the equilibrium level of national income to an initial change in planned expenditure. For an economy in which imports play an important role, the value of the multiplier is given by the formula

$$\text{Multiplier} = \frac{1}{1-(MPC-MPM)}$$

or $\frac{1}{1-MPC_D}$.

MPC_D is the marginal propensity to consume domestic output.
$$MPC_D = \frac{\Delta C}{\Delta D1} - \frac{\Delta M}{\Delta Y}$$

Multiplier effect The ability of a \$1 shift in the aggregate nominal demand schedule to induce a change of more than \$1 in the equilibrium level of nominal national income.

National income The total of all incomes, including wages, rents, interest payments, and profits received by households.

National product The total value of all goods and services supplied in the economy.

Natural monopoly A monopoly protected from competition by technological barriers to entry or by ownership of unique natural resources.

Natural rate of unemployment The rate of unemployment that would prevail if the expected rate of inflation were equal to the actual rate of inflation.

Natural resources As a factor of production, land and mineral deposits.

Near-banks Institutions that accept deposits on which cheques can be written but that are not chartered banks and not subject to direct Bank of Canada control.

Negative income tax A general name for transfer systems that emphasize cash benefits, beginning with a basic benefit available to households with zero earned income that is then subject to a benefit reduction rate of substantially less than 100 percent.

Net exports Total exports minus total imports.

Net incidence of taxation The difference between the amount paid to government in taxes and the amount received from government, calculated as a percentage of income.

Net national income Total income received by a nation's productive factors, including wages and salaries, interest and rent, corporate taxes before profits, and income of unincorporated enterprises. It is also equal to GNP — capital consumption allowances and indirect business taxes.

Net reproduction rate The inherent long-term growth rate of a population, measured as the average number of daughters born to each female child over her lifetime.

Net tax multiplier A multiplier showing how much equilibrium nominal national income will change in response to a change in net taxes.
The formula for the net tax multiplier is
$-MPC/1 - MPC_D$

Net tax multiplier A multiplier showing how much equilibrium nominal national income will change in response to a change in net taxes. The formula for the net tax multiplier is
$$\frac{-MPC+MPM}{MPS+MPM} \quad \text{or} \quad \frac{-MPC_D}{1-MPC_D}$$

Net taxes Total tax revenues collected by government at all levels minus total transfer payments disbursed.

Nominal rate of interest The rate of interest measured in the ordinary way, without adjustment for inflation.

Nominal values Measurements of economic values made in terms of actual market prices at which goods are sold.

Normal good A good for which an increase in the income of buyers causes a rightward shift in the demand curve.

Normal rate of return to capital The opportunity cost of capital to a firm — that is, the rate of return necessary to attract funds for investment from their best alternative uses.

Normative economics The part of economics devoted to making value judgements about what economic policies or conditions are good or bad.

Notice deposits Interest-paying accounts at chartered banks against which it is not ordinarily possible to write cheques.

Okun's law Each 1 percent increase (decrease) in unemployment results in a 3 percent decrease (increase) in real economic growth. Or, conversely each 3 percent increase (decrease) in real economic growth results in a 1 percent decrease (increase) in unemployment.

Oligopolistic interdependence The necessity, in an oligopolistic market, for each firm to pay close attention to the behavior and likely reactions of its rivals when planning its own market strategy.

Oligopoly A market structure in which there are two or more firms, at least one of which has a large share of total sales.

Open market operation A purchase of securities from the public or a sale of securities to the public made by the Bank of Canada for the purpose of altering the quantity of reserves available to chartered banks.

Opportunity cost The cost of doing something as measured by the loss of the opportunity to do the next best thing instead, with the same amount of time or resources.

Outside lag The delay between the time a policy action is taken and the time its effects on the economy are felt.

Par The point at which one unit of a currency is traded for exactly one unit of another currency.

Partial equilibrium analysis An approach to the study of markets along the lines of: If Event X occurs, the effect on Market Y will be Z, provided that the equilibrium of other markets is not disturbed.

Participatory socialism A socialist system under which the means of production are owned collectively by the workers of individual firms, who participate democratically in the process of management and share the profits of their firms.

Partnership A firm formed by two or more persons to carry on a business as co-owners. Each partner bears full legal liability for the debts of the firm.

Perfect competition A market structure characterized by a large number of relatively small firms, a homogeneous product, good distribution of information among all market participants, and freedom of entry and exit.

Perfectly elastic demand The situation in which the demand curve is a horizontal line.

Perfectly inelastic demand The situation in which the demand curve is a vertical line.

Personal disposable income (disposable income) Personal income minus personal taxes.

Personal distribution of income The distribution of income among individuals, taking into account both the functional distribution of income and the distribution of factor ownership among persons.

Personal income The total of all income, including transfer payments, actually received by households before payment of personal income taxes and other transfer payments to government.

Phillips curve A curve showing the relationship between the rate of inflation and the level of unemployment. Inflation, usually placed on the vertical axis of such a figure, can be measured in terms of either the rate of change in wages or the rate of change in a price index.

Planned investment schedule A graphical representation of how the rate of planned investment for the economy as a whole varies as the expected real rate of interest varies, other things being equal.

Population trap A situation in which the rate of population growth rises above the rate of economic growth, halting the growth of per capita income and aborting the demographic transition.

Portfolio balance The idea that people try to maintain a balance among the various kinds of assets they own — including money, consumer durables, stocks, and bonds — shifting from one kind of asset to another as economic conditions change.

Portfolio investment Purchase of securities that involves no control of the company selling the securities.

Positive economics The part of economics limited to making scientific predictions and purely descriptive statements.

Potential output growth The average growth that can be expected each year as a result of changes in population, and in labor productivity.

Potential real GNP (potential real output) The level of real GNP that the economy could, in principle, produce if resources were fully employed.

Precautionary motive A motive for holding money arising from its usefulness as a reserve of liquid funds for use in emergencies or in taking advantage of unexpected opportunities.

Price discrimination The practice of charging more than one price for different units of a single product, when the price differences are not justified by differences in the cost of serving different customers.

Price elasticity of demand (elasticity of demand) The ratio of the percentage change in the quantity of a good demanded to the percentage change in the price of the good.

Price elasticity of supply (elasticity of supply) The ratio of the percentage change in the quantity of a good supplied to the percentage change in its price.

Price leadership A situation in an oligopolistic market where increases or decreases in price by one dominant firm, known as the price leader, are matched by all or most other firms in the market.

Price support A program under which the government guarantees a certain minimum price to farmers by undertaking to buy any surplus that cannot be sold to private buyers at the support price.

Price taker A firm that sells its outputs at fixed prices that are determined entirely by forces outside its own control.

Principle of diminishing marginal utility The principle that the greater the rate of consumption of some good, the smaller the increase in utility from a unit increase in the rate of consumption.

Production possibility frontier A curve showing the possible combinations of goods that can be produced by an economy, given the quantity and quality of factors of production available.

Profit-push inflation A variety of cost-push inflation in which a spontaneous increase in profit margins is the initial source of price increases.

Progressive tax A tax that takes a larger precentage of income from people whose income is high.

Proportional tax A tax that takes a constant percentage of income from people at all income levels.

Public goods Goods or services having the properties that (1) they cannot be provided to one citizen without being supplied also to that person's neighbors, and (2) once they are provided for one citizen, the cost of providing them to others is zero.

Purchasing power parity theory (of exchange rates) The theory holding that the price of a unit of Currency A in terms of Currency B will, in the long run, tend to be equal to the ratio of the price level in Country B to the price level in Country A.

Pure economic profit The sum remaining after both explicit and implicit costs are subtracted from total revenue.

Pure economic rent The income earned by any factor of production that is in perfectly inelastic supply.

Pure monopoly A market structure in which one firm accounts for 100 percent of industry sales.

Rate of natural increase The current growth rate of a population calculated as the crude birthrate minus the crude death rate.

Rational expectations Expectations about the rate of inflation or other future economic events based on a rational weighing of all available evidence, including evidence on the probable effects of present and future economic policy.

Real values Measurements of economic values that include adjustments for changes in prices between one year and another.

Realized rate of interest The nominal rate of interest minus the actual rate of inflation.

Reflation An expansion of aggregate demand after a period of high unemployment and decelerating inflation, bringing substantial short-term gains in employment with little or no inflationary penalty.

Regressive tax A tax that takes a larger percentage of income from people whose income is low.

Required reserve ratio The fraction of each type of deposit that the Bank of Canada requires chartered banks to hold in the form of non-interest-bearing assets.

Required reserve ratios Legally required minimum quantities of reserves, expressed as ratios of reserves to various types of deposits.

Reservation wage The wage (adjusted for nonmonetary advantages and disadvantages of a job) below which a person will not accept a job offer.

Reserves (of chartered banks) Money held by chartered banks as cash or non-interest-bearing deposits with the Bank of Canada.

Saving schedule A graphical or numerical representation of how nominal saving varies as nominal disposable income varies, other things being equal.

Scientific prediction A conditional prediction having the form "if A, then B, other things being equal."

Short run A time perspective within which output can be adjusted only by changing the quantities of variable inputs within a plan of fixed size.

Shortage As used in economics, an excess quantity demanded.

Socialism Any of a number of doctrines that include the following tenets: (1) that some major share of nonlabor factors of production ought to be owned in common or by the state, and (2) that justice requires incomes to be distributed at least somewhat more equally than under classical liberal capitalism.

Sole proprietorship A firm owned and usually managed by a single person, who receives all profits of the firm and who personally bears all of the firm's liabilities.

Speculative motive A motive for holding money arising from its fixed nominal value, when the nominal value of alternative assets is expected to decline.

Stabilization policy An effort by government to control the level of national income and the related conditions of inflation, unemployment, and the balance of payments.

Staple product A commodity on which the economy of a settlement or region concentrates much of its labor and capital.

State capitalism A capitalist system under which government intervenes widely in the market and provides an alternative to the market as a means by which individuals and firms can win control over resources.

Static efficiency The ability of an economy to get the greatest consumer satisfaction from given resources and technology.

Stocks Accumulated quantities existing at a particular time, measured in terms of simple units.

Stop-go policy A cycle of acceleration, inflationary recession, deceleration, and reflation brought about by alternating political pressures to do something first about inflation and then about unemployment.

Subsidy price A price guaranteed to farmers by the government; if the market price falls below the subsidy price, the government pays the farmers the difference.

Substitutes A pair of goods for which an increase in the price of one causes an increase in the demand for the other, other things being equal.

Substitution effect The part of the increase in quantity demanded of a good whose price has fallen that is attributable to the tendency of consumers to substitute relatively cheap goods for relatively expensive ones.

Supply curve A graphical representation of the relationship between the price of a good and the quantity of it supplied.

Supply schedule A table showing the quantity of a good supplied at various prices.

Surplus As used in economics, an excess quantity supplied.

Surplus In referring to government budgets, an excess of net taxes over government purchases.

Target level of nominal national income (income target) The level of nominal national income judged by policy makers to be most nearly compatible with the goals of full employment, price stability, and real economic growth, and balance of payments stability.

Total rate of return to capital The opportunity cost of capital plus pure economic profit, expressed as a percentage of the capital invested in a firm.

Transactions motive A motive for holding money arising from the convenience of using it as a means of payment for day-to-day transactions.

Transfer payments All payments made by government to individuals that are not made in return for goods or services currently supplied. Social security benefits, welfare payments, and unemployment compensation are major forms of transfer payments.

Transitivity The situation where if A is preferred to B and B is preferred to C, then A must be preferred to C.

Truncation Limits placed on the development of skills and services in and by a Canadian subsidiary because they are concentrated in the parent company.

Unemployment rate Percentage of the labor force who are actively looking for employment but who are not employed.

Unit elastic demand The situation in which price and quantity change by the same percentage along the demand curve, so that total revenue remains unchanged as price changes.

Utility The economist's term for the pleasure, satisfaction, and need fulfillment that people get from the consumption of material goods and services.

Variable inputs Inputs to the production process that can quickly and easily be varied to increase or decrease output within a plant of a given size.

Very short run A time horizon so short that producers are unable to make any changes in input or output quantities in response to changing prices.

Wage-push inflation A variety of cost-push inflation in which a spontaneous increase in nominal wage rates is the initial source of price increases.

Weighted average An average that gives appropriate weights to products in proportion to their relative importance in the total basket of goods purchased.

The White Paper of 1945 Committed the federal government to the maintenance of stable, full-employment economic growth.

I N D E X